SOUTH AMERICA OVERLAND

SOUTH AMERICA OVERLAND

From New York to Tierra del Fuego

IAIN FINLAY & TRISH SHEPPARD

ANGUS & ROBERTSON PUBLISHERS

Angus & Robertson Publishers
London • Sydney • Melbourne • Singapore
Manila

First published by Angus & Robertson Publishers, Australia, 1980

© Iain Finlay and Trish Sheppard 1980

National Library of Australia
Cataloguing-in-publication data.

Finlay, Iain.
  South America Overland.

ISBN 0 207 14122 3

1. South America — Description and travel.
2. North America — Description and travel.
I. Sheppard, Trish, 1942-, joint author.
II. Title.

918

Printed in Hong Kong

*For Zara and Sean without whom none of
this would have been ... half as much fun*

For anyone travelling in Latin America there is one book which should be carried at all times, *The South American Handbook* — 1000 plus pages of invaluable information. This wonderfully helpful book added considerably to the interest and fascination of our journey as well as making it measurably easier.

AUTHORS' NOTE

Following the style we set in *Africa Overland,* readers of this book will find we have interspersed our points of view. To differentiate between them Iain's comments are in the bolder type

CONTENTS

PHOTOGRAPHS

MAPS

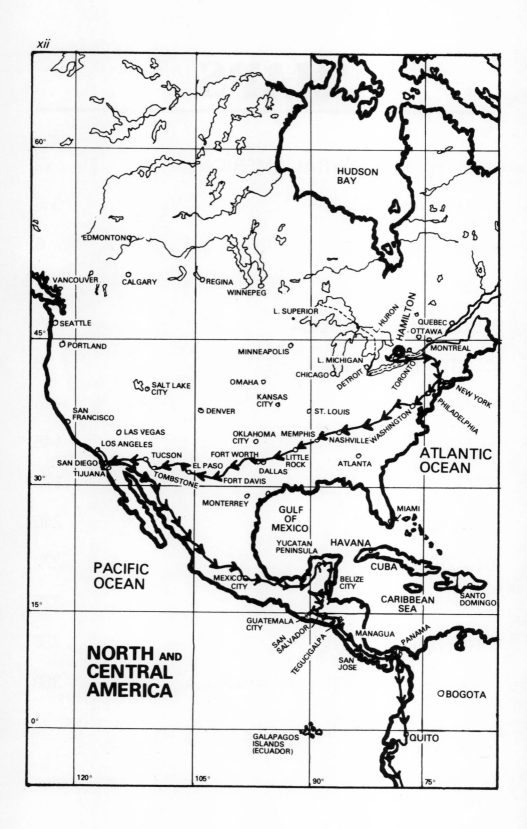

HUDSON
BAY

EDMONTON

VANCOUVER

CALGARY

REGINA

WINNEPEG

L. SUPERIOR

L. HURON

HAMILTON

QUEBEC
OTTAWA

SEATTLE

PORTLAND

MINNEAPOLIS

L. MICHIGAN

CHICAGO

DETROIT

TORONTO

MONTREAL

NEW YORK

SALT LAKE
CITY

OMAHA

KANSAS
CITY

DENVER

ST. LOUIS

PHILADELPHIA

SAN
FRANCISCO

LAS VEGAS

LOS ANGELES

OKLAHOMA
CITY

MEMPHIS

NASHVILLE WASHINGTON

ATLANTIC
OCEAN

TUCSON

FORT WORTH

LITTLE
ROCK

SAN DIEGO

EL PASO

DALLAS

ATLANTA

TIJUANA

TOMBSTONE

FORT DAVIS

MONTERREY

GULF
OF
MEXICO

MIAMI

YUCATAN
PENINSULA

HAVANA

CUBA

PACIFIC
OCEAN

MEXICO
CITY

BELIZE
CITY

CARIBBEAN
SEA

SANTO
DOMINGO

GUATEMALA
CITY

SAN
SALVADOR

TEGUCIGALPA

MANAGUA

PANAMA

NORTH AND
CENTRAL
AMERICA

SAN
JOSE

BOGOTA

GALAPAGOS
ISLANDS
(ECUADOR)

QUITO

60°

45°

30°

15°

0°

120°

105°

90°

75°

CARIBBEAN SEA

CUBA

BELIZE CITY

CARACUS

PANAMA

SAN SALVADOR

MANAGUA

SAN JOSE

GEORGETOWN

NEW AMSTERDAM

CAYENNE

BOGOTA

MOUTH OF THE AMAZON

0°

GUAYAQUIL QUITO

IQUITOS AMAZON MANAUS RIVER

BELEM

CHICLAYO ANDES

TRUJILLO

PORTO VELHO

RECIFE

MACHU PICCHU

SALVADOR

LIMA CUZCO

MATO GROSSO

CUIABA

BRASILIA

15°

NAZCA LA PAZ

LAKE TITICACA

AREQUIPPA

SUCRE

BELO HORIZONTE

GOIANIA

PACIFIC OCEAN

ANDES MOUNTAINS

SAO PAULO

RIO DEJANIERO

ASUNCION

CURITIBA

TUCUMAN

30°

PORTO ALLEGRO

VALPARAISO

SANTA FE

MENDOZA

SANTIAGO

ANDES MOUNTAINS

BUENOS AIRES

MONTEVIDEO

RIVER PLATE

ATLANTIC OCEAN

MAR DEL PLATA

PUERTO MADRYN

VALDEZ PENINSULA

TRELEW

45°

PATAGONIA

FALKLAND ISLANDS

(ISLAS) (MALVINAS)

SOUTH AMERICA

0   320   640   960   1280   1600

PUNTA ARENAS

USHUAIA

KILOMETRES

90°   75°   60°   45°

INTRODUCTION

The sensible way to approach a trip from the Northern Hemisphere to the Southern Hemisphere that is to last roughly six months, would be to plan it to start during a northern summer and to end in the following southern summer. Unfortunately, we don't seem to do things in the sensible way very often and, as you'll soon see, most of the planning for this trip, if you could call it planning, was done on the move. It was a trip that sort of grew.

Originally we had thought of making a journey from the northern parts of South America to the southern tip of Tierra del Fuego. It was as loosely conceived as that. We knew that there were a great many things we wanted to see in South America; the fabulous lost cities of the Incas, the mysterious desert lines at Nazca, Lake Titicaca, the highest in the world ... and the Amazon River, a destination that had attracted me since childhood. There was also the remote vastness of the Mato Grosso, the great cities of Brazil and Argentina, the wide pampas and plains of Patagonia and Ushuaia, the southernmost town in the world.

But, looking at the map of South America, it was difficult to decide how to tackle it. We knew, from the beginning, that we wanted this South American journey to be, as much as possible, like an overland trip we had made through Africa, from south to north, with our two children during 1976. That trip, which had lasted approximately six months, had proved to be a superb experience for us all, but particularly for Sean and Zara, who at that stage were only eight and nine years old.

On that African journey we covered some 8000 miles from Cape Town to Cairo using only public transport; local buses, trains, hitchhiking where necessary and carrying only the bare necessities in four backpacks. We saw some wonderful sights; Victoria Falls on the Zambezi River, the great game reserves of East Africa, the source of the Blue Nile in Ethiopia and Egypt's magnificent Valley of the Kings. At the same time, we went through considerable hardship; plenty of rough travelling, being arrested by the army in Tanzania and all of us coming down with dysentery in the Sudan. But the overall experience had been what we wanted: for Trish and I a new direction and a change in life-style and for the children, a wider knowledge and understanding of the world around them.

The idea for the South American trip grew from a combination of the desire to continue the pattern set by our overland trek through Africa and an unfulfilled ambition of mine to travel down the Amazon River. Just the name had always conjured up images for me of great adventure, vast, unexplored reaches of primaeval jungle, savage, blow-pipe-wielding Indians with basin-cut hair-dos, man-eating piranhas, alligators and giant anaconda snakes that could crush a man and swallow him whole. And, to lead you through this white man's hell, there was the jaded hunter-explorer type who, at the end of the day, would sit outside his tent in his sweat-soaked khaki drills, drinking too much whisky, while you stood nearby listening to the frightening sounds of the jungle, as night descended.

Is that what the Amazon would really be like? Well, I have to admit that, at this end of the twentieth century, I didn't really expect to find it quite like that. And yet ... perhaps. Maybe some of this fantasy, adventure world still remained. But I knew that there was really no way of knowing unless we went to see the Amazon and all the rest of it for ourselves. But, where to begin such a trip through South America? Would you believe, Canada.

The reason for travelling from winter to winter did actually have its own logic; that's if you believe that family emotions can be even remotely connected to logic!

My family are spread around Ontario, Canada. Dad, Mum, two sisters and a brother; with their respective spouses and children they number sixteen and that's without hanger-abouters like steady boy/girlfriends. When you add us to the crowd we total at least twenty, which number my younger sister was planning on for a Christmas dinner, proudly presided over by our Dad in his eightieth year; who could look about him and see that his fruit had multiplied and prospered!

The first family Christmas in seventeen years and the first ever white Christmas for my children. There was the fun of getting dressed up in protective clothing to go out into the sub-zero temperatures; cross-country skiing which left my legs trembling with exhaustion; and whizzing down steep icy slopes balanced upright in a yoga position on a tiny metal tray. And there was skidooing astride compact two-person motorised sleds at 65 kph through the snow drifts which collect among the trees on my sister's apple orchard.

Then there was carol-singing, open fires, a constant stream of visitors, many of them come to see what this foreign sister was like, homemade crackers and too much good food to eat and liquor to drink. Pantomimes, real holly and mistletoe, the infectious excitement of the youngest children as they put out the cookies for Father Christmas, individual stockings, piles of presents, family jokes and reminiscences and by the end of three weeks, the unavoidable internecine squabbles which are one of the reasons why one loves them and leaves them!

Slowly the idea took shape of driving overland instead of flying from Canada to South America. Basically it was because all of us enjoy these long slow voyages over vast areas of land. A further reason was the children hadn't travelled in North America, except Zara as a baby, and as we were planning on journeying through South America by land why not do the same across the USA and Central America? It's only an additional nine or ten thousand kilometres!

We made inquiries about cars and found they are considerably more expensive in Canada than in the States so we decided to hire one for the first hop down to New York and buy one there.

The family was aghast. Mum and Dad had secretly hoped that having once been re-clutched to the family bosom we would succumb to sanity and settle down, 'put those poor gypsy children into school', and all become regular guys.

'You can't leave now,' they said. 'The forecast is for severe blizzards!' This was followed by horror stories of women and children frozen to death in stranded cars.

'And even if you avoid an accident,' Dad said doubtfully, 'I can't see why you want to go to South America anyway. The whole continent is populated by trigger-happy bandits who are always busy having revolutions and selling drugs to travellers. It's dangerous, and what's more they don't even speak English.'

He laughed, but only lightly, and I thought that perhaps one reason why I wanted so badly to go was because I wanted to make sure for myself that he wasn't right!

NORTH AMERICA

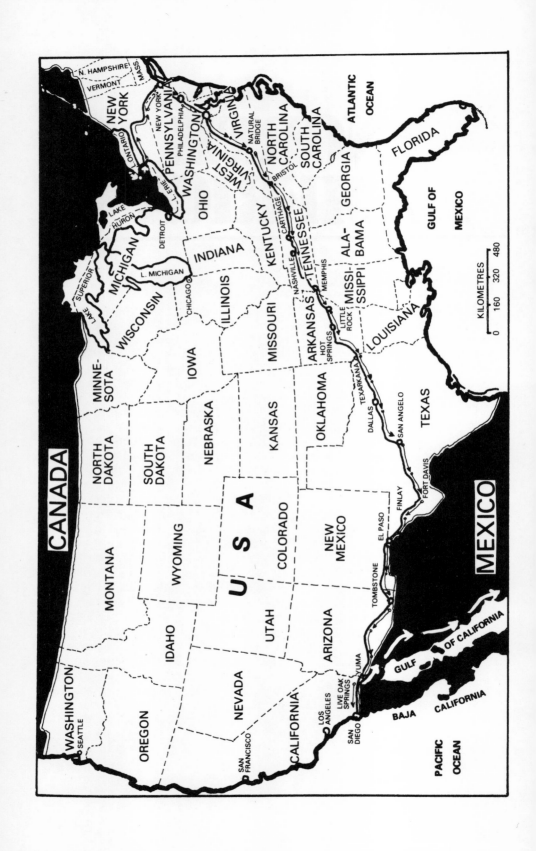

USA

1

It could only happen in New York

'Always carry a supply of candles in your car . . . they could save your life!'

This was just one of the assorted bits of 'helpful' information we were given to send us off on our journey. Evidently a single candle burning in a snow-bound car gives off enough heat to prevent the occupants of the car from freezing to death. Naturally, we were hoping not to have to put this theory to the test, but on that bleak January day when we began our trip south from Canada, it seemed a very real possibility.

True to the forecasts, a blinding blizzard was sweeping across all of up-state New York and southern Ontario. Radio announcers were issuing warnings of extremely hazardous driving conditions, 'white-outs', and 'wind-chill factors' of minus 28 degrees Celsius for anyone exposed to the weather out of doors.

With the heater in our hired Pontiac Bonneville putting out a steady stream of warm air, we felt warm, but hardly secure, as we struggled down the Queen Elizabeth Highway to Niagara, where we stood, briefly, as the only tourists of the day, I'm sure, to gaze for a few minutes at the strange beauty of the frozen falls. Then, after crossing the border into the United States, we set off along the New York Thruway.

The road was absolutely treacherous; so icy that the slightest wrong movement of the wheel would send the car into a slide. Strong gusts of wind would whip great sheets of powdery snow, edging in drifts across the road, up into the air, to cause blinding 'white-outs', where nothing could be seen, even a few metres in front of the windshield. At times we were slowed almost to a standstill and saw many trucks and cars which had slid off the road. We were tempted on many occasions, usually after a frightening slide, to leave the Thruway and stop. That would probably have been the sensible thing to have done, but we kept on driving . . . nobody talking, just staring silently ahead.

There was very little traffic on the highway and what vehicles there were moved carefully. We pushed on past Rochester, but by the time we were level with Syracuse, some 100 kilometres and about three and a half hours further on, we were ready to give up. We decided to stay in a small town, rather than in Syracuse itself and left the highway, making south towards a town called Cazenovia. I don't know why we chose it, because it was out of the way, perhaps it was just the name. Anyway it was a very attractive little town and, as we approached it, the weather suddenly improved. It stopped snowing and the wind dropped, so that the countryside in the late afternoon became calm and beautiful under deep, fresh layers of snow.

We found a small boarding house with two comfortable double beds in an upstairs room of a private home; $12 for the four of us and we all slept like logs.

The trip south to New York the next day was magic. The blizzard was gone and, apart from snow falls during the early morning, the sky was clear and blue and the countryside crisp, sparkling and brilliantly white. Low hills, open fields, forest pines laden with snow and small farms with smoke rising from their chimneys. It was the sort of day and the kind of scenery that could make it clear to anyone . . . even a non-American like myself . . . why the early settlers called it 'God's country'.

In the afternoon we found ourselves following Route 97 down along the Delaware Valley where the cliffs beside the road were covered by frozen waterfalls shining and gleaming in the sunlight, like beautiful, endless walls of glass. We stopped for gas at a tiny town and found the two attendants at the garage sitting inside the workshop by a smoky old wood stove. Trish commented to one of them that the weather seemed to be getting better.

'Yep,' said the older of the two, a bald-headed man in his sixties, with a corn-cob pipe clamped between his teeth, 'and it's going to stay that way for a while, according to this.' He waved his hand at the stove.

'What?' I said. 'The stove?'

'Yep. Tells us exactly what to expect. Good weather or bad . . . never misses. When good weather's on the way, the room always smokes up. When it's bad weather comin, there's never any smoke in here.'

The children were mightily impressed by the stove.

'How can the stove tell them that?' Zara asked as we drove off. I knew it had something to do with rising and falling atmospheric pressures, but I don't think I explained it very well.

Just before we hit New York City, we stopped at Suffern to telephone Bob Judd, a friend living in Greenwich Village. We told him we planned to check into a hotel and that we hoped we could meet for dinner shortly after.

'Karen and I will see you at the "Under the Trees" restaurant on the corner of Bleecker and Grove,' Bob said, . . . 'at 7.30.'

What followed could only happen in New York and, for me at least, was fairly convincing proof of the old cliché about truth really being stranger than fiction.

The children hardly noticed us leaving our room in the Iroquois Hotel on West 44th that evening, so engrossed were they in a TV shoot-em-up and their take-away hamburgers, french-fries and Coca-Cola. Who says kids don't know what's good for them! Downstairs, the manager, who was complaining in almost unintelligible Brooklynese that the weather was preventing him from driving south for his annual vacation in Miami, promised to keep an occasional eye on them.

Bob and Karen Judd were waiting for us, as arranged, at the 'Under the Trees' restaurant in Greenwich Village and we swopped news of events and doings that had occurred in the eighteen months since we'd last seen them. Their most momentous news, though they were, in the vernacular, very 'laid-back' about it, was that they had uncoupled; to go their separate ways. Bob, having left a large advertising company to write, on a big advance, a guide which was aptly titled, 'How to Fall Out of Love', and Karen to divide her time between editing a leftist magazine and going on archaeological digs around Mexico.

'But,' Bob said, 'we are still good friends', and they laughed.

Over the next drink, we explained that I had contacted another New York friend, Fred Kaplan, a fellow we hadn't seen since we lived in Hong Kong some thirteen years previously, and that he had asked to join us for dinner and had made it impossible for us to refuse.

Tactfully explaining one friend to another is a difficult business; especially when, having been out of touch for so long, one doesn't know what to expect. We told them that Fred was a Chinese linguist and scholar and that he was about to leave on another extended visit to the People's Republic, having just completed a comprehensive encyclopaedia of that country. Bod and Karen said it would be fine for Fred to join us.

Now that the way was paved, or so we thought, we settled down to a few drinks, but when Fred hadn't arrived by 9.00 p.m. we decided that he wasn't coming and ordered dinner.

But Fred did come . . . just as we had started our dessert . . . late as usual; at least that hadn't changed. He made his entrance in a large, black cloak and hat, bringing in tow Simone, a highly articulate, but rather abrasive woman in her late forties, and a younger black man, Peter, who wore a wide-brimmed, white cowboy hat.

Peter obviously despised initial social niceties, such as small talk, as he launched straight into a heavy conversation about always being an outsider; which is probably one of the reasons why he was.

For half an hour or so the talk was sharp and bitchy, while the five New Yorkers jostled for status and primacy as only they know how. We participated at the edges.

Fred had introduced Peter as an artist, managing to intimate that it was only because we were out-of-town yokels that we needed to be told. Simone was his agent. He had exhibited all over Europe and the USA and on Sunday he was flying to Britain on Concorde for another one-man show.

Peter let Fred continue with his publicity, while Simone, evidently having decided that Karen was not a saleable commodity, directed her conversation at Bob, who was able to lob a few returns.

Throughout this bout of verbal fisticuffs, while they were still waiting for their meal to be served, Peter made frequent, extended visits to the pay-phone at the back of the restaurant. But it wasn't until we heard the menacing wail of fire engine sirens and watched in astonishment as two of them pulled up outside the restaurant that we registered that Peter was nowhere about.

As we were sitting at a window-side table, we had a front-row view of the firemen unreeling hoses into the street and the arrival of a police car. Bob had just finished joking that he was glad that we, at least, had come early enough to have dinner before the kitchen caught fire, when one of the waiters, who had gone outside, probably in the hope of getting a closer view of any possible tragedy, came back inside to ask: 'Is that black guy a friend of yours?'

We nodded.

'Well, I think he needs you. He's in trouble out there.'

At that, Bob Judd and I left the table and went out into the street to see, a few metres away, a crowd gathering around a policeman and two firemen. A girl stood sobbing in a doorway nearby. As we pushed through the crowd, we saw Peter, face-down in the gutter, another policeman astride him, pushing one knee into Peter's back as he struggled to get his arms behind his back to clamp a pair of handcuffs on them.

'What's happening?' I shouted. 'This guy is a friend of ours. He's done nothing wrong. He was just sitting, having dinner with us a few minutes ago.'

'Keep your goddamn nose out of this buddy,' the cop on Peter's back said, 'unless you want to come along too!' His face was flushed with the effort of the struggle and his hat lay in the gutter, to one side, as the other policeman and the firemen battled to hold back the crowd of people pressing in. You could feel the tension and their nervousness . . . as if they expected almost anything to happen. I'm sure they'd been in similar mob situations where things had fallen apart. No reason why it couldn't happen here too. By this stage Trish and the others had come out from the restaurant.

'But look . . .' I started again.

'Listen pal,' the second policeman shouted venomously at me, jabbing me sharply backwards with his baton, 'mind your own fuckin' business. This guy tried to attack that girl.'

I turned towards the girl we'd seen crying on the edge of the crowd.

'He was trying to rape her and we're taking him in.'

Bob and I went across to the girl.

'Oh Peter,' she kept sobbing, 'I'm sorry.'

'Do you know him?' Bob asked, incredulous.

'Yes, yes. He used to be my boyfriend,' she cried. 'He's been phoning me constantly for the past half-hour, trying to get me to come down to talk to him. I live up there,' she pointed to some small apartments above the restaurant, 'and I wouldn't . . . until they said there was a fire in our building and I had to come out with everyone else . . . and then Peter grabbed me in the doorway here. Oh Jesus, I didn't mean this to happen.'

By this stage, the two policemen had man-handled Peter to his feet and, although he struggled violently to prevent it, he was forced into the back of the police car.

'Where are you taking him?' I shouted, as the car began to move off.

'Sixth Precinct,' the second policeman snarled. 'You can come and see him there, if you want to.'

We arrived at the Sixth Precinct at the same time as about fifty riot police, who charged past us, toting the usual array of police revolvers and batons. But these ones were equipped, in addition, with round, gladiator-style shields, hard hats and tinted, perspex face-masks. Frightening creatures, spawned perhaps by Darth Vader.

Apparently Farah Diba was in town buying up Norma Tullos, Zandra Rhodes and possibly half of Tiffany's, and some 2500 extra police were needed to protect her from violent demonstrations by Iranian students and their supporters who were angry, not so much over her choice of couturier, as over her husband's government back home in Iran, which, as it turned out, wasn't to be around for very much longer.

I wondered whether New York taxpayers should be called upon to foot the bill for the protection such a shopping spree involved, especially as the city is so desperately short of money, but right then didn't seem to be the appropriate time to bring the subject up for discussion.

Peter was there, in the charge office, slumped, silent, in a chair to which he was handcuffed like a dangerous criminal. The thin, very pale girl with lank hair, whose name we never discovered, was also there, still sobbing, 'Peter, oh Peter. I'm sorry.'

The atmosphere was super-tense, but as the two policemen who had arrested Peter were not around, and no one else seemed to be in charge of the mêlée, Bob and Iain began asking questions of anyone who would listen. Suddenly, a young officer, his sandy hair and a slight accent telling of his Irish ancestry, burst back into the room. It was the one who had held Peter in the gutter. His face was white with tension and his fist clenched and unclenched above the butt of his cowboy-slung revolver.

'How was I to know she was his girlfriend?' he yelled at us with the defiance of a man accustomed to being challenged. 'Anyway, we think it was him who called the fire brigade out on a false alarm . . . and if it was . . . then he's in big trouble. Right!'

Poor bastards. All of us, I mean; Peter, churning over a broken love affair and going to dinner with us, absolute strangers, by complete coincidence, in the restaurant beneath his ex-girlfriend's apartment; the cop, having learnt from experience to expect the worst from everyone; and us . . . all of us, living in cities which pit person against person like Chinese fighting dogs. Why couldn't we all sit down now, put away our defences; Peter his hurt, the policeman his anger, the girl her tears, and all of us our tension . . . talk it over calmly, accept one's and others' responsibilities and smooth the situation over?

But no, it had gone too far now. And once begun the game must be played to a conclusion. Peter's attorney arrived, having been called away from a late dinner, smartly dressed and smooth talking. We got the impression that this was not the first time he'd been through a scene like this. He sized up the atmosphere, talking first with Peter, then the girl, then the police. Then he turned to us and asked us to leave. 'Your presence here creates more heat than light,' he said.

So, out we went, into the cold and dirty New York streets, feeling suddenly tired and depressed.

'It could only happen in New York,' I said, avoiding the refuse spilling out from an upturned garbage can.

'You won't believe this,' said Fred, who, together with Simone, had remained silent in the precinct office, 'but I've lived in New York all my life and I've never been inside a police station.'

Peter didn't catch his Concorde flight to London and, when we left New York on Monday, he was still in custody.

Leaving New York also proved to be pretty difficult for us. There was a lot to organise. The decision about the car seemed horribly complicated. We had thought that if we bought a car in the States — a good secondhand one — we could drive it down into Mexico and Central America and sell it, and maybe even make a profit, in Panama. But all the information we received indicated we wouldn't be able to sell it legally in Panama and that we'd even have difficulty getting rid of it illegally.

We began to think about using public transport, as we had in Africa and then we remembered 'Autodriveaway', the system widely used in North America for delivering other people's cars from one part of the country to another. Trish and I had actually used it ourselves a couple of times back in the sixties. We checked with the company's New York office to see if they had any cars they wanted delivered to the west coast, and, more particularly, to San Diego, where we hoped to see two long-time friends, Simon and Virginia Casady.

'Sure,' the voice on the other end of the phone said, 'we got a '74 Dodge Dart going out to San Diego. It'll be ready in about three or four days.'

'Have you got a driver yet?' I asked.

'Not yet. You interested?'

'Yes.'

'Okay . . . just come in and sign the papers then.'

The decision had been made for us.

In the meantime, we set about organising everything else. Firstly the equipment we would carry on from San Diego after we had dropped the car. If you're travelling on public transport, carrying your own baggage all the time, then backpacks are easily the best; both hands are free for clambering on and off buses and trains. But most important . . . the kids can carry their own bags.

Obviously it's wise to keep everything light, but we knew that we would be travelling in all sorts of climates, from hot, in the jungles of Mexico, to cold in the high Andes, to hot again on the Amazon, to freezing cold again in southern Patagonia and Tierra del Fuego. We made up our minds to carry mostly lightweight clothes, and to wear them in layers as it got colder . . . no big winter jackets. We would each carry a small, feather-down jacket that could be compressed into a tiny nylon bag so as not to occupy much room in the packs when not being worn. Lightweight, windproof rain jackets, would also come in handy in the rain in temperate climates, but could be worn over the top of the down jackets when it got colder. And things like woollen hats and gloves could be stuffed into the bottom of our packs until we needed them. Jeans, shorts, a light sweater and easily washable shirts and T-shirts made up the rest of the clothes.

As for camping gear, we decided to take good sleeping bags and ground sheets, but not tents. We had read that in most places in Latin America, accommodation is inexpensive and that we would be able to find cheap lodging houses and hotels most of the time. But we knew from past experience that a sleeping bag is often essential in unexpected situations. We would also carry cooking and eating gear for times when food was either not available or too expensive.

We delved for hours through piles of this sort of stuff in the Paragon Sports Store in Lower Manhattan, selecting some and rejecting others to the mounting frustration of the sales assistant. But as he saw the pile of gear we were going to take growing, he slowly became more enthusiastic.

'Planning a camping holiday?' he said at one stage, early in the piece.
'Well, yes . . . sort of,' I replied.
'Where are you going? The New England area?'
'Well . . . no, actually we're going down the Amazon.'
I can remember at the time feeling that it sounded terribly ostentatious.

Sunday, January 15th. Tonight, upwards of 120 million people across the entire country will be riveted to their TVs, watching a duel of the gladiators, one of the great spectacles of the year, with all the colour and excitement of the Coliseum . . . and more . . . Superbowl, when the winning teams of the American and the National football leagues play off.

Bob Judd took us to an apartment in the Village to watch. The owners were friends of his who worked as clowns in New York's One Ring Circus. We were introduced, and there was some friendly chat, only for a few moments though, as this was much too serious a situation for small talk. The game had just begun. There was a table, at arm's length from the chairs, that was laid with cheese and crackers. Cans of Millers High Life and Budweiser were raised silently and seriously to the lips of the group seated around the colour TV. I could envisage this scene repeated in millions of homes across the nation.

On this night it was the unstoppable machine, the most successful team in football, the Dallas Cowboys, versus the up-from-nowhere, doormat of pro football, the Denver Broncos.

There was everything you would expect from such an event, all of the razzmatazz, brass bands, briefly-clad cheer-leaders and roaring crowds . . . 100,000 of them in the Louisiana Superdome in New Orleans, which, from the outside, looks for all the world like a giant UFO.

During the ads, Bob Judd fed us a running commentary on the relevant details: the largest enclosed stadium in the world, the largest roll-up rug (more than 8000 square metres of Astro-turf), the TV ads cost $100,000 for 30 seconds etc., etc. During the game he gave whispered advice on the strategy and significance of various moves which would be lost on us otherwise. Zara played with a cat in the corner.

By half time the Cowboys had a 13 to 0 lead over the Broncos. I went out to get some pastrami on rye and kishka from the local deli and felt great satisfaction when the guy behind the counter asked simply: 'What's the score?' and not only did I know what he was talking about, but could tell him.

Back at the game Denver managed to score 10 points, but the Cowboys notched up another 14 despite quarterback Roger Staubach's injured finger on his throwing hand, to decimate the Broncos 27 to 10. We left Bob and his friends to return to our hotel, feeling as if we had participated in a great American ritual.

Zara is always quick to tell people, 'I am an American', which further confuses people who are trying to sort out our international family. 'I was born in New York,' she says, when the opportunity arises. And so she was, at Roosevelt Hospital on W59th at the end of 1966.

On the ride downtown a strange expression of barely controlled emotion came over her face as we passed the Roosevelt. Why is it that one's actual physical roots are so important?

We spent that day 'doing New York'. Up the Empire State Building because it doesn't matter that it isn't the world's tallest building any more, it's still the Empire State Building. To the top of the World Trade Centre because it also held the record briefly. Here, with a half dozen other mid-winter visitors we could ignore the cordoned-off routes, mapped out to control the mid-summer hordes, to stare out into the dense cloud which completely obscured the view.

Then across on the Staten Island Ferry, in the bitter wind, to climb up inside the equally empty Statue of Liberty. There's something slightly obscene about clambering up inside this gargantuan lady's thigh and through the folds of her metallic robe. Is it slightly more acceptable because you know that she is a French mademoiselle, a present from the people of France, and not a liberated American chairperson?

Thank God her arm and flaming torch are closed now because of possible physical danger to those who insist on going as far as they can get with a lady. I was quite breathless enough with claustrophobia by the time we had made it through her head to peer down from the windows in her crown.

'Give me your tired, your poor, your hungry, your struggling masses yearning to breathe free.' She must have been a stirring first sight of this promised land for all those thousands of early immigrants who sailed in from Europe under her upraised arm to New York harbour. Today the skyscrapers of Manhattan look like a backdrop for a Neil Simon play.

We travelled back up to our hotel on the subway, the trains spray-painted, while standing idle at weekends, with a mixture of garish, mad designs and obscenities.

The carriages were scruffy and littered with discarded newspapers and fast-food cartons. The directions on how to use the system were so complicated they were virtually impossible for a visitor to follow. And those New Yorkers we asked for help reacted with a curtness which bordered on being rude. Probably they were so accustomed to being on their guard against the anticipated and invariable rudeness of others that they have adopted this manner as a defence. Get in there first and put down before being put down.

In travelling a long distance, from point A to point B, it seems to me that, inevitably, the journey is punctuated by a number of 'jumping off' places where you gather yourself together and organise yourself for the next hop. Looking back now on the trip across the United States it is understandably remembered as more comfortable and civilised than our later travels in Central and South America. But at the beginning of that trip, New York City still seemed to us to be a jumping off place from where we would be heading out into the blue. The fact that New York City was probably a far more dangerous place to be than almost any of the other places we planned to visit, didn't really seem to be a relevant point at the time.

On our last night in New York we stood in the wind and snow waiting in a long queue to see the movie, 'Close Encounters'. Both Sean and Zara loved it and so did we and we had long discussions afterwards as we walked back down Sixth Avenue towards the hotel on the possibility of life in other worlds.

After putting the children to bed, Trish and I went out for a cup of coffee and to take in some of the sights around Times Square and 42nd Street, which were within a few blocks of our hotel.

Despite the sleazy aspects of 42nd Street, the area has always been fascinating to me. The lights, the movement, the activity, the big, first-run movie houses, the Broadway theatres, the drunks, addicts, prostitutes, pimps, misfits . . . side-by-side (almost) with ermine-clad ladies and dinner-suited men, stepping from large chauffeur-driven limos to attend a first night.

As we wandered along 42nd Street past long-running classics like 'Deep Throat' and 'The Devil in Miss Jones', porno peep shows and strip clubs proclaiming 'Live Sex on Stage', a sad-looking man in a drab grey suit walked past in the opposite direction, with a fully-grown llama on a lead! We turned and stared in disbelief, then shook our heads and continued walking. Nobody else seemed in the least surprised . . . just part of the New York scene. Does he keep the animal in his apartment with him? Is he going to shear the wool and sell it? Is it perhaps part of some commercial promotion? We will never know.

We started to head back towards our hotel and then, feeling that there may be some aspect of life, or of our sex education that had been missed and that we might not be in New York again for some time, we stepped up, slightly sheepishly, to one of the 'live show' theatres.

'Sorry sir,' the middle-aged lady at the box office said, 'no mixed shows on at the moment.'

'Pardon?'

'No male and female acts tonight.'

'Why not?' slight disappointment on our part.

'Police orders. Vice squad.'

'You mean everywhere . . . all of the theatres around here?'

'That's right. No mixed sex. But we've got the ordinary strip show . . . and of course the films.'

'No thanks,' I muttered, slightly embarrassed. Having made up our minds to see the show, we now felt somewhat cheated. All or nothing at all, we decided. We had a cup of coffee in a nearby diner and walked home to bed.

Next day, I spent almost the whole morning going through the process of picking up the car we were to drive across country; first at the office of the Autodriveaway company, then out in the Bronx where the car was in a garage being serviced. But, once I had ploughed through all of the formalities, there I was sitting behind the wheel of a jazzy looking chocolate-brown Dodge Dart, with a golden stripe down its side, almost ready to drive some 4800 kilometres across the country.

By mid-afternoon we had checked out of our hotel, loaded our luggage, including the new backpacks, into the trunk of the car and we were off through the Lincoln Tunnel, looking for the New Jersey Turnpike. Shortly after, the car radio began issuing storm warnings. The eastern states, the weatherman was saying, were in for a real blizzard; at least ten centimetres of snow predicted for that night. By the time we reached the connection with the Pennsylvania Turnpike, on our way to Philadelphia, it was already snowing heavily.

USA

2
Across a continent

We woke on Benjamin Franklin's birthday to find Philadelphia buried under several centimetres of snow which muffled the city noises and gave the red brick colonial buildings the final touch of statuesque beauty.

The Liberty Bell had moved home since last we saw it, to a new, more open setting, so as to accommodate the bigger than normal crowds who came in 1976 to view the birthplace of the United States during her Bicentennial Year.

'Proclaim Liberty Throughout All the Land Unto All the Inhabitants Thereof.' We read aloud to the children the words from Leviticus inscribed round the rim of the large bell which was rung on the first reading of the Declaration of Independence on July 8th 1776. But the bell, which cracked fifty-nine years later, was of less interest to them than the guard who patrolled the area. On finding we were Australian, he reminisced about his war service in Brisbane and Melbourne, where, by his own account, he quaffed large quantities of Ballarat Bitter.

Another guide, who took the small band of us who had braved the winter storm on a tour around Independence Hall, excited Sean's imagination by pointing out a room in which the British had maltreated American officers.

This was the sort of history he, and Zara, were interested in and they listened closely, beginning for the first time to consciously realise that America had been a colony of Britain; that they had fought and won a War of Independence against the British.

That this country, which they have known through a process of cultural and social osmosis, ever since they were old enough to think, as the wealthiest and most powerful country in the world, could ever have been a mere colony, was an idea which they at first found difficult to fully grasp.

For a very long time a child's view of history is limited by its own date of birth! That was when the world began! As America was rich and strong, and independent then, it must always have been so. As they listened to the guide explain the First and Second Continental Congresses, talk about the original thirteen states in the Union, and tell how the people cheered when Thomas Jefferson's Declaration of Independence was first read in Independence Square, they began to make more shape from the tangible evidence they saw about them.

One of the most exciting things in the world is to watch a child grappling with a whole new concept.

The only drawback in driving someone else's car across the United States under this delivery scheme is the time factor. In every other way it's a good deal. You get comfortable, independent transportation for a very low price; the only cost is the gasoline. But, under the terms of the contract, we were given only eight days to get to San Diego, a distance of some 4800 kilometres. We could probably stretch it out to ten, we felt, because of the bad weather, but any longer would mean that the company would take a slice, or all of the $100 deposit we had left with them. Then, we thought, perhaps it might be worth it, just so we could take the extra time if we needed it. We'd see how things worked out.

In the meantime, we kept moving . . . seeing and doing as much as possible, but not wasting any time. From Philadelphia we set off on Route 95 towards Baltimore and Washington in blinding snow, but fortunately, because of the heavy traffic on the freeway, the snow wasn't settling on the road surface, only on the drifts at the edges. Driving under these conditions, though, was more of a chore than a pleasure as it was necessary to be constantly alert.

As we arrived in Washington, the snow turned to rain and the roads became a mass of brown slush. We spent half an hour or so finding a relatively cheap hotel and then, as a result of Sean's urging, went out again into the pouring rain to find a hamburger joint. Sean had become obsessed with hamburgers and the American way of eating. He applied insidious pressures on us all when the subject of meals arose, which it does with monotonous regularity at certain times every day.

'I saw a terrific restaurant (invariably a 'Burger King', 'McDonalds' or 'Hardees') just back there,' he'd say. Or, 'Can't we have hamburgers just once more?' etc., etc.

The problem is that you are constantly tempted to give in, because hamburgers are so easy, but we resolved that this tendency to become fast-food freaks was to be carefully watched; the effect on the shape of American bodies was to be seen all around.

The next morning, with the air crisp, clean and cold, we charged out into Washington with a list of things to do a mile long. First the National Geographic Headquarters on 17th Street to look through some back issues of the magazine for some material on the Amazon and Brazilian Indians. But when we arrived there, we discovered 'Explorers' Hall', the whole ground floor of the building given over to a superb exhibition, complete with models, charts, photographs and artifacts depicting the great endeavours, expeditions and adventures of the 20th century.

Sean and Zara were immediately entranced and, after rapidly completing a survey circuit of the exhibits, began plying us with, 'Dad, come and see this,' or 'Mum, you should see what they've got around here.'

One of the things they had 'around here' was a separate exhibition called 'Objects of Fantasy' . . . a collection of intricately fashioned pieces of jewellery from Tsarist Russia; priceless treasures designed by the master craftsman Carl Fabergé; golden Easter eggs, encrusted with diamonds, emeralds, rubies and pearls, which, when opened, revealed miniature photographs or paintings of the Tsar's family or of various noble families.

'Why don't they make things like this now?' Zara asked. And we talked a bit about how times have changed. Not only in Russia where these things came from, but in the rest of the world. I suppose the very wealthy still give expensive gifts ... like Richard Burton's million dollar diamond to Liz Taylor, but there's nothing quite like the Tsar's eggs, which were given every Easter for over thirty years until the time of the revolution.

They were fascinating and beautiful objects, but somehow, you can't help thinking of the moral aspects they raise; the immense wealth needed to commission them, versus the grinding poverty of the country as a whole at that time. It was the kind of situation we were to recognise often as we later made our way down into Central and South America.

Next on our list was the Washington Monument, surrounded by broad, open vistas of snow-covered lawns glistening in the morning sunlight. The Stars and Stripes fluttering from the ring of flagpoles around the base of the huge obelisk were all at half-mast for 'the happy warrior', Hubert Humphrey, the one-time presidential candidate who had died a few days previously.

Inside, as we took the elevator to the top of the monument, the operator, in National Parks uniform, filled in the details; the number of building blocks used, the height of the tower: 'Exactly 555 feet, five and one eighth inches,' he proclaimed. 'It was begun in 1841 and not completed and opened to the public until 1885.'

Forty-four years. Not long really; a little more than my own age, but what a forty-four years for the United States! At the time work on the monument to the nation's first president began, there were twenty-six states in the Union. By the time it was completed, there were thirty-eight. And in that brief, dramatic period America opened up the west, experienced a massive expansion of the railroad system, saw the development and introduction across the country of the telegraph, and fought a war with Mexico. The great Californian Gold Rush flourished and died, the Civil War burst across the pages of American history and in the year of its ending, one of America's greatest presidents, Lincoln, was assassinated. The middle years of the nineteenth century also brought the growth of the factory system and of labour unions in the United States. With this came the simultaneous emergence of the mighty business tycoons and the rapid development of the nation as a great industrial power.

Standing at the top of the Washington Monument on that cold, wintry day, looking out over a capital mantled in snow, it was difficult not to feel a sense of history. It was all there, laid out beneath us. The Jefferson Memorial, the Lincoln Memorial, the Pentagon, Arlington National Cemetery, the Capitol ... and the White House.

'Please Mr President help us! Our fiancées are being held, against their wishes, in Poland. They want to join us here. The Polish government won't allow them to leave. If you asked for them, they could not refuse. We are American citizens. Please Mr President help us to get back our fiancées. Signed, in the name of love.'

The two young men, heavily muffled against the freezing cold, walked up and down in front of the White House. Their declarations of love and belief in the freedom and power of the United States and its President, chalked up for all to see on boards hanging from their necks. We gave them smiles of encouragement.

Further along an elderly man was reaching through the iron railings to feed the half dozen or so grey squirrels who had made tracks through the deep snow in the White House garden. From the nearest trees to the railings and back again, they went with that curious epileptic gait, clutching the titbits he passed them.

'I come every day in winter,' he told us proudly.

At the other end of the garden, heedless of the temperature, was a very ordinary looking man in an open-necked shirt sitting on a pile of cardboard, from which, every now and then, he took another piece and tied it with bits of multi-coloured string alongside the ones already fixed to the railings behind him.

JFK is Not DeAD! AciA-PLoT!! HANoi KNows HoW iz it ThAt HooVER WaS ThERE ??? AnD ThE OTHER OnE?? No!! WhEN WiLL RussiA TeLL? Azk ThEM! Azk THEM !!   FRee FoReVER !

Each of the ten or so placards bore a similar scrambled message written in an amalgam of blue and red crayon with underlinings, reversed letters, unfinished words, crossings through and perverse spelling.

Zara and Sean were fascinated. Who was this man who could write like a child and get away with it? They wanted to study each placard carefully exclaiming and pointing, totally unabashed, while my adult embarrassment forced me to hurry them away.

'Is he crazy?' Zara asked hopefully.

'No, no,' I answered too quickly.

The only evidence of any official concern that all this was happening within a bomb's throw of the President's home was a solitary patrol car on the far side of Pennsylvania Avenue.

Outside the Capitol matters were a little less casual. Over a thousand farmers were gathered there to demand more support from the government in the form of subsidies. They had travelled, many of them for over three thousand kilometres, and were camping there in farm vehicles, trailer homes, and campervans which were daubed with far more precise and punchy slogans. 'Crime Pays. Farming Doesn't', 'Fair Deal and We'll Grow Your Meal'. There were a lot of personal snipes at peanut-farmer Jimmy Carter.

The demonstrators, mostly men, wore boots and dungaree coveralls, heavy plaid jackets and woollen beanies with ear-muffs. They talked in southern and mid-western accents, chewed gum and loped over the tarmac with the unmis-takable strides of men accustomed to wider landscapes.

There was a lot of good-natured chaffing, but under the holiday atmosphere a definite feeling that they were here on business. Their vehicles choked the entrance to the Capitol and when the police, who were much in evidence, tried to prevent more from joining the jam there was a fury of horns and raised voices.

By contrast the Lincoln Memorial was silent and very impressive.

I whispered to the children the beginning of the passage from Lincoln's most famous speech which is inscribed on the high walls of the colonnaded hall around his statue: 'Four score and seven years ago our fathers brought forth on this continent a new nation, conceived in liberty and dedicated to the proposition that all men are created equal.' They caught the infectious awe in the architectural magnificence and whispered back their demand: 'Read it all.' So we crossed in front of the seated Lincoln staring out forever toward the capital of the nation he presided over and spoke aloud the words he wrote so long ago.

'He freed the slaves,' Zara said.

'Like it showed on "Roots",' Sean added.

'He was a good man,' Zara declared.

'So why did they shoot him?' Sean asked.

'I did my best to explain and they asked no more questions. Children are far more accepting of senseless death than adults. Perhaps because they haven't yet learnt the pretence of trying to make sense from life.

When we walked away down the broad flight of steps in distant sight of the Washington Monument I was struck by the grand scale on which the original architects and designers of the capital thought and planned.

It was started at the beginning of the nineteenth century when the nation as such was only forty years old and still very much a struggling infant. Yet they had such bold belief in its future that they built a capital on this impressive scale.

As a child, growing up in a cramped Europe recovering from the war, it was fashionable to knock the Americans. Along with my contemporaries I was filled with the sort of unrecognised envy which causes us to deride its wealth and power as brash and empty. I didn't even want to visit the country and as for having an American daughter! Horror! In retrospect I am ashamed of such mean spiritedness and very glad that through living and travelling in the United States I've overcome my ignorant prejudices.

Like all societies the American way of life has a great many faults. But they are faults based on a surplus of enthusiasm and vitality, on an over-abundance of heart. They are errors on the positive, rather than the negative balance.

By mid-afternoon we were on our way again on a hundred kilometre drive to and into the Shenandoah National Park, which took us through some of the most beautiful scenery we have ever seen. We followed Route 211 west from Washington and, although the road was dangerously icy, we found ourselves captivated by the wonderland through which we were driving. The combination of snow, followed by rain, then by a new freeze, had covered the forest and the shrubs and trees along the road in ice, and they appeared like trees made of glistening glass. With the winter sun, low behind them, they provided a setting of great beauty.

We drove into the forestland of Shenandoah, intending to follow the narrow and winding 'Skyline Drive' down along the ridge of mountains for about eighty kilometres and to find a place to sleep once we left the park. We noticed with vague feelings of unease that we were in the only vehicle on the forest road, which was edged on both sides with high snowdrifts. Then, after only thirty kilometres, we came to a barrier across the road with a sign on it. Heavy drifts and bad conditions had forced the road to be closed further on down the Skyline Drive. So, after considerable cursing, we turned back again, to make our way through the gathering darkness to the park entrance, then west and onto the freeway . . . Highway 81, for a terrifying drive on icy roads.

It was terrifying, not so much because of the road itself, but because of the trucks that were sharing it with us. There seemed to be a profusion of them and there is nothing like a giant eighteen-wheeler barrelling past you at 125 kph on glass-slick roads to scare the hell out of you. Even the wind blast can push you into a slide, if you're not careful. After an hour of it, we gave up and pulled into a small hotel at Natural Bridge.

Man: 'Let's take a trip to Spain.'

Woman: 'Your trip will be much more enjoyable when you can meet people and make yourself understood.'

Man: 'Listen to this recording and repeat what you hear. Listen, then repeat. Are you ready to travel with Berlitz?'

Woman: 'Yes . . . Si.'

Man: 'No . . . No.'

The tape droned on for twenty minutes or so with all of us dutifully repeating the words. Then we turned it over and continued. We were listening to 'Teach yourself Spanish' for the first time as on the following morning we drove down Highway 81 through more falling snow. We felt that, as we knew practically no Spanish, a start had to be made somewhere. But this definitely wasn't it. We all found the tape absolutely boring. Whether it was the presentation or the fact that we hadn't actually arrived in a Spanish-speaking country yet, I'm not sure, but we switched the tape off and just listened to the radio.

The network news was full of the snow-storm that had hit New York. It had started just as we left and had become, according to the reports, the biggest in ten years. Over forty-five centimetres had been dropped on the city, bringing it to a grinding halt. Virginia and all of Tennessee had averaged about fifteen to twenty centimetres and it was still coming down.

The disc jockey we were tuned to was broadcasting from St Paul, Virginia:

'Well, with awl thes kinda weather fallen awl ova cree-ay-shun, ah wanna play a reckud fo ole Paul Ledford who's tooned in thes mawnin out thar on a tractor, sorta gettin people outa the ditch-lines 'n everthin . . . so heeers Kenny Dale wuth a bran noo release: 'scalled Raid Hot Memories . . .'

We crossed the border into Tennessee at Bristol, stopping for a sentimental lunch for Trish, who hails from the original Bristol, several thousand miles across the Atlantic. But Bristol, Virginia/Tennessee unfortunately was also a bit of bad luck for us. Sean lost his camera there and we didn't discover it was missing until we were many kilometres further along the road. We decided not to turn back though, and continued along Route 40 heading for Nashville.

We had to stick to the freeway even though, on many occasions, we were tempted to try the smaller roads that ran generally parallel to the main highway. They were now either in a terrible condition or completely impassable because of the snow. Even the freeway was a nightmare. We would drift and slide at the smallest movement and the snow was now being driven by a strong wind. Several times we saw trucks and cars that had slithered off the road. By nightfall we were way behind our schedule. We had hoped to reach Nashville, but conditions had become so bad, with the freeway virtually deserted, that we left it about sixty kilometres before Nashville, slipping and sliding for about eight kilometres to a small hotel at Carthage, where we staggered to bed and watched President Carter's State of the Union Address. (It was on all channels, much to the children's annoyance.) He spoke of Atom Test Bans, twenty-five billion dollar tax cuts and the Panama Canal . . . all of which sounded infinitely remote from the vantage point of Carthage, Tennessee.

Sparta. Smyrna. Manchester. Lebanon. The directions for turnoffs formed up out of the swirling snow and were lost behind us. Where were we? In some composite land grafted together from a hotch-potch of foreign soil? Was this really Route 40 slithering icily west and a little southwards through Tennessee?

Occasionally we saw, mistily through the whiteness, a huge semi-trailer creeping along in the other direction. Just as rarely, but more frighteningly, one of these giants passed us, and we held our breaths. And again more stranded trucks, like still-born monsters, marooned or overturned off to the side.

The founding fathers having run quickly through Europe (Paris and Milan were up ahead), abandoned altogether any attempt at imagination and now every town became a ville. Tompkinsville, Hendersonville, Shelbyville, Russelville, Scottsville, Fayetteville and now, the pits, Centersville. The only redemption lay, or so I thought, in Soddy Daisy, south of the Tennessee River.

We slithered through Nashville, billed, would you believe it, as the Athens of the South; the State Capitol Building being an exact replica of the Parthenon in Athens.

We drove past the new 4400 seat Grand Ole Opry House, home of the country music from which this town spins itself an incredible $300 million a year.

A few kilometres outside the town we stopped, along with the snow for a while, at Belle Mead, a southern plantation home now kept as a museum. It is closed during the deepest winter months, but to us it seemed at its most beautiful under deep snow.

I really didn't expect Rhett Butler to appear around the corner in all his sartorial elegance and sweep me off my feet, dressed as I was in boots, jeans, woollen beanie and big Korean-made anorak! Still, you know, all women have these fantasies and I couldn't help feeling a little of the Scarlett O'Hara in me as I ascended the wide front steps!

We pressed our cold noses at the window, oohing and aahing like deprived children over the period furnishings.

Two hundred and forty kilometres further on, we stopped again, this time to visit the actual home of that all-weather, all-American hero, Casey Jones, who drove his engine number 382 to legend land. In the early 1900s he worked the Cannonball Express along the Illinois Central line, covering the three hundred kilometre stretch between Memphis and Canton, Mississippi in his McQueen locomotive.

Casey became so famous for keeping time on the eighty kph schedule that they say people set their watches by the wail of his whistle. It was this pride in efficiency and punctuality which drove him into trying to make up a lost ninety-five minutes on a trip which he had voluntarily taken over from a sick colleague. With bursts of up to 160 kph he was only two minutes behind time and twenty-two kilometres from the end of the run when he swept round a curve and saw the red lights of a freight train caboose on the rail ahead.

Shouting to his fireman to jump and sounding his whippoorwill whistle in warning, he managed to slow the express down to sixty kph. They say the crash was heard many kilometres away and that Casey, the only person killed in the collision, was found with an iron bolt through his neck.

Chief among the bric-a-brac which crams Casey's tiny wooden house is his watch and an exact replica, made by Casey's son Charlie, of the old whippoorwill whistle Casey was blowing at the time of the wreck. Out back, for the steam freaks, is a McQueen locomotive, numbered 382.

From the home of one hero to that of another. In Memphis we squirmed with embarrassment as we asked for directions to Elvis Presley Boulevard.

'For the children,' I smiled and explained weakly to a fellow who looked as though he'd just finished a day's work in an insurance office. He told us the way and as I was thanking him, Zara wound down the back window, 'It's really Mum who wants to go,' she smiled sweetly.

If at some distant future date someone should want, for some remote reason, to name a street after me I think I would ask to see it first. Quite unlike what we had expected, Elvis Presley Boulevard is lined with automobile sales yards, adorned in the tasteless style at which they excel, and fast-food joints, whose décor exhibits only a slight improvement. Even the softening layer of snow couldn't conceal the sort of ugliness which typifies the worst form of urban development.

'ELVIS . . . OFFICIAL SOUVENIRS,' a flashing neon sign proclaimed. 'FREE'. Despite our cynical protestations that nothing comes free, the children insisted on making sure.

'You'll be sorry if they are giving away something, because you'll miss out,' Zara stated baldly and accurately. But even she was disgusted when they returned to the car a couple of minutes later with only a photostat copy of the marriage certificate of Elvis Aaron Presley and Priscilla Ann Beaulieu to show for their trouble.

Opposite, Graceland Mansion, up on a slight rise, was securely one hundred metres or so behind a high stone wall. Next to the gates, fashioned with wrought iron treble clefs and notes, was a guard box. Empty. The house wasn't empty though; at least there were lights on.

In the early twilight we read some of the hundreds of messages which completely covered the wall: 'Elvis we love you.' 'Gone, but not forgotten.' 'We shall meet again beyond the Pearly Gates.' 'The King is Dead.'

And so he is, the poor bastard. Destroyed by becoming a living legend, a sex idol, a phenomenon, a money-making machine, a magic factory who turned the last trick on himself. It's difficult to believe even now that the boy who gyrated his way into so many hearts was found dead on his bathroom floor. Alone.

The Malmar Hotel at Brinkley, Arkansas, about 120 kilometres on from Memphis, is an old, wooden building with a pool table in the front hall and a large, railway-style cafe through a door to one side. When we came in out of the snow, at the end of that day's driving, a few middle-aged men were sitting at a table in the centre of the cafe, talking and drinking cans of Pabst beer. A couple of teenagers hovered over an ancient juke-box, trying to decide what to play.

'Where ya'll headin?' the black woman who served our meal asked with a big smile. She was about sixty, plump and friendly.

'San Diego,' Trish replied.

'Well, I declare,' the woman exclaimed in surprise. 'Four of my boys are out there.' She pulled up a chair beside us.

She had, so we quickly learnt, eleven children . . . all of them already grown up. Seven had stayed in the Brinkley area, but the others had headed west. 'There's better jobs and pay out there,' she said. 'They all workin' as inspectors at the Sanyo plant there.'

'Will they stay out there, do you think?' I asked.

'I don't know. The youngest one, he says he's savin' to come home to Arkansas. It's just great when we all gets together, y'know. I got twenty-seven grandchildren and when we're all together . . . well! Don't we have real fun!'

It was not long since we had watched the 'Roots' programme on television, so we asked her what she had thought of it. She paused . . . only for a moment. The children leant forward.

'Good . . . good,' she said. 'We've always been very close family people . . . and though it was a mighty sad story, it was true and, well, it kinda made us proud. Proud of our history, proud to be black.'

When I was down in Louisiana . . .

just about a mile from Texarkana . . .

Well, that's how the song goes, but if you check the map, it would be pretty difficult to be in Louisiana and to be just about a mile from Texarkana, at the same time. Still, I suppose songwriters have to have some creative licence, otherwise . . . well, the song wouldn't be the same, would it?

And songs are one of the really nice things about travelling through the US. Almost everywhere you go, there's a popular song about the place . . . every town and city. Just on the route we'd been following over the last couple of days: Nashville, Memphis, Little Rock, Texarkana. And now we were heading into Texas where, believe it or not the car radio played for our entry, *'the stars at night are big and bright, deep in the heart of Texas!'*

A few minutes later, while twiddling the dial, we came across a hell-fire and brimstone evangelist preaching death and destruction for us all unless . . .

'. . . unless each and every one of you listen to and accept the word of God. Yes, my brethren, God only wants you to reach out to him . . . and he will reach out to you. Yes, even *you*, and hold you and protect you for ever. Believe me, my friends, Yaweh is just as alive and as real a God as he was in the days of Moses . . . and . . . since the dawn of creation. So now, before I say goodnight to you all until next week, let me tell you of a very special offer that will help you to find true faith in God. If you will just write to me, the Rev. Wayne Beaumont, care of this station, KZQT, Greenville, Texas, I will send you, absolutely free, with no obligation, a "Miracle Message Faith Handkerchief". Remember, send no money my friends. This is an absolutely genuine offer . . . a "Miracle Message Faith Handkerchief" will . . .'

THE PRESIDENT IS DEAD. Is there anyone over thirty who doesn't remember where they were, what they were doing and how they felt when they first heard that John Kennedy had been shot? I doubt it.

I remember it as vividly as everyone else, marooned as I was on a P & O liner, sailing to a new job in Hong Kong, listening to this unbelievable news coming, as if from another planet, over the vessel's loudspeaker system.

Right at that moment, even without the benefit of hindsight, I think people realised that his death was a turning point. No more fair Camelot, now for harsher and less readily definable realities.

We found the Kennedy Museum in downtown Dallas almost by instinct. The news photographs of the area had so impressed it on our minds, it was as though we had been there before.

It's impossible not to see the landmark on top of the Texas School Book Depository Building; the big Hertz Rent-a-Car sign which the company is trying, despite strong public opposition, to take down. Perhaps the Hertz people feel that it's bad publicity but others say it's part of history. Later, inside the museum, we were asked to sign a petition against its removal.

We drove down Elm Street, along the fatal Presidential route, to Dealy Plaza, recognisable even in the snow. There was the ramp down under the fly-over toward the Stemmons Freeway. And there was that little grassy knoll from which Emil Zapruder shot that incredible roll of 8 mm film.

Inside the museum, visitors silently filed past the glass-fronted exhibition cases, reliving again the pleasure and pain in the story of one man who encapsulated so much of the American dream; the idyllic childhood, the fairytale romance, the struggle to the top, the brief power and glory and then, the terrible death. All of it pressed into newsprint. Captured on celluloid. Jackie spattered with her husband's blood. Three year old John-John saluting at his father's funeral.

Our children, sensitive to the atmosphere, were subdued and impressed.

'But who was he?' Sean asked, and one realised with a jolt how quickly the present becomes the past and how inexorably life rolls forward. And again the same questions about why.

There were the photographs of Oswald and Ruby too, which raised more questions not only from the children but from a large number of Americans who remain unconvinced that the Warren Commission and the more recent Congressional inquiry, saw all relevant evidence and witnesses or even examined carefully enough what it did see. In every one of the years since John Kennedy was shot new theories have been published on his death.

Violence, it has been said, is as American as cherry pie. But violence is not an American preserve. Many of the countries we travel through in this book are far more violent.

But it wasn't only just the inescapable atmosphere of violence in the Kennedy Museum which depressed me. After all, if Oswald planned and executed the assassination by himself, it was the act of a solitary madman; if there was a conspiracy involving the CIA, FBI or even foreign powers, all of which has been suggested, then it was the act of a group of madmen.

No. That wasn't it. What depressed me was that I felt so overwhelmed by the reinforcement of the knowledge of an individual's total vulnerability and lack of control in the face of such ungovernable madness.

Outside, the weather matched my mood. It had stopped snowing but conditions on the early morning drive into Dallas had been, if possible, worse than any with which we had coped so far. Weather like this, heavy snowfalls and ice, is so unusual this far south, that Dallas was not properly equipped and had insufficient numbers of snow ploughs or quantities of grit and salt for the roads.

The museum had left us all quiet and thoughtful as we headed west, but by the time we reached Abilene, our spirits had lifted because we had actually begun to leave the snow behind. When we turned south onto Route 277 to San Angelo there was even some blue sky and we could see naked trees and raw earth.

The road stretched ahead, straight and empty, and the land opened up like in a western. This was the Texas where they say men walked taller, and we could believe it.

In the middle of the last century, after Texas had joined the Union and the fruits of the Mexican War had added to the United States a vast territory comprising the present states of New Mexico, Arizona and California, the 'Wild West' really was wild. It was a hostile land, ruled by Indians and there were literally tens of thousands of square kilometres of country that were completely unexplored by white men.

But, when word of the discovery of gold in California burst on America in 1849, thousands of immigrants began flowing west to seek their fortunes in the gold-fields and many of them, hoping to avoid the rugged mountains and the winter snows of the more northerly routes across the country, followed the primitive tracks that wound their way across the savannah grasslands and semi-desert plains of southern Texas.

This huge, open land, through which the southern road into El Paso ran, had been, before the coming of the white man, the exclusive preserve of the Apache and Comanche Indians. Inevitably, as the wagon and stagecoach traffic began to increase, so did the Indian raids on small farms and the attacks on travellers in southern Texas.

In the 1850s, the attacks had grown to such alarming proportions that the authorities in San Antonio decided that it was necessary to build a chain of forts in West Texas. One of the most famous of these forts was established at the junction of the North and South Concho Rivers and called Fort Concho, from which the legendary 'Pecos Bill' forayed out on expeditions into unknown lands and against the Plains Indians.

Fort Concho is today just a small part of downtown San Angelo, where we spent one night on our way southwest across Texas. But the Fort buildings are preserved as a national historical landmark; a total of twenty of them remain to recreate some of the flavour and character of the Old West as it existed over a hundred years ago.

We were the only tourists to wander through the barracks and the old Headquarters Building that cold January morning and I remember stepping through a doorway into the reconstructed office of the Fort Commander to find Sean, who had gone through the room ahead of us, wearing a cavalry hat he had taken from the head of one of the models in the room and wielding a sword he had taken from its scabbard.

'Sean!' I exclaimed crossly . . . but as quietly as possible, hoping the woman at the front door wouldn't hear and come into the room . . . 'for God's sake . . . put those things back on . . .'

'Oh come on,' Trish said. 'Don't be a spoil-sport. Take a picture of him.'
Well, what else could I do? No one wants to be a spoil-sport.

One of the more interesting aspects of Fort Concho's history and that of another fort, Fort Davis, some 400 kilometres further west, which we visited later in the day, is that they were garrisoned for much of their operational life by black troops serving under white officers. Both Concho and Fort Davis were, at different times, home to the black troops of the 9th and 10th Cavalry Regiments and the 24th and 25th Infantry Regiments. 'The Buffalo Soldiers', as they became known, apparently earned a remarkable record as Indian-fighters and scouts.

The country through which they roamed over a century ago and across which we travelled during that day, is fabulous. Well, it was for me anyway, because I like wide, open spaces. And this was real Wild West country; open plains, low sierras and flat-topped mesas in the blue distance, an occasional tall cactus and, at last, no snow and an absolutely clear sky.

But travelling fast, in the heated comfort of a '74 Dodge Dart, is a far cry from wagon-training it across those flat, dry lands and it takes a considerable mental leap to try to imagine what it was all like in those mid-nineteenth century days.

We found Fort Davis, when we arrived there, more impressive than Fort Concho, mainly, I think, because it wasn't in the middle of a present-day town. There were no modern buildings nearby and it looked just as isolated as it was when it was originally built.

The buildings already preserved and being restored by the National Parks Service of the Department of the Interior were the officers' married quarters and the enlisted men's barracks; beautiful stone buildings on either side of a huge parade ground at the mouth of a steeply-walled canyon. As in Fort Concho, there was a museum in one of the buildings crammed full of memorabilia, photographs, uniforms and the history of the fort.

We walked from the museum out on to the parade ground (once again, because of the cold weather, we were the only visitors) and suddenly an officer's voice boomed out an order. We stopped in amazement to listen, as invisible troops responded with the slap of hands against rifle butts and the crunch of boots on gravel. A recorded tape was flooding the parade ground with the ghostly sounds of marching feet and blowing bugles. It was eerie and hard to believe that hundreds of men once moved in unison to sounds like this on what was now just a deserted and lonely piece of ground.

And yet, in the officers' quarters, along one side, the picture came more easily; the cavalry captain standing out on his small verandah in the cool of the evening. Leaning against the post, smoking his long pipe, he is relaxing at the end of a long day, but still wearing his high riding boots and those blue pants with the broad, yellow stripe down the sides. His small, neat wife, in her high-necked bustle dress, is sitting beside him in a rocking chair, doing her stitching as they both gaze quietly out across the parade ground into the absolutely empty plains beyond.

The loneliness and isolation of the fort in those days must have been almost overwhelming for those who lived there. All those people; officers, wives, troops

... even the Indians, who probably looked down from the canyon walls ... all gone. And yet, somehow, because Fort Davis has been preserved in the way it has ... they're still there.

What's in a name? or, a rose by any other name would smell as sweet. Well, would it? I'm not so sure. All I do know is that we came as close as it is possible in the United States to getting lost, next morning, by driving off onto dirt roads to find FINLAY, Texas. There it was on our map, albeit in very small lettering. But all we could find was a criss-cross of tiny dirt tracks, until, after over an hour of scurrying backwards and forwards on this immense landscape, trying to keep track of our position in relation to the looming peak also named after our driver, we discovered a single, fairly beaten-up, wooden, one-storey house alongside the rail road track.

We all dutifully braved the cold wind to walk about the deserted yard. There were some coveralls blowing about on the wash-line and a child's battered red tricycle, which gave evidence of occupation. We even peered through the windows at the frozen scene of domestic chaos. But the residents of Finlay, Texas, had obviously left town for the day.

The children joshed Iain about having a not-even-one-horse town named after him. But he replied that it was far more his scene than Elvis Presley Boulevard and we all agreed.

After considerable difficulty travelling along a great many false trails, we managed to rejoin Route 10 and drove on through beautiful cottonwood country, past commercial groves of pecan-nut trees and into El Paso.

Here, we pulled off the freeway for what must surely rate as one of the most compelling views in the whole of the United States. Suburban America came down a slight hill and up to the freeway which ran along one edge of the Rio Grande River. The affluent homes were well maintained, and prosperous looking. We knew that inside these homes lived small numbers of healthy, well-fed, well-educated people for whom life's possibilities were virtually limitless.

Standing, almost on the doorsteps of these houses, we looked at the freeway, along which large American cars and trucks travelled in relative safety and comfort, and then over that and across the Rio Grande to the matching rise on the other side. There we could see the unkempt rickety wooden shacks of Ciudad Juarez, Mexico. Men were riding on donkeys or pushing heavily-laden hand-carts. Scores of obviously poor children played tag between the shanties. Because we couldn't hear their voices above the roar of the vehicles whizzing heedlessly by on this side, it was a bit like watching a silent movie of the population explosion.

We knew that by comparison to the kids on this side of the river, life's possibilities for those children were very limited. Mexico already has a population larger than any other country in Latin America except Brazil and, by the time these children, from the present population of sixty-four million, grew up, they would be competing with twice that number for employment and living space.

No doubt many of those in Ciudad Juarez would try to join the hundreds of thousands who cross the border as illegal immigrants to the United States. Naturally, no one has exact figures of how many succeed, only of those who are apprehended or turned back. In the late seventies that was a staggering one million people a year!

This contrast between El Paso and Ciudad Juarez is a sharp reminder of how wide the gap is, not only between the US and Mexico, but also between other affluent nations and those underdeveloped countries which are struggling merely to keep their equilibrium. The only physical barrier between us and them was a high metal link fence and the river. But the economic and cultural barrier involved a quantum leap.

After El Paso, Route 10 pushes north to Las Cruces before turning west again, leaving a comfortable and discreet distance of eighty kilometres between us and the Mexican border. But we left the freeway before long and, as we drove along the little back roads through the Chirachua National Park, a luminous full moon rose to illuminate the mountain passes where once Geronimo and his Apache warriors fought out their doomed battles against unstoppable intruders.

We'd travelled 590 kilometres that day and were so tired and hungry that we felt a degree of relief, perhaps a little similar to what the old-timers experienced when they rode in from the range to the tiny settlement of Tombstone, Arizona.

It was still cold enough for the footpaths to be slippery with ice and there was even a residue of snow on the wooden back steps of the 'Adobe Lodge' when we pulled in.

'The only room we have left is the bridal suite,' the diminutive Asian proprietress told us with a small, slightly embarrassed smile.

'Great!' Zara cried, 'let's take it.'

The old four-poster, complete with pink drapes and quilted coverlet, almost filled the room. Zara was ecstatic, even though she and Sean were to share a collapsible cot in the walk-in dressing room.

'Oh go on,' she said, 'you can pretend!' Much laughter.

January 25th ... Sean's birthday. He had reached double figures, and we had the happy birthdays and handing over of presents in our bridal suite before going out for breakfast. We gave Sean a watch, a book on the Amazon River and a promissory letter for a new camera (to replace the one he lost in Bristol, Virginia) when we got to San Diego.

'YESTERDAY'S TRAGEDY'

'Three men hurled into eternity in the duration of a moment.'

'Stormy as were the early days of Tombstone, nothing ever occurred equal to the event of yesterday.'

Those were the headlines and opening paragraph of the main front-page story in the *Epitaph*, Tombstone's daily newspaper, for Thursday, October 27th, 1881. It's a story that has become one of the classic tales of the Old West; the story of the gunfight at the OK Corral. Doc Holliday, Wyatt Earp and his two brothers, Virgil and Morgan against Ike Clanton and his gang, with Wyatt, Doc Holliday and co. emerging victorious.

And it's all there in Tombstone to be seen ... the OK Corral, just as it was (or so they say), with fibre-glass figures of the principal characters, in western costume, with their guns drawn, in the exact positions they were when the shootout occurred. Well, there is some dispute about the actual positioning, whether the shooting was really in the Corral or out in the street, but who cares? The atmosphere is there and not only the OK Corral, but the whole of Tombstone seems to excite your interest in those bygone days. It may be all a bit kitsch and it's certainly very commercialised, but there's absolutely no doubt that it's fun!

There's the Wells Fargo Museum, jam-packed with the most amazing junk from the Old West (probably worth a fortune) and the famous Birdcage Theatre, where many of the greatest names of the theatre and musical entertainment of the time performed.

The Birdcage is also full of fabulous old photographs and bric-a-brac. At either side of the silver and gold-leaf-adorned stage are the exclusive private boxes which could be bought, in those days, for $25 a night. There's the story they tell about the Russian count who took one of the boxes to watch the Birdcage performances every night for two years. Then he stole a horse and was hanged for it. Everyone in Tombstone apparently felt very sorry for him. He wasn't really a bad guy; in fact he was, so the story goes, a rather shy and diffident character who had always wanted to be thought of as a tough guy.

A similar desire must have been motivating the lone stranger we saw clomping up and down the wooden sidewalks of Tombstone all that morning. Dressed from head to foot in black western gear, with his spurs jangling, his gun-belt hanging low on his hip and his hat set at a rakish angle, he swaggered around with his right hand hanging loose by his holster, as if he was looking for a shootout with someone around the town. We thought he was part of Tombstone's image-making promotional activities, but when we asked the local hairdresser, who was sitting on a bench outside his salon, about the man in black, he replied, 'Him, haven't a clue who he is. He came into town a couple of days ago and he's been stalkin' around like that ever since.'

I guess he was just born a hundred years too late.

What else? Well, there's the Crystal Palace saloon, with its great wooden bar and huge engraved mirrors, the Wyatt Earp Museum and the Court House Museum, which, as it is run by the National Parks Service, is much more subdued than the other commercial museums. It is however better laid out and contains a great deal of authentic material from the Old West, including a set of gallows on which, we were told, much to the children's fascination, five men were once hanged in one day.

But the thing that will always bring back memories of Tombstone for us is a family portrait we had taken in a little photographer's studio on Fremont Street, in which we are all dressed up in cowboy gear and early settlers' clothes.

'In those days,' the photographer explained as he positioned us, 'nobody smiled at the camera, so no smiles please.'

We all look so deadly serious in the photograph . . . but, believe it or not, we were having fun.

As we left Tombstone, we stopped on the outskirts to visit Boot Hill, the town's graveyard. A walk along the rows of tombstones and old crosses there gives some idea of how difficult life must have been in the first decade of the town's existence. (It was founded by a prospector who was warned that all he would find was his own tombstone. He struck silver, though, and staked his claim in 1877.)

The epitaphs are depressing: John Burrows, died of the pox, 1883; Katherine Johnson, committed suicide, 1881; Jamie Howard, lynched, 1885; Ike Patterson, shot, 1881; lots of hangings, several killed by Indians, others murdered, and quite a few unknown bodies. Practically no one in Tombstone's Boot Hill died naturally.

But today's Tombstone is certainly not about to expire. The silver mine which was the original reason for the town's existence, has long since been cleaned out, but the gold mine of the tourist industry has ensured that Tombstone will continue . . . living up to its original motto, 'the town too tough to die'.

After Tombstone, we felt as though we were on the home stretch. We followed Route 10 into Tucson and up to Casa Grande, then along Route 8 through Gila Bend and across the Sonora Desert, organ-pipe cactuses dotting the flat, barren, but somehow beautiful landscape until we crossed into California at Yuma.

From a phone booth in Yuma I called the owner of our car in San Diego, to let her know we would be arriving the following day. Then, in the men's toilet at the gas station, I came across the first signs I had seen of an anti-Mexican prejudice that is apparently widely felt along these border areas. Amongst the sexual graffiti on the walls was scribbled the comment: 'It took a thousand spicks to kill Davey Crockett . . . what would you goddamn spicks do if you had to face 1000 Davey Crocketts?'

Only one more incident before we stopped for the night in a little A-frame cottage at Live Oak Springs in the mountains to the east of San Diego . . . a UFO sighting!

Well . . . that's certainly what it looked like. I'm really not a UFO believer, but this was definitely something quite strange.

We were approaching El Centro, a little over 160 kilometres from San Diego. The sun had just set, and in the distance we saw a bright light, motionless in the sky, probably 300 metres or so in the air. My first impression, as we continued to drive towards it, was that it was the light on top of some tall communications tower or aerial. But, through the gloom, as we approached the outskirts of El Centro, it became clear that there was no tower, or aerial supporting this stationary light. Then, as we came to within about 800 metres of where it was, we perceived that there were one or two more lights beside it, and we became even more excited and puzzled . . . particularly as the road kept bringing us straight towards the object.

Coming so soon after we had seen the film 'Close Encounters', we were perhaps a little preconditioned to the possibility of UFOs, but this one was certainly doing all the right things to fit the pattern. As we continued driving, several of the cars in front of us on the highway slowed down, evidently also wanting to get a better view of the craft, for there was no doubt in our minds now that they were aircraft of some sort. We got to a point almost beneath the lights, when suddenly they began to move off. There were now quite clearly two of them and they travelled not really at high speed . . . probably no faster than a helicopter, until they eventually disappeared behind a low range of hills silhouetted against the clear night sky.

The sensible answer, of course, is that they *were* helicopters, but we had stopped the car and jumped out as they moved off and we heard no sound of rotors . . . in fact, no sound at all. But I guess they must have been helicopters, more than likely from a nearby military base. But why would they hover in the dark for so long? And be so silent as they moved off? We were mystified and we drove on to Live Oak Springs talking excitedly about the incident and discussing with the children again the possibilities of intelligent life in other parts of the universe.

USA

3
Why would anyone live anywhere else?

San Diego! Why would anyone live anywhere else in the United States? That was our immediate reaction on driving over the mountains from Live Oak Springs and down to the coast. After that drive across 4800 kilometres of snow, blizzards and ice, it was like arriving in a little corner of paradise.

It never snows in San Diego (that could be a song), in fact, it is never cold. Nor is it ever humid and muggy like it gets in Florida and, as yet, it suffers only slightly from those lung-destroying smogs which foul Los Angeles and San Francisco. And, as we were to discover during our two week stay in San Diego, second and even later impressions live up to the first.

Immediately, like homing pigeons, or aging surfies, we headed for the beach, where we discarded our heavy jackets, took off our boots and ran about on the sand, feeling like prisoners just released from their shackles.

It was wonderful to feel natural warmth again and also to see the sea. To have traversed an entire continent and stand on the edge of it is a delirious sensation. It's not just the strong, bitter smell of the sea, or the constant and fascinating motion. It's also the knowledge that it stretches out there, empty and challenging for 13,000 kilometres! It's this combination of mental and physical excitement which gets my adrenalin pumping and makes me feel whole again.

The process of delivering our car to its owner, Mrs Vandenplatz, an elderly Jewish lady who evidently came to spend every winter in San Diego, was fairly brief and straightforward . . . even if a little sad. We had come to think of the car as ours, even though we had been driving it for such a short time. We had covered a lot of ground together, through some pretty nasty weather and she hadn't failed us, nor even once given the slightest hint of trouble.

We put her through an automatic car wash to get rid of the accumulated mud and grime of 4800 kilometres, then drove to the grand apartment building on the beach at suburban Coronado. Mrs Vandenplatz test-drove it herself, signed a piece of paper saying all was okay, which we took to the San Diego branch of the Driveaway firm to retrieve our $100 deposit, and that was that! A great way to travel!

San Diego, although our stay there was short, holds very pleasant memories for us because of the great hospitality of two of the finest Americans . . . finest people, we know . . . Si and Virginia Casady whom we had met when we had all lived in Singapore for a couple of years in the early seventies.

Simon and Virginia are both now in *their* seventies and consequently are old enough to be our parents, but they both possess a rare and precious quality, a youthfulness of spirit and attitude that makes chronological age irrelevant. Whenever we are with Si and Virginia we feel as if we are the same age as them, or vice versa. Not that we really sit down and think about it, but if the thought arises, that's the feeling.

Simon was originally a journalist and I suppose he still is, although he became a newspaper owner and publisher in the mid-fifties, when he took over the El Cajon Valley News.

In the sixties both he and the paper were centres of controversy for their outspoken stand against the Vietnam War. Si, in fact, became President of the California Democratic Council, one of America's largest grass-roots political organisations, and, as such, came under some fairly close scrutiny by the FBI.

Under the provisions of the new American laws embodied in the Freedom of Information Act, Si had, some time ago, petitioned the FBI for details of the files they held on him. They had produced copies of the files, but significant sections of them were either missing or blanked-out. While we were in San Diego, staying with Si and Virginia, Si began the process of suing the FBI and the CIA for the rest of the undisclosed information. We were somewhat amazed at the concept of being able to sue such 'august' bodies.

But this was only one aspect of life with the Casadys. We found that it also meant being swept (admittedly only as observers on the fringe) into the world of local and state politics. We were whisked off to attend seminars run by 'The City Club' at the University of California, San Diego, on such things as 'the running of San Diego' and 'the role of the media in state politics', where we would be introduced to people like congressman George Mills, or local council-woman Maureen O'Connor, or behind-the-scenes lobbyist and political hopeful, George Mitrovitch:

'Everybody wants to come to San Diego now, but, if I've got anything to do with it, we won't let them do here what they've done to Los Angeles!'

Or perhaps it would be off for the evening to hear the Indian Ambassador to the United States addressing a meeting on India's economy and the state of US/Indian relations. Or, in sharp contrast, we would be out, together with Si and Virginia, to see 'Saturday Night Fever', which we all enjoyed and which, we'd been told on several occasions, 'is where American culture is at, right now!'

For Zara and Sean, our sudden dive into these varied aspects of American culture posed no real problems. Si and Virginia had grandchildren ... the two sons of Kent (one of their five sons) living on the same street. So when the children were not with us, they were fully occupied with friends, either riding skateboards, bicycling, roller-skating, or being taken for rides in the large maroon-coloured Rolls-Royce, owned by a glamorous blonde psychologist across the road.

The best thing about San Diego's entertainments is that all the places which the children insist on visiting are also enjoyable for adults. The quality standards are very high. For instance, normally I loathe zoos, but San Diego's is superlative and, if zoos must be, then all zoos should aim for this standard.

The aviary in particular is quite spectacular. So huge that one is unaware of being inside a cage at all.

The buildings, footpaths, eating bars and facilities are immaculately maintained. The climate encourages the lush vegetation which softens all the enclosures and we spent a very full and happy day watching the wide assortment of beasts, chief among them, of course, the always-popular monkeys who did us the courtesy of ignoring us.

Sea World is the other great tamed animal experience in San Diego. It is populated by trained dolphins and seals which the children were delighted to be able to feed by hand, leaning precariously over the side of a pool and trying to entice the over-fed mammals to leap for titbits of fish. There were also some sharks, to add the necessary terror to the show, plus smaller fish and even a few ducks.

But the undoubted star was Shamu, the killer whale. Shamu is four and a half metres of svelte muscle and when he powers himself round his large sea-water pool he reaches speeds of fifty kph. Not the sort of animal you'd want to get in the way of, especially as his mouth runs in a wide grin right round his snub-nosed front half. Yet the ease with which his trainer rode him bare-back, arm flung out for balance as if on a bucking bronco in a stampede, while Shamu dove and surfaced, dove and surfaced, made it appear deceptively simple.

With one swish of that massive flat tail he could easily have broken the man's back. The audience, seated in a high-tiered semi-circle in front of the pool, cheered enthusiastically.

Responding instantly and with obvious pleasure to whistle signals, Shamu lay on his side and rolled over and over while his trainer, standing upright, kept his balance by walking him as loggers do when they bring giant logs down river. More cheers.

While his trainer explained over the loud-speaker system how Shamu had been taught on a reward system (do something right and get a fish, do something wrong and get nothing) to work with a crew of people, Shamu jumped through suspended hoops, stood on his head and slapped the water with his tail drenching those in the front few rows who shrieked with delight.

As a finale, a young woman volunteer from the audience stood, nervously, at the edge of the pool, under the very attentive eye of a crew member, while Shamu swam faster and faster round the pool before leaping up to plant a large and very wet kiss with his open, pink, tongue-filled mouth on her cheek. Most definitely the kiss of a lifetime.

'But why aren't any of them here?' Zara asked, disappointed, as we sat sipping our milkshakes in Schwab's Pharmacy on Sunset Boulevarde.

'Well, they don't all come out and parade around the streets, you know,' Trish said to her. 'Film stars have to live a private life too. And when they are not working, they like to stay at home and just do the same things as everyone else.'

'Well, couldn't we just visit some . . . one of them at home?'

'No, not really. You can't do things like that. Anyway, they wouldn't like it.'

'But why not? This is Hollywood and I thought . . . oh, look, is that one there?'

A tall, expensively-dressed woman with a Farrah Fawcett hair-do walked in to the drugstore and began talking to a group of trendy-looking people at a nearby table.

'No, I don't think so,' Trish and I said together. We could very easily have been mistaken though. Isn't just about everybody in Hollywood either a once, present, or future star?

We had driven up to Los Angeles to go to Disneyland and decided to take Zara and Sean on a quick tour of Beverly Hills and Hollywood. Up and down Hollywood Boulevarde, where Zara really expected to see stars aplenty, Grauman's Chinese Theater . . . 'Who was Marilyn Monroe?' . . . and Schwabs Pharmacy, where, so the story is, stars gather frequently for an expensive snack, milkshake or coffee. Evidently more so in the good old days though, than now.

I know that hundreds of millions of people, mostly Americans of course, but a fair percentage of foreigners too, have already discovered Disneyland to be what is probably the best value-for-money entertainment complex in the world. It's been around for more than twenty years now, but that's not going to stop me from singing its praises, because we've only just discovered it.

One of the most interesting things we noticed about the place, almost as soon as we walked through the gates, was that there were more adults than children and all of them even at 9.00 in the morning, with that expectant look on their faces . . . a look one normally only associates with children . . . wide-eyed interest, because they are there for just one reason . . . to enjoy themselves.

Since it was first opened in 1955, Disneyland has been an enormously successful money-making concern. The reasons are obvious. What makes the place eminently worthwhile and enjoyable is the really high standard of all the entertainment and the facilities and the great lengths to which they've gone to make people, as Walt Disney said, 'feel they are in another world'.

But while Disneyland is great for adults . . . it's fantastic for kids. Zara and Sean were at a loss over which things they wanted to do and see first, in Adventureland, Fantasyland, Frontierland, and Tomorrowland.

Eventually we got around to doing most things; The Jungle Cruise, the Swiss Family Robinson's Tree House, exploring Tom Sawyer's Island, seeing the Pirates of the Caribbean, Peter Pan, riding the Skyways, the People Movers, the futuristic Monorail, the Mission to Mars and, horror of horrors for Trish . . . Space Mountain.

Space Mountain is where 'only the stout of heart' board a rocket for a high-speed, twisting, turning, 'out-of-this-world' journey through space. It was pretty hair-raising and, unfortunately, it left Trish so shattered it took her nearly half an hour to recover.

But even a bad trip on Space Mountain can't spoil the overall effect of Disneyland; I'm sure everyone walks out of that huge park at the end of their day, feeling that they've had fun! We certainly did.

We had another friend who lived in the San Diego area to look up. Sally Shapiro and I had suffered through the vicissitudes of an English boarding school education together and even though we hadn't met for ten years we slipped easily into joint gear.

Sally looked well. As always, slim and darkly attractive. And comfortable to be with because her life style, and in particular her manner toward her two boys, the same ages as our children, is very similar to my own. Even when Sean accidentally threw a golf ball through a large window she didn't get heavy. On our way with Si and Virginia to the jai alai game across the Mexican border in Tijuana we discussed these similarities and decided that it must have much to do with our own similar childhoods.

Even though she had lived in San Diego for eighteen months this was Sally's first venture into Mexico, as it was ours.

'Stupid to live within forty kilometres and never go across,' she said, 'but you hear such terrible stories.'

And so you do, though with around two million Americans visiting the country every year, there are certain to be a number of nasty incidents, especially in the border towns. The further south you go, the fewer of these tales are told.

Si, who was driving the car, stopped at the border so we could show our passports. For him and Virginia and Sally, American citizens, there were no such formalities. Many San Diegans go across not for the game but to shop, go to the dentist or have repairs done on their cars, all of which are much cheaper south of the border.

Si bought Mexican car insurance, $3.50 for twenty-four hours. Surely a licence to print money, but as no foreign insurance is valid, a necessary piece of paper in this country where a traffic offence is a felony and where the judicial system treats you as guilty until you prove yourself innocent.

Virginia regaled us with stories of friends who had spent weeks in the not-so-hot Mexican jails charged with some minor traffic violation, unable to contact friends and not having sufficient cash for the large bribes demanded.

So this was the legendary Tijuana, Mexico of so many American novels and films and we were really here! Even the immediately perceivable differences between San Diego and Tijuana were quite remarkable. The condition of the roads and buildings deteriorated as spectacularly as the atmosphere of exuberant living went up. All the shops were open, brightly lit and selling a jumble of traditional Mexican artifacts, as well as gaudily advertised cheap clothing and household goods. Touts and bargain hunters jostled on crowded sidewalks. It was dirtier, noisier, less organised and more fun, at least to visit. The battered vehicles of the locals and the gleaming new models of the visitors hooted viciously as they jockeyed their way round the complex of small streets.

We parked in the 'Lighted and Guarded' parking area beside the Fronton Palacio.

'If you don't have a Mexican insurance sticker on your window,' Si said, 'it's for sure that you'll come back to find the car scratched, dented or even gone.'

The Palacio was garish, over-illuminated and crowded. It shared that same atmosphere all sporting events create and even the same smell. It was all familiar but yet there was a difference. What was it? It was a few moments before we realised. Yes! That was it! Most of the people were speaking Spanish.

Rows of hard seats, the experienced aficionados had brought cushions, reared up before the fifty-five metre long, hard-surfaced ball court which was twelve metres wide and completely sealed off from the spectators by an open-work, metal-link fence. An excellent precaution when you realise that the rock-hard pelota, the ball, travels at speeds in excess of 240 kph.

We'd never seen jai alai before so Si explained a few of the ground rules. The object of the game is to throw the pelota to the front wall so that when it returns it will be impossible for the opposing player to catch it and return it again to the front wall.

It sounds simple but apart from being the oldest-known ball game, it's said to require more skill, speed, endurance and sheer nerve than any other sport. Certainly it's a very exciting and fast game to watch.

Si and Iain immediately got with the spirit of the occasion and started betting. Jai alai is only the excuse, while betting is actually the reason why so many thousands of Americans attend the nightly game!

'Here they come, Mum,' Sean hunched forward in his seat, mashing potato chips into his mouth by the handful. The players dressed in shiny, satin, numbered shirts, made final adjustments to the ties which hold the long, curved, woven, wicker-work basket, or cesta, to their wrists. It's with this wicked arm extension that they collected and returned the pelota.

The locals jeered or hurrahed each player and the game began. Men ran, jumped, tumbled and even tried to climb the walls in order to get at the ball. The children joined in the cheering. Sally and I talked over the infinite limits and limited infinity of marriage. Iain and Si ran up and down to the betting counter, shelling out dollar bills. So a good time was had by all!

On the thirty minute drive back to the other world of southern California Si and Iain were jubilant. After being $25 down at one stage they had finally come away $8 winners. They replayed each bet in detail and decided that once you knew each player's form it would be possible to make a fortune. (But of course!)

'They come past here every year at this time,' Virginia said as we gazed intently out to sea. 'Literally hundreds of whales, within a period of a few weeks, come by on their way south to Baja California.'

We were standing high on the windy cliffs at Point Loma, at the entrance to San Diego harbour, looking westward out to the Pacific. The wind was just whipping up a few white-caps on the water, but we were able to discern, a mile or so from shore, the occasional spray from the blow-holes of what appeared to be two whales making their way southwards.

'On days when the seas are calmer,' Virginia told us, 'it's possible to go out in small boats to be right amongst the herds as they pass by Point Loma.'

'But don't the whales run from the boats?' I asked.

'No. So far they have been extremely friendly. We've had photos in the papers here of people scratching their backs with oars and scuba divers have been in the water with them!'

The whales make the long journey every year, swimming the many thousands of kilometres from the Alaskan waters where they have spent the winter, to calve and breed in the warmer waters of one or two particular bays on the Baja California Peninsula. Many years ago, they used to breed in the waters of San Diego harbour, but the growth of the city forced them further south to seek more peaceful surroundings.

From a different part of the Point Loma headland, a short while later, we watched another, more deadly, denizen of the deep make its way out into the Pacific; an American sturgeon-class nuclear attack submarine. A chart in the small park on the headland carried illustrations, as a guide to the recognition of all the various types of US naval vessels and military aircraft that can be seen coming and going from the different installations in the San Diego area.

Only in America! It's just this sort of thing that, every now and then, makes you suddenly realise that you are in the United States and not some other part of the world. After travelling in many different countries in Asia and Africa, one tends to accept a sort of national paranoia over military matters as being normal. I often recall, with considerable annoyance, being arrested as a spy in Tanzania for taking photographs in a civilian bus depot. There was a chance, I was told by the arresting officer, that I may have photographed some members of the Tanzanian army, who happened to be waiting, in their camouflage uniforms, for a bus ... and that was forbidden. Here in the United States, overlooking one of the country's biggest naval installations, not only is there no ban on photography, but they offer you a guide to the types of ships and planes you might see!

Our morning on Point Loma was our last in San Diego. We had completed the extra shopping for small bits and pieces we needed to take with us and organised ourselves so that we could fit everything we needed into just our four backpacks. The heaviest part of it all turned out to be my camera equipment and the cooking and eating utensils.

I would have liked to have carried more photographic gear, but it was impossible. As it was, I had one camera, a Nikon EL and three lenses; a 24 mm wide-angle, a 43-86 mm zoom and a 70-210 zoom, an electronic flash unit and fifty rolls of slide film. I also carried a miniature camera, a Minolta 110 for occasions when a large camera would be too obvious, and a miniature Sony cassette recorder. These all added up to a considerable weight, but I was able to fit them quite snugly into a separate compartment in the bottom of my pack.

Trish would carry most of the cooking gear, although Zara took the little collapsible stove in the bottom of her pack and Sean carried our amply-stocked medicine chest.

The rest of our clothes and additional luggage, two aluminium suitcases and a duffle bag, we would leave in storage with Si and Virginia.

San Diego had become, like New York, another jumping-off place. But somehow it seemed a much bigger one than New York. We would be, from now on, in foreign territory. Terrible really, what an immense difference language makes. I mean, after all, we are not Americans (well, Zara is ... technically ... having been born in New York) and yet, because of the language, the similar cultural backgrounds, we always feel perfectly at home in the United States.

Now, suddenly, we were leaping across a border into a different world. It wasn't really such a big deal; I guess it was just because we were facing five or six months on the road, which we knew would include some fairly rough travelling, that made us feel a little overwhelmed. And yet, at the same time we were keen to get going ... to be on the move. We felt to some extent that we had been procrastinating by travelling in the United States and spending two weeks with our friends in San Diego. After all, the object of the exercise was supposed to be Latin America ... or, in the original concept, South America, which still seemed a hell of a long way from San Diego.

We had decided to take the train across the northern Mexican deserts all the way to Mexico City. Si and Virginia offered to drive us the 150 kilometres or so to Mexicali, where we would catch the train. We would leave the next morning.

That evening, before dinner, Si produced a blender and began mixing drinks.

'If you're heading into Mexico,' he smiled, 'we can't let you go unprepared. You have to get used to the national drink. We should have started this long ago.'

He prepared a batch of Tequila Margaritas, which led to another and another ... and another. All I can say is that I enjoyed them very much while I was drinking them ... but not the next day when I felt as prickly as the cactus that the tequila came from.

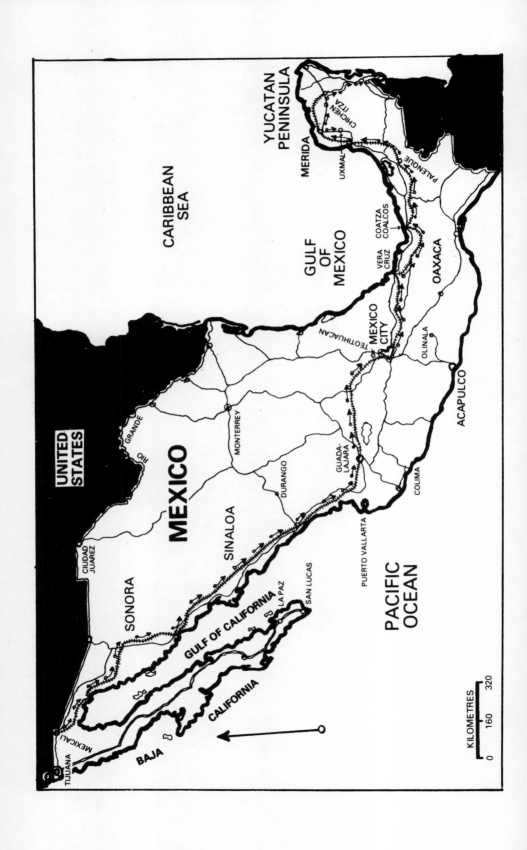

MEXICO

4
The bandy-legged bandit

When the Spanish Conquistador Hernan Cortes was asked in Madrid what Mexico looked like, he took a piece of parchment, crunched it up in his hands and released it.

'That,' he said, 'is a map of Mexico.'

From the window of our train, heading south, down the coast of the Gulf of California, we could see what he was getting at. The rugged and barren escarpment of the Sierra Madre stretched on endlessly to our left, while to our right, an arid desert ran down to the sea. Mexico, of course, is much, much more than dry mountains and deserts, as we were soon to discover, but, certainly, most of the first 1500 kilometres of our train trip into Mexico was through territory similar to Cortes' description.

To give these northern parts of Mexico ... Sonora and Sinaloa provinces ... their due, wherever they are irrigated they become extraordinarily fertile, producing a large proportion of Mexico's fresh vegetable needs and about 60 to 70 percent of all the tomatoes and cucumbers sold in the US.

We had said goodbye to Si and Virginia Casady at Mexicali on the previous day and spent that night in a small hotel there, waiting for the train the following morning. We found Mexicali to be a small, relatively poor town, just across the border from the equally small, but less poor, American town of Calexico. The names of both towns are an obvious amalgam of Mexico and California.

Mexicali is a free port and is described in the Mexican tourist brochures as 'prosperous', but after the over-abundant affluence of the United States, I suppose almost anywhere would look poor by comparison. It is a fairly solid sociological jump from southern California into northern Mexico, where the only hope most people have of a decent life, opportunity and education for their children, is to somehow, some day, make it across that border into the US. There, if they can stay long enough without being discovered, they may eventually be legalised under the occasional amnesty programs.

We had felt, as we humped our packs for the first time along the dusty, unsurfaced road to the train station in Mexicali that we were on our own now. Nobody between here and the bottom of South America that we knew ... and just public transport to get us there.

We found this a bit disturbing in some ways, but very exciting in others. Travelling in a car certainly gives a sense of security and independence, but while satisfying in that way, it also tends to isolate you from the people around . . . a bit cocoon-like. Whereas travelling on different forms of public transport immediate-ly puts you into close touch with other people.

That's not necessarily always a pleasant prospect, however, particularly in this part of Mexico where anybody who speaks English and no Spanish is automatically regarded as a 'gringo' . . . a 'yanqui'. And, as Americans are not greatly liked in this part of Mexico, and in most of Central America, in fact, we learnt that it was best to make it clear, very early in any conversations with Mexicans we met, that we were not Americans. 'Somos Australianos,' . . . we are Australian, we would say.

Actually, the Latin American reaction to the United States is probably more of a love-hate relationship than anything else. In common with almost every other country in the world, they latch on to everything American, like their cars, blue jeans, hamburgers, movies, and so on, yet resent them for their affluence and influence in the region. They also often refer to people from the United States as 'Norte-Americanos', being quick to remind foreigners that there is more to the American continent than just the United States and that, 'We also are Americans'.

As it happened, our train trip to Mexico City, which took two days and two nights, and cost about US$30 each, produced no interesting meetings and was basically uneventful; miles of desert sand-dunes and a succession of small, poor towns. A group of Americans who drank too much dominated the scene in the lounge car of the train, so we read or played cards, chess and backgammon on miniature, magnetised sets, in our compartment for most of the journey.

We felt, from the moment we crossed into Mexico, the problem of our lack of Spanish. We had to improve it . . . fast. We had bought a couple of small Spanish/English dictionaries while we were still in the US, but apart from our brief attempt with the cassette in the car, had made no real attempts to learn anything, being, like most Anglo-Saxons, intrinsically lazy about learning other peoples' languages, until the crunch was reached . . . which was now!

We attempted to order our meals in the train's restaurant car in Spanish and our woeful efforts were only successful in getting us something to eat because of the sympathetic treatment we received from the waiter. Even then, there were some surprises when he arrived with the food!

Mexico City, so the statistics say, is now, or very soon will be, the world's largest city. Now that puts it up against some pretty stiff competition, but apparently, although the last official estimate was just under nine million people living in metropolitan Mexico City, some demographers feel that the Mexican capital's 1000-a-day growth rate has already pushed it over 11 million; past Tokyo, New York, Shanghai and Sao Paulo. They conveniently leave out Calcutta, though, which hasn't had a reliable census for years, but which many, including myself, reckon could be close to twenty million already. Anyway, it doesn't really matter, I suppose . . . all we're saying is that Mexico City is a very big town!

It's also a bit overwhelming at first. We had no idea where we would stay when the train pulled in to the central railway station at about 9.00 in the morning. We carried our packs along the platform to the main hall to find a phone booth from which to telephone a few hotels, and on the way immediately felt the height. Mexico City is about 2300 metres above sea level and its air is slightly rarefied; nothing to what we would experience later in South America, of course, but we noticed it.

There were quite a few young people carrying backpacks amongst the crowds of people coming and going in the main hall of the station, but we seemed to attract curious stares and be the subject of conversation amongst the locals wherever we walked, mainly because of Zara and Sean, I think. To see two young children carrying their own packs was probably a rare sight in Mexico City.

A young Australian couple, who introduced themselves as Graham and Suzy, came up to talk to us. They had just flown in to Mexico and were heading off to the Yucatan Peninsula to roam through some of the ruined Mayan cities there. We chatted for a while, as they gave us some hints on things to see and do in Mexico City and then left us to phone some hotels. We said we might meet them again somewhere in the Yucatan; one of those polite things you say, but never really expect to happen.

After two or three phone calls, using really primitive Spanish to try to establish the cost of a room with three or four beds, we finally decided to stay at the Hotel Polanco, where we were able to obtain a room for the four of us, including a private shower and toilet, for under US$10. It was a pleasant hotel, a few kilometres from the city centre, but very close to the large and beautiful Chapultepec Park and the fabulous Mexican Museum of Anthropology.

If, even though you may be embarrassed to admit it publicly, you are as ignorant about pre-Columbian Indian culture as I was, well, stick around. First up the Museum of Anthropology.

I went in knowing names like Aztec, Maya and Inca and thinking of them as somehow parts of a whole. This overview was blurred by a hazy recollection of a very bad movie about the Aztec ruler Moctezuma in which a parody of a pidgin-speaking Indian was dressed like a cross between Julius Caesar and Queen Nefertiti. The addition of a monumental feather head-dress turned him into a strutting turkey-cock as he tore the hearts out of beautiful (of course) compliant virgins and flung them at his grovelling subjects.

I staggered out after four hours with an increased knowledge but also the realisation that I had a desperate need to read more about what was to me a whole new history and culture. I felt like a child must when first confronted with a book. All that information and knowledge, now all one needs is the key.

The first things to get straight are that the Aztecs were centred around what is now Mexico City; the Maya on the Yucatan peninsula, that fat thumb of land which sticks out from the east coast of Mexico into the Caribbean, and the Incas settled thousands of kilometres to the south on the western mainland of South America, in Peru. Although they were all around at the same time, they spoke totally different languages and had little contact.

It was just bad luck, like so much of history, for Moctezuma that he happened to be King of the Aztecs when Hernan Cortes, explorer/exploiter, hove into sight in 1519 looking for fame and glory (gold and land).

The empire which Moctezuma ruled, stretching from northern Mexico to southern Guatemala, was then little more than a century old. Older and even grander civilisations had risen, reached peaks of culture and affluence and declined, before the Aztecs arrived on the scene. I find it quite consoling to realise that these older civilisations were quite as baffling to the Aztecs as the Aztecs were to be to the Europeans.

It's the magnificent artistic expressions of these pre-Aztec cultures in addition to the Aztec and Mayan pieces, which so overwhelm the visitor to the Museum of Anthropology, surely one of the greatest museums in the world both architecturally and in its contents.

Set in the quiet of Chapultepec Park the museum has a 425-metre facade and an immense patio shaded by an acre-and-a-half concrete roof supported by a single central column. At the entrance looms the over eight metre, 167-tonne, monolith of Tlaloc, Aztec God of Rain. The story goes that when it was moved from near the town of Texcoco to the museum, there was a protesting cloud burst!

Inside, a spacious setting enables the pieces to retain much of their mystical presence. There are the stone images, monoliths, stelae (large pieces of carved stone) and sculptures of the Mixtec, Zapotec, Toltec, Olmec and Tarascan races, all of them forerunners of the Aztecs and some of them dating back 3000 years.

My favourites were the enormous Olmec heads, some of them a metre or more across, with flat faces, fat lips, slit eyes and disapproving, turned-down mouths.

That most famous piece of Aztec art, reproduced and sold in gift shops around the world, is here in all its originality; the twenty-five-tonne Aztec calendar stone; a unique combination of art and astronomical calculation more accurate than anything else about at the time. It was unearthed in a corner of Mexico's main square in 1760, two hundred and fifty years after Moctezuma's palace, in that same square, had been torn down by the Conquistadores and its stones used to build the present-day cathedral. Difficult to imagine leaving a masterpiece like that lying about so that it gets built over. Such carelessness gives the impression that there must have been a vast amount of similar beauty about for it to have been treated with such contempt.

All those reproductions do not detract from the impact of the calendar's ferocious central face of Tonatiuh, Lord of Heaven, his fat tongue stuck out, demanding to be fed blood and human hearts.

The upstairs galleries display folk costumes and life-styles of various Indian tribes through to the present day. It was here that we had one of those shocks which would repeat itself continually throughout our journey. We turned from an exhibit of Mayan clothing and came literally face-to-face with a face from the past. A young boy, perhaps thirteen, taking notes, probably for a school project. He had the olive skin, almond eyes, high cheek bones and very distinctive high sloping forehead and long straight nose which the ancient Mayas thought so beautiful that they bound their infants' heads to produce this supposedly high-class characteristic. He twinned all the chiselled and carved faces about us. Iain asked if he might take his photograph. The boy smiled, did he know why? and stood in profile beside his ancestors.

The second flash of recognition came just as we were leaving, feeling as though we had walked ourselves some centimetres shorter. There it was, the huge Quetzal feather head-dress, a replica of the one worn by Moctezuma, and by that awful actor in that terrible film which had so garbled my preconceptions of Mexico. The original was sent to Charles V and is now in a museum in Vienna.

That night we had a very good meal, made even better by the fact that it was so cheap. After the blandness of American food my taste buds went wild over spicy enchiladas, tostados, tacos and tortillas washed down with big glasses of thick, fresh orange juice.

Always a little slower than Iain (due, I tell him, to the reserve of my British heritage) I now ventured forth into execrable Spanish and amazed them all (and me too, though I tried to appear casual) when I ordered, 'una fresca y hellado por favor' and was served luscious fresh strawberries and ice-cream.

Zara, who is a sweet freak, endeavoured to take us all on a candy-shop-crawl. Both the sweets and cakes in Mexico City are a dentist's despair. Numerous shops sell wonderful concoctions including the most extravagant, multi-tiered, lavishly decorated wedding and birthday cakes I have encountered anywhere.

We were all still gooey-ed up when we climbed into a taxi, the driver of which took great delight in pointing to a high tower and claiming, 'Highest building in the world'.

Sean, fresh from his assault on the World Trade Centre, disagreed. The man turned round, ignoring the speed at which we were hurtling along through congested and seemingly unpredictable traffic, and grinned:

'Is highest. Not tallest, highest. Is tallest building in Mexico City which is highest town in world. So is highest. Si!' he laughed.

If the traffic had been lighter I might have contested his opinion of Mexico City as the highest city in the world but it seemed safer to agree and laugh, 'Si! Si!'

In the fifteenth and sixteenth centuries, at the time the war-like Aztecs ruled central Mexico, the great city of Teotihuacán was already in ruins. Even the mighty Aztecs felt a sense of awe for these ruins of a civilisation that had flourished a thousand years before them and died for no apparent reason. They called Teotihuacán 'the place of those who have the road of the gods'. They thought it had been the religious capital of the Toltecs, a race of craftsmen and builders who had preceded them. But no one since then, including the Frenchman Desiré Charnay, who first uncovered part of the twenty-square-kilometre city in 1880, and the other archaeologists who have studied Teotihuacán after him, have been able to agree on who the inhabitants of the city really were, why the city died and where its people went. Even today, nobody knows.

For the present day visitor, Teotihuacán (pronounced Tayo-tee-wuckarn), about an hour from Mexico City by car, remains one of the most remarkable relics of an ancient civilisation in the world. The two pyramids of the Sun and Moon, which are the most outstanding features of Teotihuacán, are huge. The Pyramid of the Sun is the largest artificial mound of earth on the American continent. It is about sixty-five metres high and covers almost the same base area as the great pyramid of Cheops. Archaeologists estimate that these great structures, begun at some time between 350 and 100 BC, must have taken thousands of workers at least fifty years to complete.

Teotihuacán was easily one of the largest cities in the world at the time, having a population of somewhere between a hundred and fifty and two hundred thousand. The acres of ruins that have so far been uncovered sprawl over relatively flat bush country on the floor of the great, ninety-six-kilometre long by thirty-two-kilometre wide Valley of Mexico. Mexico City itself also lies in the same valley, which is surrounded by a chain of forbidding mountain peaks and extinct volcanoes, including the snow-capped Popacatepetl and Ixtaccihuatle, both well over 5000 metres high.

As we wandered from one part of Teotihuacán to another, we found ourselves in a grove of peppercorn trees. We made our way, under the hot midday sun, through long grass, down to the banks of a stream. It had, we felt sure, run this same course for centuries. It was slow moving and algae-covered by the banks, but perhaps in earlier times there had been more water and it had been clearer. Away from the sound of the voices of other tourists on the site, it was not difficult to imagine Toltec women washing clothes or collecting water at the spot where we now stood.

Later we climbed the hundreds (we started but lost an accurate count) of steps to the top of the Pyramid of the Sun for the magnificent view of the surrounding countryside and the mountains in the distance. On the way down we passed a group of Mexican schoolchildren going up. One of the teenage boys in the group carried a transistor radio which was blaring out the music from 'Star Wars'!

'My father was a colonel in the Mexican army,' our taxi-driver, Juan Clemente, informed us in excellent English during the drive back from Teotihuacán. 'And my grandfather was a general.'

'What about you?' I asked. 'You had no desire to follow in their footsteps?'

He was a heavily-built man of about fifty, once handsome perhaps, but the condition of his clothes indicated that he was not an affluent man.

'No.' He laughed and then said with conviction, 'I can make more money as a taxi-driver.'

Our conversation was interrupted as he pulled in to a Mexican arts and crafts centre, suggesting that perhaps we would like to see onyx-carvers at work. It was obviously a planned stop, made every time he had foreign tourists aboard, but unfortunately one which brought him no commission this time. We explained that we were travelling light and that carrying onyx carvings along with us wasn't part of the plan. But the proprietor of the place wasn't in the least upset. He proceeded, with a big smile on his face, to demonstrate to the children how the Aztecs made pulque, a fiery liquid not unlike tequila, by cutting the heart out of a spiny agave plant, which is something like an aloe. At least four and a half litres of liquid forms in a day, in the hollow centre of the plant, to be later fermented. Zara and Sean were also highly impressed when he showed them the Aztec technique for making paper from the thick leaves and a needle and cotton from the spines of the same plant.

'How many children do you have?' we asked our driver, picking up the conversation again as we left the arts and crafts centre.

'Nine,' he replied with a proud smile. 'Five boys and four girls.'

'Nine!' Trish and I both exclaimed ... although really we shouldn't have been surprised. Mexicans are not noted practitioners of the art of birth control. 'But what about the country's population problem,' I said. 'You have too many people here now.'

'Hah! Never!' he laughed. 'The United States has over 200 million ... Mexico has only sixty million. And anyway, do you think my nine are going to make any difference?'

Sadly it is just this attitude which is creating for Mexico a gigantic problem which, for millions of its people in the years to come will mean just one thing: grinding poverty.

The clearest illustration for us came on the drive back into Mexico City. Our route took us past a depressing collection of slums and shanty-towns which had sprung up only recently. Similar collections of tin and wood hovels could be seen in other outlying areas of the capital.

Mexico City is the crucible, the crisis point on which the country's massive population problem centres. The city is literally bursting at the seams as squatters (campesinos they are called) leave the rural areas by the thousands seeking better opportunity and employment in the big city. But, for hundreds of thousands the move is only to another sort of poverty ... not necessarily any better than that they have left, and in many cases, worse.

The basic cause of the problem is the population growth rate; at 3.5 percent, amongst the highest in the world (Mexico City's is between 4.2 and 4.5 percent). It will, if unchecked, push the country's population to over 120 million by the turn of the century.

The government family planning services claim that the rate is going down. They say it's closer to 3.2 percent and that they hope to get it down to 2.5 percent by the mid 1980s. Most Mexicans are Roman Catholic, but fortunately the church has not raised any objections to the free family planning services offered by the government. President Lopez Portillo has ordered an expansion of the programme which already makes use of radio stations, billboards and newspapers to make the point that 'small families live better'. If the campaign achieves anything near to its objectives then it's clear that it won't only be small families but the whole of Mexico that will live better.

In the meantime, although the capital, Mexico City, may be expanding at an impossible rate and heading for tremendous problems in the future, it is still a remarkably beautiful, relatively clean (in the central areas), exciting and endlessly interesting city.

The impressively large zocalo (main square) in the heart of Mexico City has been the nerve centre of national life and the scene of historic events since Aztec times.

It is several city blocks square and all the buildings around it were built in the sixteenth century. On the north side is the cathedral, one of the oldest and largest in the western hemisphere. To the west is the Portal de Mercederes, a shopping collonade; to the south an elegant set of buildings now used as government offices, while the entire east side is taken up with the National Palace.

Standing in the middle of this square, surrounded by Hispanic architecture and roaring traffic, it takes a vast leap of imagination to visualise this same square as it would have appeared to Hernan Cortes when he first saw it.

Then Moctezuma's palace, where now the National Palace stands, rose in awe-inspiring splendour above Tenochtitlan, a planned city of 300,000 inhabitants which, when the Conquistadores came, with a mere 400 men, was the equal of any city in Europe.

Built on an island in Lake Texcoco, the city had myriad canals and paved thoroughfares which laced their way through huge markets selling everything from food to slaves. There was a botanical garden and even a zoo, the oldest in the world. There were luxurious palaces and temples, well-built dikes to prevent flooding, an aqueduct bringing in sweet water and straight, well-maintained causeways linking the island with the shore.

No wonder Cortes' men were impressed. These 'primitive' people they had come to enlighten with the word of God lived in a city far superior to the mediæval towns and villages of Europe from which most of them had come.

We left the safety of the central square, taking our chances with the crazy traffic, barely controlled by whistle-blowing policemen, to cross to the corner behind the cathedral, where we looked down into an excavation site which has revealed some of the original Aztec stonework from ancient Tenochtitlan. It disappears, tantalisingly, under the present buildings.

The xenophobic history I was taught at school explained that the right man (no one mentioned women) is produced at the right time, like spontaneous combustion in a hayrick. Thus Churchill. Even though I had niggling doubts as to the veracity of this view I knew too little then to ask, 'so how come Moctezuma?' Or did this enlightenment strike only Great Britain?

Poor Moctezuma. He found himself very much the wrong man for his time and place. In 1519 along came Cortes on his horses, which were taken to be mythical creatures of enormous power by the Indians who had never before seen such animals. His arrival fulfilled an ancient prophecy that the great God Quezalcoatl would return to claim this land in the Aztec Calendar year of One Reed: 1519 was that year. I guess it could be said that God (somebody's god anyway) was on Cortes' side.

Moctezuma was not the man to deal with this bandy-legged bandit who demanded gold, subservience to the King of Spain and wholesale conversion to a religion in the name of which he murdered a staggering quarter of a million people. Not wishing to offend these possibly divine visitors, Moctezuma gave them lavish gifts; chief among them two cartwheel size discs several centimetres thick, one of silver, the other of gold. This was a terrible mistake, for it merely whetted the Conquistadores' insatiable appetite for more and when they still wouldn't go away, Moctezuma made them welcome in his capital.

Soon demoted from host to prisoner, the forty-year-old monarch seemed to lose all spirit of resistance. When the Indians stormed the great palace in which Cortes and his men were now living, the Conquistadores took Moctezuma, dressed in all his royal finery, out onto one of the parapets to show the people that he was not a prisoner and to order them to lay down their weapons. But as Moctezuma raised his arms a howl of anger and a shower of arrows flew up from his abandoned subjects and he was severely wounded. Refusing food and medical attention, and also conversion and baptism, Moctezuma took three days to die;

whereupon Cortes sent his body out to the howling mob below. A sad story, especially in the light of all the barbarous acts with which the Spaniards followed it up.

But the other lesson history teaches is to put things in perspective. So it is as well to remember that the reign of terror spread by the Spaniards differed very little in its bloodlust from what had gone before. In fact Cortes would not have been able to march his men the 400 kilometres from Veracruz on the coast, over inhospitable terrain, if it hadn't been for the help of other Indian tribes whom the Aztecs had conquered and brutally oppressed.

The Aztecs rarely sacrificed their own people to their voracious gods; instead they tore the hearts from living victims drawn from among these subject people. At the dedication, in 1487, of a great new temple to Huitzilopochtli, 80,000 people were torn apart alive in a non-stop four-day celebration. No wonder the Aztecs were hated and that Cortes so easily found Indian allies to help him along the road of history.

Now, 450 years later, the full circle is turned and it is Cortes' turn to be reviled. On the eastern side of the zocalo, in the National Palace, there are gigantic murals by the prolific artist Diego Rivera depicting the history of Mexico since pre-Hispanic times. In them, Cortes is shown dwarf-sized, scrawny, almost hunch-backed, bow-legged, with domed forehead, large hooked nose and an open syphilitic lesion on his forehead!

A German woman tourist faints; falling absolutely face down through Mexico City's thinly oxygenated air, onto the tiled floor, smashing her glasses.

Back out in the zocalo we ask, 'Donde es il tumba de Cortes?' We might just as well have asked in English for all the too-quick replies or stares we received. Either no one knew or no one was telling where Hernan Cortes was buried. Unlike all the other conquerors and desecrators of Latin America, Cortes has no square, no public buildings and no streets named after him. Nor any statue to commemorate his life's works.

Even the usually helpful Government Tourist Bureau people looked blank and, when we persisted, one of them told us that Cortes had died and been buried in Spain. That is true, but the bones were disinterred and brought back to Mexico, where the hatred of the man has continued so intense over the centuries that his mortal remains were moved no less than three more times before finally coming to rest in the Hospital of Jesus, a church which is no longer used as a place of worship.

It's a shabby place, propped up by scaffolding. In a far corner we found the small plaque which simply read: 'Hernan Cortes, 1485-1547'. The only other visitor was an aesthetic-looking Englishman who carefully recorded his emotions into a tape machine.

Between Cortes and the Mexican revolution of 1910 ... a period of almost 400 years ... the story for the majority of Mexicans, particularly the peasantry, was one of grinding poverty and endless misery. Once the Spaniards had full control, they set about making the country over to serve their own purposes. Thousands of Indians, hastily baptised and converted to Christianity, were set to work in the gold and silver mines and on the huge agricultural holdings ... the haciendas ...

which the Spanish began to establish. The owners of these immense estates held absolute title to the land and imposed a near-feudal way of life on the Indian peasants who worked them.

Within the first fifty years of the Spanish conquest, *every* Indian in the most populous southern and central regions of Mexico had been harnessed to the getting of wealth, from the soil or from the mines, for the Spaniards. But even the winning of independence from Spain in 1821 did not change the situation greatly for the landless peasants. In fact, in many ways it probably made things worse.

Mexico began its independence under self-styled Emperor Augustin de Iturbide, but the empire only lasted a year. Then it became a republic under a series of dictators who involved the country in a succession of disastrous conflicts. The first was a war with the United States which resulted in the eventual loss of all the land from Texas to California and from the Rio Grande to Oregon. This was followed by a short period of reform, during which there was freedom of speech and of the press, the separation of church and state and the legalisation of civil marriages. But the church and conservatives, opposed to the liberalising measures, fomented a civil war in the early 1860s which brought economic collapse.

Britain, France and Spain then landed troops in Mexico to protect their financial interests and, in 1863, the French occupied Mexico City and installed the Archduke Maximilian of Austria and his wife Carlotta as Emperor and Empress of Mexico. Mexican forces eventually regained control of the country in 1867 when Maximilian was captured and shot.

All of this chaos did nothing for the poor peasants, who were badly fed, wretchedly housed and illiterate. The great landowners however, seemed only to prosper. By 1910 two-thirds of all the land in the country was owned by just over 800 individuals . . . either absentee landlords or the Roman Catholic Church. Over 300 of these huge properties were in excess of 10,000 hectares each; more than fifty of them were over 30,000 hectares, and eleven of them were properties of more than a 100,000 hectares each!

In the midst of the enormous wealth that these vast landownings represented, were the main mass of uneducated and half-starved peasants whose life could hardly have been more miserable. Many had had land stolen from them, their personal liberties curtailed and been sold into forced labour. For them, death was sometimes a blessed release. It certainly held no fear for the desperate peasants who rose in 1910 to sweep away the thirty-four-year dictatorship of Porfirio Diaz with the cry 'Tierra y Libertad' — Land and Liberty!

The most imposing building on the zocalo, standing at its northern end, is the Great Cathedral; the largest and oldest church in all of Latin America. It was first built in 1525, only four years after Cortes defeated Moctezuma and captured Tenochtitlan. Many of the stones used in its construction were, like those used in the National Palace, taken from Moctezuma's Palace, which Cortes ordered to be destroyed. The first cathedral was, however, also demolished later in the sixteenth century, to make way for a new and much more grand structure, the present cathedral, on which work began in 1573.

We approached the huge cathedral (our first church in Latin America) with a sense of freshness that was, I have to admit, unfortunately dulled considerably during the rest of our journey through Central and South America by the overwhelming wealth and magnificence of cathedral after cathedral in almost every city and town along the way.

But for the moment we stood in silent awe inside the cavernous hall of the great church, gazing in wonder at the beautiful marble floor, the grandiose architecture of columns and multi-domed ceilings (which combined Ionic, Doric and Corinthian styles) and the statues of different saints around the sides of the great hall at the Stations of the Cross. Mexican men, women and children moved around from one to the other, whispering prayers or kneeling before a particular saint quietly saying their rosary.

Zara and Sean were particularly fascinated by the statue of the Black Christ, before which several people knelt. But the huge alcove which enclosed the high altar was the pièce de résistance; sixteenth century Baroque. Incredibly ornate gold and gold-leaf ornamentation completely covered the walls and ceiling.

On the eastern side of the zocalo, opposite the National Palace, we spent a short while browsing through an amazing collection of wares in the Nacional Monte de Piedad. In Spanish, Monte de Piedad means Mountain of Pity. Colloquially it means pawnshop.

The National Pawnshop has occupied this position on the zocalo, which was once the site of an Aztec palace, since 1775 and has continued to operate under government control there to the present day. At the monthly auctions of unredeemed goods there are some remarkable bargains and some fascinating goods to be found. We saw one room filled with what appeared to be extremely valuable antique furniture, crockery and cutlery, but what really bowled us over was a life-size ceramic Nubian slave, complete in a green knickerbocker suit and a gold-fringed turban, holding a torch-like lantern. I know a few trendy types who just couldn't walk by something like that, but all we bought in the Nacional Monte de Piedad was a nylon toilet bag.

A few blocks from the zocalo, on the Avenida Uruguay, is the Hotel Monte Carlo. It's a small, but charming old colonial building with a driveway off the street leading to a central, tiled courtyard which has been roofed over. A broad wooden staircase leads up to a landing which encircles the courtyard. It has a slightly decaying, but not unpleasant atmosphere.

We glanced at the tariff, on a printed sheet of paper pinned to the wall. Two double rooms for 180 pesos; just over US$8.00; cheaper and more central than our own. However, it wasn't the price that interested us, but a little historical curiosity. This was the hotel in which D.H. Lawrence lived while in Mexico City during the late 1920s where he wrote *Mornings in Mexico*.

We stood in the hallway, before a man seated behind the desk, reading a newspaper.

'Que es el cuarto por escritor Ingles ...' I began in my fractured Spanish, hesitating momentarily, not knowing how to say D.H.

The man looked up and with a slight smile pointed to a room on the first landing above the courtyard. 'Ciento veinte,' he said. Room 120. I smiled back and said, 'Ah!'

He returned to reading his paper. I guess he gets quite a few like us.

We needed to buy anti-malaria tablets for later in the trip and Mexico City seemed the place to try because of the large number of brightly advertised, attractive 'farmacias'. The sales assistants in smart-coloured uniforms, often with the name of the shop embroidered across the back or its monogram stitched on the pocket, sold a frighteningly large array of potentially dangerous drugs without bothering about prescriptions. We bought our tablets and stocked up on antibiotics.

For a pill-popper, Mexico is paradise, but it wasn't until we talked with a young American doctor, holidaying in the Yucatan, that we heard of its hellish side. Mexico, he assured us, is used by the huge American drug companies as an unofficial testing ground for their new products, treating Mexicans as one step up from mice and guinea-pigs.

Many Mexicans may deride gringos, but they still lap up the worst aspects of gringo culture, along with the rest of the equally schizophrenic world. American TV and fast-food outlets are everywhere. McDonalds, Pizza Hut and Colonel Sanders are transplanted as complete units, right down to the disposable plates which set your teeth on edge and nasty, squeezy containers full of ketchup and tasteless mustard.

But we ignored Sean's imprecations at lunch time and ate instead from a roadside stall, tortas, flat buns stuffed with cooked ham, tomatoes and avocado. Yummy and only three pesos (36 cents).

As we munched, we watched the female population pass by. They seemed to have become stuck with the extravagant duenna-style stage make-up and fashion epitomised by Maria Callas.

Beside us was a newspaper and magazine kiosk with a large range of stock, among them Excelsior, Novedades, El Dia, El Nacional, Siempre, Sucesos. We skimmed through them, already readjusting our view of world events to how it is seen from this rarely-considered part of the world. We moved round one side and Iain squeezed my arm and pointed with a smile; here were the comparatively modest Mexican equivalents of Playboy or Penthouse.

One of them was taped open at a centrefold (I wondered if she had the seemingly obligatory degree in macrobiotics and sociology) who exhibited a very catholic amount of her luscious charms beneath a vacuous smile while beside her was pinned a full colour poster, again no detail spared, of a crucified Jesus Christ.

At the Basilica of Guadalupe, the most revered Catholic shrine in Mexico, we were treated, the following day, to another rather bizarre scene. In the big, open plaza surrounding the old church and the new circular Basilica, we were confronted, on our arrival, by the somewhat extreme sight of men and women walking on their knees across the wide-paved courtyard towards the entrance of the new Basilica. Many of them, we were told proudly by an English-speaking man at the gate, had come on their knees from their homes, perhaps several kilometres away. He offered us his service as a guide, but we declined and followed the pilgrims towards the shrine. Several of the men's pants were torn and the knees of both men and women were bloody ... but they had a light in their eyes. Soon they would look on the sacred cloth.

Legend has it that here, in 1531, the Virgin Mary appeared to a humble

Indian, Juan Diego, and told him that a church should be built on this spot. On hearing Diego's story, the Bishop asked for more proof. The Indian returned on December 12th with his cloak full of roses that the Virgin had directed him to pick; but when they opened the mantle they found instead a vivid image of the Virgin. The sacred cloth hung in the old Basilica for many years in a frame of solid gold behind a railing made from 27 tonnes of silver. It has recently been shifted across the courtyard into the giant, new, modern church, where it hangs on a wall above the altar.

Inside the huge building close to 3000 people stood packed tightly, listening to a special Sunday Mass. Hundreds of them, many weeping with emotion, filed slowly through a passageway behind the altar, where they could look more closely at the sacred picture of the Virgin and throw coins, or notes, into a large receptacle beneath it.

The church will need every penny it can get, especially if it has to build a new Basilica every couple of hundred years, which appears likely. Due to the fact that Mexico City is built on a lake-bed and has no rock foundation, the original old Basilica of Guadalupe and the chapel beside it are slowly sinking. They tilt at an alarming degree, looking like some topsy-turvey buildings from *Alice in Wonderland,* and are already dangerous to the public. The same fate probably awaits the new Basilica.

Leon Trotsky would have liked the new subway we took to his extraordinary house in Coyoacan, an old, outer suburb of the city. Classical music is played softly and continuously on all stations. The service is efficient and the trains are clean, modern and silent on their rubber wheels. Best of all, at only one peso (12 cents) for any distance, it's cheap.

Our carriage was filled with young women, shapeless in their warm ponchos, all of them with at least one child, and young men with glossy black hair. A boy walked through the carriage, shouting remorselessly to advertise the tray of combs he carried, but, surprisingly, he sold not one.

Leaving the subway we found, after a brief search, the large brick house that once belonged to Trotsky; an incongruous, high-walled, corner fortress amid soporific suburbia. It is made monstrous and ugly by turrets with gun-slits and steel shutters which cover three-quarters of each window.

This is the self-made prison into which the terrified Trotsky locked himself during the 1930s in the vain hope of escaping the unforgiving menace of Stalin's secret police, the NKVD; an arm of the Soviet Government which, while realising that Trotsky alive was a pivot around which dissent could gather, failed to recognise that a dead martyr often fulfils that role at least twice as well.

The gate through the wall was bricked up and we had to search further down the street to find a way in through the garage to the garden.

We were shown grudgingly around the grounds and inside the building by a young student, who brightened only marginally when we let drop the fact that we were not Americans who would be, from his political viewpoint, total anathema. Australia is sometimes a usefully unknown quantity.

Trotsky's was a classic case of needing no worse enemy than your best friend. On August 20th, 1940, Ramon Mercader, who was known to Trotsky as Frank Jackson . . . a close friend, was admitted past the manned gun-slits and guards, into the house. Trotsky was sitting at his desk when Jackson/Mercader buried a mountaineer's ice-pick in his skull.

As if frozen in horror, the house has remained unchanged from that time. Everything has been left exactly as it was. The smashed reading glasses and open book are still on Trotsky's desk and there are stains of what is supposedly blood on the floor.

Sean, with the morbid curiosity of all ten-year-old boys, pored over the files of clippings from newspapers written at the time, which spare no grisly detail; photographs of Trotsky's mutilated brain being weighed and measured and showing (what else did they expect?) that it was normal size. The autopsied body, complete to the last stitch, is shown going into the fire and the ashes coming out. This, perhaps, was meant as final proof that he was indeed mere man. The indignity of it all.

The student was relieved as we moved out again from the house into the tangled garden, where a deeply-cut hammer and sickle marks Leon Trotsky's simple gravestone. Two dogs, more willing, apparently, than their owner to voice their hostility, barked at us and frightened a large tabby cat into leaping over the grave.

At the exit, we paused, uncertain if we were expected to make some donation, or if that would perhaps be taken as a capitalist insult. But, by the time we had decided, the young man had turned and closed the door.

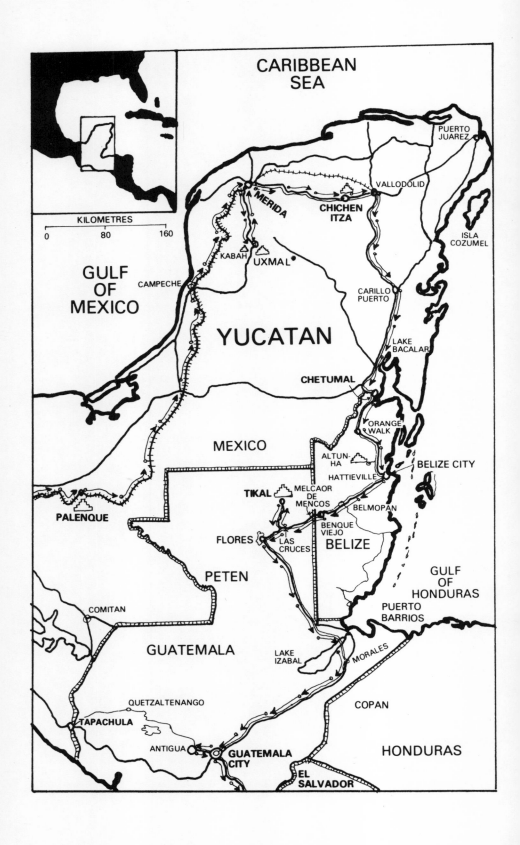

MEXICO

5
Their entire history went up in flames

We very nearly missed the night train to Palenque arriving with mere minutes to spare only because a game taxi-driver entered into the spirit of the adventure and risked having to pay penalties (or bribes) for breaking all regulations by cramming the four of us, Iain hunched down on our packs on the floor in front, into his three-seater VW Beetle.

It was a slow train, covering the 1000 or so kilometres in fourteen hours, but that gave us time to indulge in the illusion of standing still which was a relief after the crowded days in the capital. We were sorry to move on, consoling ourselves with a promise of an extended return visit, because there was so much more we would have liked to have seen and done. But what we had seen, especially in the Museum of Anthropology, had whetted our appetites for the Yucatan and also, as South America seemed still such a very long distance away, part of us was glad to be moving on.

The American-built train had no dining car, so we ate boiled eggs and fresh fruit, which were sold by vendors who pushed trays through the windows at each stop. We read, slept, wrote letters and our diaries. The countryside slipped by outside and we pleasurably shed a layer of clothes as it became increasingly tropical. By midday we stopped at Coatzacoalcos, on the wide mouth of a river which feeds into the Caribbean.

We would be here for 'dos horas' according to a fellow in a white uniform jacket, which we hoped gave him some sort of official status.

'Autobus a puerto.' He pointed to a battered vehicle. We boarded it and did a complete tour of the small town before stopping beside a pleasant open-air restaurant overlooking the river.

Lumbering pelicans and swift seagulls vied unequally for morsels thrown overboard from numerous craft which motored up and down in front of us as we consumed a large fish and prawn meal. There seemed to be nothing to do in Coatzacoalcos except sit and watch the water traffic, which would make it a very pleasant place to be marooned for a while.

Back at the train we found that a carriage full of soldiers carrying English automatic rifles had been added.

'Is there a war?' Sean asked, hopefully. Or perhaps a revolution, just to fulfil my Dad's prophecy!

Actually this picture of Mexico teetering from revolution to revolution with the aid of Pancho Villa and Emile Zapata (not to mention the Cisco Kid) is completely erroneous and is based mostly on the average Northern European's parochial belief in the superiority of his political system.

It is true that in the twenty-five years following 1823, when a republic was established, there were at least thirty changes of government, but all that is over a century ago. The thirty-year dictatorship of Porfirio Diaz ended in 1911 and six years later a constitution was established. Since then, apart from the bloody suppression of student disorders before the 1968 Olympic Games in Mexico City, the country's domestic life has been relatively tranquil.

There has been a slow but steady increase in the standard of living, especially among city dwellers, and at almost $1100, average earnings per capita are the highest in the region apart from Panama for which the figure is over $1300.

Primary education is free and compulsory, though the illiteracy rate is still as high as 40 percent. Social welfare and health programmess are sporadic and most Mexicans survive on a diet well below the minimal UN standards. The overall picture has been of a rural economy moving slowly and sometimes awkwardly into the technological twentieth century.

But there could be some very dramatic changes. In the last three years Mexico has discovered such immense reserves of oil and natural gas . . . some 200 million barrels . . . with more to come, that it is second only to Saudi Arabia in the oil stakes. This new found wealth is likely to revolutionise not only standards of living in Mexico itself, but also its relations with the economic giant to the north, the United States, which, as oil supplies from the Arab world become more difficult and expensive, is certain to turn increasingly to Mexico — its once despised poor neighbour.

Elections in Mexico are held every six years and anyone, having once held the office of President, is automatically barred from standing for that office again. Perhaps the ambivalence implicit in the name of the present ruling party, under President José Lopez-Portillo y Pacheco, sums up Mexican life most succinctly. It is The Party of Institutionalised Revolution.

Our soldiers settled down to a game of cards and we dozed our way to Palenque, arriving at the tiny unlit station a little after 10 p.m. It was very dark as we stumbled under our packs over a number of recumbent bodies huddled on the floor in the cold, doorless, foul-smelling waiting room. We felt our way outside where we peered through the light drizzle into the swallowing blackness. Even when our eyes adjusted we couldn't see any indication of human habitation; just an empty stretch of land.

After fifteen or so anxious minutes, the lights of a vehicle solidified into a beaten-up taxi which drove us five kilometres into the seemingly peaceful little village of Palenque.

The front room in the Hotel Avenida had three small beds, insufficient blankets and cold water only. And we were wrong about the peace. At frequent intervals through the night our shallow sleep was further disturbed by the roar of heavy trucks and their drivers who used our hotel as a half-hour R & R stopover.

The haunting ruins of Palenque, however, should be sufficient compensation for any sleepless night and, the next morning, by the time we had taken a ten-minute ride, in a bus labelled 'Ruinas', and were walking through the entrance gate to the ancient city, the noise-makers of the previous night were forgotten and we were beginning to feel a sense of real excitement.

For Palenque, though small in the area that has so far been uncovered, is extremely important in the story of the Mayan people ... not only as a sacred city, their most westerly outpost; where the sun 'died' each day, but because it has yielded an astounding treasure to modern archaeologists.

The ruins are set in a sea of deep jungle, which covers almost all of what was once a great city, with many thousands of inhabitants. Only two groups of eight structures have so far been rescued from the jungle's grasp, but researchers, clambering through the tangled undergrowth, have pinpointed scores of other major buildings spread over an area eleven kilometres long by five kilometres wide.

Western interest in Palenque and other Mayan cities in the Yucatan began to gather some momentum in the mid-nineteenth century, after publication of the journals of a New York lawyer, John Lloyd Stephens, who came to Palenque in 1837 with the architect and illustrator Frederick Catherwood. They spent two years uncovering its temples and carvings, writing about and drawing them.

We have a copy of those journals and it was Catherwood's wonderful line drawings, perhaps even more than Stephens' words, which had inspired us to visit the Yucatan and particularly Palenque. His illustrations of the vast, ruined Mayan city are beautifully sensual, but at the same time, remarkably detailed and accurate. They show huge, grotesque, stone faces peering out from thick, tropical jungle and intricate, very alien carvings along the surfaces of mammoth temple walls.

We were early on the site and there were no other visitors about. There was silence, serenity ... and a strange beauty about the place, which, although the air was warm, was wreathed in mist and low clouds.

Almost before we realised it, having passed along a short jungled path, we arrived in a large clearing. To our front, the so-called 'Palace' and to our right, the towering 'Temple of the Inscriptions'. (The names of the various temples and buildings at Palenque ... even the name Palenque ... are not Mayan, but Spanish. The original Mayan names are not known.)

The Temple of the Inscriptions is atop the highest pyramid, which has proved to be the most fascinating structure in Palenque and amongst the most important in the entire Mayan world.

We climbed up the wide, but extremely steep, central staircase, Sean and Zara leading the way, and then, sitting on the stone platform outside the temple at the top, catching our breath, we looked out over what was once a broad plaza. Rolling, jungled plains stretched off, under heavy grey clouds, into the distance. Turning inside the temple, we studied a wall covered with detailed and beautifully complex glyphs, the story-telling pictures, or ideographs, used by the Mayans as writing.

The other limestone walls dripped with moisture, but it is the floor ... the floor of the temple which is the key to one of the greatest archaeological discoveries of the century.

The Mexican archaeologist, Dr Alberto Ruz Lluhuillier noticed, in 1949, while in charge of the excavations at Palenque, a number of stone-filled round holes in a giant slab, set into the floor of the temple. Removing the stone pegs and employing a powerful winch, hooked into the exposed holes, he raised the slab to discover a flight of steps leading down some eighteen metres into the heart of the pyramid.

At the time, he couldn't see how far the passageway went down, because it had been purposely filled with rubble to block the stairway. But after almost three years of clearing work, Lluhuillier reached a chamber at the bottom of the steps. Outside were six skeletons, presumably guards. Inside the small chamber, he found a huge stone sarcophagus, covered by a five-tonne slab of granite, intricately carved with glyphs telling the story of the person inside the tomb. The skeleton in the sarcophagus was that of an old man with one club foot and a split big toe on the other. He was bejewelled in a jade necklace, jade earrings and a beautiful pear-shaped pearl. It was the skeleton of a king.

We descended the same stairs slowly. The walls of the narrow tunnel leading into the depths of the pyramid were dripping with water, the steps were slippery, and the gloomy passageway was lit only at irregular intervals by bare electric bulbs. We talked softly, as if there might be someone down there to hear us, but our voices boomed and echoed.

Zara and Sean laughed nervously and Sean asked,

'Are there ghosts down there?'

Eventually, at the bottom, we stood before the tomb of the mighty King Pakal, who ruled the city-state of Palenque for sixty-eight years, dying, when he was well over ninety years old, in the year 683 AD. For almost 1300 years he lay, in absolute darkness and silence, until that day in 1952 when his funerary crypt was opened and all previous theories about the pyramids of the Americas were shattered.

The discovery of Pakal's burial place came as a profound shock to modern archaeologists who, until that moment, had firmly believed that all Toltec, Aztec and Mayan pyramids were built only to support temples and not intended, like those of the ancient Egyptians, as tombs for their kings. This was the first middle-American pyramid in which an important tomb had been discovered.

Climbing up the stairway to the light again, we found that the heavy mist had turned to rain. We put on waterproof jackets and, climbing down from the high temple, wandered through the ruins of the Palace, in the cracked walls of which, tropical shrubs and even trees had taken root. It was easy to see how the jungle takes over.

We stood watching the rain trickle over the magnificent carvings in the courtyard. We were alone. It was slightly uncanny ... the almost silence ... only the soft sound of the rain drenching everything. And yet, in a way, we were glad it was like this; seeing it under these circumstances was probably closer to how the original people of Palenque knew it, as the area around Palenque has the highest annual rainfall in all of Mexico. The rain had also discouraged other visitors, so we had the ruined city almost to ourselves.

We followed a soggy, jungle track to some smaller buildings and, climbing a grassy hill to the Temple of the Sun, we stopped, surprised to hear the haunting sound of a single flute being played. We continued up to the temple and found a young girl sitting, dripping-wet, on the floor, facing out into the rain, playing her flute. She was Canadian. We talked for a while, but conversation was difficult, either because of the effects of Palenque on her, or of something else. She appeared to be somewhat 'spaced-out'.

She continued playing melancholy, but also beautiful music, while we stood for ten or fifteen minutes, during a heavy downpour, looking out towards the dense forest surrounding us. It was almost impossible to imagine that these huge, grass-covered mounds we could see, and on which we were standing, were all once gleaming-white pyramids and temples of stone and that people thronged the plazas and the streets below. And yet, that was how it was in Palenque until, for some reason still unknown, the city died around the tenth century AD when the Mayans began their mysterious migration north into the Yucatan Peninsula.

The Mayans had been in Palenque, archaeologists believe, from around 300 BC but, the beginnings of Mayan civilisation go back considerably further, to roughly 2000 BC ... a civilisation that lasted right through to the Spanish conquest of Central America in the sixteenth century. The Aztecs, by comparison, only flourished briefly for three or four hundred years.

The Mayans developed the most advanced method of writing in the New World, the complicated glyphic system, which has not been properly deciphered to this day. They practised an astronomy so precise that their 365-day calendar was as accurate as the one we use now. They used sophisticated agricultural techniques and their art, pottery and sculpture were not only of the highest standards, but incredibly beautiful. The sculptured wall panels at Palenque are considered amongst the most exquisite achievements in pre-Columbian art.

But, for us, viewing the Maya from the twentieth century, their story is one of great tragedy and mystery. Tragedy, in that an incredible civilisation was so brutally crushed by the crusading, gold-hungry, Spanish Conquistadores and that, as a result of their sweeping destruction we are left with only a partial picture of what Mayan societies were like. The rest of that picture may be a mystery forever because of the wholesale destruction, by the Spanish friars, of an entire culture.

The Spaniards were so angered by the Mayan practice of sacrifice that, under the direction of Bishop Diego de Landa, the friars carried out a systematic burning of all Mayan ideographic literature. In dozens of major centres across the Yucatan, hundreds of Mayan priests and intellectuals were forced to watch, helpless and distraught, as whole libraries ... their entire history, went up in flames.

But stone carvings were not destroyed and so far about 800 glyphic elements have been catalogued from these, although archaeologists have been unable to decode more than about thirty percent of them. Unfortunately, up to the present, there has been nothing like the Rosetta Stone, which led to the translation of Egyptian hieroglyphics, for Mayan scholars to use. The task of decipherment is slow and tedious, but there are at least some Mayan experts who are sufficiently optimistic to predict that one day the language of the Maya will eventually be fully understood.

When we began our visit to Palenque, we had felt a sense of excitement. As we left the ruins, in the still-falling rain, to make our way back to the town of Palenque, it was more like a sense of discovery; as though we had been shown another world . . . a world of which we had only the beginnings of understanding.

'Where you from then?' the rain-bedraggled man in the bush hat inquired in immediately recognisable accents, as we shared the shelter of a small porch outside our hotel.

'Same place as you, mate,' we replied laughing in the immediate, easy camaraderie which is one of the luxuries shared between fellow travellers, especially mutual nationals.

But we had even more than that in common with Will and Nora O'Shea from Sydney, for they were travelling with their eight-year-old son Jason. Jason, as I shall always recall him, of the wonderfully raucous laugh! Will and Nora were, and still are, the only people we have ever met who travel long overland distances in the company of their children. People on the road are either younger than us and therefore have few responsibilities, or older and have dispensed with their ties.

Will and Nora had sold up their home, left two older boys, one of them married, behind in Sydney and headed for London, where Will was born, by a somewhat roundabout route. Sydney to Rio and from then on by public transport overland down through the Argentine, up through Chile, Bolivia, Peru and Colombia and across into Central America. Having made it up to Mexico they were now going on into the US and over to England where they planned to work awhile. By making their money spin out as far as possible, they had already been on the road for five months and hoped to make London inside another four weeks.

We swopped the sort of hard-earned advice and cautionary tales which come by experience and are of far greater value than any guide book.

'Don't go through Colombia, unless you really have to,' Will suggested. 'It's rough. We've not met one person who's travelled through there who hasn't had some lousy experience. Robbed . . . mugged even. I had my camera snatched off my neck. You have to be constantly on your guard. And who needs that?'

To escape the steady rain we were sitting in a little café eating pancakes swimming in honey. Such a relief to be able to speak quickly in English and to be readily understood. The children, delighting in each other's company, were indulging in behaviour which normally would not be allowed, especially in public; gobbling their food, talking sideways from full mouths, balancing back on their chairs and stretching to grab drinks.

They were becoming more and more hyped-up when Jason let rip a most contagious wild laugh. This broke up our two who fell about in tears of pure joy and the more we tried to shush them up, the more uncontrollable they became and the less able we were to resist joining in so that eventually we were all guffawing like loonies.

In the exhausted lull which followed Nora told us, 'Friends thought we were mad to bring Jason on a trip like this, I guess they've said the same to you.' We nodded. 'But we've enjoyed it so much more with him than if we'd been on our own. We push ourselves to see more because we want him to see it and he is such good company.'

Jason was regaling our kids with the story of how he'd climbed to the top of the Great Pyramid at Uxmal.

'It's so steep they have a chain for you to hold on to.' He turned to me. 'People have fallen down and died.' Loud laughter from Zara and Sean. 'You won't like it.' Gales of giggles. How very right he was!

'I'm getting a bit tired of it now.' Nora, with mother-quick reactions saved Jason's chair from toppling backwards. 'Especially at night when we walk past people's lighted homes and can see them eating dinner or watching TV. Oooh, I think, what wouldn't I give to be in my own place. And I'm sick of being scruffy.'

Jason didn't care, as sockless and resembling a walking jumble sale, but still laughing, he clutched a very battered, large teddy bear as we waved them and their five dilapidated suitcases onto the overnight bus to Mexico City.

Rainwater sprayed out from under the wheels as the bus rolled away into the darkness. We followed, silently downhill to our hotel, 'Quiet, isn't it?' said Zara, in a lonely voice.

'Second-class tickets only.' The man behind the ticket grille at Palenque station was adamant. Sleeping compartment tickets could only be purchased in Mexico City.

'What about on the train?'

The man was offhand. 'No possible,' he said.

We were waiting for yet another night train, this one from Palenque to Merida, almost six hundred and fifty kilometres away at the northern end of the Yucatan.

Iain persisted, 'Can't I buy a sleeper ticket now, just in case they haven't sold them all in Mexico City? Then if there's no sleeper available I could get a refund the other end.'

Without answering, the clerk slammed the door shut across the grille.

With Iain still muttering abuse about all station clerks from Wagga to Wadi Halfa, we went along to the rather dingy cafe on the platform and joined a multi-national group of young travellers, many of them also complaining about the unavailability of sleepers. Rather as though the Holy Ghost had come upon them, they all understood one another even though they spoke in many tongues. The one who most impressed the children was a tall sun-tanned fellow dressed in elegantly casual clothes, topped by a straw sombrero. He conversed simultaneously with several people, asking questions in Spanish, replying in English, translating into French, Italian and Dutch while making asides in his mother-tongue, German.

Sean settled down at a corner table to play a version of draughts with the young daughter of the café owner who was very quick to join them as a chaperone. Sean was disgusted at losing to a mere girl.

'Anyway, she cheated. She kept making up new rules.' Good training for future relationships.

Rick McLellan had been taking a short, wind-down break from New York ('I was on the verge of flipping out') and had flown from Miami across to the Yucatan, only an hour and three-quarters away, on sudden impulse. His only previous travels had been in Europe. With the glazed expression of a punch-drunk prize fighter he kept repeating:

'What a place! I didn't know there was anything like this. I mean you read about the third world and all. But wow. The dirt and the poverty. It's awful. But it's interesting too. And so old.'

On hearing that Zara was born in New York he immediately began rummaging through his bag.

'I've got just the thing for you. Here. Take it.' He held up a black T-shirt with 'Native New Yorker' emblazoned on it in blue glittering letters.

'My girlfriend thought I might need it in Miami but it suits you better and, wow, wait 'til I tell her about Mexico. She won't believe it. What a place!'

Ever since, Zara has, with uncharacteristic eccentricity, used this declaration of her identity as a pyjama top.

Ten minutes before the train was due to arrive Iain stationed us on the platform beside our packs, at a very specific spot which he had chosen and from which he warned us not to move. The rest of the would-be travellers gathered at the far end of the platform, where the first carriage of the incoming train would be sure to halt. But Iain was adamant that we were better positioned here.

'When you hear the train coming put on your packs and follow me.'

Out of the inky blackness it came, only a quarter of an hour late, and screeched to a standstill with an open carriage door exactly where we stood. Iain leapt aboard and we obediently followed. A scowling attendant appeared, shaking his fist at us.

'No entrada.' He pointed up the train to where the seething mob were trying to board.

'Alcoba,' Iain demanded and the man's face broke into smiles.

'Ah. Si. Si. Senor.'

We followed him to an empty sleeping compartment with four bunks and he went off to arrange bedding.

By the time the other travellers had struggled through to the Alcoba (Bedroom) Carriage the children were already in bed. The ticket inspector had readily accepted the cash in hand for the increase in fare over the second-class tickets we held.

From the comfort of his bunk Iain explained that he had remembered where we'd disembarked from our sleeping compartment on arriving in Palenque and had rightly guessed that the train would stop again in the same position.

Merida, at the northern end of the Yucatan Peninsula, has the reputation of being one of the most pleasant towns in Mexico and we found that view well-deserved. Not only is it a physically attractive town, but its people were friendly, open and relaxed.

The city, which is the capital of the state of Yucatan, is known for being progressive and clean and for the beauty of its colonial buildings. It was founded in 1542, built on the site of the ancient Mayan city of Tihoo, using building material from the Mayan structures, which were torn down.

Most of the present-day inhabitants of Merida, which has a population of some 250,000, have some Maya blood and a considerable number are pure Maya. Nearly everyone speaks Spanish, of course, but it came as a surprise to us to learn that there are still many who prefer to speak the ancient Mayan language of their forefathers and to regard themselves as Mayan first and Mexican second.

In cosmopolitan Mexico City, all significant traces of the Aztecs, as a race, have been virtually swamped, but here, we really began to feel as if we were amongst a living Maya people. It was quite unexpected too, to find people wearing different clothes ... particularly the women, most of whom wore 'huipils', the long, white, embroidered robe. They also tended to braid their hair into a long pigtail.

Although there is little physical evidence of its Mayan origins left in Merida itself, it is a good central base from which to explore some of the other ruined Mayan cities in the Yucatan, particularly Uxmal (pronounced Ooshmal), about seventy kilometres from Merida, and the famous Chichen Itza, both of which we hoped to visit in the next couple of days.

Having arrived in Merida after a reasonable journey on the overnight train, we avoided several hotel touts at the station and humped our packs about seven or eight blocks to the Hotel Flamingo, which we'd seen recommended in our guide book. A room with three large beds and a bathroom; 166 pesos (US$7.50) for the four of us ... and that included a swimming pool, which Zara and Sean entered immediately.

Later, we wandered through the narrow streets, past beautiful old Moorish houses, painted in pastel pinks, blues and greens to the 'Plaza Major', the lovely main square, shaded by trees and flanked by the usual Cathedral, State Palace and City Hall. There are also several pleasant restaurants around the square, at which one can sit quietly, with a cup of coffee or a glass of wine, and watch the passers-by.

The only sour note to the Plaza Major is Montejo House, which was built in 1549; two stone Spanish knights stand on either side of the entrance to the building. Each one rests a foot on the head of a bowed Indian!

The markets of Merida are renowned for traditional Mexican crafts; panama hats, deer-skin and tire-soled sandals, hammocks, pottery ware, tortoise-shell combs, sisal baskets and beautiful filigree silverwork. The most astounding, though very cruel, items for sale were tiny black beetles about two and a half centimetres long; which had been studded and bejewelled with bits of coloured glass and then attached to a small chain which could be pinned on a blouse or jacket. The owner would then be wearing a live, glistening brooch which could wander about on his or her lapel, within the limits of the restraining chain. We didn't buy one.

We were however sufficiently tempted to buy some well-made replicas of Mayan pottery, which we planned to send off by parcel post, but unfortunately our forays into the Merida markets were cut short when Trish began to develop the crippling symptoms of what the locals call, with grim irony, 'La Vengeanca de Moctezuma' ... Moctezuma's Revenge. In other words ... the runs.

We took a horse-drawn carriage to the bus terminal to buy a return ticket for a day trip to the Mayan ruins at Uxmal for the next day, but by mid-afternoon, Trish felt so lousy, with stomach cramps, nausea, and muscle pains, that all she could do was go to bed.

Thank God, once treated, the dreaded symptoms of diarrhoea go almost as fast as they arrive. So that by the time we boarded the early morning bus for the sixty-five kilometre ride to the ruins at Uxmal, though I was feeling wobbly-kneed and disconnected, I knew I was on the mend.

My Dad always comforted my petite younger sister with the old saw, 'great things come wrapped in small parcels', and Uxmal is an illustration of the truth in this.

The main section is about 800 metres long and about 600 metres wide but within this small compass are a series of buildings which were built between 600 AD and 1000 AD when the Mayan civilisation had reached its apogee of skills and craftsmanship.

In contrast with the jungles of Palenque, the Mayan towns of the Yucatan are set in arid scrub country. Even though it was not yet 9 a.m. the dry air held the threat of great heat.

Despite this, my still uncertain muscles and Jason's vivid warning, the first thing we did was to scramble up the ludicrously misnamed Pyramid of the Dwarf. One hundred and fifty steep steps with narrow crumbling treads. I was less than half-way up when I realised, with that awful, cold, clutching at the stomach which presages fear, that I had made a terrible mistake. But it seemed safer to go on up, than to attempt the reverse.

Iain tells me that the temple at the summit has a single row of rooms, and that the stone facade is decorated with a design of entwined serpents. Also, that there's a magnificent view from the forty-five metre perch, out over the tops of the ruined buildings, across the slightly undulating landscape. He also says there was a slight breeze, but I noticed none of this through the blur of tears which came unbidden. Instead I sat hugging my knees, trying very hard to concentrate on gathering together all my inner resources. (Pull your socks up, mother of two.) At the same time watching from the outside and thinking how ridiculous I looked and how badly I was behaving. Which is exactly what anyone who has never suffered from vertigo, or fear of heights, is thinking as they read this.

I asked Iain, who, oblivious of my distress, was still pointing out things of interest, to start off before me and talk non-stop all the way down.

At this point Zara and Sean who had run up ahead of us and had gone down already, came leaping up again, 'Look Mum, no hands,' to see what was wrong and I yelled at them to go away; which they did, nimbly, only increasing my panic.

Lying on my stomach I edged my feet back over the almost sheer drop and, wiping the nervous sweat from my hands for the final futile time, grasped the heavy metal chain which lay down the steps from top to bottom. This, I guess, was put there by a thoughtful tourist department. (Dead tourists are not good for business.)

If you are insensitive enough to be chortling with disbelief at all this, now is the time to tell that a week later, in the ruined Mayan city of Tikal, a government tourist guide who had been running, yes, running up and, would you believe it, down the steep sides of the giant thirty-metre-high pyramid there, fell and, before a crowd of horrified tourists, bumped and tumbled to his death.

'Talk,' I demanded of Iain.

'The best thing is not to look down,' he began.

'Not about that, you stupid bastard,' I yelled. 'About anything else. Just talk.' Which is what he did, but, even through my suffocating fear, I could sense his justifiable anger. At the bottom he strode away without a further word, with me stumbling, my heart still thumping, after him, apologising profusely for being such a bitch.

They say that in times of stress people show their true colours! I tried to joke the incident away, but it was some time before he would even smile. By then the children had come bounding back, with the news that they had found a giant penis, made of stone, I hasten to add. It once stood, with a temple of its own, in all its three metre splendour, in front of the House of the Governor. Now it lies, broken cruelly in half, supposedly for moral reasons, not yet restored.

The Governor's House is spoken of by archaeologists in awed tones as the single most magnificent structure of all the ancient buildings in the Americas. It is an imposing 97 metres long, 12 metres wide and 8 metres high, and its three terraces are faced with 20,000 richly carved and ornamented stone blocks. The standard of craftsmanship is so high that it would be impossible to slip even a sheet of paper into the fine mortarless joints.

Behind the Governor's House is the equally impressive Nunnery Quadrangle, designated this because of its eighty-eight little rooms, by the Spaniards, whose wholesale destruction of Mayan culture left us no further clue on its original use.

Among the fine carvings on the walls in the four buildings which enclose a twenty-seven by eighteen metre courtyard is an illustration of an ordinary village dwelling. It is especially interesting because, in common with all ancient cultures, only the mammoth temples were built to withstand the rigours of time and climate so that of the simple houses of the people, nothing remains. But here it is, frozen in stone, the classic Indian mud hut with a thatched roof which we saw everywhere throughout Mexico, unchanged down all the centuries.

Uxmal is only one of the many Mayan ruins in this area of the Yucatan Peninsula, the whole of which is thick with barely revealed sites and certain to contain treasures yet undiscovered. Many of these cities were linked to one another along raised causeways which are thought to have been ceremonial roads.

At the southern extremity of the Uxmal site is a triumphal archway under which one of these roads leads off to be swallowed up by dry bush. The arch, five metres high and three metres wide is an illustration of a peculiar engineering dyslexia from which the Maya suffered, for they never discovered how to form a true arch. Instead, by placing stones on top of one another, each projecting slightly beyond the one below it until a single stone could breach the gap, they built a corbelled arch; an ungainly and awkward way to go about things.

Their other mental block, which was probably an even greater deterrrent to their advancement, was their extraordinary failure ever to use the wheel for anything other than children's toys.

On the bus back to Merida, Sean leant forward and quietly threw up. By the time we were back at our hotel he was white-gilled and silent and wanted nothing more than to lie on his bed. Iain went off to dinner with Zara, who was delighted, like all pubescent girls, to have her father all to herself. On their return, I was spared no detail of their superb Huachananga a la Veracruzana (red snapper) meal. But in the low ebb of the early morning hours, the red snapper made its reappearance as Moctezuma struck again.

It is quite a singular experience to stand in the hollow centre of a great pyramid and to gaze into the vacant, stone eyes of the terrible god, Chac Mool. I can stand a couple of metres from him in safety and, in the tiny, sweltering-hot chamber I have reached by clambering up a long, metre-wide tunnel, I can photograph this apparently innocuous, recumbent figure, which holds a stone, saucer-shaped dish on his stomach . . . without fear. And yet I feel the fringes of fear in the awful presence of Chac Mool. Behind him stands the High Priest's throne; a red jaguar, carved in stone and set with seventy pieces of jade.

How many hundreds . . . how many thousands of freshly-torn-out, still-beating human hearts had been flung triumphantly, by innumerable high priests, into that stone dish as their owners were brutally sacrificed to Chac Mool? The thought is sobering . . . and yet, 1000 years ago, that sort of scene was commonplace here in Chichen Itza.

Chichen Itza (literally: the well-mouth of the Itza people) is the most famous of all the archaeological sites on the Yucatan Peninsula. About a hundred and twenty kilometres east of Merida, the ruins of this once-great Mayan and Toltec city are one of the wonders of the world.

But to attempt to see one of the wonders of the world, spread, as Chichen Itza is, over fifteen square kilometres, in blistering thirty degree weather, when you are suffering from the dreaded Moctezuma's Revenge, deserves a medal. Yet that is just what we did. Trish and Sean had both, by this stage, fully recovered from their bouts, but Zara and I were just about zonked out. We had slept for most of the one-and-a-half-hour journey on the early-morning bus from Merida, checked into a pleasant and cheap little hotel in the village of Piste, a kilometre or so from the ruins, then flaked out in bed!

An hour later, however, we were up. We hitched a ride to the ruins and walked in, dripping with sweat. Zara and I felt utterly drained, full of aches and pains . . . without any strength. Zara said she would sit in the shade of a tree and rest. It was fiercely hot and I felt desperately like joining her, but . . . well, I told myself, I've come this far . . .

From where we stood, we could see, across the main plaza, the great pyramid, El Castillo (again Spanish, not Mayan names), the Ball Court and in the distance, in the other direction, the Temple of 1000 Columns and the Temple of the Warriors. My determination to see it all took over. I staggered off with Sean to climb El Castillo. Trish, after her experience with 'The Dwarf' at Uxmal, stayed down this time.

There are 91 steps on each of the four sides of the pyramid: 91 x 4 = 364. Plus the one big step up to the temple on the top, equals 365; the number of days in the Mayan calendar.

From the top, the view of the surrounding ruins was superb, but climbing these Mayan, or Aztec, or Toltec pyramids, it is difficult to avoid thinking about the sacrificial bodies being hurled down those steep steps after their hearts had been torn out. Gruesome . . . but that's the way it was. The Aztecs were the worst; they slaughtered by the thousands, in almost frantic efforts to placate their weather gods. Of course they couldn't continually sacrifice their own people, without decimating their population, so they were constantly at war in order to take prisoners to sacrifice. The Toltecs were not much better, but the Mayans were perhaps a little more circumspect; the numbers of their sacrifices were considerably less. One feels, though, that for the local populace, these temples must have had an aura of terror. They can hardly have been places of joy.

Still, in its heyday, Chichen Itza would have been, in many other ways, a fabulous city to see. First founded by the Mayas around 430 AD, it grew and expanded into a powerful and influential city and a major religious centre for the Maya. Then, around 900 AD, Chichen Itza came under the rule of the more aggressive Toltecs, who brought with them the dreaded Chac Mool. They remained in power until about the middle of the thirteenth century, at which time the city was apparently abandoned; no one knows why.

Sean and I descended cautiously from El Castillo, clinging to the iron chain which lies down the whole length of the steps, to enter the tunnel, at the bottom of the pyramid, which leads up into the interior sacred chamber containing Chac Mool and the Jade Jaguar.

Coming out from the inner sanctum again, we joined Trish and began walking (very slowly, with frequent rests for me, in whatever shade we could find) around some of the other structures. First, the famous, or rather, infamous Ball Court, a huge, oblong arena where players had to hit a rubber ball through a small loop of stone, positioned about six metres up on the side of one wall of the court. The winning team was, by all accounts, showered with gold and jewels, while the losers, according to a picture-carving on another wall, were often decapitated!

From the Ball Court, a broad causeway led us through the scrub to the sacred 'cenote' . . . a huge well, some sixty metres across with a drop of about nineteen metres to the surface of the water. Like Uxmal, and most of the other Mayan sites in the northern Yucatan, Chichen Itza is set in flat, dry, bush country in an area of very low rainfall. The only water supply the Mayans had was from a vast subterranean water table which was reached either by artificial wells, or through natural sinkholes . . . cenotes.

The air was absolutely still. In the massive heat of midday everything was still . . . and silent. Only mad dogs, Englishmen and we were out. We stood, a little awed, gazing into the dark waters of this huge hole, in which so many people died.

Into this cenote at Chichen Itza, hundreds of sacrificial victims were flung on various occasions, along with other treasures, as offerings to the plumed serpent-god Quetzalcoatl and Chac Mool. Many of these golden artifacts and jewels, as well as human bones have, in recent years, been dredged from the deep, green, algae-covered waters.

We continued walking (staggering on my part) from site to site. Despite my feelings of illness and fatigue, the fascination of the place was overwhelming. The city is so big, the buildings are so well preserved, you can feel its past magnificence; there are the remains of the huge Temples of the Warriors and 1000 Columns, which contain murals depicting the conquest of the Mayas by the Toltecs and another awful stone statue of Chac Mool. There is also a circular astronomical observatory which was the largest in the Americas, and the remains of the greatest and busiest market in the Mayan world where a slave could be bought for a hundred cacao beans.

In the comparative cool of that evening, as we sat quietly on the tiled verandah of the hotel, one of Sean's teeth fell out.

'Will the tooth fairy be able to find us here?' he asked with a knowing smile.

'Probably,' I said, also smiling.

Zara and I both began to feel slightly better. We had eaten no food during the day and drank only Coca-Cola, which, we have discovered, is an excellent aid to recovery from Moctezuma's Revenge. There was a beautiful full moon shining down on us ... the last we had seen had been in Tombstone, Arizona. Now, sitting here in its pale light, thinking about Chac Mool, sacrificial wells and ball games where the losers lost their heads, we talked with Zara and Sean about how lucky we are to be living now, instead of then. Although, I suppose we have our own, more modern terrors now.

Chichen Itza also left me with a striking impression of the impermanence of things. How great cities and civilisations come and go ... and that really, we can't expect our own to be much different.

On the bus to Valladolid, the next morning, we met Suzie and Graham, the young Australians we had first encountered in the railway station at Mexico City. They'd come on the bus from Merida and were on their way to find a hotel in Valladolid, after which they planned to go back to visit Chichen Itza from there. We hadn't really expected to see them again, but here we were, sixteen hundred kilometres or so further on, happily swopping stories. We were beginning to be able to make ourselves passably understood in Spanish, but it was always a bit of a struggle, so that speaking to someone in English again was such a relief, that I remember our conversations. Trish and Suzie, who is a nurse, talked about the comparative effects of psychology and chemotherapy on mental patients, while Graham set off to explain to me a theory he was developing about the reasons why the civilisations that evolved in the Northern Hemisphere were more advanced than those in the Southern Hemisphere.

'It's because they had the North Star,' he said.

'The North Star?'

'Yes. It seems to me that it was much easier for those northern societies to develop a calendar, because they had the North Star ... something which attracted their attention, because it appeared to remain stationary while all the other constellations revolved around it.'

I knew that the North Star was important. 'But,' I said, 'surely there were several early societies in the Southern Hemisphere which had pretty good calendars and understanding of astronomy without the North Star? The Incas ... and the Polynesians for instance.'

'Well, yes,' he said, 'but nothing like those of the Mayans ... or of course, the European calendars.'

Graham went on, turning in his seat to try to show me, drawing invisible circles in the palm of his hand, the movements of Venus around the sun, in relation to the earth and to explain how earlier societies recognised the fact that Venus was both the Morning and the Evening Star.

We left Graham and Suzie in Valladolid, to take another bus, about half an hour later to Carillo Puerto, a two-hour journey to the south.

The countryside was flat and monotonous; thick scrub country, punctuated occasionally with tiny settlements of poor, adobe (mud and straw, etc.) houses, with thatched roofs; subsistence farmers, trying to scratch a sorry living, growing corn, in a dry and unproductive land.

At Carillo Puerto, a nondescript town, we changed, almost immediately, into another bus which had been coming down the coast road from the popular resort areas of Cozumel and Isla Mujeres to the north. It was a large, modern, 'Greyhound' type of bus on which we would now travel all the way to Chetumal, the Mexican free-port town on the border with Belize.

We were on the move again and we felt good about it; good to be heading south. We'd been twelve days in Mexico and, although we'd crammed a lot in, and had been enjoying it all (except for La Vengeanca de Moctezuma) we were ready for the next stage now.

The bus droned on, the road was good, although narrow, and the driver held the bus at about a steady 110 kph. We were all sitting in separate seats, as the bus had been almost full when we boarded it. A Mayan woman of about twenty-five sat next to me, pressing a large, brown breast to the mouth of a child who looked old enough to go to school. Across the aisle, a wrinkled old man, with a classic Mayan hook-nosed profile, sat next to Trish, dozing quietly to the soporific hum of the bus's engine. Behind him, Sean, trying to cope with creeping boredom, began throwing his straw hat into the air and catching it. On the third throw, just as I was about to tell him to stop it, it went over the back of the seat and fell onto the sleeping old man.

BANG!!.

At that instant, the bus shook sharply and, with what sounded like machine-gun fire, the vehicle began to shake violently as the driver struggled with the wheel, trying to keep the bus from careering off the road.

All of the passengers had sat bolt upright in fear and gripped their seats at the sound of the first explosion ... some had yelled in surprise. I was surprised, when I had a chance to glance again at the old man, that he hadn't had a heart attack.

The bus slithered and staggered to a halt. The driver stepped out. We all stepped out ... a blow-out on one of the rear tires at 110 kph.

Nervous laughter, excited conversation, joking. Relief all round.

Fortunately, there had been double wheels on each side at the back, otherwise we might easily have left the road and crashed. It was the inside wheel which had blown, and therefore difficult to get at to change. But forty minutes later, after the driver and his assistant had fitted a new wheel, we were on our way again, arriving in Chetumal late in the afternoon.

We booked into the Hotel Eldorado (US$10 for the four of us), then walked to the waterfront where we sat in a nice little outdoor cafe, eating tortillas, tostadas and tacos as we watched the sun set on the Gulf of Mexico.

Chetumal has been declared a duty-free port in an attempt to turn it into the Singapore of Quintana Roo, the Mexican State of which it is the capital. The attempt is not, on the surface at least, a raving success though Mexicans do travel interstate on buying sprees and the shops sell an odd collection of expensive foreign goods; Australian canned butter, North American bottled beauty preparations and Japanese electronic gadgetry.

After a perfunctory look around the next morning, we decided to hitch out to a large, freshwater lake, Lake Bacalar, which we had seen, about ten kilometres out of town, when we had come in on the bus the previous day. Once we found the right road out of town, we didn't have long to wait for a lift.

'Oh, you are Owstralianos,' Jesus grinned and spoke in heavily accented, but easily understandable English. 'I thought you were Americanos.'

We had been stumbling along in Spanish and, though Jesus Velasquez had been kind enough to pick us up from the roadside, he had been decidedly cool toward us. Now all that changed and he continued to talk a blue streak.

'I live before, many years, in the United States. In Chicago, cold city. But I make much money. Every year I come home and work as policeman in Mexico City. I marry there and have three children, but they never come with me to the United States. I do not want my children to become Americanos.'

Jesus fulfils everyone's mental image of a Mexican. Rugged with sun-tanned, leathery features, a droopy moustache and thick black hair. He said he was forty-six, he looked thirty-five.

'Two years ago I buy land here. People are friendly, air is clean, life is simple. Only three hectares. I grow mango, papaya, avocado, pineapple, banana, coconut, tapioca, vegetables and chickens. You look.' He turned off the road sending up a shower of dust and small stones. 'Maria!' he yelled as he swung down out of the truck.

His wife, small and plump, wiped her hands on her large apron as she came out from under the shade of a lean-to shelter built against a shed. She smiled diffidently at us as Jesus gave what sounded like orders in Spanish. She brought us tin mugs of water from a rainwater tank beside a large wood-burning stove on which a big pot was bubbling.

From an old wheelless bus, which was obviously used as sleeping space, a girl of about fourteen appeared; a twin to her mother, followed by two boys of perhaps nine and four years. Again Jesus spoke to them in Spanish and they beckoned to Zara and Sean who followed them under the shade. Soon we heard cries of joy as they were introduced to dogs, cats, ducks and a parrot.

Jesus showed us around. Iain, being at heart a man of the soil, was very enthusiastic and asked detailed questions about crops and prices. Mrs Velasquez, despite our best efforts, kept a few paces behind us.

'I make a living,' Jesus told us. 'That is all, but I do all this myself and I belong to no man. I like to work hard. And I think my children should learn to do the same. We don't have television. It's a waste of time.'

The smallest child came with a request and Mrs Velasquez went with him back to the shed.

'That is Dante,' Jesus smiled indulgently. 'No more now. Three is all we can afford. I am not a Catholic. The church has made Mexico poor because it says to have children. There are not enough schools or jobs for all these people. The government says this oil they have found will make us all rich but how can it, if they go on having babies and thinking God will provide. That is the Indians who think like that. I am Spanish.' He said with pride. 'The Indians, the Maya, are lazy and superstitious. If the moon is covered with cloud, they say it's a bad sign and they don't work. I have at least twenty Mayan sites on 800 hectares I am buying further north, but I am pulling them apart and using the stone for walls. What's the point of keeping them. That's the past. What matters is the future.'

Later when Jesus dropped us off at Lake Bacalar, we found dozens of families spending a lazy Sunday afternoon. Mum guarding the remains of the picnic meal and keeping an attentive eye on baby while she knitted, Dad splashing in the shallows with the toddler. Teenage girls pretending indifference to young men who were playing ball and laughing a lot. A universal scene.

We swam out through the clear unbuoyant water, over a white granulated limestone lake floor, to a raft where we surfaced to the distinctive accents of rural England.

They came from some of those wonderful men in their flying machines who were part of the RAF squadron, based just eighty kilometres away over the border in neighbouring Belize.

'There's absolutely nothing to do there in off duty hours,' Ian McConnell from Wiltshire told us. 'So we come up here as often as possible just for a change of scene.'

When we told him that we were heading down through Belize, Ian, who has five children of his own, and was an instant hit with ours, offered us a lift in their jeep, which they had left just across the border.

'Be a bit crowded,' he warned Sean, who already had visions of himself as General Patton heading a convoy!

That evening all of Chetumal's residents were abroad enjoying the soft, warm air; dressed in their Sunday best, eating ice-creams, drinking soft drinks, riding on the miniature train, or lounging under the string of coloured bulbs hung haphazardly from tree to tree around the small waterfront square. We joined the cuddling couples dancing to the loud pop music provided by 'Pedro y su Groupo,' moving in a soporific trance around a large statue of Mexican soldiers in suitable heroic poses commemorating some long forgotten battle.

CENTRAL AMERICA

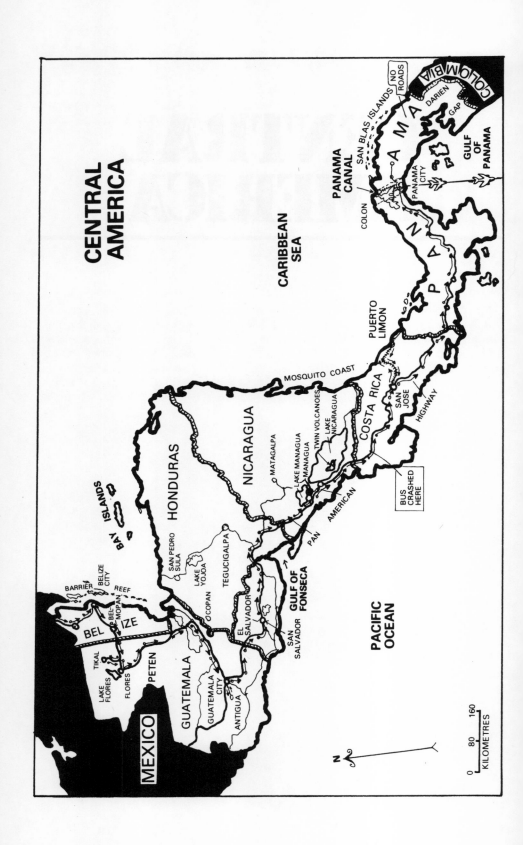

INTRODUCTION

Central America is comprised of seven countries which occupy a land area less than the size of New South Wales or the United Kingdom. But these tiny republics; Panama, Costa Rica, Nicaragua, Honduras, El Salvador, Guatemala and the self-governing British colony of Belize, strung out along 2000 kilometres of the relatively narrow strip of land separating the South American continent from the North, have had a violent and tempestuous history . . . a history which has ensured the fragmentation of the region into separate small entities, rather than staying together in a successful amalgam as a larger unit.

Attempts were made, right from the earliest days of the struggles for independence from Spain, to form a Federation of Central American States, at first voluntarily, then by force, then voluntarily again. From 1823, for a period of just on fifteen years, largely under the leadership of General Francisco Morozan, of Honduras, the Federation struggled on, slowly withering through civil war, insurrection, massacres, Indian revolts and various dictatorships. In 1838, the Federal Congress in Guatemala City passed an act permitting each province to choose whatever government it wanted, thereby officially ending the Federation.

Looking at the different Central American countries now, it is hard to see how they could have stayed together, because they are just that . . . very different.

Costa Rica, for example, has the highest standard of living and the highest rate of social and economic advancement, with one of the highest literacy rates in all of Latin America, while neighbouring Nicaragua and Honduras have amongst the lowest. There are also sharp differences in the racial composition of the peoples of Central America; Guatemalans are mainly pure-bred American Indians (descendants of the Maya and other related tribes). Nicaraguans, Hondurans and Salvadoreans are almost entirely Mestizo (a mixture of European and Indian). Belizeans are predominantly black, while Costa Ricans are almost wholly white and Panamanians are virtually a complete mixture.

They are all, however, depressingly similar in their political situations. With the exception of Belize and Costa Rica, each of the Central American republics lives either under the direct rule, or the watchful eye, of the military.

CENTRAL AMERICA

6
'We're just showing the flag'

Belize is something of an anachronism in Central America. It is the one region where English is spoken as the principal language. And it is, or was when we were there, the last remaining British territory on the American mainland.

Belize, which was British Honduras until it gained self-government in 1964 and changed its name in 1973, has always been a backwater. While the gilded spectacular of the Spanish conquest of Central and South America was played out all around it, the tiny territory of Belize, covering just under 23,000 square kilometres, was left in the wings. Its reef-bounded coast, steamy climate and unyielding jungles were apparently a considerable deterrent to all but a few Englishmen and their black slaves who came, in the early 1600s, from Jamaica and other British West Indian colonies, to log mahogany and the plentiful hardwoods on St George's Cay, a small island, just off the coast from present-day Belize Town.

The Spaniards, living to the north and south, resented the presence of the British there and, although Spain had officially granted permission for the loggers to work the area, fitful warfare between the Spanish and English continued for over almost two centuries until 1798, when an invading Spanish naval force was firmly routed by the English settlers in the Battle of St George's Cay.

After they achieved independence from Spain in 1821, both Guatemala and Mexico claimed sovereignty over Belize and, for another forty years there were claims and counter claims over the territory, protests, and counter protests, until, in 1859, an Anglo-Guatemalan treaty was signed, under which Guatemala recognised the borders of Belize. Three years later, Britain declared it a colony. Mexico eventually renounced all claims it had on the territory in 1893, but Guatemala has renewed its claim from time to time. The most recent serious Guatemalan claim was in July 1977, when they began troop movements and spoke of annexing Belize by force. This was the reason for the presence of the British airmen we had met swimming at Lake Bacalar on the previous day.

We crossed the border into Belize at Santa Elena, after a 45 peso (US$2) taxi ride from Chetumal, at about ten in the morning. We had been up early though, to call on the Guatemalan consul in Chetumal, to obtain the tourist cards we would need to eventually enter Guatemala from Belize. With relations between Belize and Guatemala so touchy, we weren't sure that we would find a Guatemalan consulate in Belize, even though the handbook said there was one. We were standing on the consul's doorstep when he opened the office at 8.30, yawning, doing up his shirt and zipping his fly (in that order). He was somewhat surprised to be confronted with business quite so abruptly but coped with the situation quite affably and issued our cards without delay.

We had arranged to meet the British airmen at 10.30 at the Belize border, where they had left their Land-Rover, preferring not to go through the hassle of taking a military vehicle into Mexico. But we were well ahead of them, as we walked over the rusty iron bridge that spans the swampy River Hondo separating Mexico from Belize. A low wooden building sat waiting at the far end, with a large Union Jack fluttering on the flagpole outside.

Once again, we experienced relief at being able to speak English. The immigration and customs officials were black ... coal black, but their lilting creole English was eminently more understandable for us than Spanish. Unlike the surrounding countries of Central America, Belize's population is predominantly black; either of direct African, or black Carib descent, or creole. There are European, Chinese, Lebanese and East-Indian minorities and a significant (17 percent) population of Amerindians, who are almost all pure Maya.

We spotted the airmen's Land-Rover parked nearby and dumped our packs beside it in the grass. There was a ramshackle hut a few metres away which showed signs of being some sort of café. Ducking through the low doorway, we discovered, in its dingy interior, that we could order scrambled eggs, bread and butter, 'cheese-whiz' (!) and tea ... brewed in a pot! We had thought, after travelling through North America and Mexico, that tea-in-a-pot was a lost art.

The Brits arrived just as we finished breakfast ... timing! And we were off, down the dusty road heading south; nine of us (three in the front, six in the back) crammed into their long-wheel-base Land-Rover.

Belize has only one or two roads worth mentioning and this, poor though it seemed, was one of them. It ran the whole 270-kilometre length of the country from Santa Elena to Punta Gorda Town in the south, but here, in the north, it had been cut through kilometre after kilometre of virtually empty, extremely hot, dry bush country. The average population density of the whole country is only six or so people per square kilometre, but, as more than half of them live in the cities, the density in the rest of the country is very low. There are some areas of the Maya mountains in the south-east of Belize, which have still not yet been explored.

As we barrelled on down the road, fine dust poured in through the back of the vehicle, coating everything and making us all look white-haired. We stopped for a break and a soft-drink, after about sixty kilometres, at Orange Walk, a rather seedy and rundown, but also colourful town, of some 6000 or 7000 people, that is evidently the centre of an expanding sugar-producing area.

Fifty kilometres further on, we turned into the jungle to visit Altun Ha, the site of another Mayan city, established some two or three centuries before Christ. The site is being excavated by archaeologists from the University of Toronto, who no doubt find it much more pleasant to spend the winter in Belize than in the blizzards of Ontario. There were however, none of them on the site at the time of our visit.

Altun Ha was smaller and less impressive than the famous sites we had been seeing during the past week or so in the Yucatan, but it had a jungle charm about it, not unlike Palenque ... and it had apparently yielded some beautiful jade artifacts from several tombs.

About three-quarters of an hour after leaving Altun Ha, we drove into 'Charlie-Delta', part of the Royal Air Force's Harrier Squadron that is based around Belize City Airport. The boys we were with belonged to the squadron, which was rushed to Belize in July 1977 as a show of force, when Guatemala started to flex its muscles and threatened a takeover of Belize.

'We were here within twenty-four hours,' Graham Collins, one of the officers in the group explained. 'At the time, it looked as if Guatemalan troops were about the cross the border. Once the British Cabinet had made the decision, we flew the Harriers and the support aircraft and equipment here non-stop ... in under twenty-four hours.'

'All the way from England?' Sean asked.

'That's right. We refuelled the Harriers in flight, from jet-tankers.'

We pulled into an area which was covered in camouflage netting. It all seemed very easy. There were no guards ... only a sun-tanned young man in shorts, who waved as we drove up.

'Look at that, Dad!' Sean exclaimed excitedly. The sleek and deadly noses of two Harrier vertical takeoff strike planes became visible under some of the netting, next to a group of four transportable living quarter units, also under camouflage.

'Are there only two?' I asked.

'No, eight altogether,' another of the group, Colin Stanaway of Cornwall, replied. 'We spread them out all over the place, so that they're not bunched up together and vulnerable.'

'And they take off from here?'

'Yep. No runways ... just straight up!'

Sean and Zara were mightily impressed. And so were we. Looking them over, it was difficult not to be impressed. They really are a remarkable aircraft; the only operational vertical takeoff combat jet in the world. To see them at such close range was a big kick for all of us. We took it in turns to sit in the cockpit while Colin and Ian McConnell, who is an electronics technician, explained some of the instruments, including a fantastic, computerised electronic map, which comes up in front of the pilot to show him exactly where the plane is at any moment.

'Have you shot any planes down?' Zara asked seriously.

'No. We're not fighting anybody ... fortunately,' Ian replied. 'We're just showing the flag. Just having the Harriers here has been enough to quieten the "Guats" down.'

'Are you going to fly them now?' said Sean hopefully.

Ian laughed. 'No. Sorry about that. They're only flown every second day ... and no weekends. We've really got this organised. That's the way to fight wars ... only on weekdays.'

Graham Collins explained that his group were not pilots, but support engineers; each one specialising in a certain aspect of the Harrier's operation; the jet engine, electronics, weapons systems and so on.

Next we were shown over the living quarters; completely self-contained units, with full toilet and washing facilities and, of course, air-conditioning, which was essential in the tropical heat. We were then presented with a very untropical, but typical English meal; beef stew, with separate carrots, peas and potatoes ... all from their tinned rations. Not as colourful or spicy as some of the food we'd been eating in Mexico, but still excellent. It was also rather pleasant not to have to worry about the possibility of the runs. We washed the meal down with huge mugs of hot, strong tea.

'What a life!' I said, at the end of the meal. 'You've got it made.'

Raucous laughter. 'Hardly!' Ian McConnell said. 'You've got to be joking. This would drive you around the twist if you had to stick it for too long. We only do six weeks here, then six weeks at home in England, then back here again ... turn and turn about ... but before long it begins to drive you mad.' He poured another cup of tea from the kettle. 'We go out onto the Cays, which are really great, to do some skin-diving, but, without your family with you, even that gets you down after a while.'

'How do you get on with the Belizeans? What do they think about you being here?' Trish asked.

'Well, they love us. The last thing they want is to be swallowed up by Guatemala. So we, the Harrier Squadron ... and the army boys who are up close to the border, are very popular.'

'How long will it go on though?' I asked Graham Collins.

'Well, Britain sure as hell doesn't want to be involved in a war over this, but you can't just let these banana republics rattle a few sabres and then take over a country like this, just because they feel like adding a few more kilometres to their coastline. Somebody has to say "stop" ... and anyway, if Britain did nothing, these people would feel that we had abandoned them.'

The end of the day was coming up fast and we had to find a place to stay the night in Belize Town. We used their field telephone set-up to reach the Officers' Mess at a different part of the field, to ask for a taxi. We all felt reluctant to leave ... we had enjoyed our day with this group of young Englishmen. There was something comfortable and friendly about their company. In a way we had felt (perhaps Trish most of all, because of her English origins) as if we had briefly visited a little bit of home.

Belize City reeks of neglected tropical empire and an inefficient sewage system ... two not entirely unconnected facts ... which give it a very definite appeal.

The Canadians, literally mopping up after Mom's sloppy housekeeping, are putting in a waste-disposal scheme. 'But that will take three years ... at least,' a local informed us, in a laconic manner bred of heat and experience, shortly after our arrival.

Meanwhile, the effluent from our bathroom in the Belcove Hotel, where we were paying an exorbitant $US22 for two spartan rooms (because there was nothing cheaper in the whole town), dropped straight into the river, which flows past the back of the building.

After settling in, we sat on a tiny wooden pier, to which the hotel owner had moored a couple of his flashy speed boats. He used them to ferry guests out to the cays, the small offshore islands.

'It's so beautiful out there,' an American woman, Jenny, who was sunning herself on the hotel's back verandah, told us. 'There are a hundred and seventy-five islands ... many of them uninhabited. And there's the biggest coral reef in this hemisphere.'

'Ours is the biggest in the world!' Sean put in quickly.

'Yes, I know,' Jenny smiled, 'but this one isn't too bad. You can fish and scuba dive, or just swim and lie in the sun. A lot of young kids go camping out there.'

'Can we go there? Can we? Can we go there ... please?' from both the children simultaneously.

'Well ...' Iain replied non-committally, 'we'll see.' It was a phrase the kids both came to regard with well-deserved suspicion. Ridiculous how we pushed ourselves on ... kept travelling, instead of staying in a place we liked, lying in the sun and enjoying ourselves.

Jenny was in her mid-thirties. She was an anthropologist and an archaeologist studying for her masters degree and she was so in love with Belize, that when she talked of it, she positively glowed. I have only once felt that way about a country and I envied her that pleasurable sensation.

'Out west,' she told us, 'the land is empty. Over the mountains, there are forests, fast-flowing rivers and big waterfalls. The Maya Indians live as they have for hundreds of years and there are ruins of their fabulous cities ... and more that haven't yet been discovered. Further south, I've seen wild horses and down there on the coast, well ...' her voice trailed off in reflection and she smiled at us. 'You know, I was just passing through here ... that was eight months ago, and I'm still here.'

Out in the town, there was the relaxed, friendly atmosphere of a tropical island. The people strolled rather than walked and there was a lot of lounging about, talking and laughing.

We wandered through the maze of little lanes which clung to each bank of the river. The unpainted wooden houses, their doors and windows open in the steamy heat, had a temporary look about them. Many of the houses were built on stilts and, we noticed that beneath a couple of the more substantial buildings on the main street, this dark space had been either fenced, or bricked in. In bygone days, we were told, this was where people, stolen from the Caribbean islands, were imprisoned until they could be sold off as slaves to work in the mahogany stands of Belize.

There was a small amount of out-dated motorised traffic and a lot of bicycles. By comparison with Mexico, there were noticeably fewer people ... actually there are about 50,000 or so living in Belize City itself, which is a little under a third of the total population. Although the birthrate is very high ... almost 3 percent (there's not much else to do in Belize), there's still plenty of room to expand, even in a country only 285 kilometres long and 109 kilometres wide.

But jobs are the problem. The unemployment rate is ten percent, at least, and an even higher percentage of people are under-employed. With a stagnant economy, vulnerable because of an over-dependence on agriculture and forestry, Belize's gross national product has been stationary for several years.

There is talk of encouraging tourism, to boost the economy along, but tourism can be very much a two-edged sword, especially in quiet backwaters like Belize, where an influx of relatively well-off tourists could easily disrupt the existing life-style. This dilemma has not yet been posed and still seems a fair way off. In the late seventies some 80,000 people a year were going to Belize; an insignificant number, compared to the more than four million visitors Mexico has each year.

Belize's relatively poor accommodation, roads and transport facilities make it appealing only to the hardier traveller. Others give it a miss and travel down the Pan-American Highway on the western side of the Central American isthmus.

In the centre of town, late in the evening, we stood at the back of a small, well-behaved crowd which had gathered to hear a·spokesman for the opposition party haranguing the government and telling of a motion to be put before the Belizean Parliament the next day ...

'We don't want independence,' he shouted. 'We want to remain a British colony.' The crowd murmured in agreement.

'He's right,' a tall, thin, very black man standing next to us confirmed. He was clearly anxious that we, obvious strangers, should get the right idea. 'The Guatemalans say, "Come to us and we'll free you", but man, they don't know what freedom is.' He laughed derisively.

'Every second person over there wears a uniform and carries a sub-machine gun. We are more free as a colony than they are as a republic.'

The fact is, Belize is an error of history; a wart on the face of twentieth century Central American politics in that it is the only colony remaining amidst a group of independent nations. As such it is something of an embarrassment to Britain at a time when the whole concept of Empire has become so outdated. Britain would almost certainly like to be rid of Belize, to let it have complete independence.

They gave the territory internal self-government in 1964 and they did at least leave a legacy of 90 percent literacy, free schooling to the age of fourteen and a legal and social system which compares very favourably with the rest of Latin America. Somehow, though, Belize seems to have missed out on the traditional compensation prizes of roads and bridges.

But now, in a time of national belt-tightening in Britain, no one would be too unhappy to see the Belizeans off on their own. No one, that is, except the Belizeans themselves. All of those we spoke to seemed proud of their British heritage and most anxious not to be given complete independence, because they feel that would certainly ensure their takeover by Guatemala.

Even so, it appears that Britain is so anxious to free herself of this historical accident that Belize will be given full independence in the very near future, buying Guatemala off with a large sum of money in 'compensation' for a Belize which the Guatemalans say rightly belongs to them. The best that the Belizeans can hope for is that Britain will stick by them, militarily, if necessary.

Back at our hotel, a British naval landing craft sailed by, down the river. Her crew, shirtless, in an attempt to have at least a sun-tan to show the folks back home, for their stint at defending the colonies, waved to us. We waved back and I embarrassed my family by shouting, 'How do you expect to run an empire with no clothes on?'

The ramshackle wooden building next to our hotel turned out to be the focus of nightlife in Belize; the 'Melting Pot', an appropriately named dive, judging by its pot pourri of patrons. Wearing tight trousers and brightly patterned shirts or short, revealing dresses, they lounged around the entrance while loud rock music blasted forth. Our bed seemed to back right onto the band stand but one of the joys of travelling is that I have learnt to sleep anywhere. So I dropped of with the room rocking about me only to wake with a start in the cool, still dark of the morning at 3.00 a.m. It took a few seconds to realise that what had woken me was the absence of noise. The 'Melting Pot' had melted away and closed.

In the morning we walked along the waterfront, breathing in the sensual perfume of frangipani, to the home of the Consulate of Honduras. It was an attractive stone house, perhaps a hundred years old on brick piers with the tropical garden climbing over the wooden balcony. The fly screen was banging gently in the slight breeze. I've often fancied the life of a Consul in one of these tucked away parts of the globe. I like the idea of being able to hand out a calling card embossed with a quite preposterously impressive-looking coat of arms and the title, in florid script, 'Consul of Honduras, Belize'.

We got our visas with no problems. Australian passports $US1. British free.

Back in the centre of town, opposite Government House, we found St John's Cathedral. (The British always had a great sense of position.) The oldest Anglican church in Central America, its diocese once stretched from here right down the nineteen hundred kilometre isthmus to Panama.

It was built in 1812 by the slaves who worked the logwood and mahogany camps and is made entirely of bricks which were imported from England as ballast. More of these same bricks were used to erect that other prerequisite of colonial life, the prison, which is also still in use.

Matins was just finishing and the parishioners, mostly elderly women in copies of the Norman Hartnell styles Queen Elizabeth wore in the fifties, smiled at us in welcome. The present vicar, whose purple cassock looked positively regal against his black skin, told us he was from Jamaica. He showed us the plaque commemorating the thirty-six year ministry of Dr Mathew Newport.

'He gave a public service of thanksgiving in 1838 to celebrate the emancipation of the colony's slaves,' the vicar smiled, 'and did you know that St John's is the only Anglican church other than Westminster Abbey, in which monarchs have been crowned?'

With a magician's timing, he waited for us to register our surprise and then, 'Ah, but these were not Kings of England, but of the Mosquito Coast in Nicaragua.' (He'd told this story before!) 'You see the Reverend Robert Shaw had been allowed to practise as a missionary in Nicaragua under the protection of these formerly heathen Indian kings and when he moved to Belize, they were so anxious to maintain their links with the British monarchy and the established Church of England, on a continent that was predominantly RC, that they followed him. Until 1845, the kings were crowned and baptised, with much pomp and circumstance, here in St John's.'

Early in the afternoon we caught the bus to Benque Viejo, where we would cross the border into Guatemala. The bus was full and I was sitting next to a spry old man who had been loudly supervising the handling of his large number of bundles which were being passed up and roped on to the roof.

Twenty-five kilometres out of Belize City we passed a sorry collection of run-down dwellings.

'Hattieville,' the old man explained, and, when I appeared puzzled, 'In 1961 Hurricane Hattie blew Belize City to pieces. There was a three metre wave.' He illustrated with his arms. 'There were many dead. Many more homeless. So the government built these temporary shelters here for them. That's . . .'; he tried counting on his fingers and gave up '. . . a long time ago and they still here. Maybe 30,000 people.'

He was going to Belmopan, the new capital which was built in 1970, eighty kilometres inland along the Hummingbird Highway. This was done partly as a precaution against the capital being destroyed again by the tidal waves which accompany a hurricane and partly I suspect, to encourage Belizeans to leave the coast and move to the undeveloped hinterland to live. Nothing is more tempting to a land-hungry neighbour than huge empty spaces.

I also think it's not too cynical to see Belmopan as Britain's farewell present. A sort of golden handshake rather in the same way that they built the new capital city of Gaberones for Bechuanaland in Southern Africa when it became independent Botswana. A salve to the conscience. Belmopan still has the look of a new subdivision, the buildings sitting uneasily amid freshly scarred land.

From here on though, the countryside was very impressive, rolling hills, mountains in the distance, lush green pastures, grazing land and forests. Very beautiful, but also very empty.

Unfortunately, the road deteriorates quickly and by the time we got to Benque Viejo, it was just red dirt. The border was a few kilometres further on, but this was as far as the bus could take us. A taxi-driver, who must have been entirely dependent on this situation for his livelihood, drove us to the border. While we were checked out by black, English-speaking, smartly-uniformed Belizeans and checked in by brown, Spanish-speaking, crumple-dressed and conspicuously-armed Guatemalans, he drove back and picked up the one other bus passenger, who was also crossing the border; a large woman with an unmanageable number of cardboard boxes. While she was being checked through, he gave us a lift the further few kilometres into Melchor de Mencos, in Guatemala. It was all very Gilbert and Sullivan.

We woke the owner of the Mayab Hotel, who, judging by his soiled, sleeveless vest and crumpled trousers, seemed to exist in a more or less permanent state of siesta. Yes, he had a room: US$1.50 for four beds!

'Do they have mattresses?' I inquired tartly.

Leaving our packs we walked back down to the river, which is the border between the two countries, to join the locals who were having their evening bath.

GUATEMALA

7
The Quetzal . . . a bird which dies in captivity

One of the things that takes a bit of getting used to in Latin America is the casual approach to weaponry. That evening, after a very pleasant swim in the deep, clear river at the bottom of the hill running out of the town, we sat in a small, local eating-house having a meal of chicken and rice. A group of civilian men sat around a table next to us. I say 'civilian' because their clothes showed no signs of them being in either the army or the police force, and yet, two of the four men had hand-guns shoved into their belts. One carried a .38 revolver, the other a small automatic pistol. They could have been plain-clothes cops, I suppose, but they looked a bit unkempt for that. Anyway, whatever they were, seeing people with all sorts of armament hanging off them always makes me feel slightly uneasy.

Our US$1.50 hotel wasn't that bad. A little primitive perhaps, but at least there were no fleas or other crawlies. We had ascertained that a bus would leave the town square for Flores, about ninety-five kilometres away, at 4.00 a.m.! So, at 3.30 the next morning we were awake, scrabbling around in the darkness (there was no electricity on at that time of night) trying to get ourselves together. Then, after waking the night watchman, who slept by the locked front door, we were let out into the dark, empty streets. At about ten to four, at the main square, we woke the driver and his assistant, who had both slept in the bus and who, with crumpled clothes and faces, set about getting the bus mobile.

Zara and Sean have become really fabulous under these conditions. They wake up, get their gear together, carry their packs through the darkness, struggle onto dirty and crowded buses, often with a wry or humorous comment, but mostly without a word of complaint.

On this occasion, the silent figures of other passengers emerged from the gloom at odd intervals over the next fifteen minutes or so to join the bus and at 4.10 a.m., we drove off. I was surprised, firstly that there had not been more passengers about and secondly, that it was so punctual. But this thought only lasted for a few moments, because it soon became clear we had only begun a long circuit of the town and the outlying districts, to pick up other passengers and their luggage. We then returned to the town square to wait for any more who might decide to come along. Eventually, we got going again at about ten minutes to five, having been in the bus for just on an hour.

Several other young foreign travellers had joined the bus also; a Scots girl, an American man of about thirty, a Canadian boy of around nineteen or twenty, and a Frenchman. We were sitting in different parts of the bus, which had eventually been completely filled, so we had little chance to talk to each other. Anyway, it was still very dark.

The road was abominable; dusty and corrugated. The whole bus, which had quite obviously suffered the torture of the trip for many years, rattled and vibrated madly. Like a tired old horse being forced to do something that was beyond it, we bounced and shook along the road, averaging no more than twenty kilometres an hour.

Trish, Zara and Sean managed to get some sleep despite the noise and motion. We were getting to be quite good at this; Zara leaning sideways onto Trish's lap, Trish lying across Zara's back. Sean put his head on my lap and dozed fitfully.

We were looking for a cross-roads about fifty kilometres from Melchor de Mencos, where we would leave the bus. There would be no town there ... just a cross-roads ... 'Las Cruces'. From there we would head north. We had one more Mayan city to see, but perhaps the greatest of them all ... Tikal.

Deep in the remote and uninhabited jungles of Guatemala's Peten Province ... although still geographically in the Yucatan Peninsula, Tikal, we'd been told, was even more dramatic, more fascinating, than Chichen Itza, and more mysterious and beautiful than Palenque.

The normal way, the easiest way to get there, is by small plane from Guatemala City, about four hundred kilometres to the south. But, we felt that, unless you go in by land to places like this, you really can't get a proper sense of their isolation. Still, so as not to make a virtue of necessity ... from the direction we were travelling, there was no plane anyway.

At about 6.30, we were dropped at the isolated cross-roads, Las Cruces ... us and about six others. The American slung a hammock in a small thatch shelter by the road and promptly went to sleep. A Guatemalan woman emerged from nowhere in the dim, dawn light to sell us oranges and warm soft-drinks and the rest of us stood around to talk and watch the sunrise. An hour and a half later the bus to Tikal arrived.

The road was even worse than the one on which we had been travelling; huge ruts, steep hills to climb, slowly, interminably. Jolting and bouncing, mountains of dust pouring in over us all the time. And hot, even at nine in the morning. But eventually we arrived at a small building with a sign indicating that it was the entrance to Tikal National Park. We paid a gun-toting guard a $1 fee in US currency (we had not been able to change any money so far, but in Guatemala, American money is at par with their own currency, quetzals, and is acceptable anywhere).

We soon discovered, however, that although this was the entrance to the Park, it wasn't the entrance to Tikal itself. That was three-quarters of an hour further on ... along the same road. Eventually we arrived at the site of the ruins where, surprisingly, we had to pass through an immigration check, producing our passports for scrutiny as several guards with sub-machine guns stood by.

Once through, we left our packs in a small lodge nearby and made our way toward the ruins, stretching our aching muscles and looking, a trifle enviously I must admit, at a small group of tourists who were walking happily from a light plane that had just deposited them on the Tikal airstrip after a comfortable, air-conditioned flight from Guatemala City.

Tikal is without doubt the greatest of all the Mayan centres. Not only because of the wealth of knowledge which it has already yielded up but also because these visible ruins are only tantalising appetisers for the gourmet archaeological feast still waiting in the impenetrable jungle.

Archaeologists from the University of Pennsylvania Museum, who have spent fourteen years working on site at Tikal, calculate that an area of one hundred and twenty-nine square kilometres was heavily populated. So far only fifteen square kilometres centring on the five temple pyramids, the tallest in the New World, have been closely examined. The statistics of what they reveal are quite staggering.

There are three thousand separate constructions, containing eighty-three stellae ... those carved stone obelisks, fifty-four altars and the finest wood carvings, mostly on door lintels, yet found in the Mayan world. More than a million potsherds and one hundred thousand tools, ceremonial objects and personal ornaments have been collected by the university group from among the ruined temples, palaces, shrines, ceremonial platforms, small- to medium-sized homes, ball courts, terraces, causeways, plazas and even a ritual sweat-bath-house!

The team says it would take a further twenty years of concentrated hard work to examine completely all the surface sites mapped so far and at least a further century to examine what lies beneath that which is at present visible. A century! But then, what does another one hundred years matter in the time span of Tikal, which began six centuries before Christ and flourished for at least a thousand years?

The fact that so many room walls and vaults are still standing is a credit to the builders of Tikal whose continuous construction over ten centuries was of such high quality that they left a multitude of tangible clues for today's experts to piece together. Even so, it would seem unlikely that we will ever know the complete answer to the biggest question mark of all which hangs over Tikal: what happened in the years around 900 AD to make the inhabitants stop building and carving and to suddenly desert the great city, leaving it to be crushed, wrenched apart and swallowed inexorably by the tropical jungle from which it is only now being released?

Was it a peasants' revolt against an over-oppressive priesthood? Was it on the orders of their gods, or for some other reason that the people trekked north further up the Yucatan Peninsula and began all over again at Chichen Itza and Uxmal?

The responsibility for the insolubility of this puzzle lies with the Catholic missionaries who burnt entire libraries of Mayan ideographic literature. Done, of course, with the most impeccable intention of saving the souls of 'ignorant' peasants by destroying their heathen scribblings, this heinous crime threw away the key to the understanding of even the non-combustible glyphs which were left, carved on stellae, walls or monuments.

We walked for one and a half kilometres along the narrow jungle tracks. Above us, aptly-named howler monkeys swung from tree-top to tree-top, suddenly halting, while executing an elegant, acrobatic feat, to swing by the tail from a liana vine and scratch most inelegantly; all the while keeping up a stream of animated chatter.

We rounded a curve in the path and were left quite literally speechless as the Great Plaza of Tikal came into view. Superlatives, no matter how florid, are justifiable and yet still inadequate when describing the two immense, sheer-sided pyramids which face each other across the 120-metre by 75-metre courtyard.

Attentive viewers of the 1977 movie box office smash 'Star Wars' would have caught a quick glimpse of the tops of these temples, gasping for air above the jungle roof and supposedly on the Rebel planet.

Their thinner profile than the pyramids of Palenque, Uxmal and Chichen accentuate their even greater height. The taller of the two, The Temple of the Giant Jaguar, is an incomparable example of Mayan architecture. Built of limestone blocks around 700 AD, its roof comb towers forty-four metres above the Plaza and is finished with stone blocks arranged to form a seated individual of monumental proportions. Unfortunately the structure is so badly eroded that this enthroned ruler can only be made out with an imaginative eye in the sunlight of early afternoon.

Archaeologists tell us that this roof was once painted cream and red and perhaps even green and blue too, and that other temples in Tikal were painted completely red. What a fantastic sight they must have been against the backdrop of lush, dark jungle greenery.

An architect friend of ours shudders with involuntary horror when I say how much I would like large city buildings to be coloured red, blue, green and so forth. He intimates that all my taste is in my mouth but I feel slightly vindicated to discover that I share this disability with the Mayans!

It was in 1963, while tunnelling in the Great Plaza beneath the Temple of the Giant Jaguar, that archaeologists discovered the grave of an obviously important and wealthy man. Unfortunately the chamber had partially collapsed some centuries previously but enough was left to discern that the body had been laid out on a woven mat fringed with jade beads and spiny oyster shells, rare and therefore valuable so far from the sea. Adorning the body was a head-dress, necklaces, earrings and bracelets, all of jade and weighing a total of seven and a half kilos. This treasure trove again confirmed the new realisation that the pyramids of the New World, just like those of the old, were also tombs for the rich and mighty.

The Temple of the Giant Jaguar has even steeper sides than the Temple of the Dwarf at Uxmal so it would be unrealistic to expect you to believe me if I said that I sped nimble-footed, up and down the crumbling treads. I didn't. I sat in the shade of a magnificent mahogany tree and tried to squelch my maternal instincts as I watched Sean and Zara follow Iain to the top.

'Say, Wilbur, did you hear that?' an American woman in her fifties, wearing colour-co-ordinated sports clothes, clutched the arm of a man wearing a pale cream linen suit. He seemed not to hear her, and stared instead in an engrossed manner, at the giant pyramid. 'The guide says that one of his colleagues fell from the top of that damned thing a week or so ago and broke his neck.'

Wilbur uncurled her fingers and without a word began walking toward the base of the temple.

'Wilbur!' her strident voice unsoftened by the thick tropical heat. 'Wilbur! Did you hear?'

Wilbur kept walking as if some irresistible force was pulling him.

'Well . . .' Mrs Wilbur was obviously unaccustomed to being ignored. '. . . I'll be . . . and in his best suit too.'

She sat down on the bench beside me, fanning herself continuously with the guide book as she told a group of about ten of her compatriots the details of the other guide's nasty demise. Every now and again she checked her story in Spanish with their young guide who revelled in the gory story. 'His back was broken in many places,' she said, apparently forgetting Wilbur, whom I watched intently as he made his slow but purposeful ascent.

At the summit he stood to gaze out only briefly and then; 'Look at Wilbur!' one of the men in the group yelled and they all gaped, Mrs Wilbur even ceasing her fanning, as the figure in the pale cream linen suit *ran* down the pyramid steps.

Indefatigable, Iain returned and then climbed to the top of the thirty-seven-metre-high facing pyramid while the children rested beside me and heard the story of the guide's deathly tumble told yet again. Then we walked through the remainder of the central cleared area, admiring the carved stellae, clambering over and through the partially destroyed buildings. Trees grew from these sites, their roots forcing a way through the ancient masonry and it was easy to see how, within a short time, the jungle growth would crush and smother all but the very highest structures.

Iain climbed with the children through the dense undergrowth to the top of one of these crumbling, swallowed temples and they all returned covered in scratches and mosquito bites to tell me of the snake which dropped from a branch beside them and slithered away into the scrub. The fer-de-lance, which is portrayed in much of Tikal's ancient stonework, is deadly poisonous and still abounds in the surrounding jungles.

On the walk back to the bus we saw Wilbur again, just about to board the light plane which would fly him, Mrs Wilbur and the rest of their group out to Guatemala City. His best suit was indeed soiled, but he looked as if he'd proved something to himself. And I suppose that was also the reason why we insisted on travelling the unmade, corrugated and potholed track sixty-five kilometres to Flores.

At one point the vehicle shuddered to a halt and one of the young fellows hanging out of the doorway dropped off to run back about fifty metres. He scrabbled around in the dirt and returned with a large metal pin. Somehow or other, above the judder of the wheels and the roar of the engine, both he and the driver had miraculously heard this drop out. The rear wheel was jacked up on a precarious pile of rocks and the young man lay, horrifyingly vulnerable, under the vehicle and pushed this pin back through the end of the leaf-spring. To complete the makeshift repair, he bound the whole joint round with a piece of coat-hanger wire.

To say that we were delighted to arrive in Flores is an understatement. The little town is built on an island in a cool, deep, clean lake and we immediately dumped our packs in a small hotel, changed and dove in, washing off the grime and sweat of a day, so long and full it seemed to encompass a week.

It's somehow quite different when you come into a country through its back door; a different feeling, I mean. It's almost as if you're sneaking up on it without its knowing. We felt a bit like that in coming in to Guatemala from Belize the way we had. All of the main population centres were hundreds of kilometres to the south, while Peten Province, which we'd just entered, was the most remote and under-populated of Guatemala's twenty-two departments. In fact the area was so impenetrable that it took the Spaniards one hundred and eighty-five years, after their arrival in Guatemala, to finally subdue the Mayan Indians in Peten. The last major battle between the Spaniards and the Mayan-Itzas was fought in 1697 on the island where the town of Flores now stands.

But even now, Peten Province, which occupies almost a third of Guatemala's land area, remains a dense jungle, largely unexplored and traversed by few roads. It is, however, potentially the richest region in the country.

And Guatemala can do with some riches. Although it is a physically beautiful land of mountains and gorges, volcanoes and lakes, and, in most parts, has an almost perfect climate, it has stayed right through to recent times a basically poor, agricultural country. In the late seventies it still relied on only a few major agricultural commodities: coffee, cotton, meat, sugar and bananas for some 60 percent of its foreign exchange. Less than half of the country's 108,000 square kilometres has been occupied, and only a quarter has been cultivated in any way. Living standards and personal income are low and more than half of Guatemala's population of seven million is illiterate.

The people, unlike those of the neighbouring countries of Latin America, are predominantly Indian; about 44 percent of pure-blood Mayan and other Amerindian races and another 47 percent of mixed Indian and European descent. Only 8½ percent of the population is Caucasian and only 2 percent of unmixed Spanish ancestry.

But Guatemala shares at least one thing with its neighbours . . . a violent and turbulent history. After it had won its independence from Spain, in a bloodless revolution in 1821, it became, during the next twenty years, through revolts and mini-wars, firstly a part of Mexico, then a member of the federation of 'Provincias Unidas del Centro de America' and finally an independent nation. But, in the one hundred and fifty years or so since its full independence, Guatemalans have been subjected to rule by a succession of powerful and often ruthless dictators. Few of these strongmen were prepared, over the years, to hand over the reins of government either voluntarily or peacefully by democratic process. Most of them were either forcibly removed from office or assassinated.

In the years since World War II the political scene has developed into a relentless struggle between left and right, which has often been marked, in recent times, by great violence. Following the assassination of President Colonel Castillo Armas in 1957, the country was launched on an anti-communist and anti-Cuban crusade. Castillo Armas had come to power with American help and the close association with the United States continued under the new extreme right-wing president, General Miguel Yidigoras Fuentes; it was primarily in Guatemala, under his aegis and US sponsorship, that the expeditionary force was trained for the disastrous 'Bay of Pigs' invasion of Cuba in April, 1961.

For much of the 1960s, guerilla terrorism was rampant in Guatemala and resulted in the murder of the US Ambassador, John Mein in 1968 and the German Ambassador in 1970. In the early years of the 1970s many prominent Guatemalans were either killed or held for ransom. But, during the presidency of General Laugerud Garcia, who assumed power in 1974, a degree of calm and stability returned to the country. No great economic advances, but tourism began to recover and grow, and foreign investment in Guatemala was on the increase.

Still, around election time, anything can happen in Guatemala and when we were in Flores, elections were only three days away. The newspapers hinted at possible demonstrations in Guatemala City, but as that was four hundred kilometres further on it seemed rather remote. From the somewhat selfish viewpoint of uncommitted tourists, we felt glad to be isolated in Flores. It was a nice place to be.

Flores remains in my memory as one of the most charming little towns in all of Latin America . . . not so much for its appearance or its buildings, which are fairly nondescript, but its surroundings and the general atmosphere, which is very relaxed. It's a small town, of only 10,000 or so people, which exists solely on the chicle-bleeding industry. Chicle-bleeding? Well, where would the Wrigleys or the Chiclets people be without chicle? Not to mention the people of Guatemala's Peten Province, which is literally covered with chicle trees.

On the day after our arrival from Tikal, we wandered around Flores doing some shopping; a pair of shorts each for Zara and Sean, we bought the bus tickets for the trip to Guatemala City the next day, posted some letters and did a little sight-seeing. Not much to see in the town itself . . . just the view; the lake, which is everywhere, and the jungled shores on the far bank. We cashed a travellers' cheque in a bank under the watchful eye of a soldier with a sub-machine gun (this was something we eventually became accustomed to as being a standard feature of banks throughout Latin America). Then back for more swimming in the delightfully clear, fresh water in front of our hotel . . . the 'Peten', which was right where the bus had dropped us on the previous day. It was clean and pleasant and we'd been able to get a room for four with bunk beds for only 6 quetzals (US$6). The quetzal, incidentally, is an almost extinct long-tailed bird, Guatemala's national symbol. It stands for love and liberty as it dies whenever kept in captivity.

Later, in a dugout canoe, powered by an outboard. motor, we sailed to another small island a couple of kilometres or so from the town, where we spent a lazy afternoon. There was a beautiful, pebbled beach from which we swam. A woman in a nearby house cooked us each a whole fish, with tomatoes and onions. A tame toucan, with a huge yellow beak, ambled about accompanied by a strange, long-legged black bird with a smaller yellow beak, both of them looking for food handouts from us as we sat eating our meal on the grass at the edge of the beach. A small spotted wildcat or maybe it was a jaguar, paced up and down outside the woman's house watching us. It was tied, on a running chain that followed it along the clothes line.

The day was very hot and quiet and we sat, rather subdued, but relaxed and happy, in the shade of some palm trees, looking out across the blue waters of the lake to the deserted far bank. Another of Sean's teeth fell out.

Everything we'd found out about the trip to Guatemala City from Flores made us feel we were crazy to do it. For one thing, the 16-hour journey (which apparently often took 25 or 30 hours) was described in guide books we'd read as a 'hell-trip', 'only for the hardy', 'extremely rough', 'uncomfortable', etc. For another, we knew that we could *fly* directly from Flores to Guatemala City for only US$20 each (half-fare for the children).

Well, the bus fare *was* cheaper (US$8), although we had to pay full fare for Zara and Sean, but once again it was this thing of wanting to do the whole trip by land, to get a feeling of the shape and size of a place ... and, in the case of Tikal and Flores ... their isolation. So, if a rough trip was necessary, then that was that. And, of course, if the local Guatemalans travelled that route, then why shouldn't we?

At the appointed hour of 'quatro y media' we were standing, waiting with our packs, in the darkness outside our hotel, for the bus to arrive to pick us up. No bus. Time went by. Fifteen minutes, half an hour, three-quarters of an hour. Had I misunderstood the man who sold me the tickets the previous day? Was the bus to come by the hotel? or was it to leave from the office of the bus company, about five kilometres away? God! At 4.30 in the morning, you don't feel like facing questions like that. We decided to wait, but I felt annoyed and despondent.

Two hours later, in the pre-dawn light, the bus arrived. No comments about why it was late, or apologies ... not that we really cared. It was here and that was all that mattered. We piled our packs up onto the roof rack and ourselves inside, where, amazingly, there were four seats reserved for us. The bus was painted red, white and blue, carried a sign saying 'Peten — Guate', was of mid-fifties vintage and had seen better days.

As the only non-Guatemalans on board, we were subjected, initially, to some curious stares and whispered comments, among which we heard 'gringo' mentioned a couple of times. We quickly made it clear that 'somos Australianos'. More chatter ... a few smiles.

The road, once we left the Flores area, was immediately terrible. It was dusty and bumpy, but fortunately at such an early hour the air was still relatively cool. The bus was full; a young girl, about sixteen or seventeen years old, sat in front of us with a small child, of perhaps three, beside her and a baby in her lap. Behind us, an old lady who looked about seventy or eighty, shared a seat with another younger woman. I wondered how they would take the trip.

The bus shuddered and rattled and jarred unbelievably. An amazing assortment of spare parts clattered and bounced around under our seats and in the aisle. Just to be on the safe side, the driver had brought along a couple of complete leaf springs, several lengths of radiator hose, jacks, spare tires and a collection of large cog-wheels which could presumably be fitted into the bus's gear-box in the unwished-for event that it might require surgery at some stage during the trip.

The countryside, however, was impressively beautiful; mountains, jungle, a winding dirt road ... remote isolation. We stopped after two hours, at a tiny settlement; a few mud huts with thatched roofs sitting on the edge of an impenetrable mass of tropical foliage. There was a stream running by. Everybody got off the bus to stretch his or her legs. We bought some questionable, orange-coloured soft-drinks in Pepsi-Cola bottles and paddled our feet in the stream.

The other passengers bought 'tamarind' ... a mud-coloured drink which they sipped through straws from a soft plastic bag. Because of our experience with diarrhoea in Mexico, we had been cautious about any drinks made with water direct from the tap. The aerated orange drink, we felt (almost certainly naively), might be a degree or two safer. As we were about to reboard the bus, the young child, the daughter of the young girl sitting in front of us, threw up on the steps of the bus. We reeled back, almost vomiting ourselves. The child had brought up a mess of wriggling white worms ... all of them 20 to 25 centimetres long and as thick as any you'd see in your garden.

Further on down the line we stopped again, at a ramshackle, wooden cafe on the edge of nowhere. There were no other houses in sight. Only the jungle on one side of the road and a line of deserted hills some distance away, on the other. An old, colour-retouched, formal wedding photograph of a man in a dinner suit and a woman in a white gown hung, dusty and neglected, on one wall of the open verandah of the cafe. Inside the two people in the photograph (but twenty-five years older) served us with lukewarm soft-drinks.

The interior walls were plastered with several yellow posters bearing the photograph of a man in military uniform. 'Vote Partido Revolucionario y Partido Institutional Democratico', they insisted. Either the PR or the PID had held power in Guatemala since 1966. But, in the elections to be held in two days' time they were running on a joint ticket. Under the photograph of the moustachioed, gold-braided and bemedalled officer was written, 'General Romeo Lucas Garcia por Presidente 1978-1982'. We realised, with some surprise, that we had seen no election posters in Flores. This was the first.

Our bus rattled on into the afternoon. It was blazing hot and, despite the dust, we had all the windows open for air. We stopped briefly in a couple of small villages, where women and children boarded the bus to come charging up and down the aisle selling tamarind drinks, oranges, dry cakes and peanuts. There were more election signs on the buildings; plenty of the PR/PID variety for General Lucas Garcia, but also some different ones; the FESC (The Social Christian Student Front) posters proclaimed, in Spanish, 'During the PR Government of 1966-70 there were 16,500 murders. During the PID Government of 1970-78 there were 23,230 murders. How many of your countrymen will die if these parties continue in power?'

In mid-afternoon we passed another bus owned by the same company that operated ours. At some stage in the very recent past, it had broken down on this remote stretch of the jungle road. It had been stripped of wheels, seats, windows ... almost everything. Our driver checked it over briefly to see if there was anything left worth taking and we drove on. We joked about the same fate befalling our bus, but nobody really laughed. By this stage we were beginning to feel the kidney-shaking effects of some eight hours on the road.

At Rio Dulce, we took a car ferry across the river and, just seeing a large expanse of water with women and children bathing by the shore, was cooling. A Guatemalan navy gun-boat lay anchored near the opposite shore. What on earth would they want a warship here for?

The journey continued. Another broken-down bus on an isolated stretch of road. Apparently it was one which left Flores yesterday. We stopped and those passengers who were still there with it boarded our bus to crowd three and four into seats intended for two, and to sit and lie in the aisle. They looked hot and tired. With the extra body heat the interior of the bus became measurably hotter and with the extra weight I wondered how long it would be before our bus also collapsed under the strain. I turned to the old woman behind me, now squashed between her original companion and a man of about forty, to see how she was bearing up. She looked grim. The young girl in front of us, her two children now both in her lap, slumped sweatily asleep against the window frame.

An hour later we reached the tarmac near Morales and a spontaneous ripple of applause and relief ran through the bus. We had covered 160 kilometres in ten hours . . . only 240 kilometres to go!

But from here on, thank God, the going would be smooth . . . well, relatively. Sixteen kilometres down the road, just as it was getting dark, the whole front windshield of the bus simply crumpled slowly in on the driver! No real reason . . . except that it was cracked already and was probably tired . . . or perhaps it was just in protest over what it had been through that day.

We drove on into the night with no front windshield and with the driver trying to protect his face and eyes from the wind and insects, which came sweeping back into the bus, by wearing first a plastic bag over his head (no good — too hard to breathe), and then a scarf round his face and sunglasses (passable).

Once he got the right system sorted out though, we began to make good time. But then we were concerned that he would go to sleep. He had driven all the way, except for an hour or so in the morning when his assistant took the wheel. But, we made it all right and, sixteen hours after leaving Flores . . . at 10.30 at night, we pulled into the bus terminal in Guatemala City. We took a cab to a small hotel and collapsed into bed, exhausted.

Guatemala City is a dump. Iain hates me to make such bald statements, but looking through my notes and fingering the leaves of my memory I can't recall anything to qualify that impression. Even photographs of the place, which, by concentrating on the interplay of light and shade can manage to give a rosier than accurate view, have a depressing pall about them.

Perhaps living in an earthquake zone creates the same feeling of impermanence and hopelessness as growing up knowing nothing other than being at war, because the wearying drabness of the Guatemalan capital constantly reminded me of Saigon in the early seventies.

The city, which has a population of just over a million, is very dirty; nasty urban dirt caused by factory pollution and exhaust fumes. The buildings are soiled and neglected and, along the sidewalks and through the paved parks, with their wilted plants, you can feel the dirt crunching beneath your feet like granulated sugar. Crumpled papers and garbage litter the streets, and the hordes of shoeshine boys wear ragged and filthy clothes.

Guatemala's last earthquake, which hit during the night of February 4th, 1976, was one of the greatest disasters of the twentieth century: in the space of a few hours . . . 22,000 dead, 75,000 injured and a million people homeless.

Now, some of these poor, homeless people beg for coins in Guatemala City, but even that they do in a hopeless, dispirited manner. They sleep in the doorways of shops which sell products they couldn't ever hope to buy, not even in their cramped and disturbed dreams. 'Wake up,' I wanted to yell, as all my anarchistic tendencies bubbled to the surface, 'throw a brick through the window and steal a pair of shoes for your child.'

The army drove by in camouflaged scout vehicles. The mounted machine-gun on one was manned by a young boy, who, under different circumstances, would still be at high school and dating his first girl. Police sirens wailed. One of the beggars moved in her sleep and, seeing us, automatically stuck out her hand. We followed the noise and the gathering crowd to the central square, over which hundreds of political pamphlets had been scattered. Tomorrow was to be election day.

We waded among multiple replicas of the same face. 'Defensor de la Familia' it said beneath a posed family portrait of General Ricardo Peralta Mendez, his plump wife and their three children. The general, in civilian clothes, had a flower in his lapel, his wife had painted fingernails and his children looked as though they never pick their noses. I wonder if the family huddled in the doorway felt defended.

People began to address the crowd. Standing on the roofs of parked vehicles, they shouted slogans and we didn't need a translator to know that they were mouthing the same meaningless platitudes and glib rubbish you can hear almost anywhere. 'Let's get rid of this general and replace him with another, who will bring down bus fares and put food in your bellies.' Knowing it was just not true made it sound like so much international vomit. The young soldier stood at the ready behind his machine-gun, while several jeep-loads of reinforcements arrived and we decided that the time had come to leave them to it.

In the early morning of the next day, before the polling booths opened, we took a small bus for an hour's drive east to Antigua. First we passed through a succession of inhuman shanty towns; hovels, put together from scraps of tin and wood, the roofs weighted with large rocks. But, as we left the outskirts of the capital, we began very quickly to climb through arid country into the volcanic mountains. At the top of a 2285-metre pass, it was chilly enough to wish that we had our sweaters with us, instead of them being stowed in our packs on top of the bus, but no sooner had we thought this, than the bus began to descend into a dramatic volcanic basin and we arrived in a warmer and much more pleasant world.

The contrast between Antigua and Guatemala City couldn't be sharper. Antigua is a fine example of Spanish Colonial architecture and was the country's capital for over two centuries. Designated as 'The Most Noble and Loyal City of Santiago of the Knights of Guatemala', it was once third, in splendour and importance, in all the Americas, only after Mexico City and Lima, Peru. From here, Spanish rule, under the Conquistador Don Pedro de Alvarado, stretched north into southern Mexico and south into Panama. But, in 1773 a massive earthquake all but devastated Antigua. Behold the works of man, how they do crumble and fall apart!

Now the city is a peaceful backwater. The few surviving colonial buildings mellow with age. Even the line of people, which stretched almost completely around the central Plaza de Armas, spoke softly as they waited to vote. The number of vehicles in the town was pleasantly small and there was even less evidence of the police and military.

We took a local bus, crowded with black-haired, almond-eyed Indians, wearing heavily-embroidered vests, skirts, belts and blouses, to the tiny village of San Antonio de las Aguas Calientes, about eight kilometres away. Here, we moved from stall to stall down the narrow and unsurfaced main street and marvelled over the intricate and colourful weavings; long-tailed quetzal birds and Indian women carrying babies in their mantas-cloths which are slung across their backs in serried rows.

These weavings hung in tempting array outside the thatch-roofed huts and, inside, were the same women, blood and flesh versions, with babies slung eternally across their backs, weaving these self-portraits on anciently designed back-strap looms.

It was another of those occasions when we had to resist the temptation to buy up, because to do so would have meant more weight in our already shoulder-shattering packs. We indulged, though, in one small wall hanging and a thick, traditionally-patterned shirt. The women pulled down from the racks several thick rugs, hand-hooked with designs of Mayan gods, in attempts to persuade us to buy more. We had to smile our 'no thanks' and take another rickety bus a few kilometres further on, over a dusty track, to Ciudad Vieja, which was also at one time, a capital of Guatemala.

In 1541 a huge earthquake also destroyed this town, which is at the base of the Agua Volcano, and the ensuing mudslide buried what was left. The newly-elected governor of Guatemala, the wife of the recently drowned Conquistador Don Pedro de Alvarado, was also buried in the mudslide.

In the ruins of the governor's palace, a bright-eyed boy in well-worn clothes, attached himself to us and insisted on reciting, parrot-fashion, in an incomprehensible language, which we assumed was meant to be English, information about the palace and the town. He pointed and exclaimed and we nodded and gave him some loose change and he smiled.

The church, which was engulfed in the slide, was later dug out intact. Built in 1534, it is one of the oldest churches in Central America. At the time of the earthquake it was apparently a beautiful pink and red building, but it is now neglected and in a poor state of repair.

Just as we were leaving the church, we heard the tramp of many feet and, around a bend in the unsurfaced street came a crowd of perhaps forty Indians; men, women and children. None of them were talking and they appeared purposeful. It was a few seconds before we realised that, in the middle of the crowd, a group of men in dark suits, shiny with wear, were carrying a little coffin. It was draped with a white lace cloth and was only large enough to hold a child of three or four years. Directly behind it walked a woman wearing a heavy, black veil; obviously the child's mother, and, beside her, five children, ranging in age from ten or eleven down to a tiny toddler. They passed us silently, without a glance and filed into the church.

Back in Antigua that evening, the polling booth was closed. Because it was Palm Sunday, there had been a street procession and the main square was now thronged with young men in long, purple silk robes . . . eating ice-creams.

For thirty cents each we went to a small cinema to see the movie 'La Spia que Me Amor', complete with Spanish sub-titles, but, fortunately for us, with English dialogue. Roger Moore's portrayal of James Bond was as smooth and bland as ever. 'The Spy Who Loved Me' could have done with a bit more of Sean Connery's rough diamond approach as he was chased around a combination of the ruins of Karnak and the Temple of Abu Simbel in Egypt, where we had been with the children eighteen months previously.

'But Karnak and Abu Simbel are two different places and hundreds of kilometres apart,' Zara complained in disappointment.

'It's just a movie,' I tried to explain.

'But it's not true,' she went on.

'Well, none of it is really true,' I said. 'They put it together like that to make it look better ... or what they think looks better.'

Oh, how well I remember discovering that the adult world was full of half-truths and downright lies. And oh, how much I want protect them from that hurtful discovery ... knowing too, that it would be even more hurtful to do so. Still, it was fun for a couple of hours to slip into a celluloid fantasy world where even the slums of Cairo are rendered acceptable.

Back in Guatemala City the next morning, there was a temporary lull while the counting of votes got under way. We visited the Nicaraguan Embassy to arrange for visas. Australian passports US$2, British, free.

We weren't really hungry, but we felt we should eat before boarding the bus for El Salvador, because experience had taught us to be prepared for unexpected happenings which could delay the next opportunity to eat. So we ordered a snack in a fairly reasonable café, but the children were unable to finish either their soup or sandwiches. We paid at the desk as we left and, glancing back to our table, to double-check that we hadn't left anything, I saw a couple of shoeshine boys gobbling up our scraps, like starving birds.

The comfortable ex-Greyhound bus followed the Pan-American Highway right down to El Salvador. This was our first ride on the 'Ticabus', the. international bus line that dominates all the traffic up and down the Central American isthmus. There were few foreign travellers on board, but, behind us, there was a couple of young American college boys discussing the difficulties of each making their $1000 stretch over a six-week vacation. Of course, it's irrelevant, but the average wage in Guatemala is around US$500 ... a year.

For both of them, it was their first visit to Central America, although one had previously visited England. His less-travelled friend, who was planning a jaunt to Britain later in the year, plied him with questions. 'Will they understand my English over there?'

To which the more experienced replied, 'Sure, if you talk slowly.'

EL SALVADOR

8
'. . . a pass to all the New York brothels'

Ed Rosenfeld is the sort of guy that makes a trip like this worthwhile. I think that meeting interesting and friendly people is probably the best thing about travelling . . . and what makes it doubly good is that it usually happens when you least expect it. We certainly weren't expecting to meet anybody quite like Ed Rosenfeld when the Ticabus pulled in to the company's terminal in San Salvador just on dusk.

We'd crossed the border into El Salvador a couple of hours previously and been passed through the customs and immigration check-point by a group of ludicrously attired officials. It takes a while for non-Latins to get used to some of the outrageous uniforms worn by the armies and police forces in Central and South America. It's certainly difficult to take them seriously. These particular officials were dressed in skin-tight pants, polished black jack-boots with jangling spurs, gold braid on their epaulets and shirts, helmets rather than hats and not only pistols slung on their hips, but swords too! At first it was all we could do to stop laughing, but many of these characters are so wrapped up in their own self-importance and imagined machismo that there's not much room for a sense of humour. So, no laughter, just the heavy, overbearing authority, some routine paperwork and a perfunctory delve into our packs and that was that . . . we were through and on our way.

But Ed Rosenfeld more than compensated for any anti-Salvadorean feelings we might have developed at the border. I can't remember how we actually met him. I think he was just sort of standing there as the bus was unloading and he started talking to us. There were a couple of hotel touts being very insistent in trying to convince us that we should come with them to such and such a hotel which was the cheapest and best etc. in town. Then we heard this deep, Bronx-accented voice.

'Hi . . . you looking for a place to stay?'

He was tall and slim, with receding grey hair . . . about sixty years old, I guess. He was wearing a pair of jeans and a short-sleeved yellow shirt. A pair of horn-rimmed glasses, with one lens held in place by a small piece of sticking plaster, kept slipping down his nose.

At first we thought he was another hotel tout . . . an American version . . . but we were soon convinced otherwise. Between the bus depot and the small hotel to which Ed directed us, we had heard almost half of Ed's life story.

'I was born in New York, but my parents abandoned me. I sort of grew up in institutions all over the place, but mainly in the Bronx, I guess. I'm Jewish you know.'

'With a name like Rosenfeld, I couldn't have guessed it,' I said.

He laughed. 'I've been down here in Central America about seven or eight years now. I was publishing a weekly tourist newspaper in Costa Rica before I came here. Not bad money in that. I could earn $400 a week like fallin' off a log. Great place, Costa Rica. The only one of all these countries that's a democracy . . . the rest are all military dictatorships.'

'What are you doing now?' I asked him as we walked along. It was rather a strange conversation, because there wasn't room for all of us on the sidewalk. So Ed and Trish walked in front. I was walking immediately behind listening to Ed's running commentary and Zara and Sean trailed behind us. It was about four or five blocks to the hotel.

'Well, I'm looking into starting up a similar newspaper here,' Ed said. 'They're beginning to build up their tourist industry and I think a little paper would do well.'

'Do you still have the other paper in Costa Rica?'

'Er . . . no. I got out of that. I felt I needed a change.'

We never found out why Ed left Costa Rica. The conversation changed to his hernia operation.

'I had to shop around a bit to get a good price. A helluva lot cheaper here than Stateside. It'd cost you thousands there, but I got both sides done for $400. Of course I had to beat the guy down. He wanted $750, but he dropped it when I told him I could get it done somewhere else for $350. I couldn't, but it brought his price down. It turned out okay, so I went back to the same guy for my prostectomy. That was pretty cheap too . . . except that it turned septic and I was in hospital for seventeen days.' He laughed. 'They wanted to charge me a packet for the extra time, but I went to court and said it was their fault I had to stay so long . . . so I didn't have to pay any more.'

It was like an instant soap opera, listening to Ed. After leaving our packs in the International Hotel (sounds very grand, but really it was pretty crummy) where we took one big room with four beds for US$12, Ed took us out for a walk around the town, during which we also hoped to find a bite to eat somewhere.

In the Plaza Barrios, the main square, Zara suddenly shouted, 'Look at the birds!' It was already dark and literally thousands of birds were sitting, asleep, on the telephone and electrical wires around the square, looking for all the world like notes on a musical score.

'They nest there every night,' Ed said. 'There are plenty of trees around for them to sit in, but they seem to prefer the lines.'

I took a photograph of them in the darkness, not feeling very confident that it would turn out. Then we went into a small cafe on one side of the square to order some hamburgers and soft drinks. Ed and I had a beer.

'They don't know how to make hamburgers down here, y'know,' Ed turned up his nose. 'If you started up a really good hamburger joint in some of these places you'd make a fortune.' He pushed his chair back and picked up his beer. 'Now I used to run a deli in Puerto Rico and . . .'

The children were unusually quiet, listening with mouths open to Ed's every word. Trish and I were too. He had sort of suddenly taken over our lives and yet he had a most engaging personality. Somehow although he talked non-stop about himself, it was relaxing and easy listening. Little snippets of information about his past life would keep popping in to the conversation and made you want to know more.

'I was all over the Caribbean for a few years. Made a packet in the Virgin Islands selling Bibles.'

'Bibles?' Trish exclaimed, 'But you said you were Jewish.'

A big smile and Ed pushed his glasses back on his nose. 'Well . . . a buck's a buck and when you've got a product to sell that people want . . . and anyway, half of it was the Old Testament, so I wasn't really going against the faith . . . not that I'm Kosher-Jewish any more, anyhow. They were forty dollars apiece and I got fifteen bucks on each one. I just took 'em round the islands and sold them by the hundreds . . . door to door through all those little towns. Very religious people, y'know, the Virgin Islanders. Amazing how much money there is around too.'

'Do you know what a Grosse Michelle is?' he said suddenly, turning to Zara and Sean, who snapped their eyes back into focus and closed their open mouths as if coming out of a trance.

Blank faces. They looked at each other and back to Ed, shaking their heads and laughing.

'Grosse Michelle is French for Big Mike,' Ed paused. 'Not a Big Mac . . . A Big Mike.'

More puzzlement.

'It's a banana. It's what keeps this country going; bananas and coffee.' This launched Ed into a discussion about El Salvador's economy and bananas, about which he obviously knew a great deal, but then he abruptly changed direction again:

'I've been to Australia, y'know.'

'Really?' Sean said, and he and Zara, neither of whom were in the least bored but were getting tired after a long day, sat up, even more attentive. 'When were you there?' Zara asked.

'During the war.'

'The Vietnam War?' said Sean.

Funny how different wars become 'the war' depending on your age.

'Hell no . . . World War II,' Ed replied.

'Oh.' Slight disappointment.

'Yeah. I was up in Brisbane with General Macarthur . . . and out in the islands.'

'Did you kill anybody?' Sean asked eagerly.

'Nope. Never even heard a shot fired. I had a terrific war . . . always hundreds of miles from the action. I was a male secretary . . . shorthand typist.'

A less likely-looking shorthand typist than Ed Rosenfeld would be hard to imagine. As he continued with more of his wartime and some after-the-war experiences in Japan as a sports-writer for the occupation forces magazine, Zara and Sean slowly began to nod off to sleep, so we took them back to our hotel to put them to bed. Then we crossed the road to Ed's hotel, where he made a cup of coffee for us in his tiny room with a small electric immersion heater that boiled a cup of water in about twenty seconds.

'How did you come to be a male secretary?' Trish asked Ed.

'It was just something I could always do,' he replied. 'In the orphans' institution I grew up in, they taught us shorthand and typing as at least some preparation for the outside world. Of course, most of the kids there never took any notice, but for some reason I liked it . . . and I worked at it. And I'm glad, because, when I got out and started looking for work I had no trouble finding it. I got a job as a secretary at the morgue in New York City.'

'Ugh . . .' I said. 'What a gruesome job.'

Ed smiled. 'Well yes . . . and no. Because it led on to another similar job with the Police Department where I ended up getting a pass into all the New York brothels.'

'You're joking.'

'No. Really.' He leant back on the bed, resting his head against the wall. 'It was the greatest job I've ever had. I used to just turn up at a brothel and show my pass and the madame would say to one of the girls, 'Okay, Sally (or Rose, or Mary, or whatever) this is Ed Rosenfeld. Do the right thing by him, okay?' And off I'd go into one of the rooms with one of the girls for about twenty minutes or so.'

I think my jaw must have dropped open in disbelief, because he laughed again. 'It's the truth. It wasn't an official pass, of course. It was organised for me by one of the sergeants on the vice squad . . . a couple of the senior guys there had it going for themselves too.'

'But . . .' I said, incredulous, 'what did the girls . . . I mean, surely you couldn't just keep turning up at these places all the time?'

'No, I had a sort of circuit worked out. I used to go to a couple a day . . . usually one during lunch-time and one after work . . . and it would take me about a month or two to get around them all, without ever going to the same place twice in that two months, so none of them ever thought I was making too much of a good thing.'

'My God,' I whispered.

Trish laughed. 'But how long did all this go on?' she asked.

'Oh, about five years. I kept going long after I'd left the job on the police force. The madames had all become so used to me that they never used to ask to see my special pass.'

'Twice a day . . . every day for five years!' I said to no one in particular, but thought to myself, no wonder his prostate packed up. Ed smiled modestly as Trish and I both looked at him with new respect.

'But you've never married?' Trish asked, bringing the conversation back to ground level.

'Nope,' he said, perhaps a little sadly. 'I guess I've never found the right girl.'

For breakfast the next morning, Ed took us to a tiny cafe he knew of where we had a terrific meal of eggs, toast and coffee for 150 centavos (about 60 cents) each. We talked a bit more about Ed's plans to try to stay in El Salvador to start up a tourist newspaper.

'It's not a bad place,' he said. 'A hell of a lot better and more advanced than Honduras or Nicaragua.'

We both had to admit to being fairly ignorant about El Salvador. In the past I can recall seeing all of those Central American republics as being a sort of general blob of seven or eight countries squeezed between Mexico and South America, but if I'd been asked to list them in their correct order from north to south, or anything very detailed about them individually, I would have been in trouble.

But it's surprising how quickly you start to pick up bits and pieces about a place when you're actually there . . . and you're receptive to all the inputs, whether they are Ed Rosenfeld, a tourist brochure, the guide book or whatever. Our first impressions of the capital, San Salvador, were reasonably good. It was a definite improvement on Guatemala City. Certainly cleaner . . . although being in a basin, surrounded by mountains, it does have something of a smog problem, mainly caused by traffic pollution.

Because it is the smallest of the Latin American republics, it seems to be more manageable than most of its neighbours. It is racially homogeneous, in fact over ninety percent of its population are of mestizo (mixed European and American Indian) descent. Only six percent is pure Indian and only two percent European.

El Salvador, we learnt from the statistics, is the most industrialised country in Central America. But that doesn't necessarily mean that everybody is better off. It simply means that a higher percentage of people in El Salvador work in industry than in other Central American countries. Unfortunately, the average El Salvadorean can only expect an annual income of just under five hundred dollars. Twenty-five percent of the population is still illiterate and with one of the highest birthrates in the region (3.5 percent), El Salvador, which is already the most densely populated country in Central America, has big problems ahead. Probably no more than the countries surrounding it, but sufficient to ensure that its turbulent history continues to be just that.

Although technically a republic where the voice of the people should be heard, El Salvador has really only ever known dictatorship, and the control of almost every aspect of life is said to lie in the hands of only fourteen families.

The current administration of President Carlos Humberto Romero has recently come under fire over the issue of political prisoners. Since coming to power in 1977, Romero has introduced the controversial 'Law of Defence and Guarantee of Public Order' which allows the government to arrest a person even on 'any presumption or suspicion' of their involvement in any anti-government activity. According to the International Commission of Jurists, the law led, even during the first six months of its implementation, to the detention of 715 people, the torture and physical mistreatment of 38, the known deaths of 2 and the 'disappearance' of another 21 people.

In late 1978 General Romero's regime was exceedingly embarrassed when one of these so-called 'disappeared' persons escaped from a police cell where he had been held in chains for ten months. Reynaldo Cruz Menjival, who was a peasant organiser for the Christian Democrat Party, was able to escape because he had been starved to the point (thirty-two kilos) where he could squeeze through the bars of his cell. His body was marked with the scars of torture and his wrists were raw from the manacles he had been wearing. He was given asylum by the Venezuelan embassy.

Prior to his escape President Romero had consistently assured the United

States that he held no political prisoners and his government denied all knowledge of the whereabouts of any of the 'disappeared' people, of whom Cruz Menjival had been one.

When you're just a tourist, coming into a country and leaving it quite quickly, it's rather hard, firstly to take in all these details, and secondly to take them seriously, because you know that you are moving on, but, unfortunately, for the people concerned, the details are deadly serious.

It is, I feel, the most disquieting and distasteful aspect of all travel in Latin America ... this undercurrent ... this knowledge that, behind the scenes, the police, the secret police, the army, have the power of life and death over individuals.

The bus from the village of Santa Tecla, thirteen kilometres west of the capital, ground its gears as it laboured over the rough and rutted steep track up the eighteen hundred-metre side of the volcano of San Salvador. It was very crowded and for the whole forty-five-minute trip Iain and Ed stood, or rather almost stood. They actually had to keep their heads bent over uncomfortably in order to fit below the low roof.

I perched beside two other women on a broken-down seat with Zara and Sean riding a knee each. Through the dirty windows I could see nothing but coffee bushes. Plantations, or fincas as they are called, ran almost to the summit. Passengers dropped off; (it wasn't worth actually stopping the bus which was climbing so slowly) to squeeze their way through and disappear into the thick shrubbery.

El Salvador is coffee and coffee is El Salvador. The two are synonymous. This tiny country, only 267 kilometres long and 106 kilometres wide, is one of the world's largest coffee producers. Because the bean is so vital to the economy of the country, El Salvador's financial situation fluctuates with world coffee prices.

The passengers were quite different from the people with whom we had travelled in Guatemala. Whereas there they had been mostly Indians, here they are almost all mestizos. The historical reason for this is that El Salvador, lying at the waistline of the isthmus, was isolated midway between the Conquistadores sent south from Mexico City and those coming north from Panama. The area had no precious metals to act as a lure for the Spaniards and the small number who did come, settled down, married the local Pipil Indians and made a living herding cattle.

As late as 1841 when the province seceded from Guatemala, after three centuries of Spanish domination, to become an independent republic, the population was still only around half a million. It was shortly after this that coffee was first planted and then, as the prosperity of the planters enriched the whole country, the population grew quickly to its present level of nearly five million. Now it is the only country in Latin America, apart from Uruguay, which utilises the whole of its land resources. As the most densely populated country on the American mainland, it is bursting at the seams; a fact which makes for strained relations with its neighbours, in particular Honduras, where many El Salvadoreans have sought living space.

Bouqueron, or 'big mouth', is as far as the bus goes. We climbed the last one and a half kilometres to the lip of the volcano crater to gaze down inside the one and a half kilometre wide, one kilometre deep 'mouth', at a smaller perfect cone left by another eruption in 1917.

There was a small army post casually manned by a few sloppily-dressed soldiers who lounged about smoking. A girl of probably the same age as Zara, though much smaller, barefoot in a skimpy cotton dress, ran up carrying a large tin plate laden with raspberries, for which she asked twenty cents.

She should have been at school. Primary school education is compulsory and free, but out in these rural areas, it would be a difficult regulation to enforce and parents cannot afford to lose the extra pair of working hands.

As we ate the fruit, Ed told us of how he once hitchhiked through Malaysia. 'I wore a solar topee and carried a rolled umbrella, both essential in that climate, and travelled the entire way in the luxury of a succession of Mercedes Benzes owned by Chinese Towkays. They thought, from my outfit, that I was British and they wanted to practise their English, which in most instances was already better than mine, but was of P.G. Wodehouse vintage; splendid fellow, spiffing type, that sort of thing, so I simply updated their slang with a few bobby-dazzlers which should go down well in the Selangor Club!'

Zara and Sean thought Ed was just great because he could make anything appear funny.

'Did you know this country went to war over a football match?' he asked them, pausing for effect. 'Fact. Probably the only time it has ever happened. It was the 1969 Central American Soccer Championship. El Salvador won. Honduras contested the decision and it was on. The Four Day War. Two days shorter than ours, yet! But it didn't get the same coverage. Like, who really knows where Honduras and El Salvador are?! They called in the OAS, closed the borders, and created a no-man's-land between them. Then Honduras threw out all the Salvadoreans living in Honduras, which was a mistake, because Salvadoreans are smarter and it was they who were keeping Honduran businesses running.' He popped a couple of raspberries into his mouth. 'Then there was Somoza. [The infamous President of Nicaragua.] He put his spoke in the wheel whenever possible, just to keep hostilities going. Why? Well, you see, he owns the ferry which runs across the Gulf of Fonseca from El Salvador straight into Nicaragua, without going through Honduras. So as long as the road border was closed, El Salvador had to ship its goods out on Somoza's ferry and he charged $200 for a private car and $800 for a truck then tucked it all away in a Swiss bank!'

Cloud began to obscure the view we had out over the edge of the volcano eastwards to the capital and began tumbling into the big mouth which swallowed it like a film of an eruption run backwards. With it came chill air and we set off to walk back down to where we could pick up the hourly bus. The young girl came shyly out again from a corrugated-tin and wooden shack and Zara handed her the empty plate, a terrible symbol of their inequality.

While we were waiting for the bus, three older men in scruffy clothes came swaying and staggering out of the undergrowth and lurched towards us, muttering in aggressive tones. We had been sitting on large boulders, but we got to our feet so as to be less vulnerable. One of them, the ringleader, despite, or perhaps because of, his drunkenness, tried to grasp Iain. He was obviously asking for money.

'Look out, Dad. He has a knife,' Sean called.

It was only then that we noticed that the man was holding a long, rusty machete behind his back.

'No comprende,' Iain kept saying to the man. 'No comprende' as we all backed slowly away from them.

One of the others muttered something which included 'gringo' to his companion.

'No, no gringo!' Ed said quickly — denying his heritage — 'Australiano. Somos Australianos.'

It had no effect though and the leader became even more insistent in his demands to Iain.

'Just get ready to run,' Iain said quietly, without turning his head. 'I'm going to push him over. He's so pissed he'll fall flat on his face, but we'd better be ready to move.'

But just then Zara shouted, 'Here's the bus!' and around the corner came the welcome sight of the old tumble-down bus which had brought us up the mountain a couple of hours earlier.

We all scrambled aboard and the conductor who swiftly appraised the situation with an experienced eye barred the door to prevent the three men from following us. The men, screaming abuse, tried to shove him aside, but he called to the driver, who put his foot to the boards and, in a shower of small stones and dust, we jolted off down the hill, leaving the men clinging onto each other for support and still shouting obscenities.

Back in San Salvador we took another bus, this time sixteen kilometres east to Lake Ilopango. Ed, undeterred, or perhaps even attracted, by our nasty adventure, good-naturedly came along for the ride. The lake is sixteen kilometres long and eight kilometres wide and is in the crater of an old volcano so the water always has an odd sulphuric smell and taste.

Sean swam out twenty metres or so to where a crowd of boys of his own age were playing around a half-submerged mass of twisted wood and metal. He was soon showing them his skill in back somersaults and they were shouting, 'Orrstraalia! Orrstraalia!'

Eight kilometres across the water, we could see the other shore rearing up abruptly. It looked enchantingly isolated.

'Some of the rich San Salvadoreans have weekenders or summer cottages there,' Ed told me. 'And there's talk of getting tourist facilities going. But it won't come to anything. Salvadoreans have this habit of grabbing at a new idea and worrying it to death, like a dog with a bone. That's how come their political life is so unstable. Some forceful personality, usually a colonel or a general even, comes up with a bright idea just before a general election and everybody votes for him. The idea collapses in the first puff of realism and the guy and his party fall into total obscurity.' He shrugged his shoulders philosophically. 'Almost all their leaders have been in the military and have been kept in office by men in uniforms. They can't even run an army let alone a country. It's sad because it's a hell of a waste of human potential. I mean, just think how much better off they all would have been if the United States had walked down here in the 1880s and taken over the whole shebang.'

Behind us, under the trees, a party was gathering. One fellow played a trumpet and a couple more strummed guitars and sang. Very quickly some of the guests had drunk enough to join in and some started to dance. Food was laid out on long wooden park tables and we were invited across.

Sean borrowed the trumpet to play 'Abide with Me', which received a round of applause. Iain drank a beer and was propositioned by an amorous young woman whose boyfriend was not amused.

'She'll get cooled in the lake,' Ed prophesied. 'Like the four virgins the ancient Indians drowned here every year to appease their harvest gods.'

'*Beautiful* virgins, of course,' I added.

'Why of course,' Ed agreed. 'If they had chosen ugly ones the women's libbers would have accused them of prejudice!'

HONDURAS

9
The original Banana Republic

The Ticabus company has Central America sewn up. They were the first people to set up a proper bus service linking the six countries from Guatemala to Panama with modern, air-conditioned vehicles that ran on schedule and guaranteed that, with a reserved seat ticket, you would actually get a seat. On many of the other buses run by other companies in different parts of Latin America, it's 'first come, first served'; a bun-fight to get a seat. Then it is invariably taken the moment you leave it, by any one of the dozens of additional passengers who are allowed to pack the aisle.

The main Ticabus service runs from Guatemala City all the way to Panama City, a distance of some 2000 kilometres. It's not possible, however, to buy a through ticket. You have to buy your tickets from capital city to capital city, or from town to town, renewing your booking as you go along.

I'm not sure whether being on the Ticabus makes it any easier when crossing borders, but the formalities at the Honduran frontier for the passengers of our bus were brief and easy. They were definitely not, though, for a young American couple with a small child and a dog we saw while we were at the border. They were really getting the run-around ... the full treatment, from the Honduran customs men. The couple had a large, well-fitted out RV (Recreational Vehicle) ... a camping van, which was towing a VW beetle. We went across to speak to them briefly and found that they were driving down from Mexico City to Panama, where the man was due to open up an office for the Associated Press wire service.

'The second car is what blows their mind,' his wife said to us, as her husband, with knitted brow and serious countenance, tried to control his patience as he went through a pile of documents with the customs officials. 'They've never seen anything like this and they say it's not permitted. If we're just towing a second car along, we must be intending to sell it in Honduras.' She shrugged. 'It looks as though we're going to have to take a customs man ... a guard if you like, the whole way with us through Honduras, and then pay his fare back to here when we leave. My God!'

We left them to their dealings as, after only twenty minutes, the whole of our bus load had been cleared and we were heading down the Inter-American Highway across southern Honduras.

Not long afterwards, the air-conditioning in the bus broke down. As it was steaming hot outside, the air temperature inside the bus rose rapidly. Everybody opened their windows, but, unfortunately, we were sitting beside a window that was fixed and could not be opened. We slowly began to swelter and drip with sweat. I tried to read an El Salvadorean newspaper and managed to decipher from the front page headlines and photographs, that there had been widespread protests against the victory in the Guatemalan elections of General Lucas Garcia. Claims of electoral fraud and ballot-rigging were being investigated, but in the meantime the General was naturally denying everything and was firmly in power.

In the burlesque world of Latin American politics, we were not at all surprised to read a few months later that Villagran Kramer, General Garcia's Vice-President, had voluntarily agreed to undergo a psychiatric examination in an attempt to refute one of the opposition parties' assertions that he was insane and therefore unfit for office!

I sat for a while, gazing out at the rolling hill country and thought of Ed Rosenfeld. We'd said goodbye the previous evening over a cup of coffee, made with his instant boiler, in his hotel room. He got out some old photographs of himself as a young man in New York before 'the' war, and some others of him in the army in the Pacific and in Japan. His hair was dark and, with the thin moustache he wore, he looked for all the world like Errol Flynn. You could see he must have been a real lady-killer in those days ... and yet, somehow it all seemed sad. He had done so much and lived such an amazing life, but here he was, in this little hotel room, very much alone ... and probably very lonely. We both urged him to write a book about his life.

'I've often thought about it,' he said with a rather absent look at the wall. 'In fact, I've even got a name for it ... but I've never got around to the actual book. I'll have to do it. I must.'

The Ticabus route we were following was to take us eastwards across the narrow southern neck of Honduras which runs down to the Gulf of Fonseca on the Pacific Ocean. The bus would not pass through the Honduran capital, Tegucigalpa, which was some ninety-five kilometres north of our route along the Inter-American highway. We had discussed staying longer in Honduras, but felt that, as some of its main attractions, like the beautiful Bay Islands, were several hundred kilometres north, off the Caribbean coast of Honduras, and we were anxious to press on towards South America, that we would move straight on through Honduras as quickly as we could to Nicaragua ... although with a civil war festering away, that didn't sound very attractive either.

As far as this book is concerned, however, we felt it would be wrong just because we passed through the country quickly, to leave it out of the narrative.

Honduras in Spanish means 'The Depths'. Christopher Columbus named the territory after the deep waters just off the coast when he landed there on his fourth and last voyage of discovery in 1502. Like much of the rest of the Central American isthmus, the land now occupied by Honduras (an area roughly the size of England) was influenced by the Mayan civilisation and Copan, in the western part of Honduras was once one of the greatest of Mayan cities. But, by the time Columbus arrived on the scene, Copan was already just a vast, empty ruin, being slowly swallowed by the jungle.

Honduras has not really had a very prosperous or happy existence since those early days. There was little in the way of gold or silver to attract the Spanish, so for almost three centuries after its first settlement, there was only a thin stream of immigrants to Honduras. Even today, although it is larger than all of the other Central American republics, except Nicaragua, it has a smaller population (three and a quarter million) than El Salvador, which is less than one-fifth the size of Honduras.

Honduras has the lowest per capita income in all of Latin America (in the mid-seventies it was under $300) and is probably the poorest country on the entire American mainland. Health conditions are amongst the worst in the western hemisphere and almost seventy percent of the population are peasants living a virtual hand-to-mouth existence. Fifty percent of all people are illiterate and, although there is a law saying that education is compulsory, for half the children in rural areas there are no schools to go to.

The only railways in the country are for the banana plantations . . . there are none in the main population centres. Even the capital, Tegucigalpa, is not served by railway.

As our bus roared on, the countryside seemed to be becoming more arid than that we had left behind in El Salvador, but it was obviously not too dry for bananas to flourish, as we passed several huge plantations.

Bananas are what keeps Honduras going. It is one of the three largest exporters of bananas in the world. Half of the country's total exports are bananas, but the vast majority of all banana production is in the firm control of two giant American companies, 'United Brands' and 'Standard Fruit', who have, in effect, a stranglehold over the Honduran economy. It is as a result of this situation in Honduras that the term 'Banana Republic' was first coined.

The two American companies own, with the government, over 60 percent of all arable land in Honduras. A further 27 percent of the land is held by little more than 600 families, leaving only 13 percent remaining for the balance of the population.

Coupled with this inequality of land distribution, the economy's desperate reliance on bananas makes it absolutely vulnerable to the slightest crop failure, hurricane damage, disease or fluctuation of the world market price. Consequently, Honduras never seems to be able to generate any real growth in its economy.

Not a happy story . . . particularly as it seems likely to continue. Honduras has had twelve constitutions since it gained its independence in 1838. For the past twenty-five years it has lived under a succession of military juntas and dictators. The elections in 1980 may bring a civilian back to power, but it's unlikely he'll stay long if Honduran history stays true to form.

NICARAGUA

10
'A revolution of possibilities'

As we were approaching the Nicaraguan border, Iain, who was thumbing through a guide, let out a little moan, followed by nervous laughter. He passed the book to me, pointing at a paragraph headed 'WARNING: Nicaraguan border officials do not like army-type clothing and may confiscate green or khaki backpacks.'

'That's just great!' I moaned also. We were each carrying a dark green backpack and, coming in a set of four we already resembled forward scouts for an advancing platoon.

There was nothing to be done at this stage except gee up the usual pep talk we always give Zara and Sean just before borders; stressing even more the dire necessity for them to say nothing, absolutely nothing, during the entire performance, just to smile a lot and please not lounge on the desks or, horror, fiddle with the rubber stamps and forms.

'Yeah, Mum, yeah.' They'd heard it so many times before and they were grumpy with the heat.

Nor was I in the mood for playing silly buggers with petty officials. My ovaries were engaged in a round of internal fisticuffs which made it very difficult for me to hold on to a balanced view of the world.

Our vehicle pulled over to the side of the road, next to a most unpromising collection of ramshackle huts and tin sheds, one of which was graced with a sagging verandah. Everyone disembarked, taking all their hand luggage with them. We found that our 'military-style' packs were under everyone else's luggage in the hold of the bus so that by the time we had them out, the single customs official had already tipped out the entire contents of several passengers' suitcases onto a long trestle table and was busy rummaging through the limp clothes as if it was a jumble sale and that he might just be able to find a bargain.

He certainly looked as though he needed one. But then perhaps he had just popped out for a break from the Managua Amateur Theatrical Company's production of 'Rigoletto'. In Nicaragua anything is possible. He was inside an oversized large-patterned Hawaiian sports shirt and crumpled baggy pants which hung precariously from somewhere round his hips and were only kept up with a piece of thick cord on which was tied a large holster which was over-flowing with a pistol. His bare feet were stuffed into broken-backed brogues. His thick moustaches drooped forlornly in the heat and he frequently wiped his forearm across his sweating brow. A very battered naval cap clung to the back of his head. And yes, to complete the caricature, the stump of a dead cigar was clenched between his teeth. We listened despondently as he shouted in Spanish at the other passengers, the majority of whom were Costa Rican.

So long ago it seems like in another life, in the time before I knew Iain, my method of dealing with border officials who showed even the slightest hesitation was to be, well, rude, there is simply no getting away from it. A rudeness, bred I fear of arrogance, an arrogance based on the fact that twenty years ago a British passport gave its bearer a carte blanche, an open sesame at almost every national front door. No one ever wanted to see your funds or asked how long you intended to stay. It was assumed that, as you were British, you had more than sufficient and that you certainly wouldn't want to linger overlong in foreign parts which were so inferior to home.

The collapse of the Empire and the rise of mass tourism and British apathy have done away with these foolish ideas. But old habits die hard and though I have allowed myself to become as tongue-tied as the children at borders, smiling a great deal while Iain does the talking (sometimes this plan backfires, as you will see later), inwardly I am often a seething mass of hostility!

Iain loathes borders but, whereas I become aggressive, he becomes positively low-key and cool. Perhaps this difference in technique is the essence of our relationship and the reason why we get along so well together! He bases his behaviour on the premise that it works! Which is fair enough. As we waited in the queue I could see him working himself up to this role, practising his used-car-salesman smile which doesn't even fool our dog, as we dragged our packs along towards our operatic friend. 'Just let him try his aria on me,' my ovaries muttered sullenly.

And then, in a flash, it was over, and we found ourselves lugging our packs back to the bus. What happened? We didn't even get to put our packs on the table. Without even a glance at our 'military-style' luggage he had waved us on in a disinterested manner and with a limp hand dismissed us as if we were merely loyal subjects come to gawp at his regal routine. Then he got back to the real business of heavying more Central Americans.

We all felt let down and were only slightly mollified when the immigration officer who conducted his business from behind a cluttered desk in one of the tiny, beaten-up, wooden shacks demanded $1.50 each from us.

'Why?' asked Iain mildly, adding 'I have already paid $5 for a visa. Here,' and he held his passport open on the appropriate page.

The man ignored him and thumbed heavily through the crowded entries.

'And I don't need a visa,' I insisted loudly from behind Iain's shoulder. The man looked up, took my passport, stamped it and, handing it back, gestured for me to move on. I glanced at Iain, who understandably looked a little miffed.

'Everything all right?' I asked a few minutes later as Iain slumped beside me in his seat just as the bus began to roll forward.

'Sure.'

'What happened Dad?' Sean persisted. 'Did you have to pay again?'

'Yes. But not for a visa. For the Managua Reconstruction Fund. Everyone paid except your mother. I think they realised in the present state of Britain's economy she couldn't afford $1.50.' Squelch!

Although the language of Latin America is predominantly Spanish and the greater part of the history and culture of most Central and South American countries has revolved around Spain and Portugal, the dominant economic and cultural influence in the twentieth century, particularly in the years since World War II, has been the United States.

As mentioned before, the United States is the object of very mixed emotions for Latin Americans: love, hate, envy, fear and, occasionally hope.

In the case of Nicaragua, one might reasonably add burning resentment, as it was the United States, which, in 1933, set the hated family of Anastasio Somoza Garcia on the road to absolute power in Nicaragua, a complete domination of the country that lasted until mid-1979 . . . a domination that was the root cause of all the violence and bloodshed that has swept Nicaragua in recent times.

The US has had its finger in Nicaraguan affairs since the late nineteenth century when they were negotiating to build a canal from the Pacific to the Atlantic across Nicaragua, but for much of the early part of this century, Nicaragua was run by an occupational force of United States Marines. American warships and marines arrived in Nicaragua in 1912 and remained active in the country's politics, administering Nicaragua either directly or through handpicked rulers until 1933. During the last five years of the American occupation, nationalist guerillas, under General Cesar Augusto Sandino, fought a bitter war against the marines, who were unable to suppress them.

When the marines withdrew from Nicaragua in 1933, they left a young general, Anastasio Somoza in charge of a newly formed, American-trained National Guard. Within a year, Somoza had captured and executed the guerilla leader, Sandino, and overthrown the liberal president, Juan Bautista Sacasa, to take control of Nicaragua himself. Once in power, Somoza did not hesitate to violently suppress any political opponents and he ruled as a dictator for twenty-two years, until he was assassinated in 1956. But his death did not mean an end to Somoza rule, because after that the country passed into the hands of, firstly Somoza's older son Luis, and secondly his younger son, also named Anastasio, who, in many people's eyes proved to be an even more ruthless tyrant than his father.

During the years following the original Anastasio's grab for power, various branches of the Somoza family spread their tentacles into every corner of Nicaragua's economy. For instance, fifty-five percent of all the country's exports and imports have been carried by a shipping line called Nicaraguan Merchant Marine, which is wholly owned by the Somoza family. They have vast land holdings and substantial interests in the four major export commodities of Nicaragua: cotton, meat, coffee and sugar. They also have large-scale investments in banks, property, the country's national airline, communications, hotels and newspaper and television outlets.

Many, if not all of these immense holdings in Nicaragua have become the subject of either outright confiscation, compulsory sale or legislation in the wake of the July 1979 overthrow of the Somoza dictatorship. A hardly surprising reaction when you consider the methods Somoza and his relatives used in acquiring them.

One would think, looking at earthquake-devestated Managua, that the Somoza family's share of the $900 million losses incurred from the disaster that struck the Nicaraguan capital in December 1972 might have proved a severe setback for them. But no. The earthquake, which brought almost every major building in Managua tumbling down, represented, as President Somoza so aptly put it, a 'revolution of possibilities'.

Possibilities of which the Somoza family were not slow to take advantage. One example: Shortly after the earthquake, Venezuela lent Nicaragua $70 million to help in the reconstruction of the capital. The interest rate Venezuela charged on the loan was a low five percent. Instead of using the money to rebuild Managua, President Somoza reinvested it through intermediaries at eight percent, making a cool two million dollars profit a year on the money.

In addition, the family raked in literally millions of dollars in construction contracts and financial operations connected with the reconstruction of Managua which were handled by the Banco de Centro America, which Somoza had set up. But the reconstruction that was carried out was in the outskirts of the capital, on the dubious pretext that this area was less vulnerable to further earthquakes. In the meantime, property owners in the devastated centre were forced to continue paying high taxes on land on which they were not allowed to rebuild. When property prices in the central area naturally fell dramatically, the Somoza family moved in. They are reported to have been by far the biggest buyers of the large areas of available land. A 'revolution of possibilities'.

Total overseas aid to Nicaragua after the 1972 earthquake was around $250 million. According to a Latin American Economic Report, 'the amount of this aid lost through corruption or theft cannot be quantified. Little of it, however, found its way into the rebuilding of Managua.'

When we arrived in the Nicaraguan capital some five and a half years after the tragedy, the place looked as if an earthquake had hit it . . . still! Wandering around the central area reminded me of those pictures that were taken of Hiroshima after the bomb; only a few buildings left standing.

The Bank of America's seventeen-storey skyscraper office block withstood the earthquake, although it was still unoccupied, apparently sufficiently cracked and structurally damaged to be considered dangerous. There were several other buildings also empty, which at first glance appeared to be whole, but on closer examination revealed huge cracks. The pyramid-shaped Hotel Intercontinental, specifically designed to resist earthquakes, did just that and was one of the few modern buildings to come through unscathed, fortunately for American millionaire Howard Hughes, who was occupying the top floor penthouse at the time. What I find amazing now, though, is to see the Intercontinental Hotel Group's ads in 'Time' and other magazines, showing the Managua Hotel. It looks positively glamorous. If only the photo showed the rest of it . . . the appalling devastation of the hotel's surroundings.

Surprisingly, several of the old colonial buildings in other parts of the central area of Managua remained standing, but for the most part the whole of the original city is a wasteland. The streets are still there, but they run between empty fields and are sprouting grass and weeds. Even so long after the event, we really felt that we were standing on the site of a disaster.

Some ten thousand people died in the earthquake, 25,000 were injured and a quarter of a million, more than two-thirds of the population of the city, were made homeless by the 1972 quake.

Any country would find it a shattering blow to be hit by a catastrophe of these proportions, but for Nicaraguans it was like being kicked in the head while you're down. Nicaragua is amongst the poorest of the Latin American countries. There is widespread malnutrition, life expectancy is just over forty-nine years and one-half of all the registered deaths are children under the age of five.

These facts are made particularly odious when considered alongside the personal wealth of President Anastasio Somoza, estimated at over $500 million. It was said he got over $200 million out of the country before he fled.

But at least the terrors and the hardships of the earthquake, dreadful though they were, could be blamed on nature . . . or God. The horrors of the civil wars of 1978 and 1979 and Somoza's brutal repression of what was obviously a popular uprising against his dictatorship, make Nicaragua's story even sorrier.

The war was begun by the Sandinistas, a revolutionary movement containing both leftists and rightists and named after Sandino, the guerilla leader who was eliminated by the original Somoza in the thirties. In 1978 the Sandinistas successfully seized the Presidential Palace, but not Somoza himself. This was followed almost immediately by a general strike and a national insurrection, in which five towns outside the capital were taken and held by the guerillas and the citizens of the towns.

For the first couple of months they managed to hold out against Somoza's National Guard until aircraft and tanks were brought in. An abundance of eye-witness accounts tell of the indiscriminate bombing and shelling of these towns and of the systematic arrest and execution of their citizens with the eventual re-establishment of Somoza's tyranny.

There was a brief period of calm, but Somoza must have seen the writing on the wall. Obsessed with the belief that he would one day be assassinated like his father, he surrounded himself with a permanent bodyguard of thirty to forty armed men while he clung obstinately to power.

In 1979, when the re-grouped and reorganized Sandinistas launched a new offensive, Somoza conducted a desperate but brutally destructive campaign from an underground bunker in the Presidential residence in Managua.

By then he had almost no friends left outside of the country. During the brief 1978 civil war he had incurred the enmity of neighbouring Latin American countries like Costa Rica, Panama, Venezuela and even Honduras, but also of the United States, because of the disruption his regime was causing in the entire region.

During both the 1978 and 1979 crises the United States took unprecedented steps to try to persuade Somoza to step down voluntarily. Most of the Central American governments feared that success in Nicaragua for the Sandinistas might lead to a communist regime there and inevitably provide inspiration for the indigenous revolutionary movements in their own countries.

When the 1979 campaign built up these demands from outside were repeated with increased pressure. But Somoza would not give in.

'If I resign,' he declared, 'I will only be replaced by a military junta.'

But even that, in most people's eyes, was preferable. Instead, as the Sandinista guerillas occupied more and more of the country, including the strategic town of Leon, Somoza ordered the renewal of conventional bombing and fire-bomb attacks on those towns and suburbs which the Sandinistas had occupied, but which also contained large civilian populations.

The country was being torn apart. Tens of thousands of refugees from the battle areas were close to starvation; forty to fifty thousand — many of them innocent women and children — were dead, but by late July, the well-equipped and apparently well-trained Sandinistas were fighting pitched battles with the once omnipotent National Guard, and winning. Parts of Managua were being overrun by the rebels. Somoza realised it was all over and flew out to seek refuge in an embarrassed United States.

Suddenly Nicaragua, battered, bleeding, poverty-stricken and hungry, was at peace — without the hated Somoza family in power, for the first time in forty-six years.

In the southern Sudan we had met a man who hunted bongo, and I had thought that was pretty off-beat. But that was before I heard of tarpon fishing in Lake Nicaragua. How's that for one-up-manship? Not that either activity appeals to me, but if people want to hunt bongo in the southern Sudan or fish for tarpon in Lake Nicaragua, well, it keeps them off street corners, doesn't it?

The lake, a hundred and sixty kilometres long and seventy-two across at its widest spot, slipped by the window of our Costa Rica-bound bus. There are three hundred and fifteen small islands in the lake and almost all of them are inhabited.

'There are sharks in that lake.' The voice had a familiar twang.

'You Australian?' Sean asked hopefully of the young man who had come to stand in the aisle beside us.

'New Zealander.'

'Oh, well. Almost.' We all laughed.

'Are they man-eaters?'

'New Zealanders?'

'No! The sharks.'

'I don't know, shouldn't think so. But they are the only fresh water sharks in the world. Lake Nicaragua used to be an inlet from the Pacific Ocean, but it was cut off from the sea by ancient volcanic and geological activity and, as the water desalinated over the centuries, sharks adapted to living in fresh water.'

Ken Stewart introduced himself and, as he perched on the arm of our seat, we talked about the importance of being able to adapt not only in the animal, but also the human world.

Like everybody else we are so caught up with the business of getting from day to day that we rarely make time to consider the immense social and technological changes which are happening even during our own lifetimes.

That's one of the reasons why I enjoy this slow and often laborious form of travel in which we indulge. There's plenty of time on eighteen-hour bus trips to stand back from life and reassess it as a whole.

Whereas basically Iain is highly adaptable and at ease with the prospect of rapid changes in the imminent twenty-first century (he and Ken were drooling over the possibilities of something called Ceefax) I am not and I have to work very hard so as not to become as separated from reality as a piece of antique fantasy in the Victoria and Albert Museum.

As my children grow older, I have become increasingly aware of this deficit because I don't want to lumber them with the same disability. I believe that this lengthy journeying with them helps to combat this; helps to make them adaptable and open-minded, able to feel at ease in any company, to realise their own potential for coping with unpleasant, difficult and sometimes even dangerous circumstances and to be interested in and questioning about every aspect of the world in which we live. All those characteristics will, I think, help them grab the new century by the scruff of the neck and ride it, not just hang on to its tail and get dragged along willy-nilly.

Ken was an air-traffic controller, surely one of the most demanding jobs imaginable. But at twenty-five, after four years of such extreme responsibility, he seemed a very relaxed and agreeable bloke, which is, I suppose, the reason he can handle the job. He had been travelling in Canada and the USA for six months and was on his way to Panama from where he was going to fly to England to join the crowd of Antipodeans who manage to make a good living at jobs and hours the English will no longer tackle.

We were now travelling almost alongside the water and we could see on the largest island, Isla Ometepe, two volcanic cones, one of which rose in a perfect shape, to loom high above the lake.

From the eastern end of Lake Nicaragua the San Juan River flows into the Caribbean Sea and at the western side it is separated from the Pacific by a strip of land a mere nineteen kilometres wide. You would therefore have to be as daft as a brush not to see it as an obvious site for a trans-isthmus canal.

The Californian Gold Rush of the 1840s brought to Nicaragua the very un-daft Commodore Cornelius Vanderbilt, progenitor of the long line of millionaire entrepreneurs. Here he was to match his financial and influential muscle against the British. The Panama Canal was yet to be built and both parties could see the vast profits to be made by whoever controlled the traffic across the isthmus between the two great oceans.

But, as is so often the case, the restless natives proved to be a stumbling block. While the US and the UK were busy signing treaties and agreeing not to seek exclusive rights to build a canal through someone else's country, the Nicaraguan government was toppled by a coup and the new leaders invited an extraordinary, colourful character, an adventurer, by the name of William Walker, to help their rebellion. Walker was less interested than fellow-American Vanderbilt in making a fortune, he simply wanted to make history and after capturing Granada, on the northwestern shores of the lake, declared himself President of Nicaragua.

Vanderbilt and Britain were so irritated that this upstart had managed to louse up their wheeling and dealing that they supported Walker's enemies who managed to depose him. He was later captured and executed in Honduras. But by this time the Brits had wearied of this particular Caribbean adventure and restored the Mosquito Coast to Nicaragua and signed a treaty giving the US undisputed right to build a trans-isthmian canal.

Although that was very far from the end of US interference in Nicaragua it was the end of that project. The Panama Canal opened eventually in 1914, but by then the Vanderbilts were milking new pastures, no doubt leaving the Nicaraguans feeling rather punch drunk.

COSTA RICA

11
One bright spot

By the time we reached the ramshackle collection of huts that formed the Nicaraguan border post, the day was already very hot. We slaked our thirst with deep gulps of Coca-Cola from a nearby stall. How often on these journeys have I caught myself thinking, thank God for Coca-Cola! A kilometre further on and we were rapidly and efficiently checked into Costa Rica.

The bus, oblivious to the change in the tarmac's national status, continued on its journey and our aisle party was joined by another fellow, this one with thick, long, blond, curly hair who introduced himself as Randy 'Beau' Lane, an American Panamanian; a difficult position to straddle, I would have thought, at this point in history. His conversation expressed sentiments I had also heard from white Rhodesians; 'I was born in Panama, it's my home, I have no other. I have dual citizenship, my Dad's American. He works on the locks in the Canal Zone. But when the Zone is handed over to the government and the Americans move out, I shall stay on. Like I say, it's my home.'

Beau, who was thirty, was one of ten children and had done a variety of jobs, including fishing in the waters off northern Peru, about which he told hair-raising stories of knife fights with the crew. He was on his way home after a working stint in the US. 'And, oh boy, am I looking forward to it. Panama is beautiful man, beautiful. The beaches are white. The sun is hot. The lobsters are huge. The beer is cheap and the hunting is good.'

'Hunting?' Zara, who up to now had been fresh with Beau as only an eleven-year-old girl knows how, sat up straight with shock. 'You hunt?'

'Sure thing.' Beau, as yet unaware of Zara's verbal talents, agreed amiably.

'What do you hunt and how?' she persisted.

'Anything wild and with a gun.'

It was on. For the next half an hour Zara did her ecology rave and Beau visibly wilted, under her steady onslaught. The family has been similarly earbashed, of course, but I had never seen Zara unleashed in public before and I couldn't help but be rather impressed!

I loved Zara and Sean when they were mewling, puking, helpless blobs, but I admit that I not only love them now, I like them too, as they grow into adulthood. We are no doubt about to embark on that highly dangerous family journey across the shifting, sinking, sands of political awareness. In my masochistic moments I quite look forward to having my approaching middle-aged political and social values challenged!

It had been very hot all day and even the slight drizzle which began to enclose us did nothing to cool the air down. The heat made the four hundred-kilometre journey seem long and I glanced down at Iain's watch so as to be able to work out a rough estimate of when we could expect to arrive in Costa Rica's capital, San Jose.

As I looked up again my eyes recorded an image of danger so imminent that I was instantaneously frozen with fear. It was like in those nightmares in which you try to call out and no sound will come and in which you try to run, but your feet won't move. I wanted to scream, 'Sean, get down,' and make a grab for him but I could do neither. In what seemed like long seconds, I had time to wonder why Iain was still reading so unconcernedly, why Zara was still haranguing Beau and why Sean was still kneeling up in his seat and facing backwards to play the fool with Ken. Why did they not see what was going to happen and why was it all taking so long? And then, CRRAAASSHH!

In the split second, after the truck hit us and we slewed sickeningly to a halt, before the realisation had impinged on our consciousness, the passengers were utterly silent and the cracking, and splintering, the crashing of glass fell in loud drops of noise. Then the constricting band of fear burst and in the instant pandemonium, people screamed and cried and my body regained its functions.

'My God, what happened?' Iain was asking as we struggled with everyone else toward the exit.

I told him how I had looked up and seen the huge semi-trailer swerving round the bend and realised that it was impossible for it to miss us. 'I was sure it would hit just where Sean was sitting and I wanted to grab him but I couldn't move.' My legs trembled still.

By the time we climbed down and moved around to inspect the damage, Sean, oblivious of his recent danger, had already wriggled his way to the front of the crowd and was enthusiastically examining the driver's smashed side window and the gaping gash along the entire bus body which looked as though it had been operated on with a giant can-opener.

Obviously the truck had been too far over on our side of the narrow winding road, but at least, once our driver realised he was going to be hit, his reactions had been quick enough to enable him to wrench the wheel hard around so as to avoid a head-on and certainly fatal collision, but not far enough to miss a heavy clip on the ear.

The truck was parked a hundred metres away on the opposite side of the road. No one had yet emerged from the cabin. Probably the poor bastard was so shaken up he hadn't the strength to move.

It wasn't until we walked round to the far side of our bus that we realised fully the very close call we'd had, and my legs became insubstantial again. Our wheels were a mere metre from the unguarded, soft edge of the road from where the ground fell abruptly away, fifteen metres, at least, into a scrub-filled valley. The skid marks in the gravel showed how terrifyingly dependent we had been on our driver's skill.

After that, everything which followed was a tedious anti-climax. The two-hour wait in the gathering darkness for the police; Beau, Ken and Iain posting themselves along the dangerous curve to slow down the traffic which would otherwise have hurtled into the stationary vehicles. The eventual arrival of the constabulary and the statements taken from the drivers and passengers; ours was refused because of our transient status. The truck driver had pulled himself together sufficiently to insist that he had not been out of his lane. This was so blatantly impossible that I guess it was said more from bravado than from any hope of being believed.

Dusk was rapidly becoming night by the time we were on our way again. Exhausted with the shock and excitement, the passengers were subdued and many of them dozed for the last hour into the capital.

When at last we arrived, four hours behind schedule, others were greeted by anxious and relieved relatives all of whom had, no doubt, imagined the very worst had befallen us.

Beau, with the stamina born of homesickness, boarded another waiting bus for the overnight run down to Panama and, as we waved him off, Zara stifled a yawn to say, 'I wish we sometimes had someone to meet us or wave us off.'

Costa Rica is the one bright spot in Central America; a real exception to the rule as far as the politics of the region are concerned, a remarkable democracy and a pleasant little country which, on paper, seems almost too good to be true.

Costa Ricans enjoy the greatest political freedom of all Central and South American countries. A study of political and civil rights by the Manhattan-based 'Freedom House' organisation puts Costa Rica on an equal footing in this respect with the United States and the countries of Western Europe.

Costa Ricans have a higher standard of living than probably any other country in Latin America and the highest literacy rate, over eighty percent, in the region. Costa Rica is in my opinion, a model social democracy, with a stable currency, a healthy balance of payments, an enviable system of social welfare, a luxurious climate and a beautifully green and fertile landscape. The sort of place you'd think everyone would want to live. And, in fact, many thousands of Americans retire in Costa Rica which only has a total population of just over two million.

All of these things are not only true on paper, but in fact. At least that was *our* immediate feeling on arrival in San Jose. My notes for the day read, 'A very nice town; much cleaner, more modern than anything else we've seen. The shops are better ... obviously a much higher standard of living ... lots of greenery ... the air is cleaner.'

And strangely enough my lasting impressions of San Jose and Costa Rica in general coincide with those initial ones, despite the fact that my notes go on to list a chronicle of annoying and frustrating situations for the next day and night.

The first night was spent in a tiny room, with no windows, in the Boston Hotel, US$10 for the four of us. At 6.30 the next morning I went to have a shower. No water. The attendant claimed that the whole town's water was shut off until 7.00 a.m. I didn't believe him. I told him I would go to the gas station across the road to try their taps. He mumbled something and went to the back of his room and turned on a tap. A few minutes later we had water ... cold water that is.

Later we took a bus out to the Panamanian consulate in a suburb of San Jose to get our tourist cards to enter Panama. The woman consul told us that we could not enter Panama without also having a ticket *out* of Panama, preferably an air ticket. As we were hoping to find a *boat* from Panama on to Colombia or Ecuador, we did not have any tickets. The only way, it seemed, was to buy a Ticabus ticket for a journey from Panama City back to San Jose, which we could use to get our tourist cards here in Costa Rica, then cash them in Panama when we eventually got tickets to leave another way.

We took a bus back into town to the Ticabus terminal, bought the necessary Panama City/San Jose tickets, then, after a meal at a small restaurant, went back out to the consulate only to be confronted with the news that, 'We do not issue tourist cards. We only issue visas.'

'But it says in our guide book that tourist cards for Panama can be obtained from the consulate in San Jose.'

A nasty look came over the lady's face. 'I said we do *not* issue tourist cards here. Only visas.'

Visas, for Sean and I, on Australian passports, would have cost US$10. Tourist cards, which serve exactly the same purpose, would have been US$4.

'The Ticabus company will issue you tourist cards,' the woman said casually.

My God. 'But . . . why didn't you tell us that before?' I said, feeling anger rise in me.

The woman shrugged her shoulders, but said nothing.

'Thank you *very* much,' I muttered through gritted teeth as we walked out.

Looking back on it, it would have been far better to have just put aside my annoyance, paid the higher price and taken the visas there and then, but we angrily bussed back to Ticabus, only to find the offices closed for lunch. Eventually it opened again and when we asked for our tourist cards, we were informed that the cards were only valid for entry on the day of travel and only for travel by Ticabus. But we had been thinking of entering Panama, not by Ticabus along the Inter-American Highway, but by rail and road from Puerto Limon over on the Caribbean coast side of the country.

By this time, I was nearly tearing my hair out.

'The easiest way,' the clerk told us, 'is to get a visa. Then you can travel into Panama whenever and however you like.'

Back on the bus again to the Panamanian consulate. But now it was also closed . . . and, as it was Friday, closed for the whole weekend! God! I was really beside myself. We had traipsed backwards and forwards for about five or six hours and achieved absolutely nothing!

It took me some time to calm down, but fortunately, on our way back to town again, we found the Museo Nacional, a charming, peaceful place with magnificent exhibits of pre-Columbian artwork; stone carvings, pottery, ceramics and weaving. Wandering through its halls I gradually forgot the hassles of the day and began to relax again.

Of course it wasn't only I who was upset by the morning's farcical running around. Situations like that are also pretty hard on the kids; getting carted back and forth between consulates and bus depots, just tagging along, not achieving or seeing anything, wore a bit thin with them too.

Anyway, we all enjoyed the National Museum, which also featured a collection of magnificent old church vestments and a number of extraordinarily gruesome, but realistic models of bleeding and dying Christs done by some fervent sculptors from the sixteenth century who must also have been sadists or perhaps masochists, I'm not sure which.

San Jose is well known for its good restaurants and nightlife, but somehow we missed out. We seemed to be either out of step, or in the wrong gear or something. Maybe our biorhythms were in the wrong phase, because, apart from a relaxing time at the museum, nothing else really fell into place properly. We finished off our day with a second-rate fast-food meal of chicken and french-fries, a second-rate movie called 'Gumball Rally' and a lousy night's sleep in a new room at the Boston Hotel.

We'd changed rooms in order to get more space and some windows, but this one was right above the street and a twenty-four-hour restaurant with cars and trucks coming and going and people making noise all night. All of which, as I said, makes it the more surprising that I think of San Jose as a pleasant and friendly town. I suppose it's got a lot to do with an unexpected change. After being confronted, in several of the other Central American republics with glaring poverty, dirty streets and feeling the constant undercurrent of tension resulting from overbearing military regimes, the sensation of comparative freedom in Costa Rica was almost enough to make one feel light-headed.

It certainly makes you think about the direction some of the other countries in the region are heading. When the majority of the people you see are under-priviledged and the bulk of the wealth is under the control of dictators and a few families . . . it would seem to me to be an open invitation for communism, and in most of these countries there *are* communist, or Marxist revolutionary organisations dedicated to overthrowing the existing power structures. And yet, in the midst of it all, Costa Rica is to me a clear example of how real democracy can work in Central America.

It's true that the country has had what can only be described as a long run of luck. It's had its dictators in the past, to be sure, but mostly they were benevolent despots and for virtually all of the nineteenth and the first half of the twentieth century, Costa Rica was peaceful. It probably would have remained so, if President Teodoro Picado had not illegally declared the 1948 elections null and void and installed his own handpicked man as the next President instead of Otilio Ulate, who had legally won the elections.

This prompted an unknown coffee planter, Jose Figuerez Ferrer, to lead a civilian uprising which overthrew the government. Figuerez installed his own junta and then, to the astonishment of his fellow Costa Ricans, he turned over the presidency to the legally elected Ulate.

Before doing so however, he abolished the army, a move that is still looked on with awe by the macho generals of other Central American countries, and drafted a new constitution for Costa Rica. Having handed power over, he then founded a new political party, the National Liberation Party, contested the 1953 elections and won, serving as President until 1958. He was President again from 1970 to 1974.

Figuerez, more than anyone else, can be described as the founder of popular democracy in Costa Rica as well as the architect of the dramatic economic and social advances the country has made over the pasty thirty years. He is universally known as 'Don Pepe' and is regarded throughout Costa Rica as everybody's uncle.

Don Pepe, who is now small and frail, still generates enormous excitement wherever he appears, but, despite his personal appeals to the people during the last elections in 1978, the candidate of his National Liberation Party, which has been the reigning force in Costa Rican politics for a quarter of a century was defeated.

Rodrigo Carazo, a former member of the National Liberation Party, led his own Unidad (Unity) Party to victory on a platform of 'change'. Unidad's ideology isn't very different from National Liberation's, but Costa Rica was in danger of having a one-party government, Carazo claimed.

The fact that the electors decided to give him and his party a chance would seem to indicate that the instinctive democratic spirit Costa Ricans are said to possess, is apparently alive and well.

Four thousand men died building the hundred and sixty kilometre Northern Railway across Costa Rica from San Jose to Puerto Limon on the Caribbean coast. Most of them were imported Chinese labourers who contracted yellow fever during the almost twenty years it took to complete the line, which finally opened in 1890.

Riding the once British-owned rails, which were finally nationalised in 1974, it is easy to see why it was such a huge task, passing, as it does, through rugged mountains and dense jungle.

The line follows the Reventazon river, a bold, pacey body of water which surges and foams over large boulders through a narrow-sided, heavily-forested valley. Three-quarters of Costa Rica's land is forested, but only 20 percent of this is worked for commercial timbers. The rest is virgin forest.

For some distance the track is laid along the narrow ledge which the labourers blasted out of the side of the mountain. The air was cool and we ate the fresh fruit, bread, cheese and chocolate which had become our staple diet on this type of short trip. It took seven hours to reach the coast.

For the last part we left the forests and coffee fincas behind and came down into luxuriant tropical growth. Here the line ran beside the Caribbean and the moist, salt-laden air and noisy surge of the surf brought waves of homesickness.

The change in vegetation had been accompanied by an equally obvious change in passengers. We started the journey with a carriage full of white-faced, rather reserved, Spanish-speaking people wearing subdued clothes. Ninety-five percent of Costa Rica's population are white; of European, mostly Spanish descent. The historical reason for this racial anomaly in Central America is that when the Spanish Conquistadores came to Costa Rica in the sixteenth century, they found very few Indians compared to the numbers in the surrounding areas. The small band of Indians which did inhabit the country were quickly decimated by European diseases. The remaining ones inter-married with their conquerors, so that now only 2 percent of the country's population are Indian and these live in isolated reservations and have almost no impact on present-day Costa Rican life.

As we came down onto the Caribbean coast however, black became the predominant skin colour and English the language, while the clothes came in riotous multi-hues, with some people even wearing brightly-striped woollen beanies despite the coastal humidity. The whites seemed to fold back into the corners of the carriages, like collapsible chairs, as the blacks filled up the seats and overflowed into the passageways. They talked volubly as they stacked up battered luggage under long bare legs and laughed loudly as a stray dog dashed through the carriage bringing down a pile of bright cloth bundles. With them came the familiar gestures and rich tang of Africa, pungent even after three centuries of exile.

Only 3 percent of Costa Rica's two and a half million people are blacks who came from British Caribbean possessions in the late nineteenth century to work the banana plantations as free labourers. Concentrated along the Caribbean coast, they almost all speak English and, among themselves, a Jamaican dialect.

Puerto Limon is built on the site of an ancient Indian village. On the waterfront is a statue commemorating the arrival of Cristobal Colon, aka Christopher Columbus who made landfall here on his fourth and last voyage. On seeing Indians wearing gold ornaments he promptly named the land Costa Rica, Rich Coast. Well, that's how the story goes, though I do find it hard to believe the supposed spontaneous ability of these early adventurers to come up with glorious name after name, as they nabbed more and more bits of land in the name of God and country.

The town had the same casual Caribbean atmosphere as Belize. Even the giant sloths hanging by their three-toed feet, with bemused expressions on their faces, from the trees in the little waterfront park seemed more slothful than their name demanded.

We paddled along the rocky shore, having been told that the town's sewage had unfortunately made it too polluted to swim. A few kilometres further down the coast the banana plantations come right down to sandy clean beaches and there's talk about this area being 'discovered' by those colonies of western drop-outs who have already been moved on by irate nationals from the beaches of Lamu, on Kenya's northern coast and Goa, on India's west coast.

The plantations are owned by Standard Fruit, the US company which is viewed with a considerable degree of ambivalence in this country and elsewhere in Central America. They produce three million bunches of bananas from this area a year. Most of them are sold on the North American market with a distinctive little 'Chica' label stuck on their yellow jackets.

It was very humid and we hugged the sliver of shade thrown down by the uneven walls of comfortingly untidy houses. Through open doors and windows we viewed cameos of thick family life which squeezed me painfully with the reminder of our self-imposed transience.

For dinner we ate at one of the several Chinese cafés. No doubt the proprietor was a descendant of one who survived the railway building ordeal. The plastic, instant-Chinoiserie obviously came from one of those companies in Hong Kong which specialise in sending complete restaurant décor to Chinese food outlets from Aberdeen to Addis Ababa. I doubted if the owner had ever visited Hong Kong, let alone China, but he spoke to his daughter, seated at the till, in Cantonese and to us, with the adaptability of his race, in lisping Spanish.

A. day later we took the hot and crowded five-hour bus ride back to the capital and, instead of checking back into the Boston, we tried another couple of similar-priced hotels which turned out to have even poorer facilities. By early evening, tired of making phone calls and of carrying our packs from nasty hotel to nastier hotel, Iain and I decided to indulge ourselves, to stay in the Irazu Hotel, a first-class place on the outskirts of town which would cost us US$33. We justified this wild extravagance to ourselves by saying that tomorrow, as the overnight bus to Panama wouldn't be leaving until 8.00 p.m. we would be able to make full use of the hotel pool and that we would also get a good night's sleep, to stock up against the next night's lack. (If only that were really possible I would readily sleep for two days of the week so as to keep a full head of steam on the other five.) We decided not to tell the children, but to let it come as a surprise.

'Where we going Dad?' Sean asked from behind his pack in the rear seat of the taxi.

'To the hotel.'

'Ooh, look at that one there,' Zara exclaimed as we circled a roundabout and the Irazu loomed up in many-storeyed magnificence.

'We won't be staying there,' Sean prophesied gloomily, as we began our approach up the drive. And then, 'Are we?' his voice lifted in hope.

When we nodded, there were whoops of joy and, 'This is the sort of place where a man in uniform opens the car door!' He settled back in his seat, nurturing dreams of grandeur, and composed his face into a 'thank you my good man' expression.

The taxi stopped and Sean peered anxiously out. The doorman was busy with an outgoing party of Americans boarding the hotel's own minibus.

'Why doesn't he come?' Sean fiddled with the door latch, impatient to be out into the big, brightly lit, thickly-carpeted lobby, which was full of shops selling toys, kiosks selling comics, and signs pointing to restaurants, snack bars and, best of all . . . a swimming pool!

Sean could not wait. He opened the door himself, charged right past the approaching doorman, tripped over the fake marble step and sprawled forward, face down, at the feet of startled hotel guests, his pack slipping up over his head to pin him, struggling, on the floor.

Bent double with laughter, which brought tears to my eyes, I was unable to assist him. The doorman, in powder blue with fringed gold epaulets, looked decidedly put out as Iain hauled Sean up and we beat a hasty retreat, first to the front desk and then to our luxurious room. Here we continued our hysterical giggles of joy as we revelled in polished floors, air-conditioning, comfortable beds, starched sheets, deep hot baths, thick towels, and a lavatory around whose sparkling seat was wrapped a notice informing us that it had been hygienically cleaned for our personal confidence. Oh for the simple joys of life!

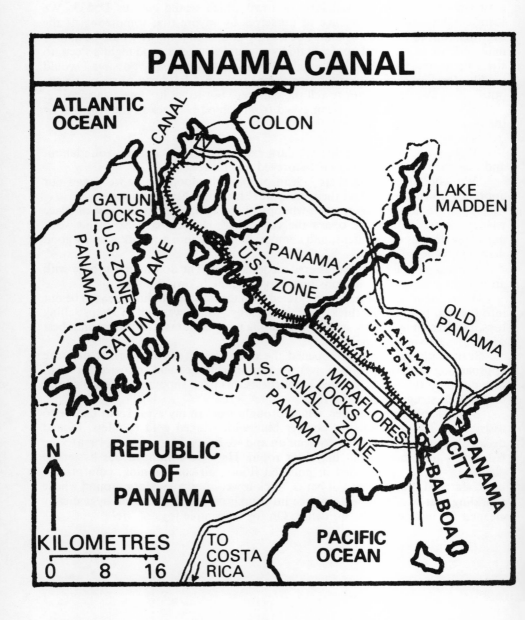

PANAMA CANAL

ATLANTIC OCEAN

CANAL

— COLON

GATUN LOCKS

PANAMA

U.S. ZONE

LAKE

GATUN

PANAMA U.S. ZONE

LAKE MADDEN

OLD PANAMA

U.S. CANAL ZONE

PANAMA

MIRAFLORES LOCKS

RAILWAY U.S. ZONE

PANAMA U.S. ZONE

N

REPUBLIC OF PANAMA

PANAMA CITY

BALBOA

KILOMETRES

0   8   16

TO COSTA RICA

PACIFIC OCEAN

PANAMA

12
The big cut

Panama is the canal. The country owes its existence to the canal. Had it not been for the construction of the eighty-kilometre link between the Atlantic and the Pacific Oceans and the wheeler-dealer machinations of the United States which preceded it in 1903, Panama would almost certainly still be just a department or a province of Colombia.

Ever since Vasco Nunez de Balboa discovered in 1513 how narrow was the distance between the two great oceans at this point, the isthmus of Panama has been of great strategic and political importance to successive generations. It has had an incredible history and is, without doubt, one of the most fascinating parts of the western hemisphere.

We were fortunate to arrive on the Ticabus from San Jose at a time of considerable historical and political importance for Panama, just two days before the crucial vote in the United States Senate, on whether or not the US would hand the control of the Canal Zone over to the Government of Panama in the year 2000.

In these days when colonialism and imperialism are equally dirty words, it would seem a fairly clear-cut issue. The Senate could hardly vote for the perpetuation of something which gave the impression that the US was either a colonial or an imperialist power. And yet, it was by no means sure that the Senate would pass the vote on the new treaty and Panama was more than a little edgy about it.

The United States has never rated very highly in the Panama popularity polls, but at this particular time, relations between the two countries were quite tense. It's always been difficult for Panamanians to think of themselves as being independent and many feel a strong resentment of the role the US plays in their country.

When you see the physical set-up, it's not surprising. Here's this tiny, 77,000 square-kilometre, S-shaped country, supposedly an independent republic with some two million inhabitants . . . and slap across the middle of it, from Atlantic coast to Pacific coast, you have a sixteen-kilometre strip of land which is wholly owned, administered, policed, defended and all the rest of it, by another country . . . the United States.

There are other more obvious aspects of this unusual situation which make Panamanians feel that their independence is qualified. Theirs is the only country in the world which uses the currency of another country as its own legal tender. The money used, not only in the United States Canal Zone, as it is called, but in all of Panama, is the US dollar. Panama makes a small gesture by officially designating these greenbacks 'Balboas', but with the faces of George Washington, Ben Franklin and Abraham Lincoln etc. looking out from them, it's difficult to think of them as anything but what they are . . . dollars.

There are no fences dividing 'The Zone' from Panamanian territory, but there are very evident divisions. Where we came in along the Inter-American Highway, over the Thatcher Ferry Bridge, or the Bridge of the Americas as it's also known, into Panama City, the road . . . 4th of July Avenue . . . is the dividing line. On one side, the American town of Balboa, on the other, Panama City. It's unfortunate that this particular entrance to Panama City takes you past, on your right, the older suburb of El Chorrilo, which is a slum; a sorry collection of two- and three-storey, rusted, corrugated iron sheds, with lots of obviously poor kids running around. On the other side of the road you are passing the well-kept lawns and clean buildings of the US Canal Zone administration offices.

The comparisons are not quite so unfavourable when you get to other parts of Panama City, which are modern and very attractive. In fact the general 'feel' of Panama is much better than we had expected. In a material sense, Panamanians are better off than all of their Central American neighbours, except perhaps Costa Ricans, having a per capita income of around US$1300 a year. Like Costa Rica, Panama has a well-developed system of social welfare and free and compulsory education. The biggest single slice of the government's budget goes on education.

But what we found most surprising and exciting about Panama was the physical beauty of the place and the variety in its architecture and people. Panama City is a contrast of modern skyscrapers, beautiful old colonial buildings, attractive houses, squalid slums, which are gradually disappearing, and an amazing mixture of races.

The beauty also extends to the countryside, which is very tropical. We'd spent most of our first day in Panama travelling past lush green fields, over rolling hills and through some very thick jungle on the way down the highway from Costa Rica. We'd driven all night from San Jose to arrive at the Panamanian frontier at 5.30 a.m. It's only three hundred and fifty kilometres, but, as the border wasn't opening until 6.30 a.m. anyway, the driver of the Ticabus took his time.

We were worried about the possibility that the border would remain closed. There had been some dispute between the Panamanian and Costa Rican governments over a stretch of road which was supposed to be surfaced by one or the other . . . we couldn't quite work out who was at fault . . . all we knew was that it hadn't been done and the officials of the town of La Concepcion, about twenty-seven kilometres inside Panama were going to close the border. We had been told it would be closed at 8.00 a.m., but what was important to us was that it opened between 6.30 a.m. and 8.00 a.m.

It did, and we continued the four hundred and sixty kilometres to Panama City without ever knowing if the townspeople of La Concepcion had closed the border behind us or not.

When we eventually pulled into the Ticabus terminal in the crowded Santa

Anna district of the capital, we decided to check straight into the Hotel Ideal, which was right next door to the bus terminal. It was certainly not the most salubrious area of Panama City; most of the more raunchy nightspots and brothels were evidently located all round us, but we were hot and tired, and the hotel looked clean and comfortable, so we took a room with two double beds and a bathroom for US$14. The clincher, though, was the fact that it had a swimming pool and, within five minutes of us having checked in, Zara and Sean were in it.

If travelling was simply a matter of getting from place to place and involved only varying degrees of physical stamina it would be as relatively simple and undemanding an experience as writing would be, if all that was involved was pushing a pen across a piece of paper.

But of course it isn't. The most exhausting aspect of moving about is the drain on mental resources and it was in Panama that I wondered if I would have enough of these to see me through.

We stayed in the hotel only long enough to dump our packs in the room and the children in the pool and then, such is the powerful allure of mail from friends and family, that we literally ran, despite the humid heat, to reach the American Express office before it closed.

The clerk pulled out a stack of blue airmail letters, 'oh, and there's a telegram too,' she said, adding it carelessly to the pile and immediately I knew.

'Bad news. Please phone me. Sara.'

I was glad my sister had put it so baldly, because in the time it took to get a call through to Canada, I had time to accommodate the first, though probably the least painful, jolt of anguish, so that I could ask uselessly rational questions and utter helplessly bland sentiments when she told me.

'Dad has cancer. They've operated. It's terminal. He knows and has come home, because he says he wants to die among the family.'

The next few days were blurred by terrifying arcs in and out of reality and unreality. Outwardly I walked and talked more or less normally, while inwardly I alternated between running and screaming, and curling up and sobbing. Grief, acceptance, anger, futility. And always the loneliness, despite Iain's support; a blend of sympathy and a determination to endure, without which I often think I would have allowed myself to be swallowed by the abyss many years ago.

We talked about going back and decided against it, because we had seen Dad well and happy only two months previously, because he had the rest of the family, because I've been preparing for this time since I left home when I was eighteen, and because I felt what we were doing was positive and life enforcing.

Even knowing for whom the bell tolls, I am yet green enough under the boughs to find in death the life-force strengthened. In that I must be my father's daughter, for some weeks later I was to receive a message from him encouraging us to go on with the trip.

As we anticipated having to wait in Panama for a little while to get a vessel in which to travel to South America, and as it is a relatively easy place in which to move about, it seemed sensible to spend some of that time accumulating the necessary visas for Ecuador, Peru, Brazil, the Argentine, and, looking far ahead, even Chile. We filled in so many forms, provided so many quite awful two-by-two mug shots and handed over so many American dollars that in one flat moment Iain pulled out his indispensable pocket calculator and worked out, that for the four of us in visas alone, we would spend almost US$150 on this trip!

The embassy I recall most vividly, though this may be coloured by the bitter knowledge of hindsight, was the Peruvian, where the secretary kept assuring an anxious Iain that he and Sean did not need visas for their Australian passports any more than Zara and I did in our British ones. We foolishly believed her. Perhaps we were too enchanted by the posters of Machu Picchu on the walls to be rational.

In each embassy, as well as in numerous shipping lines, we asked about ships to the southern continent and everyone shook their heads. Cargo boats yes, but for passengers no. 'Of course,' they all told us, 'there used to be ships.' But nowadays everyone flew. It was so much quicker and more comfortable. Why would one want to go by sea?

When we tried to explain that we wanted to travel the whole way — from Canada to Tierra del Fuego on the earth's surface and that taking the rough with the smooth was a large part of the purpose of the trip, they smiled the anxious smile I give drunks at parties, in the hope that they will move on to be sick, obscene, or violent elsewhere! When we mentioned the possibility of travelling through the Darien Gap, the bottom curve of Panama's S-shape and the final 240-kilometre extremity of the isthmus which seems, on quiescent wall maps, such a definitive link between the two continents, their smiles froze in horror.

The Gap is covered with dense tropical jungle and the Darien Indians who continue to live in primitive seclusion there are linked to each other only along narrow jungle paths or small rivers, broken up with treacherous rapids. It is possible to hire a guide in one settlement to take you on to the next and, in this way, to walk and canoe the distance in a couple of weeks. If Iain and I had been travelling alone, we would very likely have tackled the journey, but it seemed a rather heavy request to put to Zara and Sean even though they have already proved their resilience through the wasteland of Ethiopia and would no doubt have come through this similar ordeal in better shape than us!

The final deciding factor against this trek was that we would plough through the Darien only to end up in northern Colombia, the heartland of the drug-trafficking industry and an area which foreigners are wise to avoid.

On most of our forays into the bewildering hinterland of embassies and shipping agents, we left Zara and Sean happily behind in the hotel pool with the invariable request from them to 'bring us back a surprise'. It was in answer to this that one day I found a copy of *The Adventures of Tom Sawyer* as the night-time story. It gave us all a boost at the end of these enervating days. Sean in particular, laughed uproariously in anticipation of Tom's antics, his favourite being when Tom fed his fiery cough medicine to his cat, to send it flying about the room as if it had been shot from a catapult.

One piece of information which we did not glean from Panama's prolific tourist literature is that while, to you and me a 'panama' is a hat (though Panamanians don't wear them) to Mexicans a 'Panama' is a commonly-used slang term for a swindle!

Actually the story of how the Panama Canal finally came to be involves, if not technically a swindle, then some pretty nifty footwork on the part of the United States. A French company, with capital of over one hundred and fifty million dollars, working under the direction of Ferdinand de Lesseps, who had already built the Suez Canal, began construction of the Panama Canal in 1882. But after twenty years, during which time the company had gone bankrupt, another French company had taken over and a staggering 20,000 men had died through yellow fever, malaria and cholera, the French gave up and sold their rights to the Canal job to the United States for $40 million.

To obtain the consent of Colombia, of which Panama was then still a part, for the completion of the Canal project, a treaty was negotiated between the US and Colombia. But the Colombian Senate would not ratify the treaty. Not to be outmanoeuvred, the United States, which was then under the presidency of 'talk-softly-but-carry-a-big-stick' Teddy Roosevelt, encouraged Panama to secede from Colombia, which it did on November 3rd, 1903. The United States recognised the independent Panama immediately and sent along a couple of US warships to ensure that its new independence was not threatened by anyone.

A new Canal treaty was rapidly worked out with Panama and within two weeks, a hastily-appointed Minister Plenipotentiary, who was a Frenchman, not even a Panamanian citizen, had sailed to Washington to sign the new treaty on behalf of Panama. The treaty, for $10 million and an annual fee of $250,000, gave the US exclusive control of the sixteen-kilometre-wide strip of land in which the Canal was to be dug across the isthmus, *for ever!* It also gave the US the right to intervene militarily to protect Panamanian independence, to defend the Canal and to 'maintain order' in the Panamanian cities of Panama and Colon as well as in the Canal Zone itself.

Once the US had the rights tied up, they set about building the Canal, which has turned out to be, without doubt, one of the greatest engineering achievements of the modern world. But firstly they had to carry out the largest sanitary operation in history, to clear the area of the malignant tropical diseases which had killed so many Frenchmen and brought their projects to a halt. Before any major work was done, US engineers built a proper water supply, sewerage and drainage systems for the towns, surfaced the muddy roads, built gutters and spread insect-killing sprays and disinfectant everywhere.

It made a crucial difference. The 'Big Cut' as the Canal is called, was successfully completed, at a total cost of around $387 million, in 1914, some ten years after the Americans had restarted the project. The Panamanian vessel, the *SS Ancon,* made the first passage from the Atlantic to the Pacific on August 15th, 1914.

But right from the first day of its opening, to the present day, the question of sovereignty over the Canal Zone has been a persistent issue in Panamanian politics. The US used its treaty rights to intervene militarily to put down riots and restore order by force in Panama City and Colon in 1908, 1917 and 1918. But since then, rightly considering that sort of action counter-productive, the US has adopted a policy of non-intervention in Panamanian affairs . . . at least directly.

The lead-up to the new Canal treaties, under which Panama would get complete control of the Canal by the year 2000, had been fraught with problems, violent protests by Panamanians and the prospect of really major trouble for the United States through the whole of Central and South America if the treaties were not ratified by both houses of the US Congress.

The US was virtually *forced* to start talking about a new treaty back in 1964 when violent riots broke out in the Canal Zone as Panamanians protested American neglect of a 1962 joint Panama/US flag-flying agreement. The Americans had agreed to fly the Panamanian flag over the zone ... but weren't doing it. The then President of Panama, Arnulfo Arias, suspended diplomatic relations with the US and demanded a complete revision of the existing treaty. Washington announced in 1965 that the two governments had agreed on the general groundwork for a new treaty, but when the commander of the National Guard, General Omar Torrijos came to power in Panama, after a military coup in 1968, he rejected three treaties that had been drafted and laid down some tough guidelines on how any new treaty should be drafted.

The concept of real sovereignty over their own land was crucial to the Panamanians and even now they are not entirely happy with the new treaty which requires them to wait until the turn of the century before the Canal Zone becomes completely theirs. Panama does get some big sections of the Zone immediately, but for the Canal itself, they will have to wait. And there are still clauses which give the United States the right to intervene to protect the Canal's neutrality. In American eyes, the prospect of a Cuban-style, anti-American government in power in Panama is unacceptable. But the real question is whether or not Panamanians are prepared to wait for the year 2000. For most of them, it is unimaginably distant.

In the meantime, being in Panama at the critical time of the US Senate vote gave us slight rumblings of unease. Theoretically, not being Americans, we should not have expected any problems, but, as mentioned previously, to most Latin Americans, any non-Spanish-speaking white foreigners are almost invariably taken to be gringos ... Norte-Americanos. So we felt that, if any trouble developed, probably the best thing would be to either carry a flag, or be quick on our feet ... probably both.

Everywhere about us we could see the evidence of anti-American sentiment. The walls of many office buildings and housing complexes were daubed with slogans and several carried detailed and finely-executed group paintings, in the Russian-heroic style, depicting banner-waving Panamanians rising against khaki-clad American colonialist/imperialists.

During the two days before the Senate vote, many of the shops and stalls we passed in the street were carrying the direct broadcast of the debate in Washington and the newspapers were carrying full reports. It was clear that Panamanians were interested. And not only in the debate. As General Torrijos had lifted the usual censorship restrictions, Panamanians were hearing, for the first time, their military leader described in definitely unflattering terms by some of the American senators in the debate.

Most of our first few days in Panama were taken up in trekking from consulate to consulate and shipping line to shipping line with little or no success as far as the ships were concerned. We did find one line which would carry passengers to Colombia or Ecuador, but only if they happened to be shipping a car at the same time. We toyed with the idea of trying to contact someone who was shipping a car, to see if we could say that we were travelling with them and then, paying our own fares, book passage that way. But it came to nothing. We began to think that we might be forced to take a plane, particularly as we had hoped to be on the South American continent by Easter, which was now less than a week away.

We were also concerned about not having enough money to get us all the way to the bottom of South America. Although we'd been travelling and living relatively cheaply, there *were* four of us and it was costing a good deal more than we had anticipated. We had some more money in New York, so I decided to see if I could get $2000 wired to Panama. But first I would have to send a letter, so that my signature could be verified. A Panamanian woman at the bank gave me some advice:

'If you send a letter through the Panamanian post office,' she told me, 'it could take two or three weeks to get to New York. If you send it through the US Canal Zone post office, it will be there in two days.'

Taking her advice, I sent a letter off straight away, through the post office in Balboa in the Canal Zone, but, looking back on it now, I feel I must have been more than a little naive to have thought that it would be all straightforward and easy.

Another thing that had been troubling us was the prospect of running into some sort of illness in South America ... particularly hepatitis. We had met several people who had either contracted hepatitis themselves, in Colombia, Ecuador or Peru, or knew others who had. We were already fairly paranoid about dysentery, after a lousy experience we'd had with it in the Sudan in 1976, and went to somewhat extreme lengths to avoid it.

Although the guide books all say that Panama's water is just about the purest on the continent and that you can drink it straight from the tap, we continued to drink soft-drinks instead ... preferring the prospect of rotting teeth to dysentery, or some other disease from the water. Actually Panama's water *is* very good and we could have safely drunk it, but when you're going from one country where it is unsafe to another where it is okay, then on to the next place where it's not safe again, it can be confusing, so we made up our minds to just stick to the one practice ... to avoid drinking tap-water, if possible (unless purified), wherever we were.

As far as the hepatitis was concerned, we decided to each have an injection of gammaglobulin. We had read the reservations expressed by several people about the limited effectiveness of this as a preventative for hepatitis ... one article even suggested it was dangerous ... but we had them anyway, at the Panamanian Government health clinic at Boca de Caja, one of the eastern suburbs of the capital.

Zara and Sean have had plenty of injections before, but for some reason the prospect of this particular one had them in a state of limited terror. I think they were convinced it was going to be like a cholera jab, which they knew produced particularly nasty after-effects, or maybe it was the name ... gammaglobulin sounds pretty awful, I suppose, if you don't know what it is. Or perhaps it's worse when you do!

Well, there were a few tears and a bit of carrying-on, but when the needle was actually stuck into their behinds, they were pleasantly surprised that there was no pain at all and fortunately no after-effects. We had our doubts about what we were doing, particularly as the shots cost US$20 and would probably only give protection for some four weeks, but we felt safer having had them . . . and I guess that counts for something.

Whenever we stayed more than two or three days in a place, two things happened. Firstly belongings erupted from our packs and like soil dug from a hole, seemingly expanded until it appeared impossible that they would ever fit back inside again.

Secondly we established routines; a development which I found interesting because routines are one of the aspects of regular living which we say we travel to get away from!

One of the routines which we quickly established in Panama was breakfasting at a small café a few blocks away from the hotel. Fresh tropical fruit, yoghurt, fried eggs and even toast, were served by the woman proprietor whose daily change of skin-tight, bright shirts and slacks livened up the male patrons, most of whom were shop and office employees on their way to work.

But even her aura was dimmed one morning by the arrival of a most spectacular, long-legged creature, wearing thigh-high shiny black boots above which there was a few centimetres or so glimpse of fishnet tights before a brief piece of black material which passed as a skirt. A beautiful bare midriff was followed by an all-revealing little white cotton top and around this outfit was flung a long, silver-lamé, lace-fringed shawl.

Zara was not the only one who 'oohed' as the girl sauntered in, tossing her carefully tangled black hair and summoning, with actressy gestures of her bare brown arms, no less than four young men, most certainly American servicemen, who followed meekly in her wake.

A heavy night had obviously been enjoyed by all and one of the fellows, who looked about eighteen, was so exhausted that he immediately fell asleep on the counter-top, his head among the abandoned coffee cups and salt and pepper shakers! The girl, who on closer inspection was nearer thirty, seemed to be the least worn out and stood behind the men orchestrating the ordering of their breakfast while admiring herself in the large mirror behind the counter, running her fingers through her hair and rearranging her shawl.

In the middle of her performance she spotted Zara, who hadn't taken her eyes off her for one second and, perhaps aware of the impression she had made, came across and began to stroke Zara's long blonde hair. Arching her eyebrows and flashing her eyes, she murmured, 'Que linda, que linda. Beautifool, si. Aaaah.'

She reached across to Sean, who almost slipped under the table in embarrassment, 'and the brothair too. Si. Si. Lindo. Beautifoooool! Aaaaaah!' She ran her finger down his cheek.

I thought she might pass on to Iain and eventually include me too in her exuberance, but instead she stood back, arms akimbo, boots astride, tossing her long hair and then spread her ams toward us, 'Aaaaah! A family. Si. Aaaaah! A happy family. So lucky. Si!'

When their breakfast was served, she strode up and down dividing her attention between stroking her companions, not forgetting the one who still slept amongst the crockery, and Sean and Zara. At one point she sat beside Zara and wrapped her shawl around her so that Zara almost swooned in adoration and pleasure!

In between her cooing over the children we learnt from her spattering of English that she was Argentinian (rather a different image than the usual one of generals and tortured prisoners). 'I am just hair for a leetle time. I am working girl. But . . .' she wagged her finger in warning, 'you must not ask at what I am working! Si! Aahaah!'

'Is your sort of work easier to find here?' I ventured politely.

She took my square, sensible hands and curled her long, beautifully manicured fingers round them, and, for a moment, almost stopped the game. Looking directly at me, with a touch of sadness, 'In Buenos Aires,' her voice dropped an octave, 'there is my family.'

On the way across the city to the ruins of Old Panama, Zara talked non-stop, recalling the clothes and gestures in detail, 'And did you see her fingernails Mum? They were fantastic!' I had and they were. It was a Panamanian fashion, and something I have never seen done elsewhere, for women to paint nail-polish patterns of stripes and spots or a combination of both on long fingernails. We saw numerous women whose nails were decorated like this, with very complicated designs, which Zara and I, both cursed with soft, bendy, ungrowable nails, envied madly.

Old Panama is where the city began back in 1519, though Christopher Columbus had sailed round the coast as early as 1502 and Balboa had 'discovered' the Pacific Ocean in 1513.

During the 1600s Panama became the centre of conflict between the Spanish and English in the grab for land and gold in North, Central and South America. The fortified town then included a hospital, schools administered by religious orders, as well as a slave market, a dungeon where the prisoners were drowned by the rising tide, kitchens, a meat market and of course cathedrals, churches and convents. It was at one of these, the Convent of La Merced, that Francisco Pizarro and his men took holy communion and received the blessing of the church on the morning on which they set out travelling south to ravage and destroy Peru's Inca kingdom.

Gold, which came back up from Peru, was collected in Panama City before being transported across the isthmus along the stone surfaced, Las Cruces trail, to either Portobello or Nombre de Dios on the Caribbean coast, from where it was shipped to Spain.

It was this gold which attracted buccaneers like Britisher, Henry Morgan, to sack the old city of Panama in 1671. He destroyed the city completely and stole so much loot that it took a hundred and ninety-five pack mules to carry the swag across to the Caribbean coast. The only piece he seems to have missed was a massive, solid gold, intricately carved altar which the monks reputedly saved by camouflaging it with paint.

Undeterred by the havoc wreaked by Morgan, the Spaniards rebuilt the city a little further inland, on the site of the present day Panama City. But when British raids on the Caribbean coast continued, Spain finally abandoned the Las Cruces route in the mid 1700s and began trading around Cape Horn.

We wandered slowly in the humidity through the remains of the old city and under the shells of the three-hundred-year-old gothic arched buildings, stopping to admire the energy of a crowd of boys who were playing football and using the fallen stonework as goal mouths.

It was gold again which spurred men on to build an iron track along the line of the original Las Cruces trail. The US-built railroad, which took four years to construct, opened in 1853 to transport the rush of men who wanted easy access to the gold boom towns of Southern California. It was quicker to go by boat via Panama, than by stagecoach across the North American continent. But when, fifteen years later, the first US transcontinental railroad went into service, the isthmus rail traffic dried up and the line was abandoned.

It's been back in service though for some time, run by the US Government, with its carriages painted red, white and blue and carrying a stars and stripes emblem. The line runs for seventy-seven kilometres across the isthmus following the edge of the Canal for most of the way.

Through the windows of the carriage, when we made the hour and a half journey from Balboa to Colon, we were surprised and impressed by the beauty of the landscape. it was lush and green and at Gatun Lake, which was big enough to have wind-whipped waves, there was a backdrop of distant dramatic mountains.

We also found it interesting, on this trip, to be going from the Pacific Ocean to the Atlantic while travelling from east to west (see map).

Iain and Sean were fascinated by the large cranes and dredgers which are as necessary to keep the Canal open as the constant fogging with insecticides is to keep down the ever-present risk of yellow fever. It is also necessary for men in small, motorised boats to push and prod to shore, big beds of bright green water hyacinth, a weed which poses a constant, choking threat to the propellers of transiting vessels.

The Caribbean coast's twin town to Panama City is named, yet again, after Columbus and has a nasty intestinal ring to it, Colon. The town is more or less one large shop for all the passengers on ships transiting the Canal who spend up big on duty-free goodies. We visited it on a Sunday when no ships were expected, so the shop was empty and closed up. It was the last Sunday before Easter and the shopkeepers were all in the churches, their songs of thanks flowing out into almost deserted streets, past protectively shuttered window displays of cameras, watches, tape-recorders, radios and portable TV's.

On the way back across the country again, we stopped off at Miraflores Locks, which are impressive, even to a mechanical idiot like me. We sat in the large glass-fronted observation deck and watched as the gigantic 25 metre-high, 20 metre-wide, 2 metre-thick, steel plate doors, weighing 730 tonnes, swung open to allow the chamber to fill with a staggering two hundred and ninety-six million litres of water. No pumps are used in filling or emptying the lock chambers. The principle involved is simply that of letting water run downhill, since Gatun Lake, the main water supply, is twenty-six metres above sea level.

A full-time guide gave an almost continuous commentary in Spanish and English over a loud speaker system; spouting wondrous facts and figures such as, 'Every time a ship makes a complete transit, some 234 million litres of water are spilled into the sea. It is estimated that the amount of water consumed in the operation of the Panama Canal in one day would keep the city of Boston supplied for two weeks.'

Fortunately, this huge quantity of liquid is a free gift from above. Panama receives an average of 293 centimetres of rain a year.

A huge German cargo vessel, the *MV Hattingen,* moved slowly forward into the lock, in the last stage of its nine-hour trip through the Canal. Since the waterway opened, 523,000 ships carrying more than 2.8 billion tonnes of cargo have transited through from ocean to ocean. Tolls are levied on a net tonnage basis; $1.29 for laden ships and $1.03 in ballast. The average toll is $14,000 which sounds like a lot of money, but is of course a tremendous saving on what it would cost in hours, fuel oil, and wages to travel instead around Cape Horn.

There have been suggestions that by the time the Panama Canal is taken over by the Panamanian people, the waterway will be more or less redundant because some of the super-tankers being built now are too large to pass through and because the Canal is already working at full capacity, which leaves no room for expansion. Americans counter this by pointing out that 97 percent of present world shipping can pass through the waterway and by insisting that it would be an engineering possibility to increase current 14,000 transits a year to 27,000 ships.

'Did you hear what the guide said Mum?' Sean sounded impressed. 'A man swam through the Canal!' And so he did. In 1928 Richard Halliburton paid thirty-six cents, the smallest toll yet levied, for his adventure. Considerably less than was forked out by Cunard for the *QE II,* the largest passenger vessel to transit the Canal. In 1977, she paid $68,499 and forty-six cents!

To recoup from all these facts and figures we committed an illegal act by stopping off at the air-conditioned cafeteria just inside The Zone and indulging in hamburgers, french fries, cheesecake and Coke. We then compounded our crime by shopping in the large supermarket next door which sold the usual bewildering American shoppers' choice of the best and worst in food.

Both these establishments are for the use of Canal Zone residents or employees only. This is done not as a form of US isolationism; the supermarket would no doubt be only too happy to sell as much as possible to Panamanians, but to protect Panama shopkeepers who don't want to lose customers to this source of cheaper and more widely varied goods.

The cashiers do spot-checks by asking to view a permit to shop but we decided to take the risk and when they did stop Iain and ask for his card, in his best phoney American accent, he assured them that he'd left it in the car. They let him pass with a warning not to be so careless again.

Rather relieved, we went back out into the tropical heat to watch a group of Cuna Indian women from the San Blas islands. On this archipelago of 365 islands, which starts three kilometres off the Caribbean coast of Panama, the women own the land and conduct all commercial negotiations. Dressed in bright and heavily appliquéed blouses and skirts with gold rings through their noses, and bands of material wound so tightly round their legs and arms that I had fears for their circulation, they sat in groups in the shade sewing 'molas'. These highly complicated reverse appliqué designs, on cotton cloth, of mythological birds and animals, have recently been 'discovered' by the New York art world, but even so they still only cost between five and ten dollars each in Panama. So we bought several, which now brighten the walls of an English cottage and on a grey winter's day are a welcome reminder to us of tropical heat.

Painting people, scenes and slogans on buses is certainly not an idea unique to Panama, but Panamanians seem to have it down to a fine art. The elaborate and brightly coloured designs and tableaux on the backs and sides of the city buses in Panama are quite fantastic, and bus owners and drivers go to amazing lengths to try to make their buses more attractive and distinctive than those of their competitors.

Travelling back and forth by bus and taxi on our various errands and sight-seeing trips, we would see dozens of different designs every day in the course of short journeys and often recognise a bus we'd seen before. The art work is incredibly varied ... from pastoral scenes and religious motifs, to well-known landmarks like the Canal Bridge, the locks or the ruins of Old Panama, to likenesses of film and TV personalities, or even comic-strip characters.

Some of the names of the buses, painted in big, bright letters on front, back or side, sound more like titles for X-rated movies than anything else: 'Hot Pants', 'Mr Big Stuff', and 'Free Love' etc. They are usually accompanied by other fascinating phrases and sayings, mainly in Spanish, but sometimes in English, like, 'Let's forget the past', 'It's all in the game', or the rather ambiguous 'What you see is what you get.' But the one we liked best, when we eventually translated it, was 'Ruega Por Nosotros' ... (Pray for Us) which, we thought, could be taken to indicate that the bus and all its passengers were heading for some kind of disaster and would be more likely to scare passengers away rather than attract them.

In the middle of all our running around, we went back to the US Canal Zone Post Office to send a parcel back home. It contained the molas made by the San Blas islanders which we had just bought plus the woven shirt and wall-hanging we had been carrying with us since Guatemala.

We walked into the post office in time to hear the final counting of the vote in the US Senate on the Canal Treaty. The employees in the post office had a radio blaring and everybody in the room, nearly all of them Americans, had stopped to listen as the vote was announced.

There had been considerable tension during the past few days, as we had learnt a little earlier at the United States Southern Command Military Headquarters at Quarry Heights. Ed Friedman, a spokesman for the 193rd Infantry Brigade, the main US military component charged with the defence of the Canal, gave us the full treatment there ... cups of coffee, cans of Tab and reams of material on the US military role in the Canal Zone.

'Of course we've looked at a whole lot of scenarios involving trouble here,' he told us, 'and, in most cases, we think we're reasonably ready to handle the situation.'

'If the Treaty vote goes the wrong way ... that is, if the Senate doesn't okay it,' I said, 'what's likely to happen?'

'Well there'd almost certainly be trouble ... probably some violence directed against Americans.' He paused and looked at a large wall map of the Canal Zone. 'But we've had all leave cancelled and all military units on alert status while the debate has been on. We've also got a civil disturbance task force especially trained for that sort of situation, so we're not too worried.'

'And the Canal itself?'

'Well, of course the reason for us being here is the Canal and so most of our planning and preparedness revolves around it. Vital installations such as the locks and dams are potential targets for saboteurs and guerilla teams and installations such as these have priority consideration as far as defence is concerned but, realistically, that sort of threat is unlikely to arise from this situation, because Panama needs the Canal and any Panamanian who blew up one of the locks, for instance, to hurt us, would harm his own country's economy more than it would affect us.'

'Will things be a little calmer if the Treaty is passed by the Senate?'

'Oh sure,' Ed said. 'But there's still plenty of people in Panama who want us out ... who won't be able to wait until the year 2000.' He smiled and spread his arms. 'But believe it or not, there are still plenty who want us to stay.'

'Do you think it would be better for the US to stay here to run the Canal?' Trish asked.

'That's a simple question,' he replied, 'to which there aren't any simple answers.'

In the hall of the post office, we listened as the voice announcing the result of the vote came through loud and clear from the Senate chamber in Washington: 68 votes for the treaty, 32 against. A buzz of conversation and several sighs of relief swept through the customers and staff of the post office. It had been close. The vote could not have been carried unless it had a two-thirds majority, so 67 to 33 was the absolute minimum. The pro-Treaty senators had beaten that figure by only one vote.

The black clerk behind the desk in the post office shook his head and grinned as he stuck down the franked stamp on our parcel.

'Boy,' he said, 'if they hadn't passed that Treaty, you'd have seen some action around here.'

Towards the end of the ten days we spent in Panama, we got some 500 colour slides back after they had been developed by Kodak in Panama. These were all the photographs we had taken since leaving San Diego. We had debated with ourselves over whether or not to have them processed in Panama, to carry them along with us undeveloped, or to send them back, also undeveloped, either to San Diego or to Trish's sister in Canada.

Had we been moving straight on, the question would not have arisen, but since we were spending such a comparatively long time in Panama, we decided to get them done. Anyway, we all wanted to see how they had turned out. Fortunately, they were all fine and we got a great kick out of seeing them. We didn't have a projector, but just going through them carefully ... holding them up to the light in the hotel bedroom was good enough. Seeing all the shots of the Mayan cities in the Yucatan seemed to reassure us considerably and made us feel that perhaps we were achieving something. In the middle of it all, constantly moving along as we were, we often had doubts, on the one hand that we would ever make it to the bottom of South America and on the other, that it was worth doing anyway. Seeing those slides in Panama gave us a much-needed shot in the arm.

There really is a great deal to see and do in Panama, and that ten days flew by very quickly ... even though it was much longer than we'd spent anywhere else, or would spend in any of the South American cities. We found Panama City to be an interesting combination of Old Spain and American modernity, with occasional touches of an oriental bazaar.

The older parts of the second Panama City, which was built after Henry Morgan's sacking of the original town, retain some fabulous old Spanish colonial buildings and churches. Sitting on a small peninsula, about four blocks wide by about seven long, which pokes out into Panama harbour, the centre of the city in colonial days is now known simply as the San Felipe district.

A short stroll from our hotel, through narrow streets, many of them cobble-stoned and lined with houses decorated with beautiful wrought-iron balconies, brought us to several of the major colonial buildings, including the church of San Jose. This church now houses the famous golden altar that Henry Morgan's pirates missed when they burnt and looted Old Panama. The altar is the most astounding baroque edifice. Beautiful, but also very disturbing. I invariably found, when confronted with such huge amounts of gold, in Central America and later in South America that I could not avoid wondering, firstly, how much the object was worth and, secondly, couldn't the money be put to some better use . . . to help poor people, for instance?

In the same street as the church of San Jose we saw the unique and famous 'flat arch'. Part of the ruins of another church, this non-geometric curve seems to defy gravity and is proudly pointed to by Panamanians as having played a considerable part in the eventual selection of Panama as a site for the Canal between the Pacific and the Atlantic Oceans. The fact that this surprising construction, 10 metres high and 15 metres across, has remained standing through several centuries, was taken as unmistakable proof of the absence of major earthquakes in Panama, establishing it therefore as a good site for the Canal.

At the end of the small peninsula we came to the Plaza de Francia, a picturesque little square dotted with poinciana trees and a tall obelisk dedicated to the French pioneers who began the building of the Canal. Behind the Plaza, running along the rocky coastline, is a beautiful elevated promenade, named, rather grimly, the 'Paseo de las Bovedas' . . . 'The Boulevarde of the Dungeons'. The promenade runs along part of the old sea wall which was built to protect the city from pirates, and the dungeons, now empty, were underneath, inside the wall itself.

Set in one wall, next to the steps leading up to the promenade, we found a bronze plaque dedicated to someone who must be a distant relative of mine . . . Carlos Finlay. The plaque reveals that Carlos, presumably the son of a Scottish father and a Spanish mother, discovered the cause of yellow fever. Just a little late for several thousand Frenchmen, unfortunately.

Walking back to our hotel, along the Avenida Norte, by the waterfront, we passed by the Palacio de las Garzas . . . the Palace of the Herons. This is one of the most impressive buildings in the city, although more so on the inside apparently than outside. It was the residence of the Spanish governors during the colonial days and is now the President's Palace. The name 'Palace of the Herons' comes from the stately white birds that stroll freely around the fountain in the tiled courtyard in the entrance to the Palace.

Unfortunately, the herons weren't there when we saw it . . . only a few uniformed and armed members of the National Guard.

The building seemed to me unusual for the presidential palace, in that, although it covered a full city block, it was closely hemmed in by other old buildings and the only access was by narrow, one-way streets. Presidents, these days, particularly Latin American presidents, like to have a bit of space around them, to give them room to move . . . quickly if necessary.

The serenity of the elegant palace seemed untrammelled by its rapid turnover of occupants; more than thirty since the turn of the century. A rate which makes the ten year run of Brigadier General Omar Torrijos Herrera all the more surprising.

In October 1968, Torrijos, then Commander of the National Guard, led his men in a military coup which overthrew the just-elected President Arias. Four months later all political parties were abolished. A new constitution recognised Torrijos as 'Maximum Leader of the Panamanian Revolution', and vested in him virtually unlimited powers until 1978.

But what was even more surprising to most observers than his ten year term of office, was that in 1978 he voluntarily stepped down from the seat of power. This is unusual behaviour by a political leader anywhere in the world, but is even more extraordinary on the Latin American scene.

Perhaps he was modelling himself after 'Pepe' Figuerez of Costa Rica; hoping to become a sort of universal uncle and a power behind the throne in a similar way; possibly even planning a return to power at some later stage.

It was General Torrijos who jostled Panamanian opinion into a force cohesive enough to be able to pressure the United States into renegotiating the Panama Canal Treaty. So, to that extent, he is already a popular folk hero in a country where personalities, rather than ideological platforms, tend to be the dominating force.

Personality Torrijos had in abundance. He came on strong like John Wayne playing Fidel Castro. And I just loved the press photograph of him taken at a formal White House dinner during the time of negotiations over the Canal Treaty. General Torrijos, for once not wearing the obligatory army fatigues and US Cavalry-style hat, oozing macho, beside President Carter, nervously displaying his teeth. And on his other side Senora Torrijos, exposing film star amounts of brown bosom, smiling expansively at everybody's Mum . . . the well-covered Mrs Carter. What a great deal that photograph said about the difference between the two societies.

Thirty-eight year old Aristides Royo lives in the Presidential Palace now. Opponents of the Panamanian government have dubbed him a communist, but probably the best description of him is a 'torrijista' for he served his political apprenticeship under the tutelage of General Torrijos and he seems committed to the General's brand of pragmatic reformism and, above all, to the acceptance of the Canal treaties.

Even so, one would need to be foolish indeed to estimate how many more men will take up residence with the herons before the Canal finally becomes Panamanian property.

It was by now the Wednesday before Easter and on the Thursday the banks were closing for almost a full week's holiday. We didn't want to spend so much extra time in Panama, even though there was much more to see and do, but our money still hadn't come through from New York. Finally after spending $45 in phone calls to New York and watching while Iain stacked on quite an impressive turn in the manager's office, we were given the money before it had officially arrived.

It was Easter which made us make the final decision to fly. We wanted to be in Quito, the capital of Ecuador, for the festivities. After all, Easter in South America, we had been led to believe, is rather more of an occasion than anywhere else in the world and we wanted to be where the action was.

We also just wanted action. To get moving south. On our visits to the various embassies we had drooled over tourist brochures and books full of beautiful colour photographs of the snow-clad Andes, ruined desert cities, magnificent churches, Spanish colonial buildings, Amazon sunsets, Indian villages, Rio beauties, Patagonian gauchos and huge blue-white glaciers. They had made us anxious to press on.

In a way this was actually the beginning of the trip for after all it had been originally planned as a South American journey. Although we had enjoyed and learnt a great deal already, the travels so far felt to us a little like an entrée with the main meal yet to be tasted.

Somehow we managed to stow all our gear back in our packs and, glad yet sad to be wrenched from our routines, we boarded a 6.30 a.m. Braniff flight the next morning and headed south to what was for us a whole new unexplored continent.

SOUTH AMERICA

INTRODUCTION

South America, like the rest of Latin America, is to the vast bulk of the English-speaking world an unknown quantity; a huge area of the world that is all but dismissed. There *are* a few details which impinge: they speak Spanish, they grow coffee and beef and they have big, colourful carnivals. Most of the countries on the continent are run by the military and they always seem to be having revolutions and earthquakes. There seem to be quite a few bandits around and the drug-smuggling scene seems to have become rather nasty of late. What else? Oh yes, there's a lot of jungle around with piranhas and that sort of thing. And there's the mountains . . . the Andes, where that plane crashed and the survivors ate each other. And, of course, there's the Aztecs with all their gold . . . or was it the Incas?

The sad thing is that, unless you are lucky enough to have been to South America, or to have read more than the average person about it, the chances are that these will be your general impressions of a continent which occupies almost eighteen million square kilometres and contains a population greater than Europe's.

Because almost the entire continent (except for tiny Guyana, Surinam and French Guyana) speak either Spanish or Portuguese, we in the English-speaking world have been, if not cut off, then set at a distance from them in terms of day-to-day communication, through radio, television, newspapers and literature. How easy it is for there to be a continuous interchange of all this material between Britain, the United States, Canada, Australia, New Zealand and other parts of the world where English is widely spoken, such as India, Africa and Southeast Asia. How easy it is to live only within the orbit of that world and to ignore or push to one side developments in South America.

I, too, have been ignorant of South America for most of my life. This trip has made me realise how much I have missed and how important this part of the world really is. One of the countries on this continent . . . Brazil . . . is destined to play a much larger role in all our lives in the twenty-first century. During this journey we became convinced, as many Brazilians have been for some time, that their country will be a major world power within a generation.

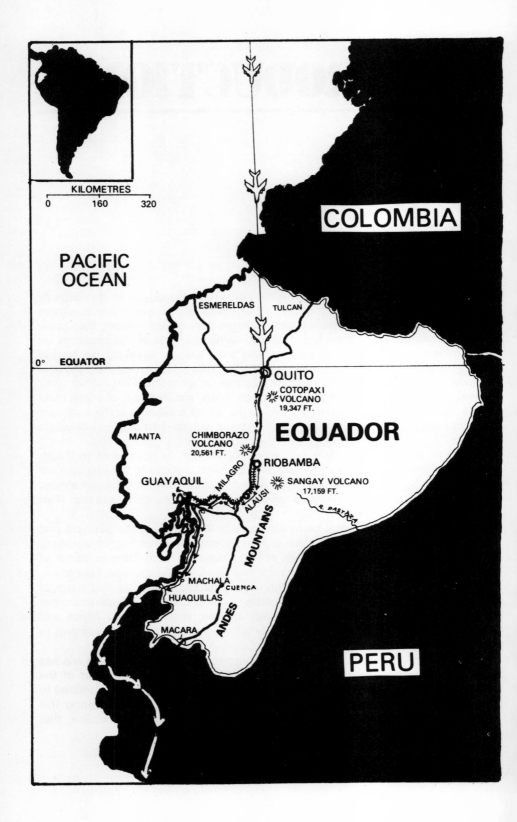

ECUADOR

13
'Chimborazo, Cotopaxi took me by the hand'

Cold! That was the first thing we felt when we arrived in Quito. Ironic as it is the capital of a country which, as its name suggests, straddles the equator. It was in fact a pleasant 23 degrees, but after our stay in Panama's muggy, sea-level heat, the instant change to spring-like air at over 2700 metres seemed like a sudden plunge into winter.

Next thing we felt was sleepy, even though we had only been up for four or five hours! So shortly afterwards, when we had found a pleasant hotel with an almost Scandinavian-style wood-panelled room with four beds for only US$7.50, the children and I lay down and were instantly and soundly asleep!

Several hours later, having done exactly what all guide books to high altitude towns suggest you should do ... rest on arrival ... we awoke with the low-level headaches which remained with us constantly while we were in Quito. But none of this detracted from our enjoyment of the town which we found an attractive, friendly, manageable-sized place whose population left no doubt at all that we were at last in SOUTH America.

Predominantly Quechua Indian, they had flat, broad faces, with complexions made ruddy by the altitude and clear, wide-spaced, almost black eyes. Both men and women wore their thick, straight, black hair in a single plait under unisex, narrow-brimmed trilbies. Many of them were disconcertingly beautiful and it seemed as though every female over the age of perhaps seventeen had an equally beautiful version of herself strapped to her back, peering out from under heavy layer upon layer of warming blankets.

In jewel-bright coloured ponchos, the men and women, even though laden with babies and baskets of produce, walked briskly up and down the steep cobble-stoned streets of the old part of town on strong muscular legs. Their short bodies had barrel chests to make room for far larger than normal capacity lungs ... a natural adaptation, over the generations of those who have lived here breathing the thin, high altitude air at this northern end of the Andes.

We puffed our way up the steep hills, stopping for some spicy empanadas, small vegetable or meat pies, and a chocolate bar which seemed to push some energy back into the old legs. Armed policemen dressed in khaki drill and white helmets added the necessary extra height to their small stature by directing traffic from large boxes adorned with advertisements for Camel cigarettes.

There was not a great deal of traffic, most of what there was being older-model, North American cars, but it took a lot of directing because the roads in this old part of town, built to accommodate horse and buggies, are so narrow that they easily become congested.

The children, who did much better than us in the altitude, kept pointing out the carelessly-heaped Easter eggs in shop windows and asking, with knowing smiles, whether the Easter Bunny would know where they were.

'Well, he found us on Lake Kariba the Easter before last,' said Sean sounding like a blasé world traveller, 'so I'm sure he won't find Quito any problem.'

'The Easter Bunny is a she,' Zara remonstrated.

Old Quito, perhaps of all the cities in South America, has retained the most reminders of its Spanish colonial history. It is rather like a living museum, unlike the other cities of the continent where new buildings have been erected, with most distressing results, amongst the old.

New Quito, with its glass and concrete edifices, indistinguishable from those in other cities or even continents, is completely separate some kilometres to the north-east leaving to itself the old town with its now somewhat crumbling colonial houses, ornate wooden balconies, and its churches, all eighty-six of them, to serve a population of around three-quarters of a million.

In the church of La Compania, we jostled with the Easter crowd who were lighting candles and praying.

'Mum! Mum! Come here! Quick!' Zara's voice was incredulous. 'Look, they are *kissing* that statue's *feet!*' Old and young men and women were brushing their lips across the recumbent Christ's feet which had been polished to a pale corpse colour by generations of worshippers. A young mother, her face in rapt adoration, held her small baby's face against the toes.

'Why do they do that?' Zara asked and I felt remiss in my parental instruction.

'Later,' I promised just as Sean squeezed his way between the bundled babies and ponchos equally agog as he informed us, 'He's bleeding! Quick,' as if it could be miraculously staunched, 'Come and see!' The realistically carved blood appeared to gush from a gaping wound in Christ's side and again I had to promise to explain later.

At the altar it was my turn to be flabbergasted. It was solid gold. Priceless. And this was not all. Several of La Compania's most precious treasures, including a painting of the Virgin Dolorosa framed in emeralds and worth at least $10 million, are kept in the vaults of the Banco Central del Ecuador and appear only on special occasions.

People were throwing small coins onto the floors of the side altars which were merely gold-plated. The heady smell of incense and the press of people made a retreat necessary. At the door, legless beggars, squatting on rags to keep out the cold, held out their hands to us.

To clear our heads we walked to the Plaza Domingo, in the centre of which was a statue of General Antonio Jose de Sucre pointing toward the slopes of the slumbering volcano Pichincha towering above the town. It was here that in 1822, after two hundred and eighty-eight often turbulent years of Spanish domination, Sucre and his men fought and won the decisive battle for independence against the troops of the King of Spain. Sucre is buried in the city's rather sombre cathedral and the whole country honours his name by calling their currency after him.

But independence did not bring the much hoped for stability. In another square, the Parque Alameda, we saw a statue of the legendary Simon Bolivar, the prophet without honour whom even today many of the people of the continent love to hate. It was he who persuaded Ecuador to join with the countries to its north, Colombia and Venezuela, as a first step toward his ultimate grand goal, a United States of South America.

He was a brilliant man, but out of step with history. The scheme was doomed from the beginning by back-stabbing, literal and otherwise, and internecine bickering. Its downfall was aided and abetted from the wings by the majority of the Indian population, who had learnt from the Spaniards themselves and probably also from the Incas and even their previous overlords across the centuries, that conquerors came and went, while their life remained unchanged in its harshness.

The alliance was short-lived and in 1830 Ecuador became a separate, independent country. And still nothing changed. The political machinations continued and the standard of living did not improve, the reason being that the country remained lumbered with an elitist Spanish colonial-style government and archaic religious fanaticism.

Religious processions have never really been my cup of tea, particularly the ones which involve people either flagellating themselves or sticking sharp instruments through their skin. I recall feeling distinctly nauseated the first time I saw the annual Tai Pusam festival in Singapore in which Indians paraded through the streets with steel skewers stuck not only through the skin of their arms and bodies, but also through their cheeks and tongues!

Fortunately the Viernes Santa (Easter Friday) procession we saw in Quito was not so gruesome, although in past years there have been some fairly masochistic entrants. There *was* a rather deformed, half-naked dwarf whose back was cut and bleeding from the cross he was carrying ... it was made from two large cactus plants ... and there *was* a four-year-old child wearing a crown of thorns and struggling under the weight of a cross his parents had induced him to carry through the streets of Quito, but apart from those two there was nothing more bizarre in the parade than hordes of people dressed in purple robes and ku-klux-klan-type hoods.

The procession was due to begin at about 11.00 a.m. at the big, open square of the Plaza San Francisco in the central part of old Quito, but it took some time to get there, because the whole town was beginning to fill up with crowds waiting to see the spectacle. We were also unable to move very quickly up the steep, cobble-stoned streets as we were still feeling the effects of the altitude. Any energetic, or too hurried movements immediately made us feel slightly giddy and short of breath. Luckily, the weather was clear, although we found that the moment we were in shade it was quite cold. Even though Quito is right on the equator, its height ensures that its climate is always temperate. It also never changes greatly throughout the year. The days are warm (in the sunlight) and the nights, which begin when the sun sets at precisely 6.15 p.m. every day of the year, are cool.

The plaza, when we reached it, was a wonderful sight. It was packed. A blaze of colour; masses of people ... full of life. Quechua Indians in their ponchos and fedora hats, old women selling peanuts and fruit, children selling pictures of Christ crucified, balloons and paper hats, shining shoes and playing, in an atmosphere more like a carnival than a supposedly pious religious festival. By the entrance to the huge church of San Francisco on the north-western side of the square, a group of white-helmeted policemen were making ready to control the crowds.

The huge assemblage seemed to be generating a mass personality of its own. Of course it was a peaceful, basically happy crowd, but there was an air of expectancy which we all felt and, despite my earlier reservations about religious processions, I began to enjoy the colour, the movement and excitement of it all.

We managed to manoeuvre ourselves into an excellent position close to the huge doorway of the church only moments before a detachment of khaki-uniformed policemen marched up and began shouting orders at everyone near the doorway to move away. The officers commanding the soldiers looked like little Mussolinis; wearing jodhpurs, polished jack-boots and spurs, with holstered pistols hanging from their belts, they stood, with folded arms, issuing orders and obviously enjoying their position on centre-stage. Several Franciscan monks in brown robes came out of the church to talk to the officers and, as they were chatting away in the empty space created by the other policemen, who had pushed back the crowd, one had a classic picture, in simplified terms, of one of the most contentious issues in Ecuadorean history and politics ... the close co-operation of church and state.

The relationship between the Roman Catholic Church and the Government of Ecuador has dominated the country's chaotic political scene ever since it won its independence from Spain in 1822. Over those years, Ecuador has had 16 different constitutions and almost 60 presidents. But, despite the constant change of political figureheads during the rest of the nineteenth century, church and state remained closely integrated. The Roman Catholic Church was granted special privileges by the Government and for a considerable period there were laws denying citizenship to non-Catholics, despite the fact that they may have been born in Ecuador.

The Conservative Party, which held power for most of the 1800s and again, for most of the years since World War II, has always been the political spokesman for the Roman Catholic Church. The Radical Liberals, on the other hand, have sought, whenever in power, to scrupulously separate church and state and, during the fifty years in which they held sway in Ecuador, after the revolution of 1895, successive liberal presidents managed to greatly reduce the political influence of the church, not least in the area of public education.

Although the military government, which took power in 1972 has adopted a theoretically neutral stand as far as the relationship with the Church is concerned, it leans, if anywhere, towards the conservative attitude and the church, under the military junta, still retains considerable power and influence in Ecuador.

The brown-robed monks hustled back into the church as the procession was about to begin. We had been in the midst of a bilingual argument with a zealous policeman over whether or not we could keep our position flush by the wall of the church. The start of the proceedings fortunately diverted his attention from us, so that we were able to stay where we were and watch it all pass us by at close range.

First came the purple-robed characters who wore tall, pointed hoods with sinister eye-slits cut in them. They all carried candles and many of them walked barefoot. They issued four-abreast from the great doors of the church and began to lead the procession through the crowds away from the square. Following behind them were people in costume representing the various central characters in the Easter story ... Pontius Pilate, the two thieves, the Roman soldier who tormented Christ on the cross and, of course, the Virgin Mary and Christ himself. The Virgin Mary was an ornate, sculpted model wearing a lace mantilla. She was carried under a silken canopy on a large, richly-ornamented, wheeled carriage. Christ was also a life-sized model depicted carrying his cross. He, too, was set atop a huge, rubber-tyred carriage which was wheeled through the streets by a dozen or so men on either side of the vehicle. People of all ages, many of them sobbing uncontrollably, pressed close to the carriages, as they passed by, to throw flower petals and coins at the feet of Christ and the Virgin.

When the last marchers in the procession had passed us, we made our way through the crowds in the opposite direction, on our way back towards our hotel, but, half-way there, we came across another street along which the procession was due to pass. Crowds were lined thickly on either side of the road and within minutes the purple-hooded figures appeared on the scene again and we saw the whole thing through once more.

By this time, however, the parade had been joined by members of the public; unofficial, independent participators, intent on displaying their own particular religious fervour in different ways. There was the little man with his cactus cross, the little boy staggering along under his wooden cross, his parents walking proudly behind him, and dozens of others who carried banners or slogans or statuettes or pictures of Christ or Mary. Many of these were also barefooted and wearing a crown of thorns.

By the time it had all finished for the second time, we felt quite shattered ... not so much by the procession, but by the combination of being on our feet for several hours and the high altitude, which continued to give each of us this pervasive background headache. At one stage Trish felt as if she might faint and had to sit for some time on the footpath with her head between her knees.

As soon as we could, we headed once again, back towards our hotel, only to be stopped this time, some four or five hundred metres from it by an intense downpour of rain which flooded the streets within minutes and forced us to shelter in a narrow doorway. But eventually we staggered, wet and weary, back to our little room, collapsing into bed to sleep ... at only 2.30 in the afternoon.

'Café Senor? Por favor.' Iain gestured at his cracked cup of hottish milk, pretending with his finger, to stir in some instant coffee.

'Café?' Iain repeated and made drinking motions followed by a simulated search. He is so much better than I am at all this sign language which generally leaves me feeling such a fool.

The young man, obviously the son of the owner of the small eatery, crammed with ponchoed Indians and their bundles of vegetables and other produce, shrugged his shoulders in disbelief that anyone, even an obvious foreigner, could be so stupid. 'Café!' he pointed imperiously at the small bottle of the sort in which cafés at home serve soy sauce or vinegar and which was standing in the middle of our table containing a dark liquid.

When the children and I burst into peels of hysterical laughter, he understandably turned away in a huff. It would have been impossible for us to explain to him that we were laughing not at him but at Iain, who for the past two days had been shaking the brown liquid from this bottle onto his morning fried eggs in the belief that it was some local brown sauce approximating Worcestershire! The fact that he managed to get in between our giggles, 'I did think that it tasted rather odd', only set us off in fresh gales of laughter.

We were still laughing sporadically an hour or so later when we boarded a battered bus, paying 160 sucres (US$6.50) for the four of us to travel just over 140 kilometres south to Riobamba.

The seats filled up first and then the aisle and when a fellow who seemed to be acting in some sort of official capacity for the bus company was satisfied that no more bodies could be jammed in, a driver climbed over bundles and babies to his seat. He started up the decidedly sorry-sounding engine, paused for a moment to collect his thoughts and then, looking upwards, made the sign of the cross. What was a trifle disconcerting was that we weren't sure whether this symbolic gesture was made to the portrait of Christ's head, bleeding and adorned with a crown of thorns, which was stuck above his window to the right, or the centrefold exposure of a nubile and very naked lass in full colour, which was stuck to the left.

Whichever it was, it did not make me feel any easier about this, our first bus trip in the Andes about which we had already been told many hair-raising stories by fellow travellers. The one which had appealed to me most, perhaps because it dwelt less on damage to life and limb than many others, was about the driver who stopped his vehicle just before descending around a particularly nasty hair-pin bend in a steep narrow track, cut into the sheer mountain face above a certainly fatal drop of several hundred metres, to take a collection from his passengers. Stepping carefully from the bus, with a dramatic gesture of supplication, he flung the money over the precipice. Then, along with all the passengers crossed himself and murmured a fervent prayer!

There may be a lesson to learn from the fact that that particular bus and all its passengers reached its destination, and then again there may not. All I know for sure is that if our driver had taken a collection from us I would have willingly contributed!

Almost all our fellow bus travellers were Indians and I experienced the same feelings I was to have every time we were with solely Indian companions in Ecuador or Peru. Perhaps it was the way they behaved toward us, not hostile, but as if we didn't exist; as if we could make no impact on their self-contained world in which being Indian came first and being Ecuadorean came a very poor second.

Forty percent of Ecuador's nearly seven million people are pure Indian. Fifteen percent of these speak Quechua, the ancient Inca language, as their mother tongue and half of these speak only Quechua. Almost all of them are subsistence farmers and live financially precarious lives. This life-style, to which they cling tenaciously, resisting all attempts at integration, ensures that they remain outside the mainstream of Ecuadorean life.

There is even a tribe of Indians, the Jivaros, living over the Andes and down in the lush jungle of the Amazon Basin, who, although they no longer keep to their very recent head-hunting ways, remain extremely wild. They have come to the type of mutual agreement with the central goverment which Groucho Marx always said he favoured with flies; they didn't tell jokes and he didn't walk on ceilings; the Jivaros ask for nothing from the Ecuadorean Government and the Government asks for nothing from them!

The Quechuas have not gone to this extreme, but as literacy is lower among them than among mestizos, they have proportionately less say in the day-to-day working of their country as only literates can vote. (Imagine the reverberations in your own society if only numerates could vote!) So one doesn't see pure-blood Indians among the grim, pale faces in the group portraits of the uniformed men who rule the nation.

Even the fight to free Ecuador from Spanish rule was led by, and in most part fought by, Spanish Ecuadoreans, and not by the indigenous Indians, who perhaps hoped that the two opposing forces would wipe themselves out, leaving the original inhabitants to take back their country. And perhaps that was another aspect of the vibrations I picked up from these Quechua Indians; even today they give the appearance of keeping their distance and biding their time.

For the first part of the day's journey, the bus travelled through rich and fertile agricultural land, most of it owned by absentee landlords and worked by Indians. The houses were comparatively substantial and it wasn't until we came into the tundra-like dry lands that there was obvious poverty. However, there were also many gum trees, able to flourish under the toughest of circumstances, which made us feel comfortably familiar with the landscape.

Considerably less comforting was the large number of wooden crosses, painted white, which kept appearing along the roadside. They were often surrounded by flowers, though where they came from, out there in that bleakness, Heaven knows. As they were almost always on a particularly sharp bend in the track, not even the children needed it explained that they marked the spots where vehicles, more than likely buses, overcrowded like ours, with fifty or so people, had slid over the edge. Each time we passed such a spot, the passengers crossed themselves frantically and so, too, did our driver, which made me nervous because I liked him to have two hands on the wheel at all times.

A sudden mass wail, as we rounded a bend and slowed almost to a halt, sent shivers up and down my spine. The driver manoeuvred past a small knot of people standing on the edge of the drop and peering down we could just see the recently crushed remnants of a bus identical to ours. Everyone crossed themselves again and out of the corner of my eye I saw Zara copying them. She grinned sheepishly but with a thrill of fear.

When I was but thirteen or so
I went into a golden land,
Chimborazo, Cotopaxi
Took me by the hand.

The jingle by Walter Turner which every citizen of the then Empire learnt at school, in those far less than happiest days of my life, regurgitated itself spontaneously, at least supplanting thoughts of driving hazards, as Cotopaxi came into a view on our left. All 5900 metres of it, snow-capped and wreathed in cloud.

Only a few miles later and Chimborazo reared up on our right, the whitened cone perfectly visible; its 6200 metres seemingly much nearer than the actual sixteen kilometres or so because of the perfect visibility through a sparkling-clear atmosphere. One of the world's highest active volcanoes, it had several violent eruptions in the nineteenth century and in 1797 the town of Riobamba was wiped out. It was moved a mere twenty-four kilometres to its present site which perfectly illustrates either the tenacity with which people cling to established patterns, or the strength of the life-force, depending on your school of social science.

Whichever it is, you'd find the present Riobamba a very pleasant and attractive town. We took a four-bedded, shared bathroom place, offloaded our packs and went to look around.

At 2400 metres, Riobamba is only a couple of hundred metres lower than Quito so, either that was enough to make a difference, which I doubted, or we were becoming more acclimatised to the altitude, because none of us had headaches.

The town has some quite unexpectedly grand stone buildings, as well as open spaces. But wherever you go you are aware of the looming presence of Chimborazo. It was rather like an irritating habit Iain has of reading over my shoulder!

We bought a little immersion heater, like the one Ed Rosenfeld had shown us in El Salvador. It was probably the best value for a single dollar on the whole trip. And then quite by accident we came across the market.

Supermarkets give me an actual physical pain in the head or make me feel nauseous. All those shelves of canned dog food and yuk breakfast cereals appear to bend towards me and close in like those awful walls in James Bond films which threaten to crush out all life. But open-air markets are totally different and are very much my scene. I can happily spend hours rifling through heaps of things I have no intention of buying. So that Riobamba market was a sheer delight; sandals, hats, belts, hand-tooled leather articles, baskets, bolts of cloth, and of course ponchos, vied for my attention. And watching the all-Indian customers was no less fascinating.

In a carnival atmosphere, they went from stall to stall with that characteristically peculiar walk/trot, ambulatory style, developed, I imagine, by almost constant pregnancy (women) and carrying heavy loads (men and women).

Iain was in danger of expiring from a bad case of 'photographer's delight', an illness brought on by there being a terrific photograph in whichever direction his camera was aimed.

The women, very reminiscent of those on shopping sprees in our own home village, insisted on pulling out the bottom bolt of bright woollen material, draping it over themselves or their friends, standing back to take in the effect, then haggling over prices. They ferreted through piles of ribbons, plastic hand mirrors, combs and hair ornaments and tried on one hat after another.

We had also noticed a change in fashion in that women's ponchos, although still in ringing clear colours were now split open down the front and held together below the neck by a single large silver stick-pin.

The men however, hadn't changed from Quito fashions and clung to their trilbies. At one stage, I was standing close to a couple who were choosing from a large selection of hats, stacked crown on crown. Fascinated by their language, but not wanting to appear too obviously nosey, I picked up one of the trilbies and looked at the label on the inside ribbon. "Made in Italy!" I wondered if they were still making them, specifically for the Ecuadorean market, or if they were a job-lot left over from the thirties, when Humphrey Bogart made sure that no man worth his salt would dare ask a lady out, without wearing his fedora.

We couldn't resist buying something, so, trying to be practical about temptation, we chose a capacious handwoven shoulder-bag bearing the design of a large mythical bird. Zara instantly named it 'FB', her abbreviation for Food Bag, a handle which stuck. She insisted that she would be responsible for carrying it, loaded with small edibles from here on in and, surprisingly, she did.

I was very glad that Zara was thus happily distracted from a scene which I knew would upset her greatly. At the edge of the market were stalls selling cooked food. In the hope of finding some delicacy, I did some forward reconnoitring and found that several of the barbeques were roasting guinea-pigs! This is an Andean speciality but, to Zara who has lovingly raised numerous of these seemingly dim-witted and outrageously sensitive animals, it would have been something akin to a menu of 'deliciously flavoured baby kitten', or 'succulent cuddly puppy'!

It had been a long and quite tiring day, so on our way back to our room, we bought a small jar of Colombian Nescafé which we anticipated would give us a boost. Back on our beds we watched with simple joy as our new immersion heater boiled a cupful of water in less than thirty seconds. 'With this little beauty,' Iain beamed, 'we could be at home anywhere!'

The journey we made from Riobamba down to Ecuador's tropical lowlands provided us with one of the most spectacular trips of our lives. The fantastic railway line which connects Quito with the major port city of Guayaquil on the coast, some 480 kilometres to the south-west, drops almost 3300 metres, in one section, in a distance of just 80 kilometres, passing through rugged mountain country along the sides of vertical canyons. Before the line was completed in 1908, it took two weeks to get from Quito to Guayaquil, or vice versa. The fast train now takes only twelve hours.

We'd read about the line in the *South American Handbook,* a British publication which is essential equipment for anyone travelling in South America. Although some of its descriptive passages weren't too encouraging ('Travellers who aren't in a hurry and don't mind unexpected delays, e.g. derailments, should take the second, slower, train, generally known as the 'tren mixto') the rest of it sounded much more interesting than a bus trip down to the coast.

So, at 5.00 in the morning we were up and, not long after, at the station, where a queue for tickets had already formed in the darkness. It was the slow train, the 'tren mixto' . . . a mixed goods and passenger train we were catching, as the faster 'Auto Ferro' only ran on alternate days and this wasn't one of them. The only problem was that there were no reserved seats on the 'tren mixto', so whoever bought their $1.20 tickets first got their seats first too.

I find that 5.30 in the morning is not the best time for me to get into these competitive situations, on this occasion especially. Firstly, it was Easter Sunday when most sensible people were remaining comfortably in bed, and secondly, my emotional preparedness had been somewhat impaired by shaving in cold water, without a mirror. But fortunately, as the train was not due to leave for an hour, the queue was not long and we managed to get seats on the old wooden carriages without any trouble. Our moods brightened slightly when the children discovered Easter eggs in the 'FB' — apparently the Easter Bunny had managed to find them in Riobamba.

The train had not changed, I'm sure, since the line was opened in 1908. The carriages were exactly the same as the ones you see in Wild West movies ... with an open platform at each end. It was necessary, when we later came to the really steep parts of the line, for a brakeman, one for each carriage, to stand on this platform and spin a large metal wheel that individually operated the brakes for each carriage. A bit archaic, but it seemed to work.

The countryside through which we passed for the first forty-five kilometres or so was lush and beautiful; rolling green hills and valleys with small Indian farms and groves of eucalyptus trees dotting the landscape. But, although the black, volcanic soil was obviously rich, the farms were equally obviously not. The houses were primitive adobe and thatch huts similar to those that are common throughout much of Africa. Most of the farms were divided by stone walls into small holdings which were clearly not sufficiently large for anything but subsistence farming.

In Ecuador, as in most under-developed countries, the distribution of land has been generally unequal and unfair. Some three hundred families in Ecuador own two-thirds of the nation's productive farmland. Land reform laws *have* been instituted and are aimed at eliminating absentee ownership and abolishing oppressive forms of tenancy, while still maintaining the principle of private ownership. But the changes have been slow and most have been effected in the tropical lowlands where the majority of the high-earning export crops like bananas, cacao, coffee and sugar are grown. In the highlands, where the main domestic crops of corn, barley, wheat, kidney beans and potatoes are cultivated, the farmers are mainly poor and uneducated. Most are pure-bred Indians who have no sense of Ecuadorean nationality and, being indifferent to commerce, have been unwilling, or at best, slow to accept changes to their traditional farming methods that could lead to better utilisation of their land and, in the long run, higher returns for them.

Cajabamba was our first stop some twenty-eight kilometres from Riobamba. The site of the original Riobamba, founded in 1534, it has never recovered from the 1797 eruption which flattened the town and killed several thousand of its inhabitants. When the new Riobamba was established, the old one died. It is still there, but it is a poor, rather sad town.

The train was climbing slowly. At Riobamba we were at about 2700 metres. At Cajabamba, some 3000 metres. After skirting a small, attractive lake, we reached Guamote and, shortly afterwards, the highest point on the line, 3566 metres, beyond which we began a gradual descent. Then the country changed dramatically. We had crossed an invisible climatic line to the coastal side of the Cordillera. No more green valleys. Suddenly the land was dry and treeless. What grass there was, was brown and tufted. The hills were barren and desolate. Occasionally an Indian woman in a vivid-red, woollen poncho, wearing a flattened white hat and carrying a baby in a manta on her back, appeared from nowhere to stand and watch the train go past.

For a short while we could see, in the distance to the south-east, the great, snow-capped cone of Sangay, which, as it continuously spews forth smoke, ash and often lava, is considered the world's most active volcano. Surrounded by impenetrable jungles on two sides and crumbling canyons of volcanic ash on the others, Sangay's 5500-metre peak is one of the most inaccessible in the world. It is also, coincidentally, one of the legendary repositories of the lost treasure of the Incas.

The story is that a vast golden treasure was buried by the Incas centuries ago in the labyrinthine crevices at the base of Sangay in order to prevent the Spanish Conquistadores from capturing it. Over the centuries, dozens of expeditions have attempted to find the treasure, but without success.

Our train trundled on and now our descent became more rapid. We were running along a barren, rocky valley with steep-sided walls. Far below, a raging, brown river rushed through the canyon floor.

I stepped out onto the platform at the end of the carriage, where the brakeman was working his wheel. A gaucho wearing sheep-skin chaps, like the American cowboys of the Old West, stood on the other platform, watching the proceedings also. He looked somehow unreal ... vaguely satyr-like, with the legs of an animal and the body of a man. The children were fascinated and did their best to try to observe this strange being unobtrusively. But the gaucho was aware that he was being watched and, with a laugh and some unintelligible Spanish, he waggled a woolly leg at Zara and Sean who were embarrassed into returning to their seats.

We were descending the very side of the canyon wall. Within a half a metre of the edge of the railway track, the precipice dropped away vertically for 300 metres or more. I wondered, rather pointlessly, if the track could stand the weight of the train. Across the valley I could see the evidence of numerous landslides. I kept thinking, how does our track stand up to this colossal weight and vibration?

As the train rounded a bend, I could see far ahead, the big, red engine, a modern, diesel-powered vehicle which looked strangely out of place pulling such an ancient collection of carriages.

'Look, Dad,' Zara shouted, pointing. 'There are people on the roof!'

For the first time, I noticed that the roofs of almost all of the carriages were packed with people and their baggage; extra passengers, presumably paying considerably cheaper fares than we had.

'Can I get up there too, Dad?' asked Sean, typically.

'No Sean. I'm sorry ... it's too dangerous.' How mundane, unexciting and unadventurous parents can be.

Some ninety-five kilometres from Riobamba, we stopped at Alausi, a mountain resort popular with people from the humid coastal towns. An impromptu marketplace beside the train sold all sorts of fruits and nuts, and tasty empanadas. But the most fascinating objects were the whole roasted pigs which were spread out on tables by the train tracks, their crackly, brown-skinned heads staring vacantly towards us. Women shouted competitive prices and sliced off great hunks of pork for the passengers who stood and ate until the train was ready to move on.

After Alausi came the big drop ... 790 metres in 12 kilometres ... a formidable engineering feat. The two major triumphs of this section of the line are known as the 'Alausi Loop' and 'The Devil's Nose', a complex series of zig-zags, or switchbacks, by which the train descends the almost perpendicular side of the canyon.

As we approached The Devil's Nose, it was difficult not to feel a trifle uneasy. Leaning out of the window, we could see straight down to the bottom of the valley into which we had to descend. The train slowed to a stop and then, almost immediately, we were going backwards, downhill on the first of the zig-zags. A few kilometres or so later, we changed direction on the second switchback and all the while there was nothing but a sheer cliff to one side of us. No one said very much. There were one or two first-timers in the carriage who, like us, peered out of the window in near disbelief, but others, who had presumably seen it all before, continued with blase unconcern to read or talk among themselves.

Shortly, we reached the bottom, safe and sound of course, and in a few minutes we were in the small town of Sibambe. After a few more minutes we left again and from there on, we were rolling along the floor of the valley following the winding course of the River Chan Chan, over bridges and through numerous tunnels ... at each one of which, the passengers on the roof all lay prostrate.

We continued to lose altitude and gradually the air became warmer and the country more tropical. Soon we were leaving the mountains and in more open country, passing pineapple, tobacco, sugarcane and banana plantations, eventually arriving, at 4.30 in the afternoon at the small town of Milagro, some thirty kilometres from the coast and only 33 metres above sea level.

The train stopped plumb in the middle of the main street of Milagro as the railway line runs right along it. As we stepped off, the crowds on the roof of the train, seeing Zara and Sean carrying their packs, gave us a cheer. It should, we felt, be the other way round ... us cheering them for their hair-raising ride!

Milagro is Spanish for miracle; but the little town was not turning on any spectaculars for us the next morning; no water into wine or even into coffee, in fact, no breakfast at all as no cafés or shops were open even by 8.00 a.m. We were glad that we had stocked up with a large dinner the previous evening.

We became very accustomed to this eating, not to a schedule, but whenever possible, because there was no certainty about when the next fuelling up would be.

This day's stretch of travelling we already knew would be a little complicated, though if we had known just how complicated we might have gone back to bed. There was no bus going direct to the place we wanted to reach, the border town of Huaquillas so, first up we caught a small local bus which was going on down to Guayaquil, the big port thirty-two kilometres away on the coast. After twenty-four kilometres, we offloaded at a cross-roads where the road headed south to Machala and Huaquillas. There were no bus stops or signs, just little groups of people who assured us that, 'Si, si,' the 'Autobus a Machala' did come through here.

Although only 9.00 a.m. it was already very hot and muggy. We sought the slight coolness of the shade thrown by a half a dozen or so wooden shacks which served as shops dependent for their trade on transferring bus passengers. One of these places, even more grubby than the rest, bore a worn sign announcing: 'Clinico Medico'. A large sow and her litter rooted under a table which was strewn with unrolled bandages, open jars of ointment and uncorked bottles of medicine. We took a photograph to send to a doctor friend back home to show him that things can get even worse than the chaos caused by on-again, off-again government medical schemes!

Then we hurried back to the roadside because we had noticed that the buses didn't stop for more than ten seconds to either put down or pick up and that all of them were very crowded. It looked like we were in for one of those hang-on-and-push-like-hell jobs. A family strategy was discussed and we decided that Zara and Sean would leap on to the steps and that, with us pushing from behind, because of their small size, they would be able to wiggle their way through. Iain and I would be flat up behind them so that they wouldn't fall off as the bus accelerated away . . . which they all did, even though there were always passengers clinging to the sides trying to find footholds.

'Machala, Machala,' we could hear the dare-devil outrider yelling as the filthy old rattletrap of a bus approached in a cloud of dust. As it slowed to a stop, we leapt. It's on occasions like these that we realise how essential it is for us each to carry our own gear and to carry it strapped to our backs leaving both hands free.

The already full-to-capacity bus seemed to expand its metallic seams to admit us. Iain and I even managed to have a foot inside the bus before it lurched off. The children had squeezed their way across to behind the driver who was sitting, not in a seat, but on a wooden box. The rest of the passengers were all mestizos; we had evidently left the Indians behind in the mountains. After a few kilometres, during which they all sifted down like sand through water into positions of relative comfort, the driver motioned to me to squeeze in on the far side of his box, between him and his shattered side-window. I eagerly accepted this offer of a real 'box seat', while Zara and Sean took turns to perch against my back, Iain crouched among a maze of legs and, when his own went to sleep, stood with his head bent beneath the low roof.

The driver was much smaller than I, and I'm not huge, so he gave the appearance of having to fight with all his strength against the recalcitrant wheel, which was shaken and spun by the bumpy road. Throughout the two-hour trip he kept a cigarette clamped between his lips, but never lit it. Every now and then he turned his brown, bird-like face toward me and grinned. Obviously he enjoyed riding this bucking metal bronco and playing dare-devil scare tactics with passengers and other traffic.

'Camino Peru,' his pardner yelled and quite as suddenly as we had been swallowed, we were now spewed out onto the empty roadside again.

'Si, si,' was his cavalier response to our anxious questions as to whether this really was the road to Peru. And then they were gone and we were left with aching limbs, suddenly lonesome and seemingly in the middle of the Ecuadorean jungle. The track stretched off in both directions empty and bordered by thick vegetation.

We were just beginning to discuss how to go about things from here, Zara having moved off to a discreet distance to meet the calls of nature, when we heard 'Huaquillas! Huaquillas!' being shouted. We struggled back into our packs, Zara still zipping up her fly, in time to board a much newer and far emptier bus in which we each settled into a separate seat. Such luxury!

The road immediately improved, so that we travelled at good speed past banana plantations and attractive tropical-styled homes in forest clearings. Twice we were stopped by police posts and both times as foreigners, we were the only passengers who had to leave the bus to show passports and papers. By the time we reached the southern tip of the continent I was heartily sick of these extra checks which have nothing to do with national borders. But this was only our introduction to this widespread paranoia, so I was excessively polite to the pistol-toting, jack-booted police officers, even filling in their own forms for them because they had no idea where to look for (ir)relevant information such as my maiden name.

Arriving in Huaquillas in the humid midday heat, our packs seemed to double in weight. We almost anticipated with pleasure the cold southern travelling when all our clothes would be on us rather than in our packs. We quaffed bottles of a sickeningly sweet local drink, Coco Rico, which only made us more thirsty.

Before we made the crossing into Peru we planned to buy a supply of Peruvian currency. It was illegal to take more than 1000 'soles' (worth officially about US$9) into Peru. But as there was an artificially low rate of exchange being enforced in the country it would be more advantageous for us to buy some Peruvian money in Ecuador, where there was a considerably better exchange rate.

Iain disappeared briefly into a dingy washroom in a small café to extract some US dollars from his nylon money-belt which he wore under his clothes and, shortly afterwards, American dollars in hand, we went back out into the street to meet the barrage of neatly dressed con-artists who describe themselves as money-changers, all of them carrying black attaché cases. These they flashed open, like nervous pornography salesmen, to reveal piles of tired banknotes. We cashed our General Sucre's namesakes for 'Soles de Oro', smiling over this suggestion that the virtually worthless Peruvian currency was backed by its weight in gold. Still the children were enchanted by the picture on the note's reverse side of the 'Ra'-like rafts on Lake Titicaca.

Iain tucked twenty-six thousand soles, which he bought for US$200 inside his undies, reminding me of the show-biz bitchery about Tom Jones doing the same with a plumply-filled stocking.

Thus equipped, we trudged in the heat through the mass of people coming the other way across the border; men pulling horse-size carts of produce and women on domestic shopping sprees. Under the Ecuadorian flag, a few scruffy soldiers were leaning against the wall of their guard post eyeing the talent. We waved goodbye to them and walked on to the Peruvian customs shed. Here our packs were given a very cursory once-over and Iain's imitation of Tom Jones went unnoticed!

The little one-room immigration post on the opposite side of the road was empty, but as we were taking off our packs, a surly looking non-uniformed fellow appeared in the doorway.

'Siesta,' he pointed at his watch. 'Una hora mas.' And left.

We groaned at this loss of an hour, especially in such uncongenial surroundings. Sean, seeing the rubber stamp and ink pad on the table suggested, 'We could do it ourselves.'

Although he had made no sign of understanding English the surly man reappeared almost immediately and without a word opened the drawer in the desk and swept the stamp and ink pad inside.

It was more than an hour before the next would-be border crossers appeared; a couple of good-looking young girls who, although they conversed in Spanish, were wearing obviously American-bought jeans and T-shirts. The sullen man came back and to our total amazement pulled out the stamp and pad and stamped their passports! Up to then we had thought he was a clerk of some sort, now we realised that he was the actual immigration officer.

Iain approached him with our pile of passports; after a less than cursory glance he brushed them aside and made to leave, apparently to resume his siesta.

'Hey,' Iain said, 'if you can stamp theirs,' he indicated the girls, 'why can't you stamp ours?' The man muttered a string of incomprehensible (to us) Spanish and walked out.

'He says,' one of the girls translated, 'that you need a visa.'

'What! Why? No. No. It's not true ... It's ...' Iain was speechless for a moment and then he ran out after the officer and, through the door, we could see him haranguing him in the dusty road, the officer keeping up a steady shaking of his head.

When he returned, Iain was a mixture of distress and anger. It seemed that the information given us in Panama had been incorrect and Australian passport holders needed visas.

The girls sympathised. We discovered that they were Peruvians who had been studying in the United States and were hitching home after a vacation. 'I shouldn't say this about my own country,' one of them grimaced, 'but if I was you I would offer him money. Good luck!' They winked as the man returned.

But it was useless. Either our inexperienced technique was wrong, we didn't offer enough, or he was that rare creature in this part of the world, the incorruptible offical. For more than an hour, in between stamping other people's papers, he kept repeating, 'No visa, no entrada.' Iain tried cajoling, he tried hectoring. I tried crying, which nearly worked, but I felt such a fool and a hypocrite in front of my incredulous children that my tears nearly turned to laughter and I dried up.

We even told him we were writing a book about his country and produced a copy of *Africa Overland* which we were carrying for emergencies just such as this. But interested though he was in the photographs of Masai tribesmen and the temple of Karnak he was unbudgable.

Quite suddenly I was filled with self-disgust. All this grovelling to a petty official of a bankrupt military dictatorship. If my Spanish had been good enough I would have told him what he could do with his rubber stamp! Fortunately Iain had come to the same decision, so we collected our packs and our battered pride and, putting on an air of not caring in the least, we swept out. The officer was of course far too busy with his stamps to deign to notice our departure.

The girls had told us that the nearest Peruvian Consulate of visa-issuing status was in Machala, eighty kilometres back, so that all we could do was to try to keep everyone's spirits up on the long, crowded, hot, two-hour bus trip, during which it rained heavily and we knew that our packs and sleeping bags, stowed on the roof, were being saturated.

My strongest memory of that awful day was not of Iain, for the first time in his life, being turned back at a border, but of Zara holding on to my hand tightly in the bus and Sean recounting his small stock of well-worn jokes to us, laughing encouragingly, each of them in their own way doing their best to brighten us up.

Looking back on it, I can clearly remember feeling, at that time, more than a little envious of those careful travellers who manage to have everything worked out ... completely organised; visas, transfers from airport to hotel, hotel reservations, buses and planes all booked before they leave home ... nothing left to chance. This was only a passing feeling of mine, of course, because I know I could never be like that. Basically I'm just not that sort of person. Neither, thank God, is Trish, although at moments like this I have wished that at least one of us was. I felt horribly frustrated and as things got worse during the next day, I wanted desperately to be able to throw the whole thing into the hands of a competent travel agent and forget it.

The Peruvian Consulate in Machala was only two blocks from our hotel. First thing in the morning, at 8.40 a.m., we were on his doorstep. The sign said 8.30 to 1.00 p.m., but there was no sign of life. We passed half an hour having breakfast in a nearby cafe, but by 9.10 a.m., when we returned to the Consulate's office, it was still not open. Asking in the shop downstairs, we discovered that the Consul had gone to Lima and would not be back for at least a week! Jesus. The nearest other Peruvian Consulate was at Guayaquil, the big port city we had been so close to on the previous day, but which was now some 190 kilometres north.

We talked about it and decided that the best thing would be for Trish and Zara to remain in the hotel in Machala and for Sean and I, who were the ones needing visas, to take a bus up to Guayaquil, get our visas and return later in the day ... if possible.

But the Consulate in Guayaquil would probably also close at 1.00 in the afternoon ... not only for lunch, but for the rest of the day, so we would need to get moving. Then we realised that we had practically no Ecuadorean money left, having changed it all to Peruvian soles the previous day. As we would now lose heavily by changing it back into Ecuadorean sucres, the only alternative was to go to the bank and change more US dollars into Ecuadorean money.

At the foreign exchange desk we stood by, driven almost crazy with impatience while the man in front, a rather nondescript fellow with a worn and baggy suit, produced a briefcase full of American $100 bills ... we counted at least one hundred and fifty of them ... $15,000! Sean and Zara's eyes were popping. The clerk then had to go through all the paperwork for the transaction; he was changing dollars to sucres, which took ages. Finally, however, he was through and then dealt with us. After pocketing some money and a hurried goodbye, Sean and I raced off, at 9.40 a.m., to try to catch a bus to Guayaquil.

With incredibly good luck we found, at the bus station only three blocks away, that a bus was leaving almost immediately for Guayaquil.

I relaxed slightly once on board the bus, which left at 9.50, but realised that, as it was probably a three-hour journey to Guayaquil, we'd be pushing to get to the Consulate on time anyway. And what was equally worrying . . . I didn't know where it was in Guayaquil, which is Ecuador's biggest city.

The bus rolled on . . . it seemed to me very slowly, stopping frequently to pick up and let down passengers while I felt it should have kept charging straight on. I kept looking at my watch and the passing landmarks, trying to figure out whether we'd make it or not. Suddenly the bus slammed to a halt. The driver and other people started yelling and several of them leapt out of the bus and into the long grass by the side of the road, where they disappeared, running in different directions. Both Sean and I, who were sitting in the back of the bus, were stunned.

For a moment I thought the bus was being ambushed, or something ridiculous like that. We were on an empty stretch of road with a small lake to our right, with long grass and reeds separating us from it. But it quickly became clear what the passengers and the driver were doing. They were chasing baby ducklings! One by one they triumphantly returned to the bus with their captured prizes, to stick them in their bags or to hold them in their laps until they reached their destination. The driver had obviously spotted the ducklings, which were presumably free-ranging and therefore anybody's property, and decided that one or two of them would one day grace his dinner table.

The whole thing only lasted about five or six minutes, I suppose, but, after the initial excitement, I began to become annoyed at the delay and impatient to get moving again. I mean really! Looking back on it now I realise how ridiculous it was for me to be like that. I should have relaxed and enjoyed it all and, even if it had taken us an extra day to get the visas . . . so what? But at the time, when we were caught up in the rush, it was somehow impossible to think like that.

The bus moved off and the man sitting across the aisle, realising we were foreigners, started to chat in fractured English. He was sitting, with his young wife, who looked about twenty-two or twenty-three years old and their four children, all under five, crammed into two seats.

'Americano?' he said, to begin the conversation.

I explained that we were Australian and that my wife and one more child were back in Machala. The explanation was one-third English, one-third Spanish and one-third hand movements. He nodded and informed us that he was a preacher from a small town near Machala and that he and his family were travelling to Guayaquil to visit relatives. He was not more than twenty-five or twenty-six . . . a pleasant man . . . open-faced and friendly, but obviously quite poor.

He asked about Australia and 'kunguru'. It was always kangaroos. I wondered if any country in the world is more closely identified with an animal than Australia is with kangaroos. He did not believe me when I told him that many Australians have never seen a kangaroo in the wild.

'Hah, hah!' he laughed, and shook his head, then wagged his finger at me. 'You are joking me.'

Our conversation, though it was very simplistic, calmed me down somewhat

... at least temporarily, until we arrived in the outskirts of Guayaquil at about 12.25 p.m.

It was much bigger than I had expected; kilometres of small industrial sites and factories, then we crossed two very large bridges over the Guayas River into a more built-up area. But, by 12.40 we were still only in the suburbs of the city. The bus was caught several times in traffic, so, as we had no baggage, Sean and I decided to leave it.

Saying goodbye to our preacher friend, we dashed into the street to try to catch a taxi. No luck for several minutes, then two stopped in quick succession. But neither of them knew where the Peruvian Consulate was. So Sean and I charged into the offices of a nearby factory, scoured through a telephone book and, armed with the address, charged out again to fortunately find another taxi which began to wind its way towards the city centre.

At 12.55 I recognised the street name I had scribbled on the piece of paper, but we were stuck again in a traffic jam, moving forward only a few metres at a time.

'Seis cientos veinte dos,' (622) I said to the driver in my best Spanish. 'Quanto quadres?' (How many blocks?)

He looked around. 'Dos,' he replied.

Sean and I paid him and ran the remaining two blocks, weaving through the lunchtime crowds, to number 622 P. Icaza, into the lobby, up in the elevator, along the hall and into the offices of the Peruvian Consulate at 1.00 p.m. A guard walked across the room past us and closed the door behind us.

We collapsed on a seat, sweating and out of breath.

But now it was all a real anti-climax. Within minutes the Consular official had stamped our visas into our passports, taken our money (60 sucres ... US$2.40 each) thanked us, seen us to the door and we were out in the street again. Three minutes later, while we were still standing on the sidewalk gathering our wits, he waved to us as he drove by in his Alfa Romeo coupe, evidently finished work for the day.

Strange to be suddenly let down like that. For a short while we were at a loss. Until that moment, all our energies had been directed at getting to the Consulate on time. Having achieved it, we found it difficult to slip into the next gear. We wandered slowly around the town for a while, asking directions, then finding our way to the bus company that ran back to Machala. Upon reaching it we were told that there was a two-hour wait for the next bus, so we continued our ramblings around the town.

Guayaquil is not really as attractive a city as Quito. It is a busy seaport and commercial city and its central area is full of modern, though often quite ugly, buildings. Much of its old colonial architecture has been razed to make way for the new. It is larger than the capital, having a population of around one and a quarter million and its inhabitants apparently tend to think of themselves as more modern and 'with it' than their compatriots in the highlands who are a little more traditional and conservative.

It's hard to imagine anyone being conservative though in a country where change seems to be the order of the day ... certainly in the political field anyway. In the twenty-two years between 1950 and 1972 for instance, Ecuador had twenty-two different governments! One President, Jose Velasco Ibarra, actually held power five times since 1934, but left his high office peacefully and constitutionally at the end of a term of office . . . only once! The other four times (the last in 1972) he was deposed and replaced by military juntas.

During most of the 1970s the constitution and any political activities were suspended in Ecuador while the country was ruled by a junta under the leadership of, first, General Guillermo Rodriguez Lara and later, Rafael Arizaga Vega. The junta promised a return to normal and constitutional political activities for the 1980s, but elections held in 1978 proved farcical, with the military attempting to influence the outcome, recounts of votes lasting months, charges and counter-charges of bribery and corruption and at least one major party refusing to accept the results.

So Ecuador seems certain to continue to be extremely unstable politically during the next decade . . . and yet it seems to me that, in a way, known and familiar forms of instability are perhaps to Ecuadoreans and other Latin Americans, just a different form of stability. For many Western countries the constant political turmoil in which Ecuadoreans live would seem disastrous, but to them it is perfectly normal . . . a way of life.

Strangely too, despite the instability of governments in Ecuador, the economy and the currency have remained remarkably stable . . . much more so than in many of Ecuador's neighbours, notably Peru. The biggest contributing factor, in recent times, has been the discovery of large quantities of oil in the remote jungle provinces in the east of the country. These have revolutionised its finances. Ecuador became an oil-exporting country during the seventies and now, having passed bananas as the major export earner, oil accounts for some seventy percent of the country's total exports. Ecuador hopes, with this relatively new development, to be able to change its status from that of a poverty-stricken banana republic to a wealthy oil exporter.

Travelling through Ecuador as we were, all we could do was to wish it the best of luck in those hopes but, without wanting to seem too cynical or pessimistic, it was difficult to believe that the future distribution of all these new-found petro-dollars would be any more equal or fair than the existing distribution of wealth and property.

Sean and I caught the 3.00 p.m. bus without any trouble or rush. The only thing to attract our interest on the way back to Machala was Guayaquil's cemetery, which we had evidently missed on the way in, due to our preoccupation with other things.

It was one of the most bizarre cemeteries I have ever seen, although I understand that for Ecuadoreans it is not in the least unusual, even though all of the bodies are 'buried' *above* the ground!

We didn't stop or leave the bus to look over it, but just from the window as we passed it by, one's first impression of the cemetery is of a vast housing complex in miniature. Rows of huge concrete structures, which look like strangely shrunken apartment blocks, filled the cemetery enclosure which stretched for some distance along the roadside. Although the top of the highest building was not more than 9-10 metres above the ground, they were 15-20 'storeys' high. The front of each 'building' was divided into three-quarter-metre squares, behind each of which a coffin was sealed. On one building I counted 30 compartments in line across the front, by 15 high ... a total of 450 bodies! And there were at least 30-40 buildings of that size in the cemetery ... probably more than 15,000 bodies ... all above ground in their own 'forever' apartment complex. I shuddered to think what would happen if a decent earthquake struck here.

With no more duck-hunts to distract us, Sean and I dozed for most of the trip back. We arrived at the hotel in Machala at 6.30 p.m. I took off my shoes, sat back and drank a large bottle of beer.

Then he put his shoes on again! And had another beer downstairs in the hotel's small restaurant. Poor fellow, he looked as though he'd been processed through an old-fashioned mangle!

Zara and I, having spent a quiet day in our cool hotel room, had plenty of energy to put into the large doses of TLC which, together with another beer and a plate of chops and chips, did eventually nurture Iain back to something resembling his former self.

Without speaking more than two dozen words to each other all day, Zara and I had both been silently happy to retreat into our own worlds; I to wade through the dense sensuality of John Fowles' *Ebony Tower* and Zara to begin work on a novel of her own: *Mr Ottermanderpuss Goes Travelling* written by Zara Finlay with illustrations (a later addition) by Iain Finlay. She stuck a passport photograph of herself on the back cover and under it wrote her short, and impressive, eleven-year biography. It was of course no coincidence that many of the places visited by Mr Ottermanderpuss had also been visited by my daughter.

The smartly-dressed, middle-aged owner of the restaurant, and as it turned out, of the hotel too, inquired if we had enjoyed our meal. When we replied with enthusiasm, he offered us a drink and joined our table. He asked where we were from and where we were going and was interested in our trip and especially in how the children reacted. 'That is my boy,' he gestured proudly at one of the four boys of Sean's age who were sitting at the next table and were fooling around in order to attract Sean's attention.

The language barrier made Sean embarrassed to join them but then I suggested he bring down his GI Joe and that soon overcame the social hurdles.

Poor Joe's predecessor had had to be left at home on a long rest and recreation leave. He'd never really recovered from the mauling he'd received by inquisitive and amazed African children on the previous trip. Balding and missing one foot and all the fingers on one hand, it was thought unkind to submit him to another arduous journey. This 'Son of Joe' was still in good nick, even though in Central America his 'Kung-Fu grip' had begun to weaken. The boys set up a crockery obstacle course and the game began.

Meanwhile Dad, who spoke enough English so that, together with our spattering of Spanish, we managed to communicate, glowed with pride when we commented on what a pleasant and friendly boy his son appeared to be. (Who said the way to a man's heart is through his stomach!)

'But he is a problem,' his face darkened and we began to mutter truthful platitudes about all children being a problem. He held up his hand to silence us and continued: 'What to do with him? Stay here or go away? Several times I have taken him and his mother to visit with friends in Israel and in North America.

They could easily arrange for us to stay in either place. Money is no problem. There he would have more opportunities to have a better education, to get a better job, to be more free.'

Zara, who has always maintained disdainfully cool relations with GI Joe, had brought down our cards and was ostentatiously playing patience. The ploy worked and Joe was deserted, sprawled like that other American soldier we'd seen in Panama, amongst the used crockery, while the boys joined her in a game of 'snap'.

'He is a bright boy,' the manager eyed his son, 'and will be wasted here. Yet,' he sighed, 'it is my home. The trouble is, it is so . . .' he moved his hands from side to side in an obvious suggestion of instability.

We tentatively made the point about the instability being so constant that the inconstancy was a form of stability and that at least the political atmosphere was alive and exciting.

He laughed derisively. 'That sort of exciting it is better not to have. And you too, if you lived here, would agree. It is like balancing always on a knife edge. It is not a good atmosphere in which to raise children. Nor is it good for business, because no one wishes to make long-term investments. Always it is the government who are having their fists into all the pies.'

I thought that the transposition of fist for finger was probably very appropriate.

'Their excuse to us is always the same. They must need more money because of war. All the time war. Now it is for fighting with Peru, a country which took much land from us in 1942 and now she threatens to take more. But she is bankrupted because she spend so much money to buy guns. Yes. It is true. So poor a country and yet she spend so much on armies.'

'Mum, Zara is cheating,' Sean announced.

'I am not,' came the vehement denial.

I gave my usual lecture about cheating being pointless because in the final analysis the cheater is only cheating her/himself but I could see that this mumbo-jumbo was having no effect and that all the boys (except Sean of course who is close enough to know better) were so impressed with Zara's self-confident air and her long blonde hair that they didn't give two figs whether or not she suffered from sleight of hand.

'Do you think there really will be a war with Peru?' Iain asked the manager, who had refilled our glasses.

'No. No. It is just a game to keep us watching and to keep the minds off the real problem. Too much government. Too many generals. Si.' He nodded vehemently. 'They think, to be a general . . . a big man,' he puffed out his chest, 'it is a necessary duty to lead a coup! Yes, really,' as we laughed, 'is true. You know every country in South America when she become independent, she declare to be a republic and then she want to be like United States. But there is big problem. At the time Spain has her Empire here, at home she has a king dictator. Yes. So that this is the way of thinking that she leave behind here. That is what we are learning. So much better it would be to have been conquered by English, like you. Then we would have learnt proper government, nòt always by generals.'

He had assumed that we were all Australians, but even if I could claim to be native born, I think I would still have had to question his suggestion that it would be preferable to be a colony of Mother England. The very idea of dumping the overflow from your prisons on the fringes of some vast and distant continent, your claim to which is fragile at best, is to me utterly repugnant.

Yet I have to admit that travelling through Central and South America I was not as burdened with national guilt as I had been in Africa. And that it was a relief to be able to say, 'I am British,' without that anxious feeling that behind me stood the ghosts of two hundred years of slave traders, missionaries, industrialists, generals, civil servants and other assorted exploiters, rattling their chains.

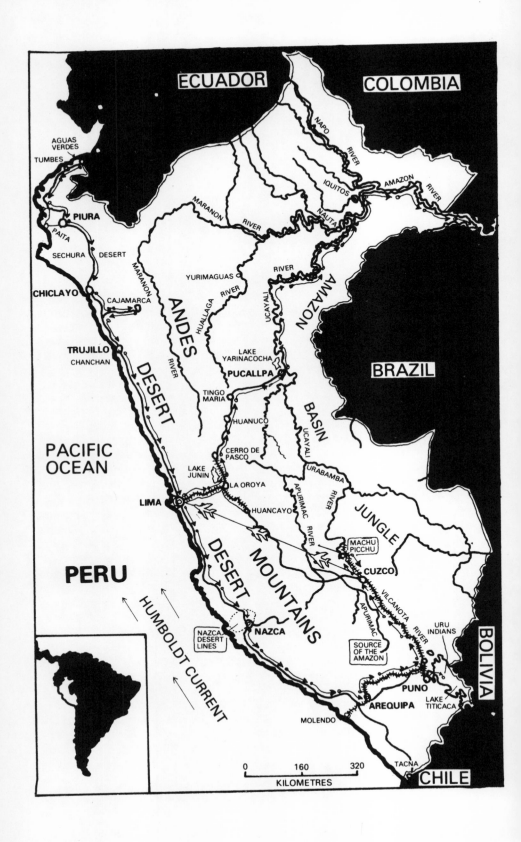

PERU

14
'One of the most atrocious acts of perfidy'

Peru must be the most fascinating of all the South American countries. It may not have the prosperity of Brazil or Venezuela, or the modern sophistication of the great cities on the eastern side of the continent, like Rio, Sao Paulo and Buenos Aires, but Peru has an aura, a mystique, and, more than any of its neighbours, there is great tragedy in its history and its soul.

These things are quickly felt by anyone who visits Peru; even those like us, with only a surface knowledge of Peru's incredible story, find the details of the Inca civilisation that existed in the past and its destruction by the marauding Spanish Conquistadores in the sixteenth century, almost too much to believe.

The Inca Empire, which was at its height around the year 1520, stretched a mind-boggling 4800 kilometres, as the crow flies, from the northern limits of present-day Ecuador, above the equator, to a point at roughly 35 degrees longitude south, almost two-thirds of the way down the long coast of Chile. This is greater, by almost 1600 kilometres, than the distance separating Hadrian's Wall in northern Britain and Jerusalem, at the opposite ends of the mighty Roman Empire. The Incas' domain covered over three and a half million square kilometres, including most of Peru and half of Bolivia, and embraced a population approaching ten million people. But even more amazing is the fact that this vast empire was built in such a rugged and hostile environment. Most of the three and a half million square kilometres in question was either in the cold and rarefied atmosphere of the high Andes mountains, or in the arid, coastal desert which runs from Peru's border with Ecuador right down into Chile.

When we crossed from Ecuador into Peru we found the physical difference between the lowlands of the two countries quite striking. Actually the geographical change from a green, tropical countryside, with an obviously adequate rainfall, to a dry, sandy desert begins just before the arbitrary national frontier, but by the time you are into Peru it is a true desert, with shifting dunes of sand and no vegetation whatever. And yet, strangely, there had been very heavy rains during the night and the border post at Huaquillas was a mudbath for our second visit. The immigration official who had given us such a hard time on the first occasion was there again, but his superior officer dealt with us this time without a hitch. We studiously ignored our unhelpful friend, who stood to one side, and we left without saying a word to him.

We found a small restaurant and Trish, Zara and Sean ate a quick meal of chicken and rice. I had nothing, as my stomach was a little upset and I had the runs ... or as they were affectionately known in this area, 'The Inca Quickstep'. Shortly afterwards we were introduced to 'collectivos', a wonderful form of public transportation which is not only fast and efficient, but cheap. Basically, collectivos are just long-range taxis which supplement the buses that travel the length and breadth of Peru, but as they are only marginally more expensive and considerably faster, they are an attractive alternative to the buses.

Most of the collectivos are big, aging American saloons which carry six passengers and leave for their destination whenever they have a full complement. We took one from Aguas Verdes, on the Peruvian side of the frontier, to Tumbes, about twenty kilometres away, then another to Piura, a further 330 kilometres south. The first trip cost us only 55 soles (40 cents) each, while the second, a four-hour journey, cost 500 soles (about $3.75) each.

For almost all of the way the landscape was moonlike; sand-dunes and stony desert. What little dry vegetation and sage brush there was soon disappeared as we drove further south. Barren, rocky mountains coming right down to the sea, with not a sign of greenery between the land and the water. Tiny, poor fishing villages appeared occasionally along the arid coastline, but apart from these, any evidence of human habitation was few and far between.

This stretch of coast, just south of Tumbes, is also the only part of Peru where the sea-water is warm. Further south, the Humboldt current, carrying water right along the western coast of South America, from the Antarctic, makes the sea for the rest of Peru's 3000-kilometre coastline icy-cold. It does, however, also bring teeming billions of fish making the waters off Peru and Chile the richest fishing grounds in the world.

The road from Tumbes to Piura, though surrounded by shifting sands and emptiness, was at least tar-sealed and in good condition, so we travelled on at high speed, a hot wind blasting through the open windows. The four of us were sitting in the back. One other passenger, a man who sat in the front, had crossed himself once, upon entering the car, and several times since, but said not a word to either us or the driver.

Just before leaving the coast to head inland, we began seeing the weird praying mantis-like machines that bob endlessly up and down, pumping oil from the ground. The whole area we were now travelling through was Peru's main petroleum-producing region and, at Talara, where the road turned inland, Petro Peru, the state-owned petroleum agency, run a 60,000-barrel-a-day refinery. Gasoline in Peru is very cheap ... at least it was at the time we were there; six soles (about four and a half cents) per litre.

We climbed a rocky pass to a high, empty plateau. In the distance the great snow-capped mountains of the Cordillera Central, part of the tremendous Andean mountain chain that reaches all the way to the bottom of the continent, came into view. In Peru, much more than in the more settled parts of the globe, one feels the immense power of the earth's natural forces at work. The Andes, as Charles Darwin discovered, contain shells from the bed of the sea that have been pushed upward to heights of over 3600 metres.

Because of these huge mountains, Peru is a country of tremendous geological contrast; desert on one side of the mountain range and almost impenetrable jungle on the other. The desert dryness is a direct result of the icy

Humboldt current running offshore. It produces so little evaporation that the prevailing onshore winds pick up almost no surface moisture and, for most of the year, the coastal regions get no rain at all. On the other side of the mountains there is a super-abundance of tropical rain.

Along the coastal strip more than fifty rivers run down to the sea, but only ten carry water all year round and not in great quantities. Wherever there is water and irrigation though, the desert blooms and these 'oases' as they are called, are ideal for cotton-growing, which has become a major export crop for the region.

Piura, our destination on our first day's travel into Peru, is one of several oases along Peru's northern coastline. With a population of about 150,000, it is one of Peru's oldest cities. Founded in 1532, three years before Lima, it is a remarkably pleasant town with attractive public gardens and parks and a number of well cared for old colonial buildings.

The small port of Paita, on the coast about fifty kilometres from Piura, is the main outlet for the export produce of the area, but is also well known as the last home of Manuela Saenz, the intriguing and powerful woman who was the mistress of Simon Bolivar during the great years of the wars of liberation from Spain. Scorned, after Bolivar's death, by the Peruvian society she had once dominated, she lived the remaining twenty-four years of her life in the tiny port of Paita, in abject poverty, making a meagre living by selling tobacco, embroidering and weaving. She died a lonely and terrible death in a small-pox plague in 1856 and all her possessions, including a priceless collection of Bolivar's papers and letters, were burnt by the town's officials in efforts to cleanse the town of the plague. Manuela's wealthy English merchant husband, with whom she had lived for only a short while, had left her a fortune, but she had declined to accept any of it.

Our hotel in Piura, the Christina, was big and clean ... and cheap; two rooms, each with bath, for a total of US$9.50. After showering and changing our clothes, we ate in a small restaurant downstairs. The food was also very good ... and cheap. Two large raviolis for the kids, Trish had whole fish and I had a prawn ceviche. Cakes and honeyed meringue for dessert, three large apple juices, a beer for me and two coffees. The bill for the four of us: just over US$5.00. I wasn't sure what all this would do for my Inca Quickstep, but at those prices I didn't really care.

We spent some time talking to Juan and Rosa Rojas, the young couple running the restaurant, who, we discovered, spoke excellent English. He was a Peruvian, she was Mexican. They had been living in Los Angeles for several years and they had two daughters who had been born there. They had come back to Peru for a visit and decided to stay for a while.

'No longer than two years, though,' Juan said to us with a sad smile. 'After that the children would have to become Peruvian citizens. We will be going back to the States before then.'

That night, contrary to the laws of nature governing Peru's desert coast, there was a torrential rainstorm.

Water is one of Peru's main problems. In common with Australia, large parts of the country suffer either from too much, or too little. This day certainly lay on the side of excess, although when we woke we found no water supply in the bathroom. Sean went downstairs to report this fact and returned with the news that the whole lobby and all the rooms on the ground floor were awash due to last night's downpour.

Grateful to have at least escaped the flood, Iain dry-shaved and we went in search of transport for the 250-kilometre trip south to Chiclayo. A bus leaving in two hours' time was already full. There was another leaving late in the afternoon but that would mean travelling in the dark for part of the trip and arriving late at night. The bus fare amounted to US$9.00 for all of us. We asked about a collectivo and found that it would cost us US$14.00 complete and that one was ready to leave immediately. We persuaded the driver to wait for us to have breakfast.

This consisted of fried eggs, fried bananas, croissants, coffee and large glasses of fresh orange juice . . . jugo naranjas (pronounced hugo naranha). Pure fruit juices are a Peruvian speciality and one to which we all became addicted. The four of us ate fit to bust and the bill came to US$1.50. When we left a tip for the waiter he ran after us into the street to return our money and when we explained that it was for him, he shook his head in disbelief. It is unavoidable for a traveller's impression of a country to be affected by costs and in this area alone, Peru looked set to enter our hearts via our pockets.

Between Piura and the next oasis of Chiclayo lie the shifting sands of the Sechura Desert. The road out of Piura started off well enough, but soon disintegrated, literally, into a quite appalling stretch of tarmac rent with jagged cracks, many of them wide enough to swallow a wheel whole. They appeared like splits in the earth's surface caused by earthquakes, but they were actually the result of tremendously heavy rains which had also washed away large chunks from the side of the road and undermined the surface so badly that it was dangerous to drive anywhere near the edges for fear of them crumbling beneath the car's weight. As the road trailed up and down and along and over the foothills of the Andes, leaving the road would have meant taking a nasty tumble.

The southern part of the Sechura Desert is witnessing a battle for the hearts and minds of the inhabitants between the Russians and the West Germans, who are financing respectively the huge Olmos and Tinajares irrigation projects. Both schemes involve channelling water from the Amazon watershed through tunnels in the Andes, one of them almost sixteen kilometres long, to the Pacific coast, eventually bringing a green revolution to over 400,000 hectares of desert.

Despite the condition of the dusty, cracked road, we were making good time and were enjoying the somewhat cooling breeze through the open car windows when, about noon, our driver let out a groan and, looking ahead, we saw a large congregation of trucks, buses and cars. We joined the back of the queue and piled out to walk the two or three hundred metres past the other parked vehicles and their occupants to find out what had caused the obstruction.

It appeared that the same unusually heavy rain which had flooded our hotel had fallen here and, in stark contrast to the surrounding dryness, a river had swollen into such a torrent that it had burst over its banks. It now swept past, carrying large amounts of debris between us and the other bank, where a similar crowd of equally disconsolate people stood viewing the impassable flood.

We joined the people lining both banks to watch a spectacle being performed in mid-river. A large semi-trailer which had obviously tried to get across at the height of the flood had been tossed onto its side by the gigantic force of the rushing water. It was now balanced precariously on the edge of the crumbling tarmac.

Two men, stripped to their underwear, were clinging to the side of the truck trying to clear away the large mass of tree limbs and branches building up between the front and back wheels of the almost toppled vehicle. The engine was not submerged and if they could prevent the build-up of debris and keep the river flowing through under the wheels with no obstruction to press against, it just might be possible that they could save the vehicle.

It was very dangerous, difficult work and no one offered to help. I hoped that at least they owned the vehicle and that they were not risking life and limb for some trucking company which would almost certainly be covered by insurance.

It was very hot, still and humid. The heat, reflected from the mass of flood water all around us, seemed to double its intensity. There was no sign of any habitation and the only relief offered was from the driver of a large truck full of semi-ripe oranges which he was selling off rapidly to eager buyers.

We sat on a small bank watching the two men fight with the river, and, even as we looked, it began to recede a little. But the earth was soggy and crawling with small, wiggly maggot-like worms, no doubt washed up by the flood. We had visions of either having to turn back to Piura or of camping in this nasty place, but after half an hour or so a decision was made on the other side to risk a crossing. A huge truck was chosen in the hope that its large wheels would give it enough clearance for the river to rush under the body.

Everyone cheered as it started off. Everyone that is except the men in mid-river, for the passing truck came within centimetres of them and the ensuing wake threatened to sweep them and their stranded vehicle into the torrent. Encouraged by the success of that crossing, a line of vehicles formed up on the other side, all of them high-wheel-base trucks followed by a bus loaded with passengers. The luggage hold of this vehicle was emptied and the bags taken inside. The hold doors were propped open and, as it crossed, the river was still high enough to pour, thickly-brown and swift, right through the open compartment.

Another half an hour of these dangerous crossings passed before the first car ventured in, cheered madly by all watchers. By now the river was perhaps a third of a metre lower than when we had arrived and it was the turn of the vehicles on our side. Our driver had managed to squeeze his way to near the front of the queue, although this was one time when I wouldn't have minded staying in place. Not lacking in imagination, I was very scared. The driver lit a cigarette and held it between his teeth and Zara and I held hands, playing the traditionally passive female role! Sean leant out of one window waving to the onlookers as if he were a royal personage, and cheering as if he were not, while Iain balanced through the other side taking photographs.

We made it, with our wake washing over the tired legs of the two men still struggling in mid-river. As we slipped and slithered up the roadway on the far side past the cheering spectators, our driver grinned as if he had felt no fear, but I noticed that his cigarette was almost bitten through. When we stopped at the first roadside shack a few kilometres further on, he had a stiff drink while we quaffed quantities of coconut milk and chewed the soft white meat of the fruit.

Two uneventful hours later we reached Chiclayo, a town of 160,000 people, in the middle of the country's largest rice growing area. It's a pleasant town with a big central square where, that night, after dinner, we wandered through the open-air market. Here Sean was delighted to come across a young boy of his own age leaning against a lamp-post, the light from which threw a ghastly glare on a large cloth spread at his feet. Arranged on this, in neat row upon row, were sets of plastic teeth; the incisors sharpened and lengthened to Dracula dimensions. The boy grinned to display his own pair of vicious fangs and of course Sean bought a set for himself which he flashed, always at unexpected times, throughout the rest of the journey with always hilarious results.

When Francisco Pizarro and his tiny band of armoured Conquistadores; one hundred and six foot-soldiers and sixty-two cavalrymen, started their march into the mountains of Peru about sixty-five kilometres south of Chiclayo, they were possessed of what can only be described as lunatic nerve. Their aim was no less than the conquest of the Inca Empire, an Empire, as has already been pointed out, of close to ten million people. Armed only with thin steel swords, a few guns and crossbows, the men, in their own words, wet their pants in fear as they approached a meeting with the Inca army. And yet, on Saturday November 16th, 1532, at the unimportant town of Cajamarca, the Spaniards achieved their aim in little more than forty minutes, without the loss of a single man. There were, however, according to Pizarro's record of the incident, 6000 Incas killed.

The great historian William Prescott, in his *History of the Conquest of Peru*, describes Pizarro's ambush and capture of the Inca King Atahualpa as 'one of the most atrocious acts of perfidy on the record of history'.

Pizarro and his men had approached the rendezvous with the Inca ostensibly as friends ... as visitors to the Incas' land. They had arranged a meeting for dinner on Saturday evening in Cajamarca, which had been left totally deserted by a terrified populace who thought (as it turned out, with considerable perception) that a battle was to take place there. Atahualpa, who had only just won the Inca throne after a long and bitter war with his brother, Huascar, which resulted in his brother's execution, came to the meeting with Pizarro accompanied by some 6000 unarmed attendants.

Atahualpa's intelligence about the white-faced, bearded strangers was inaccurate. True, they rode on huge, snorting beasts, the like of which had never been seen before, but these monsters, according to the Incas' information, were ineffectual at night and, if a rider fell off, then both were finished. At first the Incas had even believed that the horse and rider were joined together as one. As for the Spaniards' guns, Atahualpa had been told that they were only thunderbolts and that they could not be fired more than twice. Their thin Toledo swords were about as useful in a fight as children's toys. And so the Inca King had no real fear of this puny force of strangers. It would be interesting to meet them.

Pizarro, on the other hand, knew that if he could but capture the Lord Inca ... Atahualpa himself, then the rest of his army would collapse.

When the Inca and his host of attendants arrived, Pizarro had laid a complete ambush around the town square. There was a farcical confrontation when one of the two monks travelling with Pizarro had approached the Inca King, who was carried on a magnificent feathered litter, and handed him a Bible saying it was the 'word of God'. Atahualpa, who, like the rest of the Incas, knew nothing of the concept of writing, held the book to his ear and, hearing nothing, threw it to the ground.

Then Pizarro gave the Spanish war cry 'Santiago!' Guns thundered, bugles blew, horses charged, swords slashed. The terrified Incas attempted to flee. The Spaniards pursued them and many hundreds, probably thousands as the Spaniards claimed, died. But in that one infamous and treacherous engagement, Pizarro had won the empire. The Inca Lord was captured.

At 4.30 a.m. we were up, showering, shaving, etc., so as to be ready to leave by collectivo at 5.00 a.m. for Cajamarca. It was a 190-kilometre diversion from our route down the main north/south coastal road, but we felt it would be well worth the effort. Driving parallel to the coast for the first sixty-odd kilometres, we were in absolute darkness. The landscape was flat and featureless all around us, so that when an occasional bus or truck approached from the opposite direction the glow of headlights could be seen at such a great distance that it almost looked like a sunrise, and when they were past us and gone it was as if we were travelling alone and in space, so dark and empty was the land. But then, even when the *real* sunrise came, it was quite weird ... like no other sunrise I have ever seen. A soft, electric-blue light slowly suffused the desert. No brilliant reds or oranges ... just a gradual but crystal-clear lightening of the eastern sky beyond the mountains.

As we headed inland, at first we were passing giant sand-mountains and then, quite suddenly, as we entered the valley of the Jecutepec River, there was greenery about us. We began to climb, slowly at first, then steeply, around hairpin bends, then levelling off for a while, then winding again along precipitous walls with what appeared to be crumbling sides. There was ample evidence of various slippages and landslides all along the way.

We passed tiny villages and settlements from time to time. Generally they were small farming communities which had terraced and cultivated the steep valley walls, in some places, almost to the top. We stopped for breakfast at one small village and had orange juice, fried eggs, fried bananas and coffee. The bill for the four of us totalled 240 soles (about US$1.70).

The scenery, as we continued the climb, became more and more spectacular, with sides of the valley showing evidence of tremendous geological turmoil; great strata of different rock formations broken and turned on their sides and then exposed by the tumultuous shifting of entire mountains. The road was no longer properly surfaced and the rain had made it dangerously wet and slippery.

At just over 3000 metres we crossed the pass and began the long descent into the valley of Cajamarca. Thirty-two kilometres from the town, while traversing a steeply-walled cliff-face, we came to a huge landslide which had covered and closed the road. A long queue of buses and trucks had been waiting for several hours for a bulldozer to arrive, on the other side of the slip, from Cajamarca, to clear a route through. With unexpected good luck, one arrived within about ten minutes of our arrival at the site and fifteen minutes later we were on our way, arriving in Cajamarca not long after.

When Pizarro had captured Atahualpa, the Inca was able to rule his Empire for almost eight months from what was in fact a prison. Pizarro held him captive in Cajamarca while the greatest ransom in history was assembled to secure his release. To his millions of far-flung subjects, Atahualpa, like all Incas before him, was God ... the Son of the Sun ... and his word was law. So when he offered to collect for the Spaniards enough treasure to fill a room six and a half metres long by five metres wide to the height of his upstretched hand, once with gold and twice with silver, his subjects obeyed his call.

Throughout the Empire vast quantities of Inca gold and silver were collected; idols, necklaces, breastplates, crowns, chalices, plates and even full-size replicas of plants and animals, beautifully and intricately wrought in gold and silver by master craftsmen, were assembled and sent on their way to Cajamarca. Over the months an exquisite treasure was brought from the four corners of the Inca kingdom, over hundreds, in some cases thousands, of kilometres to Cajamarca.

The room, the 'Quarto de Rescarte', or ransom chamber, was finally filled to the appointed level with gold ... then with silver. There were twenty-four tonnes of gold alone! At 1979 prices for gold bullion, some three hundred and thirty million dollars worth!

As the Spaniards came to realise that they would never be able to carry it all out in its original form, they built nine huge forges, which worked for months to melt down the priceless works of art into crude metal ingots. Each horseman was allotted 40 kilos of gold and 80 kilos of silver. At 1979 prices that would represent about $575,000 in gold and $40,000 in silver for each rider. The foot-soldiers' allotment was exactly half, because that was all they could conceivably carry anyway.

The honourable and thankful Pizarro then put Atahualpa on trial on a charge of treason ... treason against the invaders of his own land ... Atahualpa was found guilty ... and garrotted.

Cajamarca is now a beautiful little city of some 35,000 people. It is very Spanish in physical appearance. There is the town plaza (the same in which Atahualpa was ambushed, although of course the original buildings have gone); there are cathedrals and churches and the warm sulphurous, thermal springs known as 'Los Banos del Inca' and, less than a hundred metres from the main square, one of the few remaining relics of Cajamarca's period of infamy, the 'Quarto de Rescarte'.

For a small fee, we entered the stone room and stood for a while pondering the huge treasure which had once filled it. But even being right there, on the spot, it stretched our imagination, trying to picture it.

We sat on the Emperor's stone chair on the hill above the town and wandered about for another couple of hours before taking off in another collectivo to retrace our route back to the coast again. Once there we turned south for a hot, dusty ride one hundred and twelve kilometres to Trujillo, a city of some 200,000 people (Peru's third largest), which was founded in 1536 by our friend, Francisco Pizarro.

A chapter of *Tom Sawyer* was a nightly ritual on which the children insisted no matter how long or tiring the day had been. Perhaps it gave them a sense of continuity in the midst of constant change. We too found it a calm ending to busy days and, as we had been up since 4.30, the book was hardly closed before we were all in deep dream-filled sleep. I find that I dream far more vividly when we are travelling, probably because my mind has to sift through so many new experiences.

We were jarred awake by the terrible, piercing ring of the bedside telephone. It was dark and my first thought was that it was already the morning of April 1st and that this was some lunatic's bad joke. But it was only 11.00 p.m. and when Iain replaced the receiver, he muttered, 'It was the girl on the desk offering to show us around the ruins,' and was instantly asleep again.

Early next morning the girl, Therese, became a reality and so too did the ruins, the vast and eerie remains at Chan Chan a few kilometres outside Trujillo.

The story of the Spanish destruction of the Inca Empire is so poignant and dramatic, so redolent of fate, greed and the lust for power that it often eclipses the lively history of all those people who had settled the area long before their arrival.

Ten thousand years ago, shortly after the retreat of the last great ice age, adventurous travellers from Asia had crossed the Bering Straits to Alaska and settled the whole of North America and South America down the entire length of the Andes. Evidence has been found of complex, well-developed civilisations existing on this stretch of the coast as far back as four thousand years ago.

There are also very convincing theories, developed by Thor Heyerdahl through the incredible voyages of his reed boats, *Ra I* and *Ra II* across the Atlantic and *Tigris* across the Indian Ocean, that South America was reached and settled by people from the civilisations of ancient Egypt and Sumeria. His ideas are given weight by the amazing similarities between the pottery and stonework of the pre-Columbian American peoples and that of Middle Eastern societies of several thousand years ago. He also makes the point that the pyramids of ancient Egypt and the Ziggurats of Iraq, Iran and the Indus Valley are almost identical in design and construction to the gigantic pyramids of the Toltecs, the Mayas and the Aztecs in Central America.

As it happened, while we were travelling down through Peru and visiting the ruins of Chan Chan, Heyerdahl was nearing the end of his long journey on *Tigris* which took him and his crew down the Euphrates River, the Persian Gulf and across the Arabian Sea to Djibouti at the entrance to the Red Sea.

Chan Chan was built by the Chimu, whose empire lasted from 1000 AD to 1500 AD and stretched for nine hundred and sixty kilometres along the coast from Ecuador almost to Lima. The ruins are now only a huge adobe skeleton in one of the driest and bleakest regions of the world.

As we approached the seven and a half metre high mud walls, a black-haired mongrel puppy hurled himself at us, delighted to have early morning playmates.

'Down. Down, Mochica-Chimu!' Therese ordered and was totally ignored. Zara and Sean were as happy as the puppy and, as they fell to cuddling him, asked, 'What did you say his name is?'

'Mochica-Chimu,' Therese explained. 'The Mochica people were here from around 400 to 800 AD. Then came the Chimu. So you see, Mochica-Chimu!'

The puppy, unfettered by his name, galloped ahead along the crumbling lower mud walls and then, executing a tight turn, came charging back, wagging his tail madly and prancing about in front of us hoping to start a game of tag.

Inside the enclosing wall were more and more walls, stretching off in what appeared at first to be a complicated jumble, until the eye began to make some shape of them. They make up nine walled compounds each containing storerooms, audience chambers and the crumbled remains of a platform mound, each the tomb of a Chimu king.

Revered by their subjects as god kings, these men had wealth enough to rival Egypt's pharaohs. When Pizarro arrived he found a doorway in the city slabbed with silver worth half a million dollars in today's currency. Convinced by the sight of the door that there must be more to be unearthed, the Spaniards went to the incredible lengths of diverting the Moche River, so as to wash away a huge mud brick ancient pyramid. The loot they netted from it would now be worth at least $10 million!

But before being too scandalised by the Spaniards' behaviour it is well to realise that what they ravaged was also a brutal, elitist society. Only the king and his courtiers lived inside the spacious splendour of the walled city. His 50,000 subjects, little better off than slaves, were confined in cramped conditions beyond, out of sight and out of mind, as long as they did not break the harsh laws. Thievery was a capital offence. Disrespect to any shrine resulted in being buried alive. Adulterers were flung to their death from high cliffs. And if a herbalist's patient did not respond to his treatment, then the physician was stoned or beaten to death.

When a king died, no sacrifice of wealth or human life was too great to ensure his return to the gods and a comfortable life in the hereafter. In one of the royal tombs archaeologists unearthed the neatly stacked skeletons of at least three hundred sacrificial victims, all of them young females. Sealed in with his wealth and his slaves, the king's former palace became a tomb and shrine so the new king had to have another adjacent high-walled domain of his own built by an army of workers.

Mochica-Chimu continued her game. She would race ahead and bound back with the children in hot pursuit, or play hide and seek though the maze of walls, appearing unexpectedly in the narrow doorways barking with pleasure at our expressions of surprise.

Therese, an attractive young woman, squeezed into jeans and a revealing shirt, addressed all her commentary and information to me. Being a fellow woman (if you see what I mean) I realised that she was doing this in her anxiety to let me know that she was not chatting up Iain. I kept trying, in those devious ways by which women communicate with one another, to let her know that I didn't feel threatened, but it was really rather an amusing situation because Iain, as so often happens, was blissfully unaware of the undercurrents. He kept calling Therese across to point out some archaeological detail and ask its meaning, whereupon she would walk back and give me the information!

We were the only visitors to Chan Chan that morning and, as we walked through the ruins under an absolutely cloudless light-blue sky, the ageless silence was broken only by the constant, soporific roar of the sea wearing away at the beach less than eight hundred metres away.

We stopped beside a wall to marvel over the lively stylistic representations of a boat-load of men about to catch a large fish which, in turn was about to swallow a squid. The design was repeated over and over again along the wall's entire length. Digging at the site has brought to light blackware pottery and delicate weaving both bearing the same easily recognisable designs.

By the crumbling corner of one courtyard we saw the remains of a huge walk-in well. It was the Chimus' astonishingly well-engineered irrigation system, which tapped the Moche River, that made it possible for them to build a city as large and magnificent as Chan Chan in an area which receives less than two centimetres of rain a year. One of their canals snakes for eighty kilometres through barren sand dunes.

Today's farmers still use some of these waterways to irrigate their fields and despite the fact that Chan Chan is an historic site ostensibly protected by the government, more than a third of the area has been ploughed under by local farmers.

What is amazing is that despite the continuous plundering which has gone on since the Incas overran the Chimu Empire in 1470 and the Spaniards continued the destruction shortly after, there are still so many of its buildings left. The Incas, who were sun-worshippers, borrowed heavily from the moon-worshipping Chimu culture, incorporating many of their legends and skills into their own. They took master craftsmen back with them to Cuzco to enhance their own capital. It was left to the Spaniards to physically ravage the city of Chan Chan. This pillaging has continued right up to the present day when many local men, farmers by day, turn grave robbers at night and dig haphazardly and therefore destructively, in the ruins in the hope of finding instant wealth.

The only digging we saw was being carried out with meticulous care by a man working with a small trowel and soft brush. Obviously an official employee or an archaeologist, he peered with disapproval at us and most especially at Mochica-Chimu who showered him with dust as she continued with her mad antics.

When we left, Therese would not accept more than the government set fee of $1.50 and when we asked her how many visitors there usually are in a day, she told us, 'perhaps ten and perhaps only one. There are three other guides and we must all take our turns. I doubt if today I will have any more people. That is why at night I work at the desk in the hotel.'

And that is why, during the bus trip to Lima that afternoon, I made sure to put her name down in my notes so that when you go to Chan Chan, you will know to ask for Therese at the Hotel San Martin. And please don't forget to give Mochica-Chimu a cuddle for Zara and Sean.

On the eastern side of the Plaza de Armas in Lima is the city's large and magnificent cathedral. It contains silver altars, superbly carved cedar wood stalls and a beautiful seventeenth century choir loft. But probably the most intriguing sight the cathedral has to offer is in a small chapel just to the right of the entrance. A marble coffin with a glass window running along its entire length displays the shrivelled and dehydrated remains of Lima's founder, the conqueror of Peru, the one-time Viceroy of all Spain's South American possessions, Captain General Francisco Pizarro.

After the murder of Atahualpa, Pizarro, at the head of an army of newly arrived Conquistadore reinforcements, set about subjugating the rest of the

Incan empire. It was a task he never lived to see fulfilled. While conducting his war against the Incas, he founded the city of Lima on the coast in January 1535 and began the construction there of a grand capital, which he dubbed the 'City of Kings'.

Despite his and the other Conquistadores' attempts to surround themselves with the trappings of civilisation and religion, the Spanish soldiers were no better than cruel and ruthless barbarians. They were greedy, deceitful, treacherous and violent in the extreme, and there were constant bickering and struggles for power among them.

In 1538 one of Pizarro's original Conquistadores, Diego de Almagro, was put to death after he had tried to turn some of Pizarro's army against him. De Almagro's attempted coup was the first in South America, but not the last. In fact it set a pattern that has been repeated over the years *ad nauseam.* Although de Almagro had failed to topple Pizarro, and died for his pains, within three years his son had gained revenge. He stabbed Pizarro to death in his own palace just across Lima's Plaza de Armas from the cathedral whose foundation stone he had carefully laid and which now holds his mummified body.

'Yuk!' was about the only response the crumbling remains of the illustrious Conquistadore drew from Zara and Sean. And I had to agree. They were rather ghastly. Bits of bone poking through worm-eaten, dry skin; the skull, with tatty pieces of hair hanging from it, is held together with pieces of wire. The mighty Pizarro!

What is interesting about Pizarro's chapel though is the fact that it is lavishly decorated in gold and blue and carries a huge replica of the Conquistadore's grandiose crest and a mural depicting an armour-clad, heroic Pizarro leading the conquest of Peru. We found the glorification of the Conquistadore in stark contrast to the vilification heaped by Mexicans on Cortes, Pizarro's equivalent there in the conquest of the Mayan and Aztec empires. Nowhere in Mexico City was there to be found any tribute to or glorification of the Conquistadore who brought Western culture and religion to Mexico.

In the wake of Pizarro, Lima grew to be, for many years, the greatest city in the Americas. From its founding in 1535, until the South American republics won their independence in the early nineteenth century, Lima was the capital of all Spanish South America. The Vice-Royalty of Peru, as it was called, situated in Lima, embraced Colombia, Ecuador, Bolivia, Peru, Chile and Argentina. There were few cities in the New World which could compete with Lima as it was then. It was a remarkably rich and beautiful city with fine colonial buildings and houses, parks and open plazas.

Much of the old charm remains today ... particularly in the central district, even though Lima, as the fifth largest city in South America, after Sao Paulo, Rio de Janeiro, Buenos Aires and Santiago, now has a population of around three and a half million and more than its share of dismal shanty towns on its outskirts. In the business district, there are tall skyscrapers and modern hotels, but fortunately, the major old buildings of the colonial era are still there ... many of them truly magnificent. On the facade of the Archbishop's Palace, on the Plaza de Armas, for instance, are what must be amongst the most beautiful carved wooden balconies to be found anywhere in the world.

For anyone remotely interested in the bizarre, Lima has a lot to offer. And as ten and eleven-year-old children invariably fall into that category, we managed to see some of the city's more esoteric and unusual sights. Probably the most odd was in the Church of San Francisco, about two blocks from the Plaza de Armas. We visited the church on a Sunday morning on our first day in the capital while mass was being held. But we heard the booming sounds of the organ and the raised voices of the choir and congregation not in the great tiled nave of the church, but from the grim, dark catacombs immediately beneath it. In these winding, dusty passages are collected the skulls and bones of some forty thousand people.

Apparently there's nothing very unusual about them being there. They are simply the remains of former members of the congregation of the Church of San Francisco who, upon their death, were kept in the catacombs instead of being buried, a practice widely followed in the early days of Lima. But the truly bizarre feature of these catacombs is that the bones of this vast horde of past parishioners are not left as individual skeletons, but collected up as thousands of separate tibias, femurs, clavicles, ulna, pelvises, skulls, etc. and are all neatly stacked in their own categories in great brick bins.

Obviously at some stage someone had been around, either breaking up skeletons, or picking up the pieces as they fell apart to put them all into their various huge piles. There were many other bins containing only jumbled mixtures of thousands of broken skulls and pieces of bone. There was no smell . . . only a general air of mustiness. Sean and Zara, who had at first been a little in awe and speaking in whispers, soon lost what fear they may have had and began picking up skulls and bones to examine them. It's rather difficult to feel reverence for the dead when they are spread around in such a way.

The exhibits were only dimly lit by an occasional electric bulb, so from time to time, as we moved quietly through the honeycomb of brick-walled passages, we were in semi-darkness. For some reason, we spoke only in whispers until suddenly Sean, who was slightly ahead of us, yelled, 'Dad, Mum . . . come quickly . . . look!'

He was leaning over a deep, circular, brick-lined pit which contained the pièce de résistance of the catacombs. At the bottom of the pit, bones and skulls were arrayed in decorative style in a circle; skulls in the centre, then a ring of thigh-bones like the spokes of a wheel, then a ring of skulls, then upper arm bones radiating out, then more skulls, and so on . . . hundreds of skulls, thousands of bones. I felt sure the souls of the past owners would be happy to know that their bones were so decoratively arrayed.

We had only planned to spend a few days in Lima before heading towards Cuzco, the former Inca capital, about 950 kilometres to the south-east in the mountains, but we found Lima such an agreeable place to be that we knew, right from the start, that it would be difficult to get moving . . . there was so much more that we wanted to see and do.

We were fortunate to have discovered a great little hotel . . . a single-storey building about two blocks west of the Plaza de Armas; the 'Residencial Roma' on Ica Street. It was clean and quiet and our one bedroom, with four beds and bathroom and toilet attached, cost only US$6.00 a night for us all.

But while we may have gained some pleasure in finding such cheap accommodation, it was dimmed considerably by the cost of having our laundry done. Trish had taken on the role of washing out the small things, socks, underpants, handkerchiefs, T-shirts and so on, each night where possible, but heavier things, like jeans, had to wait until we were somewhere where we would have time to get them dry before moving on. Either that, or put them into a laundromat. Laundromat?! What's that? They are so rare in Central and South America that no one knows what you're talking about if you ask for one.

But we found one in Lima ... or so we thought, until they told us it was not self-service. We had to leave our washing with them, to be collected later. Foolishly we didn't ask for a detailed and itemised costing before we left, so glad were we to be able to dump our washing on someone else. I think we also felt that, as everything else in Peru had been so cheap ... the washing would be too.

When we came back to collect it the next day, we found to our horror that our laundry, which would have cost no more than $2.00 to wash and dry in an Australian or an American laundromat, cost 1,560 soles ... US$12.00!

One of the first things we did in Lima was to phone back to Canada to find out how my Dad was doing. We had picked up our mail from American Express. Thank God for friends. There were wonderful words of support in reply to my written outbursts of blackness. But there was no news from my family, although we reasoned that this was probably because of the pressure of the situation.

The scene in the central telephone office for international calls in Lima is about what you'd expect. Jostling crowds of people accosting harassed clerks, raised voices, distorted loudspeaker messages and a general air of chaos from which I was resigned to accept that no order could possibly be made.

When, after over an hour of waiting, a clerk, gesticulating wildly, indicated that I should enter a glass booth, the last piece of this puzzle of insanity slotted into place. Through the sound-proofed walls I could see, but not hear, the crowd continuing its antics only now they appeared like a silent movie. From the phone I heard the strained tones of my sister's voice coming from the peaceful emptiness of her comfortable Canadian lounge room. She told me that Dad was home and that while the end still seemed close and inevitable, in his determination not to give in he was doing remarkably well and that the message from him urged us to continue with the journey.

Another priority in Lima was to buy some anti-histamine for Zara, who had been awake on and off for most of the previous night coughing, wheezing and finding frightening difficulty in breathing. The attack had come on suddenly and for several hours we anxiously discussed what the cause could be and whether we should take her to a doctor.

White-faced with the air rasping in her chest, she sat up in bed clutching a little toy llama which she had bought from a street stall that morning. That was it! In a flash of realisation we understood the reason for the speed of this unexpected attack. The llama. I almost snatched it from her arms. Made from vicuna wool, the stuffed toy was silky soft and Zara, who never does anything by halves, had throughout the day continually snuggled up to it, as she does with any and all compliant beasties, with quite often the same allergic result.

The anti-histamine helped immediately but Zara would not be parted from her llama. She did, however, take the precaution of swaddling him in a little cotton blanket before propping him on her shoulder from which vantage point he kept up his end of their conversation while she wrote her diary and added to her growing novel.

While we were in the pharmacy we took the opportunity to buy the local remedy for altitude sickness in anticipation of our coming visit to Cuzco and Machu Picchu and some more quinine, the anti-malarial precaution which we had been taking since entering Central America. We were also given the address of a clinic where we could have another shot of gammaglobulin. Thus re-equipped, we took a cross-town bus through the usual mindless jumble of inner city suburbs to the Museum of Anthropology which we had been told was the best museum in town.

It had been quite fascinating during our trip southward through Central America to watch the children begin to grope with knowledge they had acquired through observation and osmosis and to sift it into a graspable intellectual cohesion. Many of the national museums we had visited in various cities had graphs, diagrams or three dimensional models to illustrate the evolution of human society and where various cultures fitted into the sweep of history. And these exhibits invariably made the story much clearer for the children.

'I see,' Zara breathed in excited recognition, as she followed the coloured bands showing Asian migration marching from Asia, across the Bering Straits and down the west coast of North and South America, dropping off little groups of settlers as it went.

Beside each group were examples of primitive weapons, jewellery and cooking utensils. Very early on in the centuries these utensils had become works of art and the museum had hundreds of examples of this Indian pottery. Made in the shapes of birds, animals, plants or human beings, they were glazed black or dark brown and decorated with red designs, all showing great vitality and humour and some of them quite open sexuality. There were examples from Chan Chan, where we had just been and Nazca, where we were going, as well as from even earlier cultures. Almost all were pre-Inca because the Spaniards had so resolutely destroyed Inca artifacts.

Some of those which had survived we saw downstairs in a large walk-in vault guarded by an armed fellow in uniform. These were some of the gold treasures which escaped being melted down. Finely beaten tunics, elegant vases and magnificent jewellery, all of it so beautifully crafted they made us ache over the terrible loss the world has suffered in the destruction of the rest.

Sean, who was naturally very impressed with being inside a safe, was even more delighted with what he found upstairs again on our way out.

'Oooh!' he pressed his nose against the glass, 'just look at that!' The skeleton lay still wrapped in a fine red cotton cloak heavily embroidered with multi-coloured wools and on its skull there was a feather trimmed turban. It had been found near Nazca where it had been buried around 2000 years ago. The flesh had shrivelled away, but the dry desert sands had acted as a perfect preservative of the rich clothing.

On the bus back across town, a boy of probably the same age as Sean, wearing a torn T-shirt and shorts, barefoot and grubby, came aboard and, standing in the centre of the aisle, burst into song. He kept up his mournful dirge, which I supposed to be a folk song, for at least five minutes, staring straight ahead, from under his heavy black fringe, with no display of any emotion, which only made his performance all the more passionate. Zara and Sean watched in silence. When he had finished he walked to each seat with his hand out. Almost every passenger gave him a little money and, as he stepped down, the conductor smiled at him, ruffled his hair and added his bit.

When we stopped in the centre of town, Iain suggested an afternoon tea at the Hotel Bolivar. This was more than a little up-market for us but though we were surprised at such extravagance, we all gladly agreed. The attractive old hotel is in the same elegant tradition as the late and lamented Shepherds in Cairo and the Raffles in Singapore. It is studded with faithful retainer types in black trousers and short white jackets who linger discreetly behind the potted palms and appear only when wanted, to attend silently and swiftly to one's every need.

We ordered tea, soft drinks and cakes which came served with forks and napkins on fine plates and we ate at the edge of the main lounge under a multi-coloured glass domed roof. Iain insisted on taking a photograph of us which we thought odd and odder still when he asked the waiter for a brochure about the hotel's facilities.

'We're not thinking of staying here, are we?' Sean was agog at the impossibility of such an idea.

Iain smiled and shook his head, 'No, not us,' and then I realised.

'Aah! It's Joe who is going to stay here. Yes?'

Iain nodded.

'Who's this Joe?' Sean demanded, suspicious that we were hoarding a secret friend. 'Do we know a Joe here?'

'Not very well, yet,' I agreed and Iain laughed. 'But we surely will!'

'Tell us. Aw, come on . . .' the children insisted.

'He's a man Dad just met,' I explained. 'He's looking for a secret horde of Inca gold!'

'Ooooh!' Sean's eyes widened.

'Oh, no!' Zara gave one of her crushing sighs, together with a withering look. 'He's in your next book. Right?'

We nodded.

'You mean he's not real!' Sean was disappointed.

Zara shook her head, and with a deprecating grimace, dismissed poor Joe.

Sean swallowed the remains of his second cake. 'What I want to know,' he said with his mouth full, 'is why this Joe gets to stay in the Hotel Bolivar when we don't.'

Peru, unfortunately, despite its outstanding attractions and its fascinations to any visitor, is politically similar to its other Latin American neighbours. Military coups d'état and occasional wars and assassinations have regularly punctuated the Peruvian political scene ever since it won its independence from Spain in the war of 1820 — 1824.

The country owes its independence to three of the most famous generals of the South American liberation armies: General Jose de San Martin, who landed in southern Peru and proclaimed independence on July 28th, 1821, General Simon Bolivar, who defeated the army of the Spanish Viceroy, La Serna, at

Junin in August 1824, and General Antonio Jose de Sucre who, in the decisive battle of Ayacucho in December, 1824, finally put an end to Spanish domination on the South American continent. None of these great generals, however, was a Peruvian. Bolivar was Venezuelan, Sucre was Ecuadorean and San Martin was Argentinian. What is even more unfortunate is that Peruvian generals seem to have been trying to make up for that apparent lack of involvement ever since. There have only been the briefest periods since the liberation in which Peru's political life has not been dominated or dictated by the military.

For the past dozen years Peru has been governed by a military junta which seized power in 1968. Composed of the president (since 1975, General Morales Bermudez) and the commanders of the three armed forces, the junta has ruled by national decree. Both houses of the congress were disbanded in 1968 and all political parties denied any role in the government.

Looking back over the administrations of past military rulers, it is difficult to deny that, in some instances, genuine attempts at good government have been made by them and that, in certain respects, direct power methods have often proved more effective in bringing about necessary reforms, than party platforms.

Under the rule of General Manuel Odria in the 1950s for instance, the Peruvian economy flourished, foreign trade prospered and agriculture, industry and education were stimulated by modernising measures. Under General Juan Velasco, who was the first president after the coup of 1968, long-awaited land reforms were announced. He introduced the so-called 'Inca Plan' under which Peruvian society was to be reorganised into state-owned, worker-owned, or joint owner-worker-owned enterprises.

But in the latter part of the seventies scandals and allegations of widespread corruption in the armed forces led to civilian cynicism and distrust of the military on an unprecedented level. The effects of this were so apparent throughout Peru that the military government introduced new legislation making it a criminal offence to be tried by court martial and punishable by imprisonment for a civilian to insult or offend in public, any member of the armed forces.

The move did little more than unite the entire political spectrum *against* the military government.

At the stroke of noon a sequence of shouted commands and then the sound of marching feet was heard. We all pressed closer to the thick, vertical bars of the high iron fence in order to get a better look. From tall archways on either side of the gleaming white presidential palace building facing onto the Plaza de Armas, soldiers dressed in high black boots, scarlet pants, white tunics and glittering brass firemen's helmets topped by red tassles, goose-stepped out onto the parade ground.

The changing of the guard at the presidential palace is a regular midday ceremony in Lima and small crowds of tourists gather every noon to watch and photograph the brief proceedings.

'Jeez, they look like bloody Nazis, marching like that!'

At the sound of the broad Australian accent behind us, I turned to identify its source. A short, bald man in his mid-fifties had spoken without removing his eyes from a movie camera, which kept whirring away.

'More like little tin soldiers, I reckon,' said his companion, a tall, thin man of about the same age. 'I'll betcha they couldn't fight their way out of a wet paper bag.' They both laughed.

'Oh, Tom,' a woman, who was clearly the tall man's wife, said, 'don't be so nasty. I think they look really nice.'

The soldiers completed their marching manoeuvre and lined up to take a salute from a senior army officer on the steps of the palace.

'Watch out for these bloody jokers behind us,' the little bald man said to us, and anybody else who cared to take his advice. He inclined his head towards two or three Peruvians who were standing at the rear of the group of tourists, who were all intently watching the events on the parade ground. 'They're all flamin' pickpockets, so our guide told us. Just keep your hands on your wallets . . . and your cameras.'

His advice was probably accurate. We had also heard that the changing of the guard was a favourite haunt for pickpockets and the characters behind us certainly didn't look as if they were mightily interested in the activities on the parade ground. They seemed more than a little shifty. But with everyone suspicious of them, it would have been exceedingly difficult for them to have tried anything.

As the ceremony finished and the crowd began to move back from the fence, I overheard a conversation. The little bald man was talking to a Peruvian, who obviously did not speak English well, but was trying hard.

'Where you come from?' he asked the Australian.

''Strailyer,' was the reply.

'I am sorry. I do not understand.'

'Oztrailyer,' the little bald man said, apparently amazed that the other man did not know what he was talking about. 'Oztrailyer,' he said again and he flapped his hands, like wings . . . 'you know . . . fifteen hours . . . long way . . . Oztrailyer.'

The poor Peruvian said nothing. He smiled and moved on, shaking his head.

'Iain? Iain Finlay?' another voice said from amongst the group of tourists, and almost immediately I recognised a face I had not seen for probably twenty-five years. I had known Brian Westmore in Melbourne when I was about 18, but, after moving away from Melbourne, I hadn't seen him again, until this moment.

Brian had become a successful dentist (are there any that aren't?) and he and his wife, Joy, a television actress, were on a six-week flying tour of South America. We sat with them outside the very pleasant Haiti Cafe, an outdoor restaurant just off the Plaza, and talked for an hour or so before they had to leave to catch a plane. It was good to meet up with people from home and to speak English for a while. They were interested in how we managed to travel with our children as they had left their four at home.

'Do you want to see my cry-case?' Joy asked pulling out a concertinaed wallet of photographs. As we all looked at the smiling teenage faces, Joy said how much she missed them.

'I get this out every night and have a little weep,' she said, 'and wish that they were sharing all this with us.'

But when Brian and Joy talked of the places they had already been to and were going to, after Lima, we couldn't help feeling twinges of envy at the ease with which they would accomplish it all, travelling on their own and by air. Our methods of ground transportation involving four people seemed so long-winded and difficult by comparison.

But then, they kept saying how envious they were of us and the way *we* were doing it, so we felt a little better. There had been several times when we had felt that we must be crazy to do it the way we were, and the occasional word of encouragement, like those from our meeting with Brian and Joy Westmore, were very welcome.

Pizarro's shrivelled remains and the neatly stacked bones of 40,000 people in the catacombs were neck and neck (pardon me!) contenders for first place on Sean's list of Lima attractions. That was until we found the Museum of the Inquisition, after which they were relegated to the position of very poor also-rans.

The infamous Spanish Inquisition was, for some reason, able to extend the sphere of its horrific activities from Spain to Lima, where it conducted its nasty inquiries, inhuman tortures and brutal murders in the Palace of the Inquisition! This large house which, during over two hundred years of terror, witnessed the aberrant acts of minds brutalised by religious fanaticism, is not the sort of museum which I would visit from choice. But travelling in a group demands a great deal of give and take and as Sean was quick to point out, 'I've been to all the museums and churches you wanted to visit, so now you should come to the one I want to see.' Fair enough.

The large room off the main entrance to the building has been preserved intact; the quite magnificent carved wooden ceiling, an equally beautiful large table and behind it, high backed chairs, the apogee of Jacobean skills ... beautiful artistic products of an age which ironically also produced minds so warped and terrible as to be beyond our mental grasp.

Sitting in those very same chairs, men stared stony-faced across that table at their fellow human beings and, god-like, judged them, condemning thousands to horrifying tortures and eventual merciful death.

On the right is the heavy door with an eye slit through which the accused were peered at by witnesses whose identity was never revealed. Very often they were not even told with what specific crimes they were charged.

On the left, rooms led off, one after another, each surpassing the previous in its horrors. Men being literally torn apart on the rack, roasted over open fires, hung interminably by their hands or feet, blinded, maimed, or branded, crushed under heavy planking, or merely shut up in cages too small to even kneel in and starved to death. They were beaten, bruised and bashed in the name of God and I felt sick.

The fact that they were all made of plaster of paris and not flesh and blood, as were those they represented, did little to alleviate the horror. Zara and I were very quiet while Sean asked question after question about when and why and Iain tried to answer. The thick stone walls were damp and the musty smell made me gag. On one end wall scores of names, dates and messages had been scratched by former prisoners of this chamber of horrors.

How is it that even in such circumstances men and women find reassurance in seeing their name? Can they still care whether people will come after and, seeing these memorials, remember their martyrdom?

The single engine of the little Cessna 584 roars as the pilot moves the throttle and continues carefully through his checklist. It's all very quick and simple and, sitting beside him, I feel, for the umpteenth time in my life that I would like to learn to fly and annoyed with myself that I have never gotten around to it. As we begin to move, I turn around to look at Trish and the children who are crammed into the two rear seats. Their faces are alive with excitement.

The plane bounces over the stony desert runway, then lifts, wavering slightly in the hot updrafts of air, climbing, then turning north. Immediately we can see the starkness of the contrast between the green oasis of irrigated land we are leaving below and behind us, and the arid desert to our front. On our right a barren mountain range rises abruptly out of the flat desert floor. It had been swelteringly hot on the ground, but now, with a little altitude and some air coming into the cabin, we feel much cooler.

'There,' the pilot says after we are only a few minutes in the air. He banks the aircraft slightly and points down . . . 'That is the whale.'

Looking out of the window of the plane, we see, marked out on the desert, the huge figure of a fish. A few minutes later we are over a weird set of triangles, then a strange human figure with a round head and big circular eyes. Then, several kilometres further on, a giant pair of hands and the design of a tree, all of them laid out in huge proportions on the desert sand.

'You see that line?' the pilot points. The desert below is now patterned with an incredible geometrical melange of triangles, trapezoids, quadrangles and lines. But the one the pilot is pointing to stands out from the rest, because it continues, straight as a die, never deviating from its course, up a hill, down a valley and up another hill into the distance. 'That one runs for nearly eight kilometres . . . absolutely straight,' he says.

These are the famous lines of Nazca and they are everything that we had expected; probably the strangest messages ever left by ancient man. Drawn in large pebbles and stones across the desert wastes of the coastal strip near the tiny town of Nazca in southern Peru, these lines, and a veritable zoo of giant birds, reptiles, monkeys, spiders and other creatures represent one of the world's great mysteries.

The markings were laid down, over some 500 square kilometres of desert, by the Nazca Indians roughly 1500 years ago . . . long before man could fly . . . and yet the lines and the figures can only be properly seen from heights of over 300 metres above the ground! Why would the Nazcas create these immense designs that even they could never see in their entirety?

This is the question that has puzzled scientists and archaeologists ever since the lines were first recognised from the air in the late 1920s. Before that, although people knew they existed, it was impossible to know what they were, or to appreciate the extent and complexity of the designs.

Until recent years no one ever visited the markings. No one, that is, except Maria Reiche. For more than a quarter of a century this lone German woman was the only person seriously interested in the phenomena at Nazca.

We had read of her studies and seen photographs of the lines and decided that, on our way to Lake Titicaca, Cuzco and Machu Picchu, we should include a visit to Nazca. We had travelled by bus down the coast road from Lima . . .

another extraordinary journey through extremely inhospitable desert country; sea on one side, for most of the way, and craggy, dry mountains on the other. Fortunately, the road was well surfaced and we travelled fast. We did not, however, arrive in Nazca until well after darkness fell and we had experienced a frightening drive through narrow passes, steep ravines and gorges.

At the tiny, white-painted Hotel Nazca, where we took two clean and comfortable rooms for US$6.00, we were told more about the famous lines by the owner of the hotel. He looked more like a retired professor or an amateur archaeologist than a hotel proprietor . . . and he might well have been both, for his office was cluttered with antique pottery, shards, small stone carvings and charts of the region. It was he who convinced us that the only way to see the lines and figures properly was to hire a light plane.

As the cost was 9000 soles (US$68) for the four of us, we hesitated the next morning before heading out to the little desert airstrip run by Aero Condor. But it was a decison that could really only go one way, and once we were in the air there was no question that it was money well spent.

The lines and the animal figures are quite awe-inspiring. Most of the figures are composed of a single line of small stones which, though it may follow a complicated and circuitous route, never crosses itself. A 180 metre-long crocodile, a 136 metre seabird, a monkey whose left hand alone measures more than 12 metres across and lines, lines, lines, straight as an arrow . . . everywhere.

'It is,' according to mathematician Maria Reiche, 'the most important astronomical monument in Peru . . . and perhaps the world.'

Maria Reiche, now seventy-seven years old, has spent half of her life trying to unravel the enigma of the lines. In her tiny, cluttered room in the Hotel Turistica in Nazca (provided for her at no charge by the government-run hotel), she pored over her lighted drawing-board explaining to us her charts and maps of the lines. She wore a pair of broken tortoise-shell glasses, the bridge of which was held together by wire. Her sun-tanned face was deeply lined and leathery in testimony to the countless thousands of hours she has spent roaming around in the desert, brushing stones, measuring arcs and radii, pacing beside kilometre after kilometre of the lines and figures, mapping them . . . trying to understand them.

'It is all a scientific jewel,' she said in still heavily German-accented English, 'and yet nobody but me studies it. I see it as literally the largest astronomy book in the world.' She pointed to a figure. 'Here,' she said, 'did you see this from the plane this morning? Did you see the monkey?' She directed the question at Sean.

'Yes,' he replied.

'Well, this long arrow connected to the monkey pointed to the main star of the dipper . . . or the plough, in the year 900 of our era. And these lines here, are symmetrical to north/south, so they could have pointed to the star's setting place.'

She went on, her pale blue eyes bright, to describe more intricate and complex aspects of the lines' astronomical connections and functions.

'Do you give any credence to the theories of Erich von Danniken?' I asked, 'that the lines are in some way connected with visits, in ancient times, of creatures from other planets?'

She looked at me with a condescending smile. 'How can I respect the opinions of someone who simply doesn't know what he is talking about. That is all rubbish.'

Even so, Maria Reiche admits that she herself does not know all the answers to the mystery of Nazca . . . not quite.

'I'm almost a hundred percent sure I know it, but proving it to the world is another matter. There is still much to know. I am crazy to know all about it. That is what has driven me all these years . . . curiosity. It has been a marvellous adventure. And even now I am still curious.'

The lines and figures have remained almost unchanged for over a thousand years. The area around Nazca has been one of the driest on the globe, averaging about half an hour of light rain once every two or three years. But, according to Maria Reiche, the climate is changing . . . even since she's been there . . . and more rain is falling now, slowly eroding the desert markings. But the greatest destruction of the lines has come from man; the car tracks of curious visitors now criss-cross the lines and, in some places, have already obliterated them.

'Time is very important,' Maria Reiche said. 'I have tried to get regulations passed to protect the lines, but it is difficult and, when I am gone, I fear there will be no one else who will care enough. What I need to find is a young woman to carry on. A woman with a fanaticism like mine.'

PERU

15
The Lost City of the Incas

Sometimes I get tired just reading my notes on this trip! All the new people, places and all the constant movement. Almost every night my scribbles finish up, 'absolutely exhausted', 'tired beyond thinking', 'totally buggered'.

On our arrival in Arequipa they read, 'We all get immediately into one bed to keep each other warm! Sleep as if dead for three hours.'

Hardly surprising really, for we had gone straight to the small hotel, through the dark streets, after the bus had pulled into the deserted little terminal at four in the morning. We had just made a ten-hour overnight trip from Nazca firstly through more coastal desert, then, in the final stages, up into the Andes.

During the ride we had attempted to sleep on each other's shoulders or laps and at one point, when the number of passengers thinned out, Zara, Sean and Iain moved forward and each grabbed a double seat while I shared the larger back seat at the rear of the bus with two Quechua-speaking Indian girls who were both about ten years old. One of them had long, thick hair which I had cause to bless because, in my semi-conscious state, curled up against the unexpected cold, I registered that my feet were the warmest part of me and realised that the child had fallen asleep with her hair spread over them like a blanket.

Occasionally I would need to sit or stand up in order to stretch my cramped muscles and I would stare out of the window into the pitch blackness. There was no moon, but the sky was clear and stars twinkled harshly-bright through the crystalline atmosphere. But it was still a disconcerting view because the track was so narrow and winding and the fall away so precipitous, that several times I had the sensation of being suspended on a tightrope as I glimpsed the bobbing lights of a local fishing fleet a few hundred metres below us.

Arequipa, when we did surface in time for a large breakfast, turned out to be an attractive, rather elegant town. An ancient Inca settlement refounded by an emissary of Pizarro's in 1540, it is now the second city of Peru with a population of a quarter of a million, who guard their independence from the capital very jealously. It has the best collection of well-preserved colonial style buildings in the country, except for those in Cuzco, and many of them are exceptionally attractive because they are built of sillar, a pearly white volcanic material, which is abundantly available in the area.

The city itself, at a literally breathtaking 2400 metres above sea level, shelters at the foot of the 5700 metre volcano, El Misti. On either side there is the slightly higher Chachani, and the slightly lower, Pichu Pichu. All three volcanoes are capped with snow; beautifully threatening.

There is also the invisible, but nonetheless constant, threat of earthquakes. In 1958 and again in 1960 the town was severely damaged and it is noticeable that none of the churches have tall towers or spires and that the houses, which are mostly one-storey buildings, do not have the ornate but vulnerable balconies we had seen in profusion in Lima.

It was at breakfast, for which I ate a large plate of 'ceviche de corvina' (fish heavily seasoned with lemons, onions and hot peppers ... and it makes my mouth water just to write of it) that we met the Raymonds. Barry and Gloria and their two small sons came into the restaurant for a snack. We immediately recognised their Australian accents, even though, we were to find out, they had lived in Canada and not been home in fifteen years.

We commented on Arequipa being an attractive, quiet town and Barry laughed. 'You should have been here a couple of weeks ago. It wasn't so quiet then. The bus drivers were on strike. Other workers came out in support of them and that square,' he pointed to the large grassy park outside, 'was crammed with demonstrators, until the army came along with sub-machine guns and arrested dozens of them!'

We had heard a little of this industrial unrest in the south, but Barry explained some of the background to it. 'It's still going; on one day and off the next and basically it's over conditions of employment. There had been a law which stated that within the first three months after being taken on at a job, an employee could be dismissed without notice and with no redress. Bad enough. But then the government arbitrarily extended the period of three months to three *years* and all hell let loose. Rightly so.'

We talked more about employment problems in Peru and this naturally progressed into discussing similar issues as they affected Canada and Australia. Barry is a physiotherapist and Gloria runs their home one hundred and twenty kilometres north of Toronto in a very attractive area on Lake Simcoe.

'What are employment prospects like back home?' they wanted to know. 'It's not that there is any reason for us to leave Canada, we have everything going for us there, but, well, we'd like to see the beach again.'

We talked about Australia's industrial and union problems.

'Well I guess we'll just have to take our chances,' Barry laughed again. 'It can't be as crazy as this part of the world. You wouldn't believe the worries we've had trying to drive through here in our campervan. First off we had to get it in at Guayaquil port. What a scene that was. Everyone had warned us not to leave the van there overnight, or it would be completely vandalised, but by the time it was offloaded it was almost the end of the day. There was one other fellow and his wife shipping in a van and I passed on these same warnings to them. Then I just peeled off thousand sucre bills in all directions and was through in less than two hectic hours. I could see that the other couple disapproved of my tactics and were determined to play it straight. We saw them the next day. They'd just come back from the port and looked sick to their gills. They'd left their van there overnight and it had been emptied, completely. They'd even taken the tyres, the wing mirrors and the steering wheel.'

On a map we looked at the route they'd followed from Ecuador and hoped to follow down through Chile and up through Argentina to Brazil. From there they would sail across to Europe and eventually drive on overland to Australia.

'This,' Gloria pointed to the narrow road which winds up from Arequipa to Lake Titicaca and which we had been told was a nightmare stretch of deep ruts and gigantic boulders, 'is where the van snapped in half!'

'What!' we chorused.

'Yes. Really. It's true. A hundred and sixty kilometres out of here in the middle of nowhere, the chassis cracked in half and we slumped to a halt, like a man with a broken spine.'

'But what will you do?' we asked, amazed at their casual manner.

'Oh it's all right now. It's being repaired. A truck driver towed us all the way back here. For free! Wouldn't accept anything. And the local garage man says he can simply weld it all together again and get us back on the road by the end of the week!'

'It must be costing a fortune?' Iain asked without any embarrassment.

'Yes. All of forty dollars!'

'Forty dollars? You're kidding.' We could hardly believe it. 'Why so cheap?'

'It might not even be that much,' Gloria said. 'The fellow who runs the garage has his eye on a pair of old binoculars we are carrying. We've had them for years. They can't be worth much more than twenty dollars, well perhaps thirty dollars. But no more. And he has dropped heavy hints that he would like them and would be willing to fix the car and give *us* a bit of extra cash for them!'

We smiled at their good fortune.

'It's all a great experience, isn't it?' Barry said.

'And good fun, too,' Gloria added.

The railways of the Andean countries are quite extraordinary. In most cases they have had to overcome almost insurmountable difficulties of terrain to link the flat coastal regions with the rugged mountainous areas of the interior. On one railway line, the highest point reached is higher than the top of Mont Blanc, Europe's highest mountain! Our train route from Arequipa to Puno, on Lake Titicaca, would not quite equal that, but at 4500 metres, it would come close.

Most of the railway lines were laid down around the beginning of the century and, until World War II, or just after, many of the lines were still run by the British companies which built them. We don't know if it's true or not, but we were told that, for many years anyone travelling in Peru on a British passport could use the British-run lines free!

As the trip we were on was to last all day, we had splurged on buffet seats (US$30 for the four of us), having heard that the second-class carriages were unheated. Once the train reached the altiplano, the temperature would be bitterly cold. When the train pulled out from the small station at Arequipa, there were very few other people in our carriage, and, from their appearance and dress, most of them appeared to be foreigners.

For most of the early part of the morning, we wound our way deeper and deeper into the mountains, climbing all the time, but on no occasion on as steep a track as the cliff-hanging switchbacks we had traversed in Ecuador. However, the surrounding terrain was no less dramatic. We spent quite a long time passing around the base of the huge volcano Chachani, with El Misti rearing its snowy cone majestically in the background.

As we climbed, the desert landscape we had been used to gradually disappeared, but it was, nonetheless, desolate and forlorn country; a bleak, open tundra across which icy winds swept with mindless ferocity. Sitting in a heated carriage eating a hot, thick brew of Sopa Criola (Creole soup), was the best way, we felt, to appreciate the aesthetics of such a scene. And yet, there seemed to be a great many people living in this forbidding region. We had passed several small centres of habitation; Socasani, and Pampa de Arrieros were just two . . . and we had seen great numbers of llamas and alpacas on the open range everywhere about . . . also many Indian women wearing the red shawls and bowler hats traditional to the area.

At Alto Crucero (high crossing), we reached the highest point on the line, 4500 metres. We all felt slightly headachey and short of breath and tried, for the first time, the mate de coca mixture the Peruvians use to alleviate, to some extent, the effects of *siroche* . . . altitude sickness. It is made simply by putting the leaves of the coca bush in hot water . . . like tea. But the weak brew that results from this infusion has a definite lessening effect on the uncomfortable symptoms of siroche. Coca is of course the same plant from which cocaine is derived and, although mate de coca is only a very weak cousin, there is obviously a connection between its comforting effects and those of cocaine.

Alto Crucero is less than 240 kilometres westward in a straight line, from the coast of Peru and the Pacific Ocean and yet, we were astounded to learn that once past Alto Crucero, all water . . . all streams and rivers flow eastward into the *Atlantic* Ocean, not the Pacific. From the area in southern Peru in which we were, that meant a staggering 6400 kilometre journey via the tortuous network of rapids and raging rivers leading to the mighty Amazon. In fact, within eighty kilometres of us, on a 5500-metre mountain near the little town of Cailloma, lay the farthest identifiable source stream of the Amazon, the river on which, within a few weeks, we hoped to be travelling.

The most pleasing aspect of our train trip to Puno though, was the people we met on board the train. The first was a bearded man wearing a Peruvian poncho. He was sitting alone several seats down the carriage from us. Sean, who had been wandering restlessly up and down the train, sat down, at one stage, to talk to him and, as we overheard with horror, proceeded to give this stranger a potted family history of us all within minutes of the conversation starting.

Shortly, however, Michael Hogan, as he introduced himself, joined us and we began to learn a little about him. He was a Canadian, engaged to a Peruvian girl and running a small business exporting Peruvian and Bolivian artifacts, weaving and handicraft, to Canada. He was on his way to catch the ferry across Lake Titicaca to Bolivia and La Paz.

We talked for some time about Peru.

'I really love the place,' he said. 'But it's crazy . . . and frightening.'

'Frightening? How do you mean?' Trish asked.

'Well, the economy is just going down the drain. And inflation is going haywire here. How much have you been getting for a dollar whenever you change money?'

'About one hundred and thirty soles,' I said.

'Yeh. Well six weeks ago the official rate was only eighty. Now there's already talk of it going to one hundred and eighty to the dollar. That's an inflation rate of well over one hundred percent in a matter of months or weeks . . . and that's disastrous.'

Michael also told us about the wars looming between Peru and Bolivia. . . . and between Bolivia and Chile over land-locked Bolivia's desperate need for a corridor to the sea. (At the time of this writing, the war hasn't happened and will continue, I guess, to loom.)

We were joined, not long after we had met Michael Hogan, by two young Americans, who were also sitting further down the carriage. They were Larry Platt and Carl Campbell, who were to become friends and travelling companions for the next week.

Larry was from Philadelphia . . . about twenty-three or twenty-four years old . . . and was due to start shortly into law school in the United States, but for the past few months he had been working on some sort of study of Paraguay's export potential in agricultural products.

'Sounds more like some CIA project,' Trish said jokingly. It takes some people a while to get used to Trish's jokes, but Larry didn't seem put out at all.

Carl was from Washington. He was about twenty and just out of college. He'd been working with a religious aid organisation for several months in Ecuador and was now on a short holiday in Peru before returning to the States.

We all sat around for the rest of the afternoon, as the train rumbled on across the altiplano, discussing South America; from Peruvian politics to the Paraguayan dictator's close friendship with South Africa. But the most animated conversation revolved around the plight of the peasants in Peru and, in particular, those in these southern, high sierra regions. It was a subject on which Mike Hogan became very vociferous.

He banged the table. 'The lousy conditions the peasants live under now,' he said, 'is directly attributable to centuries of oppression and exploitation by the church.' There was a pause, but nobody said anything. He went on. 'These people were kicked into the gutter by the Conquistadores, and the church, despite all its patronising words, never allowed them to get up again.'

There were two other passengers sitting directly behind us. They were both men, who appeared to be foreigners, probably North Americans, but there was no way of being sure. They shifted slightly and looked at each other on hearing Mike's outburst, but said nothing.

I commented to Mike that we also had felt that there was something morally wrong with the church having such incredible wealth tied up in elaborate solid gold altars and ornaments instead of putting it to better use by investing it in educational or social welfare programmes, although we realised that it did already run schemes like this.

'Listen,' Mike said vehemently. 'I am a Catholic . . . or at least, I was brought up as a Catholic . . . and in Canada, that can be pretty strict stuff. But I tell you, it's very difficult not to be turned off by what you see here. I know that there are good people . . . many good men in the church. But what has gone on here in the past . . . with the Inquisition here for two hundred years . . . and the way the church milks these poor people even now, it's a wonder anyone accepts it. The sad thing is that they do.'

The two men behind us were quiet . . . obviously still listening.

'But I thought that, in Peru, the church was very politically active . . .' I said, 'and often takes the side of the extreme left wing in pushing the case for the peasants.'

'Well, that's true, in some cases and some areas,' Mike said. 'It's for sure that the church is very politically active. But depending on where you are, in South America, their support could be for the extreme left, the extreme right . . . or anywhere in between. It's really just playing the same old power game, that's all.'

At about 5.30 p.m., the train pulled in to the small market town of Juliaca, about forty-five kilometres from Puno. Mike said goodbye to us there, to take a collectivo on to Puno. Having done the trip several times before, he knew it was faster that way.

'I'll be there about an hour before you,' he said with a smile, as he left. There was not much we could do about it, and having bought our tickets right the way through to Puno, we decided to stay on the train. But the two men who had sat listening to us in the next seat, also left the train at that point.

After waiting an hour in Juliaca, the train eventually moved off slowly in the direction of Puno and one hour after that, we arrived on the shores of Lake Titicaca. We made our way to the Hotel Monterey, which Mike Hogan had recommended to us. It wasn't bad, but unfortunately the only water available was ice-cold . . . providing somewhat of a disincentive to showering.

Mike wasn't in when we arrived, but Larry and Carl met him later in the evening, in a café. He told them he had shared his collectivo from Juliaca to Puno with the two silent men from the train. They turned out to be American Catholic priests who had been working for the Peruvian church with the peasants of southern Peru!

'Our Father, the Sun, seeing that men lived like wild animals, took pity on them, and sent to earth a son and daughter of his, in order that they might teach men the knowledge of our Father the Sun, and that they might know how to cultivate plants and grains and make use of the fruits of the earth like men and not beasts. With these orders and mandates our Father the Sun placed his son and daughter in Lake Titicaca.' So wrote Garcilaso de la Vega, the son of a Spanish Conquistadore and an Inca princess, in his *Royal Commentaries*.

As soon as you see the lake you realise why the ancient Indians endowed it with such magical spiritual powers. It lies like a huge puddle of spilt, deep-blue ink in a giant fist of crumpled brown paper. There is, about its still depths, an air of unreality which borders on the frightening. Four kilometres above the sea, it appears to have drained the life from the barren, sheer-sided mountains which ring it.

This impression was probably only the result of my febrile brain, affected by the oxygen-thin air which gave to the landscape an unnaturally sharp and over-clear three dimensional effect. Whatever the cause, it's a fact that I felt a little overstimulated as the launch we had hired left Puno harbour and headed out toward the watery horizon.

I tried to calm myself by being practical; rubbing a thick coat of zinc ointment on Zara's nose. She objected, 'it's not hot'. No, in fact, it was cool. But I had seen several visitors with very bad facial sun-burns. At this height there's considerably less filtering of the sun's dangerous ultra-violet rays.

I tried my self-soothing practicality on Sean by recounting a piece of technical detail of the sort on which he thrives. Combustion engines, I informed him, lose efficiency at the rate of more than two percent for every three hundred metres of altitude which meant that this boat was most likely operating at thirty percent below its sea-level capacity.

'Where'd you read that?' he demanded, distrustful of a female with facts. 'Is it true?' he turned to his father to verify.

'Sexist,' said Zara, apparently also over-alert today.

Undeterred by the attempted undermining, I told them both that even before the railway reached Puno a hundred years ago, there were steamships on the lake which is the highest navigable body of water in the world. They were built in England, sailed around Cape Horn to Peru, taken apart and were carried, piece by piece, along mountain trails by mules all the way from the coast up to the lakeshore where they were reassembled.

'Look how clean the water is.' Zara leant over to trail her hand. 'It's cold.'

'Are there sharks?' Sean asked and Zara quickly sat up.

'No, but there are lots of fish,' Larry said, telling us about a Canadian outfit which introduced trout into the lake. 'Being carnivorous, they very quickly multiplied and grew fat by eating up the smaller fish and for some years visiting fishermen set records for the number and size of fish they caught. They even opened a cannery to export fish to Europe. There was a sort of fish-rush for a few years but, like most booms, it bust and the cannery shut up shop.'

The lake is 196 kilometres long and 76 kilometres wide and, on the other side is Bolivia. But we weren't going that way today. Three-quarters of an hour out, we began to approach what looked like a large piece of floating debris, but gradually materialised into one of the floating reed island homes of the Urus Indians. The little launch nosed its way along a channel through the totora reeds and bumped to a standstill beside several conical piles of the drying vegetation.

We were all rather embarrassed and reticent about going ashore because we were conscious of being intruders. But the women (there were no men to be seen) who were sitting outside reed huts as simple as a child's drawing, beckoned to us and we stepped gingerly ashore onto the spongy island which sagged gently beneath our weight. In a couple of patches the reeds had rotted through and we sank into wetness but, for the most part, the continually replenished layers of fresh reeds made safe, if rather oddly moving ground.

One of the women grabbed me by the arm and almost pulled me through a low doorway into a hut where there was a wooden crate half-covered with a cloth on which was propped a tarnished cross, some wilted flowers and an over-coloured picture of Christ. I felt pressured into dropping a few coins into the old tin at the entrance.

The Urus, like the Aberdeen Boat People in Hong Kong, live their entire lives on the water. They eat mainly fish and water birds and chew the stems of the totora reed. The ubiquitous reed which is used as floor, house and food is also crafted into boats like *Ra I* and *II* which Thor Heyerdahl sailed across the Atlantic. It was Indians from Titicaca who helped Heyerdahl build not only the *Ra* boats but the *Tigris* which was constructed on the Euphrates River. Heyerdahl flew a team of Indians all the way from Lake Titicaca to Iraq to direct the operation. Several of the long, narrow reed boats rested at the water's edge not far from the village huts, so Iain, of course, insisted that we have a ride in one. A young ruddy-faced, bowler-hatted woman poled us out from the island while a small child played hide and seek behind her layers of skirts. The soggy instability of the craft made me instantly grateful to be on the relative safety of flat-calm Lake Titicaca and not in the rollers of the Atlantic Ocean.

Back on 'land' Sean bought a model of the boat, which now 'sails' across his bedroom windowsill, and we boarded our more conventional craft for the trip back to Puno.

'Ti-ti-ca-ca,' Zara was trailing her hand again as she spread the syllables. 'It sounds like ... what d'you think it sounds like?'

'I don't know what it sounds like,' Larry said. 'But the Inca meaning is Rock of the Puma. I've seen a photograph of the lake taken from a satellite, a few hundred kilometres up and it actually looks like a crouching puma. Interesting eh?'

Had we been able, we would probably have gone straight on from Puno, the following day, to Cuzco, but, being Sunday, there were no trains. Monday would have to do. Not that Puno wasn't a pleasant enough little town ... it was. But we seemed to feel, whenever there was a slight pause like this, that we were wasting time. It was a ridiculous attitude really and we had to consciously fight against it whenever it occurred and, once resigned to the fact that we could not move on, we would generally settle down and relax to enjoy the place, or the situation in which we found ourselves.

It was a pattern to be repeated often in the days ahead. On this occasion in Puno, we made use of the opportunity to do some washing and to hang it out on lines on the flat roof of the hotel. Then, after a breakfast of eggs fried in rather fishy oil, we wandered, with Larry and Carl through the markets of Puno. The market stalls were almost all run by women, dressed in what seemed to be a uniform of several short, flaring woollen skirts worn one over the other in layers of different colours. They all, of course, wore the ubiquitous bowler hat, in either grey, brown or black.

We found that we were sorely tempted, as we had been in other Central and South American market places, to take advantage of the superb bargains that were offered. Here there were beautifully hand-knitted alpaca sweaters, scarves, gloves and hats. They were knitted and crocheted almost exclusively in the natural browns and fawns of the raw wool and in intricate Peruvian patterns. The sweaters would have been an attractive buy even at normal western prices, but when we discovered that the going price was about US$4.00 each, they became almost impossible to resist.

It wasn't the price that posed problems for us however, but the space. Our packs were practically overflowing already. But telling ourselves that it would be mid-winter by the time we got to Tierra del Fuego, we bought ourselves a sweater each and also some of the traditional, crocheted Peruvian hats ... 'chillos' they're called ... with ear-flaps and a tassle on the top. They provided the locals with a laugh or two when we wore them in the streets of Puno.

By this stage, we were becoming a little acclimatised to the altitude, although we still resorted occasionally to a drink of mate de coca, which was offered in all of the local cafes, to clear our heads slightly and give ourselves a bit of a lift. The Incas, incidentally, also knew of the effects of the coca leaf centuries ago, although its use then was strictly supervised. Only the Inca royal family or physical labourers engaged in building construction or arduous agricultural work were permitted to chew the leaf or drink the tea.

One of the great tragedies of the Andean countries is that, with the downfall of the Incas, the controls over this powerful drug disappeared. The defeated Inca peoples, initially seeking relief from the cruel tyranny of the Spaniards, turned more and more to the coca leaf, which, though it brought them some solace, sapped their will and, over the years, brutalised millions of people.

After a short afternoon siesta, we walked slowly through the town to a high place on the outskirts, from where we could see Puno laid out beneath us and the great lake stretching away into the distance. Such an immense body of water . . . over 8000 square kilometres of it, almost four kilometres above the sea. Ringed by mighty mountains, in the dramatic late evening light, there was an aura of majesty and mystery about it. It looked as if it could very easily have been what the ancients believed it to be . . . the birthplace of the gods.

Puno also gave us the time to assess and plan our onward route. The logical thing, if you have as an ultimate goal the tip of South America, is to keep heading south until you get there . . . and that is what we had been doing, up until now. But at Puno, we were about to turn and head north, not just for the 400-kilometre trip to Cuzco and Machu Picchu, but 1600 kilometres or more. To travel down the Amazon, which was very much a part of our plans, it would be necessary for us to go into reverse and travel in the opposite direction (although not covering the same tracks) for some considerable time. I mention this now only because at Arequipa and Puno, we were further south than we would be again until we reached Brasilia and Rio de Janeiro, on the other side of the continent, almost seven weeks later.

Bang! Bang! Bang! Oh my God, I thought, this altitude headache is getting worse. Then I realised that the banging was not in my head but on the door of our room.

'It's Larry. Wake up. We'll miss the train. The fellow forgot to wake us and we've only got twenty minutes.'

Groans and moans as we all came to and began, in the early morning gloom to silently and swiftly dress and tie up our packs, carefully avoiding any contact, physical or verbal, with one another. These pre-dawn departures had become so common a ritual, that we each knew better than to make any demands of the other three at this time and we were already jog-trotting down the deserted street toward the station before we bade 'g'day' to each other.

There was a little crowd around the window of the ticket office and we joined in the good-natured jostle, eventually buying tickets in the second-class compartment. This soon filled up, almost exclusively with foreigners (we were back on the tourist route again), who spoke a variety of languages. Behind us, yet again, sat the men we now knew to be Catholic missionaries. Remembering our ravings of the other day, I smiled rather weakly at them and they, in their Christian charity, nodded back.

It hadn't taken the children long to come fully awake, and by the time the train drew out of the little station, to run for a while along the shores of Lake Titicaca, they were already demanding a game of cards. An hour later, and still before 9.00 a.m., I felt that I had fulfilled my motherly obligation and threw in my hand, to retreat to *The Four Seasons of Manuela,* Victor von Hagen's very well-researched and highly-readable account of the life of Simon Bolivar's woman, Manuela Saenz. And what a woman! It made me think even more highly of him. He must have been quite a fellow, firstly for such a woman to be interested in him and also that he should have taken on such a passionate, intelligent and forceful partner in an age and society when, if you wanted to remain in high public office, you did not make public your love affair with an already married woman.

The children coerced Larry and Carl into further games of cards and I was amused to watch a couple of Peruvian girls, city-slickers, probably from Lima, approach the missionaries with a pack of cards. They settled down to a game, during which the young women giggled a lot in that tedious way too many of them do when they are being skittish and hopefully seductive. I didn't think much of their chances.

Outside, it looked cold and we were very glad for the central heating in the carriage. The sun was bright in a clear, blue sky and, having left the lake we climbed even higher. The track ran for a good while beside the very fast waters of the Vilcanota river which tumbled and plashed over boulders; catching the light and sparkling in the thin air.

I looked it up on our map and was amazed to find that this same river flowed on beneath the mountain fortress of Machu Picchu to become the Urubamba and then, joined by other streams, changed names to the Ucayali, the very same headwater which we planned to travel on downstream till it became the mighty Amazon. Incredible to realise that the sliver of lively water I saw now, bounding along at 4200 metres above sea level, would first travel north and then east across the entire continent; a 6400 kilometre journey, to end in the waters of the Atlantic Ocean!

Llamas grazed in twos and threes and occasionally we saw vicuna and alpaca. A few kilometres or so from the track, the mountains reared up their barren brown sides. Sometimes as we edged a little closer I could see primitive stone huts and behind them ancient cultivated terraces or pata-pata. Maize and grain crops will not ripen at this altitude, though they are grown as forage for cattle. But for centuries before Europeans arrived, the Indians used these small, stepped gardens to grow 'papas', a tuberous vegetable indigenous to the Andes which has passed into our culture as the humble staple, potato.

Also, centuries before our modern technology had developed the process, the Indians had perfected a method of freeze-drying which they still use to store their potatoes. They leave them out to freeze for several nights. Next they tread on them, gently, to squeeze out the moisture, then they lay them out in the sun to dry completely. Preserved in this manner, the potatoes last through from crop to crop and can easily be reconstituted when boiled up into the sort of soup which we were now served in the compartment of the train. Delicious.

'Pardon me, but do you think this is safe to eat?' a pleasant-faced woman in her fifties asked with a southern drawl.

'I assured her that it was. Of course, I didn't know if it was safe or not, but if she was as hungry as I was, all she really wanted was to pass the responsibility for her stomach on to someone else.

'Well,' she drawled, 'I guess if you let your children eat it, it must be safe.' She took a tentative sip. I didn't bother to tell her that my children have been in circumstances where they have eaten what looked like a tired, dirty dish cloth and been grateful! We talked of other things and she told me that her son, who was sitting beside her and looked like a long drink of water, had been working as a Mormon missionary in Argentina and now that he had finished his service, she and her husband had joined him for a flying trip to see some South American highlights like Cuzco and Machu Picchu.

At this point Larry, who had been sitting beside me, excused himself abruptly and left me struggling through a difficult conversation. I can mostly chat along with anyone quite comfortably but her particular brand of spiritual smugness, indulged in vicariously as a result of her son's activities, was beginning to get up my nose and I was glad when the train stopped in the middle of a huge, open, grassy space and I could make the excuse of joining my family who, along with everyone else, piled off to walk about and relieve themselves.

As I climbed down the stairs, I could hear her, behind me, introducing herself, 'My son's a Mormon missionary,' to the two Catholics. I thought it would be interesting to be a fly on the wall and listen to their conversation.

Larry and Zara were engaged in light-hearted banter when I approached but Larry immediately became serious, 'Terrible people,' he said to me.

'Who?' I asked, startled.

'Mormons.'

Larry himself had Jewish parents who had brought him up as a non-conformist Christian. We had talked quite a bit about religious bigotry and he had until then seemed to me to be very open-minded.

'Last year,' he told me, 'the Mormons opened a huge, and I mean huge, temple in Washington. Six million dollars it cost. They had an opening ceremony or whatever you'd call it. Interdenominational. Anyone could go inside and look. It's a quite magnificent place. All white stonework. And do you know that after this special service they ripped out all the brand new carpets on which non-Mormons had trod, and burnt them, because they considered them defiled. They even went to the lengths of purging some spots, which had been touched by non-Mormons, with fire and, from then on only Mormons were allowed in. They consider themselves holier than holy!'

Back on board, we settled down to more card games and reading and after several hours we made a stop at a small village where tradespeople swarmed aboard selling model reed boats, hand-knitted sweaters and caps, empanadas and fruit. They shouted their wares up and down the aisle. Through the window I watched women wearing layers of skirts, bright ponchos and bowler hats, carrying babies in their mantas, talking together and spinning alpaca yarn as they walked along.

One never sees idle women in the Andes, though there are numerous idle men. I was pondering this fact when I felt a nudge and looked round to see an older Indian woman with a very lined, brown face proferring a basket of mandarins. She pointed to Iain's camera, to the bulging FB and to the litter of cards and books all of which were on the small table in front of us.

'You watch,' she ordered, 'plenty bad men,' and before I could buy any fruit she had moved on down the crowded aisle.

We were in the act of moving our things to the safety of our seats, when there was a little scream followed by a shout and we looked up to see a young blonde girl push her way wildly past our table. At that moment the train gave a jolt, began to move forward and the girl, now with tears running down her cheeks waved her arms and yelled wildly as she hung out from the metal steps. She was joined by two other travellers, obviously her friends and, through her sobs, it became gradually clear that her handbag, which she had left hanging on the edge of her seat, had been lifted by a well-dressed man who had passed quickly down the carriage with his jacket over his arm — although she had run after him he had jumped down onto the rails and disappeared into the crowd. The bag had contained all her money and travellers' cheques as well as her plane tickets and passport!

An official was summoned, but he merely shook his head. It was such a common occurrence and yet what could he do about it? She should have been more careful. A high-ranking, judging by his flashes and tabs, Peruvian military officer who was sitting toward the middle of the carriage, made no move or offer of help. The girl slowly calmed and, as she became more coherent we understood that she was an Austrian air-hostess working for Saudi Airlines and was in Peru on a three-week holiday. She had the numbers of her travellers' cheques so she would be able to claim on them and as she was travelling with friends they would be able to see her through back to Lima where she could apply for a new passport. Even though all this would take valuable time out of her holiday, she was relatively fortunate.

Other travellers gathered round and began to relate their own personal horror stories. One mightily attractive young German girl, who wore a baggy khaki overall, yet still managed to look sexy and who was travelling alone, told of being set upon by three men in Colombia and beaten up because she didn't have anything worth stealing.

An American couple recounted having their packs, while on their backs, slit open and ransacked on a crowded train. Some talked of tying their packs and loose bags to their wrists, while others suggested that this was dangerous because thieves would simply slice off the hand to get at the bag. At this point I took Zara and Sean, boggle-eyed with horror, back to our seats where we found Larry sunk in a deep depression. After much coaxing I managed to wheedle out some of his feelings.

'I can't bear to think of people reduced to such acts,' he said. ''I like to think of life as full of beauty and happiness, not desperation and crime.' He refused to speak any further, staring out into the gathering darkness. Even when a crowd of men touting for Cuzco hotels came aboard he wouldn't join in the haggling.

As it would be dark when we arrived and we had already been warned that Cuzco station was a favourite haunt of thieves and pickpockets, we decided to settle on a hotel whose promoter promised a free taxi ride direct to its luxury of hot water and fine restaurant. Six dollars for the four of us. Four dollars for Larry and Carl. Of course we didn't really believe him but quite honestly on a trip like this, your standards have to be so adaptable that as long as a room doesn't have fleas and is not too noisy, you can count yourself lucky!

The fact that the water was cold enough to turn you blue and that the lobby and even the minuscule restaurant smelt of urine and that the insufficient blankets meant adding sleeping bags to the covers to keep warm, was par for the course. We ignored it all by eating a large bowl of soup and snuggling down with *Huck Finn*, who had now replaced *Tom Sawyer* as our bedtime reading.

The great square in the centre of Cuzco is called, as in most other Spanish South American cities, the Plaza de Armas. It was however a plaza, or the Inca equivalent, long before the Spaniards ever set foot there. Cuzco, in the Quechua language, means 'navel'. It was, for the Incas, the centre, the capital, the Holy City of their great Empire, for hundreds of years prior to the conquest. In fact Cuzco, according to archaeologists, is the oldest continually inhabited city in all of the Americas.

Standing in the big square now, there is superficially no indication that it is anything but a purely Spanish plaza. And yet, if you simply walk to one side of the square and look at the stonework foundations on which the Spanish churches and other buildings are set, there is ample and very impressive evidence of the Incas' occupancy of Cuzco. Nowhere in the entire world can finer stonemasonry be found. Yet the Spanish Conquistadores, when they arrived in Cuzco, found the temples and other Inca holy places offensive and, in their religious fervour, set about destroying them. They were able to demolish only the super-structures. They found the bases and foundations of the buildings so formidably strong and superbly built as to be virtually indestructible.

This has been borne out during the four hundred and fifty years since the Spanish conquest. Two major earthquakes have sent Spanish churches and buildings tumbling down, but the Inca foundations on which they stood have not moved.

Walking through the streets of Cuzco, many of which are the original thoroughfares of the Inca city, these walls and foundations are a marvel to see; not perhaps exciting in the sense that the magnificent Egyptian rock carvings at Abu Simbel or Karnak might be, but tremendously intriguing because of their massive size and wonderful craftsmanship. You may have read, at some stage, the stories of how it is impossible to put a razor-blade between these stones and in many of the finer walls about Cuzco this is absolutely true.

There is no mortar between the stones, many of which are of huge proportions, with up to twelve and fourteen corners exposed on the face, all finished entirely by hand. The secret of their tremendous strength and stability, without the use of mortar, is that each stone is individually 'keyed' to its neighbour by small notches and grooves on the inner surfaces of the stone ... somewhat like a jig-saw puzzle.

We spent a very pleasant morning, with Larry and Carl, walking around Cuzco after an enjoyable English breakfast of fried eggs and bacon, toast, with *real* marmalade, and coffee at a restaurant facing onto the Plaza. If you get the impression that we always seem to be looking at buildings or churches or eating at cafes on the Plaza de Armas, I can only say that that's the way it is in South America. The Plaza de Armas ... which means 'the place of the arms' ... is literally the centre of all activity in just about all Spanish-American cities.

We didn't visit the cathedral on the main square. It was large and I believe it is magnificent inside, but we were beginning to feel that we'd had a surfeit of churches. We did, though, look through the nearby Santa Rosa convent, which the Spaniards built on the ruins of the Incas' Temple of the Virgins of the Sun. This was only one of many convents in Cuzco as, in the early days of the Spanish occupation of Peru, the eldest daughter of every family was expected to enter a convent.

This particular one was still occupied by twenty-two nuns and was full of religious paintings and murals of the colonial era as well as a rich collection of woven gold vestments and silver and gold chalices, salvers and other church ornaments. But the major object of interest was a solid-gold monstrance, studded with 1500 diamonds, 600 pearls and countless emeralds and rubies. It is used in processions and festivals not more than two or three times a year and is regarded as one of the most perfect specimens of gold-smithery in the world. It contains almost 23 kilos of gold, which at 1979 market prices would bring over $320,000, but as a work of art, it is probably priceless.

Less than three minutes walk from the convent of Santa Rosa is Callejon Loreto, a narrow street lined on both sides by magnificent Inca stone walls. And there, blind Indian beggars sit on the pavement beneath the walls, plucking mournful Quechua tunes from ancient stringed instruments, hoping for a handout of a few soles from tourists or passersby.

Two blocks further on, the remains of the once mighty Temple of the Sun lie hidden behind the Spanish colonial walls of the Church of Santo Domingo. Here, apparently only lately realising the wealth of their Inca heritage, the Peruvian government is excavating and revealing more and more of the walls and chambers of the massive temple which the Conquistadores sought to destroy and cover with their own temples. In the Temple of the Sun, we met Carlos Iruri, a young Quechua student of archaeology at the University of Cuzco. He was about twenty-three, very knowledgeable of Inca history and obviously proud of his own links with his distant Inca forebears.

'You see what the Spanish did!' he said, pointing to a beautiful Inca stone wall which was partly covered. 'They plastered over it and painted religious murals on it . . .' he made a sneering gesture . . . 'trying to hide what they could not equal.'

Carlos led us from chamber to chamber, then out onto a small paved terrace next to one of the outer walls of the temple. The symmetry of the stones in the wall was quite stunning. Pointing to a broken section, Carlos explained to us the keying system of tying one stone to the next and how the sloping angle of the wall gave it the strength to resist earthquakes. Then he gestured to an open area of ground, just beneath the wall, which contained some temporary tin sheds. These, according to Carlos, were being used by archaeologists. There were a number of large stones bearing cataloguing numbers that were lying about.

'That is the famous garden,' Carlos said.

'Garden?' I queried. 'What garden?'

'The Inca's golden garden,' Carlos replied. 'It is from here that much of Atahualpa's ransom was raised. Before the conquest, the garden was full of plants and shrubs and animals, even full-sized llamas, all in pure gold.'

'Did they leave them out all night . . . in the rain and everything?' Sean asked.

'Yes, they were quite safe,' Carlos said. 'They were in the temple grounds and no one would have dared to steal them. Only the Inca king was permitted to own gold. It was a crime for anyone else to have it.'

Zara turned back from looking at the garden. 'Did the Spaniards take it all?' she asked Carlos.

'No. They took much, but it was only a fraction of the Inca gold.'

'What happened to the rest?' I asked.

'No one knows. It is a great mystery.'

Carlos came with us in the afternoon on a taxi ride for several kilometres up into the hills around Cuzco. We talked about a fee for him to 'guide' us through some of the ancient Inca fortifications outside the city. He was reluctant to set any figure at all, but, as he was a student, we knew he could do with the extra cash, so we decided on 1300 soles ($10) between us. Carlos was happy and so were we, as he turned out to be better than any tour guide could ever have been.

We visited four ancient Inca sites, the first of which was Tampumacchay, a sort of spa, a place for ritual bathing for the Inca nobility during their time of rule. Crystal-clear, cold mountain water still runs through the hand-carved rock channels there. We all lay down on our stomachs to drink deeply from the sparkling rivulets ... something we would not have dared with the twentieth century water coming from the taps in hotels or restaurants anywhere else in Peru.

Next on our tour were Puca Pucara, a small fortress and Kenko, an Inca amphitheatre not unlike those of ancient Greece or Rome. At each place, Carlos proved to be a fund of information about the significance of certain rock carvings, altars and the like. At Kenko, he pointed out a long, zig-zagging channel that had been cut into the sloping surface of the granite.

'It is a lightning bolt,' Carlos said. 'They used to pour chicha, a fiery drink made from maize, up here at the top of the channel, and the Inca nobles would drink from the channel as it flowed past them.'

But the greatest sight of all, on that afternoon trip, was the remnants of the looming fortress of Sacsahuaman, (closest English pronunciation; sexywoman), which sits on a hill, overlooking Cuzco. It is one of the Incas' most remarkable achievements and certainly one of the most amazing feats of construction in the world. The first Spaniards to see it were speechless in astonishment and the noted historian Sir Clements Markham has said of it, 'There is nothing in the whole world to be compared to this fortress.'

The walls of Sacsahuaman are built of rocks so huge as to strain the imagination. Single rocks, some of them more than six metres high, by six metres wide and weighing more than three hundred tonnes, each finely shaped and cornered to fit perfectly with those above and beside it. The main wall, which also forms a zig-zag, lightning pattern, is almost unbelievable. How did the Incas, who never, despite all their other achievements, discovered the wheel, get these gigantic stones to this site and manoeuvre them into place? How did they work them so finely with only stone tools? There are plenty of theories, but no one really knows.

'The Inca Manco laid siege on Cuzco from here,' Carlos said. 'That was in 1536, after the Spaniards had taken Cuzco. When the Spaniards killed

Atahualpa, they set Manco on the throne, thinking he would be a puppet, but he led a revolt and occupied Sacsahuaman for six months before the Spaniards finally forced them out, into the mountains.'

Suddenly Carlos began singing. We were all slightly taken aback. We stood quietly and listened to him. He was singing in Quechua.

'This is a song my people sing,' he paused for a few moments from his song. 'It tells the story of how they defied the Spanish to hold the fortress of Sacsahuaman.'

Carlos continued. It was quite a long song and although none of us understood a word of it, we stood transfixed and silent ... first in amazement that Carlos had given voice like this, and then, simply by the power of the emotion in his words. It was clear that it was very important to him. At the end of the song, Carlos smiled, but I felt that he was near to tears.

That evening, we ate with Larry and Carl at the Restaurant Roma. It was, as you may have already guessed, on the Plaza de Armas, but it's worth a mention if only for the fact that it is the only restaurant in the world that can claim an entire interior wall, some six metres high, that is part of an original royal Inca palace, the Palace of the Inca Pachacutec. But if there was irony in that, we felt there was even more in the fact that the restaurant overlooks the place where the last Inca was brutally put to death by the Spaniards.

There were four more Incas after Pizarro's execution of Atahualpa. First, as we've just said, there was Manco, a young prince, one of Atahualpa's nephews, whose tenure of the Inca throne and rebellion against the Spanish lasted many years. The Incas established a secret mountain retreat, deep in the jungled valleys of the Urubamba River. The Inca city was originally called Vitcos, though contemporary writers refer to it as Vilcapampa.

After Manco's death, in 1545, his three sons, Titu Cusi, Sayri Tupac and Tupac Amaru, all had a turn on the Inca throne over the next twenty-five years. During that period, relations with the Spanish, by now headquartered in Lima, remained tense. There were brief periods of peaceful though cautious contact and others of outright war. But during all of this time, the Spaniards never penetrated the Incas' mountain labyrinth, nor discovered the whereabouts of the secret city of Vilcapampa.

But by 1572, almost forty years after the original capture of Atahualpa, a new Viceroy, Don Francisco de Toledo, had arrived in Lima. He ordered the extermination of the Inca royal family.

A Spanish expeditionary force fought a battle with the Incas in the rugged mountains somewhere near Vilcapampa. A small group of Incas led by the last Inca King, Tupac Amaru, was cut off and fled into the jungles. The Spaniards remorselessly tracked them down and finally captured the Inca, bringing him back to Cuzco for a mock trial. Toledo, whom the history books describe as 'savagely bigoted, cruel and pitiless', travelled to Cuzco to enjoy the spectacle of the trial and the punishment of the captured Incas.

In the middle of the square, onto which our restaurant faced, Tupac Amaru's chiefs were tortured to death with fiendish brutality. His wife was mangled before his eyes and his own head was cut off ... before thousands of his weeping and wailing subjects, to be stuck up on a pole, by the Spanish, in the great plaza ... the Plaza de Armas.

Top: Heading south on the New York Thruway. 'The road was absolutely treacherous.' USA

Centre: Making for Shenandoah National Park. 'A wonderland, like trees made of glistening glass.' USA

Right: Finlay, Texas, 'a not-even-one-horse-town.' USA

Left: A 'no smiles please' family portrait, Tombstone, Arizona. USA

Below: The new Basilica of Guadalupe when '3000 people stood tightly packed, many weeping with emotion.' MEXICO

Above: Teotihuacán, 'a remarkable relic of an ancient civilization.' MEXICO

Right: 'The old Basilica of Guadalupe and the chapel beside it are slowly sinking.' MEXICO

right: Trotsky's house, 'an incongruous, high-walled, corner fortress amid soporific suburbia.' MEXICO

below: The ruined city of Palenque gave us a sense of discovery, as though we had been shown another world.' MEXICO

right: While climbing the one hundred and fifty steep steps with narrow, crumbling treads to the top of the Pyramid of the Dwarf at Uxmal, Trish suffered a bad attack of vertigo, or fear of heights. MEXICO

Top: Chichen Itza. 'How many hundreds, how many thousands of freshly-torn-out, still-beating hearts were brutally sacrificed to the terrible god Chac Mool?' MEXICO

Centre: The waterfront at Belize City. 'The City reeks of neglected tropical empire.' BELIZE

Right: Our bus to Tikal. 'Jolting and bouncing, mountains of dust pouring in over us all the time.' GUATEMALA

Left: Woman and child bathing at Rio Dulce on the road to Guatemala City. GUATEMALA

Below: The temple of the Giant Jaguar at Tikal, 'the greatest of all the Mayan centres.' GUATEMALA

Above: Children of San Antonio de las Aguas Calientes. 'We moved from stall to stall and marvelled at the intricate and colourful weavings.' GUATEMALA

Below: The Panama Canal. Since it was opened over half a million ships have passed through — and

Above: The solid gold altar in the church of San Jose which Henry Morgan's pirates missed when they sacked Panama City in 1671. The monks had reputedly camouflaged it with paint. PANAMA

one swimmer who paid a toll of 36c in 1928. In 19.. the *QE 11* paid $68,499 and 46c cents. PANAMA

Above: The Viernes Santa (Easter Friday) procession in Quito, 'hordes of people dressed in purple robes and Klu-Klux-Klan-type hoods.' ECUADOR

Below: A Quechua woman and child in the Riobamba market, 'a photographer's delight.' ECUADOR

Above: The countryside near Riobamba was lush and beautiful, but the small holdings not large enough for anything but subsistence farming. ECUADOR

Right: 'Looking from our train down "The Devil's Nose" switchbacks it was not difficult to feel a trifle uneasy.' ECUADOR

Below: Havoc brought about by a flash flood in the Sechura Desert. PERU

Left: The Quarto de Rescarte or ransom chamber. Atahualpa's ransom filled this room, once with gold and twice with silver. PERU

Centre: Beautiful carved wooden balconies on the facade of the Archbishop's Palace on the Plaza de Armas. PERU

Below: 'Uru Indians live their entire lives on their floating island homes on Lake Titicaca.' PERU

Left: Quechua woman and friend. PERU

Centre: The view from Huayna Picchu with the Urubamba River far below on its long, winding journey to the Amazon and the Atlantic Ocean. PERU

Below: Machu Picchu, The Lost City of the Incas. 'We sat entranced. It was a quite mystical, almost spiritual experience.' PERU

elow: Zara and Sean look at beautiful multi-loured butterflies and huge and ugly black rantulas displayed on a Lima street. PERU

ight: Main street Pucallpa, a quagmire in the wet. ERU

bove: The waterfront at Pucallpa. 'Small, nvas-canopied dugouts, powered by tboard motors, ferry passengers back and rth from nearby villages.' PERU

ght: The *Campeon,* our floating home for ght hundred kilometres down the Ucayali ver. PERU

Above: In an Amazon village Zara watches a Jivaro Indian with his blow-gun. PERU

Below: A Jivaro Indian sharpens a deadly bamboo dart. Sean eventually traded his green rubber ball for the gun and a quiver of darts. PERU

above: The *Adolfo,* built in Glasgow and used to carry passengers on the upper Amazon since 1909. PERU

below: Iain wades through a flooded jungle track to Monkey Island which we had been told was surrounded with electric eels.' COLOMBIA

right: Sean, snake-wrestler Mike Tsalickis, and a four-metre anaconda. 'They're not poisonous, but they can give you a very nasty bite. That's why you've got to hold them tight, right behind the jaws.' COLOMBIA

Top: 'It's like the very first day,' said Zara as the Amazon River turned on another of its spectacular early morning scenes for us. BRAZIL

Centre: A tiny farm clings to the edge of the Amazon, behind it millions of hectares of virgin jungle. BRAZIL

Right: Our bus stops in an outback town on the Mato Grosso. Five million pioneer Brazilians have migrated here, opening up the potentially rich lands of the west. BRAZIL

Top: Women on the beach in Rio de Janeiro. BRAZIL

Left: 'Suddenly we saw our first gaucho. It was strange to see once again someone dressed so casually in traditional costume.' BRAZIL

Above: One of the many old cars still running in Uruguay. 'It was like being on a 1940s movie set.' URUGUAY

Left: The Moreno Glacier, 'huge and blue
Every few minutes the silence of the
deserted place would be broken by
thunderous tearing and cracking sounds.'
ARGENTINA

Centre: Sunset at Rio Grande, 'the most
magnificent we had ever seen —
anywhere.' ARGENTINA

Below: The shoreline at Ushuaia. 'The
Channel was so still it reflected and so
doubled the dramatic beauty. Everywhere
we looked there were mountains covered
with snow.' ARGENTINA

There was yet another early morning train to catch, but this time at least, we were not running late and could take our time to puff laboriously up through the already busy vegetable market to Cuzco station.

Almost as soon as we pulled out, we began to traverse the mountain above the town on a series of four switchbacks which lifted us from Cuzco's 3380 to 3800 metres above sea level, from where we could survey the whole of the city nestling in a saucer-like basin. At this point, four ancient Inca cobble-stone roads take off in separate directions, one of them heading for Quito, 2400 kilometres away to the north, and another for Lima, 800 kilometres north-west where it becomes part of the comparatively modern Pan-American Highway.

We settled down for the three-hour trip at the end of which we would be gratefully almost 1200 metres lower than Cuzco and, still, unimaginable as yet, at Machu Picchu, the fabled Lost City of the Incas. Could it be true? Could I be going to see Vilcapampa/Vitcos/Machu Picchu call it what you will, does it matter? It certainly didn't matter to Hiram Bingham, who at twenty-seven, led the Yale University expedition which in 1911 discovered, what every archaeologist in the world had dreamed of finding, and what he was certain was *the* Royal Inca City. He called it Machu Picchu because that was the name used by the Indian guide who led him to it. It means simply, Old Peak.

For at least four hundred years its location had been a secret. Certainly the Spaniards never found it and, after all we had seen so far in Peru, it was going to be a pleasure to visit a place which they had not managed to defile.

Ever since Bingham's almost accidental discovery, scholars have disputed the purpose of this high mountain fortress. Was it the happy home of the first Inca, Manco Capac? Was it the final bitter retreat of the last Inca, Tupac Amaru before his capture? Was it a nunnery for the Virgins of the Sun, young women whose life was dedicated to honouring the chief among the Inca gods, the Sun itself. This theory is lent credence by the fact that, of the one hundred and forty three bodies as yet recovered from the cemetery, at least eighty percent of them are of young females. Or is it, as others have suggested, one military post in a series of such Inca defences, a sort of Andean Maginot Line? This though is a theory difficult to accept because no other comparable site has yet been found, even with the use of such revealing aids as satellite photographs. All such speculation remains just that, educated guesswork. It is because of the fact that despite their high level of cultural achievement, the Incas left no written language, that scholars have as yet not found the key to Machu Picchu.

Iain was looking distinctly seedy. His face resembled rumpled bedclothes. I like this business of aging together. When we are in our eighties we shall know how each of our wrinkles was come by. They will be like a map of our lives drawn together. Still, despite such affectionate musing, I thought that he did look particularly lined that morning and asked how he felt.

'Bloody terrible. I was awake until after four o'clock!' This is almost unheard of, as Iain's ability to fall asleep mid-sentence is notorious. I thought he must be sickening for something. But no. 'I reworked the entire plot for the Inca gold book! Want to hear it?'

Through the carriage window I could see the torrent of the Urubamba lashing over the huge boulders on its downhill course. The ancient, but still cultivated, Inca terraces at the base of the sheer, snow-capped mountains reared up on both sides of the narrow valley through which we wound, and the comforting familiarity of eucalyptus trees, which grew in large numbers.

Beside me Iain told his story and we shared one of the greatest joys of fiction writing; getting to know the intimate details of those characters who people the pages.

We were so wrapped up in our world of make-believe that the train was pulling to a halt before we realised that we had arrived. Hurriedly we shouldered our packs and jostled out onto the platform where we peered upwards in the vain hope of catching a first glimpse of the secret city. Nothing. No wonder the city remained a mystery for so long. It was just over 600 metres up the mountain but there was absolutely no sign of it from the bottom of the valley.

This is the very spot where Hiram Bingham crossed the Urubamba and began his difficult ascent. Looking at the sheer face of the mountain it was amazing to me that he even attempted it. Several buses were filling quickly and we scrambled into back seats for the tortuous eight-kilometre ride up a winding road, which was built in 1948 and opened by Hiram Bingham himself. It took fourteen hair-pin bends in order to climb to the top of a saddleback ridge. And still we could not see any sign of the ruins.

We had asked on the previous day in Cuzco at the State Tourist Hotel about accommodation at the only hotel in Machu Picchu, which is also owned by the government, and had been told that the Machu Picchu place only had room for thirty guests and was fully booked. But when we had expressed very great disappointment, the clerk in Cuzco had said that if we wanted to, we could sleep on the floor of the lobby for a mere three-quarters of the regular tariff. No doubt this went straight into staff pockets but this was not our worry and we gratefully accepted the solution.

So, at Machu Picchu, we told the desk clerk that we were the roomless people and arranged to leave our packs behind his counter. The rest of the visitors all filed into the dining-room for lunch. But even Sean, the ever-open mouth, was not going to waste time eating. That was not what we had come for.

The feeling I had now in the pit of my stomach was somewhat akin to stage fright. I could very easily have got on the bus and gone back down to the train. It had to do with the fear of being disappointed. Fortunately none of the others seemed to be likewise mentally crippled and they were raring to go.

'I'll be first, I'll be first,' Sean ran on ahead up the small track which led through a wooden gate-house and disappeared around a sharp bend. Larry, Carl, Iain and Zara talked animatedly and I trailed behind silently praying to some unspecified god, that now that I was here at last, the reality would not be too much of a let-down.

For years I had seen photographs on posters, in magazines like National Geographic and in books on South American civilisations, of the ruins of this dramatic Inca retreat high in the jungled mountains of Southern Peru. It had been one of the world's remote places I had always dreamt of visiting. Could it possibly live up to my expectations?

Through the wooden gate-house and turning a bend, I hardly dared to look and then ... well what is there to say when words are just not adequate? The impact of the stupendous beauty of that place stunned us all into momentary silence. Machu Picchu is, without qualification, the single most dramatically beautiful setting for a city on the entire face of this globe. Your imagination can soar no higher. No wonder Bingham died convinced that he had indeed rediscovered the fabled city.

The roofless ruins of two hundred and fifty stone buildings were spread out before us across the two hectare site. Behind it, forming a dramatic backdrop, from whichever direction we looked, was the towering peak of Huayna Picchu, New Peak. Built on terraces hewn from the mountainside, it is estimated that this, the ultimate self-sustaining fortified city, was home for around one thousand people. Its water supply, brought in from natural springs, has now been diverted to supply the nearby hotel. Three thousand steps incorporated into a hundred staircases interconnect the separate districts.

We climbed up and down from the Palace of the Princess to the Temple of the Sun, on to the Royal Tomb and the Temple of the Three Windows. All such prosaic names for such fine displays of craftsmanship and great imagination.

'What's that noise?' Iain stood still. 'It sounds like people chanting.'

It was. We came down to the Principal Temple to find that a group of Japanese, led by a priest in a white kimono, had set up an altar and were making obeisance and praying. At first we were startled, but then we remembered that Shinto, the main religion in Japan, was like the ancient Inca religion, a worship of the sun. So it should have been no surprise that they were here in the Holy of Holies of the Empire of the Sun, but it was.

Carl decided that he was going to climb Huayna Picchu. The rest of us chickened out, promising ourselves that we would do so tomorrow, though I personally doubted that I would allow myself to be persuaded. As we continued to walk around, we caught an occasional glimpse of Carl's yellow T-shirt getting further and further up the 600-metre-high green pinnacle. We waved and could just make out that he was waving back.

The day-trippers had gone by now, returning to Cuzco on the train which left at 3.00 p.m. and we had the whole city almost to ourselves. Zara found a couple of real llamas with whom to commune. Sean squirmed his way on his belly through the long grass, stalking an imaginary foe and revelling in the all-too-rare physical freedom. Iain took Larry back to the Royal Tomb to do some measuring which would be an intrinsic part of Joe Sawyer's adventures and I lay along a stone wall scratching at the pale gold and green lichen.

It was very peaceful, that is my strongest memory of Machu Picchu, the peace. The constant muffled roar of the river, six hundred metres below us, was so soothing to the ear, and the greenness of the sheer mountains on all sides, set off to perfection by their snowy peaks, so visually satisfying, that the whole combined to create a wondrous sense of completion.

We were awake before daybreak and, not long afterwards, ready and waiting at the entrance to the ruins for them to be opened at 6.30 a.m. We had woken Larry and Carl, but they were still showering and dressing and said that they would follow us shortly. We were the only ones at the gates when the attendant opened them and, once inside, began immediately to climb the narrow path and steps up to the area known as the Cemetery on a high point above the ruined city. This, so we had been told, was the best vantage point from which to watch the dawn break over Machu Picchu.

It was eminently worth the effort of rising early and climbing the hill. In all my life I have never seen such a wonderful spectacle. And it lasted for almost an hour, changing continuously. When we arrived at the little thatched hut, we sat down on the grassy verge of the hill which fell steeply away to the ruins below. We were completely alone and there was a beautiful silence about the place. There was no wind and it wasn't cold, yet the whole of the ancient city and the valley below were wreathed in mists. But they were more than mists . . . they were clouds. And all around us, beyond the closer circle of jungled mountains and steep, black cliffs, we could see the majestic, snow-covered peaks of the Cordillera Vilcabamba on which the sun was already shining.

Suddenly, as if some unearthly signal had been given, the clouds beneath us began to move, to rise, to sweep across the ruins. Heavier clouds then moved in from a neighbouring valley and engulfed us in wet, white fog. But after only a few minutes in this ghostly and silent enclosure, the cloud passed by to reveal the city below us once again. As the brilliant ball of the sun appeared over the tips of the surrounding hills, we had the unique experience of seeing our own shadows projected onto the white clouds to the west and below us, with a completely circular rainbow around them . . . like a halo.

We sat entranced. Zara and Sean, who under different circumstances might have run off on their own missions of discovery, were quite happy to stay quietly with us and just watch. Even their words of appreciation like 'wow!' and 'isn't it fantastic?' were whispered. It was a quite mystical . . . almost spiritual experience.

We had been joined, after about the first fifteen minutes, by Larry and Carl who also felt a sense of awe at the sight. It was as if we were an audience at a show which had been put on especially for us. I tried to picture what it must have been like for the people who once lived at Machu Picchu. I wondered if they felt the same sense of appreciation and privilege at being able to wake each morning to this wondrous happening. This beautiful valley, I thought, has been like this forever. Long before man . . . before the Incas . . . before us. And it will go on like this long after us . . . forever.

With the rising sun, the sounds of hundreds of birds singing and calling to one another signified that the day proper had now begun. The magic show was over. It was time to get down to more serious things.

From our point of view, about the most serious thing that we could think of at that stage, was breakfast. So, leaving Larry and Carl, we returned to the hotel to eat a hearty meal of eggs, toast and coffee, before making our way back into the ruins to continue our explorations.

About mid-morning we met up again with Larry, who, not to be outdone by Carl, was heading off to climb Huayna Picchu. After a couple of minutes' discussion, we decided that we couldn't really come to Machu Picchu and *not* climb it. After all, if the Incas could construct terraces and grow food on the almost sheer rock faces at the top of the pinnacle, we surely could get up there and down again. There was a steep path, which Carl had followed the day before, but the guide book described it as precipitous and extremely dangerous. In the event Sean made the decision for us.

'I'm going,' he said, with a determined look in his eye, 'even if you're too scared . . . I'm not! I'm going with Larry.'

So off we went all together, walking in single file, following the narrow track, through dense undergrowth to the foot of the pinnacle, which rose some 600 metres above us, but which stood a good 1200 metres clear of the valley floor and the raging Urubamba River below.

The path, which had originally been cut by the Incas, probably six or seven hundred years ago, followed a tortuous, zig-zag route up the practically vertical south face of the mountain. At times the path had been cut out of the solid rock and, although only thirty or forty-five centimetres wide, had a cliff-face on one side and a drop of a three hundred metres or more on the other. The only saving grace was that, in most places, thick grass and bamboo grew in great tufts on the precipice side so that we weren't constantly confronted with the stomach-churning view of the huge drop beside us. There was also some comfort, small though it was, in the thought that, if you slipped, you would have something to grab hold on to.

It was steamy and hot as we climbed and we stopped frequently for a breather. Even so, it only took just over an hour for us to reach the amazing terraces the Incas had built just below the summit of Huayna Picchu. Why they should have gone to such extreme lengths to build gardens in such an inaccessible place has puzzled most archaeologists. The only explanation, tied in with the fact that there are tunnels and ruins of other constructions, believed to be temples, near the top, is that these were sacred gardens for the priests who stayed in the temples.

We reached the summit and sat on the highest point, a huge boulder, gazing out at the panorama of mountains and Machu Picchu spread out six hundred metres below us. From where we sat, we could see the Urubamba River describing a great arc, almost full circle, around the base of our mountain. It was supremely quiet.

We went back down from the summit to one of the small terraces thirty metres or so below and relaxed there for half an hour amidst a profusion of wild flowers. After ten minutes or so, we heard someone else come climbing up the track. He was an American, about twenty-seven or twenty-eight years old. He smiled, said hello, and we talked for a few minutes before he continued on up to the summit. A few minutes later, he came back down again to sit with us, gaze at the view and chat.

It's terrific to meet people under circumstances like that, particularly when they are pleasant and interesting like Peter Nahan. He came from a farm on the shores of Lake Superior in Michigan, but for the past four months or so he had been working as a mining engineer in Ecuador. We talked of Ecuador and the Galapagos Islands, which he had also just visited, but strangely what we found most interesting were some of the tales he told of his childhood as one of a family of fifteen living by the lake. Life had been full of horses and dogs, racoons in the forest and canoeing, and I thought of how vital it is for children to have experiences like that to remember. Certainly it's important that they should grow up being able to cope with life in the city . . . the competitive rat-race, if you like, the hurly-burly, the pressures and all the running around. But something of that soft, country background makes all the difference to a child's . . . a person's life, I think.

We made our way carefully down the mountain again, taking only forty minutes for the descent, then sat around on the verandah of the hotel, drinking 'Inca Cola' and 'Jesus Mineral Water' until the time came to board the buses that carried us down to the small railway station on the floor of the valley where we were to take the train back to Cuzco. It was difficult to think that, in a few hours we would be there and by tomorrow, back in Lima. In many ways it was an unwelcome thought. None of us really wanted to leave. Machu Picchu had been a magic place and I think that more than anything else, what I shall always remember most strongly is the great aura of peace and solitude which surrounds it.

PERU

16
Stuck in the mud

Welcome back to Lima; to the omnipresent stench of human urine; some streets, even worse than others, appear to be established as public open urinals; to the low-lying pall of pollution and to the quite astonishing degree of noise which any sizeable cluster of people creates.

After only ten days away, the big city was an insult to the senses. Yet Lima was also friendly in its superficial familiarity. It was a rarity for us to travel backwards; to recognise street patterns and to check into the same hotel. This was pleasure in the known.

We said goodbye to Carl who was going to stay with friends on the outskirts of the city. In the jostle of the crowded streets, we were already becoming strangers.

Among the mail at American Express there was a letter from my Dad, written in a painfully obvious attempt to appear normal and cheerful and another telegram. With a dread, dulled by anticipation, we opened it to read, 'Trouble with house. Please phone. Jan.' The real world seemed to be inescapable on this trip. Back at the hotel we fetched the insurance papers for the house from our portable office in the lower 'shelf' of Iain's pack and put in a call to Sydney.

While we waited, we discussed the endless list of possible horrors which might have struck number twenty-five and how we would react.

'What do you think we should do if there's been a landslide and the house has slid into the sea?' Iain voiced our joint number-one horror.

'Well . . . what do you think?'

'No, I asked first. You say.'

Pause.

'Let's both say together at the same time,'

The children followed our tense conversation like a tennis match.

'Keep going!' we both said together, and then laughed with relief.

'Just let the mortgage build up?'

'Yes. After all the bank can hardly put it up for sale if it's swilling about on Bilgola Beach!'

'Then sort it all out after we've done the trip?'

'Right. After all, if we don't go back for my old man, I'm not packing it in for a bloody house.'

We were agreed and prepared. So when Jan's voice informed us, that, 'the electrical wiring has gone haywire and only a couple of lights are working, what shall I do?' we laughed with relief and asked her to please find an electrician to fix it!

Of course, it was only imagination but I could hear the surf and feel the sand and smell the sea in her voice. An earlier letter from her had told us that she was excited to be pregnant with their second child.

'Congratulations!' the children and I yelled into the joint handset. Jan laughed then chatted pleasantly for a minute or two and was gone, putting the phone down like a lid, shutting out the familiar and I was left to wonder why we travel.

Outside in the main street, we gawped at glass display cases in which were exhibited huge and beautiful multi-coloured butterflies and huge and ugly black tarantulas. We were tempted to buy some, but knew there was no hope of them arriving unsmashed and had visions of my sister opening a parcel for customs clearance in Toronto, to be confronted by a hairy-legged, bulbous-bodied spider! Instead we bought a carved gourd and, back at the hotel, we wrapped it up along with a stack of research material.

On the way we found the address which had been given to us of a place where we could take our phials of gammaglobulin and have a professional shoot it into our systems. 'Injectables' the faded and stained sign was not a good omen. Silently we trooped up the filthy wooden staircase and in the gloom, tripped over broken, formerly beautiful tiles on the landing floor as we felt our way from door to door searching for the right number.

Iain knocked and it was opened by a dishevelled woman to reveal a domestic jumble of considerable proportions, the smell of which reached Sean, who without another word fled downstairs, followed hastily by Zara. Iain stammered his apologies along with the word 'injectables'. The woman nodded. We gathered that the injector was out and would be back this afternoon if we cared to call then. Thank you. We backed over the tiles and turning, scuttled downstairs after the children. Sean, standing on the sidewalk tensed, as if ready to make his escape, was adamant.

'I am not going back in there for an injection!' But he need not have worried. We were unanimous. We'd look for another place.

'Perhaps we should learn to give it to one another,' I suggested. There was a horrified silence. It seemed that practising our hairdressing skills was one thing, but boning up on medical practice quite another.

That evening we had a farewell dinner with Larry. We'd only known each other for a week or so and yet because we'd shared that high-point of our life, Machu Picchu, together, it was like saying goodbye to an old friend. One of the difficulties of having a collection of friends who live in different parts of the world, is accepting a constant background sadness. How many times have I wished that a particular friend, whom I knew would enjoy a special aspect of what I was seeing or doing, could be transported instantly to share it with us. There never has been and never will be a time when all the people I care for deeply will be in one place at one time. I day-dream of being so wealthy that I could fly my friends in for gigantic get-togethers. But the pessimistic realist in me knows that, just because I love each one separately does not mean that they would even like each other! So saying goodbye to Larry was a sadness which only our common weal as a family could comfort.

Next morning in subdued moods, Zara most of all because she had developed a hacking cough during the night, we searched for and found another 'Injectables' clinic which by comparison was rather more acceptable. At least the woman wore a cleanish white coat and she did wash her hands. We handed over our gammaglobulin, together with disposable needles, which we had bought in the hope of reducing, as far as possible, the risks of infection.

When it came to my turn to pull down my jeans and bend over, I didn't feel the plunge of the needle at all because I was so embarrassed to come eyeball to eyeball with a brightly-hued picture poster of Christ who stared back at me with a baleful expression, not from sympathy with me over my vulnerable position, but because in his hand he held a bright red St Valentine's Day card caricature of his heart which dripped clots of blood.

One of the most pleasant aspects of our brief return to Lima was the 'Chez Giselle' for breakfast. The 'Chez Giselle' was a tiny cafe around the corner from our hotel. It was run by Giselle, an aging (I guess about sixty or sixty-five-year-old) Frenchwoman who had, at one stage in her youth, apparently been reasonably well known in European theatrical circles as a dancer and singer. The walls of her little restaurant were festooned with photographs and press clippings of Giselle in her spangled tights, Giselle in top hat and tails, Giselle in a chorus line, Giselle shaking hands or being hugged and kissed by hordes of different personalities and smiling out of group photographs at the tables of various nightspots in different European cities.

And, here in Lima, Giselle hovered about us on the days we ate breakfast there, ensuring that the croissants and milk coffee were just as we would have had them in Paris. But also, we felt, she was pleased to have the opportunity of using her English again. There was, though, a touch of sadness about the restaurant. Giselle, on the surface, seemed perfectly happy with her life in Lima, where she had lived for more than twenty years. But underneath, we could sense great homesickness.

'Ah, Paree . . .' she said, on more than one occasion, '. . . zose were ze good old days.'

While in Lima this time we spent almost a whole day stocking up on foodstuffs and medicines. Fortunately, as in most Latin American countries, doctors' prescriptions are not needed to buy pharmaceuticals. I mean fortunately for us, because, as travellers, the business and the expense of finding doctors and getting prescriptions every time you need medicine would drive you crazy. It also poses difficulties when you want to buy several courses of antibiotics to carry just *in case* you need them. It may *not* be fortunate for those living permanently in these places to have such easy access to powerful drugs, but that's another argument.

We bought a number of courses of the broad-spectrum antibiotic Penbritin and a couple of bottles of Tetracycline tablets. I suppose there will be doctors reading this who may shudder and shake their heads, but all I can say is that these pills served their purpose very well, when they were eventually used . . . with no ill effects. We also bought more malaria tablets, iodine (an additional water purifying agent), germicidal soap, disinfectant, antibiotic powder for festering cuts etc., a variety of other medicaments as well as stacks of insect repellent of various kinds.

Several of the places for which we were heading in the Amazon jungles were described as swarming with mosquitoes, so we felt it would also be prudent to carry a mosquito net each, to use at night. But, as Lima is virtually mosquito free, being so dry, we found it practically impossible to buy mosquito nets there. Eventually we had to settle for the alternative of four large sheets of tulle, which we could rig up over our beds, bunks, hammocks or whatever.

We knew that food would be a problem, once we got to the river, so we bought enough supplies of various tinned and dry food to fill a couple of medium-sized cardboard boxes to carry with us. It would be awkward, but, we hoped, worth it. I tied them securely with thick twine and then made handles for them both so that Trish and I could carry one each, in addition to our packs.

Ever since we had left San Diego, we had been carrying a tiny collapsible stove which burnt benzine, or dry-cleaning fluid, or white gas, as the Americans call it, but, up until now, we had not had occasion to use it. In fact we didn't even know if it *would* work. We discovered that in most parts of South America, chemist shops stock benzine, so we bought a large bottle of it and determined to have a practice run with our cooker.

We had another parcel of books, reference material and the few souvenirs we had bought along the way, which we were hoping to send off by post before we left Lima. But it was the weekend and the post office would not be open until Monday. By waiting to post the parcel on Monday, we would unfortunately miss the Monday train that was to take us on the first leg of our journey towards the Amazon. There was, however, another train on Tuesday and we would have to settle for that.

In the meantime we took off to look at some of the other areas of Lima, in particular, the Miraflores district which is a relatively affluent suburb of attractive homes and shopping centres in tree-lined streets which run down to steep cliffs overlooking a long, pebbly beach on the Pacific Ocean. We wandered about the area for some time, simply sight-seeing and people-watching. Looking down from the high cliffs above the beach, we saw a beautiful, blue swimming pool which attracted Zara and Sean's attention and they begged to be allowed to swim there. I felt sure that it was a private swimming pool, but undertook, if we returned the next afternoon, to try to talk our way in.

After a rest on the lawn in the shade of a palm tree in a park above the beach, we went by bus to another nearby suburb, where we visited the famous Lima Gold Museum. For the past couple of months, we seemed to have been in and out of so many churches, temples, ruins and museums that, although we had enjoyed them, we were beginning to feel that we had had enough. But I think we more or less realised that this one would probably be the last of this type of institution we would see for quite some time, so we made the best of it.

The Spaniards, as we've said frequently here, apparently felt no appreciation of the great artistic value of the Inca golden treasures they seized and proceeded to simply melt them down to gold ingots. But this state-owned gold museum in

Lima contains a beautiful collection of some of the marvellous Inca golden artifacts which escaped the Spaniards. They are not many when compared with the huge hoard the Conquistadores took, but the collection still represents a large fortune and gives at least some indication of the fineness and beauty of the Inca and pre-Columbian craftsmanship in golden necklaces, vests, mantles and cloaks, woven in spun gold, gloves made of finely beaten and intricately designed gold and dozens of small golden human and animal figures.

The following day, Monday, we set out early, in order to post our parcel of books and odd souvenirs. Two hours later, we walked out of the post office in a lather of perspiration and frustration, having only just completed what should have been a simple task lasting five or ten minutes. Our parcel, which we had neatly wrapped and tied the previous day, had to be completely undone. A customs officer had to be found to examine what we were sending *out* of the country and then, after we were told that there was *no export duty* to pay on the goods!!, a postal officer informed us that the parcel would have to be wrapped in calico and sewn up before they would accept it. We had to go off to find a shop which sold calico, then return and sew up our parcel, by which time we were close to exploding and Zara and Sean were completely fed up.

Anyway, once it was finally accomplished, we took the bus back to Miraflores and managed, by slipping the swimming pool manager a small bribe, to talk ourselves into the 'Waikiki Beach Club' pool, the one we had seen from the cliffs on the day before. As it was a normal working day for most people, the pool was virtually empty, so we had a quiet, relaxing afternoon ... at least Trish and I did. Sean and Zara ran and swam themselves to a standstill ... before returning to our hotel to get our gear ready for the train trip in the morning.

Before going to bed that night though, I tried out our portable benzine-powered stove/cooker. It was a great success and continued to be so for the rest of the entire trip.

'Col. E A Haine. Author.' The card made the announcement with military precision and the dapper little man who proffered it smiled with boyish enthusiasm. 'Coming aboard?' he asked as if the train for Oroya standing in Lima Station that early morning was his own private vehicle. And as we settled into our seats, 'I can hardly believe I'm here. Keep pinching myself to see if it's really me. Promised myself all my life that I would travel on this line and now ...' he looked about, barely able to prevent himself whooping with joy, 'Well, here I am.'

He stowed his one bag under his seat as he asked, 'You railway enthusiasts too?' When we shook our heads, he looked sorry for us. 'Pity. It's a masterpiece you know, this line is. It reaches the highest altitude of any standard gauge railway in the world, 4800 metres. Higher than any mountain in Europe. The ruling gradient is 4½ percent and along its whole length there are sixty-six tunnels, fifty-nine bridges and twenty-two switchbacks.' He announced the figures with pride. 'Unbelieveable. It was started in 1870. The brainchild of the great American railway engineer Henry Meiggs and it took twenty-three years to complete. Of course the construction was financed by a British company and the work actually done by imported Chinese labourers.'

'And are you going to write about the railway?'

'Yes. Yes.' The Colonel was emphatic. As if there could be anything else in the world worth writing about. 'My trip is financed by the club to which I belong. We are all railway enthusiasts. Very keen.'

The carriage had begun to fill up. Right on the scheduled time, it jolted forward as the train began to move and I thought the Colonel might actually pass out with excitement. Almost as soon as we left the outskirts of the city, we began to climb steadily and in less than half an hour we were at Choisica, already over seven hundred and sixty metres above sea level and well above the cloud and smog-bank covering Lima. This is where the well-heeled Limans have their weekenders, and many attractive modern houses could be seen through the windows clinging to the hillsides.

Then we really started to climb. At times the mountains appeared to jut out and almost overhang the tiny train as it traversed the first of the zig-zags. Backwards and forwards we went through tunnels and over bridges from canyon to canyon. The ever-changing view was spectacular; deep ravines and towering peaks.

At San Bartholome station the tiny platform was crowded with Indian women in layered skirts and ponchos, but by the time we reached Casapalca we were into lead and zinc mining country and the passengers were mostly Indian men rugged up against the cold, their pinched faces peering out from under their thick caps.

'There! You see!' The Colonel's shout made me jump. 'The flag! That must be Mount Meiggs.' A metal flag painted with the Peruvian colours of red and white, frozen in perpetual national pride, like the American astronauts' moon flags, was stuck, not on top of the highest mountain in the area, but on the one through which runs the longest tunnel, an impressive 1200-metre hole cut through solid Andean rock.

Beyond was Galera, the highest railway station in the world. Nothing more marked the spot than a single, unattractive shed bearing the name Galera and a sign saying 4,781 metres, 15,681 feet. It was plonked down in a raw scene bereft of any other building or evidence of life. Naturally we all tumbled forth to be shocked by the cold and left wobbly-kneed by the lack of oxygen. Colonel Haines was a truly fulfilled man.

Back on board, we trundled off again through the bleak barren landscape and a steward began to bring round bowls of steaming-hot, tasty soup. Colonel Haines asked us to inquire if there was anything else to eat. 'I don't speak anybody else's lingo you know,' he confided with a touch of pride. This admission conjured up pictures of him bumbling through countries and across continents clutching a railway timetable and oblivious of everything except the size of the gauge and the quality of the track!

I couldn't take more than a sip of the delicious soup because as in Puno and Cuzco my olfactory senses seemed to be so oversensitised by the altitude that my nose forced me to reject what my stomach yearned for! So while they sipped, I told the Colonel of our trip on the Tanzam, Chinese-built railway in East Africa. He was green with envy and couldn't hear enough about the perfection of the blue metal embankment on which the track runs for over sixteen hundred kilometres.

But even these reveries had to cease, because we had come to Oraya and the parting of the ways. The Colonel was staying with the train which turned south here to Huancayo and we were changing to catch one going north to Cerro de Pasco. We said our farewells and wished him luck with his writing.

On the cold platform of Oraya Station we all ferreted through our packs for sweaters and extra socks and shoes. The train we were to catch was already waiting in a siding. It was far less comfortable than the one we had just left, but at least there was an empty carriage and we could spread ourselves out for the start of a hundred and twenty-odd kilometre run.

This happy situation did not last. The rattling train made frequent stops to pick up groups of Indians. Again all of them were pinched with the cold and it was perhaps because of the climate, that there was also a strong smell ·of unwashed bodies!

Snow-covered mountains formed a constant backdrop, the snow occasionally even coming down to the track. For the entire journey the landscape was barren and inhospitable. For much of the time we were crossing the Junin plateau, one of the world's largest high-altitude plains and the battle-field where Simon Bolivar defeated the Spaniards in 1824. What a fearsome place to do battle and yet,· if people must fight, perhaps they should be confined to areas of bleak desolation such as this.

Several of the men who had boarded the train, miners by the looks of them were already inebriated and continued to swig away, passing a bottle around among their large group of friends. Their conversation became increasingly loud and slurred and their faces reddened by a combination of the cold and the liquor. Their women, mountainous under heavy cloaks and voluminous skirts, continued to knit, crochet or spin as they looked on indulgently. In the bleak, thin, grey light the few carriage lights which functioned illuminated a scene very reminiscent of a Hogarth painting.

It was dark and even colder by the time we pulled into Cerro de Pasco. It was also snowing and there was slush underfoot. We crammed ouselves and our packs onto a bus, built, it would seem, for dwarves. Hunched over in ridiculously uncomfortable positions, we travelled the short distance to the centre of town. Here the only hotel we could find was decidedly dirty and thankfully full up.

At this height, 4370 metres, the packs which at sea level were fairly hefty, had become very nearly unmanageable. Our load had also been made far worse by having to carry the additional leaden weight of two cartons full of canned and boxed food.

We were told that the one other hotel was in the newer part of town, a few kilometres away, but when we found it, squatting in a wasteland of partially completed buildings, it looked very deserted and when we entered, we found it as cold inside as out.

In what passed as a reception room we found the manager, at least we thought that's what he was, huddled round an ineffective little heater with a group of men. No one spoke and the atmosphere was heavy with unwelcome. But we persisted that we needed a room and while Iain haggled with the man, who finally pocketed our money, I gazed at the pin-up pictures of naked European women cavorting under the glass top of his desk and wished that I was in a climate where I could divest myself of so many garments. Perhaps the manager did too and that was why he was so offhand.

The room he took us to had only two beds and was bitterly cold. Its two-bar heater, he warned us, must be turned off when we slept because it would eat up the all-too-precious oxygen and we could easily asphyxiate ourselves. There was hot water. Scalding hot. And only a little trickle of cold water. So it wasn't possible to regulate the shower to a bearable warmth. This necessitated us bobbing back and forth into the too-hot water and out into the too-cold air. There were one and a half thin towels. The kids didn't even mention food because there obviously wasn't any.

We shared our single beds and lay our sleeping bags on top for the extra necessary warmth. In an attempt to comfort ourselves, Iain started on a chapter of *Huckleberry Finn* but had to stop because he had a raging altitude headache and couldn't get his breath to read. Huddled against the cold we lay awake listening to the difficult breathing of the children and eventually dropped off to sleep ourselves.

I awoke with a heart-lurching start and lay awake almost trembling waiting to catch the sound of the children's breath. Nothing. Two minutes in the low ebb of the night feels like two hours. Panic rose and I reached out to touch their bodies, terrified that I would discover them to be already stiff and coldly dead from lack of oxygen. Of course they were warmly pliant, but after that I dozed only fitfully for the rest of that nasty night and was aware that Iain too was tense and breathless in his shallow sleep waiting for the morning.

The following day was one of those rare ones in which, as it progresses, everything seems to get better and better. Mind you, with Cerro de Pasco as a starting point, it would be difficult for things *not* to get better. My memories of the place are anything but pleasant; we found ourselves wondering why the hell anyone would choose to live in a place like Cerro de Pasco when, within a distance of only thirty-two kilometres or so, the climate and countryside are a thousand percent more attractive and within ninety-six kilometres and a drop of some 2400 metres, there is the pleasant and comfortable little town of Huanuco. It's one of those aspects of civilisation which I find infinitely sad; that people should make traps for themselves, or so willingly accept the traps of custom, convention, employment, family and so on that prevent them from moving, often only very small distances, in order to change their lives for the better. This, of course, applies all over the world, not just in Peru and Cerro de Pasco.

I'm sure the residents of Cerro de Pasco didn't want any sympathy from us and, if they were asked, they'd almost certainly have said that they were perfectly happy where they were, thank you very much. To which, I suppose all I could say would be 'good luck'.

As for us, we took off at the earliest possible opportunity in a collectivo, which, for US$2.50 each, took us on the two-and-a-half-hour run to Huanuco.

The journey was like a tonic. As the road descended through rugged and bleak mountain passes our altitude sickness began to disappear. We saw trees again, then rich, green, beautiful valleys. We were winding constantly downwards beside the tumbling torrent of the Huallaga River, which like us, was on its way to a rendezvous with the Amazon.

Stopping in Huanuco about mid-morning, we felt as if we were in a different world, as though an oppressive load had been lifted from our backs. Although it was still some 1900 metres above sea level, it was warm and sunny. People wore brighter clothes and their faces were not grim with the cold. After a big breakfast of fried eggs, toast and tomatoes and hot coffee, we continued on, in the same collectivo, for another two-and-a-half-hour run to Tingo Maria.

At Tingo, as our driver affectionately called it, we were another 1200 metres lower, the climate and vegetation had become lush and tropical. Under these conditions we would have been happy to sleep in a tent, but the State Tourist Hotel, on the outskirts of the town by the river, was just too good and too cheap to pass up. It was a low, rambling, jungle bungalow-style building with a big, open verandah running right around it, and it was set in truly beautiful surroundings. On the other side of the Huallaga River, which, at this point, ran past the hotel fast and deep, green hills rolled off into the distance.

Apart from us, there were not more than half a dozen other guests in the hotel. We took two double rooms for a total of about US$8.00 and set about enjoying the rest of the day; beginning with a swim in the outdoor pool during an absolute downpour of torrential, but warm rain. Tingo Maria has upwards of 305 centimetres of rain a year. Then there was table tennis with Zara and Sean and afternoon tea on the verandah. All very civilised. As we sat there, two men in a dugout canoe came into view on the river, working their way tortuously upstream, paddling against the powerful current and gradually succeeding by sticking as close as possible to the far bank.

We felt as if we were on holiday ... suspended in time for a brief moment. Tingo Maria had won us completely. Nowhere on the trip so far had we found such a pleasant little place. That evening, we ate a meal of steak and chips on the verandah and, though we were in the open, there were no mosquitoes or insects.

After putting Zara and Sean to bed and reading two chapters of *Huck Finn,* Trish and I sat on the verandah again in the dark, velvet warmth of the night, sipping on pisco sours, looking out into the blackness and listening to the sounds of the river.

The fact that the collectivo, which we had arranged to pick us up at the self-indulgent hour of 9.00 a.m., finally arrived at eleven did not augur well for the rest of the day. And when, less than eight kilometres out of town the noisy, old, blue Chevrolet had its first flat, we should have taken the hint, turned back, and waited until the next day before heading off on the two hundred and seventy kilometre trip to Pucallpa.

But being unquenchable optimists, we helped the driver change the tyre, which left us with no spare, and pressed on along a moderately good road which climbed out of the tropical greenery to the watershed, the Cordillera Azula, between the Huallaga and Ucayali Rivers.

Iain sat in the front, with Sean between him and the rather surly and very macho, dark-complexioned driver who seemed distinctly cavalier about having our lives in his trust! He appeared not to speak or understand any English and made no attempt to help us communicate in Spanish, so after a while we abandoned the effort. Zara and I shared the back seat with a friendly middle-aged woman of enormous proportions who was laden with quantities of overflowing handbags. She told us she was a salesperson for a fabric company and was going on a selling trip to Pucallpa. She stroked Zara's blonde hair.

'Linda!' she said as she rummaged in one of her bags to give to her a small plastic Peruvian coat of arms and me a calendar printed on a small square of material.

The pass we were making for was the Boqueron Padre Abad, named after a priest who had found the route through the virtually impassable mountains back in 1757. The location of the pass was lost for generations but, after a long search, rediscovered around the beginning of this century. The pass, which is about four kilometres long and 1980 metres below the tops of the jagged peaks around it, crosses the divide between Peru's deserts and mountains and her Amazonian jungle interior. Our Chevrolet, which had coughed its way to the top, now ground its teeth on the way down. There was an immediate deterioration in the condition of the road and I was reminded of the change which occurs at Gretna Green as you leave England and enter Scotland and realise why the Scots talk of devolution. I wondered if we would find that those who live in the Amazonas region of Peru were similarly motivated.

The road was now unsurfaced and deep runnels had been worn into it by heavy downpours of tropical rain. The Aguaytia River raged through the canyon and we followed beside it, fifteen metres or so above its boulder-strewn course, gawping at the spume it sent up and the rainbows which formed as the light caught the fine sparklets of water.

'Stop! Stop!' Iain called, 'I must get a photograph of that.' A jet of water spurted over the top of a sheer canyon wall and plumed down perhaps 450 metres to dive beneath the swift surface of the river. The driver slithered to a halt in the loose shale and we all scrambled out, glad also for a chance to stretch and walk. At first there appeared to be total silence but then we realised that it was just that the roar of the river obliterated all other sounds. Iain tried the impossible task of capturing the scene on film and we had begun to reload ourselves into the car, when Sean called out: 'We've got another flat tyre!'

The driver, who was already seated impatiently behind the wheel came round to the back to stare at the offending piece of equipment and then, with an air of resignation prepared to jack up the vehicle. Half an hour later and two tyres, the spare and the recent casualty, in hand, he thumbed a lift on a truck going in the direction of Pucallpa. From what we could gather the nearest place where it would be possible to have them repaired was Aguaytia which was forty-eight kilometres and therefore at least an hour away over such poor road conditions.

We made a mental adjustment and accepted the fact that we would not reach Pucallpa by nightfall and contemplated the possibility that we might not reach there at all on this day. Zara and Sean went off to explore. Iain took more photographs. I moved to let our travel companion snooze in the back seat while I sat up front and finished Graham Greene's *Travels with My Aunt* and immediately began William Stevenson's *A Man Called Intrepid*.

When Zara and Sean returned, we occupied ourselves by walking about 400 metres or so to a bridge which crossed the river and there we played Pooh Sticks. For those deprived folk who have never read Winnie the Pooh, it should be explained that this game consists of dropping sticks off one side of the bridge and rushing to the other there to wait anxiously to see whose stick appears first. This also involved a great deal of shouting, 'It's mine.' 'I can see mine.' 'Mine was first,' and more in similar vein.

The game tends to bring out the beast, or rather the Pooh in people, even grown-up ones; Pooh sulks when Piglet wins, so after we had been at Pooh Sticks for awhile, it was a welcome diversion when several flocks of bright yellow birds flew down the gorge and we all tried to follow their flight through the luxuriant growth of tropical ferns and dense foliage that clung to the sheer precipice sides. At least for a change it was a beautiful place to be stranded in. It was neither too hot nor too cold and after four hours, we were discussing the possibility of breaking open our river rations when our driver dropped off the back of only the third vehicle to come by since his departure.

The tyre was quickly on and then, feeling safe in the luxury of a spare, we were on our way again. Well, at least we covered a hundred metres before an ominous thumping from the front offside told us that the original spare was flat again! The tyre must have had a slow leak and been deflating even during our wait. The driver, dirty and dishevelled from climbing in and out from under the car, could not believe it. In typical Latin fashion, he threw his arms in the air, muttered, no doubt some unprintable abuse, and once more changed tyres, leaving us again with no spare.

We drove off, leaving the close confines of the steep canyon walls, across the bridge and into a tunnel cut through the base of a mountain. Shortly we found ourselves passing through less mountainous country and we realised that from now on the Andes were behind us and we would be heading down towards the vast jungles of the Amazon basin.

The horizon of the late afternoon began to fill with steel grey thunderheads which bulged out toward us with frightening rapidity. Lightning illuminated, in stupendous zigs and zags, the rutted, potholed road, putting to comparative shade the luminosity of the almost full moon.

It was close to dark when we reached the small settlement of Aguaytia and the driver pointed to the place where he had had the tyres fixed. There were no lights, it was obviously empty and there was no value in trying to get the spare repaired. He pulled up outside a square, tin-roofed building with open sides; the local café, and we only just got inside when the skies opened and a tropical downpour bucketed down; the separate drops of rain so fat they burst against the verandah like water-filled balloons at a children's birthday party.

We felt like ancient cave-dwellers as we ate our chicken and rice while staring out from our protected place into the deluge only a couple of metres away. The storm subsided even more quickly than it started just as if a giant shower had been turned off. We regained the road and resumed our journey, having taken eight hours to cover only one-third of the distance.

An hour later there was an ominous groan from the driver and once more we pulled to a halt at the side of the jungle road. I didn't even bother to get out. Iain's shout of dismay was enough. The rear offside tyre was almost flat, due to another slow leak; our fourth flat in one day. Iain was incredulous. There was no place nearer than Pucallpa where it could be filled let alone fixed. We were all sitting disconsolately in the car and I was about to unroll the bags to soften the seats for sleeping when the total blackness of the sky was illuminated by the headlights of an oncoming vehicle, the first we had seen since our dinner stop. The gods must have been smiling on us.

The driver turned our car lights on and flashed them continuously as a May Day message, then, when the truck, which seemed huge as it loomed out of the night at us, was a hundred metres away, he planted himself mid-road. The oncoming truck ground its gears and pumped its airbrakes as it slowed painfully. After a conversation, shouted above the noise of the idling engine, the truckie's mate dismounted with an airhose. They attached one end of this to our slowly flattening tyre and the other to a small air compressor which they carried with them for emergencies just such as this. But the relief we felt was only slight because such makeshift provisions seemed unlikely to be adequate to see us through to the end of the road. So, as soon as we were moving again, I submitted to a wave of fatigue, cuddled up to Zara and dropped into a deep sleep.

'Look out! Stop! Stop!' Iain's shouts woke me just as there was a terrible thud. The children and I came instantly awake to see that we were right in among a herd of cattle. We had obviously hit one and the sweating driver was trembling so much that he couldn't manipulate the gear shift into reverse. When he did, with much grinding, he accelerated wildly backwards and we felt and heard a sickening mangling beneath us and then saw in the headlights, the bloody, torn remnants of a baby calf.

The children screamed and I yelled, 'Stop!' The animal was horrendously dead, but the least we could do was pull the broken body to the edge so that it would not suffer the indignity of being splattered flat by other vehicles. Also it would reduce the risk of other cows, crowding as they do round the sick and maimed, also being hit.

But he wouldn't stop. He looked like a man possessed by devils as he threw the wheel violently over and almost drove off into the thick grass to get past the broken herd.

'Stop! Stop!' Zara cried, the tears pouring down her cheeks as with both hands she hit the driver about the head. 'You killed it. You murderer! You bastard!' she sobbed. A hundred metres or so further on, when he regained the road, the driver put up his arm to fend off her blows and I tried to quieten her, though in my own anger at the driver, it was difficult.

'How did it happen?' I asked Iain.

He answered from the front without turning around, his voice low with emotion. 'He was travelling fast. It was very dark because of the clouds, and suddenly we were on them. The calf was trotting along close to its mother, the mother swerved to avoid being hit and we hit the calf.'

'You murderer!' Zara shouted again.

The driver, who until that moment had showed no understanding of English at all, suddenly spoke quite clearly in English. 'Not my fault. They go in front of me. I cannot stop.'

'But you could have at least let us move the body,' I insisted.

'No,' he declared. 'If police catch me, I must pay and I am poor man. And if farmer catch me ...' he rolled his eyes and made a throat slitting gesture, '... dead!'

Thankfully there were only another eleven kilometres to Pucallpa to be covered in an air of tense hostility. The travelling saleswoman, as distressed as we were by the incident, suggested that we stay at the hotel she always patronised, the Tariri. We arrived at 11.00 p.m. and took her advice, and there were only three other happenings before we finally slept.

Firstly Iain, while trying out the lock on our door, locked us into our room and himself out and we had to shout out of the windows overlooking the street until the owner came to our assistance. Then I swept Zara's watch which was lurking under a towel onto the tile floor and smashed the glass and finally, as I was dropping off, I realised that I had left my book, *A Man Called Intrepid* in the collectivo. As my notes put it, 'quite a day'.

I can remember, long before we left home to head for South America, looking at a map, trying to decide which would be the best place from where to start a river trip down the Amazon. Technically the Amazon starts where the Maranon and the Ucayali Rivers meet, but by that stage is is already a very, very big river. Better then, we thought, to start the journey from further up one of the mighty river's tributaries. Even at that distance, I recall thinking that Pucallpa, some 800 kilometres up the Ucayali, above the Amazon, looked as good a place as any, although its description in the *South American Handbook* did not sound too encouraging: 'An unattractive town, still in the pioneer stage with unpaved, but lit streets, and no adequate water or sewage system.'

Now, here we were in Pucallpa at last, hoping to find a boat to take us 1000, 2000, maybe even 3000 kilometres down the river. There was, I should say, nowhere else to go. Pucallpa was the end of the line. Except for the road back, the one on which we had just come, there was no other way to travel except down the river ... or up, if you wanted to, but there was even less to look for upriver.

Even on first impressions, Pucallpa turned out to be a much more interesting place than the prearrival image had led us to expect because, if nothing else, Pucallpa had colour and character.

During our first night in Pucallpa it rained heavily and continuously, so that when we emerged in the morning the town was a mudbath, an incredible mudbath. It's almost unbelievable that a town with a population pushing 100,000 has no paved streets whatever. When it's dry, Pucallpa's streets are blown by a fine, red dust. When it's wet, they become quagmires in which vehicles of all shapes and sizes become bogged. We took our sandals off and walked barefoot through the mud to look around the town. Any other form of footwear, other than wellington boots, would have been pointless. Cars and trucks were hopelessly stuck in several of the streets. Two heavily-laden trucks were actually bogged to the axles, back to back, like copulating dogs. The second one had backed up to the first in an attempt to transfer its load and in the process became stuck itself.

On our way to the port we bought four large, clear sheets of industrial plastic and, cutting holes in them, used them as improvised raincoats. Then, at the Libraria Verdad (Truth Bookstore) we met Martin Cross, an American evangelical missionary who has been working in Pucallpa for fourteen years. We were buying a couple of notebooks and pens there and also trying to find a town map of Pucallpa. Picking us as obvious strangers, he came out from his office to speak to us. He was a stocky man of about forty-five with dark hair and a boyish face. He told us that there were no maps available, but he was able to give us directions to the Port Captain's office and the port.

'The actual port has shifted,' he informed us. 'It used to be just down from here,' he pointed out of the window towards the Ucayali River, which ran by, broad and muddy, about a hundred metres away, 'but the mudbanks have all shifted and collapsed, so they have had to move the port about three kilometres down the river.'

'What's there?' I asked.

'Well, it's just a collection of riverboats and tugs pulled up against the mudbank and they load and unload their cargo there . . . or, I should say, try to unload, because, under these conditions,' he waved his hand towards the road and the rain which was still falling heavily, 'it's practically impossible.'

'Why haven't they done anything about the roads?' Trish asked. 'It seems amazing that in a town this size . . .'

'They've had the money to seal the roads four times,' Martin said, 'but each time something has happened; either it's gone into some politician's pocket, or it's been spent on something else.'

'But surely people complain. Can't they do anything about it?'

The missionary smiled. 'When I first came here, I thought like that. After a while, you begin to realise that it is a pattern of life the people here are used to. You can't change it. If something gets done . . . well, that's lucky. If it doesn't . . . well, that's just too bad. Maybe next time.'

Nelson Munio Rios is short and dark haired. He was born in the Peruvian province of Amazonas thirty-two years ago. He has served for fourteen years in the Peruvian navy. Now he is Captain of the Port of Pucallpa.

'I have been to Germany,' he informed us as we stood talking in his office, '. . . and America . . . Miami. Very nice.'

The Port Captain's office is, unfortunately, due to the shifting river's whims, no longer anywhere near the port, but the bureaucracy is unwilling to shift to the port's new location which is little more than a shanty town. So it remains in its original position overlooking the muddy river bank where shallow-draft boats can still approach to land fruit and vegetables for the town's market and small, canvas-canopied dugouts, powered by outboard motors, ferry passengers back and forth from nearby villages.

Here, fishermen carry gaping-mouthed, piraiba catfish of gigantic proportions; 50 to 100 kilos, on their backs up from the river to load into trucks. Shipibo Indian women with their black hair cut in straight bangs across their foreheads, wander through the market crowds selling patterned bead necklaces and armbands and everybody seems totally unconcerned with the hundreds of large, black vultures . . . or buzzards . . . which continually swoop low over the bustling waterfront to land in the street, whenever the opportunity of dropped garbage, rotting fruit, or a piece of fish presents itself. When they are not in the air, or on the roadway, these ominous-looking birds perch on the roofs of the town's two-storey buildings, hotels and houses; they are particularly fond of the Ristorante Internationale, just watching everything . . . and waiting.

'There are no boats going to Iquitos for several days,' Captain Munio informed us after consulting a big wall chart in his office.

'What about other ports downriver?' I asked him.

'There are no other ports,' he said. And then, 'Well, there are a couple of small villages, but no real towns.' He scratched his head. 'Perhaps there will be something tomorrow. Come back tomorrow. Or maybe you should also go to the port. Yes. You could try there.'

The driver of the rickety cab who took us to the site of the port proper declined to drive down the small hill to the end of the road by the river. He knew that in mud like this (we had slipped and slithered for just about all of the three kilometres to the port area) he would not be able to get his cab back up the hill again.

There was no joy for us at the riverside when we eventually sloshed and slurped our way down to it. It was a scene of unbelievable chaos; barges, boats, launches of every description tied by hawsers to large stakes, as thick as telephone poles, which had been driven into a huge, soft, black mudbank. Trucks laden with goods for shipping out by river, or loading up with goods that had come from the riverboats, were slipping helplessly about, trying to get in and out of the area with little success. Three or four of them were bogged down hopelessly. We went from boat to boat along the entire length of the mudbank. Nothing going downriver. And no one knew when there would be anything going.

'Great! We could be here for weeks,' I muttered disconsolately as we made our way back up the hill to look for a bus or taxi back to the town centre.

During the afternoon we bought a few more food supplies and medicines and then had a siesta ... just lying in our hotel reading and sleeping. All the shops closed up in the early afternoon, and with the sun now shining down from clear skies, the town had become a steambath. In the evening we ate a Chinese meal at the Chifa Man Keong in the Hotel Mercedes (all Chinese restaurants in Peru are called 'chifas'), then went to a terrible movie called 'The Adventures of Captain Nemo', starring Omar Sharif. Even the children, who are usually prepared to give the seal of approval to any movie with a bit of action and excitement, thought it was awful. So it must have been bad. The only thing Trish could think to say about it was that, 'Omar Sharif must have needed the money'.

There was only one other movie showing in Pucallpa while we were there, and a small van patrolled the streets, once the mud began to dry out, blaring advertisements for it through a loudspeaker. We didn't bother to see it. After Captain Nemo, we didn't want to chance it and anyway, the title was enough to put anyone off: 'Madre Porque Me Abandoneste?' ('Mother, why have you abandoned me?')

That night Zara's cough, which she had been nurturing since Lima, became worse. It kept her awake for some considerable time and in the morning we debated whether or not to start her on a course of antibiotics. We were reluctant to do so and, as she seemed much better after a good breakfast in a nearby restaurant, we decided not to.

Back at the port again, in sunny, but humid weather, we had our first stroke of luck ... or so it seemed. Another vessel had pulled in to the shore and was, we were told, heading downriver soon. It was the motor vessel *Campeon* ... a steel-hulled boat of probably 100 tonnes, which looked something like a large tug, with two or three cabins and a verandah along its upper deck. A large, iron barge was moored alongside.

We swayed across the plank linking the boat to the shore and met one of the crew, a mean, florid-faced man with a bristly moustache, who remained swinging in a hammock on the deck of the barge as we spoke to him.

We found that we could communicate at basic levels with almost anyone now in our Spanish ... broken and primitive thought it may have been, but this man was decidedly unhelpful and made no effort to speak either slowly or clearly to us. However, we did eventually discover from him that the *Campeon* would be heading for Yurimaguas, a town on the Huallaga River, within a couple of days. Quickly consulting our map, we pinpointed Yurimaguas and, although at first glance it appeared to be hundreds of kilometres from where we wanted to go, we saw that, to reach it the *Campeon* would have to travel some 800 kilometres down the Ucayali, almost to Iquitos, then turn to sail up the Maranon to get to its destination. Perhaps we could disembark somewhere near where it would leave the Ucayali.

'Where is the Captain?' I asked the man in the hammock.

'In one hour he will return.'

We wandered off to fill in time, looking at the activity along the banks of the river. Scores of sweating mestizo Indians ran barefoot back and forth from the barges to trucks, carrying huge loads on their backs; bags of flour, bags of sugar, bags of cement ... non-stop. Fifty metres back from the water an impromptu market had been set up to sell all sorts of fruit and vegetables as well as other food and drinks to the waterfront workers. We walked over to buy some soft drinks.

'Hello, senor,' a voice in English made us turn. 'How are you today?'

It was Captain Munio, the Port Captain, who had just driven up on a small motorcycle. 'I am inspecting,' he said, without waiting for a reply, 'inspecting the cargoes of the boats.'

'The *Campeon* ... ' I said, 'the *Campeon* is going soon. We hope to travel on it.'

'The *Campeon*? Ah yes. But she is going to Yurimaguas ... no?'

'Yes, but perhaps we can leave it at the Maranon River. On the map there is a town there.'

'Yes.' He paused a moment. 'That is correct ... Nauta. The Capitan will stop for you there.' Another pause. 'Capitan Gomez. You have speak with Capitan?'

'No, not yet.'

'Come. I know him. I will speak to him for you.'

We explained that the captain would not be back for at least another half an hour, but he insisted that we should return to the vessel with him anyway. The man in the hammock, who we discovered was the first mate, was considerably more polite this time. He got out of the hammock and spoke with some deference to our friend. The Port Captain insisted that the mate take us on a tour of the boat, during which we were shown a dingy cabin, about two metres long, by two metres wide, by two and a bit metres high into which four bunks were crammed.

'This will have to be painted for you,' the Port Captain said and issued a string of high-speed instructions in Spanish to the mate, who nodded, but said nothing. He looked at us with obvious dislike.

'But, this is not necessary ...' I began.

'Of course. You cannot travel in this cabin. It is too dirty. They will paint it for you.' He shrugged his shoulders. 'It is no problem.'

Perhaps not, I thought, but I'm sure it's not going to make us wonderfully popular with the crew . . . and the mate in particular. The mate left us shortly and we stood at the stern of the vessel making conversation with Captain Munio in a combination of our awkward Spanish and his awkward English. A huge splash near to the boat made us all turn towards the river.

'Look! Look!' Zara cried, 'a porpoise . . . a porpoise!'

'A porpoise? Here?' I said. 'No.' But then, one jumped clear of the water again and it obviously was a porpoise . . . or a dolphin of some kind. It was smooth and grey, about a metre long and had a blow-hole in the top of his head.

'Yes,' Captain Munio said. 'Amazon dolphins. There are many of them here. They are freshwater dolphins.'

'Do the fishermen catch them?' Sean asked.

'No, they are sacred. It is bad luck to catch them.'

At this point Captain Gomez returned to the boat and we were introduced. He was a tall, rugged-looking man in his mid-fifties, with a thick black moustache. Unlike his first mate though, he smiled.

'A drink?' he said in Spanish, 'you will have a drink.' It was more a statement than a question.

It was only ten in the morning, but when the Port Captain accepted, we all trooped along to the Captain's cabin where he produced a bottle of what was obviously homemade liquor. The cabin was too small for us all to fit inside, so we stood outside on the deck to sample it. Trish politely declined, but he poured a couple of fingers into a glass for himself, me and the Port Captain. Captain Gomez tossed his down in one gulp. I tasted it. It was firewater.

I smiled and said, 'Very good. You make this?'

'Yes,' the captain replied proudly.

'It comes from the trees,' Captain Munio explained, draining his own glass and smacking his lips.

Wood alcohol! I thought to myself as I managed another smile and drank a bit more. Rotgut. This stuff can kill you. 'Very nice,' I said, wondering whether he fortified himself with it while steering the boat at night.

'These people are coming with you to Nauta,' Captain Munio told Captain Gomez, who nodded and poured himself another drink.

'They will need their cabin painted.'

Captain Gomez nodded again . . . but more slowly this time. Then finished his drink.

'How much will the fare be?' Captain Munio asked.

There was a pause while the captain did some calculations. Four thousand and five hundred soles,' he said.

'For all of us? . . . all four?' I asked.

'Of course.'

Thirty-five dollars for an eight hundred-kilometre trip that would take four or five days.

'Okay,' I said. 'Fine. When do we leave?'

'On Tuesday,' the captain replied.

Today was Saturday. Only three more days. That's not long to wait, we thought. Ah, if only life was so simple and certain.

It became the daily routine to go immediately after breakfast to check at the Port Captain's office on possible departures. No boat can come into or leave Pucallpa without permission from this office. Even though we had the *Campeon* lined up, if another boat on which we could travel had been leaving before she did, we would have taken it. It would have been foolish not to, because in these parts a boat actually moving downriver is worth more than two still moored to the bank.

From the Port Captain's office we walked to the Verdad library to pick up a new title. Choice was limited to Barbara Cartland or Morris West, a combination which I thought would give local readers an interestingly distorted view of European modes and manners.

I stuck with Mr West because even though his plots seem manipulated to pose as many Christian moral dilemmas as possible, this at least makes the reading marginally more stimulating.

Neither the port office nor the library were open on Sunday, so we took a bus so small it looked as if it had been amputated from an ancient Greyhound coach, to Lake Yarinocochca, thirty minutes outside town. Beside the deeply-rutted road, the lallang grass grew high enough to hide a guerilla army or your most secret desires. The one-roomed Tupac Amaru Primary School, which we passed on the way, was deserted and so too was a tiny cinema whose corrugated iron walls were plastered with expired advertisements, illegible in their undulations.

I fought to keep my seat from being taken over by a thickset aggressive man in order to offer it to a tired-looking, pregnant woman who turned out to be the man's wife! For one mad moment I could see her considering giving it up to him.

At the lakeshore there was a small market where Zara tried her hardest to persuade us to buy a small monkey who stared fearfully out of large round eyes and clung tenaciously to her with its surprisingly strong muscular tail.

We hired a hollowed-out log canoe and went a couple of kilometres or so along the shore to the Summer Institute of Linguistics, an American-financed interdenominational religious foundation with an international membership, which has similar centres in several parts of the world. The one hundred and fifty or so people who live at this one, in outback Peru, use it as a base to go out into isolated settlements in Ecuador, Brazil and Colombia as well as Peru to study the multitude of complex Indian languages, some of which are spoken solely by communities with as few as a couple of hundred members.

We were interested in seeing how the school operated and we had been told that visitors were always welcome. Ruth Cowan, the young American woman who opened the first door on which we knocked, after clambering up the bank and into the compound, lived up to that reputation. She invited us into her simple but comfortable communal living room which she shared with three other women, all of whom had gone water-skiing for the day, and offered us, luxury of luxuries, a glass each of ice-cold drinking water. 'We have our own water-purification plant,' she assured us, 'so drink up, it's absolutely safe.'

Though she didn't know us from Eve and though we were simply casual visitors, Ruth answered all our questions about the institute and offered to take us on a look-see around the grounds.

'On first sight,' Ruth said, as we followed along the neat paths between residents' low-slung homes set among a tropical riot of gardens, 'we probably appear to be purely a teaching body because we are teaching these primitive Indians how to write down their own spoken languages, many of which are almost extinct. But we are actually far more of a learning body. We are all learning all the time from these wonderful people.'

Ruth's prim, Sandra Dee-style gingham frock unintentionally accentuated, rather than concealed, her attractive curves. Her hair was pulled severely back into a neat old-maid's bun, and she wore thick, sensibly-framed eye-glasses which emphasised thoughtful grey eyes that had about them just a trace of the manic.

Ruth's parents were missionaries and she was born and grew up in Mexico, where her parents were spreading the gospel. 'We have four of our own light aircraft,' she told us, 'one of them a seaplane, so that we can get into most of the remote areas, but even so, a few are still only accessible by paddling your own dugout up a narrow tributary. People may go out from here for months at a time and we have to air-drop in supplies and keep in contract by two-way radio.'

'Are any of the Indians cannibals?' Sean asked with a journalistic determination to get down to basics!

'No,' Ruth assured him. 'They don't kill other people just to eat them,' and then added with a maiden's unawareness of a child's blood-thirsty instincts, 'but many of those who do kill in intertribal fighting, shrink their victims' heads.'

'Oooh!' Sean was enraptured, but then let down when Ruth didn't supply more technical detail. 'Has anybody from here been killed and shrunk?' he persisted.

Ruth gave him a quick look and then the benefit of the doubt.

'Yes. Two men were killed, quite unexpectedly and for no apparent reason. But their bodies were brought out and given a Christian burial.'

I spoke up quickly hoping that it would distract her so that she wouldn't notice Sean's facial expression of thwarted hopes. 'When was that?' I asked.

'Some years ago,' Ruth said, 'and since then two women, two brave women, have gone back into the same area, alone, and re-established contact with the tribe who did the killing.' One was the widow of one of the murdered men.'

In the neat, air-conditioned reference library, Ruth showed us primers written in some of the ten languages which have so far been transcribed. They put James Joyce to shame. One of them was filled with words half as long as our average sentence and was comprised almost entirely of consonants!

'We are working on forty-three languages,' Ruth told us, 'and they are as different from one another as Chinese is from Greek. It's an immense job, but one day we shall have the New Testament translated into each of those languages and after that the entire Holy Bible. We have one lady working here who is in her late seventies. She has spent thirty years on one language and has almost finished the New Testament.'

'Have a look at this,' Iain was examining the shelves of books. He pulled one out and read its title, *Tariri,* that's the name of our little hotel back in town.'

'Aah, you're staying there,' Ruth smiled, 'then you should know that Tariri is our greatest success story. He was a head-hunter, living a desperate existence in the jungle, until he met our people who persuaded him to come in.'

Out of the cold, like a spy, I thought but didn't say. Kill a commie for Christ. Win a heart for Jesus. It's all very confusing.

A couple of days later; still stuck in Pucallpa's mud, we visited other foreigners living on the lake. A young American couple, he an architect and she a nurse, both turned hotel-keepers. Connor and Mary Nixon had dropped out of affluent American west-coast living to build their own version of a tropical paradise in the form of several thatched-roof, A-framed huts and a large circular eating area, also thatch-roofed and built on two and a half-metre high stilts to avoid being underwater in the wet season.

Their six hectares of lake frontage land cost them a mere $1000 and, as local labour is cheap, they had been able to erect their hotel, which was only just becoming functional, at pretty rock-bottom prices. Even so it's banking on rather a long shot because Pucallpa is hardly a tourist boom-town.

Connor, loose-limbed and tall, showed us around with justifiable pride. It's no mean achievement to conquer any sizable piece of land in these parts. It needs an abundance of stamina and imagination and a driving impulse that Connor was unable to verbalise.

'I felt cramped in California. I wanted to feel free,' he said in answer to my query.

Cramped in California? ... the most free-wheeling state in the most free-wheeling country in the world!

Mary, noticing my scepticism added, 'It's an adventure!'

Aah, now, that's more like it. All these people purposely putting themselves to the test, beyond the support of their own familiar society; Ruth Cowan for God, Connor Nixon for freedom, Mary for adventure. But there was still more to it than that. More even than their sum total. More yet than I can express ... but I know it interests me.

When we got back to the Tariri that evening there was a message from the Captain of the *Campeon* asking us to be aboard the next morning at 11.00 a.m. Leaving, we thought, at last! No more Morris West, but also no more showers for a while. In preparation, we had an extra good scrub up and hair washing and were on board the following day well before the appointed hour.

Having scrambled about to be there in good time, there was a consequent sensation of disappointment when we could see that there was no way that we would be leaving before noon. And when, by 2.00 p.m., it was obvious that we weren't going anywhere at all that day, we consoled ourselves by trooping back into town for one more visit to the library Verdad and to post off more letters. It's as much of a sanity-saver to write letters as it is to receive them.

In an odd way I had grown rather fond of Pucallpa and thought it would be nice to share it with my friends by sending off some picture postcards of it taken on a good day, showing the buzzards grubbing through the rotting garbage and the rutted mud streets to their advantage. These pictures were strange enough, but I wasn't really prepared, when thumbing through a collection in the general store, to come across ancient, glorious colour pictures of a scantily-dressed Jayne Mansfield in various pin-up poses. Standing in that grubby little shop, I could think only of her horrific death, how many years ago? Beheaded when a sports car, driven with its hood down, by her young boyfriend, went right under the tailgate of a truck. Yet here she was in Pucallpa, the rear end of Peru, looking so full of life.

We decided that we might as well sleep on board the *Campeon*; it would save on hotel bills as we were sure the Captain couldn't charge us more than we had agreed. We would also be ready to start the trip in the morning without the hassle of getting all our gear back into our packs. So that night we rigged up our bags and mosquito nets in the tiny cabin. Before turning in, we went ashore again for a drink at a very seedy waterfront bar.

It was really no more than a rotting wooden shack squatting on the mud and lit only by a couple of candles. The patrons were either too lazy or too drunk, or both, to go outside to urinate but used instead a dark corner of the room where there was a hole in the rotting floor board.

Iain ordered a beer and some Cokes and it wasn't until the waitress slow-wiggled back with them that we realised she was a he. Then, as our eyes adjusted to the dim light, we saw that the few other patrons were also all men dressed as women. They made me feel sad because their imitation was so pathetically bad. They were cumbersome and awkward on their high wedge heels, lumpily padded, too-heavily made up over beard-roughened skin and squeezed into poorly handmade or covertly bought, tacky, out-of-date fashions.

Both Zara and Sean watched them in silence for a while and I was wondering what they were thinking, and what sort of mother took her ten and eleven year old children to such a decidedly nasty gay bar and what I should say to them, when Zara turned round to me and asked, quite matter of factly, 'What would you do if Sean grew up to be like that?'

Zara's cough had not improved since we had been in Pucallpa, so that night, as we went to bed, we decided to start her on a course of Tetracycline tablets. Her cough was bad during the night, her throat constricted and her breathing difficult, but when daylight came and she was up and about, it seemed to improve and we hoped that, once the antibiotics had begun to take effect, the condition would clear up. In the meantime, she looked pale and subdued and, with a whole batch of mosquito bites on her legs which had come up in itchy lumps, she felt miserable.

I asked the first mate, whose name we had learnt was Chavez ... Ricardo Chavez, when we would be leaving. Eleven o'clock, he told us ... another two and a half hours. Perhaps this would be it, at last.

Trish wanted to get another book from the library, so we made a quick trip back into town to borrow Morris West's *The Ambassador,* explaining to the American woman there that we would post it back from Iquitos. But, back on the *Campeon,* eleven o'clock came and went with no sign of the boat moving and with no sign of Captain Gomez.

Towards noon, huge black thunderclouds built up in the sky all around us. The heat was oppressive and we were all sweating profusely, but soon, the air began to cool somewhat when the rain started coming down in buckets. Zara stood in her bikini on the metal deck, aft, and showered in the warm rain, washing the bites on her legs with germicidal soap. Then a strong wind blew up and the rain became slanting and fierce, almost like hail, and we retired to our little cabin to sit, with the door open, watching the rain pelting down in sheets past us to give the entire waterfront yet another drenching.

We made some sandwiches of salami, cheese, peanut butter and honey (not all mixed together) and I brewed up some tea on the cooker. Not long afterwards, the captain appeared to inform us that everything was ready for us to leave except for some 'paperwork'. Then he left the boat again to return to town, apparently to straighten it out.

The afternoon dragged on with alternate bursts of blazing sunshine and torrential rain. We lay in our cabin for most of the time and read except for one brief excursion, during a break in the rain, when we plodded ashore through the mud, to buy some soft-drinks.

At last, at about 5.00 p.m., Captain Gomez returned, accompanied by Nelson Munio, the Port Captain. They were both drenched to the skin from a shower of rain that had caught them between where a taxi had dropped them at the end of the road and the boat.

The Port Captain, acting in his official capacity now, checked various aspects of the *Campeon,* the big barge that we would be pushing in front of us and its cargo. It seemed as if we were about to leave. It was hard to believe. There was an air of excitement and activity developing and we felt good at the thought of being finally on our way again. If we left now, it would be exactly a week since we had arrived in Pucallpa.

Suddenly the activity on the boat became more frenetic. People started running around. There were shouted commands from the Captain and the first mate. But something was wrong. They were clearly not making preparations to leave. It was something else ... something quite simple. The lights didn't work!

In the gathering dusk, the Port Captain had asked Captain Gomez to switch on and test the big spotlight above the wheelhouse. It didn't work. Neither would any other light on the whole ship. The engineer worked frantically on the auxiliary generator. They started up the boat's powerful diesel engine. But still there were no lights. An electrician would have to be called. We would have to wait until morning.

We were all bitterly disappointed. Having geared ourselves up to leaving, the thought of yet another delay made us feel that we would never get away. We already had some candles, but we went ashore and bought some more in a small, waterfront store, then, after a light meal back on board, we all went to bed and I started reading some more of *Huckleberry Finn* to Zara and Sean.

At about 8.00 o'clock, there was a knock on the door. It was Captain Gomez. He wanted me to come with him. I was reluctant to interrupt the reading, not only because the children wanted to hear more, but I was enjoying it myself. The Captain kept saying 'Capitan del Puerto'. ... the Port Captain? I didn't know what he meant, but I got up, dressed again and, somewhat mystified, went out to see the Captain, who was waiting outside the cabin. He was obviously more than a little drunk, but motioned for me to come with him.

I followed him as he staggered across the plank to the darkened mudbank and up toward the shanty town that lay on the fringes of the port area. I wondered what the hell was happening, but kept close behind the Captain as we approached a dim and dingy bar. Inside, one of the first things I saw was the Port Captain and another man; a stranger, seated at a table in the centre of the room, well and truly drunk.

'I am sorry,' the Port Captain said to me, motioning to a chair beside him. 'I am sorry you cannot leave tonight. But with no lights it is very dangerous on the river.'

I agreed and, out of politeness, accepted a glass of some dark liquor which the Captain had poured for me from a labelless bottle. It tasted like rum, but I wasn't sure. Captain Gomez and the other man mumbled to each other while I carried on a rather strained and not very effective conversation with the Port Captain, going over the same thing, about the ship's lights, again and again.

It wasn't a situation I wanted to continue late into the night, so, after half an hour, I managed to excuse myself and made my way back to the *Campeon,* where Trish and the kids were already asleep. Zara's throat condition and cough had improved considerably so that, for the first time for several nights, she slept well. At least something seemed to be going right.

We were up early in the morning and, on being told that we would probably leave by 10.00 a.m., we went into town for breakfast and to return *The Ambassador*, which Trish had already finished reading, to the library.

Back on board the *Campeon*, the appointed hour of departure once again came and went without any sign of the Captain. In desperation, I went for a quiet walk along the mudbanks to look at some of the newer boats and barges that had tied up there during the last twenty-four hours. After I'd been away about ten minutes or so, one of the young crewmen from the *Campeon* came running after me. 'We go! We go!' he shouted.

On board again, I found a man in khaki uniform was checking everyone's papers. He wanted also to see our passports. It struck me as a funny time to be doing it. The passengers had all been on board the boat for several days now. Anyway, it was obvious that he could not read English, but he went through the formalities of leafing through our passports and muttering some sort of approval before leaving.

Five minutes later, we heard, with satisfaction, the deep, throaty roar of the *Campeon's* big diesel engine as it started up. We were casting off. Everybody was smiling. The Captain was pacing the deck outside of the wheelhouse issuing orders as we backed out into the fast-flowing stream. As we manoeuvred to turn the big barge, which was lashed to the front of the boat, to face both it and the *Campeon* in the right direction, Pucallpa was already moving past us and slipping away. With a couple of blasts on the *Campeon's* fog horn, we said goodbye and headed downriver.

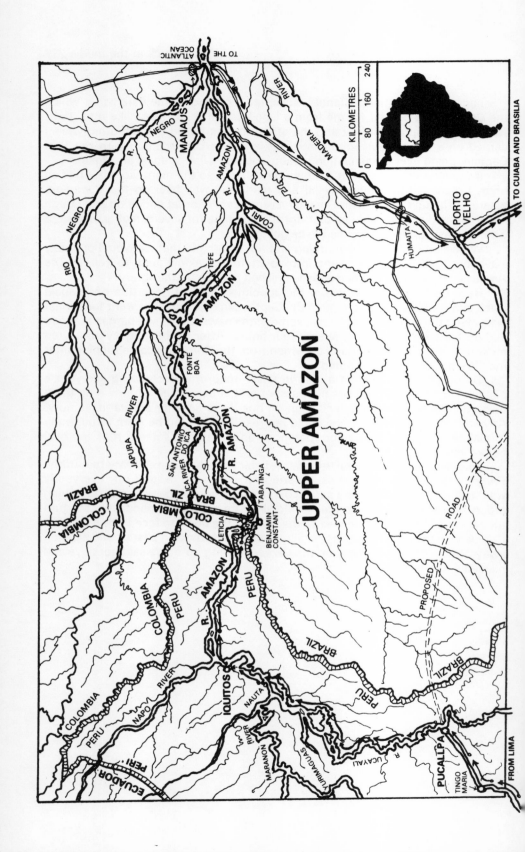

PERU

17
A bump in the night

As we sailed off, I promptly went into a steep decline, perhaps it was withdrawal symptoms from Morris West novels, but more likely simple fatigue, brought on by the release of tension from actually being on the move at last. I retired to my bunk and slept deeply for a couple of hours.

When I awoke, restored to normality, the river, a 400-metre width of liquid mud, was carrying us along at a cracking pace past an unchanging view of dense jungle foliage which began abruptly at the river's edge and went on from there to cover thousands of square kilometres with the same impenetrable growth.

There were no mosquitoes, so after we'd eaten some lunch, Zara and I sat in the narrow walkway outside our cabin and I wrote letters while she knitted away at a brightly-striped vest, her first attempt at a total garment.

'Mum?' The word seemed to carry a note of anxiety, so I stopped scribing, 'that man at breakfast ...'

I knew immediately that she was referring to the strangely-behaved fellow who had sat at the little table next to ours in the café in Pucallpa and ordered only a coffee and then stirred and stirred and stirred it, as if he hoped, that by doing so, it would turn into something else. We had all commented on his obsessive behaviour; three stirs to the left, three to the right, left, right and so on.

'Uh-huh,' I hoped I sounded receptive.

'Well ...' Zara paused ... 'well, I know how he feels. I mean when he stirs like that. In a pattern. He has to because ... it's a game with himself ... it's like ... well, it's like ...?'

'Like having to have the bed-sheet turned over the blanket exactly thirteen and a half centimetres all the way across? Or your clothes for the next day stacked neatly by the bottom left-hand leg of the bed, always in the same order; shoes, socks, pants, jeans, T-shirt and so on? Or your various different foods completely separate on your plate; your vegetables never touching your meat etcetera? Is that what it's like?' I asked with a laugh as I referred to just a few of Zara's minor obsessions.

She laughed too in self-acknowledgement. 'The thing is,' she became sad, 'I don't want to do those things, but I can't stop myself. Do you think that means there's something wrong with me? What can I do?'

For a while as dusk was falling we discussed such quirks of personality and were unable to reach any conclusions beyond the fact that they were not important, so long as one was aware of them, talked openly and even joked about them. I was feeling, as I often do with Zara, the terrible loss I endured in not having a mother at her age, when the Captain called out for us to come and eat.

I waved my hand to intimate a 'no thanks' and hoped that my broad smile would lessen the insult. Iain came up from the barge and went through the same pantomime. The Captain finally shrugged his shoulders and joined the rest of his crew at the small table on the piece of covered deck at the aft end of the boat.

This not eating with everyone else was an initial embarrassment because we felt that it made us appear rude and stuck-up; as if we thought that their food was not good enough for us. But one look at the cooking arrangements and another at the end product had been sufficient to make us decide that being polite and eating the food prepared on board would have been an act above and beyond the call of duty.

Down below, right at the tail end of *Campeon,* behind the open engine room and beside the lavatory, a story in itself, was an open fire, burning in a grease and grime-encrusted pit and blackening everything around it, which was perhaps the reason why the old woman who tended it wore all black clothes.

She was assisted, loosely, by the youngest crew member, a lad of maybe fourteen who, in between wiping oily rags over the engine, wiped his oily hands over carcasses of dried fish of similar man-sized proportions to the ones we had seen offloaded at Pucallpa waterfront. These he chopped into chunks and threw into a greyish broth of water scooped from the river, which the old lady stirred in a large pot over the fire like a witch in 'Macbeth'.

Behind them, lying on the greasy floor, were dozens of unripened bananas, still on the limb. When unzipped, they revealed themselves as the same grey colour as the broth and tasted hard and wooden. Drinking water was obtained by throwing a bucket on a line off the side into the river and hauling the contents back aboard. The resultant liquid was brown and thick.

Three times a day the crew and other passengers sat down to the same meal of grey broth containing floating grey lumps, grey tough bananas and brown muddy water.

So you see why we decided to stick to our own food. It was a joke though to see us crouched on our bunks, while Iain hovered over our little stove which was set up on the floor of our metal-walled cabin. Perspiring like mad, because we kept the door closed, in a hopeless attempt to appear less obvious, he cooked up a succession of surprisingly tasty meals.

Not that I think for one minute that the cook took any offence. She was too flat out feeding up the crew and the other eight passengers to have time to spare a thought for us.

When we had watched all these extras pile aboard at the last moment, we'd wondered where on earth we'd all fit because we occupied the only spare cabin. But a family of five, a plump friendly woman and her almost blind husband and their three small children, built a sort of shelter on the rear deck space with their pile of bags and slung a hammock which they took it in turns to inhabit. Two short-haired young men who looked like soldiers on home-leave had come onboard with only a small grip each and at night they simply put these under their heads when they lay down on the metal floor in the passageway to sleep. Finally, an incredibly beautiful part-Indian woman, with her five or six-month-old baby, slung her hammock over the table. I don't recall ever seeing her except lying in it asleep like a madonna, day and night.

After we'd eaten canned meat and vegetables, fresh bread and fruit, a piece of chocolate and a cup of coffee, we carried our utensils and platters down to the lower deck and across the plank linking us to the barge. Here, by the light from our flashlights, we washed first them and then ourselves; taking it in turn to strip off, soap up and be splashed down with water pulled in from the river. We cleaned our teeth, rinsing out with rainwater and finally had a pee over the side, one of the few occasions when I would have preferred to be a man.

Then in the cool of the evening we leant against the side of the barge for a while, enjoying the river flowing by silently, and a peaceful sense of fulfilment.

Then we read a couple more chapters about the adventures Huckleberry Finn and Tom Sawyer had on another great river, the Mississippi, before we dropped off to the soporific chug of the *Campeon's* diesel engines.

We hadn't been asleep long when both Trish and I awoke again, sensing that the engine had slowed. Looking out to the starboard, from our cabin door, we could see absolutely nothing, it was so totally dark. We couldn't even make out the difference between the sky and the top of the jungle on the far shore, but, slipping some clothes on and moving forward towards the wheelhouse, we saw that someone was playing our big searchlight onto the left bank of the river for short intervals. We heard the Captain's voice. It seemed as if they were looking for a place on the shore at which to stop . . . a particular place . . . and yet, there were no lights on the shore anywhere.

Before long we pulled in to the edge, coming to a soft slithering stop as the barge ran into the mudbank. There was suddenly more activity. Voices and lights down on the barge and a few small flashlights moving on the shore, which seemed, in the flickering, dim light, to be nothing but impenetrable jungle; there was no sign of any habitation whatever. We stood on the upper deck, watching from the darkness as men ran back and forth from the shore to the barge, carrying some sort of cargo on board and stowing it in the hold of the barge. What the cargo was, or why they should load it in almost total darkness, in such a remote place, I can't say with any certainty, but, in all probability, it was either marijuana or cocaine. Both are grown in large quantities in this part of Peru and, so we'd been told, almost every river boat plying the Ucayali and the Maranon would, at some stage, carry these drugs down towards Iquitos. From there, they would find their way to Leticia, a small town further down the Amazon River in Colombia, and then they would travel through established Colombian pipelines to the United States.

As soon as our business, whatever it was, was completed, we were on our way again. Trish and I stood for a while outside the cabin in the darkness, talking softly and just feeling the river go by. It was a strange sensation. Under what was probably a very heavy cloudbank, we were in almost total darkness. Occasionally, the powerful searchlight would stab ahead to ensure that we were on course and that there were no obstacles, but for the rest of the time, we were sailing along in a black void, as if through space. The only sound was the steady, heavy throb of the big diesel engine and although there were plenty of other people on board, for a while we saw none of them, so that standing there on the top deck in the cooling breeze, there was a wonderful sense of isolation.

After twenty minutes or half an hour we went back to bed, but we had only been asleep for a couple of hours I suppose, when we were awakened by a tremendous din from the cabin next to us, which was occupied by four crew members, including a young mestizo Indian with a portable record player. The machine was turned up full blast and distorting like hell as it played some Peruvian rock band's version of 'I can't get no satisfaction'. Someone, I guessed it was the record player's owner, was doing his utmost to outsing, or outshout the singer on the record. As our two cabins were only separated by a sheet of three millimetre-thick steel, we got the whole lot at full volume. In fact the wall was vibrating with it.

I looked at my watch. Just after midnight. I let it go on for a while. Trish was awake, then the kids. I staggered down from my bunk and put my jeans on, then out of our cabin and looked about. The boat had stopped again. We were pulled in by the shore, next to what was even more dense jungle than we'd seen before. Huge trees with great hanging vines towered above us, but they disappeared into a deep mist which shrouded the boat. We were in a thick fog and obviously could not travel because of it. Turning, I stepped into the next cabin and a nasty confrontation.

The young Indian was standing next to his bunk, on which the record player was resting. He was dressed in a pair of tattered, greasy khaki pants. His face and body were dripping with sweat and he was almost totally drunk. The other crew members lounged on their bunks on the other side of the cabin. They were also drunk and eyed me silently. I felt the situation had all the possibilities of lurching out of control, yet I had to do something.

The young Indian looked at me vacantly. His head moved slackly and a thin trickle of saliva shone in one corner of his mouth.

'Musico . . . abajo.' I made downward motions with my hands and pointed to the player. Music . . . down, I was trying to say, but, either my Spanish was too bad, or he was too drunk, or what was more likely, he just didn't want to know. He turned his head away and did nothing.

'Los ninos,' I said, putting my hands by my ears and closing my eyes to indicate sleep. The children are asleep. He looked at me unsmilingly, but still said nothing. He adjusted the position of his feet on the floor and faced me. I reached across in front of him and turned the volume control on the record player down. He immediately and defiantly turned it up again.

I felt my spine tingle and my stomach tighten. I reached again and turned it down . . . this time shouting at him in English, 'Leave it down!'

He paused for a moment and looked at the end of his bunk. I followed his gaze. There were a pair of jeans there. The belt in them had a leather sheath with a knife in it. One of his companions shouted at him, I think telling him to leave the player turned down. He waved his hand at me and shouted something in Spanish. I turned and walked out, not really knowing if the volume was going to go up again or not, but thinking that perhaps this was the time for discretion, rather than valour.

As it happened, the volume didn't go up because other, far more interesting events overtook the little drama that had been developing between me and our next-door neighbour.

I had only taken one step out of the Indian's cabin when I was almost sent flying by the first mate, Chavez, who had come stumbling heavily along the narrow deck past me. He stopped and, finding his balance by leaning against the railing, looked at me with what seemed like hate in his eyes. It was difficult to tell, however, because his condition was even worse than the young Indian's. He was paralytic!

His normally florid face was even more flushed than usual, and the sullen, brooding look with which he went about his job during the day, had deepened into an attitude of brutish aggression. Then, within seconds, all hell broke loose. The *Campeon's* engineer suddenly appeared, having run up the steps from the deck below.

It was the engineer who, whenever weeds or plants clogged up the cooling water intake on the bottom of the boat's hull, would go under the muddy water, while the vessel wallowed without power in midstream, and clear the blocked intake. And he, it seemed to us, was the complete opposite of the mate. He was a reasonably good-looking man, about thirty-eight or forty years old, who was always happy, smiling and friendly. And now, on this occasion, the contrast was even more pronounced because he, unlike the mate, was perfectly sober.

He shouted something at the mate, who let out a roar and lunged at the engineer, sending him flying backwards along the companionway to the aft deck-space where other passengers slept, either on the floor or in hammocks. The two went sprawling into one of the hammocks, belonging to the mestizo woman with three children. Both she and the hammock collapsed to the deck. She let out a scream, then she and her half-blind husband who was lying on a blanket nearby, struggled up and to one side as the two figures of the mate and the engineer lunged and tore at each other.

It was obvious that, unless the engineer could get clear of Chavez, who seemed possessed of wild strength, he would not be able to gain any advantage. The others, that is the passengers who had been sleeping on deck and the other drunken crew members, including my young Indian friend, had all now gathered around to watch.

The two men suddenly separated and were on their feet. The engineer let go a right which connected with a terrible crack on the mate's left eye. He went down like a nine-pin. The engineer was on him in a flash and, before anyone could move, had delivered eight or nine smashing blows to the face of the now unconscious Chavez.

It was the roar of the Captain's voice which stopped the engineer and broke everything up. Captain Gomez was anything but sober himself, but no one was going to stand up against him, so, within fifteen minutes or so, the mate was in his cabin, soon to be asleep and heading for an almighty hangover, the young Indian was in his cabin, with the record player switched off and there was, once more, relative peace on board.

In the morning, when we saw Chavez, he appeared very sorry for himself. He had a huge black eye, his bottom lip was badly cut and he had a nasty gash on his right cheek. Both he and the engineer were closeted in the Captain's cabin for some time. We could hear angry words, and they were all the Captain's.

After breakfast and cleaning up our cabin (four people in a confined space make an unbearable mess) we slung our hammocks on the barge again and lay in them reading and chatting.

It was a wonderful relief not to have to catch trains or buses, not to need to make decisions. It was like a return to infanthood when all decisions are made for one. We had no control over where we went or when we stopped. It was all someone else's headache and so a real holiday for us.

Occasionally the air would become very still and we'd know that within seconds a squall would hit us. This happened several times during the morning but they were so brief that they brought very little rain. Towards midday we decided that, as our own purified water supplies which we carried in two 18-litre plastic containers were running low, and we couldn't rely on there being sufficient rain, we should start to think about purifying some river water.

A couple of years before, in the sparsely inhabited deserts of the Southern Sudan, Iain had very nearly died of dysentery. Once you've had as close a call as that, you don't take any chances of a repeat nasty performance. Or if you do, you're a fool.

Firstly, we pulled up a bucketful of water from the river and let it sit for an hour so that a lot of the silt dropped to the bottom. Then we carefully poured off the water, which was still muddy brown, through a cloth, to filter it. This we then boiled and left to cool by which time there was a further thick layer of mud in the bottom of the billy. Careful not to disturb this we decanted the boiled water into our water containers and added not only a few drops of iodine but also a couple of drops of household bleach!

The result, when we tasted it about half an hour later, was about as repulsive as much of the tap-water I have drunk in various parts, but I bet it was safer and, when it was brewed up into tea or coffee it was perfectly potable and even enjoyable!

During the whole day we had passed no settlements and had seen only two boats. One had been hugging the shore, trying to avoid the current as it pushed against it upstream and one was floating with it and trailing in its wake a large quantity of logs. These were prodded and pried apart by men who walked on them with as much ease as I manage along a wide footpath on a good day. We waved in admiration and they waved back.

On several occasions the river narrowed so much that we could stretch out our arms and almost touch the vines hanging from the trees which were packed tightly together, jostling one another for space and light. When I consulted the rather good map which we had I realised that we were actually passing not river banks, but large islands. Because of this ridiculous desire which most European travellers have to know where they are at all times, I took the map up to the battered first mate who was at the wheel and asked him to point out where we were.

He squinted at it from his puffy, red-rimmed eyes and shrugged. A couple of other crew members in the wheel house looked at it too, running their fingers over the convoluted blue streak. One of them suddenly stabbed with his finger and cried out 'Orellano', the name of a settlement which I thought we might have passed in the night. The others exclaimed in query, 'Rio Ucayali?!'

'Si, si!' I nodded realising for the first time that they hadn't even known that they were looking at a map of the river they were navigating. More interest was shown then, but only in seeing the familiar names printed on paper, as if that was a proof of their existence. I had the feeling that none of them had ever looked at a map of the Amazon and her tributaries before, which, when you stop to think about it, is not so surprising. After all, do commuters ever look at a map of the route they follow each day to and from their place of work?'

'Mum! Look!' Zara called up from the barge and I glanced around to see a quite magnificent, bright-blue bird darting along between us and the jungle. Then another and another. They gained and lost height with enviable total ease. They were obviously kingfishers because their beaks were adapted for diving into the river for food. I tried to capture them on film but it was hopeless because they were so fast and camouflaged by the vivid greenery.

I returned to the barge to find Iain up to his elbows in bubbling soap powder scrubbing away at a pair of his jeans. He scooped water from the river to rinse them and then looped a rope through the legs to hang them up to dry; which they did eventually, but so stiff with silt from the river water, it was as if they had been starched and could almost stand to attention unattended.

Late in the afternoon the *Campeon* pulled into the bank and we went ashore to a little village, too small to be named on my map. It had perhaps a hundred and fifty inhabitants who eked out a very basic existence from subsistence farming and selling food to passing boats. Their poverty was obvious not only from the bellies of the children which were swollen by malnutrition, but also the apathetic manner of the adults who slumped on raised platforms under attap roofs, picking through their children's hair for lice, or swinging listlessly in hammocks.

Despite the dozens of fowls running about between the shacks vying with the skeletal dogs for scraps, everyone we asked for eggs shook their heads. Here were all these hens laying free range eggs in the nearby undergrowth and no one could be bothered, or had the energy or the sense to collect what could have provided a very much needed source of protein.

We bought some over-ripe squishy papayas and then, back on board, we watched the crew carry on half a dozen or so loudly-squawking hens which they cooped up in a tiny hutch on the hot metal roof of the barge. No doubt these were due to supplement the repetitious diet of fish. More of which was also brought on board and dragged down to the kitchen; great sides of unrecognisable fish slap, slap, slapping along the filthy floor and down the metal steps, slop, slop slopping past the lavatory to be thrown in heaps beside still more unripe bananas.

I was so very glad that Iain was turning out another of his gourmet dinners that night and while he cooked, I plucked up enough courage to withstand the incredulous and disapproving stares of the cook lady and did what I had been wanting to do ever since leaving Pucallpa. Descending the stairs to the lower deck, I took the cap off a large bottle of disinfectant and emptied the entire contents, throwing it at the walls, over the floor and down the pedestal of the satanic lavatory!

After dinner, more *Huck Finn* and then we all went soundly to sleep, until, in the middle of the night: BANG! In the total blackness of our cabin we all four sat up, instantly awake.

'Dad!' Zara yelled with panic in her voice.

'What is it?' Sean called out, still sure, in his childish innocence, that adults have all the answers.

The boat gave a great shudder. Several small things which we had propped on the cabin's iron ribs, clattered to the floor. There was a terrifying rumbling noise and the whole vessel shuddered again as the noise swelled and thundered toward us gathering speed. Before we could think, let alone act, it had rumbled and roared right beneath us and on out into the night leaving a little gasp of silence to be filled with the raised and startled voices of other passengers.

Iain got down from his bunk, put on his jeans and went out on deck, returning a few minutes later to tell us that we had hit an enormous log, probably a whole tree, which we had then run over.

'They don't know if there's been any damage,' he said. 'It seems that the mate didn't have the spotlight on, or perhaps he had dropped asleep. Whichever it is he's in the stink again. We're coming into the shore and we're going to stay here for the rest of the night, but the mosquitoes are gathering for the kill.'

So they were, but we were ready for them. We lit a mosquito repellent coil, the delicious heady aroma of which always makes me homesick for Malaysia. We sprayed the walls and ceiling and even the floor with Baygon, a lethal insecticide, and our exposed parts we covered with repellent. Then we lay down, careful not to disturb our precariously rigged mosquito netting, and went to sleep again.

No doubt we burnt a spot or two on our lungs, raised the toxicity level of our blood and destroyed part of the ozone layer. If, like Iain, you are hardly affected by mosquitoes, you will be muttering, tut-tut. But, if like Zara and I, you come up in big, red, furiously-itchy weals and penny-sized blisters, you will be more tolerant!

I guess even mosquitoes must have their place in the great overall scheme of things and I'll live and let live along with the best of them, so long as I am not attacked without provocation ... in which instance there's nothing in my rule book against as much defence as possible.

I don't know what that stuff had in it, but it was mighty powerful. In the morning, the floor, the window sills, the mosquito nets, everything was covered with literally hundreds of mosquito bodies. The thought of that horde getting stuck into us gave us the shudders, and we were just thankful that we'd had the right things with which to fend them off. We were discovering that the situation as far as mosquitoes was concerned was unpredictable. In some areas there would be flying armadas of them, in others ... or really most of the time while we were sailing, there were none at all. But once they found the boat, they often hung about and took some time to get rid of, even when the boat got under way again.

Fortunately, near the front of the barge, where there was always a breeze blowing, there were very few and we spent most of the next day there, swinging in our hammocks, reading and watching the shore on either side. At times, making use of the changing current, as we followed the winding course of the river, we would be close to one shore and then the other. There was very little sign of human habitation; an occasional village of half a dozen thatched-roof houses or a tiny 'peque peque' dugout canoe with a lone paddler in it, would be all we would see for hours.

There were about three or four small settlements marked on the map for the 880-odd kilometres separating Pucallpa and Nauta on the junction of the Maranon and the Ucayali Rivers. These were Contamana, Dos de Mayo, Iberia and Requena. But we were not stopping at any of them. We just kept sailing on down, past endless kilometres of trackless jungle. On almost any part of the trip down the Ucayali, if we had been able to get off on the right hand shore and head in a straight line due east, which would have been impossible anyway, unless we'd been flying, we would have been able to travel for hundreds of kilometres without the slightest sign of civilisation. A few Indian head-hunters maybe, but nothing else but jungle; some of the densest, most inhospitable jungle in the world.

Even more than enclosing jungle, we felt the enormous power of the river. The Ucayali, though not well known outside South America, is one of the greatest rivers in the world. One of the major tributaries of the Amazon, it brings immense quantities of water, melted snow from the high Andes, on a rampaging course down through mountain valleys and gorges to the Amazon basin. This big, brown river on which we were now sailing, was carrying water from the same clear and sparkling Vilcanota River which had leapt and tumbled beside us as we travelled by train from Lake Titicaca to Cuzco. And the water that charged through the Urubamba gorge beneath us at Machu Picchu, was now with us in the Ucayali, heading for the sea, still some 4800 kilometres distant.

In their first mad rush for the sea, nearly all of the Andean rivers drop an average of over five metres for every one kilometre the river travels, a staggering 4800 metres in the first 960 kilometres! Then, over the next 5000 kilometres, they fall only five centimetres for every one and a half kilometres of river . . . a total of only 200 or 240 metres over all that distance.

Yet over this long flat run the river is anything but sluggish. Pucallpa, for instance, is 195 metres above sea level, some 4800 kilometres from the sea, but the river there, though wide and deep, is moving fast, probably six or eight kilometres an hour. It is the great weight of water behind, which pushes it remorselessly onwards, toward the Atlantic. And all the way down, for the whole of that 4800 kilometres, the pace never slackens, because more and more great rivers keep feeding into the Amazon right until it makes its last exit into the sea.

During the afternoon, we had seen a number of heavy rain squalls in the distance. Occasionally they would come near to the boat, but no rain had actually fallen on us all day. We were hoping that we would run into some rain, because it would allow us to replenish our water supply with really fresh water, so that we could avoid going through the tedious process of purifying the river water again.

About four in the afternoon, the sky ahead began to really darken, the clouds were absolutely black and it was apparent that this was one we were not going to miss. I ran to collect our big plastic water containers and stood waiting for the rain to hit. We could see it coming fast across the water, upriver, towards us, slightly to one side of our course. It was like a sheet of foam on the surface.

Soon we were in it. It was pounding like a million tiny hammers on the roof and pouring in great streams off the sides of the roof. I emptied one can I had laboriously filled with treated river water and held it under one of the streams of water. Within minutes I had it and the other can both full.

That evening we cooked up a packet of beef almondine which we had been carrying with us all the way from San Diego. We had bought several packets of freeze-dried food, which were very light and compact, but so far hadn't used any. All that was needed to make a tasty dish from them was to add a cup and a half of boiling water and wait five minutes. We ate our beef almondine with a tin of meat balls, a can of green beans and a slice of bread and butter. Then finished it off with a tangerine, a piece of toffee and a cup of coffee ... A meal fit for a king!

We woke the next morning to a world of water. It was falling in opaque sheets of grey from a grey sky into a grey river. It looked as though it had rained from the beginning of time and would rain till the end. We climbed back into our bunks and would have lain there for some time, but for the fact that Sean was awake and kept up a perpetual request for breakfast, until we capitulated and got up to make it.

'Media dia,' was the captain's reply when we went to his cabin to inquire what time he expected to arrive in Nauta, where we would be getting off. Noon was still a couple of hours away and to raise his spirits in the face of the torrential downpour, the Captain was having a mid-morning tipple. He invited us to keep him company. Just the fumes from his home-brew were enough to pickle my brain, so I left it to Iain, who has a stronger constitution, to uphold the family honour.

Captain Gomez's cabin, right behind the wheelhouse, had an air of bachelor freedom. Shirts and pants, only slightly cleaner and less rumpled than the ones he wore, were strung forlornly on ropes around the walls. Papers, most of them scribbled over and crumpled up, overflowed from a makeshift desk onto the floor, where they covered several pairs of decrepit sandals. A very old typewriter and a slightly younger adding machine were the only symbols of authority.

Between them was a large glass jar which seemed to contain grey insects or ... I stepped closer to examine it and Captain Gomez, quick, despite the alcohol, noticed.

'Aaah,' he picked up the jar and presented it to me saying something with obvious pride. I didn't need to understand his own very peculiar brand of Spanish to recognise the stiff grey shapes for what they were. Nail clippings! Captain Gomez's very own home-grown product.

A psychiatrist would have a field day. I know because I have boned up on people with this particular fetish. Sean, you see, puts up a tremendous scene every week on nail-cutting night, begging to be allowed to grow the nail on his pinky and to store the clippings from the rest. I am cruel enough to disallow both, and no doubt this will cause my son to cherish a resentment toward me. Too bad! Far rather that than jars of dirty, dead, nails stacked in his room.

To change the subject, I smiled at the Captain as if in admiration of his achievement and picked up a photograph of an attractive woman propped up amongst the clutter. I correctly guessed this to be Captain Gomez's wife. What I hadn't bargained for was a seemingly inexhaustible supply of photographs which he then produced from a drawer. All of them, it appeared, were his wives!

Putting his arm round me and squeezing tight, winking and leering, he gave us to understand that, like all sailors of repute, he kept a wife in every port along the river. He was a roughly-attractive man with an interesting air of mixed authority and vulnerability and he definitely gave the impression of being a bit of a lad, so I was sure that his was not an idle boast.

I thought that the most effective way to ease out of his clinch was to appeal to his ego, so I suggested that we all go round to the wheelhouse and take some photographs of the Captain in charge. This idea he eagerly accepted, performing like a professional and following instructions exactly. He was in the middle of telling us where to send copies of the photographs when there was a loud cry of alarm from below us, on the barge in front and the mate, his bruised face now purpling, gesticulated wildly and shouted up at us. Gomez, the Last of the Great Lovers, immediately became Gomez the Captain again and, loosing his arm from my waist, began calling out instructions to crew members who tumbled out of their cabins in to the still sheeting rain.

They assembled at the end of the barge closest to the ship and began hauling up the cargo from below decks. Zara and Sean who had been fishing from the front, where they were sheltered beneath a canopy, came back to enjoy the drama.

'We're sinking!' Sean yelled up at us, grinning with pleasurable anticipation.

'No we're not,' Zara shoved him in the ribs. 'We're just leaking.'

Several of the crew started passing up buckets of water which were dumped overboard making no impact at all on the moving flood around us.

'It's soap!' Zara announced as the cargo began to ooze from its cardboard boxes making the metal decks dangerously slippery.

After an hour's continual labour the leak in the barge was repaired, but the pile of sodden boxes spilling their slippery cargo must have meant a considerable loss in revenue for Captain Gomez, though he showed no sign of being particularly upset. Probably such an event was very common.

He propped his bottle of rotgut in front of him as he took the wheel to bring us into Nauta. To do this we had to make an almost 180° turn, leaving the Ucayali to go up the River Maranon for about a couple of kilometres. It was a tricky manoeuvre, because we immediately felt the tremendous force of the river trying to push us backwards.

To add to the hazards, we were still struggling against the current when, as if in honour of our arrival, we heard a loud explosion, which sounded like a pistol shot, and a horde of small dugout boats powered by outboard engines began to charge toward us. As they burst through the curtain of rain and passed us by, we leant over the side waving and shouting, but they didn't pause to reply. Each was intent on winning what was clearly some kind of race.

From the bows of the boats there fluttered thin red pennants which were echoed in much larger red flags hanging wetly from poles from almost every window along the small waterfront, which was also lined with spectators.

'It's a May Day race,' I exclaimed, 'It must be May the first.' And so it was. Another month gone, never to return or be repeated.

The *Campeon* moored as best she could beside the flooded banks and we said our goodbyes before wading ashore. The main street, the only street, was paved. After Pucallpa, a miracle. We asked around in stalls and shops about boats for Iquitos and learnt that there was a ferry leaving that night, but not until 9.00 p.m. It was now only one o'clock in the afternoon.

On the waterfront we found a small, clean café with attractive polished-wood walls which was run by a Chinese, who no doubt regarded May Day and any other day of rest as a complete fantasy. Here we sat all afternoon playing backgammon, reading, drinking Coke and coffee and eating a rather nasty mess of fried bananas squished up with tough minced meat.

The *Campeon* sailed by about mid-afternoon after having unloaded some cargo and loaded up with more. We waved, feeling the wrench one always experiences when moving on. She would continue on up the Maranon and then turn into the Huallaga and on up to the small river port of Yurimaguas.

The rain kept up and I thought about a girlfriend of mine whose baby was conceived on A Wet Afternoon in Dubrovnik. I had always thought it would make an intriguing title for a novel. I could see that there would also be little else to do on A Wet Afternoon in Nauta!

We took it in turns to make forays out into the little town, but there was really not much to see. A few well-kept one-storey houses, some small shops and a church. The people were predominantly Spanish-speaking Peruvians of European extraction, or mestizos. There were comparatively few Indians. Most were reasonably well dressed and looked like fairly average working people. No one took much notice of us, although Zara and Sean carrying their packs caused comments and odd looks from some people.

Through the open sides of the café we stared out at the river which had doubled in width. The Ucayali, on which we had been travelling, had been joined here by the Maranon River which was carrying not only the waters of the Huallaga River, which we had last seen back at Tingo Maria, but also those of the Rivers Tigre, Pastaza, Morona and Santiago whose snow-fed waters came from the volcanic slopes of Sangay in central Ecuador where we had been six weeks previously.

Here I was, little Trish from Bristol, sitting around playing backgammon at the start of the mighty river sea, the longest river in the world, the Amazon. Good one!

At the table next to us a well-dressed woman in her forties; what Australians, who are not known, thank God, for their subtlety, call 'an oldie but a goodie', began to flirt outrageously with Iain. She wiggled in her tight white trousers, gesticulated a great deal with her hands (which, as Zara was quick to notice, had a ring on every finger), talked loudly and smiled a lot in our direction encouraging us to join in the group with whom she was sitting. I liked her. She was full of beans and nerve and reminded me very much of a similar woman in our home town whose extravagant behaviour always makes me feel happier, wanted, even necessary. And isn't that what we all enjoy?

At five we made what turned out to be the right decision, when we boarded the ferry which was at that stage an empty hulk. We slung our hammocks on the covered upper deck aft and Zara and I stayed aboard to keep an eye on our gear, while the fellows went off to buy something for dinner.

By the time they returned, the rush had begun in earnest and in less than an hour the entire intestines of the vessel was a swinging mass of occupied hammocks. At least a hundred hung like agitated, trapped insects and the noise of human babble was made even more deafening by the acoustics of the hollow steel ship.

Aft, Cook Finlay impressed the locals hereabouts not by his culinary skill, though *we* appreciated that, but by the ease with which he lit up, used and then folded away our portable stove. He had to give several curtain call encores to demonstrate how it worked to the sizeable crowd which had accumulated.

As there is no other way to travel to Iquitos from Nauta; no roads, no air connections, everyone has to go by river and, this being the only ferry, the cross-section of travellers covered the gamut of Peruvian society: Indians, mestizos, businessmen, students, the obviously poor and the conspicuously wealthy. It was the most democratic experience we had on the entire continent.

Only two hours late, pretty good I thought for this part of the world, we departed, motoring out into the blackness, swinging in our mosquito-netted hammocks at the start of our Amazon adventure.

Six restless hours later, in pre-dawn gloom, we slipped into Iquitos, where we waited until the rush ashore had subsided before we followed to find, within about half an hour, a cheap but pleasant room on the first floor of the Hotel Peru, in the centre of town.

PERU

18
Alligators, piranhas and electric eels

Peruvians have long regarded Iquitos as their Atlantic seaport, because, although it is some 3700 kilometres up the Amazon from the mouth of the river, it is served regularly by ocean-going cargo vessels from all over the world. Within Peru, it is connected to Lima and the rest of the country only by the river and by air. All roads leading out of Iquitos disappear in the jungle, petering out after only a few kilometres. Iquitos is isolated; an island in a jungle sea. It is nonetheless a fast-growing city of over 150,000 people.

In its earliest days it was a military garrison, until the rubber boom of the late nineteenth century turned it, almost overnight, into a thriving city of luxury hotels, clubs, elegant tiled buildings and attractive houses. During the day, fashionable ladies in the latest dresses from Paris, strolled the colonnaded promenades with men in white linen suits. In the evening, there were dances and balls, recitals and concerts.

Then the rubber boom burst and Iquitos died ... well not exactly died, just went to sleep, I suppose. The Peruvian government tried to awaken it in the 1960s by offering tax incentives to new businesses, with some success. And then suddenly, in the seventies there was oil in the Iquitos area ... in big quantities and the town was back on the map and growing like Topsy.

Through all its ups and downs, Iquitos has remained the financial and trading capital of Peru's jungle region, mainly because there's been no other town to take its place. It's also remained a basically interesting town with an amazing assortment of international characters making some sort of living or non-living in the region. There are Americans buying chicle for chewing gum, Frenchmen making jungle jewellery, and running sidewalk cafes, Greeks running a bar near the Plaza de Armas (there it is again), Chinese organising alligator hunting expeditions, a German chef, a Swiss exporter of tropical fish and so on.

The central part of the city sits on a high bluff overlooking the Amazon. In the main commercial area there are several pleasant parks and the streets are paved and clean. As there was no rock to be found in the region, the first 3000 tonnes of gravel to pave the streets of Iquitos were brought by naval landing craft from Lima ... via the Panama Canal to the Atlantic Ocean, then up the Amazon River ... a journey of 11,260 kilometres between two cities only 1000 kilometres or so apart.

After a shower and a clean-up at the hotel and arranging for our laundry to be done ... this time more cheaply than it had been in Lima ... we went out to eat a big English breakfast in the pleasant dining-room of the Hotel Turistica, which overlooks the Amazon.

There were several large, international ships moored in the port, a little downstream, but we had heard that none of these carried passengers. Anyway, the smaller trading boats and launches were more what we wanted. They would be more likely to stop at the small towns and villages along the way.

At the Port Captain's office we were told that virtually no Peruvian boats traded or took passengers into Brazil. They all left either from the Colombian town of Leticia, about 480 kilometres downriver, or the Brazilian towns of Tabatinga or Benjamin Constant, just across the border from Leticia. But, we asked, how could we get to any of them? After consulting a blackboard, on which the names of several vessels were chalked, one of the officials in the office explained that there were a few boats going within a week or ten days, but that over the next day or so, there was only the *Adolfo*.

The *Adolfo?* We soon had her tracked down. She was moored on the river bank less than 100 metres from where we had breakfasted at the Hotel Turistica, in fact, we had seen her but as there was no sign of activity we had not investigated further. She was a large, old-fashioned passenger ship with two open decks. She looked more like a Nile river steamer than anything else but, though she was old, she was gleaming under a new coat of red and white paint.

When we returned to her both Zara and Sean were excited at the prospects of travelling on such a jazzy-looking vessel. 'Fabulous,' Zara said. 'Can we go on that?'

I had to agree, she did look fabulous. But there must be a catch somewhere I thought. And there was. After going on board the *Adolfo* and eventually finding a crew member, we learnt that the ship was sailing in two days' time on an Amazon River cruise that would end in Leticia five days later. She was under charter to an American-run organisation called Amazon Safari Camp, who had an office a block or so away on the Plaza de Armas.

As it happens the company's office is in one of the most unusual buildings in the world and therefore worth a mention. It is an all steel building designed by the French architect Alexandre Gustave Eiffel, of Tower fame, and constructed in Paris for the 1889 exhibition there. It was then dismantled and transported across the Atlantic and up the Amazon to be erected in Iquitos where it became the exclusive Clube Social Iquitos.

Inside this building we met Paul Wright, a friendly American in his mid-forties who founded and now runs the Amazon Safari Camp organisation. We had a brief chat, but within minutes we realised that the *Adolfo* was out of the question for us. It was to be a luxury trip, all things being relative, six days and five nights, all inclusive: good food, accommodation and travel, including a number of excursions up some of the smaller tributary rivers to visit interesting Amazon Indian tribes. The cost: just on US$300 per person!

We walked away gloomily wishing that we had money to burn. It would be a great trip, but there was no way that we could pay that sort of money.

Then Trish suddenly said, 'Why don't we try to do a 'contra' with them? We'll be writing about the whole trip anyway ... and maybe a couple of extra magazine articles ... you never know ...'

We both thought that the idea had possibilities. We went back to the hotel and got out a copy of our book about Africa, which we had been carrying with us, and took it back to Paul Wright with a proposal for a 'contra' deal; a trip on the *Adolfo* for us, if we wrote about it.

He tossed it around for a bit, but seemed unwilling to make up his mind. 'I'll think about it,' he said. 'Come back about 5.30 or 6.00 this evening.'

There was a slight possibility, we thought, as we left his office for the second time. But we weren't really very hopeful so we continued to look for other vessels, trying the offices of several shipping companies without success. After a ham and cheese sandwich each for lunch we staggered back to the hotel for a siesta. The heat and humidity had become almost overwhelming so, turning on the overhead fans, we collapsed in just our underclothes onto the beds and slept like logs until late in the afternoon.

When we went out again the sky over the town was black. Huge thunderclouds covered the sky to the north-west. It was warm but there was a feeling of imminent rain; it was something in the quality of the light or the stillness of the air or maybe it is that the human body can subconsciously sense the changing atmospheric pressure. Whatever it was, there wasn't long to wait for the rain. The skies opened up and down it came in torrents. The pavements steamed and people ran, jumping across puddles, to shelter.

We sat in a small café and had a Coke each and, by the time we were finished, so was the rain; about fifteen or twenty minutes, that was all. And by about 5.45 ... as we walked back towards Paul Wright's office, the sky was almost clear again and the air was fresh and cool. I'm not being pedantic by saying the time was 5.45. It was impressed on our memories by an extraordinary spectacle which, we learnt, takes place in Iquitos every evening at exactly that time.

Just as we were nearing the offices of Amazon Safaris, Sean cried, 'Look!' He pointed to the sky where thousands of birds, we later found out they were swallows, were wheeling and diving in formation, following what looked like a single leader. They formed a great, thick, black, arrow-headed wedge, that became wider towards its tail-end, but which dived and swooped, almost like a long piece of material being waved across the sky. We stood on the pavement and stared in amazement. One second the leaders were diving to within six or so metres of the ground above the tree-lined Plaza de Armas and the next they were sky-rocketing upwards hundreds of metres into the sky again, with thousands of other birds trailing behind them playing follow the leader. Then at exactly 6.00 p.m., as if someone had given a signal, they all swooped down into the trees in the Plaza and amidst a cacophony of tweeting and chirping settled down within a few minutes to their night's rest.

'It happens every night, regular as clockwork,' Paul Wright told us when we stepped into his office, still open-mouthed in amazement, a few minutes later. 'They go off into the jungle during the day to feed, but I guess they feel safer back here at night, or,' he laughed, 'maybe they like the company.'

'But what about all the swooping and diving?' I asked. 'Does that happen every night?'

'Sure. Just showing off I suppose. Some sort of ritual they have. They really seem to enjoy it.'

We talked a few minutes more about the birds and other generalities but what we really wanted to know was what decision he had come to as far as the trip was concerned.

'I've thought over your suggestion,' he said. 'And we'd like to have you along with us . . . but . . .'

As he spoke we had felt like jumping in the air. Zara and Sean had been about to let out a whoop but his pause, and then the 'but' made our stomachs sink.

'. . . but we can't let you travel completely free,' he went on.

Okay, I thought, so far so good. But how much?

'Transportation and accommodation we can give you,' he said, 'because we have a spare cabin on the *Adolfo,* and there are no other paying passengers waiting in line. But we will have to charge you for food. How about seventy-five dollars?'

For six days and five nights and a 480-kilometre cruise down the Amazon? It wasn't a difficult decision. We celebrated that night with a big Chinese meal at the Chifa Man Keong which was run by the same people who owned the Chinese restaurant in Pucallpa.

By the middle of the next day, we were at a Safari Camp about an hour up river from Iquitos. This was part of the package the other cruise passengers were getting, so although the *Adolfo* was not due to sail from Iquitos until the following day, we thought we might as well join in on the proceedings as soon as possible. During the morning we had organised our gear, checked out of the hotel and obtained, from the Colombian consul, the tourist cards, in lieu of visas, we thought we would need on arrival in Leticia. Then after the main group of the *Adolfo's* passengers had arrived at the company's offices on the Plaza, we were taken with them by bus to a wharf on the river then in launches up the nearby Momon River, a small tributary of the Amazon, to the Safari Camp.

The bulk of the passengers, about twenty altogether, had just flown in to Iquitos from Lima and had come straight from the airport. They were American college students from Fulton, Missouri. Two teachers and two parents were also travelling with them. Apart from the four of us, there were only two other individual passengers; Chuck Edwards, an advertising executive from Los Angeles who arrived the following day and Syd Hastie, a New Zealander whom we met on arrival at the Safari Camp.

At this stage we had some doubts about whether we were doing the right thing and about how we'd get on with the students, most of whom were about nineteen or twenty years old. It was a very 'touristy' way of going about things and generally we liked to avoid large groups like this. But then we felt that we'd had a reasonably hardy run down from Pucallpa on the *Campeon.* A bit of soft travelling was probably in order.

The Safari Camp was a rambling set of rustic wooden structures connected to each other by thatch-covered walkways elevated above the ground on stakes to avoid flood-waters. It was set on a narrow stretch of the Momon River, no more than fifty metres wide, in the midst of dense jungle. The buildings were also on stilts to cope with the apparently big fluctuations in the river's level during the rainy season. The main building, also thatched-roofed, was surrounded by a large verandah which looked out over the river and was furnished with simple but comfortable chairs. In the out-buildings, linked by the walkways to the main structure, there were small cabin-like bedrooms each with an adjoining closet containing a chemical toilet. As there was no electricity in the camp they were lit by kerosene lanterns. It was a beautiful place ... wonderfully quiet and peaceful and as there was a swimming area in the river immediately in front of the lodge, Zara and Sean fell for it immediately.

In the afternoon we went for a walk along a jungle path with one of the members of the lodge's staff. He led us to a small village, about a couple of kilometres or so from the camp, which was occupied by a small community of Jivaro Indians. Their village huts, which were in the middle of a large clearing, were also on stilts and though they too had thatched roofs, their sides were completely open.

Naked children scurried away from us, but then, after only a momentary pause, returned to circle curiously around us as we entered the village area and the guide from the camp led us across the open ground to introduce us to a group of men wearing long, sarong-like pieces of material and round feathered head-dresses. Criss-crossing their torsos, like bandoliers, they wore dozens of beaded, black necklaces made from tiny seeds and in their hands each one carried a long blow-gun.

After the formalities, the adults tended at first to ignore us, but the children, who ran off to get various artifacts and handicrafts returned to run amongst us, constantly laughing, shouting and badgering us to exchange and barter with them.

We had been told that the Indians are not greatly interested in money and much prefer to exchange goods for goods; sharp knives, mirrors, scissors and tools of almost any kind were what they wanted. The children though, naturally enough, preferred fun things and Sean, who was carrying a rubber ball, became the focus of their attention. They all wanted the ball. Eventually we traded it for a small blow-gun and a quiver of darts, non-poisonous of course! The darts incidentally are made from thin slivers of bamboo about fifteen centimetres long and just before he places the dart into his blow-gun, the Indian wraps a tiny ball of natural kapok, also carried in a separate pocket on the quiver, around the tail-end of the dart. This not only gives something to blow against when he's firing the gun, but imparts stability to the dart in the air.

The adult men were then persuaded by our camp guide to demonstrate what they could do with the blow-guns they carried, which were all roughly two metres long. Someone pinned a hundred-sole note, worth around seventy-five cents, onto a tree about ten or fifteen metres away. At a word from one of the Indian men, five of them quickly placed the thin darts into their blow-guns, raised them to their lips, aimed briefly and blew. All five of them hit the note!

A few minutes later, one of the men pointed to the top of a nearby tree. A tiny humming bird was hovering, extracting juice from a flower some fifteen metres above the ground. Within seconds, before any of us had time to say 'No', it was on the ground, dead ... with a dart through its neck. We had not asked for the demonstration and there were some of us who had felt a little cross about it, but there was nothing that could be said or done once it had happened. It was however a very convincing demonstration of the deadly accuracy of a blow-gun in the right hands. With poison tipped darts it would make a formidable weapon.

That evening after a very good buffet dinner of chicken, rice and salad washed down with Peruvian beer, we sat on the verandah of the camp and talked to Syd Hastie, the New Zealander. Syd was a dairy farmer from Te Puke in the South Island of New Zealand. But over the past ten years or so he and his wife Molly had done some pretty extraordinary non-dairy-farming things such as: travelling by Land-Rover overland from Cape Town to London, then from London overland to Bombay. After that they travelled by campervan through the United States, Central and South America and followed that by travelling across Russia on the Trans-Siberian railroad and then spent almost a year digging for opals in the Australian desert.

Molly wasn't with Syd on this trip, but he was hoping to fulfil a long-held ambition, to travel down the Amazon to the mouth at Belem. Not a bad run for anybody really, but what made Syd Hastie a little out of the ordinary in doing all this, was the fact that he was seventy years old!

Sean was delighted to regain his physical freedom. He suffers more than the rest of us from the restraints of bus and train travel, so by the time we awoke and made our way to the riverside, he had already swum in the river and was paddling a canoe towards us through the mists which hung over the water; he called for us to join him.

Zara was still asleep, so Iain and I joined Sean in the narrow canoe, balancing nervously behind one another, to set off upstream.

It was incredibly still, cool and beautiful. Giant trees sprang up at the water's edge to a height of 15, 25 and 30 metres. From them hung a profusion of vines, tree ferns and, surprisingly delicate orchids. The varying shades and textures of green were as visually challenging as the most outrageous riot of colours.

Our paddles picked up water that was black from rotting vegetation. It was a sobering thought that in a couple of million years time, when we would not even be a faint hum in the electricity of the universe, all this would have compressed into coal and that by then there would probably be no one around to think of it as a source of energy. The droplets of water fell back into the river as if never disturbed, to continue on their long journey to the sea. We were most insignificant.

Resting on our paddles, the three of us were awed into silence. In the increasing heat, the mists on the water floated away like a belly dancer's veils, and we heard the very foreign calls of birds, harsher and more insistent than the melodies imprinted in childhood. Occasionally there was the screeching chatter of monkeys.

Immediately we had stopped paddling, the river pushed us backward at quite a pace. We let it carry us for a while before making a slight diversion into a small backwater channel. Here we came with a sense of shock on another human being, fellow intruder into this world of vegetation and animals. He sat silently upright in a tiny canoe, fishing. We passed by close enough to make verbal contact unnecessary and simply nodded our best wishes which were returned in similar fashion.

Out into the main river we swirled again and at the lodge we had to make an un-seaman-like grab for the verandah to avoid being carried on downstream and missing a delicious breakfast.

The Safari lodge launch broke down twice on the way back downriver to Iquitos and it was during these pauses that I began to realise that if you are going to travel with a group of any sort you can't do better than to go with young students.

There had been a few older people at the lodge who were on another tour organised by a New Zealand travel agency. Several of them had complained about the 'primitive' toilet facilities, accommodation, food and even the presence of mud! I had overheard one po-faced woman remarking that, as far as she was concerned, one river looked much the same as any other and that the Amazon might as well be the Ganges or the creek that ran through her property back home.

Travel is wasted on people like that. They should give their tickets and funds to more imaginative and hardy folk like the young Americans we were with. They at least made jokes about getting out the oars, swimming or pushing even and when we drifted out of control into the bank, they examined the leaves of the trees we struck, the insects which came aboard and collected specimens of ferns.

In Iquitos we bought some more knives and scissors as trading goods and boarded the *Adolfo* to be shown around by George Kreisselmeyer. He was described as the Cruise Director, whereas he rather more resembled that white hunter whom Iain had anticipated meeting!

George, who was even more hirsute than Iain, was in his fifties, and had been 'floating around South America' as he expressed it, 'for more than thirty years.' If one was unkind enough, like me, to work out specific dates, it seemed more than likely that George, German by birth, had left his native land towards the end of or just after the last war, and sought sanctuary in the only continent which had remained friendly to Germany. He had worked in various unusual capacities in the Argentine, Brazil, Paraguay, Bolivia, Ecuador and now Peru; surviving coups, counter-coups, anarchy, fanaticism and plain incompetence. Through it all he had kept his accent, his own teeth (but only just because what remained of them were not in good shape) and an engaging manner.

He was the sort of token European, the one who on other river trips, when the passengers were either older wealthy Americans or Europeans, would have to take the heavy flak of their piddling complaints. He was probably also the authority figure who smoothed over the inevitable differences which arose between members of the crew. A 'PR man', that was our George.

He introduced us to Steve Mosquaera, a Napa River Indian, exceptionally good looking, in his thirties, who was equally at home on the river, in the villages or the jungle. Steve would be our guide and interpreter.

The third member of the upper deck team was Edgar Enriques, twenty-two, from Lima and already well on his way. Six months earlier, Edgar had been the male prop in a series of fashion photographs taken for 'Vogue' at Machu Picchu. You know the sort of thing: ludicrously useless and invariably unflattering clothes which could only be worn by a matchstick-thin, over-made-up model in a spectacular setting.

The photographs caught the eye of the sister (or sister-in-law, it was difficult to ascertain for sure) of Canada's Prime Minister, Pierre Trudeau. So when she visited Peru she asked to meet Edgar, who was also a rather attractive fellow, and now Edgar would shortly be emigrating to Canada. He already had a place in college lined up to study tourism, was learning French and planned to use his knowledge and abilities to lead tours of French Canadians back to Peru.

Life aboard the *Adolfo* was luxurious after the self-sustaining system we had operated on the *Campeon*. Meals were all served buffet style. The freshly-caught fish, a giant variety called 'paiche', was particularly delicious. There were fourteen cabins on the top deck. Our cabin had four bunks with foam mattresses, light bedding and mosquito nets. The crew of fifteen slept on the lower deck. The toilets, showers and wash basins were always clean.

The thirty-six-metre-long ship was skippered by a small, dapper fellow in his sixties with the most curious light grey eyes which seemed less human than animal. This was Adolfo. He had been named after the ship, which his grandfather had had built in Glasgow and which had been shipped over and had been used to carry passengers on the upper Amazon since 1909.

In the afternoon we pulled ashore beside a Yagua Indian village. I didn't like the atmosphere. It was reminiscent of a zoo. There were no men, as they were off fishing or tending their crops. The women stayed behind to supplement their income by being gawped at by people like us. Not that we gave them money, we just swapped knives again for more necklaces. Like the villagers we had seen on the Ucayali River, they also were obviously malnourished. Not starving, just not eating enough of the necessary foods. So amazing really, when surrounded by such a profusion of lush vegetation.

We all looked huge by comparison. The college boys in particular, for they were all, without exception, over 1.8 metres tall. It's one of those unexpected shocks you receive when you go to the USA or Australia from other parts of the world; the general impression of height. Each succeeding generation is slightly taller. A result perhaps of the improved high-protein diet. Sometimes I wonder if there is a physical limit to how tall a human being can be.

Zara and Sean had left our sides, each attaching themselves to the most extrovert member of the group of each sex. Zara hung, full of open admiration, around Cliffie Wesson, who had a large suitcase of fashionable though still very functional clothes and the sort of attractive poise which comes from being the daughter of a family of some resources.

Sean stuck close by Rick Keppelman, the tallest, blondest, most athletic of the young men.

Occasionally I would catch a glimpse of Zara, wearing one of Cliffie's shirts, talking animatedly, her face glowing with excitement. Or of Sean, arm-wrestling or looking through magazines, with Rick. Neither had the time or interest to spare me a nod.

I showered before dinner, looking out as I did so through the open side of the bathroom across the great river, now three kilometres wide and growing, at the jungle and a most dramatic, deep-red sunset. Then I wrapped a sarong around myself and pinned up my hair and felt more presentable than I had for quite a while!

After eating, when the bar was open, people swung in big comfortable hammocks at deck's edge, reading or playing cribbage, backgammon or chess, or just talking. It was all so very pleasant.

In the soft confidence-inducing air, I talked with Chuck Edwards who, apart from Syd, was the only other 'stray' traveller. Very overweight and very West Coast American. He was from Los Angeles and had the dry laconic wit which helps one to survive in that bitchy, tough community.

Next morning when we awoke at about 6.00 a.m. we found that the *Adolfo* was not moving. She had stopped during the early hours of the morning at a place called Pijuayal, which was a Peruvian military base ... well, a check-point really, rather than a base. We were still within Peruvian territory, about 128 kilometres from the border with Colombia on the left bank of the river and 225 kilometres from Brazil on the right bank. But for some reason the Peruvian authorities required all boats to check in at Pijuayal before proceeding further down river.

It wasn't much of a place: a few small, grey-painted, naval launches moored to a mudbank, some decrepit tropical bungalows sitting on top of the bank, with the jungle pressing in on their backs and one or two Peruvian naval ratings moving about, doing their chores in a dispirited fashion. Evidently River Fleet postings like this are not particularly popular with either ratings or officers. In the early days, officers from Peru's Pacific Fleet who fell into disfavour were 'banished' to the river postings where they were left to 'rot' in the jungle backwaters.

Nothing much seemed to be happening to us either. They were apparently waiting for the right officer to arrive to deal with us and nothing could proceed until he showed up. On board the *Adolfo*, however, everything went on as usual. We got up, showered and had breakfast. The whole routine seemed so very civilised compared with life on board the *Campeon.* Breakfast on the open-sided deck was a real pleasure. Buffet-style, help-yourself: papaya, scrambled eggs, sausages, bacon, toast, all sorts of spreads and coffee or tea.

Not long after breakfast we were cleared and left the military check-point to sail only a short distance to where a small tributary flowed into the Amazon. It was the Ampryaco River and, following the right bank a little way upstream, we came to a small town called Pevas. It was a poor, but quite well-cared-for Peruvian town with a church, some paved streets and a number of concrete houses. Its population of only three or four hundred, were all Spanish-speaking but I should imagine the greater percentage of them were mestizos.

Our visit to Pevas was not exactly a success. It had been intended that we pay something of a diplomatic visit to the governor of the district who coincidentally owned one or two of the local handicraft shops which we should also visit. But the governor was in Iquitos and we discovered on our arrival that virtually the whole town was in mourning. Evidently one of the most popular young men in the town, a youth of just twenty-three, had only the night before committed suicide by taking the dread poison, curare, which is extracted from the bark of a tree.

As we came up the steps from where the *Adolfo* had moored, we were confronted by the boy's wailing mother and relatives. At first it took some time for us to work out what had happened and even then we could only establish that it was all because of what they called 'an affair of the heart'. There was nothing we could do to comfort the mother who was completely distraught. A doctor was being brought from the military base to perform an autopsy on the boy within the hour. There was a blanket of sadness over Pevas and it took some time for any of us to be able to think or say anything positive after leaving the little town.

Sailing further up the Ampryaco River we stopped to visit the neighbouring villages of two different Amazon tribes, the Huitoto and the Boras. They were quite different from those we had seen nearer Iquitos and although the Huitotos and the Boras lived only a very short distance apart, they too were different from one another.

The women of both tribes wore a sort of lap-lap made from pounded bark fibre, but were naked from the waist up and many, like the men, wore feathered head-dresses. The designs painted onto their bark clothes by the Huitotos were more elaborate and complex than those of the Bora. The Huitotos on the other hand used little or no body decoration, while the faces of all the Boras were painted with a black, moustache-like slash across their mouths.

Both groups were extraordinarily friendly and we took photographs and traded small goods with them for half an hour or so in each village. In Iquitos I had bought a couple of large, sharp kitchen knives especially for an occasion like this and had no trouble disposing of them, one in each village, for a small, brightly coloured head-dress and a large, brown, ku-klux-klan-type mask made of beaten bark. It was, I was told, a witch-doctor's mask for use in ceremonial dances.

The Bora village chief obviously fancied the Mexican straw hat which Sean had been wearing and carrying with him ever since we had bought it at Chichen Itza, the ruined Mayan city on the Yucatan Peninsula. There was no possibility of communication between them because although I thought the chief looked as if he may have had some Spanish blood in him, he spoke only his own Bora dialect. But he motioned back and forth with his hand to Sean's hat and to his own feathered head-dress. Sean got the idea and within seconds they had swopped and the chief, now the proud wearer of a rather battered Mexican straw hat complete with a small hole in the top, looked as happy as Larry.

After we had left the two villages and rejoined the Amazon, most of the rest of the afternoon was spent just cruising down the river. We swung in hammocks on the upper deck and read. I played cribbage for a while with several of the students then spent an hour or so chatting with Syd Hastie, Chuck Edwards and Jack Cooke. Jack was the president of a bank in Fulton, Missouri and in his late fifties. His son Steve was one of the students in the group. Jack was quite taken with Syd ... we all were, I guess. Syd was a great raconteur and he had a never-ending supply of jokes. Whenever he got talking he had everyone in peals of laughter with stories of some of his hair-raising experiences on the road in different parts of the world. Obviously he had made quite a bit of money as a dairy farmer, enough to enable him to do all the travelling he did. But he wasn't going to just let things stand.

'I'm going to make a million soon,' Syd told us at one stage, 'out of Kiwi fruit and avocados.'

'What about the dairy farm, though?' I asked.

'Oh, I'll still keep that going, I suppose, but Kiwi fruit, Chinese gooseberries, you call them, that's where the big money is. I've already switched about eight hectares over to avocados and the same to Kiwi fruit and I'm going to do a lot more when I get back. Make a fortune!'

There's nothing stopping some people and whenever Syd was around, I couldn't help thinking, I hope I'm still like that when I'm seventy.

At about four in the afternoon we turned from the Amazon into the Cochiquinas River and stopped after only a few kilometres at a deserted jungle lodge called Tambo Pirana. At one time it had been used by travellers and tourists, but for some reason, probably economic, had fallen into disuse. The buildings, which were similar in construction to the safari camp where we had stayed before leaving Iquitos, were all competely empty, though in reasonably good condition. The jungle was already beginning to encroach on the cleared land on which the buildings stood and if they continued to remain unused, the jungle would soon take over.

We were not going to use the buildings, but just moor alongside them. The stream where we stopped was deep, dark and fast flowing, but we were told it was safe to swim. Within minutes of receiving this information, half of the students were in the water and led by Rick Keppelman and John Gray, both of whom we discovered were star college divers, we all began jumping and diving from the roof of the *Adolfo* into the water below.

It was quite a height, probably eight metres, and though it took a while for them to work up courage, both Zara and Sean went off the top. It was only after we had finished swimming and were standing around helping ourselves to the buffet dinner that someone asked, 'Why do they call this place Tambo Pirana?'

'Because of the piranha fish here,' George said.

'What!' about six voices exclaimed at once. 'Piranhas? In that water?'

'Sure,' George said casually. 'There are plenty of piranhas about here all the time. It's a fallacy about how dangerous they are.'

'Yeah?' Chuck Edwards said disbelievingly. 'Well, here's one guy who's not taking any more chances, that's for sure.'

'No, seriously,' George persisted. 'They won't attack humans at all unless there's blood in the water.'

'That's great . . . thanks very much,' someone said sarcastically. 'It's nice to feel so secure.'

About an hour after dinner we joined a small group to go out with Steve Mosquaera hunting caimans . . . or alligators. Not hunting with guns, but spotlights. We lashed two flat-bottomed aluminium boats together and after all donning life-jackets, set off into the night, the single outboard motor chugging away behind us. There were about a dozen of us altogether. Zara and Sean were sitting in the front of one boat, while Trish and I were in the rear of the other. Everyone was quiet as we left the comforting lights of the *Adolfo* behind and turned off the Cochiquinas River into a smaller, narrower stream and almost total darkness.

Steve, who was standing at the bow of one of the boats, would occasionally shine a strong flashlight along the swampy shores of the jungle on either side.

The sky was clear and filled with stars, which were reflected in the dead-calm water. But from the top of the trees down to the water there was nothing but absolute blackness. We sensed from the brief flashes of the torchlight, that the stream was becoming narrower still. The walls of thick foliage were now closer on both sides. Suddenly Steve signalled and called softly to the crew-member on the tiller behind us to stop. The engine was slowed right down.

'See,' Steve whispered, playing the beam of torchlight onto the shoreline. There were several exclamations of excited surprise as we all saw four or five pairs of bright red eyes shining back at us from where the jungle met the water. We shut the motor off and as we were already pointed towards the shore our momentum kept carrying us in. The fiery eyes continued to gleam back at us more brightly the closer we came. There were a few whispered comments of concern . . . niggling fear. One of the sets of eyes turned and disappeared with a soft splash . . . then another. Steve, who remained standing on the bow of the boat, kept the flashlight shining directly on the remaining animals. Two more of them slipped away. There was only one left. We were within about three metres of the shore. We could see its long, brown body, maybe two and a half metres long, half hidden under some low-hanging shrubs. Then there was a splash and he was gone, disappearing under the weeds and lilies which now surrounded the boats.

We started the engine and moved off again. Then, 'thump', we hit something fairly solid in the river. A log? A caiman? Whatever it was it broke a sheer-pin on the outboard motor and we started slowly drifting with the current, with no control. Soon we were coming close to the shore again and the darkened jungle loomed high above us. Someone gasped as a long, hanging vine brushed against her. One of the boys in the other boat grabbed a tree trunk to push us off, but found his hands covered with stinging ants. But at last the sheer-pin was replaced, the engine restarted and we were off again with sighs of relief.

We continued for almost an hour more upstream, spotting half a dozen or so other alligators on the bank, before turning around and heading back for the *Adolfo*. Just as we turned, we heard the distant sound of drums. We stopped the motor and all sat quietly in the darkness listening. It was strange. They were several kilometres off, and were probably just part of some village celebration or ceremony, but the sound sent a shiver of excitement down my back.

The excitement kept up on the next day when we took a walk in the jungle. Again we went in the *Adolfo's* flat-bottomed aluminium dinghies, this time so that we could push our way in through the foliage. Steve told us that the river was at present in flood and the water level was up to six metres above its normal height.

When we came to a stop, in amongst thick bushes, the water was still knee-deep. In my defence all I can say is that I have a primaeval horror, probably conceived in the womb, of walking on oozing mud in water through which I cannot see to the bottom. In short, Iain carried me to dry ground, to the accompaniment of 'boos' and derogatory remarks!

High above us, the trees disappeared to meld together into a deep green ceiling. It was raining, quite solidly, but none of it penetrated the jungle canopy beneath which it was oppressively humid and hot. Again there were the creepers and vines, the ferns, fungus and flowers. The Drs Howard and Louise Hinde, both of them heads of biology departments at their separate small private colleges, were just about going ga-ga over the vegetation. He was collecting spores and she was making notes and both of them were raging on like children at Christmas!

'Everything grows so much bigger than at home,' Louise kept saying. 'It sure is different from Fulton, Missouri!'

We were following behind one another in single file, along the narrow jungle path, when there was a yell from up ahead and the word was quickly passed back, 'Snake!' It seemed that a metre-long effort had slithered right across Rick's sneaker, as he led the way faithfully followed, as always, by Sean.

There was indeed a snake and it was indeed a metre or more, at least, long. But it was even more frightened of us than we were of it. It had slithered up a nearby tree trunk and draped itself over a branch in the hope of passing muster as a vine. After everyone had taken a photograph, we left it to its self-delusions.

Above the chatter of the monkeys we heard the repetitive call of a pair of orioles and on the way back Steve cut down a baby palm tree. Everyone had a piece of 'heart of palm', that expensive piece of cuisine snobbery served in all the best international restaurants which is absolutely tasteless, unless doused with salad dressing. I'm sure it is only considered a delicacy because it is so exotic, so difficult to come by and because it necessitates destroying a whole tree, to prise out the very centre. If one could buy it for forty cents a kilo in the local green-grocery no one would want it. Aren't people odd?

We made only one stop on the return trip and that was at a collection of huts which didn't even qualify as a village. Steve and Edgar climbed up the steep bank to where we could see a thin coil of blue smoke rising from an open fire. We followed them and had our over-developed Western sensitivities upset when we discovered that a whole monkey was being roasted. Worse still, the monkey had been a feeding mother and her tiny baby, chattering with fear, was tied to the wooden stilt of a hut watching and smelling the procedure.

Steve bought the roasted meat, a delicacy he assured us that the crew would enjoy, though we weren't sure that it wouldn't be served to us. And one of the engine room crew paid a few soles for the trembling baby monkey which Zara immediately appropriated.

The *Adolfo* motored on and at about 4.00 p.m. made an unscheduled stop, at George's behest, at a small illegal sugarcane distillery hidden from river view. If it wasn't illegal it should have been because the cumbersome makeshift machinery was so old and dangerous, and because the alcoholic content of the liquid produced there was so high as to be almost lethal. Most people had a sip of the raw, potent, freshly distilled liquid and George carried off a couple of boxes filled with bottles of the demon stuff.

That evening, our last on the *Adolfo,* we had a bit of a bash. Steve, who had not mixed over much with the passengers, preferring the company of the crew below, set up a blow-gun competition using his own very long and unwieldy pipe. When we had all proved what miserable failures, though what good sports, we were, Steve took his turn and of course, to the manner born, his darts hit the board dead-centre every time. We all cheered, partly I suspect because he looked as if it were important to him. The two best efforts among the passengers, one boy and one girl, were ceremonially crowned. Then Captain Adolfo came out with a pair of castanets to accompany the guitar and drums played by Edgar and Steve.

Dancing and drinking and generally good-natured kid-type fooling around followed, finishing in a conga line which stretched right round the top deck and snaked up onto the roof from where we all stared out at the Southern Cross, which seemed to be taking a break, reclining on the jungle roof.

When I checked the kids, who had finally collapsed an hour or so before, I found Sean asleep flat on his back, his arms spread, as if he had simply keeled over, still wearing his feather head-dress. And in Zara's bed there were two rather than one, for snuggling up in her armpit was the tiny monkey. The long white fur on its jowls made it appear like a miniature lion. He had wound his tail round her protective arm, like a handcuff.

I remember getting up a couple of hours later to find out what all the noise was about and staring sleepily over the side at the diminutive figure of Captain Adolfo who, in his pyjamas, was running back and forth along the muddy bank, against which we were moored, waving his arms and shouting in a very excited way, 'Peligrosa, Peligrosa,' (danger) at a couple of stout men who were struggling to bring aboard tanks of petrol. Zara and the monkey — and everyone else — slept on.

We only made one more stop before the end of the cruise and that was at Monkey Island which is on the left-hand side of the river going down, or if you prefer, the north bank. By then this was Colombian territory, though the right hand, or south, bank was still part of Peru.

And Island of Monkeys it certainly is. Twenty-five thousand of them live on it! A population explosion caused by the fact that their owner, Mike Tsalickis, a Greek-American adventurer, had his licence to continue exporting them to the USA, where they were invaluable in cancer research, cancelled by the Colombian government.

Due to timidity, Zara and I stayed near the shore talking to the macaws, who looked like pieces of strutting rainbows, while intrepid Iain and Sean ventured further.

It was only a short walk along a jungle trail similar to the one we had been on the previous day but on this one sections of the narrow path were flooded up to knee and thigh-depth. Several of the students were about to turn back, but Steve, who was leading the way, kept insisting that we continue. There was something he wanted to show us.

Nobody felt very happy about wading through the water. We had been told that the streams and pools on the island abounded with electric eels. These snake-like creatures, often two metres long and more, pack a lethal charge of several hundred volts of electricity in their bodies. They can easily knock a man unconscious which is usually a nasty thing to happen to you in the water, and if you're unlucky they can kill you in one hit.

'Just keep your eyes open for them,' Steve had said. But in the muddy water it was impossible to see anything. Sean stuck close behind me as we waded through the last flooded section of the track which led straight to a beautiful pool that was surrounded on all sides by thick jungle.

'There,' Steve pointed to the pool. 'Lilies.'

In front of us, the pool was covered by gigantic lily pads, the huge 'Victoria Regia' water lilies up to two metres in diameter that are the biggest in the world. They are so strong they can support the weight of a seven-or-eight-year-old child.

I was glad to have seen the lily pads; they were really quite something, but still standing in water up to our knees, kept us feeling somewhat edgy. We took some photographs and then turned to make our way back towards the *Adolfo,* feeling a considerable sense of relief when we left the flooded section of the track and were back on dry ground again.

After leaving Monkey Island, there was only another hour or so cruising downriver before we arrived at the end of our trip on the *Adolfo.*

To avoid the bureaucratic problems of Colombian paperwork, she moored off the Peruvian settlement of Ramon Castillo, a collection of perhaps a dozen shacks and we took it in turns to cross over to Leticia, in Colombia, on the far side of the river in the ship's powered aluminium dinghies.

The water was choppy enough for us to ship quite a lot and I thought how foolish we were to be crouching there under our heavy packs. If we went overboard, an idea not to be lightly dismissed, the packs would drag us down. Iain looked grim. I tried to soothe him by suggesting that we wiggle out of our packs so as to be better prepared for swimming.

'That's not what's on my mind,' he seemed distracted. 'I'm worried about all the film in my pack getting ruined.'

At that moment we heard the droning of an engine and, squinting up through the spray, we saw a battered Colombian airliner, an antique DC4, circling prior to landing. What took my mind off our own worries was that only three out of the four propellers were turning!

We landed at a small wharf and walked up into the town to book into the Colonial Hotel, the cost of which was included in the river trip package, at least for one night anyway. But although we had landed in a different country, Colombia, there had been no sign of any customs or immigration officials and when we asked about this, George said casually, 'Oh, don't worry about it. Nobody gets too concerned with formalities like that here. It's a very easy-going town.'

So with us and the precious film safely and illegally ashore, Iain immediately went off in search of another boat to carry us the next sixteen hundred kilometres downriver to Manaus. He came back triumphant. 'A beauty' called *Dominique* was sailing in three days time; sixty dollars for all four of us for the estimated five-day voyage.

Drs Hinde and their students were flying out to Bogota in the morning. I didn't tell them about the plane with the defunct propeller. As it had flown in that way it would probably manage to fly out and there seemed no point in adding fear to their luggage.

Waving them onto the little airport bus was one of the most difficult goodbyes I've ever made, for both Zara and Sean stood beside me, tense and only just holding back their tears. The moment the crowded vehicle disappeared from view, leaving only a cloud of dust and the fading shouts of farewell, they both burst into heart-wrenching wails.

Intermittently throughout that day and the next, despite my guilty attempts to distract them, they would come to a halt, stand still and weep unselfconsciously. In trying to say the right words of comfort to them I only managed to upset myself. This was one of the very few times on the journey when I asked myself if I was doing the right thing by my children and the answer didn't come back clearly and loudly in the affirmative.

BRAZIL

19
Half the world's fresh air

Although Leticia is in Colombia, we're including it here, under Brazil, for the simple sake of convenience. It's the only part of Colombia we get to talk about and anyway it's a pretty international town. It's just across the river from Peru and it has a land frontier with Brazil which is only a couple of kilometres or so from the centre of town; a land frontier which anybody and everybody crosses freely in both directions, in cars, trucks, buses, on bicycles, or on foot, without any formalities.

In fact, there is nothing to mark the border and you have to look very hard to even seen an office that would deal with immigration or customs procedures. The road, the telegraph poles and the street lights continue between Leticia in Colombia and Tabatinga in Brazil, as if there was no territorial distinction between them. The only difference, we were told, is that up to the invisible border the power for the Colombian street lights comes from Leticia, while the power for the Brazilian ones comes from Tabatinga.

When we eventually found a Brazilian immigration office at which to get our passports stamped, the official filled them in as if we had already entered Brazil, even though he knew we were staying in Leticia for a couple of days before going by boat into Brazil. Then we went straight back to Leticia, Colombia, which we had neither officially entered nor left.

In Leticia we also found that in most shops and restaurants any one of the three currencies, Colombian, Brazilian or Peruvian, was generally quite acceptable. This took some getting used to; Colombian pesos were 36 to US$1.00, Brazilian cruzeiros were 18 to $1.00 and Peruvian soles were 130 to $1.00. But it tended to get confusing when you learnt that it took 10 cruzeiros to buy 18 pesos. Which was the stronger currency?

Despite these minor worries, the three days we spent in Leticia were pleasant, relaxing and interesting. It was an attractive town; much cleaner than the average Peruvian town, we thought and with tree-lined streets, well-kept parks and sidewalk cafes, it was not a difficult place in which to pass a few days.

Syd Hastie and Chuck Edwards were still in town and were sharing a room at the Anaconda Hotel. We had moved on the second day into the Hotel Allemanas (the German Hotel) which was run by an elderly German couple and was considerably cheaper than the Colonial and the Anaconda. Syd had decided to join us on the trip to Manaus on the *Dominique* and as Chuck was not due to fly out to Lima until the day our boat sailed, for the few days we were in Leticia we more or less all stuck together.

It's almost impossible to visit Leticia and not meet Mike Tsalickis. It's *definitely* impossible to be there and not *hear* of him, because he is Leticia's leading citizen; he owns just about half the town and is one of the great characters of the Amazon. Mike is a Greek-American from Tarpon Springs in Florida. When we met him, I guessed him to be in his mid-forties, but he first came to the Amazon when he was in his early twenties, collecting animal species for zoos and research establishments. And that, along with leading jungle safaris, is how he made his name in the area.

Now his home and office are on the main square in Leticia. The Booth Line Shipping Agency, which is his, is next door. Immediately behind his house, is his jungle animal complex, in which a huge assortment of wild animals, monkeys, jungle-cats and snakes, are kept. Beyond that, sprawling over a couple of hectares, is Mike's Parador Ticuna Hotel and swimming pool. In the centre of town, the newest and most prestigious hotel, the Colonial, where we stayed one night, also belongs to Mike, as does the brick factory, the ice-plant, the airport guide service and 'Turamazonas', a jungle tour organisation which can organise almost any kind of safari into the wilds of the Amazon and its headwaters.

But Mike Tsalickis is probably best-known as the slightly crazy guy who wrestles with giant anaconda snakes. Magazines all over the world have featured photo-spreads of him swirling in muddy waters, with the massive, thirty-centimetre-thick coils of an anaconda wrapped around him as he struggles desperately to hold the animal's head away from him.

'They're not really as bad as they look,' he said to us one morning as we stood looking down at a four-metre specimen, lying on the grass in Mike's animal compound. 'Once they've had a good feed, they become very sluggish and if you know what you're doing, you can handle them okay. They're not all that dangerous.'

'What if they bit you?' Sean asked, not taking his eyes off the great brown snake which, though it lay still, stared back at us and flicked its forked tongue in and out of its mouth incessantly.

'Well they're not poisonous,' Mike said, 'but they've got sharp fangs and they can give you a very nasty bite. That's why you've got to hold them tight . . . right behind the jaws. Like to try?'

We all involuntarily stepped back a pace. 'Not on your life,' Trish muttered, retreating along the wall of one of the compound sheds.

'Aw, come on,' Mike insisted, 'there's nothing to it.'

'Are you game to have a go, Iain?' Syd Hastie suddenly said to me, 'because if you do, I will.'

I paused a moment. Syd was older than my father. If he can do it, I thought, I can too. But I knew I was being 'shamed' into it. 'Okay,' I said. 'I'll have a go.'

Mike Tsalickis made a lunge at the anaconda's head with a long forked stick and held it tightly. Then, with the help of an aide, he manoeuvred it across to me and passed its head into my hands so that I could grab it behind its jaws. When they both let go and stepped back, there were two things I felt immediately. First its weight. The snake must have weighed between 70 and 90 kilos . . . maybe more, some of them grow up to 11 metres long and weigh 225 kilos. I went down on my knees for better stability under its weight. Then I felt its tremendous strength. As its thick, cold coils writhed and wrapped themselves around me, it took all of my strength, not only just to stay upright, but also to hold the animal's head as it tried to force its way free from my grasp. I held on as if my life depended on it.

'Don't strangle the poor bugger,' Mike laughed as the others stood back and took photographs. 'He's worth a lot of money.'

'Okay,' I said after a couple of minutes. 'I've done my bit. Now it's your turn, Syd.'

Mike and his helper quickly released me from its clammy embrace and passed it to Syd, who insisted that I capture it on his movie camera for Molly and the folks back home in Te Puke. And he did it! Without any problem whatever. Held a live, four-metre anaconda . . . which is more than most seventy-year-olds can say.

We spent that afternoon swimming in the pool of the Parador Ticuna Hotel. Although we weren't staying there, we were permitted to use the pool because of some arrangement Mike Tsalickis had with the *Adolfo* Cruise people. It was there at the pool that we met Sam Poole (with an 'e'). Sam was large, blond and about fifty. He had just finished manoeuvring a seaplane on wheels into Mike Tsalickis' backyard and was angry as hell. Not with Mike but with just about everyone else.

'Some bastard was trying to steal my plane,' he told us, chomping aggressively on a cigar. He obviously wanted or needed to talk to someone and as we were the most convenient . . .

'Thirty-six hours ago I was in Miami,' he went on, 'when I got a phone call from here saying that some Canadian joker was crating my airplane up and shipping it out. Well, I got here just in time. I had the guy arrested last night at the airport . . . and now the plane is safe . . . here.' He waved his arm towards the animal compound and the rear of Mike's house.

Apparently Sam Poole's seaplane had been held under some government lien or legal restriction for several years and Sam, who runs an airport in Florida, had been trying sporadically to get it released through official channels.

'Well, they released it all right,' he said, 'but the bastards didn't tell *me* anything about it. So the next thing I know, the airport manager here has sold my plane to this Canadian guy . . . who's about to ship it out.'

'But surely they can't do that?' I said. 'It wasn't his to sell.'

'Ah ha . . .' Sam leant back in his chair, relaxing a little, '. . . small formalities like that don't bother people around these parts. I used to run an airline down here back in the fifties. In sixty-one the Colombian Government expropriated it . . . just like that. I lost a million bucks and I've been suing them ever since . . . seventeen years. In seventy-three I won a $500,000 judgement in the Colombian courts but they still haven't paid me.' He shook his head and laughed. 'I mean, can you believe that? The courts order the government to pay it, but they just won't do it.' His face became serious again. 'Now I'm suing 'em not only for the $500,000, but for five years' interest on it as well!'

We don't know what happened to Sam Poole's lawsuit, but from what we'd heard about corruption in high places in Colombia, I didn't like his chances. It's drugs, though, that are the really big corrupter in Colombia. Sam Poole's plane was pretty small potatoes when compared to that scene. While we were in Leticia, we learnt some of the statistics relating to Colombian marijuana, which is apparently regarded as the best in the world.

The grower gets around $10 a kilo for his crop. The man who packages it up, ready to ship it out gets another $20-$30 a half kilo, bringing it up to say $40. By the time it leaves Colombia, however, the cost is $140 a kilo. The additional $100 has gone into the pockets of the various officials, politicians and generals who have sanctioned its movements within the country. But when it hits the streets of New Orleans, for example, or other towns in the southern United States it is already up to $500 a kilo and in northern US cities, like New York, well over $1000 a kilo, and yet ... even at those prices, there are literally tons of Colombian pot being shipped to and sold in the United States every day. Big money.

While we were in Leticia we had most of our meals with Chuck and Syd and on two of the evenings ate in a very pleasant little outdoor restaurant which served basically Spanish food. We all had steak on both occasions, finding the meat much better than we had eaten for some time. But it was the atmosphere which made the meals memorable. First there were the sunsets, which each evening were incredibly spectacular. On the opposite bank across the river great, blue-black rain clouds would hang suspended over a golden and red sky beyond. Then after dusk as we sat outside the restaurant in the warm, humid air, sipping a beer before our meal arrived, the rain would come pelting down on the canvas awning while we, comfortable and dry underneath, would just sit listening to its deafening roar and watching it pour in thick rivulets off the sides.

On the day that we left Leticia, we said goodbye to Chuck in the morning and took a small ferry, about lunch-time, across and down the river to the tiny Brazilian town of Benjamin Constant. On board, just before we left the wharf at Leticia, we were startled to see a very muscular, long-haired man wearing little more than a leopard-skin loin cloth and a few beads around his neck. He had a large knife strapped to his arm and was making sure that we and the other half-dozen or so passengers took good notice of him. I found myself looking around to see if I could spot a film crew anywhere. He looked so much like the screen version of Tarzan, Colombian style. We never really found out who he was because as the little ferry pulled out, he leapt back on to the wharf with a flourish and a wave and that was all we saw of him. An Amazonian eccentric.

We were taking the ferry to Benjamin Constant because our boat, the *Dominique*, had sailed the previous day to have some repairs carried out in a small boatyard there and we had arranged to board her there instead of at Tabatinga. We couldn't help feeling a slight twinge of anxiety. What if the boat had gone without us? If the Captain had misunderstood the arrangements, or if he'd just decided to take off with our fare deposits of $50 which we had left with him.

When we docked by a small concrete ramp running down into the river at 'Benjamin', as the locals called it, there was no sign of the *Dominique* and when we tried to find out where she was, we suddenly realised we couldn't speak the language. We had become so accustomed to Spanish over the past three months or so, that we had thought we would also be able to manage Portuguese. But it might as well have been Russian! In fact it did sound like Russian to us. We felt a wave of depression over having to start right from scratch again.

Eventually, though we managed to find out that the *Dominique* was berthed about 800 metres upriver and after a short, motorised ride in a dugout peque-peque we pulled up alongside and clambered aboard, passing our packs up to a crew member on the deck.

We had only seen her at night before and had not really looked her over very thoroughly. Now however we went on a tour of inspection, not that there was really very much to see. She was a sturdy, good-looking cargo vessel of about thirty metres. She appeared to be relatively new and was very solidly built of wood with the cargo holds occupying the forward parts of the ship and the wheelhouse and the crew and passenger accommodations aft. She was bigger than the *Campeon*, but considerably smaller than the *Adolfo*. But what immediately appealed to us was that she was gleaming with fresh paint and was clean everywhere. Our cabin, though it only had one small window with a sliding wooden-louvred shutter, was lined with pine-timber panelling and the four bunks had comfortable, foam-rubber mattresses. We settled ourselves in, sliding our packs away under the bottom bunks, then read or slept during the afternoon, until we were ready to leave.

We sat in the wheelhouse, just before sunset, watching several children swimming in the backyard of their home next to the boatyard. It had been flooded by the rising waters of the river, although the house itself was still some metres above the water level, being built like most houses in the town on stilts. The floodwaters were playing havoc with the family's garden . . . if they ever had one . . . but the kids loved it.

While we were watching, the diminutive figure of our captain, Captain Nieto, climbed on board from a peque-peque. A short while later the *Dominique* manoeuvred out into the stream and, sailing down past Benjamin Constant, its powerful searchlight sweeping the water in front of us, headed confidently off into the night.

It seemed quite normal to wake around 6.00 a.m., lie listening to the now familiar early morning shipboard noises and look through the window of our cabin at the continuous band of jungle which seemed to have been unrolling along the horizon for a very long time and at still the same massive body of water moving inexorably onward.

Each of the boats on which we had travelled was different; the *Dominique* was workmanlike and efficient. But even though they were of different nationalities and going about dissimilar businesses, they had an indefinable quality in common; perhaps an atmosphere created by plying up and down the world's largest river.

I'm not a good sailor and when Iain enthuses over his plan to island-hop on local boats right across the Pacific, my stomach heaves in anticipation and I suggest that he may have to find another travelling companion for that trip. But a river; that's different. It has all the excitement of water travel and none of the sickening disadvantages. So I lay there, with my family slowly surfacing around me and schemed of having my own boat in which to trade up and down a great river. It's a way of life which has a tremendous appeal for me.

At 6.15 we were called to breakfast. We had again brought our own food supplies, but decided, having surreptitiously inspected the kitchen, to give the cook the initial benefit of the doubt. Very sweet coffee and small unsweetened biscuits were laid out on the table on the deck below. We brought down our own bananas and shared them around.

Captain Nieto was just getting up too and joined us with his son, Marcos. Six years old, he was a bit of a tiger and unmistakably his father's boy. The same slightly pinched physique, same strutting gait and same husky voice in which he talked loudly and non-stop in unintelligible Portuguese. I felt a quite irrational anger over the fact that Portuguese was so totally different from Spanish. My first impulse was to refuse to learn it!

The Captain who was in his early thirties, told us that he had only owned the *Dominique* for three months. She was thirty-six metres long with a four and a half metre beam, and two and a half metre draft.

It seemed that apart from the cargo of tapioca and chickle, the raw product from which chewing gum is manufactured, we were also on a bottle-run; picking up empty beer bottles which would be exchanged in Manaus so that full ones could be delivered on the way back up.

We had to keep reminding ourselves that all the various-sized communities along the river were totally dependent for supplies on these river boats. There was no road, of course no rail links and air freighting goods would be prohibitively expensive. No, the river was their only lifeline.

They perched on its banks totally surrounded by jungle which seemed to be only biding its time before swallowing them in one gulp.

Back upstairs we sat for a while beside the man at the wheel. It was already warm and threatening real heat. The river was a few kilometres wide but as we mostly stayed near to one bank, the distant shore looked as though it should belong to another country. There was as yet no other traffic and sitting there behind the glass windows, which could be let up and down, looking out over the tarpaulin which covered the length of the ship's deck to protect the cargo, I had a satisfying illusion of proprietorship.

Behind us on both sides of a narrow passageway were the cabins, two a side and at the far ends lavatory/shower rooms. Then came a small covered aft deck with a big, open bay window reminiscent of a suburban English home, only this one gave onto an unobstructed view of the river to the rear. It had tarpaulins which could be arranged to give shade or shelter. There were a table and chairs, and a little handbasin and mirror. This was our living-room.

After morning ablutions it was still only 7.30, so we sat and read. I started into Syd's copy of *Roots*. Syd himself was ripping through our books at great speed, in between keeping us amused with stories of his adventures on five continents. 'I remember once in Leningrad . . .' he'd begin and we'd all sit back in happy anticipation.

By 9.30 a.m. I thought I would have an afternoon nap! I dozed off only to be woken at 10 a.m. to be told that lunch was served! Obviously the *Dominique* had her own distinctive time schedules! The well-cooked meal of as much fried beef, spaghetti and rice as we could eat made us realise that we needn't have brought our own grub.

In the afternoon we stopped at a small settlement called Sao Paulo de Olivencia and here three more passengers came aboard; two young men who turned out to be what they looked like, soldiers and a girlfriend of one of them.

Later the children and I swung in the capacious hammocks in the wheel house. They were recovering from their unhappiness with the incredible resilience of all children, though they were still rather tired from all the excitement. They lay one on each side of me and we watched the splendid drama of the setting sun, as we discussed home and homesickness, friends and friendsickness.

'I liked them,' Sean said, referring to Rick and the rest of the American students, 'because they were old enough to know a lot and be interesting, but young enough to still be good fun.' Sean doesn't express himself much, but when he does it's worth waiting for!

In the middle of that night there was a most tremendous rain squall. The noise of the heavy drops on the roof was only centimetres from my face where I lay in the top bunk. I got up to go to the loo and found the mate sitting at the wheel in a heavy sweater, the rain lashing against the windows. It looked like a scene from a North Sea gale; except that all around him in hammocks swung the sleeping bodies of the rest of the crew.

When the Spanish Conquistadore, Francisco de Orellana sailed down from Peru onto the Amazon in 1542 and followed its waters another 3000 kilometres to the sea, his tales of battles with warrior women, similar to the Amazons of Greek mythology, gave the river the name by which we know it today. And it's hardly surprising that the giant river has tended to be the stuff of legends. It is by far the greatest river on earth. The volume of water flowing into the Atlantic Ocean at its mouth exceeds the *combined flow* of the next eight largest rivers in the world! The Amazon's outflow is, for example, *60 times greater* than the Nile, 11 times greater than the Mississippi. The incredible Amazon basin, from which more than a thousand major tributaries feed the main river, spreads over almost six and a half million square kilometres and when you lay a chart of the river network over a map of the United States, or Australia, for instance, it almost completely covers either country. More than 80,000 kilometres of these tributary river systems are navigable and ocean-going steamers can travel more than 3700 kilometres up the Amazon. The river, where we were travelling on it now, some 3000 kilometres from the sea, was almost three kilometres wide and about 45 metres deep!

For most of the morning of our third day, we cruised beside the left bank of the river, stopping at a few small settlements to load crates of empty beer and soft-drink bottles. Earlier, we'd had a good breakfast of bread and butter and a superb, locally-made coconut marmalade, with beautiful, hot, black, percolated Brazilian coffee. Being able to come up with coffee like that on the upper reaches of the Amazon not only endeared us to the cook, but convinced us that Brazilian coffee amply deserves its great reputation.

We found that there was a simple, if rather lazy, routine developing for us on board the *Dominique*. After breakfast we would shower and clean up, then either swing in a hammock and read, sit in the little recreation area, aft on the upper deck, and play solitaire, or just sit on the foredeck and watch the river and the shore go by. This last was one of the most soothing and relaxing occupations I have ever experienced.

In the afternoon we stopped at the township of San Antonio de Ica, at the confluence of the Amazon and the Ica rivers. It was only a small settlement, built for safety from floods, high on the embankment above the river, but its streets and gutters were concreted and clean and the gardens of its simple houses were a profusion of tropical greenery; hibiscus, flamboyants and frangipani. The four of us had gone with Syd for a walk through the town to escape the stifling humidity on board the ship. While we were travelling along, there was always a cooling breeze, but once we stopped, the temperature on board quickly became uncomfortably hot.

At a little wooden general store, we bought a large bottle of cold 'Bare', a sort of sweet local ginger ale. It cost ten cruzeiros or about sixty cents. While we were standing there drinking it from five small glasses provided by the storekeeper, a young man came into the shop and ordered a different sort of drink. The proprietor poured a stiff shot of a clear liquid into a small glass. The man tossed one cruzeiro (six cents) onto the counter, then downed the drink in one swallow. I looked at the bottle. It was cane spirit ... twenty-one percent alcohol. At that rate, the locals could get blind drunk and I imagine many of them did, for half the price of a bottle of ginger ale.

For the rest of the afternoon, we cruised downriver, turning north, towards the end of the day, to travel up a small tributary to a town called Amatura. There, while they were loading crates on board, several of the crew dived overboard, into the dark river waters, for a swim.

This was one of the 'black-water' rivers. Strangely, nearly all of the rivers which flow into the Amazon from the north ... Colombia and Venezuela, are black; all of those from the west ... the Andean countries, Peru and Ecuador, are muddy and brown, while those that flow from the south ... from Brazil itself, are blue. These black-water tributaries which we were seeing, are made black by the darkening stain of rotting rainforest vegetation in their headwater regions. But when you look at the water closely, it is a clear black, rather than opaque. A glass of it, when you hold it up, seems clearer than weak tea, yet to us, simple travellers, it appeared dark, mysterious and dangerous.

But, it had been a boiling hot day, so, overcoming our misgivings, Zara and Sean and I put on swimming costumes and dived in, to find the water cool and refreshing. Trish, however, would not be persuaded. We frolicked about in the water for a while, but we didn't stay long. Refreshing as it was, there was a strange taste to it and we did not feel comfortable.

The *Dominique* pulled back from the shore shortly after our swim and sailed back down the tributary towards the Amazon just as the sun was setting. It was wonderful. Dusk on the river seemed always to be a magic time. In addition to the numerous photographs I took of the beautiful succession of sunsets on the trip, I have a collection of mental images which I hope will remain with me forever. Nowhere have I ever seen such grand and dramatic sights as the sunsets on that river.

That evening, although we had been perfectly happy with the meals the cook was preparing, we told her we would be cooking our own food for one meal that night. It was not only for a bit of variety that we decided to do this, but to use up some of our supplies, which, it was now clear, were far more than we needed. I made frankfurters and corned beef in tomato paste, with green beans and noodles. For dessert we had fresh papaya, washed down with a cup of tea. Syd joined us and we cooked and ate on the table in the aft cabin compartment on the upper deck. It was a great success. With a cooker like that, I felt, you could rule the world.

After cleaning up, Zara and Sean went to bed and, having finished *Huckleberry Finn,* we started into *Lassie Come Home,* reading the first two chapters. Being read to had become a nightly ritual which they really looked forward to. There was no television, but nobody cared in the slightest. Zara and Sean were also reading other books on their own ... Zara would bury herself for ages in *Swallows and Amazons,* while Sean was reading a boys' thriller called *There's No Escape.*

We woke the next morning to find ourselves alongside a small village called Porto Montezuma. We had travelled almost continuously during the night and stopped, according to the captain, at about 3.00 a.m. Now, after loading crates, we shuttled to three or four little landings within a couple of kilometres or so of each other, doing more of the same. At one of them, a big, green iguana sprinted across the mudbank, frightened by the approach of our boat.

The villages we were visiting now were no longer those of Amazon Indians. The people were nearly all purely Brazilian ... that is, Portuguese-speaking. To see more tribes from this part of the Amazon, one would have to leave the main stream and follow the tributaries away from it. Not very far though, depending on which river one followed.

But it was obvious to us now that we were well and truly on the main highway, the great thoroughfare of Brazil's northern territories, and, even at this distance, so far from the sophisticated and civilised centres of Brasilia, Rio de Janeiro and Sao Paulo, we began to see and feel evidence of Brazil's great size and economic power. What was difficult to visualise or accept was that we were separated from these major cities by thousands of kilometres of virtually untouched land; trackless, virgin rainforest and the open plains of the Mato Grosso, one of the emptiest pieces of land on the globe.

Even though Brazil's population is over 120 million, the whole of the Amazon basin has a population density of less than one person per square kilometre and most of these people are congregated along the navigable rivers, so the remainder of this vast region is all but uninhabited.

There is considerable disagreement over the future of the Amazon basin; whether or not it could be an almost limitless foodbasket for the world's hungry millions. Generally the feeling is that in this vast, humid tropical rainforest, just about any seed you throw down will grow. To a certain extent, that's true, but agronomists have shown recently that rainforest soils are rarely very rich in a nutritional sense. The huge trees of the jungle keep alive from the combination of sunlight, large amounts of rain and the self-made humus of fallen leaves and rotting vegetation on the jungle floor. The same applies to the rest of the flora, an incredible hotbed of thousands of exuberant species of plant life. They survive and prosper in the damp compost heap of the natural jungle, but clear that all away to plant food crops and, so the tropical agriculturalists say, the soil will be exhausted within two years, unless subjected to large-scale and therefore expensive fertilisation.

There are many who are convinced of the Amazon's great future potential. One in particular is the seventy-five year old American billionaire Daniel Ludwig, who has started doing some pretty amazing things in the Amazon basin. He began in the late sixties by buying 200,000 hectares of jungle on the Jari River, a tributary of the Amazon, about four hundred kilometres from the mouth. Putting 2500 men to work, they cleared 100,000 hectares of rainforest and planted eighty-one million fast-growing trees for pulp paper processing. Then, at a cost of two hundred and fifty million dollars, he had one of the most modern and highly-automated paper-making factories in the world constructed in Japan, as a complete entity, on a huge, floating barge. This gigantic facility was then towed 24,000 kilometres across the China Sea, the Indian and Atlantic Oceans and up the Amazon and Jari rivers to his jungle site, where it is now going into operation, churning out up to seven hundred and fifty tonnes of pulp paper a day.

Ludwig's project will probably be a success, but before it ever turned over a penny, he had put some five hundred million dollars into it. With a personal fortune of about three billion dollars, I suppose he could afford it, but there are very few *governments,* let alone individuals, who could plan to utilise the Amazon region on that scale.

Another and probably far more important aspect of the Amazon basin is that it has long been recognised as a vital 'lung' for the whole world. Its huge contribution of fresh oxygen, from countless trillions of air-breathing trees, into our atmosphere, has been estimated as over fifty percent. Half of all the world's oxygen supply coming from this one area. Environmentalists, warning of the dangers of destruction of the rainforest, go so far as to claim that without the Amazon basin, life on earth would not survive.

Travelling down the river, as we had been for so many days, it was difficult to imagine anything that man could do being able to have a significant impact on this immense, untouched land. And yet, we all know that in other parts of the world, mankind has managed to wreck his own environment on a terrifying scale, so, presumably, it's possible on the Amazon also.

In the late afternoon there was a move by everybody on board except the man at the wheel, to find a spot near the bow from which to view the sunset. Captain Nieto, his family and crew must have witnessed this spectacle many, many times so I found it a pleasant surprise that they hadn't become blasé or numbed by its extravagant beauty.

I took along a pair of Iain's jeans, the cuff of which needed sewing up because he, along with the rest of us, had lost so much weight, that they kept slipping down from his waist, so that the cuffs were rubbing on the floor and fraying.

We sat staring forward in absolute silence, a scene of Amazon domesticity. In homes all over the world families sit like this transfixed by television. What we viewed was considerably more fulfilling.

Above us, great orange and raw-gold flares screamed along the jungle roof, which was thrown by the contrasting shade, into a featureless blackness. The painfully vivid colours were doubled in the three-kilometre-wide flat constancy of water beneath us, so that it appeared as though we were sailing forward into a receding, all-encompassing inferno.

For at least twenty minutes the display continually changed until, at last, just at the point when I felt almost satiated with beauty, the light began to fade. No one had spoken throughout the entire quite mystical experience.

After dinner, which Iain cooked again, for the variety as much as to use up some of our supplies, we were sitting around the table in our aft living space when the *Dominique* began to rise and dip like a ship at sea.

After weeks of flat calm sailing it was an unnerving sensation and we quickly lifted the tarpaulin and looked out to see close behind us a very large oil tanker. She had obviously just passed us and we were riding in her wake.

This was the biggest ship we had seen so far on the river and it reminded us, with something of a jolt, that we were on an international waterway which had been declared open to ships of all nations by the Brazilian president in 1866.

When the children were on their bunks, Iain read some more of *Lassie*. Of course I'd read the story when I was a kid and then I had thought it sterling stuff. Now I found it so full of class-consciousness and snobbery that it made my gorge rise.

In the early morning the river turned on another of its spectaculars for us. We awoke to find ourselves moored beside a little settlement and the mist rising off the water surface like a person, once made timid by rebuttal, slowly revealing his innermost thoughts.

It was Zara, at eleven, quite unafraid of appearing sentimental, or of purple prose, who sucked in her breath as she looked over the side and said, 'Oh Mum! It's like the very first day.' She stared into the moving wreaths of water vapour. 'This is exactly the picture I get in my mind when I hear that music, you know, it goes ...' and she hummed the first bars of the music which accompanied the opening shots of the movie '2001 a Space Odyssey'. 'Thus Spake Zara Thustra'.

As we moved off from the settlement, a flock of kingfishers, hundreds of them, an iridescent blue cloud, flew out of the jungle toward us and then on seeing us, stopped, hovering in midair for a second before wheeling round to fly back.

And that wasn't all. As the mists finally evaporated we began to see large floating islands of bright green weed, probably the size of a football field, crowded with elegant white herons, who disdainfully ignored our presence as they floated on downriver.

Then without the usual warning of stillness we were hit by a sudden squall, so fierce that it whipped up little waves topped with white foam. In the wheel house the crew lowered the tarpaulins and closed all the windows, bar one through which the mate, standing well to one side but with his arm outstretched to hold the wheel, navigated by taking short glimpses of the river which was now all but invisible through the barrage of driving rain.

Like all the squalls we experienced on the Amazon this one was sharp but short and in less than half an hour the sun was out and climbing higher, becoming so oppressively hot that between breakfast and lunch I had taken three showers in an attempt to cool off.

In that time Iain had been active too, managing to win two hundred and fifty dollars! He sat alone, hunched over the table on the stern deck, needing only a green eye-shade to complete the picture of a nineteenth century Mississippi riverboat gambler, playing himself at solitaire. He paid the bank an imaginary fifty-two dollars for the pack and then won himself an imaginary five dollars for each card he got out. Beside him he kept his little pocket calculator so that he couldn't cheat or be cheated!

The off-duty crew and the other passengers were intrigued by this display of schizophrenia and gathered round the table to watch. This encouraged Iain to get out the children's pack of trick cards which they had bought in Disneyland and with which he had been practising in flat moments! I was so impressed by his growing skill that I didn't want to know how he did the tricks because it would spoil the fun.

'If we run out of money,' Sean suggested, 'you could do like those two men who held Huck and Jim prisoner on their raft and put on shows at the places we stop at.'

The two soldier passengers, not to be outdone, then put on their own display which consisted of snapping five-centimetres-thick pieces of wood in half, executing neat karate chops with their bare hands.

The crew kept urging them on, so, fearing they would do themselves a damage just in order to keep up their macho image in front of me, the only woman around at the time, I retired to our cabin.

Here Sean and Marcos were now engaged in a bilingual war. Marcos had produced a GI Joe, in rather better shape than Sean's 'man', together with a large tin full of Lego construction pieces.

Having built fortresses and caves from the Lego they were now intent on demolishing them to the accompaniment of Portuguese and English war-type expletives which needed no translation to be understood by both sides. The most interesting point for me was that the Germans and the Japanese remained the traditional enemy.

Sean imagines that by adding, 'hausen' to any English word, it translates into German so his dialogue went something like this: 'Achtung! Thishausen prisonhausen destroyedhausen! Eeeeeek! Bang!' and he'd crash his 'man' down on a multi-coloured hideout, sending Lego pieces everywhere. Marcos would then follow up with his own garbled Portuguese-German, ending in a similarly spectacular explosion.

Zara, flushed and breathless with excitement, put her head in to announce that she had found 'the most gigantic beetle'. And so she had. A rhinoceros beetle measuring over seven centimetres without counting the monstrous great horn sticking out the front of his head. He had probably flown aboard at the last stop for he looked pretty exhausted as he posed for photographs.

At midday we stopped at Tefe, an unattractive little port town where we all went ashore to stretch our legs and get a change of scene. But after a slow look around, during which we bought some fruit and eggs, the debilitating heat drove us back aboard to swing back and forth in our hammocks in an unsuccessful attempt to create a little breeze.

The Captain and his wife and son went ashore and we took this to mean that we might be here for a while, so I had yet another shower and finished *Roots* (not in the shower!). I found it a powerful story told with great skill and made twice as enjoyable for me by Alex Haley's postscript explanation of how and why he came to write his personal history book.

I also finished the vest I was knitting and sewed up Zara's multi-coloured one, which looked super though, in this heat it was impossible to imagine it ever being cold enough to wear it.

By dinner-time there was still no sign of the Captain and I felt so exhausted by the heat, that shortly after dinner I retired to my bunk where I was reduced to reading Syd's copy of 'Readers' Digest'; that soporific magazine which, along with 'National Geographic', gives the impression that all is right with the world and that every third world country has a rising middle class!

I dropped off to be woken about midnight, finding the *Dominique* still anchored and hearing a screaming match going on below. The Captain and his lady wife were hurling abuse and loose objects at one another. Having been reduced to similar comic behaviour in my time I felt a great sympathy for them.

I thought that perhaps all of us were beginning to show symptoms of what Canadians, in their minus thirty-seven degrees Celsius snow-swirled winter isolation call, 'cabin fever'. The only cure is spring, or getting ashore.

We awoke to find that we were still in Tefe ... alongside the mudbank we had berthed at the day before. After breakfast, for which we fried the eggs we had bought, we asked one of the helmsmen what time we would be leaving. Ten o'clock, we were told, but from past experience, we decided to believe it when we saw it. Neither the Captain, nor his family were about and after the fracas of the previous night, we were wondering what was likely to happen between them.

There was nothing for us to do in the town, so we stayed aboard, continuing to pass the time, reading, playing cards and showering every hour or so as the heat became more and more intense.

'Where the hell is the Captain?' Syd exclaimed on a couple of occasions when his impatience got the better of him. We were all beginning to feel frustrated, sitting in the one spot. Not that we really had any desperate deadlines or meetings to make, but just sitting around in Tefe for ages was not what we had planned.

'We've been here twenty-four hours already,' Syd said in annoyance. It was 1.00 p.m. and we were standing in the wheelhouse, looking ashore and up the street that ran towards the town from our berth.

'Come on Captain!' Syd said suddenly, grabbing the rope, hanging from the ceiling, which was connected to the ship's foghorn, giving it three sharp tugs. The horn blasted out loudly over the whole waterfront. I jumped and so did two crew members who, rudely awakened from a quiet nap in hammocks on the deck below, came charging up the steps. They began to berate us in rapid Portuguese for blowing the horn, so I thought the best defence was for us to be a bit aggressive also.

'Onde estar o Capitaon?' Where is the Captain? I said firmly in very rudimentary Portuguese. 'Porque no partir?' ... Why aren't we leaving?

They were put on the defensive and one of them explained what we already knew ... that the Captain was not aboard, but from a couple of words picked out of their commentary ... 'problema' and 'banco', we gathered that the Captain had some difficulties to sort out.

'I hope they don't come and seize the boat and leave us stranded here,' Syd said with a laugh. But it wasn't all that funny. After some of the things that happened to delay our boat in Pucallpa, I'd believe almost anything was possible.

As it happened, Syd's blasts on the foghorn did at least excite some action from the crew who had been shaken out of their torpor. They got the *Dominique* under way and, after backing her out into the stream, during which time we wondered what was happening, they sailed her across into the middle of a small bay, about two or three hundred metres from shore, where there was a big barge moored as a floating petrol station to supply fuel oil and other requirements to river boats calling at Tefe.

We thought that this seemed a positive move and that, after refuelling, we would soon be on our way. But no, we sat there all afternoon, on occasions fuming with frustration, but the rest of the time simply resigning ourselves to the situation.

During the afternoon, we were told that we would be leaving at about 6.00 p.m. and when, at 5.00 p.m., we sailed back to our original berth, we thought the information might be correct. When the Captain arrived back on board at just after 6.00, we felt sure we were on our way. But he had returned without his wife and son and was more than a little drunk. Nevertheless, we were elated when the engines started up and we began to move again.

However, our excitement lasted only a few minutes. The *Dominique* headed out to the floating petrol station again and there, after it had tied up alongside, the Captain went aboard the barge and sat down in a cane chair to join the man who ran the station and his wife in a heavy drinking session. All we could do, for the next hour or so, was just sit on the deck of the *Dominique* and watch, while the Captain got thoroughly plastered.

But nothing lasts forever and eventually, at about 8.00 p.m., Captain Nieto staggered back on board and with a wave of his hands gave orders for us to get under way. So, after some thirty hours in Tefe, the *Dominique*, giving another three blasts on its horn, finally moved out to rejoin the Amazon, flowing fast, wide and deep past the town and to leave the lights of the settlement to grow smaller and dimmer behind us, eventually to be swallowed up by the night.

Later, after we had eaten, we showered again and went to bed reasonably early. I read a couple more chapters of *Lassie* to the children and then dropped off while I was reading *Travels with my Aunt.* I had a bad cold coming on. My chest felt tight and I had aches and pains in my body. I was hoping that it would only be a cold . . . and not a bout of flu just as we were coming up to Manaus.

We all awoke in the middle of the night to the sounds of an incredible rainstorm. If it seems, during this narrative, that we spend a disproportionate amount of time talking about rain, it is because there is so much of it on the Amazon and it is never soft and gentle. It is always dramatic. Now, with the river wide and open, storms could be not only dramatic, but also dangerous. Many a ship has been lost in an Amazon storm, where big waves can be whipped up by fierce winds in a matter of minutes.

On this occasion, the *Dominique* was suddenly in the midst of a violent thunder storm. Brilliant sheets of lightning were intermittently whitening the jungle shores and the river with each deafening crack and explosion of thunder. The *Dominique*, driven by the blinding fury of the rain, ran to shelter by the shore until the storm had passed.

At breakfast, disaster struck. I took a hearty bite at some spaghetti sprinkled with largish lumps of a hard cereal called farinha, and broke a tooth. Not just a chip came away but the whole back half of a molar on the upper left side which had been holding a sizable filling. All I was left with now was the remnants of a hollow, pointed fang.

I was distressed. Well, actually that is an understatement! I ran upstairs into our cabin and when Iain followed to try to pacify me, I shouted at him and he wisely left me to sob. I'm a bit hung up about teeth, having had mine butchered by national health dentists from an early, impressionable age.

Before we'd left home I'd had a thorough checkover and quite a bit of dental work done. So I thought it unfair that this should happen now, way out from 'anywhere'. I have a morbid fear of being stuck somewhere inaccessible with raging toothache. And one can hardly call the Amazon River, just above Coari, accessible! Sure, Manaus would have dentists and I could well imagine what they would be like! No thanks. But, as we were anticipating a fairly arduous overland trip across the Mato Grosso, would I be tempting fate to try to hold on till Brasilia?

Of course, initially, it felt like an enormous hole, but once I had calmed down enough to apologise to Iain and let him examine the gap, I realised that at least the nerves were not exposed. I decided to wait and see how it was by the time we reached Manaus before committing myself to some local dental practitioner.

Sean, under threat of loss of pocketmoney and sundry other dire promises, submitted to having his hair cut, which is for him as great a trauma as nail cutting but fortunately needs to be done less frequently. During our journeys Iain had, from necessity, become so expert with the scissors that even when we are in 'civilisation' he continues to be the family barber. He even does his own.

We made one more stop, our last of the trip, at Coari, again, not a town to write home about. We went ashore and found a large open-air fruit and vegetable market where we bought papaya, pineapple and bananas which were later made into a delicious fruit salad.

Then it was foot-to-the-boards for Manaus. We could sense that the Captain and his crew were as anxious to get there as we were. We spent the afternoon restuffing our packs and collecting a sizable pile of now useless and cumbersome items; a large billy, a plastic washing up bowl, cloths, bottles of disinfectant and some canned foods, all of which we gave to the cook.

This was our last night on the river. Syd was going on the further sixteen hundred kilometres to the mouth, but he had decided that he'd had enough of a good thing and that he'd fly the rest of the distance. We were leaving the river at Manaus to head across the comparatively little-travelled Brazilian outback, the Mato Grosso.

We talked over our journeys on the MVs *Campeon, Adolfo* and *Dominique* with a touch of sadness now that it was almost all over. Even if we did come back one day, perhaps nothing much would be changed, but we wouldn't be the same. And one never again can capture the freshness of the first image.

It had all been great fun. The primitive conditions for the eleven hundred kilometres on the *Campeon,* the fight and the leaking barge; the comparative luxury of the four hundred and eighty kilometres on the *Adolfo;* the infectious enthusiasm of the students, the Indian villages, jungle walk and caiman hunt; and the beauty of the scenes during the sixteen hundred kilometre stretch on the

Dominique, the unforgettable sunrises and sunsets.

We had travelled down 3,200 kilometres of the longest river in the world. The river which contains one-fifth of the entire world's supply of fresh water and which daily pours out into the Atlantic Ocean at Belem enough fresh water to supply the needs of Sydney for a quarter of a century!

I often think how privileged I am. To be alive is a privilege, to be healthy is another, to be happy is asking too much and to travel as we have done is almost an impudence.

In the morning, the fish were biting in such numbers that a piece of bread dropped over the edge brought so many to the surface that they turned it into a thrashing foam.

The river was sixteen kilometres wide, the opposite bank a mere pencil line on the horizon and we were in the busy, exciting port of Manaus, saying goodbye to the *Dominique* and sadly at the end of a chapter in our journey.

BRAZIL

20
Pioneer territory

Wandering through the great auditorium and marbled halls of the Teatro Amazonas, the Opera House of Manaus, the outstanding sensation one experiences is disbelief. How can this incredibly grand and elegant structure be sitting here, in the jungle, sixteen hundred kilometres up the Amazon River? And yet, here it is; its rococo reception halls, overhung with crystal chandeliers and floored with mahogany parquet brought from Portugal, its balconies in the main auditorium enclosed by elaborately wrought and gilded balustrades, its ceiling decorated in Renaissance style with nymphs and goddesses. All in remarkably good repair and condition for a building which was opened in this steamy, tropical climate, in 1896 and whose hey-day has long since passed.

The story of the Manaus Opera House is really the story of Manaus itself. It is the most magnificent remaining symbol of the city's past glory ... a glory which flourished for roughly thirty years from about 1885 to 1915, during the great 'rubber boom'.

Up until the late nineteenth century, the trees from which latex or rubber was extracted, grew only in South America and most of them were in the Amazon basin. The combination of Charles Goodyear's invention of the vulcanisation process in 1848 and Dunlop's development of the rubber tyre in 1888, created an enormous demand for rubber, on which Brazil had a virtual monopoly. Rubber prices rose astonishingly and Manaus became, within almost no time, one of the richest cities in the world. Its per capita income, it has been calculated, was higher than that of any other city in all of the Americas and the general standard of living of its inhabitants could be matched only in the richest cities of Europe.

Attracted by the city's splendour, doctors, lawyers, engineers, writers, artists and agriculturalists flocked to Manaus from all over the world and by the turn of the century a simple riverside settlement had become transformed into a modern city of imposing buildings, with electricity, telephones, water and sewage systems, efficient dockyards and other facilities equal to those in the most sophisticated cities in the world.

When the Opera House was opened, it attracted the most famous performers of Europe and North America. The great Enrico Caruso performed there, as did Sarah Bernhardt and the immortal Pavlova.

But the fatal flaw in this little oasis of civilisation in the middle of the jungle, was that its prosperity was based on a product which was inefficiently harvested from rubber trees which grew randomly over great areas of the Amazon rainforest.

In 1876, an Englishman, Henry Alexander Wickham, who was living on the Amazon, quietly gathered 70,000 of the best rubber tree seeds and 'smuggled' them (so the Brazilians say, although there was no law against it at the time) out of the country to England. Nurturing them there, in the huge greenhouse in London's Kew Gardens, he soon transported them to Malaya, where they were planted symmetrically in groves.

When the Malayan rubber began to come onto the market, followed by new plantations in Ceylon, Java and Sumatra, prices fell dramatically and the Amazon's bubble burst. The Brazilian rubber barons could not compete with the more efficiently harvested rubber from the East. Manaus all but died. The Opera House closed . . . everything closed. And the rich and fashionable fled in droves.

But after a long period in the doldrums, Manaus began to thrive again in the late sixties when the Brazilian government declared it a free trade area . . . a duty-free zone which brought business and investment flowing back into the city on a big scale. Manaus has grown from a city of around 300,000 people at the beginning of the seventies to over a million at the start of the eighties.

On our first morning in Manaus we set off, accompanied by Syd, to have a look at the city. On leaving the *Dominique*, we had found, after a short search, a simple little hotel, the Fontaleza, about a block from the waterfront, where we took a room with four beds for $16. Syd also moved in to the same hotel, but his room was cramped and dark and he said he would move out as soon as he could.

The temperature was over thirty degrees and extremely humid, and as we walked about the city, we were sweating profusely, so we took things slowly and, on several occasions, stopped to drink cold bottles of Pepsi-Cola. We wanted to do some sight-seeing . . . in particular, we wanted to visit the Grand Opera House, of which we had read so much, but there were also several other things that had to be arranged.

Firstly, there was Trish's tooth. Would we try to get anything done to it here in Manaus . . . or leave it till we reached Brasilia, or Rio? They seemed a long way away from here, so I suggested we look about for a dentist. But Trish insisted that, since the tooth had broken, its jangled nerves had calmed down and was causing no pain, so she would leave it . . . at least until we reached Brasilia.

Next there was our onward transportation. We wanted to head southwards across the new road which linked the Trans-Amazonian highway to the West Brazilian town of Port Velho, some thousand kilometres south-west of Manaus, on the edge of the Mato Grosso. The road, so we'd heard, had been pushed through a huge section of virgin jungle, but the only advance information we had about it was from the *South American Handbook* which said that the road had been 'virtually completed' and that there were 'no buses on the route yet, but trucks are running.'

Fortunately things are happening fast not only in this part, but all of Brazil. We soon discovered that a bus line had already started operating on the run to Porto Velho; a fairly spartan service in a Mercedes Minibus, but when we checked the schedules and learnt that there was a bus leaving at 9.30 the next morning, we decided to take it and booked four tickets at US$12 each with no half-price fares for children.

With that settled, we then went with Syd to try to sort out some money problems. He wanted to get more money sent to him from California and had apparently cabled from Iquitos to arrange for a draft to be sent to Manaus. But we had been told that any US currency coming into Brazil must all be cashed at the official rate into cruzeiros, and then cannot be changed back or taken out again in dollars.

Also, if Syd collected it in Brazil, he would lose considerably by changing it all at the bank instead of through money changers, whose rate of exchange was invariably higher. He decided to try to alter the original arrangement with the people sending the money from California and have it sent instead to Monte Video, in Uruguay where there would be no problem getting it in dollars instead of having to change it to the local currency. Eventually, after several international phone calls, he managed to get it all organised, and we set off to see the Teatro Amazonas.

We stood first, to admire the building, in the great open plaza in front of it. The pavement is intricately decorated in black and white wave patterns made from millions of small mosaic tiles, while the building itself looms ahead, an enormous domed structure with Grecian columns at its entrance.

Inside, we found a ballet company rehearsing its routines. After years of closure, the Opera House is enjoying a new lease of life, and is open regularly for all sorts of live theatre performances, although Grand Opera is rarely, if ever, performed there now.

We wandered through the place without a guide, but listened in to another one, with a group of American tourists telling them some of the stories of the rubber boom and the opera house itself. One story he told, was about a group of French actors who were brought all the way from Paris, in the early 1900s, to perform a play at the Teatro Amazonas. It took weeks for them to get here by ship, but on their arrival they were put up in the best hotel and fêted by local society. Then they had their rehearsals and gave *one* performance of their play before an audience of *four* of the wealthiest rubber barons and their families. The rest of the huge auditorium was empty! The four millionaires had not only paid the actors' fees and for their trip, accommodation and expenses, but they had also bought up every other seat in the house!

The group of Americans who stood listening to the guide tell this tale seemed impressed. They had just flown in by jet, direct from the US to Manaus, which incidentally is equipped to handle supersonic aircraft, and were staying at the luxurious Hotel Tropical outside of town.

We couldn't help comparing the way they had reached Manaus with the way we had. The two routes couldn't have been more different; one from Miami by plane in six hours ... the other from Lima by road and riverboat in four weeks. We felt decidedly superior!

In the afternoon we were all so drained and sapped of energy by the heat, that we collapsed on our beds in the hotel with the fans blowing across us, intending to have a short siesta. Instead, we didn't wake until about 5.00 p.m. Out in the town, again with Syd, we found, miracle of miracles, a bookshop which sold some titles in English. We had all but exhausted the books we'd been carrying with us on the boats, so we bought a few more paperbacks.

On our way back to the hotel, we also discovered a small café which made very good pizzas which we washed down with Brahma Chopp, a fine Brazilian beer, before going back to bed again.

We felt rather anxious saying goodbye to Syd. On the river he had appeared as a self-confident, bold adventurer but in the hubbub of Manaus he looked suddenly frail and old. Even though he had travelled so much and under such arduous conditions, it had always been with his wife, Molly, who by all accounts was quite a gal, and in their own vehicle; a totally different prospect from being alone and relying on the vagaries of public transport.

We soothed our consciences slightly by arranging to leave messages at the Australian or British embassies in Brasilia which we hoped to reach inside a week and where Syd was flying on to from Belem.

At 9.00 a.m. it was already crushingly hot and humid. On the way to the small bus depot we saw baseball style caps advertising the Copa Mundial (World Cup Soccer) and bought one in Brazilian colours and one in Argentinian colours for the children.

Funnily enough, it was buying those caps advertising matches which were about to get under way sixty-four hundred kilometres by road south which made us realise that although we could congratulate ourselves on how far we had already travelled, we had yet to cross a vast land mass to reach the Atlantic coast and then still travel down through Uruguay and Argentina to reach our goal at the tip.

The first thing we were to discover when we boarded the compact bus which had been battered into early senility by hard travel and which was already packed to the gunnels with people and property, was that the journey would not take the anticipated fifteen, but rather twenty-two hours. This would mean travelling through the full day and night and arriving in Porto Velho around 7.00 a.m. the following day.

The next thing we found was that we had bought the worst seats in the bus, the four non-reclining ones right at the rear. All we could do was make some mental readjustments.

We left promptly at 9.30, a good sign, but then took all of three hours to clear town, which entailed everyone being carefully checked through a police post, then taking the ferry across the sixteen-kilometre-wide confluence of the rivers Amazon and Negro. Coming from the north, the waters of the Rio Negro were black and menacing and where they met the brown, muddy and somehow more friendly waters of the Amazon, such was the tremendous force of each river, their difference in temperature and consistency, that for some kilometres they ran completely separately, side by side, black and tan, a watery apartheid.

As the ferry bumped to a halt on the far side and we took our last look at the Amazon, a porpoise broke the surface, twisted and dove back, for all the world as if it were waving goodbye. On leaving the ferry, our bus then stopped immediately at a rather rough-looking eatery and all the passengers disembarked to consume a hearty meal, though how they could in this heat was quite beyond me.

We just drank Coke. When we are stationary, I hardly ever touch the stuff, finding the taste too strong and the effect too heavy. But there have been times when we are moving that I have dreamt of the flavour and longed to guzzle a large bottle!

When we started off again, the intense midday heat was magnified by the reflection from flood water which stood in large areas on both sides of the track.

A couple more times we crossed little arms of water on smaller ferries and on each occasion we'd get out in order to catch the breath of a breeze while clinging to the minuscule line of shade thrown by the bus.

Beside one of these ferries we spotted a makeshift stall selling what at first we thought were. . . . well, actually we had no idea what they were. We examined the six and a half centimetre-long, white and grey, 'U' shaped pieces of rough-surfaced, hard material which all had a definite curve to them as well as bright red tips.

'Paiche,' the woman stall holder said, making fish-type swimming motions with her hand.

'My God!' Iain said, 'they're fish scales.'

Gigantic fish scales and therefore obviously from a gigantic fish.

'I could make a very dramatic necklace for you with those,' he said. So we bought twelve of the freaks but I've noticed that after showing them to other people, it seems only he and I really appreciate their monstrous beauty!

With no more ferries, we started to cover some of the 1000 kilometres to Porto Velho at a pace, bumping over the dusty road which, whenever the sudden and frequent rain bursts hit us, became a red mudbath through which we would find ourselves slithering dangerously.

The showers were too slight to be cooling and when the sun was out again, it beat vengefully down and sucked what little energy we had left from us. I pulled the tattered dust-stiffened curtain over the open window in order to filter the direct rays, but that only stopped what slight breeze our forward movement created. Zara and Sean sat motionless between us, stupefied by the heat.

Occasionally we passed small clearings, created by the timeless, primitive 'slash and burn' method of farming. Some were planted with bananas and pineapples. Often the patches had been left go and the jungle had quickly reclaimed them. But for much of the time we travelled along a monotonous narrow ribbon between high walls of impenetrable thick green jungle.

Anyone thinking of taking up land out here, even at the give-away prices offered as inducement by the government in an attempt to open up the red heartland, needs more endurance, spirit, stamina, courage and imagination than most people can muster in a lifetime.

The bus droned on and I had plenty of time to examine our fellow passengers. All of them had that tough look of pioneers and all of them were mestizos. No blacks, Indians or Portuguese, but the mixture of all. The ones with nothing to lose and everything to gain. Some of them would be optimistic gold miners, working on their own, battling the odds against malaria, dysentery, loneliness, primitive living conditions and even attacks by hostile Indians, in the hope of finding 'instant' fortune. But most of them would be trying to make it in a more conventional way, by tending however much ground one person could manage on his own.

Around half of the thirty passengers were women and over one-third of them were visibly pregnant. One of them, who looked at least five months pregnant, stood, up at the front of the jolting bus, in the crowded aisle for seven hours. Her bare feet spread wide for better balance, she stared out at the changeless view of jungle like an anxious urban commuter not wishing to miss her stop. When, scores of kilometres from any other habitation, she signalled to the driver that she wanted to be dropped, the bus shuddered to a halt and she hoisted a full sack onto her back and clambered down. Through the swirl of dust, which our departure created, I looked back to see her begin to climb a steep muddy bank to a wooden, straw-roofed hut which perched on the top of a rise in a clearing hacked from the all-surrounding jungle.

The relief everyone felt when the sun disappeared behind the jungle horizon was obvious from the way they all began to talk to one another. It was as if, before the sun went, they had been held prisoners of silence by its stunning power.

We stopped once more, for dinner at a small roadside eating-place, but again we managed only half a sandwich each, washed down with quantities of Coke. While the others ate, we looked through a set of white fibreglass living units which resembled nothing so much as igloos. We asked the owner about them and were told that they were manufactured on the coast and trucked up here as accommodation for the road workers. They were also rentable as overnight accommodation for five dollars apiece. Good value for a clean, womb-like room with two beds and a shower recess. I think that probably the only way to make a living in these pioneer situations is to get in on the ground floor of the service business like this man had done.

Then on we went into the dark moonless night, trying to sleep upright, our heads jolting forward and every muscle cramped. At three in the morning we came to a halt and looking out I saw a large bridgeless river. After consulting with other passengers I found that this was the Madeira, just this side of Porto Velho, but that, as the ferries didn't begin running until 6.00 a.m., we'd be here until then. With the bus standing still I did manage a little sleep during those last three hours. I do distinctly remember though, waking once with the thought that it was almost four months since I had been inside a private house, a comfortable, friendly place with a lounge and easy chairs, a convenient kitchen and a fresh-smelling bathroom.

Our approach to Porto Velho was not inspiring. At first glance the muddy, unfinished roads and the dirty, dilapidated bus terminal in a field on the outskirts of town, made us feel that we were arriving at a poor imitation of Pucallpa. But when we eventually got closer to the centre of town, things improved considerably, with sealed roads, several parks, modern buildings and some interesting old colonial structures.

The business district of Porto Velho is on a hill that slopes down from a high bluff overlooking the river Madeira, which flows into the Amazon about a hundred and sixty kilometres below Manaus. Had we wanted to, we could have taken a riverboat up the Madeira from Manaus to Porto Velho, although it would naturally have taken a great deal longer than our twenty-two hour bus trip.

The town, which has a population approaching 100,000, is the capital of the huge Brazilian territory of Rondonia, named after Marshal Candido Mariano da

Silva Rondon, who explored much of Brazil's wild western territory in the early part of this century and built the telegraph lines which linked the remote area with the rest of Brazil. The Indians called the telegraph line 'Lingua Mariano' or Mariano's tongue.

At the moment Porto Velho is a rapidly developing communications centre for the vast, untouched hinterlands of jungle that Brazil wants to open up. But not telegraphic communications this time ... now it's the government's vast road-building programmes that are changing the face of the land. In the past ten years, almost five million pioneer Brazilians, most of them coming from the over-populated and job-scarce areas on the east coast, have moved into tropical outback areas of Western Brazil. Spreading along and out from the new highways, taking advantage of generous land grants and taxation concessions, they are the forerunners of what the Brazilian Government hopes will be a great migration to the rich lands of the west.

As far as we were concerned though, on our arrival in Porto Velho, all we wanted to do was collapse and sleep. We were absolutely shattered after our twenty-two solid hours in the bus, although it appeared that what lay ahead of us was not going to be any better. At the terminal we had checked on buses to cover the next sector to Cuiaba, and it wasn't a very pleasant prospect. Cuiaba was the next major town of any size and it was just on 1600 kilometres away, across the Mato Grosso, on a dirt road. There were only four other small towns showing on the map between Porto Velho and Cuiaba ... and three of those towns hadn't even existed five years previously. It was truly pioneer territory, once you left the river systems and travelled cross-country.

The bus we were to catch was expensive ... 520 cruzeiros (US$29) each and again no half-fares, but there wasn't any alternative. I remember thinking that, after all, 1600 kilometres was a long way, and perhaps it wasn't really too bad a price. That was before we made the trip. The bus was to go direct from Porto Velho to Cuiaba stopping only for meals and fuel. Forty-eight hours! Theoretically we could have left the bus to break the journey at one of the new settlements along the road, but there was really no point, so we decided on the through-trip. It was not something any of us were looking forward to though, particularly as we would have to leave Porto Velho that same evening, at 6.30 p.m.

It was then just after 7.00 a.m. so, as quickly as possible, we sought out a hotel, at which to 'crash' for at least part of the day, settling on the *Vittoria,* a low, rambling, concrete hotel with not much to recommend it, except for the fact that it was only about three hundred metres from the centre of town. After a slight hassle with the manager over the fact that we only wanted one double room (for $11) even though there were four of us ... just for the day, we moved into a tiny room and tried to sort ourselves out.

We washed some clothes and strung them out on a line across the room then, to try to get some sleep, we stretched out, two to a bed, end-to-end, but it was so hot and steamy, that even with an electric fan going, we were continually perspiring just lying still. It wasn't long, however, before we had all dropped off to sleep, despite the conditions.

Waking, about three hours later, in a lather of perspiration, I got up and showered, then went out into the late morning heat with Sean to try to change some money, only to receive a rather rude shock. None of the banks in Porto

Velho were prepared to change either US dollar travellers' cheques, *or* US dollars in currency notes.

'They're making it difficult,' I remember saying to Sean, with a slight sense of despair, which increased as I tried unsuccessfully for almost an hour to find a money changer in the commercial centre of town who was prepared to change foreign money. I tried several shopkeepers and trading organisations which, I had been told normally exchanged foreign currencies, but not one was prepared to give me cruzeiros for my US dollars.

Do they know something I don't? I kept thinking. I knew that the value of the US dollar had been going down slightly, but this was ridiculous. It had been some time since we'd read a newspaper. I wondered if there'd been another Wall Street crash or something. But at last I found a jeweller who was prepared to change $100, at 17 cruzeiros to the dollar, instead of the going rate of 18.50, because he needed some US money to send to his sick mother in Miami. Poor dear.

Back at the hotel, we slept some more during the afternoon. Again, it was a sweaty and fitful sleep, but we knew that, over the next few days, we'd be needing every bit of it we could get.

The people who boarded the six-thirty bus were a tough looking, motley crew. When people live under more or less battlefront conditions, unless they are actually run as an army, they very quickly abandon much of the social behaviour which makes for civilised living.

So these passengers reminded me of nightclub patrons seen in the full glare of daylight. They were grubby, unkempt and shabbily dressed. Apart from one black woman, who had three children under five, they were all mestizos.

Our kids were delighted to find a couple of empty seats, so that they were able to stretch out across two seats and manage a little sleep before midnight when we stopped at Arequimas, the largest settlement on the run, where a whole crowd came aboard.

Among the new passengers was a fellow who was obviously drunk and who tried to eject Zara and Sean from the one seat which they had now moved to occupy jointly. When he changed from badgering them verbally to actually hauling them up by their arms, both Iain and I shouted a sharp and effective rebuke. Whereupon he moved his attention to the three black children who were curled up all together, fast asleep, in the seat behind. Shaking them awake he bundled them out and then sprawled in the seat himself, to fall fast asleep immediately while they clambered onto their mother who had done nothing to prevent his behaviour.

So we moved off again into the night, sleeping uncomfortably on each other's shoulders or collapsing into each other's laps as the bus continued to travel across Rondonia. The territory, as we have said, was named after Marshal Rondon, who also carried the dubious title of 'The Great Pacifier of the Brazilian Indians'. But unfortunately, or fortunately, depending on your point of view, the Brazilian Indians are anything but pacified.

The problem is that, as settlers expand into the jungle, whether prospecting for gold, planting bananas and rice, or growing timber, they naturally come into conflict with Indians, many of whom prefer to keep to their own hunter-gatherer life-style and resent the intrusion of the twentieth century.

One example: the savage Atroari-Waimiri tribes which massacred twelve roadworkers and an expedition between 1968 and 1973. Another: when the 140-strong Txukahamei tribe were selected for relocation, an intertribal fight over the decision resulted in the death of seven members.

It's a problem which has continued since Brazil was first settled by Europeans and which, until a hundred and fifty years ago, was handled simply by slaughtering anyone who stood in the way of change. In that way the world has lost a multitude of micro-cultures and is the poorer for it. Although it quite often doesn't seem that way, the value that man places on his fellows has somewhat increased since the days of wholesale massacres of natives in North America, Africa and Australia and it is no longer possible to ignore world opinion over questions of how a nation deals with its minorities.

The answers are only easy however if you haven't seen the problems close up for yourself and the inescapable, but none the less heartrending, truth is that there is no one solution as to how to cope with the inevitable conflict that occurs when simple, self-sufficient people meet a complex interdependent society.

FUNAI, Brazil's National Foundation for the Indian, insists that the Indians of the area 'must enter the mainstream of Brazilian national life'. The government has set aside parks or reserves for Indians who want to keep to their traditional way of life. The international press have carried stories that these reserves are little better than concentration camps in which tribespeople are herded together and die off from unchecked, simple Western diseases such as measles, influenza and that inevitable Western panacea, alcohol.

Casual visitors are not allowed to enter these parks, so all we could do was to judge from conversations we had. These gave us the overwhelming impression that Brazil is a dynamic society led by a pragmatic and hard-headed government, which at times is ruthless and has no tolerance for what it sees as soft-minded, woolly thinking.

It's within this framework that they have developed a policy which they think is the best answer for their small, primitive Indian communities and which at the same time is best for the overall development of Brazil's resources and her people.

Nothing is done on a small scale. The opening up of the outback, with its promise of tremendous future wealth, and hence power, have involved the relocation into the Amazonia area of at least a hundred thousand families.

These people come from urban areas with a population density of hundreds, sometimes thousands, a square kilometre, or so, into an area where they will share one square kilometre with an average of only one other person. But to help overcome the natural feeling of isolation, the government is constructing 'planned' villages and towns in an effort to create a sense of community.

The journey in the following day's heat took us through some of these settlements, all of them very simple, with a single main street of wooden-fronted shops with verandahs looking very much like the Wild West must have in the 1880s.

The country's coastal sophisticates refer, with a touch of contempt, to these pioneer people as 'faroestes' or 'farwesters'. We found many of them appeared tired and worn by their struggle with the environment and hardly responded to our attempts to strike up a conversation. This was an expected trait which I've seen before among isolated people. A solitary life presents little or no opportunity for speech and, unused, the facility falls into disrepair and people come close to forgetting how to communicate verbally.

By contrast with our travel on the previous day through the claustrophobic green tunnel of jungle, the view had now opened up slightly as the land had been cleared for a couple of hundred metres and more back from each side of the narrow dirt road. This exposed land wasn't cultivated, but lay like an ugly open red wound, baking in the intense heat.

Sean was unnaturally quiet and when asked, said that he had a raging headache and sore throat and that he hadn't bothered to tell us because he realised that there was nothing much could be done right now! We had antibiotics, but they were in the medicine box in Zara's pack which, along with the rest of the luggage, was stored in the reddened bowels of the vehicle.

The bus was becoming distressingly more and more like a moving trash can, with people coughing up their spit onto a floor already strewn with smelly food scraps, fruit peelings, discarded sweaty clothing and assorted other rubbish, over all of which hung a smell of infant's urine.

Every seat was taken and passengers who got on and off at stops along the way, to travel relatively short distances, like three or four hundred kilometres, had to stand in the aisle.

Naturally they would endeavour to slump down on a vacant arm rest and, selfishly, but perhaps understandably, all the passengers, us included, kept our arms along the rests to prevent this happening because when it did, it meant being leant against by a lump of hot sweating flesh.

The fact is that twenty-four hours non-stop travel in a hot, crowded, smelly bus is not guaranteed to bring out the best side of anyone's nature.

Particularly when you've got another twenty-four hours to go! We were really beginning to feel it by this stage and the prospect of another sleepless night was not in the least appealing. But, to make matters worse, during the day Sean's headache and sore throat had not improved and he had also developed a temperature. Looking inside his mouth we were horrified to see how inflamed his tonsils were. We gave him some aspirin which, after it had had time to take effect, made him slightly more comfortable, which was more than we could say for ourselves as we tried desperately to find positions in which to sleep. Zara and Sean lay across our laps for some time, but with the constant thumping and bumping over absolutely appalling roads, it was impossible to sleep properly.

To top everything off, just before midnight some idiot standing half-way down the aisle began talking loudly, although shouting would be a more accurate description of his 'conversation' with two other men, which seemed designed to make sure that whoever else had managed to doze off to sleep was now wide awake. It wasn't long before we realised that the man in question was the drunk from the night before. We had seen him during the afternoon tippling regularly from a bottle he carried with him.

There were several loud 'SSSHHHHHH's' from other passengers. But he went on talking even more loudly for ten minutes or so. We had also tried some 'Sshushing', but to no avail until suddenly Trish, who values her sleep highly, leapt out of her chair, clambered down the aisle over several people's baggage and tapped this character hard on the chest, saying firmly in English, 'For God's sake shut up! Everybody else is trying to get some sleep . . . now shut up!'

He looked at her in stunned amazement, obviously not understanding a word she had said, but fully comprehending her meaning. He shut up.

I couldn't help laughing to myself as Trish, who was now also smiling, manoeuvred herself back to her seat. I'd often heard that it was a British maxim when they were starting new colonies and building their Empire that, 'If they don't understand English, just shout.' Obviously it worked!

There was once again a brilliant moon shining down on the vast, empty landscape and for a while, having been well and truly woken by the little drama with the drunk, we sat and looked out of the windows. The land was flat and open as far as the eye could see and in the pale, ghostly light, looked at times as if we were passing through a barren desert instead of grasslands.

On several occasions in the early hours of the morning, we found that we were suddenly in the midst of heavy rainstorms. The road, when this happened, became almost instantly hazardous, as the powdery, red dust turned in minutes to mud. We would slip and slide alarmingly when we ran into these storms and although on a few occasions the driver would slow right down to negotiate a particularly boggy section, for the most part he just charged on in such a hair-raising manner that even if we had been able to find a position comfortable enough in which to sleep, we were too tense to attempt it anyway.

Not long after dawn we stopped at another roadside restaurant for a meal and a clean-up. It was a part-concrete, part-adobe building which sat, like a block-house, alone in the middle of the prairie. At a long communal tin wash-basin that was attached to one outside wall of the building, I managed a shave of sorts, in cold water. What toilets there were, were blocked or out of order, so the passengers from the bus were weaving off into the distance to use the meagre cover of a fence post, some sage brush or the long grass, behind which to relieve themselves.

I asked the driver if I could get our packs out from the baggage compartment. He was reluctant but when I said 'medicin', he unlocked the cover and helped me extract Zara's pack, where our medical kit was stowed. All our packs were completely blanketed in thick layers of fine, red dust, which I had to slap off before I could even start to get at the kit. I extracted a bottle of Tetracycline tablets, one of which immediately went into Sean's mouth to start him on the course of treatment.

For the rest of the day the country through which we were passing remained unchanged . . . the vast Mato Grosso. This was the land which had swallowed up the great British explorer, Colonel Percy Fawcett. His expedition to find the secret city of 'Z', the ancient and mythical capital of some race of Atlanteans he believed existed in the Mato Grosso, set out in 1925 from Cuiaba, heading northwards across the territory we were now approaching. Neither he nor any member of the expedition was ever seen again.

This section of the Mato Grosso has no major settlements which could be called towns. Instead there are numerous truck and bus stopping places which, presumably, if Brazilians continue their migration to these remote hinterland areas, will become towns themselves before very long.

One thing we noticed as we went along, getting steadily nearer to civilisation, was that the food and drink at these stops became not only more varied and interesting, but cheaper and of better quality. By the time we reached Cuiaba, however, we were beyond caring. We were all bone weary, worn out, grubby and like the rest of the passengers, showing signs of the strain. At 6.00 p.m. (having 'hit the tarmac' to some jubilation a little earlier), we arrived at Cuiaba.

Somebody, with not enough to do I guess, has worked out that Cuiaba is in the dead centre of the South American continent.

After forty-eight hours straight travelling in that manner any place would have appeared as a beckoning oasis on the far side of a mirage, so Cuiaba with its street lights and shops looked pretty damned good to us.

We bought tickets at the bus terminal for the next day's nine-thirty morning trip to Goiania, then found a nearby hotel where we slapped some of the heavy layer of red dust from our packs before opening them up to retrieve some clean clothes, all of which also had a fine coating of the same colour.

Then came the much anticipated, long shower at which point we were introduced to one of the more unusual aspects of travel in this part of the world. The water for the shower was heated at the point where it fell from the showerhead by passing directly over an electric element carrying 240 volts, which had been plugged in and switched on at the wall! As, when you shower, you can hardly avoid getting your feet wet or standing on wet ground, in this case bare cement, you become a perfect conductor, which turns taking a shower into an exciting game of Russian roulette. If that's your bag well, that's fine but, coward that I am, I found this method of heating water, which we were to find in almost universal use throughout Brazil and Argentina, even in reasonably good hotels, rather took the edge off an otherwise enjoyable dousing.

Once we were all spanking clean and refreshed, we even felt we could eat again. In a café which opened out onto the main street, we had a steak, though mine had to be cut into tiny pieces and eaten gingerly with my good front teeth only! The accompanying crisp salad, tomatoes and spicy rice was absolutely delicious after two almost totally foodless days.

The waiter was young and black and beautiful. He gyrated his way to us between tables to the reggae rhythms coming from the radio. Then he stood under the front awning looking out into the streets, which were livening up with the evening trade, swaying hypnotically and dreaming I bet of one day making it to Rio.

Rio. Even this far, 1900 kilometres away, we could sense its allure. The walls of the café were decorated with travel posters showing girls in those marvellous, brief bikinis, Sugar Loaf Mountain and Copacabana Beach.

The waiter swivelled back toward us carrying our dessert fruit but all the time he was planning what he'd wear at Carnival.

In the morning we had a light breakfast at the bus terminal which was the best we had seen so far in South America and we thought hopefully a good sign. Here we struck up a brief conversation with a Polish man of about fifty. He was a diesel mechanic and told us he'd been living in Brazil for almost thirty years. He had no family, but he lived now in Manaus and normally worked on repair and maintenance jobs up and down the Amazon. For the past few weeks though, he'd been on a contract job in Cuiaba and was waiting to take a bus back over the 2400 kilometres we'd just covered. We sympathised with him.

When our bus pulled in to the terminal, we were agog. It was a huge, modern Mercedes Benz job with a special body built in Brazil. It had big, clear windows, beautifully comfortable seats, a toilet in the rear of the bus, with a clean wash-basin and soap, a bed for the use of the driver or co-driver, when either of them was not at the wheel, and wonder of wonders, the drivers wore uniforms ... with white collars and ties! The drivers on the previous buses had been more like cowboys than bus drivers and this sudden change was a bit much for us. It was also a surprise to find only eight other people on the bus when we pulled out of the terminal. We gathered more as we stopped at various towns during the day, but it was clear that we weren't in for another ordeal like the Porto Velho to Cuiaba trip.

In fact, we were beautifully comfortable. The sky remained overcast, keeping the temperature outside down and with the air-conditioning working for a change, we were travelling in some considerable style. The road was wide and well surfaced for most of the way and over many stretches, was even a dual carriage-way.

Sean's tonsilitis began to show rapid improvement, although the tablets were unfortunately making him drowsy and a bit weepy, but at least his throat was looking better and his temperature had come down. But then Zara began to complain of earache and as the day progressed her nose became stuffy and it was obvious that she was developing a nasty head cold. We couldn't win.

But even Zara, although she was 'down', felt the difference between this day's travelling and the previous three. It was fast and comfortable and the scenery had changed dramatically. We were still in the state of Mato Grosso, which is approximately twice the size of New South Wales or four or five times the size of the United Kingdom, but the land was now filled with deep, verdant valleys and as we went on, climbing gradually to a high plateau, we passed vistas of beautiful canyons and flat-topped mesas surrounded by endless kilometres of lush vegetation. It was not the dense rainforest of the Amazon basin, but it presented a picture of a huge and enormously rich land.

Understandably this feeling of the immense size of Brazil had been growing over the past few days. Since entering Brazil, at Benjamin Constant, we had travelled 1600 kilometres by river, now we'd come another 2400 by road and we'd still only crossed half the country. I hadn't realised, although I probably learnt the statistics years ago at school, that Brazil is the fourth largest country in the world after Russia, Canada and China, its almost nine million-square-kilometre area surpassing the land areas of either the continental United States or Australia.

We were also beginning to feel the excitement generated not only by its physical bigness but by the size and variety of its population. One hundred and twenty million in 1980, Brazil will have reached two hundred million by the turn of the century. Apart from the United States, it is the most powerful country in all of the Americas. So far we had only been seeing the outback ... the boondocks.

But before long we'd be seeing the other Brazil; the sophisticated cities, the industrial and commercial centres of Rio and Sao Paulo and with every kilometre, we could feel it coming.

All of the bus stops along the way were now modern terminals like nothing we had seen before ... even the Greyhound bus terminals in the United States could not complete. These all had restaurants of a high standard, toilet facilities and shopping centres geared specifically to the passengers on the big bus lines, which throughout this area provided the fastest and most efficient form of transportation. There were now several major bus lines operating on the route we were following and the contrast with what we had experienced on the run down from Manaus could not have been greater.

These buses were all as good, if not better than the best American or European passenger buses. We were impressed. But I can remember feeling depressed also, as we approached Goiania. There were aspects about one or two of the cities and towns which had reminded us of home. There were nice comfortable-looking houses. Through the windows we could see lights and people moving around in their own homes, living normal lives, eating meals, going to bed, getting up in the morning to go to work, while here we were, always charging by in buses and trains or boats, seemingly forever on the move, never stopping. We felt left out ... a bit lonely ... a bit homesick. We seemed to have been on the move for a hell of a long time.

The trip from Cuiaba took us exactly the fifteen hours that the company's timetable had promised, an average of 53 kilometres an hour over 800 or so kilometres. But it brought us into Goiania at thirty minutes past midnight, so once again, although this trip had been easy by comparison with the others, we were still tired.

Nevertheless, we decided to book our onward tickets to Brasilia immediately we arrived, before we found a hotel. It may seem strange that we always did this, instead of say, booking the whole thing from Manaus all the way through to Brasilia, or Rio. To which I can only say that it is impossible. It just isn't done that way and there's no way you could organise it like that.

On this occasion, we discovered that the only bus we could take the next day left at 8.15 in the morning, unless we wanted to wait in Goiania until the late afternoon. We quickly opted for the early bus and went straight off to book in at the nearest hotel just across the road, hoping to get into bed quickly, so as to grab as much sleep as possible. As we checked in I noticed that the time on the clock above the reception desk was different to that on my watch. I had ten to one. The hotel clock said ten to two. We had moved into a different time zone and lost an hour.

Coming into Brasilia like we did was rather like sneaking into the palace through the tradesman's entrance. We had already travelled more than four thousand kilometres across territory which the majority of Brazilians, let alone foreigners, think of as not worth visiting, before we reached the country's capital.

It hadn't been pleasant or easy travelling but it was important, if we wanted to get any perspective at all, of a country which is determined to enter the big league within the next quarter of a century. Visitors to Britain get to know very little about the nation if all they see is London and visitors to the United States learn even less of that country if all they see is Washington or New York.

It's the same in Brazil, major cities tend to give a distorted view. Brazil is a huge country and Brazilians know it. Consequently their national character and behaviour is influenced and shaped by the innate confidence that comes with bigness. Size means power and there is no way that Brazil will allow itself to be thought of as a fifth-rate banana republic at the beck and call of European or North American powers. Brazilians intend to be reckoned with.

We covered the two hundred kilometres from Goiania to Brasilia, once more in the luxurious comfort of a big modern air-conditioned bus, complete with reclining seats and a washroom. These magnificent machines outnumbered private vehicles on the superb roads by around two to one and were without doubt the best buses we have travelled in anywhere.

The bus was full of middle-class Brazilians who had about them far more the air and look of Europeans than do South Americans from the other side of the continent. But what I remember most about that morning ride across the wide open landscape with its distant hills and pockets of forested land, were the stops we made at the bus terminals.

The nearer we came to the capital the more superlative these became in design and content. The only trouble was that it had been so many weeks since we had been under big city pressure that I found myself unable to respond to the instant demands of the counter staff, who huffed and puffed at our slowness to understand the complicated system of ordering and payment.

On our second stop, when we were still fumbling for words at the counter, a kind French-Brazilian woman took us aside and explained that it was necessary to first pay the cashier for food, by telling her what you required. She would then give a little numbered receipt which should be taken to the service counter where the uniformed staff handed over the snacks or meal or whatever.

That would probably have worked very well if we had been in these places before and knew what we wanted to buy in advance and could speak the language, but none of those qualifications applied to us. We had to first, ask the rather impatient catering staff what a particular delicacy was called in Portuguese, so that we could relay this information to the cashier who was equally brusque about our ineptitude. It was all very confusing and, oh yes, the twentieth century is wonderful, but God help you if you aren't fast on your feet and quick with the words.

It's hard to believe when you first see it, but before the late 1950s there was absolutely nothing where the brilliant city of Brasilia now stands ... just the rolling savanna grasslands of a 1200-metre-high plateau in the central Brazilian state of Goias. At that time a rancher by the name of Gama was the only person who lived in the region. Now there are more than 300,000 people living in a modern city of skyscrapers, wide boulevards and parklands, with another million more in seven satellite townships which surround the capital.

For almost 200 years Brazil's capital had been Rio de Janeiro. But with the capital and all the other major cities on the coast, or very near it, Brazil's rich, untouched interior remained that way. It had long been a dream of Brazilians to develop their unknown western territories, but nothing had been done about it until 1956 when President Juscelino Kubitschek came to power. He was one visionary who recognised that opening up the hinterland was more than just a dream for Brazil . . . it was an urgent economic necessity. He revived an old plan, formulated around the turn of the century, to create an inland capital as the spearhead of a massive expansion into the great, empty lands of the west.

The government announced plans for a competition for the design of the new capital and when it was won by Professor Lucio Costa, they simply rolled in the bulldozers and set about building it. With 40,000 men on the job, non-stop for three years, Brasilia was ready to take over as the country's capital on April 21st 1960.

Not everybody agrees that it *was* ready just then. It was a pretty raw sort of place, from all reports. True, there were sweeping modern highways, office blocks, government buildings and apartment buildings. The architecture was grand . . . impressive; the whole place was laid out in the shape of a drawn bow with an arrow pointing westward. Most people thought it looked more like a huge bird, with a sixteen-kilometre wingspan. But whatever it was, there was no greenery. The place was like a great, red dust-bowl.

Who, the critics asked, would want to leave the beauty and pleasures of life in Rio to come and live here? But the opening ceremonies took place that April in 1960, the government departments began shifting from Rio and the civil servants began settling in to their huge, new apartment blocks, or 'super-quadres' as they are called. Four of these 'super-quadres' form a neighbourhood unit, each with shops, cinema, playground, club and primary school. Brasilia was under way and since then, it has just grown and grown. Now most of the bare earth areas are grassy lawns and the capital, though it probably lacks the sophistication and excitement of Rio or Sao Paulo, is definitely there to stay.

In fact, the Brazilian government is hard-pushed to keep its population down. It has a planned maximum level of 500,000, but for the overall area, this has already been exceeded. To keep the population of the Federal District as low as possible, the government imposes stringent controls on any new buildings and requires extremely high standards. The measures have effectively precluded any families earning less than $10-12,000 a year.

What this has done though is to encourage the rapid growth of the satellite towns on the borders of the Federal District where, with less restrictions in force, there are already quite large shanty towns developing.

By comparison, these are relatively minor problems because Brasilia has already proven to be just what it was intended to be . . . a spearhead. The extent and power of Brazil's headlong drive to open up its own interior is enormous. The road-building programme, which was launched in the early seventies, is considered one of the greatest projects of its kind to be undertaken anywhere in the world this century. Some 12,800 kilometres of new roads are being pushed through the Amazon jungles and across the Mato Grosso; a network which will eventually link up the developed, populated and industrialised regions on the coast with the most remote areas of Brazil.

Brazil, like China, sees itself as being one of the world's great powers by the turn of the century. And this is by no means a remote possibility for Brazil. It has two essential ingredients: people . . . some 200 million by the year 2000, and the raw materials . . . immense natural resources of land and vital minerals.

Coming in to Brasilia as a stranger you sense this latent might. Although it is a young city ... still raw in many ways ... it is exciting. I felt the dynamism, the power and the energy of Brazil more than any country I have ever been in, apart from my own and the United States. That feeling grew, with every day that passed.

Despite being surrounded by all these dynamic vibes we unfortunately had a number of mundane things to organise on our arrival in Brasilia. For a start, Sean's passport was full so we would have to see about getting a new one from the Australian Embassy. We needed to find a bank to change some travellers' cheques and then look for a hotel. When you're carrying packs around, these things can get complicated. So, Trish and Zara stayed at the Rodoviaria ... the bus station, to mind all four packs, while Sean and I went off to change the money and locate the Embassy. Having done so, we then all checked into an hotel.

By our standards the hotel at US$25 a night was not cheap but we had no choice unless we went out to one of the satellite townships, a considerable way out of town. All the hotels in Brasilia are grouped in several separate areas, close to the inner-city area, and they are all similarly priced, except the really luxurious ones, which are naturally much more expensive.

Having settled ourselves, we then went out to spend what was left of the afternoon looking around the city. We dropped Sean's passport off at the Embassy with an application for a new one, went to the tourist office for some information about some of the city's sights, then wandered around photographing several of the extraordinary buildings in the capital.

After an excellent meal at a Lebanese restaurant in one of the big shopping complexes, we returned to the hotel and a mammoth clothes-washing chore. We had a huge amount of dirty washing to do, after our almost non-stop run down from Manaus and across the Mato Grosso. We had checked during the afternoon at a laundry and received a rather nasty shock to discover that if we wanted all of our washing done, it would cost between $35 and $40! We estimated we could have done the same amount of washing and drying in a standard Australian or American laundromat for no more than $3 or $4.

So there we were, scrubbing away in the shower, in the bath and in the basin, until finally, at about 9.30 p.m., it was all done. I strung up lines from one corner of the room to the other and back again and by the time we were finished, with washing hanging in every conceivable part of the room, it looked more like a Chinese laundry than anything else. If anybody from the hotel had walked into our room ... they'd have thrown us all out, I'm sure.

We read two more chapters of *Lassie*, then went to bed, but none of us slept well. Sean and Zara and I all had colds and Trish had bad toothache. The tooth she had broken on the Amazon was really beginning to give her trouble now.

Despite my toothache, that night in Brasilia was quite an occasion for Iain and I because we shared a double bed for the first time since leaving Panama, over two months ago! All of the other hotels in which we stayed were equipped only with single beds. This was just one of the additional strains which South American travelling puts on a marriage! I can only assume that it was because the hotels in

Brasilia anticipated having a high percentage of overseas guests that they pandered in this manner to what was probably considered a strange foreign habit; cohabitation of a sleeping space I mean!

In the morning, we collected Sean's new Australian passport and after establishing that there had been no messages from Syd left for us, we took the opportunity to leaf through some back issues of the *Sydney Morning Herald*. Same names, same faces, same situations even. They told us nothing that we would have liked to have heard about, for what we missed was not the stuff that can be compressed into newsprint, but the smells and voices, the space and the light and above all our friends.

Then it was necessary to get Sean's visa for the United States which was valid for four years, transferred across into his new passport. But by the time we arrived at the American Embassy, stopping en route to buy bus tickets for that night's overnighter to Rio, it was closed for lunch.

All this time we had been carrying around two bags of damp clothing which had not dried overnight in our room. We had hoped to find a laundrette where we could finish it off in a dryer but the people at the Australian Embassy had assured us that no such modern conveniences existed in Brasilia. So we took advantage of our enforced pause and walked a discreet distance away from the American Embassy into what was soon to be a new subdivision. Here we spread out our clothes on the grass to dry in the sun. The roads into the sub-division had been well surfaced, kerbed and guttered and the view the future residents would have of the artificially created Lake Paranoa would be pleasant enough, but I wouldn't like to live there in Brasilia, an artificially created town, any more than I would care to live in a new house. I like my environment to have developed slowly and somewhat haphazardly.

The children sat in what might one day be garage space for a large limousine and trapped huge bull ants for closer inspection, while I read a current issue of 'Time'. The world really had caught up with us. With the clothes dry and Sean's visaed passport in my pocket, we made another Embassy stop. This time with the British, to leave a message for Syd. But he had beaten us to it.

'Oh, yes,' the lady at the desk with the refined voice looked up at our query. 'We have indeed heard about Mr Hastie. It seems that he travelled down the Amazon and went on alligator hunts.' She looked impressed. 'Such an adventurous old gentleman! No, he hasn't left a message for you. In fact, he didn't come here at all. He went direct to the Embassy residence and spoke with Lady Strathallan. Lord Strathallan is away on business, but it seems that Her Ladyship was most taken with Mr Hastie.'

We could well imagine Syd regaling Her Ladyship with his adventurous tales! We have heard from Syd since he completed his trip and he is now back in Te Puke planting his Kiwi fruit and he and Molly are planning more travels.

We spent the afternoon admiring Brasilia's architecture, much of it the inspired work of the country's internationally reputed architect Oscar Niemeyer. For an overall view we took the elevator to the top of a high observation tower from where we could see the suburban satellites of the capital stretching off into the empty landscape.

It was here that my toothache became so acute and unbearable that I made

Iain promise that no matter how much I lied and fought and conned and cajoled he would force me to a dentist in Rio.

The distance between Brasilia and Rio de Janeiro is just a little more than 1200 kilometres, which meant that we were in for another journey of roughly twenty-four hours. We were beginning to feel that Brazil was so huge that none of the major centres in the country were less than a day's bus travel from each other. At least we had the comforting thought that all of the buses were now the ultimate in luxury. The huge, modern bus terminal in Brasilia was a hive of activity. There were three or four companies operating the run to Rio and each of them had buses leaving every half an hour. Two of the companies, trying to handle an evening rush, had departures for Rio every fifteen minutes!

Our bus was one of the big Brazilian-made Marco Polo vehicles which seem to dominate the field as far as buses are concerned. Brazil has become, since the 1950s a major automobile manufacturer, the largest in all of Latin America. The industry employs well over a quarter of a million factory workers directly, and provides more than a million and a half more jobs in related fields. It produces well over a million cars a year with most of the European and American auto-manufacturers being represented, either in the full-scale manufacture of cars and trucks or local assembly of imported parts.

The biggest producer by far is Volkswagen. The Brazilian company makes its own VW 'Brasilia' and is now the only VW plant in the world still producing 'beetles'. There are only just over fifty German employees in the company compared to over 40,000 Brazilians, who churn out almost 2000 vehicles a day ... accounting for close to one-quarter of Volkswagen's total world-wide production.

The road out from Brasilia took us, after several kilometres up a long, shallow escarpment, from which, looking back, we could see the lights of the capital laid out like an illuminated carpet in the distance. Then we plunged off at high speeds on an excellent highway south-east, towards Rio. The bus stopped on about three occasions during the night, but all of us managed to get reasonable stretches of comfortable sleep.

Throughout all of the following day, we continued our run to the coast. The countryside of rolling green hills was remarkably rich and beautiful. The farms and towns became increasingly middle class, affluent and civilised in appearance. The bus stops also continued to amaze us with the wealth of sophisticated foods and products they had for sale, although we still found the system of buying anything ... having to have a docket first ... most irritating.

About midday we passed through Belo Horizonte, the capital of Minas Gerais state and the third largest city in Brazil. We had given some thought to stopping briefly in 'Belo', as it is said to be an attractive city of wide, tree-lined avenues which radiate outwards, like the spokes of a wheel, from the city's centre. It was Brazil's first planned city and features a large number of ultra-modern, glass, marble and concrete buildings. But Rio was a stronger magnet, so we had made the decision to press straight on.

In the late evening, just around sunset, we began to enter the rugged, granite hill country that surrounds Rio. The highway running through this territory becomes quite dramatic, passing through some impressive tunnels and over bridges spanning deep gorges. The highway at one point clings to the side of an almost vertical cliff, built out from it on great buttresses.

Then there came the long, slow descent into Rio. There were lights everywhere, below and around us. Gradually as the traffic built up, there were houses, buildings, factories. Soon we felt that we must be near the centre of town, but it went on and on and on. We were all very excited. Reaching Brasilia was one thing. It had been civilisation. But here ... at Rio, there was the Atlantic. We had crossed the continent.

At the bus terminal, once again, enormous and mightily impressive, we wasted no time. Retrieving our packs from the locker beneath the bus, we took a taxi immediately to the Hotel Ingles in the suburb of Flamengo, about twelve or fourteen kilometres away. We knew nothing about where to go, where anything was, how far various places were from the centre, or which hotel to choose. All we had was the *South American Handbook,* which listed so many hotels that we didn't know where to start. But the 'Hotel Ingles; $5 a double with bath, good breakfast' looked a reasonable place to try.

Unfortunately, there was an unpleasant shock for us when we arrived at the hotel. Despite the fact that our guide book was only nine months old, the tariff had gone up to US$25 a double ... ... or US $50 for the four of us! Brazilian inflation. Anyway, it was full. A few doors along the same street, however, we found the Hotel Perola which had a large, pleasant, groundfloor room with four beds and bath, available for US$11 a double.

We took it and after a shower ... again the terrifying, electrifying version ... we went out for a walk along the Praia Flamengo, the broad boulevard lined with beautiful lawns and parks, which runs for a couple of kilometres or so along the southern harbour shoreline. After walking about 800 metres of it, past shops and hotels and restaurants, we stopped to have a pizza each at a pleasant little out-door cafe, with white-aproned waiters bustling busily about between the tables on the sidewalk.

It was amazing to be suddenly among 'beautiful' people. All of the other patrons were sun-tanned and well dressed in sporty-type clothes, or fashionable denims, laughing and chatting animatedly amongst themselves about anything and everything. We couldn't understand, of course. We just looked and listened, in a sort of awe ... almost as if we were country hicks. We felt as if we were suddenly in a place where everything was happening. Which it was. We liked the feeling, but I think it was all a bit much for us. We made our way back to the hotel and went to bed.

BRAZIL

21
The most beautiful city in the world

Rio! Just the name is exciting. An expression of exhilaration. Just thinking about the place I find myself smiling and have to restrain myself from getting up and doing a little dance!

We were told that Brazilians say, 'In six days God created the world. The seventh he spent on Rio.' Residents of Rio, who affectionately refer to themselves as 'Cariocas' an Indian word meaning 'house of the white man', didn't actually rush up to us and repeat that apocryphal phrase, but I wouldn't have been surprised if they had. In Rio, the feeling was that anything might happen and what is more it would be fun.

There might be times when this sensation of frenzy, bordering almost on madness might be overwhelming, threatening even. But we were in the mood for it. After a month on the river and in the outback, we were ripe for stimulation and just walking in Rio's central district was enough to get the adrenalin racing and the pulses jumping.

Eight million sun-, fun-, pleasure- and luxury-seeking Brazilians live in this city which sweeps for nineteen kilometres along a waterfront whose beaches, bays and mountains make it without doubt the most beautiful city in the world and whose buildings and inhabitants make it worthy of its setting.

'Cariocas' cope with the overcrowding, the pollution, the noise and the frequent breakdowns of even such basic services as electricity, in an exuberant Latin manner.

Public resources are stretched well beyond their capacity yet growth goes on. Immigrants from Europe and the United States come to Brazil seeking the good life. The newest national group to arrive are the Japanese who already number well over a million, making up the largest colony of Japanese outside their own islands. Showing typical resourcefulness they are already growing one-fifth of the nation's coffee, thirty percent of its cotton, all of the tea and are well into the market gardening business.

For all these immigrants, Brazil spreads wide her beautiful, brown, bare arms and takes them in. When they re-emerge they have been Brazilianised, adding yet another flavour to the multicultured, multihued melting pot.

We took a bus from our hotel in Flamengo to the centre of town which was full of brightly dressed people all in a hurry to get to where they knew they were going and we seemed to get in everybody's way, as we ogled the ultra-modern city buildings, which stood side by side with century-old, iron-balconied beauties.

We admired the parks with their tropical palms and plants and the softly pleasing curves of the wave-patterned mosaics built into the sidewalks. All we could ask was, why aren't more cities so attractive?

At out-door tables, shaded by bright umbrellas, gesticulating people were already having their first drink of the day. Many of them sipped a 'cafezinhu' a demi-tasse of black coffee, so thick that the grounds took up a third of the cup. I found that as a coffee addict, I needed two to get enough to satisfy thirst but, that I had to revert to drinking only one at a time because the brew was so strong.

In all this bewildering mêlée, we at last found the American Embassy, which we had relied on to provide a list of possible dentists.

'Of course we can't recommend any one dentist in particular, that would be unethical,' the clerk's finger paused fractionally in its sweep down the list and I immediately asked about the name on which it rested.

'Balthar. This one here. Abillio de Souza Balthar. What's he like?'

'Well, he's the one all the Embassy staff visit.'

'He'll do.'

We found Mr Balthar in a tiny room on the Avenida Rio Branco. Rents, commercial and private, are exorbitant in Rio, so the size of his surgery didn't worry me. A quick once over told me that while he did not have the very latest in dental equipment, of which I am a connoisseur, it was near enough not to be a worry. And yes, he could look at my shattered tooth.

Half an hour and two injections later I was trying to straighten the wobble of relief in my knees by sucking inelegantly at a 'cafezinho' through my half-numb mouth, and it was all over. Mr Balthar said that until I found myself in a place long enough to have a cap fitted, the temporary one which he had attached with great skill would do the job, and he was right.

While he had drilled and filled, Mr Balthar had complained about the high cost of living in Rio and the country's forty percent inflation rate. But then, when he'd done and charged me thirty-two dollars, he informed me that I was the last patient of the day and that on that afternoon, as they did on almost every afternoon, he and his wife, who was also his nursing aide, would be on board their yacht, either sailing or just messing about in the sun. Rough!

At American Express, we collected a pleasingly large pile of mail and for a change none of it was bad news so we spent a happy couple of hours reading over the gossip from friends and family. Dad, who was out of hospital after a major operation, was as well as could be expected and was looking forward to seeing us again.

It was then with a large degree of relief that we realised we had only two more visas to obtain, for Uruguay and the Argentine. The Uruguayan Embassy was closed, but we found the Argentinian office open and we were told there to 'fill in these forms, then take them, with the correct amount of American money to the Banco Argentina. When they have stamped your forms, bring them here again and we will issue the visa.'

The bank was half an hour away through crowded city streets.

'But why can't I just pay here?' Iain asked, sounding as though he hadn't spent the last four months facing up to such Latin American madness.

'No, sir. We cannot take your money. It must be paid at the bank.'

'When does it close?'

The clerk studied his watch. 'In less than half an hour.'

The clerk didn't seem in the least put out by the fact that, not only did the acceptance of nothing but US dollars mean that Argentina obviously had a pretty poor regard for its own currency, but that being prohibited from handling the money transaction themselves meant that the government evidently didn't trust their own Embassy employees!

We added ourselves to the gathering rush hour traffic, made the bank with less than two minutes to spare and after an equally hectic return trip, walked out with our visas into the pinkening evening light.

It was a beautiful evening and we decided to stroll back to our hotel along the harbour foreshore and through Flamengo Park.

We watched pleasure cruisers and yachts idle drowsily back into Guanabara Bay and above them the cable car inching along its all but invisible lifeline to the familiar cone-shaped peak of Sugar Loaf Mountain. It was that time of dusk when anything solid becomes intensely three dimensional, just before seeming to disintegrate into thousands of fat molecules of darkness.

There was a couple cuddling down by the high-tide mark, indicated by a not unpleasant broken line of nautical debris. There were people walking their dogs and several more coming towards us, shimmeringly insubstantial in the luminous, fragmented light, jogging in shorts or tracksuits.

The one hundred and twenty hectares of Flamengo Park was reclaimed from the sea during the last reclamation project in 1960 and is the biggest landscaping project so far carried out in Brazil. It now contains three large museums, large pieces of commemorative sculpture and a couple of children's playgrounds, in one of which is a grounded DC-4 where kids can act out their dreams of being airline pilots.

At the far end of the park, opposite the street in which our hotel was situated, we sat for a while under the street lights and watched the local neighbourhood team play a casual game of 'futebol'.

Throughout the day we had noticed that whenever half a dozen or so young men got together they seemed to burst spontaneously into a game of 'futebol'. It's a national obsession though treated, we were to find, with far more humour than in Argentina, where it is something altogether different than a mere ball game.

The lights came on at the base of the huge statue of Christ which stands in perpetual benediction on Corcovado Mountain, high above the city. And across the thirteen kilometre elegant span of Niteroi Bridge, which links Rio with the city of Niteroi on the eastern side of Guanabara Bay. Opened in 1974, it is another beautiful piece of evidence that Brazilians think big.

That evening we ate steak and rice in a small bar in the central area and then window-shopped and people-watched up and down the wide streets, which were still milling with effervescent crowds. Fatigue made it necessary for us to pack it in at about eleven, just the time when, we were told, 'Cariocas' really start to get into top gear!

About fifty metres from our hotel on Avenida Silveira Martins there was once a wide road called Rua do Catete. Some day soon it will be a road again, but when we were in Rio, it was nothing but a huge, fifteen-metre deep channel, a jumble of machinery, cement mixers, cranes, girders, heavy construction equipment and great mounds of earth. It was also, for twenty-four hours a day, seven days a week, the scene of non-stop activity: construction workers moving back and forth under arc lights, the sparks of arc-welding machines, the sound of jack-hammers, pile-drivers and compressors. It was part of the route of Rio's new underground railway . . . the Metro.

The city's traffic problems in the seventies became so acute that the planners finally decided that an underground system was a necessity, come what may. And they've charged into the project with typical Brazilian abandon, ripping up streets right, left and centre, to dig the tunnels for the new lines. Once laid, the tunnels will be covered in again and the streets will once more be usable and by the early 1980s, 'Cariocas' will probably be travelling back and forth to work in one of the most modern Metro systems in the world.

On the morning of our second day in Rio, we manoeuvred along the edge of the Rua do Catete, scrambling over piles of earth, squeezing past the streams of people who crammed into the narrow walkways on either side of the excavations, making our way towards a nearby post office. We had packaged up all our odds and ends; extra books and research material we had collected since we left Peru and we were hoping to send them off in two parcels, one by seamail to Australia and the other, containing most of the research material by airmail to Trish's sister in Canada, which we hoped to be able to pick up after we had completed the trip. We almost missed the post. Five minutes later and the parcels office would have been closed for the weekend. I sort of wish we had missed it. It cost us thirty-two dollars! The same price as Trish's tooth.

In the afternoon we took a bus out to the Cosme Velho region to see the famous statue of Christ the Redeemer on Corcovado, one of the huge outcrops of sheer rock that seemed to sprout up from the city in several places like giant thumbs. Rua Cosme Velho is just a normal suburban street which winds and climbs its way up the gently sloping base of Corcovado, but although the ordinary city buses travel along most of its distance, they cannot go all the way to the top of the big granite mountain.

To get there, visitors usually take a little funicular railway, but when we were there it wasn't operating, so the owners of about half a dozen minibuses were competing for the business of taking people up by a steep and narrow road which stopped about sixty metres below the base of the statue. We piled into one of them, which took off like a racing car and though it was very steep, we roared around the tight corners to the top in no time. The driver said that he would wait for half an hour for us and four other passengers who had come up with us.

Unfortunately, on our way up, several large clouds had moved across the sky and by the time we were climbing the steps up to the base of the massive statue, we were shrouded in mist. A battery of strong spotlights were playing onto the figure of Christ which was built in the early thirties and stands almost thirty-nine metres high. We could just see his outstretched hands and the top of his head, but even that was sometimes obscured in the mist. It was quite a weird sight, because the whole figure seemed to be constantly changing, coming and going, appearing and disappearing in the cool, damp fog.

Under normal conditions, the statue of Christ the Redeemer is one of the most dramatic sights of Rio ... it can be seen from almost anywhere in the city and conversely, you can see almost any part of the city from the vantage point of Corcovado. But today, it and we were all but hidden from below by the clouds ... and the wonderful panorama of Rio, spread out below, was also largely obscured to us. We could see to the beach areas of Ipanema and Copacabana, but it was all very vague and misty. We returned to our minibus disappointed, but at least glad that we had seen the statue.

The trip down again was terrifying. Our driver was bad enough on the way up, but going down, freed from the restraints of gravity, he became a maniac, not the last we were to encounter in Brazil, who only knew two speeds ... flat out and stop. We skidded and careened the whole way down seeming at any moment as if we were going to crash through the retaining wall and plunge over the cliff-like wall of the mountain. But we made it.

After a few minutes recovering on a roadside seat, we took a more leisurely bus ride back into the centre of the city, where we had hoped to go to the movies to see Woody Allen in 'Annie Hall', which was up on the billboards in Portuguese as 'Noivo Neurotico, Noiva Nervosa' (The Neurotic Bridegroom and the Nervous Bride). But on attempting to buy the tickets, we discovered it was a restricted movie ... children under sixteen were not admitted.

However, just around the corner, there was another movie theatre which was showing a comedy thriller ... 'Mr Billion', which was unrestricted and which Zara and Sean both wanted to see. So we split the difference. They went to 'Mr Billion' and Trish and I saw 'Annie Hall' ... in English, with Portuguese sub-titles.

The only way to get to know a big city is to walk around its heart. That was how, on a Sunday morning, we discovered all the colour and excitement of a big meat, fish, fruit and vegetable market in one of the side streets of Rio, near our hotel.

Sun-tanned shoppers in bum-revealing little shorts or shirts open to the waist, or both, haggled amenably over the price of delicious fresh fruit and vegetables, mouth-watering heaps of which covered stall after stall.

The prices were only a little less than we would pay at home and the choice was the widest we had seen since being on the road. The meat and fish, which were of the same high quality and variety, made us all wish that we had our own little beachfront apartment where we could have a big cook-up.

Residents of Brazil's big cities are accustomed to being able to buy the best of anything and everything they want. So far their economy, even accounting for its staggering annual inflation rate, has a yearly growth rate hovering around eight and nine percent which has been able to support their demands, though not without there being an unusual amount of luck involved.

For all its headlong rush into industrialisation over the last twenty years, forty-four percent of the nation's people are still rural workers, even though polished urbane Brazilians would like to see themselves striding into the twenty-first century as an industrial giant.

The main problem is that Brazil still has a single commodity agricultural economy. Over the years that commodity has changed from brazilwood to livestock, sugar, gold, rubber and coffee. Where luck has played a big part is that a fortuitous combination of international situations has ensured that with each change Brazil has led the world production in that specific commodity.

In each case Brazil, when challenged by other sources of supply where more intensive methods of production have been used, has simply relinquished her supremacy and moved on to the next boom crop.

The most recent of these boom crops has of course been coffee, a beverage which became synonymous with Brazil. Then on a July night in 1975 disaster struck in the form of an exceptional drop in temperatures. Eighty percent of the nation's coffee plantations were ravaged. Leaves withered on the trees. The harvest was lost. Farmers were ruined. Farm workers packed up and many joined the pioneers in the outback states and territories.

In Parana State alone, which until then had produced eleven million bags of coffee a year (more than Colombia's total production), over half the trees were killed and 150,000 plantation workers were forced to move off to find employment elsewhere.

In that one night the two dollars-a-kilo bag of coffee went the way of the five cent cigar.

When they got over the immediate shock, many former coffee farmers looked around for another crop. They began instead to plant soy bean and in under three years Brazil has become the world's second largest soy bean exporter after the United States!

This ability to be able to move on to the next pot of gold when, for whatever reason, the bottom drops out of the market, is something of a two-edged sword. So far it has worked. But this lack of any compelling reason to intensify and stabilise in any one region of the nation's economy has encouraged a generally opportunistic attitude to investment which leads to a fundamental economic instability. It's okay just as long as the 'Force' is with you and the karma is good. But it's the sort of dangerous living which gives the gnomes of Zurich heart attacks (which is okay anyway, in my book!)

On a superficial visit to Rio none of these undercurrents are felt and I am sure it would be possible even on a longer term basis to live the life of Riley, unaware of such economic bogey-men. I've never heard Great Train Robber Ronald Biggs complain about living in Rio and for a while on that Sunday we came very close to making the decision to join him; finish the trip south and then return to Rio to settle down for a while.

Back out on the harbourfront road again we caught a bus, which cut across through Botafoga and dropped us at the far end of Ipanema Beach. Although as it was May and the beginning of winter, very few people were actually swimming, the beach was still crowded with slim, healthy-looking, oiled bodies soaking up the sun in swimwear so brief as to make nudity look prudish.

Bodies beautiful played energetic ball games, did press-ups, exercises, jogged and ran while only a few actually lay about, insolently indolent.

Everyone of course has heard all about Antonio Carlos Jobim's bossa-nova 'Girl from Ipanema', but what are not so widely publicised (and who's to say that's not discrimination) are the boys from Ipanema, who are equally wowee! in their tiny figure-hugging bathers which leave NOTHING to the imagination. On occasions I think I am a voyeur. This was one of those occasions!

We walked the two kilometres length of the beach over the attractive wavy designs in the sidewalk which runs right beside the sand. None of that quite awful, British-born, Australian-inherited, habit of allowing a car-filled road and hideous public lavatories to obstruct the view of the beach. Instead plenty of room to stroll, to avoid energetic children on tricycles, to stop and buy an ice-cream from a vendor or talk with groups of friends. Civilised.

At the far end of Ipanema we rounded the point and began to walk along Copacabana. Immediately the atmosphere changed. It was rather less exuberant, rather more sophisticated. The people were no less beautiful and wore no more clothes, but they were older. Instead of doing press-ups and playing ball they had improvised tables from piled up sand, covered with a towel and were playing cards, backgammon and chess. They had brought bottles of wine, but no slurping, oh no, they had also brought the right tumblers.

Again the same wavy sidewalk for the entire two or more kilometres, with the strollers greeting one another and staying a while to chat before moving on. Not a bad way to spend Sunday.

Back from the beach are the attractive blocks of highrise condominiums some of which sell for as much as a cool one million dollars. Around this area, in which the wealthy live cheek-by-jowl with ten thousand other people per square kilometre are some of the most exclusive hotels, restaurants and boutiques in the world.

Iain and I fantasised about a time when the chidren have grown up and quit home, when we could have an apartment here and live in a rather genteel, self-indulgent manner, between visits from grandchildren!

A rather less wild dream which we have promised to make come true soon is to revisit Rio during carnival; that four day pre-Lenten festival when a staggering five million costumed people take to the streets.

In the hundreds of samba schools all through Rio, people practise their complicated dance routines all year. They build huge, elaborately-lit and decorated floats and make stunning costumes. All for the ephemeral joy of competing in the three simultaneous eighteen-hour street parades.

What can you say about people who annually convulse themselves into one of the most spectacular shows in the world except Rio! Caramba! We must return!

Andre Goncalves, the commander of one of the sailing ships in a fleet piloted by the great navigator Amerigo Vespucci, is said to have been the first Westerner to have had the privilege of sighting Guanabara Bay shortly before sailing past Sugar Loaf Mountain into the great harbour on January 1st 1502. Thinking that they had discovered the mouth of a great river, they named the place 'River of January' ... Rio de Janeiro. They described it as 'the most beautiful and agreeable bay in all Brazil'.

Since then, there have been many who have broadened the description to 'all the world'. Charles Darwin wrote in 1832 after he had sailed into the harbour on board the *Beagle* that, 'its magnificence exceeds everything which the European has seen in his native land'. Standing on the top of Sugar Loaf Mountain, the steep-sided 365-metre-high, treeless pinnacle of rock which sits like a sentinel at the entrance to the harbour, we could only agree. The view is so spectacular, so stunningly beautiful and impressive, that you could stand for hours, just looking.

We had come to Sugar Loaf directly from Copacabana Beach, having first taken a short bus ride to the cable-car station at Praia Vermelha at the foot of the double-coned peak. Modern, Italian-built cable-cars, each capable of carrying seventy-five standing passengers, lift you in two hops to the summit. The first stage is to the top of a lower, half-way cone of rock called Morro da Urca. The second, swaying out over yawning emptiness, to the peak of Pao de Acucar, which is the Portuguese for Sugar Loaf. The name is said to have originated from an Indian expression describing the feature, 'Paund Acuqua' which means 'high, low and pointed islands'.

'You're not getting me into one of those things,' Trish exclaimed when we arrived at the base and saw the swaying cable-cars. Our last experience in anything similar had been in Cape Town where we had taken the exhilarating ride to the top of Table Mountain and back again. On that occasion I recall Trish saying, 'Never, never again!'

But now, here we were, waiting to go to the top of Sugar Loaf and one of the greatest sights in the world and she was saying she didn't want to come.

'Come on, Mum,' Sean said. 'It won't be too bad. It isn't as bad as it looks.'

She didn't take much convincing. 'Oh all right,' she said, 'but I'm not standing by the window.'

So on we got, with Trish standing right in the middle of the crowd of people who entered the car, staring at the floor the whole way. But as each section of the trip only lasts about three minutes, there's not really much time to be frightened.

Just as we reached the peak of Sugar Loaf, we saw two mountain-climbers with full equipment: crampons, steel spikes, fixed ropes, the lot, clinging precariously to the vertical rock face on their last approach to the summit. As we sailed by above them, into the cable car station, an American tourist beside us in the crowded cabin laughed, 'Hell, the lengths some people go to avoid paying a fare.'

Whichever way you get there, Sugar Loaf is eminently worthwhile. Looking to seaward, the view is of the great golden crescent of the beaches of Ipanema and Copacabana, with the blues of sea and sky joining together on the distant horizon. Inwards, across the harbour, there is fantastic scenery with the city of Rio laid out beneath and stretching off along the shore against a backdrop of mountain peaks, islands and the blue waters of Guanabara Bay.

This magnificent setting was, for the first two hundred years or so after its discovery by Goncalves, the scene of many bitter and violent battles over its possession, between the Portuguese and the French, who occupied the city for several periods.

Portugal, in those early days, was operating in the New World at some considerable disadvantage. In attempting to colonise Brazil it was theoretically hampered by a papal bull ... a decree issued by Pope Alexander VI in 1493, just one year after Columbus's first voyage of discovery to the Caribbean. The Pope, in effect, divided whatever territory or spoils there might be in the New World between Spain and Portugal ... with Portugal getting the short end of the stick.

The Treaty of Tordesillas, approved by Pope Alexander, gave Portugal all territory west of the Cape Verde Islands for a distance of '370 leagues' (about 1750 kilometres). Most of that territory, as you'll see if you consult an atlas, is

Atlantic Ocean. There is the eastern bulge of Brazil marked by a line drawn roughly from Belem to Sao Paulo . . . but that is all. All of the rest of South and North America . . . although at.that stage the Pope didn't know that they were there . . . was given to Spain.

But then, taking another look at the map, it's pretty clear that Portugal didn't take a great deal of notice of this edict and from their earliest days in Brazil attempted to claim and secure as much territory as they could realistically hold. They travelled to the far headwaters of the Amazon and its many tributaries to do so.

Portugal appointed a Viceroy to Brazil in 1640. His seat of government was initially in the north-eastern city of Bahia, but after 1663 it was moved to Rio de Janeiro. The colonial economy was based mainly on a number of huge estates run with slave labour. But in Brazil, unlike in the Spanish colonies, the slavery was not so brutally repressive, taxation was lax and there was little general regimentation of the colonists from Portugal.

Nevertheless, Brazil, like most of its Spanish South American neighbours, was more or less forced into independence during the early part of the nineteenth century by Napoleon's disruption of Europe. King Joao VI, the Portuguese royal family and some 15,000 supporters fled to Brazil in 1808. In 1821, when the King returned to Portugal, he left his son, Dom Pedro, in charge in Brazil.

In Portugal the parliament mistrusted the arrangement and called on the young prince to return home. He refused and assumed the title of 'Perpetual Defender and Protector of Brazil'. Before the year was out he was challenging Portugal with the cry, 'Independence or Death!' and being crowned the constitutional Emperor of an independent Brazil.

His reign lasted only ten years as in 1831 he was forced to abdicate in favour of his son, Dom Pedro II, who at that stage was only five years old. For a further ten years Brazil was governed by a Regent, but when the young Dom Pedro II was just fifteen, he took over the crown and, surprisingly, led Brazil into a golden age of growth and enlightenment.

He proved to be, during a reign of almost fifty years, one of the wisest rulers in history. He promoted literature and the arts, vastly expanded education and communications, encouraged immigration and the development of agriculture. He fought two successful wars against oppressive tyrants in neighbouring Paraguay and Argentina and brought about the final abolition of slavery in Brazil.

But, a sad comment on human nature, it was this last achievement which caused his downfall. The rich and powerful landowners turned against the Emperor and in November 1889 Dom Pedro was overthrown and a Republic proclaimed. Two years later, Brazil's greatest leader died, poverty stricken, in a second-rate Paris hotel.

In 1922, during the centenary celebrations of their independence from Portugal, conscience-stricken Brazilians brought back Dom Pedro's remains and interred them in the cathedral at Petropolis on the outskirts of Rio.

It was with a great sense of relief that we collected our Uruguayan visas in the morning. There was still a great deal of border crossing and recrossing, showing and reshowing of passports, to come, but at least there were now no technical reasons why we shouldn't be able to reach the tip of the continent.

The requirement of a visa hangs a veil of uncertainty over everything and the obtaining of them brings one into unwelcome contact with bodies of authority, the majority of whom are, at best, obstructionist. It was good to know we were done with them.

We repacked our gear, sad to be moving on after too brief a visit, and Iain went to the far end of the street, to the main road, there to flag down a cab for the cross-town trip to the bus station. He found one easily enough but when the driver pulled up outside our hotel and saw us waiting with our packs he suddenly turned nasty, shouted abuse and refused to take us.

Iain, surprised more than anything else by the swift change in manner, yelled abuse back. Quite a little scene developed, ending with Iain slamming the taxi door and loudly offering a few pertinent suggestions to the driver as to where he should put his vehicle!

The children naturally enjoyed this bit of real-life drama and were full of support for their father when, as the driver roared off waving his fist and shouting, he rejoined us and our packs.

We were still nursing Iain's injured dignity when, 'Hey!' a man called from the front seat of a VW campervan which had just pulled up alongside us. We ignored his shout, sure that he was about to hurl more abuse. 'Hey!' he repeated. 'Come! I give you a lift. Where are you wanting to go?'

The young man, in his late twenties, shovelled a litter of children's toys onto the floor of the van and took our packs from the astonished four of us, all the while keeping up a verbal attack on rude taxi-drivers.

'You know,' he turned back to us having already stacked our gear, 'you must not think we Brazilians are all like that.'

Over the top of our profuse exclamations that we certainly didn't and that on the contrary, we had found Brazilians to be friendly and helpful, he continued, 'Maybe he has trouble with his wife, or perhaps even with the police or the government.' He shook his head. 'There are plenty who do.'

It was a half-hour trip through heavy city traffic to the bus terminal and we kept apologising and thanking him for going out of his way, and he kept assuring us that it was his pleasure.

He was interested in our journey, especially the Amazon trip, because he had never been outback in his own country. His English was fluent and when we commented on this he said, 'I have a number of foreign friends and I have visited Europe several times. In fact, I am on the point of leaving to live there permanently.'

'Oh, but why?' I exclaimed. 'How can you bear to leave such a fantastic place as Rio?'

He smiled grimly. 'For you, a visitor, it is fantastic. For me, no longer. My father is in prison for his political views and my brother is a political exile in Sweden. My choice is to join one or other of them and I think I can achieve more for my country outside prison.'

It all seemed so unreal. Such a contrast with the good life in evidence around us. And yet we knew that Brazil has this very dark side in common with the majority of countries in Central and South America.

The amnesty movement in Brazil, which is increasingly well organised, believes that two to three hundred prisoners have died under torture since 1968 while another fifty to sixty have 'disappeared'.

They also say that there are at present at least a hundred and twenty political prisoners and between six and ten thousand political exiles, many of whom would have to face trial if they returned to Brazil.

Eunice Paiva, the widow of an opposition party deputy, Ruebens Paiva, is at present threatening to sue the state. She believes that her husband, who was arrested in January 1971, was thrown out of an airforce plane over the beautiful Guanabara Bay we had so admired from Sugar Loaf, and Corcovado.

President Jimmy Carter's statements about this type of alleged human rights violations in Brazil have angered many Brazilians. 'Norte Americanos should keep their noses out of our internal affairs,' many of them say.

It's another of those situations where the United States is caught in a cleft stick. She is very glad that her largest and most powerful neighbour in South America shows no imminent danger of becoming a communist state, as happened in Chile and is on the cards for Peru, but none the less she doesn't want to have to voice much support for Brazil's heavily military-orientated government.

At the time of writing, this military government is headed by President Ernesto Geisel, and although his term of office is scheduled to end soon his successor General Joao Baptista Figueiredo, has already been handpicked from among the top echelon of generals. So there is unlikely to be any change in government policy or any loosening of the strong hand of military control in the foreseeable future.

'Norte Americanos can only talk,' our new friend commented when we made mention of President Carter's public admonition. 'It is up to Brazilians to do more than talk. We must return to a democratically elected government.'

But to return, as he suggested, would be difficult because Brazil has had over fifteen years of military government. A generation has grown up with no experience of democracy and it is frightening how very easy it is to get out of the knack of coping with the responsibilities freedom brings.

'Do you ever seen your father?' Zara asked.

The young man shook his head. 'No, not since the secret police picked him up. He was imprisoned with no trial and I doubt if I will ever see him again. Even if I did, I probably wouldn't recognise him. It's been five years and they do terrible things to people in there.'

'What would happen to your brother if he came home?' Sean asked.

'He would join my father in prison, again with no trial.'

'What did he do?' Sean persisted.

'He was a supporter of the Allende government in Chile. He was shot and wounded in the fighting during the final days of that government and he was warned against ever returning to Brazil, because he had openly supported a communist government.'

Iain asked, 'Are you a communist?'

The young man laughed. 'To be a communist in South America is different from being a communist in Europe. There I would be a social democrat. Here there is no other viable alternative to the generals' total power. I think I am more a nationalist, but for the time being I support the communists because they are the only ones who will give us enough financial backing to enable us to have any impact on the military machine which controls us at present.'

I commented on the extraordinary contrast between a people so obviously into hedonistic pleasures and the social and intellectual repression of a military government.

Again he laughed wryly, 'Not so extraordinary. We Brazilians tend to leave our spiritual welfare to the tender mercies of Mother Church and our political welfare to the not-so-tender mercies of Big Brother Army, so that we are then free to get on with the more important things of life, like lovely women, good food, happy music and lying in the sun.'

At the bus terminal we found that although several companies were operating services on the 400-kilometre run to Sao Paulo, on a one-every-fifteen-minute basis, they were all fully booked up for the next three and a half hours ... until 2.30 p.m. We bought our tickets (110 cruzeiros, or US$6 each) and had a small snack at one of the terminal restaurants.

We all felt sorry not to be staying longer in Rio. There was so much more that we would have liked to have seen and done, but time and money were beginning to force the pace for us. It was already the end of May and we felt that we should try to be in Tierra del Fuego, at the bottom tip of the continent by the end of June, which meant only a month to cover some 8000 kilometres.

The bus trip to Sao Paulo was a fast, straightforward and comfortable run of some six hours in one of the COMETA company's giant Greyhound-type cruisers, a model which is aptly called 'the Dinosaurus'. The road was a super-highway almost all the way through very attractive tropical-green countryside.

About eighty kilometres inland from its main port of Santos, Sao Paulo sits on a 760-metre plateau enjoying a pleasant Mediterranean-type climate. Although we knew what to expect, we weren't really looking forward to Sao Paulo in quite the same way we had been to Rio. Its reputation was a big one, but not for the same things. While Rio's was for its great beauty and for the gaiety and happy-go-lucky way of life of its people, Sao Paulo's fame rested on such things as size, economics, power, industrial output and the restless energy and dynamism of workers and businessmen. All very admirable, but not as interesting and exciting as Rio's qualities.

Nevertheless, we were mightily impressed with Sao Paulo which is an extremely modern, sophisticated, fast-moving city of skyscraper office blocks, apartment buildings, freeway systems and enormous factories and industrial complexes.

The city of Sao Paulo, with a population of ten and a half million (Greater Sao Paulo is considerably larger still) is the biggest city by far in South America ... and maybe in *all* of the Americas, surpassing Mexico City, New York and Los Angeles. It's also, so they say, the eighth largest in the world and it's estimated that by the year 2000 its population will be 20 million, although I must admit statistics like these tend to be confusing, if not contradictory. In Mexico City they say they're about to be the biggest city in the world. In Tokyo they claim it, then there's Shanghai, Calcutta and New York. Why they want to compete over something like that, I don't know. Anyway, as far as Sao Paulo is concerned, it's right up there in the big league.

It is the powerhouse of the Brazilian economy, employing forty-five percent of the country's total workforce and is responsible for fifty percent of all production. Sao Paulo produces more than half of Brazil's chemicals, pharmaceuticals and textiles and more than three-quarters of its rubber goods, machinery and electrical materials. Because of Sao Paulo's great wealth and productivity, it is the fastest growing city, with the possible exception of Mexico City, in the world ... not just from increases in the population due to the birthrate, but from large-scale immigration of workers coming from all over the country, as well as from other parts of the world seeking their fortunes. For them, Sao Paulo is the city of promise where there are large rewards for initiative, enterprise, imagination and hard work. Certainly, 'Paulistanos' as the residents of the city are called, seem possessed of an almost vicious energy in their pursuit of material well-being.

Sao Paulo is also probably one of the most cosmopolitan cities in the world; one of the greatest racial melting pots, with over seventy percent of its inhabitants of foreign immigrant stock. There are large numbers of Italians, Chinese, Japanese, Lebanese, Syrians and, of course, Portuguese and Spanish, not to mention a considerable number of the descendants of North Americans who left the United States for Brazil at the time of the Civil War.

Sao Paulo's early growth depended largely on the vast agricultural riches of the region, but the tremendous expansion of its industrial output stems from one important factor: the availability of virtually endless supplies of cheap electrical power. Large-scale hydroelectric schemes within Sao Paulo State have for years provided ample power for the growth of the city and its industrial complexes. But Sao Paulo's growth is already almost outstripping the supply.

So Brazil has embarked on the world's largest power-generating scheme. Some 20,000 men have been working continuously for the past three years on the vast Itaipu Hydroelectric Scheme to dam the Parana River on the Paraguayan border near the Iguacu Falls. By the time it is completed, in 1989, it will have cost over $6 billion, but it will churn out more 70 billion kilowatt-hours of electricity annually ... over three times the output of American's Grand Coulee Dam. Even then, the Brazilian forecasters say, they'll be short of power again, so fast is the growth of consumption.

Consequently Brazil is also charging headlong into nuclear power production and has under way one of the world's most ambitious programmes for the construction of atomic power plants. Its first nuclear power station began operation in 1979, but by 1990 Brazil plans to have completed the installation of another seven nuclear reactors, more than one of which will have the capacity to produce plutonium, the fissionable by-product of nuclear reaction necessary to construct atomic weapons.

This development, in which Brazil is receiving technical assistance from West Germany, has been strongly criticised by the United States, which is opposed to the spread of the so-called 'fast-breeder' nuclear reactor technology. Brazilians themselves however seem all for it; there is virtually no opposition to the plans for the expansion of nuclear power and they have, in effect, told the United States to mind its own business. Brazilians are intensely nationalistic and their attitude is that if these things are necessary for their country to achieve the goal of becoming one of the world's major powers by the turn of the century, then that's okay with them. Looking at Sao Paulo, it's not difficult to see it happening.

Sao Paulo presented us with a particularly aggravating run-around when we arrived there trying to find a place to stay the night.

Stepping off the bus at 8.30 p.m., we tried a hotel opposite the terminal, but all we saw were some not very salubrious accommodations for $20 a night, so we decided to look elsewhere. After a $5 cab ride into the centre of town, we next saw a very plain, cramped room and bath in a somewhat better hotel at a somewhat higher price ... $50 a night! Fifty dollars! And then another for a similar price. We were horrified and decided that Sao Paulo was going to prove to be what everybody had said it was ... expensive.

So we grabbed another cab and hightailed it back to the original hotel near the bus terminal only to find that it was now full up anyway. But we soon realised that there were several other hotels nearby and before long we had found one in which the rooms were bigger and better ... and cheaper than any of the others we'd seen. Sixteen dollars for the four of us. Dearer than we'd been paying way back in Peru, but a hell of a lot better than fifty dollars.

Another thing that takes you by surprise about Sao Paulo is its newness. A hundred years ago, when London and New York were already big cities, Sao Paulo had a population of a mere thirty-five thousand! This means that all the city's commercial and industrial buildings are new; the majority of them built since the last world war. So that a journey across town is like visiting an architectural trade fair.

I have never seen so many impressive modern buildings amassed in one area. It's impossible to visually register them all individually but the overall impression is of shapes, surfaces and materials used in new and exciting ways to present almost a space-age scene.

Not even in the United States had I seen such a conglomeration of modern factories and office buildings. Such buildings are not constructed without a sound and large financial base. These buildings represented wealth, not just in bricks and mortar, but in investment, shares, future plans and development.

While in beautiful Rio money is spent, in Sao Paulo money is made. This was capitalism rampant. The knowledge that, in that free-for-all, anyone with enough energy and nous could succeed and sometimes succeed on a large scale, laid an air of excitement over the city.

Iain's New York publisher had asked him to call in at their Sao Paulo offices to have a first look at his novel which they had just produced and were due to publish soon. It wasn't there. It had been lent by the manager, who was away in Europe on business, to a colleague who was looking at it with an eye to the possibility of translating it into Portuguese. This colleague was also out of town and the copy of the book was at his home in a distant suburb.

We arranged by phone with the man's wife that we should call in to have a look at it but before we left the publisher's office, Iain phoned his New York editor and agreed to his request for Iain to be in New York for publication the first week in July.

That was it then. A date, by which time the trip had to be finished, was struck. Outside pressures were beginning to close in.

Roberta da Silva opened the door of her home and welcomed us into a comfortingly familiar scene of domestic life. Sitting in easy chairs in a lounge for the first time since leaving California, I hardly registered her apologies for the absence of her husband. I was too happy drinking in the surroundings.

The rows of books in Portuguese, Spanish, German and English. Roberta's husband worked in the management of the city's telephone company, but was a graduate linguist. Then there were paintings, personal collections of mementos and artifacts, newspapers and magazines, childworn toys and puppy-chewed table legs. There was no way I could have explained to Roberta, who had lived all her life in middle-class Brazil, how comforting a scene this was.

In the small front garden, their two boys, aged three and one and a half, warred with a visiting gang of toddlers. In the kitchen a black maid made us coffee.

To our queries, Roberta, who was in her late twenties, answered in fluent English, 'I have my own practice. I am a dentist. I go in every day from 1.00 p.m. to 5.00 p.m. I drop the boys off at a playgroup on the way and pick them up on the way home. It all fits in very well. Most of my girlfriends of a similar age have their own careers. It's less common among older women. Our maid comes every morning so that takes a lot of the pressure off having both a family and professional life. Most of the families in this street have maids. Some have two, one to do the cleaning and one to care for the children. Some of them live in, although I don't care for that.'

It was a quite ordinary street, nothing pretentious. But being rather crass and inquisitive, we asked the price of homes in the area.

'We bought this house eight years ago for 720,000 cruzeiros,' she said.

Between us we worked that out to be $40,000.

'But,' Roberta went on, 'prices have sky-rocketed and there's no way we could possibly afford to buy it now if we had to start from scratch, because it must be worth three times that now . . . at least.' A very familiar story, these days, certainly not unique to Sao Paulo.

She brought out Iain's book. A slightly fraught moment it is when you see for the first time that which has sprung from your mind, through your hands onto paper, actually down in print and bound between covers. It stares back at you as if it were the final truth, which it isn't, thank God. After looking through it carefully, with great pleasure, Iain signed it self-consciously and gave it back.

Back at the bus terminal, which had the most stunning, massive, multicoloured, translucent, plastic roof, supported on stainless steel struts so that it resembled modernistic stained-glass windows in a new cathedral, we boarded the bus for the seven-hour trip south along the coast to Curitiba.

It could have been a relaxed enjoyable journey through the green, intensely-cultivated, rolling land. Instead it was turned into an exhausting terror-trip by the crazy antics of the driver, who insisted on travelling at high speed astride the dividing line, painted down the centre of the road, or continually swerving across into the opposing lane.

A few times I felt so incensed by his selfishness that I wanted to haul him bodily out of his seat and drive the giant vehicle myself.

By contrast with the traffic into Brasilia, down to Rio and on to Sao Paulo which had been dominated by huge buses, there were now less of these and more private cars and trucks. We experienced also the very definite feeling of moving away from the heart of Brazil and out again into the body.

There was one last thing we wanted to do in the country. Something we had been anticipating since long before leaving home when we had seen a documentary film on the waterfalls of Iguacu.

Foz do Iguacu are one of the greatest sights in the whole of South America, probably the world. On the Brazil/Paraguay border, a hundred and twelve kilometres from Curitiba, the Parana River plunges in an amalgamation of two hundred and seventy-five waterfalls across a frontage of more than two and a half kilometres over a drop of 60 metres.

From the documentary film and from what we had read, we knew the falls were stupendously beautiful. But, ever since entering Brazil and even before, we had been hearing the disheartening news that they were at the moment almost completely DRY.

They were, at any rate, the driest they had been in over forty years due to a series of seasons of unprecedented dryness caused by lack of rainfall in the areas of the upper tributaries of the Parana.

It was a difficult decision, but finally we concluded that rather than see them disappointingly barren, we'd add the falls to the growing list of reasons to return to Brazil.

The driver, having been unsuccessful in his suicidal mission, brought us in after dark to Curitiba, a city with a population of more than a million, which is held up by Brazilians as a modern and attractive example of planning for people as well as progress.

When the driver released the hydraulic pressure on the door of the bus and it swung back to let us out, we received a very nasty shock. It was cold.

Looking back on it, Curitiba was something of a turning point on the journey. It was certainly the end of the warm weather. From here on, as we went further south, it got progressively colder. We hadn't expected it to happen quite so suddenly. It seemed only a few days ago that we were sweltering in 38-degree heat on the Mato Grosso and on the Amazon. But now, as we headed south on the run from Curitiba to Porto Alegre, everything seemed different, as if we'd been transported overnight to Europe.

The countryside was covered with pines and deciduous trees which had lost their leaves for winter. The houses in the towns and on the farms were of a totally different design and structure than those we had become used to seeing in other parts of Brazil. These were mainly of wooden construction and had a distinctly European style. Many of them looked like houses you might see in Switzerland or Austria. It was a remarkable transformation.

As the day progressed, the weather slowly deteriorated. In the morning when we had dashed to the bus station with only minutes to spare having overslept, the skies were clear and blue even though the air remained crisply cold. But as we drove south, heavy, grey clouds gradually covered the sky, threatening to bring rain before long.

About midway through the morning, we stopped at a small town for a coffee break and to pick up some passengers and suddenly we saw our first gaucho. There he was, standing by the open door of the bus in high, polished black leather boots that were concertinaed at the ankles in shiny folds, a thick and obviously warm, grey woollen poncho and a flat, wide-brimmed, black gaucho hat. With his droopy moustache, he completely fitted the stereotyped image I had always had of the South American gaucho.

It was strange to suddenly see once again someone dressed so casually, as his normal attire, in a traditional costume. We realised that, ever since leaving the Andes, where the Indian men and women nearly always wore their distinctive traditional costumes, including the bowler hat or Italian fedora, that we had not seen anything similar until now. Everybody in between, except for the Amazon Indians, had worn normal, European-type clothes.

From here on we began to see more gauchos. Technically speaking the term gaucho applies to the South American cowboys of mixed Indian and European blood, who ranged over the vast open Pampas during the last century, making a living from the huge herds of wild cattle which roamed freely over much of southern Brazil, Uruguay, Paraguay and Argentina. But now, *all* of the residents of Rio Grande do Sul, Brazil's most southerly state, are affectionately called 'gauchos' even though they may have nothing to do with cattle farming or ranching.

This southern corner of Brazil which covers over half a million square kilometres and includes Rio Grande do Sul and two other states, Parana and Santa Catarina, has great areas of excellent cattle country; rolling hills and open, well-watered prairies. It is also the major wine-growing area of Brazil, having been settled by large numbers of German, Slav and Italian immigrants during the last century.

Shortly after midday we stopped at a very pleasant German-style roadhouse for lunch. The standard meal, at quite reasonable prices, was a fabulous assortment of shish-kababs that were brought around, on long swords, by the German owner and his wife. They were of sausage, beef, pork, chicken, lamb, bacon and onion, served with a steaming-hot soup which was ideal for a cold day.

We arrived in Porto Alegre, the southernmost city of any size in Brazil, at about 8.30 p.m. Porto Alegre, which is just on 1600 kilometres from Rio, is the capital of Rio Grande do Sul; a big, modern metropolis of over a million people. We had planned to stay only overnight in Porto Alegre and to hopefully take a bus south into Uruguay later the following morning. So, just prior to our arrival in the city we had checked the list of hotels and boarding houses in our *South American Handbook* and found one or two that we thought would suit. But we decided that, before leaving the bus terminal, as it was our usual practice, we would book our onward tickets.

Shock. The only bus that ran south, across the border into Uruguay, was leaving at 10.00 o'clock that night. There were no buses running during the day, which meant that we would either have to take the one that left in little over an hour's time or wait a full twenty-four hours for the one that left the next night.

This posed a problem for us. We wanted to be in the Uruguayan capital, Montevideo, on the Friday so that we could get to a bank there. We had arranged for some money to be sent from the United States to a bank in Montevideo. Uruguay, as we have said, is one of the few countries in South America to which it is possible to transfer US currency and get it paid to you in dollars instead of having to accept it in local currency. Today was Wednesday so, if we waited in

Porto Alegre until the following night, we wouldn't arrive in Montevideo until possibly midday Friday, to find that the banks closed for the weekend within a couple of hours, if they hadn't already done so. It would be cutting things a bit fine.

On the other hand, we were all very tired and looking forward to sleeping in a good bed that night so the prospect of travelling straight on in another bus was not attractive. But in the event, that's what we did.

So at 10.00 p.m., after a quick snack and without even a look at Porto Alegre, we boarded a Uruguayan ONDA Lines bus, which was just as big and luxurious as the Brazilian buses, and took off moving south again on our way to Uruguay.

As we left, the co-driver, complete with suit, white shirt and tie, came down the aisle with a tray of sweets. Not long after the lights were dimmed and as the bus was only half full we were all able to shift to double seats, stretch out (well, a little bit) and try to sleep. As it was, we were so tired anyway that we didn't have any trouble.

At about 4.30 a.m. the co-driver came down the aisle again waking everyone up with a cup of coffee and a biscuit, to tell us that we were at the Uruguayan frontier.

URUGUAY

22
They were all white!

Going from Brazil into Uruguay was like stepping back in time from an all-action Saturday Night Fever in 1981 into a work-to-rule, Wet Sunday Afternoon in 1953. The contrast could not been more startling.

'Where is everyone?' Zara asked as the bus drove along the deserted road which curved round the bay into Montevideo. The buildings facing the bay presented grim, blank faces. The sidewalks were devoid of people and our bus was the only vehicle in sight on the wide road.

'Uruguay is closed!' I joked. The country had shut, at least for winter and perhaps, by the look of it, for good. 'A notice in the Times personal column,' I improvised,' reads, 'Due to poor public response the last performance of Uruguay will be given this evening.'

Travelling from the border town of Chuy, where we were given a perfunctory inspection by customs and immigration officials and ate a small breakfast served by a waiter who, thank God, spoke Spanish again, we began immediately to feel that we had come into a quite different country.

The second smallest on the continent, after French Guyana, it is about the same size as England and Wales combined, and has a population of just under three million.

One of the first things we noticed was the much larger proportion of older people. Uruguay's average life expectancy, 70.2 years, is one of the highest recorded in Latin America. Degenerative diseases, such as cancer and heart conditions, rank higher as a cause of death in Uruguay than in most Latin American countries. Causes of death are now accepted as a valuable indicator of living standards.

The bus driver and his mate were in their late forties, the border officials in their fifties and the waiters in their thirties. In most of the other Latin American countries through which we'd travelled all these jobs would have been done by people in their twenties.

Partly as a result of age and partly because of the wintry weather, the Uruguayans we saw were also noticeably more conservative in their dress and manner.

The three hundred-kilometre route from Chuy to Montevideo goes through the beautiful coastal resort area centred on Punta del Este to which 300,000

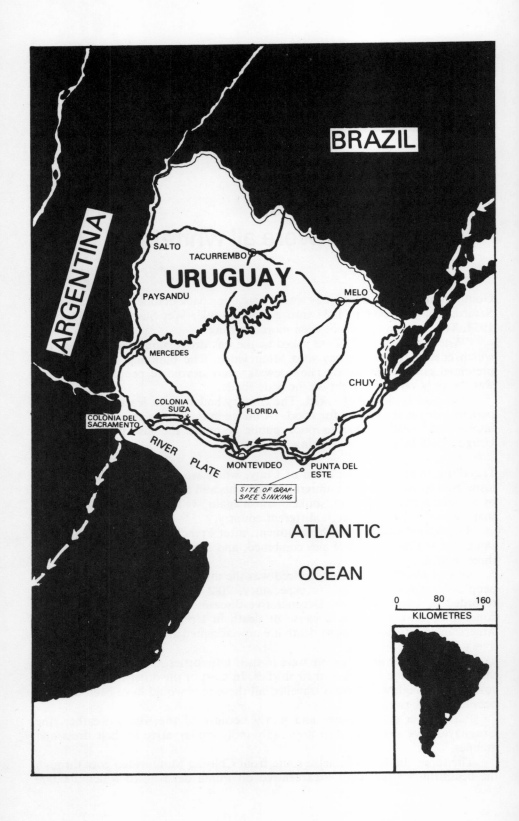

BRAZIL

ARGENTINA

SALTO
TACURREMBO

URUGUAY

PAYSANDU

MELO

MERCEDES

CHUY

COLONIA
SUIZA

FLORIDA

COLONIA DEL
SACRAMENTO

RIVER

PLATE

MONTEVIDEO

PUNTA DEL
ESTE

SITE OF GRAF-
SPEE SINKING

ATLANTIC

OCEAN

0   80   160
KILOMETRES

visitors come every year to swim and fish, surf, ski and lie in the sun. Wooded, gently rolling country reaches down to the sea which, when we saw it, was slate grey and forbidding as only the Atlantic can look.

Easy in that weather to visualise the menacing grey hulk of the German pocket battleship the *Graf von Spee,* which was defeated by the British South Atlantic Squadron in full sight of the point at Punta del Este in the famous Battle of the River Plate, a confrontation which occurred in December 1939. The German commander scuttled his ship in order to avoid capture or possible loss with all hands . . . and then shot himself. Incidentally, it took another five years before Uruguay finally got around to declaring war on Germany in February 1945.

In among the pines and gum trees were some very elegant and spacious private homes set in immaculately tended lawns; small, neat, white-painted wooden cottages for summer rentings and a couple of very large hotels with the European four-star look. Even from the outside, they spoke of deep pile carpets, a reading room, solid furniture, chambermaids who unpacked cases, room stewards who polished shoes, dressing for dinner and regular patrons cossetted by faithful, long-serving staff.

Odd to realise that many of these and the newer luxury hotels too are owned by the state. In fact Uruguay is practically owned by the state! It is the only welfare state on the entire continent.

A quarter of the entire workforce is employed by government and state-run corporations and work only a statutory thirty hour week. Apart from hotels, the government runs its own theatres, casinos and of course banks, which open for only four hours a day. It controls telephones and broadcasting and subsidises the arts. Electricity, railways, tramways and waterworks have all been nationalised.

A maximum forty hour working week, a minimum wage, holidays with pay, liability insurance, free medical service, old age and service pensions and unemployment pay are all guaranteed by law. Women have the vote and the vote is secret. Capital punishment has been abolished. Divorce is legal and illegitimate children have equal rights and status. Education is free and compulsory.

It is the cradle-to-grave security which some people find sinister and others find comforting. I just find it stifling. On paper it all looks good, but in practice this tight control has led to an inflexibility of economic and industrial policies that have resulted in social stagnation and recession.

Uruguay was tremendously hard hit by the oil crisis and resultant world wide inflation of the mid-seventies. This added to problems already caused by the loss of a traditional beef market when Britain joined the EEC.

In 1974 inflation reached the staggering figure of one hundred and three percent! Even though it has dropped from that, it has nonetheless remained horrifyingly high ever since, so that despite the fact the per capita income is the third highest in the continent after Venezuela and the Argentine, the population fell by 100,000 during the first half of the seventies as people emigrated, mostly to more free-wheeling Brazil, in search of better job prospects.

It's not really surprising that Uruguayans accepted so readily the concept of cradle-to-the-grave socialism. Their whole history has been fraught with strife; see-sawing battles between the Spanish and the Portuguese over ownership of the territory, long and bitter civil wars, repressive dictatorships and continual intrigue. So when the opportunity presented itself for their lives to be slightly more stable, organised and secure, they probably accepted the change more out of relief than anything else.

Even in a continent renowned for the violence and traumas of its early history, Uruguay stands out, although in the beginning things were a little slow. After the Spanish explorer Juan Diaz de Solis landed in 1515 near the site of present-day Montevideo, practically nothing happened in Uruguay for over 160 years. One Spaniard, Hernando Harrias, did try unsuccessfully to land settlers in 1580. Some of his cattle escaped to form the beginnings of the huge herds of wild cattle that later roamed the Uruguayan pampas, but there was no further European impact until 1624 when Jesuit and Franciscan missionaries landed. Even so, their effect on the territory was largely confined to pacifying a few Indians rather than developing and colonising the land.

It wasn't until the Portuguese suddenly showed an interest in the region, pushing down from Rio de Janeiro in 1680 to establish a town at Colonia, just across the River Plate from the Spanish town of Buenos Aires in Argentina, that things began to hot up.

The Spaniards immediately attacked the Portuguese and for 148 years, until 1828, Uruguay was fought over. First, as we've just said, it was between the Spanish from Argentina and the Portuguese from Brazil. But when both gained their independence from their mother countries, they continued to fight over Uruguay, each side controlling the territory for different periods. Britain even got into the act when it attacked and occupied both Montevideo and Buenos Aires in 1806. It withdrew, however, the following year.

For the next twenty years or so there were continuing battles until, in 1828, both Brazil and Argentina formally relinquished all claims over Uruguay and the country became independent.

But independence brought no respite from trouble. The country was almost immediately plunged into long periods of civil war between the two main political factions, the Colorados (Reds ... no connection with present-day communist 'reds') and the Blancos (Whites). The conflicts lasted for most of the nineteenth century and coincided, unfortunately for the long-suffering Uruguayans, with the heavy-handed excesses of a series of ruthless dictators, so that by the time it was entering the twentieth century Uruguay was in a wretched condition.

However, when Jose Battle y Ordonez gained the presidency in 1903, the Uruguayan scene was set for great changes. Battle was a distinguished states-man and a man with considerable vision. In his two terms of office, 1903 to 1907 and 1911 to 1915, he truly revolutionised life in Uruguay in every way, initiating reforms that transformed the country into South American's only welfare state.

From our point of view as casual visitors to Uruguay, the most notable effect of all this stability and security was, as Trish has said, the apparent conservatism of the people. As we walked about in Montevideo, it was as if we were in Europe. The people's clothes: leather jackets, fur coats and hats ... everybody was rugged up. But what was more noticeable than anything else ... they were all white!

Coming down through Central and South America, we had become accustomed to a polyglot racial mixture in all the countries ... except for Costa

Rica. But we hadn't expected quite such a dramatic change in Uruguay. The reason for the high percentage of whites is that virtually all of the indigenous Charrua Indians were wiped out in the early colonial days and the only immigration allowed to Uruguay was from European countries. The resultant breakdown of ethnic origin of the present population is 95 percent European, which is split 60 percent Spanish, 30 percent Italian and 5 percent Portuguese and British. The remaining 5 percent are of Indian or mestizo descent.

With close to one and a half million inhabitants, Montevideo contains virtually half the population of the whole country. It struck us as being a relatively quiet, clean and pleasant city with a number of wide, tree-lined streets and avenues and several large and well-kept parks and gardens. But in the cold, windy conditions that prevailed for the couple of days we were there, we realised we were not seeing it at its best. A touch of summer sunshine and leaves on the trees would have made a world of difference. But even in winter, it was still an interesting city to be in.

We had checked into the Hotel Balfer, near the Plaza Liberdad, one of several large squares spaced along the length of the Avenida 18 de Mayo. Our accommodation was one room with four beds, a bathroom and ... most important ... central heating and hot water. Suddenly, within the space of a couple of days, these two facilities had assumed a very different degree of importance in our day-to-day arrangements. And from now on they would have a considerable effect on how we viewed the places through which we were passing.

We spent a good deal of that first day chasing after the money we had asked to be transferred to Montevideo. It wasn't there. After several fruitless calls to the bank during the afternoon, we gave up for the day hoping that it would be there by tomorrow.

That evening we had a very good meal of steak and french-fried potatoes at a colonial-style restaurant on one corner of the Plaza Liberdad. The steak was beautiful; the best we'd had for a long time. Also reasonably cheap (about $1.50), but the big shock was the hot chocolate drinks that we all had with the meal. When the bill came we almost fell over; 40 pesos (about $6.50) just for the hot chocolates. Coffee was about 30c a cup.

'There must be some mistake,' I said to the waiter, pointing to the item on the bill.

'No sir,' he replied, 'it is correct. Chocolate is very expensive in Uruguay.'

'You can say that again,' I mumbled, making a mental note to avoid hot chocolate in future.

After dinner we went to the movies, responding to some desperate pleading by Sean to see a farcical war movie called 'Kelly's Heroes', which involved Clint Eastwood, Telly Savalas and Donald Sutherland pulling off a bank-robbery behind German lines in World War II. It was corny, but entertaining and with plenty of action; Zara and Sean loved it.

During the next morning we sat in our room and wrote letters; some to friends and some business letters. Sean, who is not the most energetic of letter-writers, fulfilled his duties as quickly as possible and then asked for his pocketmoney. We had been giving both the children, US$1.00 each week, or its equivalent in the local currency. At least that was the way things were intended to be, but crossing borders and changing currencies often tended to confuse things and sometimes they would forget to change their own money as we crossed a border and they would be stuck with it ... or I should say, Trish or I would be stuck with it, because we inevitably had to change it for them. Consequently, we now have a large collection of small denomination notes and coins from all of the Central and South American countries we passed through.

'What are you going to do?' I asked Sean as he put on his jacket, preparing to go out.

'Oh, I don't know,' he replied, 'I think I'll just go and "ravel" through some shops.'

We all laughed, but the concept of Sean 'ravelling' through some shop (and we knew which one it would be, as he had discovered a well-stocked toy shop nearby) only evoked in us a sense of pity for the poor shopowner. The word 'ravel' has since passed into the family dictionary as the most apt description of Sean's attacks on cupboards, drawers or whatever.

Towards noon, we took off to wander through the older part of the city, partly on foot and also by tram car. Sidewalk vendors were selling hot, roasted peanuts in their shells to people bustling back and forth to their jobs and doing shopping. The air was chill and our breaths came misty from our mouths as we walked along. We had extracted most of our warmer clothes from the bottom of our packs and were wearing sweaters and wind-proof jackets.

We managed to sort out the non-arrival of our money during the afternoon. The draft was eventually traced to the head office of the state bank, the Banco de la Republic, a gigantic, marble-columned edifice in the old part of the city. Once again, however, it cost us almost $20 in international telegrams and phone calls to get it.

By the time we had finished collecting the money, getting it changed into US dollar travellers' cheques, which in itself took an hour, it was almost dark. Sunrise and sunset were now noticeably closer together. In the past ten days we had travelled south some thirty-five degrees of latitude from just below the equator, so that we were now on roughly the same level as Cape Town and Sydney, but with another twenty degrees of latitude and some 3200 kilometres still to travel southwards.

In the deepening dusk we walked down onto the great boulevard which winds its way for kilometres along the city's metropolitan waterfront, the Rambla Naciones Unidas, which changes its name in different sections of the road, to Rambla Francia, Rambla Gran Bretana, Rambla Republica Argentina, Rambla Republic de Chile and so on. There was a cold wind blowing by now and we were alone on the beachfront. It was again as it had been when we arrived, deserted; very few cars and no people in sight anywhere, even though the Rambla was lined with tall apartment buildings with lights shining in the windows. Everybody was inside ... out of the cold.

Back at the hotel a little later we joined the crowd of guests in the small lobby to watch our first World Cup football match on TV. The elimination matches were just beginning, even though we'd been subjected to the build-up for weeks. All the way down from Mexico, but more particularly in Peru and Brazil, whenever we passed a news-stand there were always pictures and posters of the World Cup soccer teams which would be playing in Buenos Aires. Now it seemed as if we'd be there in Buenos Aires right in the middle of the play-offs.

The match we saw on TV in Montevideo was Argentina versus Hungary. It was a brilliant match . . . really good soccer. The score was tied 1:1 until the last three minutes of the game, when Argentina scored a goal. The crowd went crazy and the announcer yelled himself hoarse. We had been thinking of trying to get to see one of the matches in Buenos Aires, but by the look of the size of the crowd in the stadium it would be all but impossible. Anyway that was for the future. Tomorrow we planned to move off again. We went to bed, but before going to sleep we finished the last two chapters of *Lassie Come Home.*

Colonia Suiza, some one hundred kilometres west of Montevideo, is described in the tourist blurbs as being in the heart of the 'Switzerland of Uruguay'. This did nothing to recommend it to me because Switzerland in the original leaves me cold and transplanted imitations I could do without.

But Colonia Suiza is only a few kilometres from Colonia del Sacramento from where the ferries and hydrofoils leave to cross the River Plate into Argentina. So we decided that it would make a pleasant rural break before continuing on our journey south.

I was relieved to find no one dressed up in leather shorts, braces and Tyrolean feather-trimmed hats, slapping their thighs and yodelling. We were however assured that we could buy locally-made Swiss cuckoo clocks from the 4500-strong Swiss community. It was also very refreshing to be away from cities and buildings again. I am very much a country girl.

The bus we took from Montevideo dropped us in downtown Colonia Suiza which consisted of a small park and four or five empty roads. In the one-room bus depot, Iain phoned one of the only two hotels listed in our guide book. He blanched, then, putting his hand over the mouthpiece, almost staggered as he reported, with glassy eyes, 'seventy-seven dollars for the the four of us!' The alternative place offered accommodation for four at fifty dollars.

'Mas barato?' Iain asked plaintively of the fellow who ran the office. 'Some place cheaper?' The man suggested the del Prado, 'Muy barato,' he assured us. At nineteen dollars for the family, it was indeed cheaper than the others and we accepted with alacrity a tariff which we would normally have rejected in other places.

The Hotel del Prado turned out to be a big family house outside of town and set back some distance from the gravel road. Formerly an estancia, it had become uneconomical to run and had been converted to a small hotel. But it still had the welcoming appearance of a place accustomed to children and animals.

We were the only guests and because no more were expected now until the spring, the radiators had been turned off in the bedrooms. But the family who owned and ran the del Prado busied themselves bringing blankets and towels, turning the heat on and inviting us to join them in their part of the house to watch the television coverage of another World Cup soccer match; this one between Peru and Sweden.

Sean and the two young boys of the family went off to scout about in the grounds while we all settled round the set.

'You are going to see the Copa del Mundo,' the proprietor, a fellow in his mid-thirties stated rather than asked. He was surprised when we told him that our visit to the Argentine had nothing to do with the World Cup.

'We've come overland through the United States, Central and South America, down through Brazil to Uruguay,' Iain explained in Spanish.

'And who do you think will win the Cup?' he asked doggedly.

'Brazil,' Iain said, taking a stab in the dark.

The proprietor nodded, said 'Aha!' but made no further comment.

His wife served coffee and after Peru had won, they asked us if we would like a lift into Colonia del Sacramento. When we explained that we would be catching a ferry from there tomorrow and that we would prefer to look around the immediate area, they suggested we go to the Club Artesanos. We weren't at all sure what this was or where it was and the more we asked, the more confusing the explanations became, so we gave up and just set out on a walk.

The hotel was some distance from what passed as the town centre. There were no shops, and between the widely-spaced houses were areas of grassland. There wasn't even a church.

This lessening in the number of churches was one of the things which I had immediately noticed in Uruguay. We'd become so accustomed throughout Latin America to seeing small roadside shrines and crosses, large illuminated crosses at the entrance to towns of all sizes in Brazil, and churches of varying size and splendor everywhere, that it was with almost a sense of bereavement that I registered their absence in Uruguay.

The reason for this difference is that Uruguay is the only Latin American nation which approaches religious pluralism. Constrasting with the ninety percent formal Roman Catholic affiliation in other Latin American countries, only sixty-two percent of Uruguayans list themselves as Catholic. Many claim no church membership.

Wandering along the deserted lanes and small roads, happy to be away from big towns, we came quite by accident across a squat one-storey, but largish building labelled 'Club Artesanos'.

Judging by the number of people clustered around the main door and the flurry of activity with children running about, there appeared to be some sort of party in progress, so we decided to investigate further.

Inside there was a bar, a large dining-room and comfortable lounge in style and fittings reminiscent of a British working men's club or Australian RSL, minus the poker machines. These rooms had only a few patrons, older men having a quiet beer, but from the noise we guessed that the party was under way below stairs.

Feeling like gatecrashers, we followed a number of children and descended the stairs to find ourselves in the midst of celebrations under a banner which proclaimed, 'Centenario d'Escola'. Colonia Suiza's school was a hundred years old and the party was just like the many given on various occasions by Sean and Zara's school at home.

Trestle tables laden with cakes and manned by Mums who looked just like Mrs Robb and Mrs Williams. Games of skill and chance supervised by Dads almost identical to Mr Sinclair and Mr Sheather. It was uncanny, like being magically transported to Avalon Junior School.

There was an initial momentary nervous pause, a mutual sizing up, a challenge to the territorial instincts and then two young boys came out of the crowd to seize Sean. Zara, not wanting to be left out, went too.

For the next hour Iain and I drank hot chocolate (having first ascertained that it was thirty cents and not a dollar sixty-five a cup!) and ate homemade cakes while we examined the school's group photographs taken over the years, which were exhibited on the walls, and explained to the continually changing group of parents where we came from, where we were going and why.

It was so pleasurable to step into the ordinary everyday lives of people much like us and our friends. People whose lives revolve around the endless details of making a dollar, feeding the dog, organising the kids' soccer matches and ballet lessons, homework, housework, shopping, changing the sheets and remembering to put out the garbage.

'Would you like to visit our town?' The question was asked by one of the parents . . . a stocky, dark-haired man in his mid-forties who had been participating in the rather difficult half-English, half-Spanish conversation that we had been having alongside the tables of food.

'Come . . . come with me,' he insisted, already moving in the direction of the door, 'I will show you.'

We could hardly refuse. Sean however stayed at the party while Zara, Trish and I travelled about the streets of Colonia Suiza with Senor Uruguay Miranda in his immaculate 1964 Plymouth.

'Uruguay? Your name is Uruguay?' I asked.

'Si,' he laughed. 'Muy patriotico.' He puffed out his chest, like a would-be candidate in the Mr Universe contest. 'I am Mr Uruguay.'

His two young boys, Roberto and Daniel, sat in the back seat with Zara and Trish while Senor Uruguay, who was, we learnt, an official in the Port Administration at Colonia, regaled us, in a mixture of Spanish and English, with the salient features of his little town. First there was the main square with the statue of the local hero, then various large houses, and public buildings, the local dam and lake and finally the two hotels which we had fortunately been able to avoid on our arrival.

But the most fascinating aspect of Mr Uruguay's guided tour were the old cars. There were scores of old-model cars about the place, either parked by the roadside or driving by. Cars from the 1950s for instance, many from the forties and quite a few from the thirties and even earlier. We were astounded. We had noticed in Montevideo what seemed to be a disproportionate number of old cars in the streets, but this was almost like stepping back in time several decades . . . or like being on a 1940s movie set.

We saw, for example, two separate model-T Fords in good working condition, driving by on the street, a 1928 Chevrolet, several A-model Fords, a 1936 BMW, a number of World War II-vintage Fords and Chevrolets, two post-war Nash cars, a 1947 Loewy Studebaker and a Kaizer . . . all apparently in good order.

Mr Uruguay, once he realised that we were interested, proceeded to take us all over the town, showing us various old cars he knew of.

'But why?' I asked. 'How is it that these cars are still on the road?'

He laughed. 'Do you know the price of a new car in this country?' When I shook my head, he went on, '60,000 pesos (US$9000) for a VW Beetle from

Brazil; almost 80,000 pesos (US$12000) for a VW Golf; 325,000 pesos ($50000) for the cheapest Mercedes Benz.'

'But that's impossible,' I said.

'Si, of course . . . is impossible. So . . . everyone keeps the old cars.' He patted the dashboard of his own car, which he had bought ten years previously and lovingly refurbished.

'But these old cars,' Trish said from the back seat, 'you could get a fortune for them from collectors in the United States and Europe.'

He shook his head. 'Is very expensive to take out old cars from this country. Also difficult. Uruguayan government will not always give permission. Then, even with permission, you must pay for export tax . . . maybe three, maybe four, maybe five times the price of the car.'

'And this car?' We had stopped and were looking at a 1935 A-model Ford in reasonable condition. 'How much could I buy this for?'

He looked at it briefly. 'Perhaps 4000, perhaps 4500 pesos.' Six or seven hundred dollars for a car almost forty-five years old. Then the export tax . . . say $3500, on top of the original price and at least seven or eight hundred more to ship it somewhere, bringing the total to something between four and five thousand dollars! A figure that would tend to make anyone think twice.

Unfortunately though, this extraordinary number of old cars in Uruguay is more than just a quaint and interesting feature of local life for tourists to photograph. In real terms they represent a very visible symbol of the serious lack of any economic progress in Uruguay over the past couple of decades.

Uruguay may have begun the twentieth century with progressive social welfare reforms, but so far the story of its experience in the second half of the century has been one of a steadily deteriorating economic situation. Although the average earnings of Uruguayans are the third highest in Latin America, the general standard of living has been declining for some time as a result of chronic inflation. The Uruguayan peso was devalued thirty-one times between the beginning of 1972 and the end of 1974 and by the late seventies, consumer prices were 13 times higher than they were in 1970 and almost 300 times higher than they were in 1960.

The main problem is that Uruguay has not moved with the times. Its wealth in the early part of this century rested almost entirely on the pastoral industry; cattle and wool. For many years Uruguay was second only to Argentina as a meat and meat-product exporter and even up until the mid-seventies more than eighty percent of the country's foreign exchange came from the export of wool, frozen and canned meats, hides and skins.

But the development of industry in Uruguay stagnated and became ineffi-cient. As a result, most manufactured goods have had to be imported and as there is a lack of foreign exchange to pay for them the country's balance of pay-ments has not been strong for many years. Consequently there have been rigid restrictions and high duties on many imports . . . cars being a prime example.

Wages and salaries have tended to drop in relation to prices and the changing situation has led to a great deal of social disaffection and economic instability. This has been followed by a corresponding degree of political instability which has brought about a distinct move away from what has been accepted during this century as traditional liberalism in Uruguay, towards more autocratic government.

On June 27th, 1973, the then President of Uruguay, Juan Maria Bordaberry dissolved the Congress and instituted a period of executive rule. The constitution was suspended and any political activity banned. Bordaberry was ousted from the Presidency in June 1976 by Uruguayan military leaders. He was replaced by President Aparicio Mendez who had the backing of the military.

Since then the influence of the military has expanded rapidly into all areas of public life. All state-run enterprises, including the central bank, are now headed by military officers and any chances for a lasting return to civilian rule seem remote.

Not an altogether happy scene. Uruguay had seemed to us at first to have been a country that was considerably better off than many of the others we had seen in Latin America, but sadly the signs for the future are not good.

ARGENTINA

23
'Do we look frightened?'

Argentina was the least happy of the countries we visited on the South American continent. Having said that it's then necessary to explain what, specifically, gave me that impression and why it should be so. That's more difficult.

A country is its people and perhaps one of the main reasons for this aura of unhappiness is that many Argentines don't feel at home in Argentina. (One small indication of this is that they are forever comparing their capital, Buenos Aires, with Paris.) They feel more like the lost tribe of Europe condemned to live in an alien continent.

They suffer from a common European malaise, a sense of superiority, over the original inhabitants of the land and even the people with whom they presently share the continent. It is quite common for an Argentinian who is going to visit another country on the continent to remark, 'I am going to South America.' This is said only partly in jest, as Argentines don't think of themselves as having anything in common with Peruvians, Ecuadoreans, or even Brazilians.

This attitude has sadly inhibited them from allowing themselves to meld into the scene, to become a part of their landscape and has condemned many of them to being strangers in their own land.

The eighth largest country in the world, Argentina was not so much founded as straggled into existence almost by default. Both the Rio del Plata, River of Silver, and the word Argentina itself, which is based on the Latin word, argent, also meaning silver, were named by sixteenth century European explorers who, on seeing the local Indians using what they fondly imagined to be objects of silver, had glorious visions of vast untapped wealth.

But their greed-coloured spectacles deceived them. There was little silver to be found and, as they were only interested in the minerals of their age; they were not impressed by the less glamorous deposits of lead, copper, zinc and tin which have provided Argentina with considerable wealth in the twentieth century.

Disappointed by the lack of either silver or gold and discouraged by the strong and effective resistance of the Indians, the Spanish mercenaries, who included Sebastian Cabot and Diego Garcia, retreated.

In 1543, Peru, which Spain had already ravaged and held in control, was given the Viceroyalty over all Spain's South American possessions. All instructions to settlements in Argentina and Uruguay had to travel a distance of 9600 kilometres, via Cape Horn, or 13,600 kilometres up through Panama and down the east coast from the powers that were, in Lima.

This unwieldy system somehow worked for two hundred and seventy years, during which time the Spanish emphasis on Lima was so great that Buenos Aires remained an insignificant outpost. Spain even prohibited it from taking part in any overseas trade until 1778. By that time its population was still only a mere 24,000, who made their living mainly by smuggling. Buenos Aires was regarded as nothing more than a Spanish military outpost kept for the purpose of rivalling the Portuguese garrison of Colonia del Sacramento.

We crossed the River Plate from Colonia to Buenos Aires in an 'aliscafo', a hydrofoil. Even at the high speed it travelled, it took an hour to cross what is hardly a single river, but more a wide bay or estuary of the rivers Parana and Uruguay and their tributaries. Mud and silt make the water an opaque brown and necessitate constant dredging to keep the channel open for ocean-going vessels.

Such are the unforeseeable fluctuations of history that Colonia del Sacramento now has a population of ten thousand while Buenos Aires is one of the largest cities in the world with a population of eight million spread over an area of 185 square kilometres. As recently as 1806 the British, following Spain's alliance with Napoleon, extended the battlefield of Europe to include the New World by invading and capturing Buenos Aires. But neither Spain nor England could have visualised the tremendous potential of this city and its hinterland.

That would have required as vast a leap of the imagination as is needed now, when visiting either Spain or Britain, to recall that less than three hundred years ago the inhabitants of these tiny nations thought they had the God-given right to divide up the world between them.

The 1806 attack by the British was a turning point for Portenos, the name taken by those born in the port of Buenos Aires. For when, a year later, they rid themselves of the British, they felt confident enough to do the same with the Spaniards.

The Spanish Viceroy was deposed. Spain retaliated by threatening invasion from Peru and by blockading the River Plate. But in 1816, high on courage, the Portenos declared their independence. The man who led them was a selfless patriot called José de San Martin. At the head of an Argentine army, he crossed the Andes to free Chile. Then he went on north in support of Simon Bolivar's grand vision for a United States of South America and captured Lima, which began the freeing of Peru from Spanish colonial rule.

It would be pleasant to be able to relate that on his return home San Martin was given a hero's welcome. This might also have been the point at which Argentina could have turned aside from their Spanish legacy of intrigue and treachery and begun to build a democratic tradition.

But the sadness is that General San Martin found his country torn apart by internal power conflicts in a game of divide-and-rule learnt from its former masters. Worn out and disillusioned, San Martin retired to France. It was an understandable, but weak, decision which set the scene for the arrival of one of the nineteenth century's most brutal dictators, General Juan Manuel de Rosas. Rosas' methods of dealing with rivalry between centralist and federalist factions in Argentina was a seventeen year tyranny so absolute and bloody that it even shocked Europe, which had been inured to most horrors by its own terrible revolutions and Napoleonic wars.

It also tore wide, rather than healed, the political breaches and when Rosas was finally turfed out in 1852 he left a political vacuum so complete that Argentina was doomed to enter the twentieth century in a state of continual chaos.

An ironic footnote to history is that General Rosas, exiled in Britain, farmed quietly for a further twenty-five years before dying in Southampton.

From the hydrofoil port, where we were checked through customs and immigration, we took a taxi to the Hotel Florida. We had rung from the port and been offered a family room with its own bathroom for US$11 a night. So far so good. Of course we had no way of knowing what the area in which the hotel was situated was like, except that on the map it showed as being very central.

When the cab driver dropped us on a corner and told us this was the closest he could get to the hotel we were pleasantly surprised to find that we were in the heart of a classy uptown area and that the hotel faced onto a street which was closed to traffic and given over as a pedestrian mall.

We put on our packs and began to move along Calle Florida in the direction the street numbers indicated would lead to the hotel and straight away were confronted with the unnerving experience of being the centre of attraction for the hundreds of pedestrians who filled the street.

They moved slowly forward as if in procession, face after face after face, all white and all staring at us, some smiling, but all commenting about us to one another.

It was Sunday afternoon and this was the custom; to promenade in the fashionable area in best winter clothes, elegant leather coats, fur hats and trilbies. They moved at an ordered pace, keeping to the right-hand side of the road to go in one direction and the left for the other way. It was as if there were signposted rules.

For as far as we could see, forward and behind us, the road was a mass of people and they all seemed to be staring.

'Why are they staring at us?' Sean asked in embarrassment.

'They're not really,' I lied stupidly as if by doing so I could pretend it wasn't happening.

'They are' Zara insisted, blushing.

It was the children I think who attracted attention. The fact that they were carrying their own packs. Also that we were so obviously foreigners. In our casual, bright-coloured clothes we stood out like beacons.

It was with relief that we found the hotel and with even greater relief that we found it was clean and warm with big beds and a decent bathroom.

During a wash and brush up, Zara discovered that she had left her watch at the Hotel del Prado back in Uruguay. As she is usually very careful about her possessions she was so upset at the loss that we said we would try phoning back to the friendly family hoteliers who had given us their address, when we left that morning, asking us to keep in touch.

It took a while to get through because, although it was only back across the river, it was in another country. But with some translation assistance from a woman who was also waiting for an international call, Iain did eventually get through at about 7.00 p.m., speak to the owner who told him that, yes, they had found the watch and that they had already parcelled it up ready to send off! A month later we picked it up in Canada.

The streets of the capital were still full of promenaders when, a couple of hours later, around nine-thirty, we walked out of one of the many movie theatres in the central area. We felt refreshed by the happy, innocent entertainment of 'Oh God!', a movie which fruitfully uses an unlikely combination of the talents of John Denver and George Burns.

We ate a light dinner at one of the many busy cafeterias and were on our way home, still attracting some attention even without our packs, because it was apparently still obvious that we were foreigners, when a middle-aged foursome stopped us.

They asked us where we were from and this was quickly followed by an inquiry as to what we thought about Argentina. As all we had seen was the centre of Buenos Aires and that only for part of a day, we made the usual and expected flattering noises.

In common with many Argentines, all four spoke excellent and fluent English. 'It is very important,' one of the men stated emphatically, 'that when you leave here you tell the people of the world that we are happy.'

His request made us sound very important. As if the people of the world wait for the pearls of truth and wisdom to drop from our lips! But we could see from their faces that they were not joking. The other three nodded energetically in agreement.

'And free,' a woman who was obviously his wife added. 'They are saying such stupid lies about us,' she continued hotly, 'that it is not safe for us to walk in the streets at night. That there are secret police, political prisoners, murders and tortures. It is quite ridiculous. Do we look frightened?'

Quite a little crowd had grown round us, craning their necks to see and hear better; some of them nodded their heads in approbation as the other couple joined in.

'We are very glad the government has cleaned up the country and rid us of these people.'

'You tell them,' the first man said insistently, 'that we are free.'

The crowd murmured its agreement.

Apart from being a rather awkward situation, it was also a little odd that these people should accost us in this manner and that the crowd who hung around should encourage them. If it had turned out to be an isolated incident, we might have dismissed it as not having much significance, but it was only the first of several such insistent demands from total strangers that we should tell outsiders, foreigners, the rest of the world, that Argentinians are free and happy.

Because of the 'Mundial', the World Cup soccer matches, Argentina had found itself during this time under the scrutiny of the world's media, and it didn't like some of what they considered the non-sporting coverage they were getting.

In our beds that night we heard a crowd of exultant soccer fans parading through the central area blowing whistles, shaking rattles and shouting AR-GEN-TINA, AR-GEN-TINA. Perhaps it was only because I was tired, but it seemed that the ardent nationalism of the fans and the crowd who had wanted us to spread the good news of freedom and happiness was a case of protesting too much.

In the course of this narrative I suppose we've made quite a few sweeping generalisations, so one more won't really make much difference: Argentina's greatest problem . . . one that it has had from its earliest beginnings and one that has prevented it from ever emerging as a complete identity . . . as a real country, is that just about every *man* in Argentina has always thought he could run the country better than the man doing the job at the time.

I know that sentiment is also quite a common one in many Western democracies, but in Argentina it invariably includes a large flock of generals and admirals, either active or retired, who think seriously of themselves as potential presidents and who are prepared to go to great lengths, usually unconstitutional and undemocratic, to achieve their ends.

And it's *men* rather than women that I'm talking about because, although Argentina has had one woman president in recent years, women generally in Argentina are very much on the next rung down. This situation derives from the so-called 'macho' tradition which dominates male-female and male-male relationships in Argentina and the rest of Latin America . . . inherited of course from Spain. This attaches to all males the mystique of dominance and imbues many men with attitudes of either real or affected superiority and aggression. All of which is pretty bad news when it comes to trying to run a country on democratic lines and developing viable economic policies.

Politically, Argentina has been a disaster area for most of this century. There has been a succession of dictators either seizing power or being put in or removed at the whim of the military hierarchy of the time. The tragedy is that very few of them have been able, or if they were able, given the chance, to do anything positive about making Argentina into the rich and prosperous nation it could be.

There is an exception. In this century one name stands out in Argentina more than any other: Peron. Juan Domingo Peron, who ruled the country as an absolute dictator between 1946 and 1955 and again, after almost eighteen years of exile, from 1973 until his death in 1974.

Peron at least had the opportunity and the time to do something and the impact of his leadership on Argentina was enormous. Perhaps the most significant long-term effect is that he left 'Peronism', a vague sort of political ideology, as a legacy. The 'Peronistas' were, during his long exile and are now, after his death, an immensely strong and influential political force in Argentina.

Peron's own political ideology was a strange, highly-personalised mixture of fascism and socialism. Just before World War II he spent several years as an Argentine military attaché in Italy when Mussolini was in power and he returned to Argentina full of fascist ideas. But when he came to power in 1946, in free elections, he introduced sweeping political, social and economic changes, which greatly benefited the working classes in Argentina. Although Peron ran a complete police-state, in which all opposition was brutally crushed, he and his second wife Eva (Evita) Peron, a former dancer and showgirl, were enormously popular with the great mass of Argentine people.

Peron raised minimum pay levels for the working class, reduced working hours, gave women the vote (a radical step in Latin America), greatly expanded education programmes and legalised divorce (even more radical).

Evita, who died of cancer in 1952, was almost certainly the most colourful woman in Argentina's history. Reviled, envied, hated and feared by Argentina's upper classes, she created a sort of class warfare between rich and poor, herself taking the side of the under-privileged, while at the same time living in extravagant luxury far beyond the means of even the richest people in the country.

Evita was always at the centre of every charitable fund-raising function, every effort to raise the living standards of the poor and indeed did a great deal of good in this respect. But in the interests of accuracy it must also be pointed out that she also raised her own living standards to the tune of many millions of dollars. She was an attractive blonde and when she dressed herself up in her jewels and finery for the multitudes, they would cheer her at every step. Her following was enormous.

After Evita's death, something of the mystique of Juan Peron seemed to slip away. He made a number of bad errors of judgement in economic measures and took a couple of foolish steps which undoubtedly led to his downfall in 1955. One was the seizure of the newspaper, La Prensa, the influential Buenos Aires daily which had been critical of him. The other was his legalisation of divorce, which antagonised the church and a large section of the predominantly Roman Catholic community. The act was later repealed, when Peron was not in power.

During the years of his exile in Madrid, where Peron married again, this time to Maria Estella (Isabel) Martinez, a dancer, there were eleven different administrations in Argentina. These included five military juntas, three presidents who were appointed by the military and three who won power through democratic elections. But none of the elected presidents left office without being removed or forced to resign. During the whole period of his exile, the shadow of Peron was over Argentinian politics. To the dismay of the military, who had forced Peron into exile, at every election that was held, Peronista candidates won sweeping victories.

Finally in 1973 the aging Peron was called back to his homeland, receiving a tumultuous welcome and three months later, a landslide victory in presidential elections. But he was old (almost 79) and tired. Within nine months he was dead.

The fairytale continued . . . a little longer. When Juan Peron won back the presidency, his wife Isabel became his vice-president. So when he died, she automatically assumed the presidency. Isabel was a powerful, strong-minded woman, but she wasn't Peron and she wasn't Evita and in the year after Peron's death the country went into a steep slide towards chaos. Argentina experienced runaway inflation of 335 percent! There was a renewal of guerilla violence and severe political instability. Revolutionaries and criminals went on a kidnapping spree resulting in an average of $10 million a month in ransom demands.

In March 1976 Isabel was removed from power by a military junta headed by General Jorge Videla, who, at the time of this writing still holds the presidency. He instituted firm military control over the country and ruthlessly cracked down on all dissidence. But he also is no Peron.

Two items of news coming from Argentina, also around the time of this writing, I think provide interesting comments. Firstly, on the future of President Jorge Videla's administration and secondly on a general state of affairs in Argentine politics. The two extracts speak for themselves.

Nov. 14: The former Naval Commander, Admiral Emilio Massera, on his return from a visit to France, launched into a bitter attack on the government of President Videla. Admiral Massera, who is reported to have presidential ambitions and to be seeking some agreement with the Peronistas, warned that: 'if the government persisted with its policies, it would be bound to produce social tensions in the country'.

Dec. 12: Admiral Emilio Massera narrowly escaped death today in a machine-gun attack on his office in central Buenos Aires. He was unhurt.

Argentinian presidents and juntas have always, it seems, been prepared to resort to pretty heavy tactics in order to stay in power and during the latter half of the seventies the military in Argentina have cracked down hard on dissent of almost any kind. While ostensibly suppressing the extreme violence and terrorism that erupted in the wake of Peron's death and during Isabel Peron's presidency, the army and the secret police have arrested and held thousands without trial and kidnapped, tortured and 'eliminated' many others.

At the end of 1978, the families of 'disappeared' prisoners presented a list of 1542 names to the Supreme Court, demanding an investigation into their fates. There have, however, been few signs that their efforts will find much response. These 1542 people have simply 'disappeared' from the face of the earth. They are either dead with no explanations likely to be made, or mouldering in some foetid Argentinian prison.

Being in Buenos Aires during the World Cup soccer finals it was understandably difficult to sense much of this. The city is very smooth and sophisticated. The people in the city itself are well dressed and apparently reasonably well off by any Western standards. For the time being, at least for the duration of the World Cup, whatever underlying tensions there may have been had been put aside, if not forgotten.

We also had something else to distract us from any serious thoughts while in Buenos Aires. By an extraordinary coincidence, we met, while walking by one of the main squares in the city, the son of some close friends of ours who live in Sydney. Twenty-two-year-old Johnny Dabron, who had been roaming around all of South America on the cheap for the previous twelve months, happened to be in Buenos Aires at the same time as us. We had no idea that he was there. His parents, John and Enid Dabron, *had* told us that he was in South America and that if we were to run into him, to buy him a meal or two, but they had no way of knowing how or when or where we might meet him, because both he and we were constantly on the move.

On our second day in the Argentine capital, we were walking along one side of the Plaza San Martin, heading for the tourist office on Santa Fe Street. Trish and I were in the midst of an argument over something (neither of us can remember what) when suddenly, from nowhere, Johnny Dabron appeared, running up from behind us, grabbing and hugging us and trying to say hello and everything else at once. It was amazing. An incredible coincidence that made that old cliché 'it's a small world' ring absolutely true.

Johnny had had some extraordinary adventures; from being thrown in jail in Ecuador for trying to sell watches in a local market ... to camping next to the great herds of seals on the shores of Patagonia. Now he was hoping to get a job on a ship heading for Europe.

Trish and I immediately forgot our argument and we spent the rest of the day with Johnny wandering about the city ... first to the tourist office, then looking over some of the sights. After a pleasant lunch together we took a bus out to the offices of the Automobile Club of Argentina where we obtained a set of superb maps to cover the last part of our trip through Patagonia and Tierra del Fuego. In the English-language section of a large bookshop we bought some more paperbacks, including *The Lord of the Rings* which Trish and I had both read many years ago, but which was now to become our bedtime reading for Sean and Zara.

That evening, together with Johnny, we all had a chicken dinner followed up by pancakes and beer (Cokes for Zara and Sean) and then just sat around talking in our hotel room until 11.00 p.m. Johnny had a lot to tell us about Patagonia and the South. He had travelled through the beautiful mountains and visited the lakes and glaciers at the foot of the Andean spine along Argentina's western border. We were, of course, looking forward to seeing some of these on our way south ... with one reservation; Johnny had been travelling through southern Argentina in glorious mid-summer weather. We would be doing it now, in mid-winter. Madness.

The centre of Buenos Aires has a pleasing number of parks, varying in size but all well kept, which breaks up the stolid turn-of-the-century architecture. There are very few buildings left from the colonial era.

The Casa Rosada, the Government House where the President conducts official business and holds cabinet meetings, is an exception. It is on Plaza Mayo and as the name suggests was built of rose-coloured stone during Spain's colonial period. It's an attractive building and after we had walked along the front of it, inspecting the guards in their toy soldier outfits, we crossed to the park in the middle of the plaza. This gave a distant view of greater realism, for then we could see quite plainly the two fellows on the roof wearing camouflage fatigues and carrying automatic weapons.

Iain and I were busy, stealthily changing lenses so as to get a shot of these men, and trying to look nonchalantly as if we were doing nothing of the sort, when a loud shout made us jump, guiltily.

We turned to see a man in a park-keeper's uniform waving his arms and yelling angrily at Zara and Sean who had been rolling about on the grass in mock battle. He shooshed them onto the path and they ran across to us. Zara, unaccustomed to being chastised by strangers, for a fairly normal display of high spirits, was flushed with emotion.

We commiserated with them, under the keeper's glare, and then distracted their attention by pointing out the men on the roof.

Having taken the shots which we wanted, we went on across the park to the cathedral on the other side, passing on the way the same keeper, still trying to prevent intruders from defiling his perfect lawns, only this time they were pigeons!

'He's mad,' Zara pronounced, still aggrieved.

A little perhaps, but it was again only the first of several incidents in which the children, behaving as children do, brought incredulous stares from people used to only ultra-formal behaviour.

The cathedral was not very attractive from the outside or ornate inside, with the exception of the massive, yet elegant, tomb of the liberator, General José de San Martin, honoured in death as he had never been in life. It is guarded perpetually by soldiers in the nineteenth century red and blue uniform of San Martin's Grenadiers.

What's interesting about the cathedral and other churches in Buenos Aires is not what they contain, but what they do not. In June 1955, at the end of Peron's time in power, there were very nasty anti-Catholic riots and severe damage was done to church property.

In the Church of San Ignacio de Loyola, the oldest colonial building in the city, all religious ornaments were smashed beyond repair and the vestry was burnt to the ground. The invaluable library at the Archbishop's Palace, which contained historical records of the River Plate since 1660, was completely destroyed. Colonial archives, ornaments and precious vestments were smashed and burnt in churches throughout the city in a night of terror which shocked even Argentines, accustomed to excess. The rampage did Peron's image irremediable harm.

The rest of the morning was spent gathering information with which to plan our onward trip. We had at this point to decide whether or not to go across the country to the south west, sixteen hundred kilometres or so to the famous winter resort of Bariloche, at the foot of the eastern slope of the Andes and on the border with Chile. Because roads south from Bariloche to Tierra del Fuego were, by this stage of the winter, closed with snow, it would be necessary to return from Bariloche across the country to the eastern coast in order to continue south.

The alternative to this was to stick to the east coast and visit instead the desolate Valdez Peninsula, fourteen hundred kilometres south, where there were wild herds of sea elephants, seals and penguins.

But either way we were in for an awful shock. At the railway station, we discovered that tickets for the one-and-half-day trip to Bariloche were US$40 each, no reduction for the children. Reeling from that blow we approached the bus depot only to find that the twenty-four hour trip to Puerto Madryn, from where one took off onto the Valdez Peninsula, would cost us US$27 each!

We checked the current guide book which put the cost of these journeys as a manageable US$17. Perhaps there was a mistake. Maybe we were being quoted in old pesos, a disconcerting habit we'd come to be wary of. But no. The government tourist bureau and a couple of private travel agents confirmed these prices as correct. When we asked why the jump in price, the staff in these offices just shrugged their shoulders. 'Inflation.'

We began to get twinges of consternation. While we had done well with the hotel and fairly well with the meals so far, it seemed that something drastic had happened to transportation costs. When we met up with Johnny he confirmed this and spread more gloom by stating that the further south we went the higher the costs would go. If we had known then just how very right he was, how very high they would go, we might even have been tempted to call it a day right there in Buenos Aires. As it was we decided to give Bariloche the miss, seeing it was more or less just a fashionable and beautiful skiing resort and plump for the unusual wild animals of Valdez.

To try to take our minds off money, we visited the Colon Theatre. Urban Argentines are very culturally sophisticated people. The city is the publishing centre for South America; it has many bookshops and several newspapers and periodicals which are highly-regarded internationally. There are also more than a dozen theatres of which the Colon is the great grand-daddy. It is one of the world's great opera houses and has its own National Symphony Orchestra and probably the finest season in Latin America.

It seats two and a half thousand, with standing room for another two thousand and still keeps to a peculiar habit commented on by Charles Darwin who visited in 1833; two of the seven levels are reserved; one for men only and one for women only. In the other five tiers, which go to create the overall effect of a red plush and gold tasselled wedding cake, men and women cohabit!

The stage looks almost as large as a football field, especially from the stained glass dome ceiling, which we reached by a nerve-racking climb up and over the iron innards. We were the only visitors and our guide let us sit in the circular pit over the giant chandelier sometimes occupied by part of the opera chorus.

The acoustics are superb and the slight delay caused by placing some of the performers separately at this distance from the stage gives an interesting musical effect. The only effect it had on me, peering down to the proscenium almost thirty metres below was that it took my voice away.

On our way back to the hotel we met the Somali crew of a Greek ship which had been based in Western Australia for a year. In our odd combination of languages we conversed and found that their ship was now on its way home to Europe, so Johnny arranged to visit the ship down at the port in the morning to see if he could work his passage over with them.

It seemed ridiculous for us to be in Argentina at the time of the World Cup soccer finals and not try to see a game. Sean had played a few seasons of little league soccer back home and was keen to see the world's best players in action. But it wasn't going to be easy.

We were in Buenos Aires in the week of the quarter-final elimination games, during which sixteen national teams; ten European and four Latin American, would be reduced to eight. But even for these preliminary matches there were no seats available for any of the games being played in the huge River Plate Stadium. It may have been possible to find seats at some of the other matches being played in stadiums in other Argentinian cities, but the only game we could realistically try to see was the Argentina versus France match in Buenos Aires on June 6th. When we tried to obtain seats however it was impossible . . . booked solid. There were several cinema houses in the city centre which would be showing live, wide-screen, colour, tele-projections of the game, but they were also booked out and had long queues waiting for games several days away.

The city was in the grip of 'Mundial' fever and all 'Portenos' seemed to have caught it long before their country even looked like getting anywhere in the Cup. As Trish has said, mobs of chanting and flag-waving fans were common sights in the city streets and from every record shop and on every radio blared the latest Argentinian hit record with the chorus . . . 'AR-GEN-TINA, AR-GEN-TINA'.

In the end we decided to take our chances at the stadium itself on the night of the game, on the off-chance that there might be some scalpers selling tickets.

Unfortunately I was late getting back to the hotel from the bus station where

I had gone to buy our tickets for the trip south the following day to Puerto Madryn. So by the time we set off for the stadium it was 6.45 p.m. and the game was due to start at 7.30. Because there were no taxis to be found, we had to walk ten blocks to the Retiro railway station and took a twenty-minute train ride to an outer suburb, then walked another six blocks through streets closed to traffic, to the River Plate Stadium, arriving at 8.15 p.m., by which time the first half was almost over.

It was quite strange as we approached the stadium, because around the outside of the enormous building (we made a circuit to see if there was anyone selling tickets) there were not more than twenty people ... apart from the officials and armed policemen who stood at the gates ... and yet we knew and could hear that upwards of 100,000 people were inside the huge concrete structure, chanting and roaring their approval or dismay at whatever turn the game took.

A few minutes after we arrived outside the stadium, the half-time bell rang and we were told that the score was Argentina, one, France, one. We begged to be able to buy a ticket and even tried to bribe one of the officials on the gate. I made rather obvious gestures with an American ten dollar bill, but the officials seemed incorruptible. At one gate, however, a young man was more helpful.

'Diez minutos,' he said. Come back in ten minutes.

So in ten minutes time after the game had just started into the second half, he looked about to see that there was no one else watching and gave the four of us and three other people who had been standing by, the nod to run up the stairs into the stadium. I offered him the ten dollar bill as we moved past, but he smiled and refused. 'No necesario,' he said.

We wound our way right into the upper stands. Naturally there was no way of finding a seat, and we had to stand behind a crowd of other people who had crammed into the aisles and walkways in order to see the field. But it was all brilliantly lit by arc-lights and with Zara and Sean on our shoulders we all had a chance to see some of the action.

The lights of a big 747 lumbered across the night-sky above us, the captain of the aircraft probably purposely making a pass over the stadium. I could imagine him saying over the intercom as everybody craned to look out of the windows, 'and, on your right, below us, is the River Plate Stadium, all lit-up, where at the moment Argentina is playing France ...'

Something like 1000 million people in 91 countries around the world watched the World Cup matches on television and they almost certainly had a closer view of the game than we did, but it was terrific to actually be there in the midst of it all. It was superb football; wonderful passing and brilliant goal-keeping on both sides. The entire crowd was in a state of high excitement. Great booming chants of 'AR-GEN-TINA' would roll across the enormous stands. The pressure on the French team, playing in the face of such massive pro-Argentina support, must have been tremendous, yet they kept Argentina at bay until five minutes before the final bell, when Argentina scored.

The crowd became almost hysterical and in fact, quite frightening. They were on their feet ... 100,000 people ... chanting, 'AR-GEN-TINA'. But with each shouted syllable they were either stamping their feet or jumping, so that the massive concrete stands ... the giant pre-stressed, suspended balconies ...

were actually rocking and vibrating. I had visions of the whole damned stadium coming tumbling down.

A minute before the final bell, we left, running quickly down the staircase from the top levels to make our way out into the roadway. At the bottom of the steps we heard the final bell, but we were well in front of the great crowd that came pouring from the stadium and after making our way back to a main road where there were lines of taxis waiting, we took the first one on the rank and within less than half an hour we were back in our hotel room.

But if we thought we had seen a World Cup soccer match and that was that . . . we were wrong. Mobs of shouting and singing Argentinians took over the streets of the city and we could hear cries of 'AR-GEN-TINA, AR-GEN-TINA' until well after 3.00 o'clock in the morning.

ARGENTINA

24
A wild and desolate place

We delayed leaving for the bus depot in the morning for as long as possible, having arranged with Johnny that he would come by and tell us whether or not his meeting with the ship's captain had been successful. But when he hadn't arrived by eight-thirty, we had to leave a message for him at the desk and take a taxi across town to the suburb from which the bus for Puerto Madryn left at a quarter past nine.

It wasn't until six months later that we heard from Johnny's mother that he had persuaded the captain to take him on and that from Lisbon he had cycled up through Portugal, Spain and France to turn up on relatives in the UK.

Beyond the immediate central areas of Buenos Aires the houses, factories and offices became scruffier and the streets less well kept. The airs, as in all big cities and despite the city's name, were far from good. Buenos Aires sprawls on for thirty kilometres or so, but even after that it was some time before we finally shook ourselves free of the overbearing big city presence and began to experience that swell of excitement which comes when horizons open out. And here they really did!

This was the Argentine pampas, the flat land which spreads out in a great semi-circle for six hundred or so kilometres from Buenos Aires and is the economic heartland of the nation. It covers only a fifth of the total area of the country but 67 percent of Argentines live in it. It contains 86 percent of the land used for cereal (mostly wheat), 65 percent of the cattle, 40 percent of the sheep and 90 percent of all the industrial production.

It was the taming of the pampas which was directly responsible for the growth of the Argentine. When the Spanish first saw the area it was covered with two-and a-half-metre high tussocks of coarse grass. In gratitude for virtually exterminating the Indian population during the genocidal wars against them between 1878 and 1883, the government, which had no money with which to reward its soldiers, awarded them instead vast tracts of land. This was how the traditional pattern of huge properties, run on paternalistic lines, with near-slave labour, came into being. To this day descendants of those army officers still own the great estancias.

Cattle and horses, which the Spanish soldiers had brought with them, were turned loose on the land and multiplied with a rapidity almost comparable to the rabbit explosion in Australia. Finer European grasses were imported, along with English bulls to upgrade the herds. The same was done with sheep by bringing in English rams. But still, all this would have created little financial reward but for the introduction, in 1877, of the first ship with refrigeration chambers. This made it possible to send frozen meat to the burgeoning European population and from that point Argentina's economy was on its feet and running.

The estancia owners, almost all Spanish-born, saw themselves as an aristocracy rather than just farmers. When some of their tenants began to plant wheat, they regarded this contemptuously as peasant-labour.

Such was the rigidity of their snobbery that this attitude holds true to this day, even though Argentina's large wheat production is now at least half of the reason why the country has the second highest standard of living in Latin America, after oil-rich Venezuela.

Gentlemen grow beef, farmers grow wheat and Italians and Yugoslavs grow vegetables. This is the attitude which still prevails in Argentina today. They have almost as fossilised an (anti-)social (de)structure as the British.

Around midday we stopped at a small cantina which looked like a deserted child's toy in a gigantic spread of flatness. We ordered from the menu, cautious now to watch prices. Soup, salad, tea and bread. It was not good, being either cold, limp or stale. We had worked out that the bill should come to about 3900 pesos (just over US$5), so when the waiter brought a scrawled list which added up to 5700 pesos (US$7.60) we protested.

The waiter was adamant. More staff came across. We were embarrassed but determined to stick to our guns: 3900 pesos was already too much for the lousy food; 5700 was exorbitant and unacceptable.

Eventually one waiter, who spoke more clearly and precisely than ours, who no doubt was shouting in a rapid-fire manner because he was cross with us for questioning his bill, explained to us where our calculations had gone wrong.

Yes, the charge for the actual food was indeed 3900 pesos, but here was the catch; there were two additional amounts to be added: a 20 percent service charge, steep but fair enough, and a 22 percent charge for the use of knives and forks! Presumably if we had brought our own, or drunk our soup from the bowl we could have avoided this fee. Only then did we understand why the other passengers had all eaten sandwiches!

The next stop, in the early evening, was at Bahia Blanca. Here we changed buses and braved another canteen, this time ordering ham and cheese rolls. At the time of our visit the Argentine peso was valued at between 750 and 770 to US$1.00. One result of a peso being so worthless was that it was necessary for waiters, even in small canteens like this one, to carry enormous wads of ten, twenty, fifty, hundred and thousand peso bills in order to give change.

Sean, who shows definite signs of incipient frugality bordering on tight-fistedness, thought he'd died and gone to heaven when his collected pocketmoney was changed into a pile of these dirty, tired notes, many of them worn into holes and patched together.

He'd pull them out of his pocket and flourish them like the last of the big spenders. Licking his fingers, he'd flick-count them like a bank teller, or Scrooge.

That night, as the bus continued on across the flat landscape, it became very cold. Although there were enough empty seats to allow us a double each in which to spread out, we couldn't sleep well because the bus had no heating and the raw chill kept us awake.

On one of the few occasions when I had managed to drop off I was roughly shaken awake and sat suddenly bolt upright to come face to face with a soldier dressed in a heavyweight khaki uniform. Somewhat in a state of shock, my mind raced with hideous possibilities, only to find that we had been stopped by a road block.

The soldiers came down the aisle methodically checking the locals' IDs and our passports. The unnerving thing about them was that, unlike the illiterate rag-tag mob who'd done the same thing in Ecuador, this bunch was smartly dressed, knew what they were doing and were efficient enough to have a list against which they checked all the passengers' names.

It sent shivers down my spine to think that if my name had been on their list there was no way I could have avoided the consequences.

On July 28th, 1865, the stretch of coast where Puerto Madryn now stands was nothing more than a deserted beach backed by seemingly endless kilometres of open pampas, most of which was hostile Indian territory. And yet, on that day, a hardy group of Welsh pioneer immigrants stepped ashore, aiming to push inland across the dry plains to start a settlement in the Chubut River valley. The nearest other Europeans were some 320 kilometres to the north, at Patagones, on the mouth of the Rio Negro.

The intention of the colony was to start 'a little Wales beyond Wales'. After the first settlers had established themselves they were later reinforced by other immigrants from Wales and the United States, but always the Welsh language was taught and preserved, so that now, in the fifth generation, although the language has begun to die out, there are still some seven or eight thousand people in Chubut Province who speak Welsh as their first language and Spanish second.

When we pulled in to Puerto Madryn at 9.30 a.m. we were greeted by a group of about a dozen soldiers armed with automatic rifles. They were all very young National Servicemen . . . no more than 18 or 19 years old, except perhaps their officer who was about 21 or 22. They were all pink-faced with the cold, as there was a bitter wind blowing, and steel helmets don't do much to keep your head warm.

As we disembarked, they inspected everybody's travel documents and searched some people's baggage. I asked the officer why they were carrying out the search and received the rather disarming reply . . . 'Futebol'.

Football? When I persevered and tried to establish what he meant, he just smiled and continued with what he was doing without replying.

The bus station, our introduction to Puerto Madryn, was also the railway station; a small, lonely Victorian-looking building on an open piece of land across which the train line stretched off towards the south-west.

After a cup of coffee in the heated snack-room of the station we made our way towards the centre of the town through cold and relatively empty streets, looking for the Hotel Vasconia, which the woman in the snack-room had recommended to us. Finding it, we checked in to a small, bare room containing four beds. There was a separate bathroom across an open courtyard, but at least it had hot water . . . we'd checked on that before we moved in. There were only two other guests in the whole hotel, which was fairly primitive, having no heating other than a small, antiquated kerosene heater which the manager gave us to put in the room. He sat most of the day in front of a wood-fire, burning in the jumbled front room which combined as a dining room, lounge and bar with no set divisions between them.

After settling in and having a nice, hot shower, we went for a walk about the town, which, being small and flat and laid out in squares, was very easy to look over quickly. There were no buildings higher than two storeys and the streets were wide and well-sealed. But at 11.00 a.m. that Thursday morning they were still empty. It seemed that we were the only tourists crazy enough to visit Puerto Madryn in mid-winter.

In summer of course the place would have been packed out. We had seen some of the brochures and had had a quiet, little curse to ourselves. One of them for Puerto Madryn said, 'The town is the centre for all touristic activity and underwater diving on the Valdez Peninsula. It is situated at the lower end of the Golfo Nuevo with a sea-view of great beauty. It is lit in summer by eighteen hours of sunlight each day, endowed with a dry climate and temperatures of up to thirty-two degrees celsius.'

In the frosty conditions we were experiencing it was hard to believe. But still, at least the seals and sea elephants out on the peninsula wouldn't be worried by the cold . . . we were reasonably sure of that. So we set about trying to find out how to get out there to see them. It would involve a 160-kilometre round-trip to the far east coast of the peninsula, with nowhere out there to stay.

In the summer for $3.50 each we could have taken a bus, but now there were no buses running. We asked about car rentals . . . nothing doing. It would be possible, we were told, to take a taxi for the day but the quoted price, 80,000 pesos ($105) was way too high for us.

At the offices of Centro Nacional Patagonicos, a sort of regional administration organization, a man called Tito told us to talk to a man called Gustavo who might take us out onto the Valdez Peninsula in his van for a fee. Gustavo, when we eventually found him at the address given us by Tito, was a pleasant-looking moustachioed young man of about twenty-five.

'Yes,' he said, he could take us out to the peninsula on the following day for 40,000 pesos ($52.50), exactly half the taxi fare. It was still very expensive compared to the summer bus fares, but there was nothing else to do. We accepted and arranged for him to pick us up at eight in the morning.

Later in the afternoon we bought some bread and cheese and various tinned foods at a small store and back at the hotel produced our little stove again to cook up a hot meal of frankfurters, corn, green beans and tomatoes. Then, climbing into our sleeping bags, as the room, even with the kerosene heater going, was still cold, we started in to reading *Lord of the Rings*.

My cold was continuing to hang around and although it hadn't bothered me much during the day the cough returned that night. Then Zara began coughing badly also. We gave her some cough medicine and just crossed our fingers with the hope that it would not deteriorate into the type of severe chest-cold she had had back in Pucallpa at the start of the river trip.

The Valdez Peninsula is the largest on the Atlantic coast and juts out into the ocean like a gigantic hammerhead, almost enclosing, to the north, the Golfo San Jose and to the south, the Golfo Nuevo.

Because these bays are so very nearly encircled, the effect of the ocean waves is greatly reduced and the waters in them are calm and transparent to a depth of a thirty-six metres. Forests of gigantic seaweed and kelp thrive there and herds of sea wolves, sea elephants, whales, killer whales, dolphins, seals and an immense variety of other sea life are attracted to the region.

French explorer and 'oceanologist' Jacques Yves Cousteau has declared that the area is one of the prime spots in the world for engaging in underwater sports. The Argentine government has set the entire peninsula aside as a protected wild life reserve.

It was still dark when Gustavo's Dodge truck, large enough to seat ten people, picked us up. It was so cold that even though we wore layers of clothes under our anoraks we still sat inside our sleeping bags in the truck. But a little under three hours later, after we had covered the one hundred and sixty kilometres of totally deserted gravel road crossing the flat, barren scrub to Punta Norte, on the northern-most tip of the peninsula, the sun was up and the chill lifted from the air.

I had never seen sea elephants before, not even in a zoo, so I wasn't prepared for their enormous bulk. The males must have been all of three metres long and the females were not much smaller. There was no way of telling, just by looking at them how much they weighed and I have since searched around and been unable to come up with that information, but it must be at least nine hundred kilos. Great cumbersome, unwieldy lumps of flab, they slumped on the sand, mountains of heaving blubber.

We got to within six metres of them, having been told that they only became aggressive if cut off from their retreat path to the sea. They were very impressive in their obese bulk and I could quite happily have spent a whole day watching their antics. Animals in the wild bear little resemblance to those in captivity. Here we visited on their terms and there was none of that air of degradation and desperation which hangs over zoos.

They watched us as we watched them. Occasionally one would lumber a little closer as if wanting to get a better view of our odd bodies. Several of them flopped down to the sea, there to become immediately transformed into svelte, sleek, elegant and beautiful swimming machines; as totally at ease in the water as they were totally uneasy on land.

Punta Norte is the only place on the continent which has a colony of sea elephants. They are of the Mirounga Leonina species and come here to have their cubs and to mate. Their name derives from the growth which the males have on their snout and which they can expand to over half a metre. It certainly doesn't add to their beauty, but it also doesn't seem to be any hindrance, for they are all polygamous and one male may have harems of up to as many as eight or ten females which he defends ferociously from other male intruders.

Zara and Sean were of course enchanted and tried calling to them in the hope of getting them to reply, for when they did struggle up onto their flippers and open their cavernous mouths, they emitted a most thrilling, harsh scream and gave a tremendous view of their large teeth and gulping throats.

On the sand dunes above the beach, we sat outside the ranger's solitary stone house and made up some sandwiches. The ranger's wife came out to hang up some washing and her four-year-old daughter brought their black and white cat and their white terrier to be introduced to us. What a magic childhood she will have to remember ... living there within metres of those magnificent sea creatures.

Back across the peninsula on the Golfo Nuevo, we stopped at Porto Pyramides. It was a small settlement of only a few houses and one hotel which must do good business in the summer. Gustavo dropped us there while he went to visit a friend in the village and we talked to the hotel proprietor.

He was interested in our trip and while showing us around his attractive little hotel, asked us the inevitable questions about what we thought of Argentina and how it compared with other countries in South America. We churned out the expected banalities and were only critical of some of the high prices. He was surprised and said that he didn't think things were so expensive. Then he charged us just over five dollars for two coffees and two Cokes!

When Gustavo returned, we drove on to the top of a cliff from where we could look down on a large colony of seals, some twelve to fifteen metres below. Being considerably smaller than the sea elephants, they were far more agile. They bunched together in lumps of convulsed flesh, barking at and clambering over one another.

It was by then early afternoon and in the comparatively warm air, the sunlight reflected on the constant motion of the ocean so that it sparkled. Fluffy-furred babies stayed close to their mums while dozens of teenagers basked in the clear water or seemingly raced against one another, diving and surfacing with enviable ease.

It was a nourishingly happy scene made complete by a small band of penguins who were probably visiting from the large colony which nests at Camarones, about three hundred kilometres to the south. It is suggested that these endearing birds, with their Chaplinesque gait and fabulous aquatic skill were first named 'pengwyn' or 'white head', by a Welshman who in 1586 was a member of an expedition which landed some six hundred kilometres south of the Valdez Peninsula. Another theory is that the name derives from the Spanish word, pingue, meaning fat. Whichever it is, they are tremendously entertaining to watch and it was interesting that two quite separate species, bird and mammal were so willing to share the same environment.

Again we could have gone on happily watching their antics for hours and hours, but Gustavo was sensibly anxious to get home before dark. On the way we stopped once more, this time on the isthmus which connects the peninsula to the mainland. Here, on an 800-metre-square islet about 300 metres offshore, thousands upon thousands of cormorants, gulls, herons, seagulls and ducks come to nest in spring. But the shore was deserted now in winter, so we wandered along the water's edge admiring the shells and searching rock pools for tiny sea creatures.

A little to the west of us was the natural estuary of the Rio San José which has an incredible difference of nearly twenty-seven metres between high and low water mark.

It was chill again and the shadows were lengthening as we began the journey back to Puerto Madryn. We had seen no other cars all day and felt that sort of quiet calm which comes only from natural sources of pleasure.

Getting up early in the morning is not nearly so odious if the weather is warm and it soon becomes light. But when it is freezing cold and dark it's a hell of an occupation. A quarter past six in the morning is not all that early, but in Puerto Madryn it seemed like the middle of the night.

We made ourselves some cheese and salami sandwiches and a cup of coffee, then headed for the bus depot at about 7.30, but even then the streets were dark and deserted and swept by a biting wind. It seemed more and more, the further south we travelled, as if all of the inhabitants of the towns we visited had gone into hibernation. And I didn't blame them.

The same young National Servicemen were on hand at the bus station (again pink-faced and shivering with cold) waiting to meet the bus coming south from Bahia Blanca which we would be catching. They smiled at us in recognition and we smiled back. We were not required to pass a second check by them as they were apparently only interested in incoming passengers. Not exactly a fun job at the best of times, but in this weather, just about the bitter end. The Argentine Army is a national militia in which all males between the ages of twenty and forty-five must give at least two years full-time service. Checking people's baggage was obviously part of it, but I can think of better ways to pass two years.

Within twenty minutes or so our bus had arrived and we were on our way south for what was to be an eight-hour run to Comodoro Rivadavia. For the first three-quarters of an hour or so we were travelling in darkness and we read by the small reading lamps above the seats.

Just after dawn we arrived at Trelew, another of the areas in which the early pioneers from Wales had settled. As we stepped off the bus to get a cup of coffee during the brief stopover, we were once again met by helmeted and armed soldiers waiting to inspect documents and check baggage. Their interest in us, however, was only perfunctory and we were quickly passed over. As we moved off in the direction of the small cafeteria, a voice in fluent English said from behind us, 'Are you English?'

We turned to see an elderly woman who had been a passenger on the bus, but who was obviously leaving it here at Trelew. We briefly explained our various origins and then, interested in what another foreigner was doing in these parts at this time of year, put the same question to her. Of course she wasn't English, but Welsh, and as soon as she spoke a little more, we could hear the pleasant lilt in her voice. But she was quick to make the point about herself and others like her that, 'No, we're not Welsh any longer. We are Argentinians.'

'But you still speak Welsh, don't you?' I said. 'I've read that there are still whole communities here that have kept the language.'

'Oh, yes,' she said, 'I speak it . . . and there are still quite a few others who do, but . . .' she paused and looked around. There was just a touch of nervousness about her. 'The government does not want to encourage it. It would prefer that the language died out . . . that we all spoke only Spanish.'

Beryl Llewellyn was a small grey-haired woman of about 65, I would guess. Her face was round and pale, but her blue eyes were lively and alert.

'You are from Australia . . .' she said to me. 'I always wanted my son to go there . . . to emigrate to Australia. But he has married an Argentinian girl and they have gone to live in the Chaco.' (the vast, forested plains in northern Argentina). She seemed disappointed as she said it.

'Do you have other children?' Trish asked her.

'Yes. A daughter. She lives in Buenos Aires. I have been visiting her there. Have you been to Buenos Aires?'

'Yes,' I said. 'We also have just come from there. We are on our way south.'

'It was very calm, don't you think?'

We weren't quite sure what to say, particularly as we had felt that the city had been in a state of high tension over the 'futebol'. 'Yes, I suppose so,' I said. 'Why do you say that?'

She looked around again; the soldiers had moved away. 'No army,' she said softly. 'I saw no soldiers. There was no trouble the whole time I was there. No killings.'

'Are there normally?'

Her eyebrows raised a fraction and she gave a sort of resigned smile. 'All my life there has been violence and revolution in Argentina. I used to live in Buenos Aires, but when my husband died I came down here to get away from it all.'

'Do you live in Trelew?' I asked.

'No, I have a farm about twenty kilometres away. It's only a small place . . . about fifty or so head of cattle, but it keeps me busy and most of all I love the space here . . . and the freedom.'

The road, as we pressed on southward, was a dead-straight ribbon of tar that cut across a landscape absolutely flat from horizon to horizon; immense dull-brown, grassy plains, on which even the occasional low salt brush stood out sufficiently to attract attention.

Patagonia, the vast, low plateau across which we were now travelling, covers some 770,000 square kilometres, yet has a population of little more than 600,000. There are large areas which average less than one person for every seven square kilometres. It is a wild, desolate place, generally blown, in both summer and winter, by strong winds and yet there is very little rain . . . only 20 or 22 centimetres, most of which falls during the winter.

We had actually entered the territory of Patagonia a few days previously, when we were coming south to Puerto Madryn. Patagonia's official northern boundary is the Rio Colorado, but it extends almost all the way to the southern tip of the continent. The name Patagonia comes from the nickname given by Spanish explorers to the original Indians who inhabited the land in the extreme south. They called them 'Patacones', meaning 'big-feet', because that apparently is what they had. These Indians were almost entirely wiped out during the so-called 'Indian Wars' of 1878 to 1883 which should more accurately be termed the Indian Eradication Programme.

The parts of Patagonia that are used for agriculture are generally devoted to sheep . . . some fifteen million of them. But there is also a wide variety of wildlife which seems to flourish under what most of us would regard as not very attractive conditions. These include guanacos (a creature not unlike a small llama) and rheas, or ostriches. We saw scores of these big birds grazing on the open plains almost side-by-side with groups of guanacos. They would run off at high speed as the bus passed by.

The coastline of Patagonia, or rather the Atlantic Ocean next to it, is also exceptionally rich in sea life and yet there is no Argentinian fishing industry of any size along the coast. The reason? Apparently because Argentinians are such big meat-eaters — consuming more meat per capita than any other country in the world, in comparative terms — they are just not interested in fish.

For most of the afternoon as we barrelled along over that wide, brown land, I found it difficult to take much interest in my surroundings. My head was completely blocked, my nose was running and I felt absolutely lousy. Zara's cough was somewhat better, but she certainly didn't feel a hundred percent.

At about 3.30 in the afternoon the road turned sharply eastwards, heading down from the plateau towards the coast. The sky had a clear, transparent look about it; it was a pale, weak blue, streaked at tremendous altitudes by thin, white cirrus stratus clouds that were misty at the edges. Within fifteen minutes or so we were pulling in to Comodoro Rivadavia.

Comodoro Rivadavia is not a place I would care to be stuck in for any length of time. Not wishing to be negative I have searched my memory and my notes for something pleasant to say about the town, but I'm afraid that I've failed to come up with anything. At the time, I thought it must surely be the lowest spot on the trip, but I was wrong, there was one worse yet to go.

The town, which has 70,000 inhabitants, looks surprised to be there. It's a jumble of ill-matched buildings whose main reason for existence is a nearby petrochemical plant and the fact that 28 percent of Argentina's oil production comes from wells just forty kilometres inland. A pipeline also carries the natural gas from here over sixteen hundred kilometres to Buenos Aires.

Iain and Sean braved the howling, bitter wind to find a hotel but had to try eight before finding one with an empty room. The general lack of accommodation in the town was due not to a horde of visitors (again we were the only ones visible), but to the influx of employees of the petrochemical plant. But at least the room, when we got to it, was buzzing with warmth from the central heating.

From the bar downstairs and the small 'supermercado' next door, where we bought some food to cook up in our room, it was obvious that Comodoro Rivadavia also had an army base in the vicinity. Dozens of callow youths, their ears and necks painfully exposed to the cold by short-back-and-sides haircuts and wearing bulky uniforms, eyed us, obvious foreigners, with suspicion.

Despite the fact that Argentines like to imagine that they are the white bastion on a continent of polyglots, in Comodoro Rivadavia and from there on south, it was obvious that many of the people had Indian forebears. They were smaller, with sturdy widespread legs, heavy brows, very black hair and had the same barrel chests we had noticed among Andean Indians in Ecuador and Peru.

That night in the bar, we watched the live television coverage of the quarter-final World Cup game between Italy and Argentina. The room was crowded with young servicemen and older men who looked like very regular patrons. Zara and I were the only females.

The complicated method of adding up the goals scored in the matches so far meant that no matter whether Argentina won or lost this match, she still would go on to play in the semi-finals, whereas if Italy lost she would be out of the competition.

So naturally, from the outset I thought it would be nice if Italy could win. This feeling was reinforced when after each team had scored a goal early on in the match, the nationalistic tension in the bar room was positively electric. Anyway, I've always been one for the underdog.

To the Argentines this was more than a mere football match. On the shoulders of those eleven men in blue and white striped shirts rested the honour of their country. It didn't matter that they didn't need to win this match, they wanted not just to win but to rub everybody else into insignificance.

Ridiculous. I loathe playing any game with the sort of person who must win, to whom a game of Scrabble is a threat to their ego. Childish and boring.

All this muscle-pumping nationalism was beginning to get up my nose, but then the Argentine team finished themselves as far as I was concerned. With the score even and the final whistle drawing near they were desperate to get extra time, so on every occasion when there was any little scrimmage one of the Argentine players would fall to the ground clutching his groin, or his stomach, or knees, or even his head and lie writhing in a pretence of agony in the hope of getting a penalty kick or some additional penalty time.

It was so blatant a ploy that I began to groan loudly and even to boo. It was this unsporting behaviour on the part of the team and the equally unsporting behaviour of the almost totally Argentinian crowd in the stadium, who cheered their team and booed the Italians, that propelled me from my seat to give a hearty cheer when, less than five minutes before the final whistle, Italy scored a second goal.

Well! The atmosphere in that room full of Argentine males, nursing their shattered machismo, was so silently frosty that, despite the central heating, we were in danger of getting chilblains. But when Italy retained their lead to the end, I was so delighted that I didn't care if I had upset them. I was so pleased that I didn't even mind Iain throwing a wobbly once we were upstairs about my partisan bad manners.

Actually I excused him not only because I was so happy over the result, but also because I knew he was feeling lousy with his heavy cold. The next day it was no better. One side of his jaw ached, and the adjacent ear and nostril blocked, so that I feared he had a severe sinus infection.

Despite this, after breakfast in our room, we decided that as there were no buses going on south until the next day, we would try hitching. There was nothing for which to stay on in Comodoro Rivadavia so we loaded our packs, which were considerably lighter now that we were wearing so much clothing, and took a cab to the edge of town.

We propped our packs neatly side-on to the roadway, so as to make them appear as small as possible, and stood by, ready to smile at the drivers of approaching vehicles. The trouble was that hardly any approached and those few which did smiled back and indicated that they were turning off on a small dirt road a few hundred metres further on, which we guessed led down to the petrochemical plant.

It was utter madness, but for an hour and three-quarters we stood in below freezing temperatures and a bitter wind hoping for a lucky break. We were each wearing T-shirts, long-sleeved shirts, sweaters, padded anoraks and on top of all that lightweight waterproof jackets which were supposed to be wind breakers, but which did nothing to break this wild one. Sean had even succumbed to Zara's and my habit of wearing two pairs of nylon tights under his jeans, but still he was shivering.

We tried telling jokes, asking riddles, playing five stone and hopscotch, all in an attempt to keep our minds off the cold. But it was futile and finally we ran out of enthusiasm and began hoping that one of the others would suggest giving in. I can't remember who eventually made the suggestion, but we all quickly agreed and caught a lift at a nearby garage back to the same hotel, only to find that the central heating had packed up.

I would have been quite happy to spend the rest of the day in my bed, reading and writing because, as I said before, there is nothing special to see or do in Comodoro Rivadavia, but if Iain is in a new place, an irresistible urge demands of him that he must inspect it. So, despite his aching face and the biting cold, we went out again heading in the direction of the waterfront.

En route, Sean, who was just about going bananas with being shut up in buses and hotel rooms, kept challenging me to sparring matches. Well, it helped to battle the cold and anyway I give myself only another year, at the outside, before he will be too strong for me to take on. So, working on the principle that I should establish my position of power while still able, I played along. Every couple of hundred metres we'd have a mock battle, land a few harmless punches and chase one another along the sidewalk, leaping out from shop doorways or from behind low walls.

After several blocks of this tomfoolery I saw, up ahead, a man in a heavy overcoat cross to our side of the street. As Sean dashed by him, he put up his hand to stop my pursuit.

In good English he asked, 'You are his mother?'

As Sean and I were wearing identical brightly-patterned anoraks, this was a fairly obvious assumption and I didn't seriously think that he could be anxious that I was a complete stranger. So I replied, 'Yes, sure.'

'Aaah!' he nodded, seemingly satisfied, 'and you are English.'

It was a statement, not a question. He was sure that only a foreign mother behaved like this in public with her son. It's for sure that an Argentinian would not.

At the risk of sounding repetitive, I have to relate that once again we rose early, in the dark, to catch a bus. But this particular morning sticks just a little more in the memory than all the others, if only for the fact that 'early' on this occasion meant 3.30 a.m.! We had to be at the terminal which was about 800 metres away by shortly after 4.00 a.m.

All I can say is that fumbling around a darkened hotel, packing our gear, whispering so as not to wake anyone except the night-watchman to let us out into . . . here it is again . . . cold, dark and empty streets, at ten to four in the morning, when you know that sunrise is a good five-and-a-half hours away, is not the sort of act I want to repeat too often. We knew that there were more early bus rides ahead of us. I just hoped there wouldn't be too many 3.30s.

At the terminal we had time for a drink of hot chocolate each before the bus left. In Argentina these were called 'submarinos' as they were made by dropping a bar of chocolate into a cup of boiling milk. They were also considerably cheaper than the ones we had been shocked by in Uruguay.

When the bus pulled out at 4.30, we all promptly went to sleep. Fortunately there were a few seats left vacant so Zara and Sean were able to stretch out in double seats. As for me, I could have slept standing on my head and with at least five hours of darkness ahead, none of us had any trouble dropping off.

A little after dawn we were awoken as the bus pulled in at a bleak and lonely roadhouse and petrol station. It was the only structure for as far as the eye could see; a stopping-off place run by the Automobile Club of Argentina, called Tres Cerros (Three Hills . . . although there were no hills to be seen anywhere). After coffee and a piece of cake there we pressed on.

Looking back over my notes they read, 'the land, the sky, everything is dull and featureless.' The only thing to do in surroundings like this was to read or sleep, but both became impossible when the driver of the bus brought his cassette player into operation. The sound system from the player by his side was piped through the bus and there was a speaker immediately above our heads.

However it wasn't music he hit us with, but poetry. We never found out who the poet was, but he sounded like Argentina's answer to Brendan Behan. Of course it was all in Spanish and way beyond our limited powers of comprehension, and with the level turned right up high, we could not only not sleep or read, but we couldn't talk to each other either. The tape ran for half an hour, then he turned it over for another half an hour. Ah, relief, we thought at the end of the second side . . . maybe a rest now. But no. He produced another tape . . . this time Argentina's answer to Bill Cosby; a stand-up comedian who went on for another hour, telling jokes which were completely lost on us because of the language, but had the rest of the bus in fits of laughter, so I guess he must have been good.

At San Julian, about 400 kilometres south of Comodoro and more than half-way to Rio Gallegos, we stopped for lunch. It was a small, unattractive town with wide, dust-blown streets. As the bus-driver had told us that we would be stopping for three-quarters of an hour, we walked about the town to stretch our legs and, finding a small cafe, stepped inside out of the cold, dry wind for a snack.

Trish and I shared a plate of mussels and a piece of dry cheese, then had a cup of coffee each. Zara and Sean each had a ham roll and Coca-Cola. The bill came to 6500 pesos . . . just under US$9.00! We could hardly believe it. When I queried the bill, the woman behind the counter made me feel like a real cheapskate . . . as if I'd just crawled out from under the cheese. She showed me someone else's bill with similar items on it and babbled away at me as if I should know the prices . . . and anyway, what was wrong with them?

Well, I suppose there's nothing wrong with $1 for a coffee and $1 for a Coke if you're having them at the Savoy in London, or the Plaza in New York, but in a run-down little cafe in Patagonia . . .? Once again it was one of those situations were we couldn't really argue so we paid it. But the sad thing is that things like that tend to colour your whole attitude to places and people.

Back on the bus a little later in the afternoon, we met Oscar Coffey, who, to some extent, made up for our bad experience in San Julian. He got on with a friend called Roberto about a hundred kilometres further down the line at a place called Commandante Luis Piedra Buena, or Piedra Buena for short. Oscar was from Chile. He was short, had dark, curly hair and was about twenty-five years old. He had been working in Tierra del Fuego and more recently in San Julian as a waiter. He was on his way to Rio Gallegos to renew his visa with the immigration office there. He spoke English reasonably well and once he discovered that we did too, there was no stopping him. He talked about himself, Chile, Argentina, the state of the world, whatever subject was raised. He was both interesting and entertaining and from our point of view, a vast improvement on the taped entertainment of the morning. Roberto, who was much younger than Oscar, about fifteen or sixteen I guessed, and who spoke no English whatever, sat quietly and listened with considerable admiration while Oscar held the stage.

But there was something wrong. It was soon apparent that Oscar was not a happy man. It was not from anything he said . . . just the way he was. He pulled a bottle of brandy from his bag and offered it to us to drink. Trish said no thanks and so did Roberto, but I took a swig, more out of politeness than anything else, as drinking brandy from a bottle in the back of a bus is not actually my scene. Oscar wasn't an alcoholic. He wasn't even drunk. It seemed to me almost as if he had bought the bottle of brandy and set about drinking it in this manner because that was the accepted thing to do when you're . . . when you're what?

Was Oscar trying to forget something? We never really found out. During the conversation he occasionally gave the impression that he had been hurt recently . . . hurt emotionally. But that was all. For the rest of the time he provided a real lift for us all . . . although I'm sure that he was in far more need of a lift than we were.

During the afternoon Trish had begun to develop flu or whatever it was I had and while I seemed to be improving, she began to slide downhill so fast that by the time we reached Rio Gallegos at about 8.30 at night, after sixteen hours in the bus, she was feeling dreadful; headache, sore throat, aches in the body.

Oscar had told us he knew of a good, cheap hotel, so upon our arrival, we trekked off with him and Roberto to go to it. But under the weight of her pack, Trish was fading fast. We reached the hotel, only to find it full, so Sean and I went off with Oscar and Roberto to find another hotel, leaving Trish and Zara to mind the packs.

We found one . . . the Rio Turbi, where we could get two double rooms, share bathroom for 13,000 pesos (US$17).

'No extras?' I remember saying to both the clerk and Oscar, who helped with some translation, 'complete . . . 13,000 pesos?'

'Si, si,' he replied.

The rooms were good and they were centrally heated. So, knowing Trish was in such bad shape and waiting for us, I didn't hesitate. I booked in and then, thanking Oscar, who was going off with Roberto to stay with friends, Sean and I hurried off to pick up Trish, Zara and the packs.

Half an hour later we had all had beautiful hot showers and collapsed into bed with not an inkling of the drama to be faced in the morning.

By the time I surfaced, groggy and unrested, Iain had already been out and about to find details of how to travel the 320 kilometres inland to Calafate on the edge of Lago Argentina, which we hoped to visit in order to see our first glacier.

We had been warned that in the winter, travel in the area was very restricted, so Iain's news that there were no buses going in that direction for two days wasn't a great surprise.

'But there is a twice-weekly flight which happens to go across this morning,' he said. 'Let's take it.'

'Let's take it,' the children immediately chorused, so fed up were they of travelling by bus.

'And the twice-weekly bus comes back from there on Friday,' Iain went on. 'So that would give us almost three days there. Apart from anything else, the plane trip is a dollar cheaper than the bus. What do you think?'

I didn't think. I couldn't. I didn't have the wherewithal to do anything except lie like a lump. 'You decide,' was all I could manage.

'Well, I don't think it's cheating to fly, as long as we come back here by bus.'

Iain sounded like there was some great judge in the sky who would award us a demerit if we didn't keep our promise to ourselves to do it all on ground level. What is this flagellating madness? I asked myself, feeling at that moment like burrowing under a stone and staying there until spring brought the bluebells.

So Iain went off to get the tickets and Zara and Sean tagged along too, anxious that he wouldn't change his mind.

It was when he returned and we went to check out, that the drama occurred. A different clerk was on duty and he produced a bill for 26,000 pesos, exactly twice what we had anticipated. When Iain said that there must be some mistake, he immediately became very aggressive and threatened to call the police.

At this point Oscar appeared and I thankfully took my aching limbs and throbbing head to a chair and left the fellows to haggle. It seemed that the night-clerk was only a casual employee and that he had got the tariff wrong. Instead of the equivalent of US$17 for two rooms it should have been $17 for each, so that we now owed $34.

'But,' Iain argued, 'I wouldn't have taken the rooms if I had been told the correct price.'

'Too bad,' countered the clerk, 'and anyway how do I know he told you the wrong price. Maybe you just didn't understand his Spanish.'

'No. No.' Oscar intervened. 'I was here with him and I heard the clerk say definitely 13,000 pesos for two rooms.'

The man glared at Oscar as if he was a traitor for siding with these foreigners. 'The price,' he insisted, 'is 26,000. That is final and you cannot leave until you have paid. If you try I shall call the police and right now I am going to call the owner.'

He made his call and then for another ten minutes the discussion continued before Iain stated that we had a plane to catch and that we had to leave or we'd miss it. There was nothing the clerk could do, really, nor even the owner, who arrived just as we stepped into a cab. They tried to insist and we just refused and drove off, but it was all very nasty and not the sort of situation which I felt up to coping with in my present poor condition.

Oscar came with us to the airport because he wanted to make sure that

Roberto also caught the plane. While Roberto went off with Zara and Sean to give the squad of soldiers patrolling the runway the once over, Oscar asked, 'Please keep an eye on him. He is going back to his father in Calafate. He had sent him to his mother who lives in San Julian, but she has a new man and doesn't want her son around. Nor does his elder sister and her busband. He is being pushed around like an unwanted parcel. He is only fourteen and very unhappy.'

Poor kid. Just three years older than Zara and Sean and already having to cope with the harsh realities of an adult word. No wonder he was so quiet and pale. Oscar himself didn't look much better. He was shivering and because he wasn't wearing a top coat I expressed concern about him being cold.

He shook his head. 'I shiver more from nerves than from the cold. I am a sad man. I am trying to forget.'

As we hardly knew him, I didn't press him about what or who he was trying to forget. But he was so open and vulnerable that when a voice over the crackling sound system announced our flight, I gave him a big hug and kiss and wished him well.

Apart from the soldiers, there had only been another dozen or so people in the desolate airport lounge. Ours was the only flight in or out of Rio Gallegos all day and our plane, a Fokker Friendship, was almost empty.

This was a flight by Lineas Aereas del Estado, LADE, the Argentine government airline whose pilots are in the air force. It's not a bad system really. It means that internal flights come out of the defence budget, the airforce gets plenty of practice and their planes don't sit around on the tarmac costing money.

The disadvantage is that service pilots, in my experience anyway, tend to be a little gung-ho. They find regular flying pretty tame and may be tempted to take risks just to liven things up a little, which is okay as long as it's not my life on the line.

I suppose it was fortunate that I was too sick to get myself into much of a state about all this. Although my residual brain did persist in bleeping out warnings about being landed in snow and ice on a tiny runway by a would-be Air-Vice-Marshal.

The steward very kindly asked us if we would like to visit the cockpit, but I declined and offered Sean instead and he returned full of enthusiasm for the splendid views of snow-clad mountains. It was less than an hour before we came in to land on the flattened top of a small hill. It was so like flying into a snow-covered Toytown that I wouldn't have been surprised to find Noddy in the little hut on the field.

There was only a ten minute walk down the side of the hill into the main street of the little settlement and Iain left me in front of the open fire in the airport hut to go with Roberto, Zara and Sean, while he looked for a place for us to stay. I had to fight off a strong urge to curl up in the foetal position on the floor, but within half an hour he was back with the news that Roberto's father had met him, but also that all the hotels in town were shut for the winter.

'I've persuaded one to rent us a couple of rooms though. They aren't heated but there's piles of bedclothes and you can just hop straight under them.'

He carried my pack and I stumbled behind him. By now I knew I had tonsilitis and Iain confirmed this when he looked down my throat and made a disgusted face. White pustules crowded on both sides.

Fully clothed, I crept into bed and after taking a couple of aspirins, fell asleep. An hour later Iain woke me to give me some 'Penoral' tablets, an antibiotic he had just bought, and also to tell me that he had found a fellow who would drive us out to the glacier tomorrow.

Again I slept and woke to have dinner cooked by Iain on our stove set up in the bathroom. More pills and sleep and through the haze I realised that Iain was washing out some clothes and hanging them round the room to dry. He had already read to the children, who were asleep.

I tried telling him that it was on occasions like this that I realised why I love him, but I was too dopey to get the words out. In the middle of the absolutely silent night he woke me to take another tablet and I must have felt a little improved because I remember laughing at the picture he presented, having just got out of his sleeping bag, wearing nothing but his woollen beanie to keep his head warm!

Argentina's Moreno Glacier, according to the brochures, is the only glacier in the world that is growing. All other glaciers in other parts of the world, although they may be moving in a particular direction, are apparently diminishing in overall size.

From our point of view this particular statistic about the Ventesquero Moreno, as it is called locally, wasn't really important. As it was our first glacier, we were so impressed and awed by it that we couldn't have cared less if it was growing or shrinking. Just the fact that this giant mountain of ice was there, sitting huge and cold and blue, filling an entire valley directly opposite us, was enough.

We had made the trip to the glacier despite the fact that Trish was still not well. The antibiotics had made some difference to the way she felt, but she was still very rinsed-out and weak. We had discussed waiting for an extra day or so, but the weather forecast was for snowstorms soon and there was the possibility of the road to the glacier, some eighty kilometres from Calafate, being closed, so we decided to go as soon as possible.

We were standing on a sloping hillside about 100 metres away directly in front of the 1000 metre-wide face of the glacier. Separating us from it was a narrow strip of milky, blue-green water which was filled with floating ice-floes or miniature 'bergs' that had 'calved' from the 45-metre-high face of the glacier. Every few minutes or so the silence of the deserted place would be broken by thunderous tearing and cracking sounds, both from the interior of the glacier and from the front, as gigantic pieces of ice broke away from it and tumbled into the water.

On occasions in mid-summer the ice-falls from the glacier have been so great as to fill the gap between it and the promontory on which we were standing. When that happens it effectively cuts the lake (Lake Brazo Rico, which is an arm of Lake Argentina) in two. Then one half of the lake, deprived of its only outlet, the Rio Santa Cruz, fills up to dangerous levels and begins to flood the surrounding countryside. In winter though the colder temperatures tend to keep the face of the glacier slightly more stable, even if, from a tourist's point of view, the weather is somewhat inhibiting.

When we stood opposite the great glacier, gazing at it in awe, the weather was bitterly cold. There was the feeling of snow in the air and we were understandably alone ... except for Carlos. Carlos Alsuri was a hotel-owner in Calafate who had offered to drive us to the Moreno Glacier. He had done so partly for the money of course (about US$50 for the day-long round trip), but also, I think, to relieve the boredom. With his hotel closed down for the winter, the cold, dark days in Calafate must seem endless to him and those others who live permanently in the town. A trip like this represented an ideal opportunity to get away from it.

We had covered the eighty kilometres to Moreno, firstly along the empty southern shore of Lake Argentina, then across flat, open prairie country towards Lake Brazo Rico and finally over a rough mountain road to a point about two and a half kilometres from the glacier itself.

Carlos, who was driving his own Peugeot 504, didn't want to take it any further as the road, although it continued on to a point almost opposite the glacier, was now very muddy and was beginning a downhill run, which Carlos felt might have been difficult to get back up again on the return trip.

We left the car and walked the remaining distance through a forest of trees which were covered and hung with a clinging grey moss. The wind, once we had climbed to a high headland, was icy and I became worried again about Trish. But we were all well rugged up and she insisted that she felt all right, so we pressed on towards what Carlos had told us was the best vantage point from which to view the glacier.

Carlos was wearing only a shirt and a thin sweater and we were anxious that he would develop pneumonia or something, but he laughed off our expressions of concern. Thinking back on it, we had good reason to be worried. He was anything but a health buff. At over fifty he was overweight and out of condition. He puffed and huffed and held his heart when we had to climb a couple of hills, so that on a few occasions when he stopped for breath we thought he might be going to have a heart attack.

He could have stayed in the car and waited for us to walk and see the glacier, but he preferred to stagger through the freezing wind to accompany us, feeling, I should imagine, an understandable sense of pride in what is not only a local, but a national beauty spot of majestic proportions.

The Moreno Glacier is one of ten large glaciers in Glacier National Park, a 400,000 hectare reserve created by the Argentine government in 1937, along the edge of the Andean foothills forming the country's western border with Chile. Most of these tremendous glaciers, filling entire complex valley systems, hundreds of metres deep with ice, extend across the border into Chile, which has also declared vast tracts of their own glacier territory as National Parks.

We moved about on the hillside opposite the glacier for probably twenty minutes or half an hour, admiring and photographing it. We were struck by the incredible luminosity of the blue shadows in its deep crevasses. It also seemed to be lined, diagonally across its face, with quite bright blue streaks, while the top of it, stretching off into the mist-clouded distance of the 800-metre-wide valley, was unbelievably jagged and broken. It is apparently all but impossible and certainly extremely dangerous to cross on foot.

What impressed us most though was the stupendous size of it all; countless billions of tonnes of frozen water ... tens of thousands of years old ... remnants of past ice-ages in which entire continents were reshaped and moulded by glaciers which would probably have dwarfed this one.

Both Zara and Sean were, like us, greatly impressed and I recall feeling embarrassed at my own ignorance when asked by Zara,

'How do they get there?'

'Er ... well, you see, they've always been there. That is, for thousands of years anyway.'

'But why don't they melt in the summer, like all the rest of the snow and ice around?'

'Well, I guess it's because there's just too much ice there to melt and it sort of acts like a giant refrigerator, keeping the air about it so cold that the heat never gets to the ice deeper down. It creates its own sort of mini-climate.'

But I wasn't really sure of what I was saying. I didn't really know and I certainly didn't know why this particular glacier, distinct from all the others, should be growing bigger. I decided to look it up in an encyclopaedia as soon as possible.

On our return to the car I extracted our little stove from a small pack we'd brought along with us and proceeded to impress Carlos mightily by cooking up a brew of hot soup which we all had with hunks of bread and cheese and then finished off with a cup of coffee. We took off shortly after for the return drive to Calafate, immensely glad that we had made the effort to see the Moreno Glacier.

The enforced day of leisure in Calafate was just what the doctor ordered. The antibiotics had started on their miracle cure (even though we normally use them with respectfully sparing caution, I would loathe to battle through without them) but I still felt very under par and only sleep would put that right.

So I spent most of the day in bed, dozing and reading, while the others made occasional forays into the cold. There were no banks open and the few shops which were; a chemist, baker and small grocery, did so for only a couple of hours around the middle of the day.

Iain continued, with his culinary skill, to turn out meals cooked on our little stove in the bathroom. Not very hygienic perhaps, though I think any germs would have had a tough struggle to exist in those almost arctic conditions.

Zara and Sean read and worked on their project books which were filling up with the oddest assortment of facts and figures about the continent. Naturally they complained whenever I pressed them into adding to them; Sean in particular, because he finds writing a considerable chore and prefers to draw what he sees and thinks. I didn't mind which method they employed to store information, just so long as they made some effort. I'm sure I would not enjoy formal teaching, especially of my own children, but I persevered with this minimum requirement and of course, since the journey, they have said they are glad to have their own record of it.

Zara's novel was burgeoning and she also spent many happy ego-sustaining hours practising her signature and came up with a very swanky product. How very well I remember doing exactly the same myself a quarter of a century ago!

Calafate cannot receive television transmissions because of the surrounding mountains, so we could only hear and not see the next gladiatorial round in the World Cup between Argentina and Poland. Even with our limited Spanish it was quite obvious who was winning. The eventual score, Argentina 2, Poland 1, left the announcer very nearly in a state of apoplexy.

By the next day I was well on the mend, the awful stuff in my throat had gone and I was ready to face the world again, this time a whitened one, for overnight it had snowed and the coating on the mountains had crept down into the village.

'You were lucky,' the lady of the house commented as we paid our bill, 'this snow will have closed the road to the glacier. You were the last people to get through. No more will go now till spring, perhaps in September or October.'

The six-hour bus trip back to Rio Gallegos was across monotonous, barren scrub under a grey, snow-laden sky. The little, poorly-heated bus was only partially occupied and Sean entertained himself and us by sitting up near the driver, lighting the cigarettes the man chain-smoked, cleaning the windows and talking into a rolled up magazine as if he was communicating over his radio with the rest of his squadron who were under attack, by the Germans of course. Occasionally he'd swap sides and talk to his Hun companions in his own brand of German.

The only thing of note which happened on the trip was when a couple of riders galloped in from the horizon, accompanied by their sheep dog, to intercept us. It was difficult to be sure, because they wore so many clothes, but I think it was a man and a woman. The bus halted and they rode up to the driver's side window. He handed out a parcel and they handed in some mail. Then they rode off, dog at heel, back into their lonely world.

Back in Rio Gallegos, late that afternoon, we checked in at a different hotel which really did cost US$17 for the four of us and was equally as good as the place over which we'd had the fight.

Before the bus station would issue tickets for the next day's trip on to Punta Arenas, which is in Chile, we had to obtain a police permit to leave Argentina. Again, as we had seen before with Argentinian police, this was no mere formality. Even though we were foreigners, our names were checked against a list of people whom I could only suppose were wanted by the police. The officer who issued the permits, which were written in triplicate, took the information down correctly; all of which made me very glad that I was not on the run. Invariably in many of the other Latin American countries these border checks are little more than an irritating nonsense, just a way of occupying a few troops or police. But in Argentina they were very much for real.

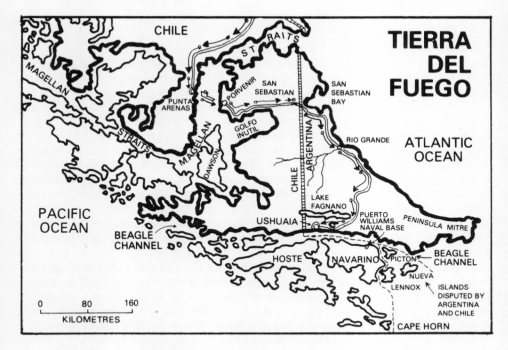

TIERRA DEL FUEGO

CHILE

ST RAITS

MAGELLAN

PUNTA ARENAS

STRAITS

MAGELLAN

DAWSON

PORVENIR

SAN SEBASTIAN

GOLFO INUTIL

CHILE

ARGENTINA

SAN SEBASTIAN BAY

RIO GRANDE

ATLANTIC OCEAN

PACIFIC OCEAN

LAKE FAGNANO

PENINSULA MITRE

BEAGLE CHANNEL

USHUAIA

PUERTO WILLIAMS NAVAL BASE

HOSTE

NAVARINO

PICTON

BEAGLE CHANNEL

NUEVA

LENNOX

ISLANDS DISPUTED BY ARGENTINA AND CHILE

CAPE HORN

0   80   160
KILOMETRES

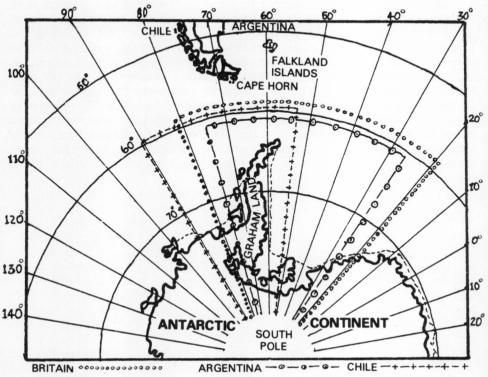

90°   80°   70°   60°   50°   40°   30°

CHILE   ARGENTINA

FALKLAND ISLANDS

CAPE HORN

100°   50°   20°

110°   60°   10°

120°   70°   0°

GRAHAM LAND

130°   10°

140°   20°

ANTARCTIC   CONTINENT

SOUTH POLE

BRITAIN ○○○○○○○○○○○   ARGENTINA ─⊙─⊙─⊙─   CHILE ─+─+─+─+─

CHILE/ARGENTINA

25
A land of fire

During the next three days we were in Chile, travelling down to Punta Arenas, the most southerly town on the actual continental landmass of South America and then through the Chilean part of the big island of Tierra del Fuego. However, as this represents only a tiny fraction of the whole of Chile, which stretches from this southerly tip, some 4300 kilometres to the north, we do not intend to devote a separate chapter to Chile or to give anything more than our own impressions of the Chile we saw and the Chileans we met in this 'southern cone' region.

We had left Rio Gallegos at 9.00 a.m. in the dark, heading for the border with Chile about fifty kilometres to the south. But even before we left town, we came to an Argentinian police check-point where, after a cursory inspection of the passengers, we were permitted to continue. Five minutes later we were stopped again and then a third time a few kilometres further on. We thought, at that stage, that we were finally clear, but about fifteen kilometres out of town the bus was stopped again. This time by the army.

We sat in the bus while one armed soldier slowly moved his way down the aisle, methodically checking the identity and permission to travel papers of every single passenger ... a process which took just under an hour! Then, half an hour after leaving that check-point we were at the border and once more being checked over by Argentine officials ... this time the immigration authorities.

When we were finally through, we trundled down the road a short way to the Chilean post. It was quite a surprise; very straightforward, no big show of arms or intimidating checks on anyone. Their immigration and customs offices were tidy and clean ... much more civilised and restrained than the heavy military approach on the Argentine side.

Our surprise was due to the fact that there has been considerable tension and ill feeling between Chile and Argentina for some time, particularly in this southern region which is the centre of an extended territorial dispute between the two countries.

There seemed to be a marked difference in the way the two were handling the situation. Obviously the endless police and army checks, on the Argentinian side, of passengers travelling to and from Chile resulted from a sense of paranoia. Why the Chileans weren't similarly affected, we couldn't work out.

But if there was a difference between the two countries in this respect, there was certainly none in the landscape when we crossed from Argentina into Chile

... it was unremittingly bleak; a flat, open tundra supporting no vegetation other than tufted brown grass and an occasional sagebrush tumbling across the road, blown along by a strong, cold wind.

There was a good deal of snow about, but it did not cover the ground completely. Flocks of sheep were foraging in exposed places for grass and ranging free amongst the sheep, competing with them for the clear bits of grass, were large numbers of wild rheas, or ostriches. The giant birds seemed to get on quite well with the sheep and vice versa.

After about an hour, we stopped for a snack at a large house, sitting on its own in the middle of an empty plain. A woman in the typical black and white uniform of a French maid, complete with miniature apron and frilly white hat, came out of the front door to greet the bus on its arrival. After a cup of coffee there we reboarded the bus and within fifteen minutes or so had our first view of the Straits of Magellan.

They appeared broad, grey and, surprisingly, were flat-calm. As gale force winds sweep the whole region for much of the year, but particularly in the winter, the Straits are rarely so calm. On this day, although there was a good wind blowing, it was far from a gale. There were even a few patches of blue in the sky.

In the distance, to the south-east, across the 24-kilometre-wide stretch of water, we could see snow-capped mountains rising on Tierra del Fuego. By tomorrow we hoped we would be across the Straits and onto the big island, but in the meantime we just kept rolling along, following the shoreline of the Straits over an unsurfaced but reasonable road until we arrived in the late afternoon at Punta Arenas . . . a most surprising town.

Well, surprising for us anyway, because it was much larger than we had expected any town this far down towards the bottom of the world to be. Punta Arenas is a busy and prosperous city of some 75-80,000 people. It is neat and tidy and, while most of the older buildings are made of wood, there are many modern office and residential buildings of concrete and brick. It is the capital of Chile's Magellan province and the so-called XII Region. But, more importantly, it is the centre of a sizeable oil exploration and production industry in the area, which is responsible for all of Chile's crude oil production.

Up until the discovery of oil, sheep breeding had been the main industry, with flocks for the region numbering about three and a half million or about thirty-five sheep for every person.

As we left the bus terminal in the Port Authority's facility on the waterfront; carrying our packs in the direction of the town square a few blocks away, we were approached by an elderly man who was curious to know what we were doing in Punta Arenas. His name was Milo Stojadinovic, a Jugoslavian immigrant to Chile . . . one of many thousands who settled in Southern Chile after World War II.

'I take you to good hotel,'' he insisted in passable English. 'Very cheap. Is hotel of Jugoslav lady . . . friend of mine.'

Five minutes later we were climbing a steep flight of stairs in an old wooden building to the 'Residencia Selecta'.

'Yes, there are rooms available,' we were told by the owner, a dark-haired woman in her mid-forties. Two double rooms for 600 Chilean pesos (US$20 . . . cheap?). But no, unfortunately they are not heated. But, yes, we can borrow a small kerosene heater and yes, the communal bathroom has hot water . . . really hot water. We hesitated, went and felt the water and decided to stay.

After a wash-up, we went out for a walk about the town, changed some money at the rather more plush Hotel Cabo de Hornos (Cape Horn), then, at a Punta Arenas version of a fast-food joint, bought some empanadas, french-fried potatoes, beer and soft drinks.

Finishing our meal, we returned, licking our fingers, to the hotel where we went to bed to read a couple of chapters of Frodo's adventures in the *Lord of the Rings.*

Of course it was still dark when we got up and of course it was very cold. It was hard to imagine that it could ever be anything else.

The military authorities at the port where the bus had dropped us on the previous evening had told us that the ferry across the Straits of Magellan to Tierra del Fuego left at 8.00 a.m. But when we eventually found it, beached on an empty stretch of shoreline in the deserted outskirts of the town, it was in darkness and looked abandoned.

As we walked down towards it, carrying our packs, the wind came off the Straits to slice through us like a cutlass of polar ice. The vessel was a large, open, front-loading vehicular ferry, not unlike an oversized, Second World War landing craft. The bow loading ramp was down but there were still a couple of metres of coldly lapping water to jump before we were on board and looking around for some nook or cranny where we would be less exposed.

The cold metal hulk was little comfort, but at least, hidden from the rapacious wind, we could discuss what to do because it certainly didn't look as though the ferry was going to run that day. Iain thought he'd better do a recce of the vessel to see if he could find anyone who could give us any further information. The three of us stayed shivering with the packs.

He was at the far end of the ferry, which was about forty-five metres long and though we couldn't see him in the dark, we could hear him stumbling around and trying doors. Suddenly one of these burst open and a man came through it, from a lighted cabin beyond, to yell at him and order him ashore. Iain stood his ground until he ascertained that the ferry would be running today but not for another hour or so. No, the man said, we couldn't wait on board.

From the deck below we almost begged the man, 'Muy frio, muy frio,' we shivered and clutched ourselves. 'Los ninos,' I pointed to Zara and Sean as a last ploy. But he was not to be won over and continued shouting at us to leave.

Muttering abuse, we stacked our packs in a dark dry corner and jumped back ashore into the terrible wind. Two hundred metres from the water's edge we could see the lights of a factory which was surrounded by a high wire fence and had, at the main entrance, a guard house.

We blundered across through the dark and cold and began shaking on the big gates beside which was a sign bearing the initials of the large petroleum company, ENAP. A guard, rugged up in heavy overcoat, boots and cap with ear flaps, came out and didn't even wait for the finish of Iain's halting explanation before opening up and inviting us into his room.

Oh, the wonderful warmth! All four jets on the gas stove were blazing away, adding to the heat already put out by a big oil-burning stove. The guard made us a large cup of hot coffee each and joined in our bitter complaints against the ferry crewmen who wouldn't give us shelter in this temperature.

An hour later we could see through the guard-house windows, although it was still dark, other passengers who must have gained their information from a more reliable source, beginning to arrive. We thanked the guard who was delighted when Iain took a photograph of him with a flash outside his post and promised to send a copy.

Leaving our packs where they were, we went, once on board the ferry, through into a little cabin where the crewman who had been so inhospitable, on seeing us again, at least had the grace to slink away. There we laid claim to a small space. By the time we left the shore there were about twenty-five passengers in this compact area, most of them having to stand. We watched as below us in the forward hold crew members lashed together two trucks and three private cars with strong ropes. We none of us commented on this precaution but each knew the other was thinking that this did not augur well for the crossing!

The craft had been built on Clydeside, though the plate didn't give the year, and was very similar to ones in which I have crossed from England to Ireland, or France. Naturally all the instrument directions were in English and though the pilot spoke only Spanish he didn't have any problems throwing the right levers and switches.

It was nine-thirty when we left the mainland of South America; the sun was just up and struggling unsuccessfully to break through the leaden skies. The Straits, thirty-two kilometres wide at this point, were the same colour so there was no demarcation of horizon.

It wasn't until we were well clear of land and still with no sight of Tierra del Fuego, that the ferry began to plunge and rise, plunge and rise. Occasionally this sickening switchback motion would be broken in mid-stroke by a current or wave on her side and then she'd judder fit to break.

The wind was coming from the south across the remote and desolate Dawson Island some miles away where, we were told, the Chilean military junta had incarcerated the majority of the country's political prisoners. In bitter weather like this life on Dawson Island must have been almost as unpleasant as in Siberia's Gulag Archipelago.

As the seas became more mountainous, with vicious, wind-whipped white caps and the tired vessel creaked and groaned, I tried to console myself by thinking how much worse it must have been on board Magellan's little wooden boat in which he found a way through here to the Pacific in 1520.

Iain took Zara and Sean, who had begun to feel very queasy, out on deck and suggested that I come too. But I pursued my usual mode of operation under such circumstances; to stay totally still, not even moving my eyeballs and to hum loudly to myself. Hymns are best . . . the ones which are full of vigour and determination. Above the noise of the engines and waves crashing with huge force over the bow, drenching the captive vehicles which strained at their bonds, I was sure no one could hear me. Even if they could I wouldn't have cared!

Several other passengers took to the deck, hoping desperately that the fresh air, even though it was so terribly cold, would dispel their nausea. Anxious that moving would make matters worse, I stuck it for as long as possible, though the fact that a large albatross landed on the side rail outside the cabin and surveyed the seething scene with a malevolent eye, did not make me feel any happier. I had no desire to finish up like the Ancient Mariner and when we went down one particular trough, so large that the total view was of green surging water and then up again, so that all we could see was grey sky, I made a dash for the cabin door.

The shock of the cold was extremely effective and we all stayed out on deck until we saw Tierra del Fuego appear as a flat strip of land. Not long after, the water calmed considerably and it was at this point that we saw the only other vessel on the entire trip, the wreck of a French ship which had gone aground within sight of port. She looked in a sorry state, lying over on her side with the constant pounding of the sea gradually reducing her to flotsam and jetsam.

Porvenir is the capital of the Chilean half of Tierra del Fuego and is a kilometre and a half inland from where the ferry docks. If you remember I said that I thought Comodoro Rivadavia was the pits, but I was to discover there was one rung further down yet to go. Well, to that rung clings Porvenir. For some reason I find totally inexplicable, there is a breed of people who have decided to spend their lives in the most inhospitable places. About four thousand of these have found their masochistic haven in Porvenir.

Because there are no trees on this part of the island, most of the houses are thrown together from tin and a few from stone. They have a very temporary appearance, as if the inhabitants are on the point of packing it in and moving on to more equable climes. Admittedly its only in the mid-winter that the sun rises at 9.45 a.m. and sets again at 3.15 p.m. In the summer the days are correspondingly long. But the island is never warm, it quite often suddenly snows in mid-summer. Charles Darwin described it as having 'the bleakest climate on earth.' And that from an Englishman! The wind blows all year and on most of the island there are no trees to soften the flat grey-grassed land, to green it, give it shade or shelter.

The bus driver who had brought us in a dilapidated old vehicle from where the ferry had docked, to the centre of town, told us of a private home which rented rooms. Following his directions, we set off walking through the unsurfaced and icy streets . . . once again the only people out in the bitter weather . . . until we eventually located the place.

The unheated room in the tin and fibre-board walled house had two three-quarter beds. For this and a shared bathroom, we paid twenty-four dollars. But, as it included three meals a day each and as the bus we would be taking to cross the island didn't leave until early the next afternoon, we thought this was a reasonable price.

At least the family room where we ate our meals was well heated and the other guests were friendly. There were several young girls staying in the house. They were nurses at the town's small hospital, so that all together, with them and their boyfriends we had a convivial dinner.

One thing which I found surprising was that none of them knew anything about, or were in the least interested in, the World Cup which was approaching its hysterical climax in the country next door. This was probably because Chile had long since been knocked out of the competition.

That night, we all slept *in* our clothes, *inside* our sleeping bags as well as *under* the pile of bedclothes provided. As we surveyed each other, we were overcome with a fit of giggles because only our heads protruded from this mass of coverings and all of us were wearing our woollen beanies!

'I've never before realised,' Iain said, 'why years ago, people wore those long tasselled bedcaps. I always thought it was an eccentric fashion. Now I know. It was to keep their heads warm!'

Tierra del Fuego seems the complete opposite of a 'Land of Fire' ... especially when you land there in mid-winter ... and yet that is what Tierra del Fuego means in English. Its name, however, has no connection with either weather or temperature, but derives from the fires lit along the shoreline and carried in their canoes by the primitive Yahgan Indians who inhabited the bleak and hostile island at the time the first European explorers began visiting the area in the 1500s.

Shaped like a rough triangle, it covers more than 90,000 square kilometres of sparsely populated, rugged territory at the very bottom of the South American continent and is divided, approximately in half, by a north-south borderline separating Chile on the west and Argentina on the east.

Most of the land is given over to sheep and estancias on both sides of the border raise huge herds. But oil, also in both the Chilean and Argentine sections of the island, has become the most important product of Tierra del Fuego. There are only two or three towns of any size in each half of the island and none of them with more than 10,000 inhabitants.

When we left Porvenir at a little after midday, we were heading east on a 220-kilometre trip to the Argentine town of Rio Grande, on the Atlantic coast. This was the only way we could reach Ushuaia, the most southerly town in the world. Our bus was a considerable come-down from the modern monsters we'd been travelling in Brazil and northern Argentina, but it was by no means a rattle-trap. We rumbled along on a dirt road across a flat, empty plain, bounded on the southern side by a large bay, which I discovered, after consulting a map, was called, 'Golfo Inutil', or Useless Bay. It certainly looked pretty useless.

And yet, although Tierra del Fuego presents this seemingly hostile and inhospitable picture to humans, it abounds with wildlife, both on the land, in the seas around it and particularly in the air. There is an astonishing variety and quantity of birds that live on the island. They include owls, ducks, geese, herons, starlings, ibis, woodpeckers, kites, finches, kestrels and all manner of sea-birds. Not all of them are migratory and there are many that remain, surviving even the harshest winters.

The driving of our bus was shared between a young man of about twenty-five or so and a grey-haired man who may have been his father. The older one, who I think was probably the owner of the bus, told us that, like Milo Stojadinovic, whom we met on our arrival in Punta Arenas, he was from Jugoslavia, and that Porvenir was a predominantly Jugoslav town.

At about 4.00 p.m., just on dusk, we reached the Chilean frontier post at San Sebastian. It looked for all the world like an abandoned sheep station; empty shearing sheds scattered about the place and only one sorry three-roomed, brick building with antiquated kerosene lighting and heating, which served as the immigration and customs office.

I took a photograph of the sunset and, turning back to face the opposite direction, was changing lenses in order to photograph a huge, golden moon which was coming up over a low range of hills a few kilometres away across the plains, when a Chilean soldier walked quickly towards me.

'No, no!' He was waving one finger at me, as if to a naughty child. 'Prohibido. Prohibido. No fotografia.'

I pointed to the moon. 'La luna,' I said, 'solomente la luna.'

'No. No posible,' he persisted. 'Muy estrategico.'

I put my camera away and looking about at the gaggle of empty huts, pondered the immense strategic importance of San Sebastian. It seemed that, as we came nearer to the area of contention between Chile and Argentina, the Chileans too were becoming paranoid.

About eight or nine kilometres further on from the Chilean post, we came to an equally remote and forlorn Argentinian one, through which we passed, after a time-consuming delay, with no problems.

Not long afterwards, we reached the coast, with the Atlantic glistening cold and white under the light of the full moon. There was now considerably more snow on the ground, but fortunately the road was in reasonable condition and we continued south at a good pace along the uninhabited coastline, with a tape of Chilean music blaring loudly through the bus's speaker system.

Sean sat up at the front of the bus, near the driver, Zara slept and Trish and I tried to read by the dim glow of the overhead lights. It was made doubly difficult by the rolling motion of the bus on the uneven road. (A note in my diary at this point reads, 'getting heartily sick of buses.')

By 7.30 p.m. we had arrived in Rio Grande, a small town of around 5000 people, squatting flatly on the coast, facing straight out into the South Atlantic. On leaving the bus, we walked directly, through icy and slippery streets, to the Automobile Club's Alberge, which was also a Youth Hostel.

To our surprise, the place was clean and modern. The rooms, which were fitted with two double bunks, were panelled in pine, the whole place was centrally heated and the tariff was only US$10 for the four of us.

Anyone planning on raising a little extra cash by robbing a bank would be well advised not to try to do so in Argentina, because there seems very little chance of getting away with it. All banks are guarded by uniformed men armed with automatic weapons. This is fairly universal practice in all of Latin America, but Argentina goes one better. Bank guards there don't stand at the entrance or lounge around the banking hall, where they might be vulnerable to pot-shots. They stand inside steel turrets with gunports and survey the scene from the safety of an eyeslit.

Each bank has its own style of turret placed in strategic positions but the one in the one small bank in Rio Grande was particularly menacing because it sat directly behind the counter. This meant that while I was checking the pile of crumpled dirty notes which the teller had exchanged for my travellers' cheques, I was uncomfortably aware of being scrutinised by a pair of disembodied eyes and the evil muzzle of a presumably loaded gun.

What if he had just discovered that his wife had been unfaithful to him and felt that he would rather die than live dishonoured and that he might as well take a few of us with him. Stranger things happen every day.

It's ironic that all these heavy precautions against bank robberies should be taken in a country whose currency is hardly worth the paper on which it is printed and which is totally valueless beyond its own borders. A great bank robber in Argentina is certainly not going to be able to turn up with his swag in Rio there to live out the life of his dreams.

The port of Rio Grande is a little more substantial looking and attractive than Porvenir, but stuck, as it is on the edge of a wasteland of sheep grazing country, it is really little more than a seasonal service town.

Again there was no bus for our final destination, Ushuaia, for a further two days, so we were very pleased that our room in the Youth Hostel was so warm and comparatively comfortable.

After we had been to the bank, and looked around the place, we did a bit of shopping at a small grocery store, paying exorbitant prices for some tinned food to cook up later in the day. On the way back to the hostel, we passed a schoolhouse filled with young pupils who, instead of a uniform, wore a white smock over their street clothes.

Fortunately for Sean there were two sessions of school a day; the younger ones starting at 7.30 a.m. and going till lunch-time and the older ones going in the afternoons. This meant that Sean could spend most of the morning careening about over the icy backyard of the hostel on sleds with a couple of boys of his own age. He tore the knee of his jeans and only came inside when the wet and cold had penetrated to his skin, all of which meant that he had had a good time.

Zara had stayed inside reading, while Iain and I did our repetitive domestic chores. I was getting heartily sick of washing shirts etc. by hand in often confined conditions, especially as it was always the same shirts. I had just finished a pile and was lying on my bunk reading, when Iain, who had also been washing and was now sorting through some research material, suddenly leapt up, scattering papers and made a rush for the door yelling, 'My watch. . . .'

But it was too late. It was gone. He had taken it off in the communal bathroom and put it beside the sink while he washed his sweater. Then he had forgotten it was there and taken the sweater to the boiler room, just down the hall and spread it out to dry. After that he had come back to our room where he had been for less than five minutes before remembering his watch.

Naturally he was very upset. It was a good watch; a hefty Seiko stop-watch, which he used for timing tapes, but I think what distressed him most was that it had been a present from me eight years ago.

The manageress of the hostel, a woman in her thirties with a small girl, was also upset. 'I have been here for five years and nothing like this has ever happened before,' she said. 'I must call the police.'

There was only one other guest in the hostel, a fellow of about twenty-two. It was difficult to imagine how anybody else but he could have taken the watch. In that short space of time, nobody else had come into the hostel . . . that was certain, because the manageress, whose room was opposite the double front door, which was the only entrance, would have seen them.

It was a very embarrassing situation. We couldn't just let the watch go without trying to recover it. We tried not to be too heavy with the fellow and to give him plenty of opportunity to say he had found the watch, or to put it back some place where we would quickly find it. But I guess he felt he had his back against the wall and that he would try to bluff his way through.

The police arrived; two constables and an officer. They questioned us and the manageress, searched our room and hers and then started on the young fellow whom they also obviously suspected. They turned his room upside down and inside out, gave him a body search and even examined the snow-covered ground below his window, I suppose in case he had thrown the incriminating watch away. Nothing.

Details of the watch were taken and the manageress said she would put a description and an offer of a reward out over the local TV station. It was a large and rather unusual watch and therefore very conspicuous, so whoever did eventually end up with it, wouldn't be able to wear it around a small place like Rio Grande, without it being noticed. Iain had to go round to the station to give a signed statement and the whole episode left us with a nasty feeling of personal violation.

What was so maddening was that it should happen then, not in all the places in which we had been warned to be careful, but there, one day before reaching our goal.

The only thing to relieve our depression was the fact that on that evening, almost as a consolation prize, we were treated to the most magnificent sunset we had ever seen — anywhere.

We were only one stage away from our final destination ... Ushuaia, 220 kilometres to the south, on the Beagle Channel and this day's bus trip would, we hoped, be our last. Once we headed northward again, from Ushuaia, it would be all by plane.

The bus for the journey to Ushuaia was a small one, a fifteen-seater Mercedes Minibus similar to the one in which we had travelled from Manaus to Porto Velho and I think this one must have been meant for that route, because it had no heating ... which tended to make things a little difficult. In fact things generally were a little difficult on that trip because, after we had travelled south alongside the coast for about forty-five kilometres or so, the driver, a young, dark-haired man in his mid-twenties (again with an older co-driver) pulled the bus to one side of the dirt road and stopped. There was something wrong with the left-front wheel.

There were only six other passengers, apart from us, on board the bus and we all piled off to see what had happened. We soon saw, on examination of the offending wheel, that four of the six bolts holding it on had simply sheared off.

The road at this point was running along a high, rocky cliff. It had been many kilometres since we had passed the last signs of habitation and from the look of the map, it was just as many more to the next sheep or cattle estancia. The temperature outside the bus was freezing. There was snow on the ground all about us, but fortunately there was almost no wind. The sky was clear, but the sun was pale and held little warmth.

The young driver set about trying to rectify the situation, but without bolts to replace the broken ones, he was up against it. Nevertheless, at the end of an hour, he had done it and we were left with the thought that whatever faults Argentinians or Tierra del Fuegans may have, they (and this fellow in particular) deserve full marks for improvisation.

He took one bolt from each of the other three wheels and after laboriously removing the sheared bolts from the front wheel, fitted the borrowed ones so that each wheel now had five bolts instead of six. That might sound a deceptively simple and rapid piece of repair work, but I can assure you it wasn't. He worked, without a jacket or gloves, in freezing weather on the grease-covered parts of the wheel assembly with ice-cold metal tools. The grease on his hands was the only thing that prevented his skin from bonding to the tools he was using.

During the whole time, there was little, apart from passing things to him or pumping the jack, that the older co-driver, I or the other passengers could do to help him. When it was eventually all fixed and we got under way again, his clothes and hands were covered in grease and he was shivering with the cold.

Shortly afterwards, we left the coast, heading inland, where the roads immediately became more icy and the drifts of snow were piled higher on the sides. About fifteen kilometres down the road we came to a petrol tanker which had slid off the road and was unable to get back onto it. We stopped to see if there was anything we could do, but it would have been well beyond the powers of our bus to pull the tanker back onto the road, so we continued on, telling the tanker-driver that we would send help back to him.

A further forty-five kilometres or so and we arrived at a big roadside hostel run by the Argentine Automobile Club on the shores of Lake Fagnano, the largest (ninety-five kilometres long, by about fifteen kilometres wide) lake on the island of Tierra del Fuego. The hostel is evidently extremely popular with tourists who come in droves during the summer to fish and hunt on and around the lake, but it was all but empty now.

The countryside for some time before we reached it had been becoming less barren. There were more hills and considerably more trees and, as we approached the hostel, which was built like a Swiss chalet, there were stretches of country which were heavily wooded with trees that were covered in the same grey, hanging moss we had seen near the Moreno Glacier.

At the hostel, the driver was able to wash and warm himself up while we had coffee. The co-driver also made use of the time to borrow a portable butane-gas heater which was lit and placed in the aisle of the bus. We were all very pleased to see it, when we reboarded, but although it looked warm and cosy, it did little to heat the bus, which seemed to be full of draughts. We all moved forward into other seats closer to the heater, but only those who were right on top of it got any benefit from it.

As dusk came on we began to enter some very attractive country. The empty plains were now gone completely. The low hills had become mountains and the mossy trees had been replaced by beautiful pine forests, laden with freshly-fallen snow. The road looked as if it had been snow-ploughed that afternoon, so, although we were not travelling fast, the road was still driveable.

After passing another smaller lake ... Lake Escondido, about forty-five kilometres from Ushuaia, we began to descend through the spectacular Garibaldi mountain pass. About half-way down, we came to a stop. A semi-trailer had jack-knifed on the icy roads and was now blocking the way completely. There were several other cars and trucks there and a bull-dozer, which had just arrived, was in the process of pushing the truck temporarily to one side, so that the half-dozen or so vehicles, including our bus, could pass. Just over an hour later, we arrived in Ushuaia.

As we stepped out of the bus, which dropped us at a small terminal on the waterfront overlooking the dark waters of the Beagle Channel, we heard the sounds of car horns blowing . . . dozens of them. Every car that came past was blowing its horn; 'Too-Too-Tootoo.' The whole town was a cacophony of sound . . . like five minutes past midnight on New Year's Eve. It was almost as if they were being blown to welcome us. It took us several moments before we realised that 'Too-Too-Tootoo' was 'AR-GEN-TINA' and that Argentina had obviously just won its scheduled semi-final World Cup match with Peru.

Despite the chaos that reigned, we managed to hail a taxi to take us in search of a hotel. The young driver was so ecstatic that, as soon as we were in the car, he drove off without knowing where we wanted to go and just blew his horn and shouted 'AR-GEN-TINA' out of the window at whomever he saw in the street for at least three or four minutes before asking our destination.

Apparently Argentina had needed to beat Peru by at least three goals to clinch one of the two top positions. The score was a walk-over: six goals to nil, which meant that Argentina would now play Holland for the Grand Final, a match which, four days later, Argentina won. We asked the driver to take us to a Youth Hostel which was listed in the guide book and, as we drove along the waterfront, the honking and blaring of horns continued. If it was like this in Ushuaia, we thought, imagine what it must be like in Buenos Aires right now.

There was no room at the Youth Hostel, but they gave us directions to the Hotel Fernandez which was nearby, on the western edge of the town and there we found ourselves a warm, comfortable room, with four beds, for 12,000 pesos (US$16). We dumped our packs on the floor and sat on the beds for a couple of minutes just looking at each other.

'Well, we've made it,' Trish smiled.

After we had cooked up a meal and read a couple of chapters of Frodo to Zara and Sean, Trish and I went for a short walk outside. The moon was up and, with the streets and houses covered in snow and reflecting the light of the moon, the town was lit with an almost unearthly pale glow. There was no wind . . . just a crisp, cold stillness. Warm, yellow lights shone from the darker silhouettes of houses and, with dramatic, snow-capped mountains forming a back-drop to the town, we felt as if we could easily have been in the Tyrolean Alps instead of at the bottom of the world.

Ushuaia is an attractive little town. The houses, many of them wooden, have steeply sloping roofs and cling to the bottom slopes of the mountains which rise abruptly from the Beagle Channel.

On this particular winter solstice the Channel was so still, it reflected and so, doubled the dramatic beauty. Everywhere we looked there were mountains, all of them not just capped, but covered with snow. One remarkable peak on the eastern edge of town had a profile very similar to the Matterhorn and what made the scene visually complete were the forests of trees. A national park full of then spreads from the town westwards right up to the Chilean border, just eight kilometres away.

In the summer it must be even greener, though it is never really warm. Tour ships bring visitors from Brazil and Argentina to shop here on their way to visit Antarctica, a mere eleven hundred kilometres south; much closer than Buenos

Aires. To cater for this trade, there are attractive small restaurants and little gift shops in one of which we bought a colourful map of the island and a dozen postcards each, which we sent off to good friends to say, 'Wish you were here'.

A number of the public buildings in the town as well as the banks and the several hotels are well constructed and there is an air of comparative affluence, all of which came as a pleasant surprise and a break from the monotony of the ramshackle, impermanent atmosphere of the other settlements in this southern cone.

From almost everywhere in the town there is a view of the Beagle Channel and it was not difficult to imagine, on this calm day, why the wide stretch of water named after the ship on which Charles Darwin voyaged around the world, must have looked like a haven of safety to him and the crew of the little vessel. It had taken the Beagle a whole month, battling against mountainous seas, to round Cape Horn before finding the entrance to these protected waters.

There was another 'namely' reminder of Darwin's voyage; a gift shop closed for winter but with a board swinging in the wind above its door proclaiming in florid style, 'Jenny Buttons'.

Jemmy (the shop had transposed 'n' for 'm') Buttons was the name given to one of the three Alacalufe Indians; two men and a woman, who had been taken aboard by the Beagle's captain, Robert FitzRoy on a previous voyage. The choice of Jemmy's name, it appears, came about from his ready acceptance of the buttons and bows, then in the height of fashion, which he was given to wear in England when FitzRoy took the three Indians there to be given the highly doubtful benefits of an English education.

At his own expense FitzRoy tried to impose a veneer of what he saw as Christian civilisation on the three Indians in the incredibly naive hope that they would return to Tierra del Fuego and there convert the rest of their tribe to the greater glory of God; FitzRoy's version of God. In mitigation it should be remembered that in FitzRoy's age, the British (and a surprising number of other people whom they had persuaded) believed God to be an Englishman. FitzRoy saw his plan as an act of great charity.

Only Darwin, of all the men on board the Beagle saw it for what it really was; a monstrous cruelty. The three Indians journeyed out with them from England and were put ashore on their home territory. A year later, on the Beagle's return voyage, FitzRoy was desolated to find no sign of the other two Indians and that Jemmy had returned to his native ways; the only ways which were of any value at all in such a harsh environment.

It's easy to forget that Darwin extended his theory of natural selection to include members of the human race. Minority races could only survive, Darwin said, if left alone, free to adjust themselves to their own environment. If this flow was artificially tampered with, then the people died. At the time of Darwin's visit in 1833, the Alacalufes numbered around 10,000. Today there are less than a hundred.

Later in the day when the short appearance of the sun was at its highest low point, we went up on the snowy slopes behind Ushuaia to take some photographs of the town which is quickly dwarfed into insignificance by the majestic towering mountains.

Below us, in the Channel, we could see an oil tanker and when the sun began to set, at around half past three, it painted the snow and the water in a dazzling display of harsh pinks through to soft purples so that the ship seemed like a phoenix arising whole again from the fire.

The view across the Beagle Channel from Ushuaia presents a distant view of snow-covered mountains on the large, but virtually empty islands of Navarino and Hoste, both of which are owned by Chile. Chile also owns the barren, uninhabited rocky island, some one hundred and thirty kilometres south-east of Ushuaia that is Cape Horn, the most southerly point of the continent. For most of the past one hundred years, the relationship between Chile and Argentina and certainly between the peoples of this remote and rugged 'southern cone' region has been basically friendly and definitely peaceful. But over the past few years, a dispute over three small islands, Picton, Nueva and Lennox at the entrance to the Beagle Channel, has brought the two countries to the brink of an all-out war . . . a war that could only be disastrous for both sides.

WAR CLOUDS OVER CAPE HORN . . . ARGENTINA-CHILE CONFLICT LOOMS OVER BEAGLE CHANNEL were the sorts of headlines that newspapers were carrying at the time of our visit to Ushuaia. Both sides were putting up a show of force and playing a game of nerves. CHILE BOLSTERS NAVAL FORCES AT PUERTO WILLIAMS and ARGENTINE FORCES ON FULL ALERT AS FOREIGN MINISTERS CONFERENCE FAILS were two more.

By the time this book is in print, the issue may have been resolved, although there has been so much intransigence on both sides, it could continue well into the eighties, even though from the outside it appears to be quite a simple dispute to decide and a pathetic thing over which to sacrifice lives.

In 1881, 1892 and 1902 agreements were signed between Argentina and Chile dividing Tierra del Fuego in two and the ocean to the south of it by a line drawn down 67 degrees of longtitude, with Chile agreeing to stay in the Pacific Ocean and Argentina in the Atlantic. Under this arrangement, as can be seen by the map, the three disputed islands would have come under Argentinian control, but Chile occupied them . . . admittedly with only a dozen or so shepherd families and their flocks, but it was a thorn in Argentina's side which aggravated the dispute over the years.

In 1971, both countries agreed to allow Great Britain to arbitrate in the dispute and in May 1977, Queen Elizabeth awarded the three islands to Chile. Chile promptly occupied them with troops and issued maps extending their claims over territorial waters from the islands, three hundred and twenty kilometres out into the Atlantic. If accepted, these claims would effectively have closed off the Beagle Channel to Argentina and prevented, for example, the resupply of its naval station at Ushuaia.

The Argentine position, during the time we were in Ushuaia, was that they were prepared to let Chile have the islands, if Chile would drop its extensive territorial waters claim. Chile had refused to do so . . . hence the crisis.

The other area of contention between the two countries lies in their overlapping claims to Graham Land, the huge peninsula jutting northwards from the continent of Antarctica to a point only eleven hundred kilometres from Ushuaia. All Chilean maps show Chilean Antarctic territory as covering all the land and sea between latitudes 53 degrees and 90 degrees west, including the peninsula, which is called Tierra de O'Higgins, after O'Higgins, the liberator and first leader of an independent Chile.

The Argentinian maps cover all sea and land (including the peninsula) between latitudes 25 and 74. Neither country seems at all concerned that on all British maps, the territory from latitude 20 to latitude 80 degrees west, overlapping both Chile's and Argentina's claims and also including the Peninsula, is designated as *British* Antarctic Territory.

On our last night in Ushuaia we cooked up a 'feast' in our room at the Hotel Fernandez. We still had two of the freeze-dried foods from San Diego left at the bottom of our packs; Shrimp Creole and Beef Chop Suey. These, served with tinned tomatoes, corn and green beans, followed up with tinned pears, a piece of cake and cups of hot chocolate and coffee made what was for us a gourmet's delight.

We had never gone hungry at any stage on the trip, yet we had all lost weight. Both Trish and I were a good five kilos under our normal weights, Sean was only a little below what he should have been, but Zara was quite a bit underweight . . . so much so that on one or two occasions, when she was ill, we had been worried about it. But now, we hoped to be able to get it back on again, before long.

So that was it then. We'd done it. Forty thousand kilometres to the southern tip of the world. Tomorrow we were going to do an about-face and head north again to fly over in three days what had taken us six months to travel by land.

Not all we had experienced had been as I had anticipated. The societies of Latin America were more complex and the interweaving of their past and present more important to understand.

If there was one over-riding feeling with which I was left it was that English-speaking people are the losers in their ignorance of this Spanish and Portuguese-speaking continent which is home to three hundred and fifty million people.

We knew too that we had only touched the surface of it. Very often during our journey we had wondered about the rationale and the point of doing a trip from point A to point B. The major failing of the concept as far as we were concerned, was that, in the process of getting from start to finish, we discovered so many places that deserved more attention and more time than our schedule or money would have allowed, if we were going to complete the original trip. But at the same time, alongside that failing was a major factor on the positive balance: If we hadn't done the whole trip, we wouldn't have discovered so many places . . . places which will hopefully one day get the attention they deserve.

Travelling, I think, gives the illusion of extending time. The multitude of new experiences turns a day into a week, a week into a month and a month into a year. Extended constantly in this way it should be possible to cram at least three lifetimes into one. Perhaps it is travel then which is the secret of eternal life!

In the morning, after rising at the deliciously late hour of 7.30 a.m., we prepared our packs and ourselves for departure. It was a great feeling not to be catching buses any more. After a breakfast of rolls and coffee in the tiny front room of the hotel, we took a cab over snowy roads to the airport on the small peninsula jutting out into the Beagle Channel next to the town.

At ten minutes past ten, the LADE Fokker Friendship lifted off the runway and within seconds was climbing up and out over the waters of the Channel. Ushuaia, to our left, suddenly looked very small and vulnerable. Blanketed in snow and backed by a string of colossal, rugged mountains, extending in serried rows far off toward the northern horizon, Ushuaia seemed totally isolated and lonely.

Ahead and to our right, the white-capped waters of the Beagle Channel stretched wide, cold and empty towards the Atlantic.

As the plane banked to the left and headed northwards over the mountains and Lake Fagnano, we relaxed into our seats, feeling what I think was a great surge of relief.

How very much we were all looking forward to being able to talk without having first to translate our thoughts. With what pleasure I was anticipating the quiet joy of sitting peacefully in my own place. Home never looks so good as when you are away from it and isn't one of the greatest joys of travelling the anticipation of going home.

Right at that moment I was sure that never again would I want to catch another train or bus, haggle with another border or consulate official, let alone visit another museum, church or ruin. Except of course . . .

As for Zara and Sean, we felt really glad to have been able to have completed the journey with them at this stage of their lives. Travelling with them as we did had made the trip much more complicated and expensive, but really, in the long run, so much more interesting and rewarding .. and so much more fun for all of us. They brought their own views and enthusiasms into almost every aspect of the trip and we were able to share in that enthusiasm and in their sense of discovery.

Yet I think that even a year or so later the same journey with them would have been much more difficult. It may even have been too late. Sean at the end of the trip was ten and a half years old and Zara was almost twelve and, although they enjoyed the excitement and adventure of it all, they had become much more independent persons than the eight and nine-year-olds they were when we travelled together through Africa two years previously.

There were times when they longed to be at home with their friends and, for all the benefit they received from a burgeoning general knowledge of the world about them, we knew that in a very short time, as they entered their teens and high school, there would be a great many other things to occupy their minds . . . things that, at that stage of their lives would assume far greater importance than tearing about with the 'oldies' doing ridiculous things like crossing Russia on the Trans-Siberian Railroad, going down the Colorado River in a rubber dinghy or island-hopping across the Pacific.